Windows Visualization Programming with C/C++

3D Visualization, Simulation, and Virtual Reality

Lee Adams

Windcrest®/McGraw-Hill

New York San Francisco Washington, D.C. Auckland Bogotá
Caracas Lisbon London Madrid Mexico City Milan
Montreal New Delhi San Juan Singapore
Sydney Tokyo Toronto

NOTICES

Lee Adams™	Lee Adams
Pizazz™	Application Techniques, Inc.
Borland® **Borland C++**™ **TLINK**™ **Turbo++**™	Borland International Inc.
Intel®	Intel Corp.
Windcrest®	McGraw-Hill, Inc.
Microsoft® **MS**® **MS-DOS**® **QuickC**™ **Visual Basic**™ **Windows**®	Microsoft Corp.
Zortech®	Symantec Corp.
WATCOM™	WATCOM Systems, Inc.
Paintbrush™	Zsoft Corp.

Other brand names or product names mentioned in this book are trademarks or registered trademarks of their respective owners.

FIRST EDITION
SECOND PRINTING

© 1994 by **Lee Adams**.
Published by Windcrest, an imprint McGraw-Hill, Inc.
The name ''Windcrest'' is a registered trademark of McGraw-Hill, Inc.

Library of Congress Cataloging-in-Publication Data

The name ''Windcrest'' is a registered trademark of TAB Books.
Adams, Lee.
    Windows visualization programming with C/C++ : 3D visualization, simulation, and virtual reality / by Lee Adams.
      p.   cm.
    Includes index.
    ISBN 0-8306-3813-X   ISBN 0-8306-3812-1 (pbk.)
    1. Computer graphics. 2. C (Computer program language) 3. C++ (Computer program language) 4. Windows (Computer programs)
I. Title.
T385.A344 1993
006.6′762—dc20   93-32093
                                           CIP

Acquisitions Editor:	Jennifer DiGiovanna
Editorial team:	Mark Vanderslice, Editor
	Susan Wahlman, Managing Editor
	Joanne Slike, Executive Editor
Design team:	Jaclyn J. Boone, Designer
	Brian Allison, Associate Designer WP1
Cover design & illustration: Sandra Blair, Harrisburg, Pa.	4115

This book is dedicated to the memory of my sister, whose quest to be a free spirit has finally been realized.

Contents

—————————————————— *PART ONE:* ——————————————————

INTRODUCING GRAPHICS
PROGRAMMING

_____ PART TWO: _____

INTRODUCING 3D PROGRAMMING

_____ PART THREE: _____

INTRODUCING ANIMATION PROGRAMMING

_____ _PART FOUR:_ _____

INTRODUCING SIMULATION
PROGRAMMING

Appendices

Introduction

This book can help you master the programming skills you need to build Windows applications that use applied animation. You'll learn how to put 3D animation to work for you in simulations, visualizations, and virtual reality. You'll discover practical ways to increase your prowess as a programmer and as a developer. You'll be better poised to take timely advantage of today's exciting opportunities in software, shareware, and freeware. Whether you program for a living, or live for programming, this book is for you.

Getting the most from this book

You'll want to get the most from the book. Why? Because competitiveness is more than a buzzword in today's world, it's a fact—and it's right here, right now. Being competitive puts you on the fast track to success. Helping you achieve success by helping you get the most from the book is what this Introduction is about.

Welcome to graphics programming

Welcome to the exhilarating world of computer graphics programming. It's a field rich with challenge and reward, and it's waiting for you to explore.

Why graphics?

Graphics is an important trend in software applications, especially Windows applications. But, more important, graphics is a trend that is here to stay. Industry analysts are predicting that the computer graphics market will swell by 10% each year leading to the turn of the century. The worldwide market surpassed $40 billion early in the 1990s. These are impressive figures and they affect you directly, whether your project is software, shareware, or freeware. The importance of graphics in the marketplace is a bellwether guiding you to success.

Opportunities for success in today's global arena are found in biotechnology, design, computers, entertainment, information technology, communication, and other emerging fields. Computer programming and application development play central roles in these areas of opportunity, which can germinate in traditional corporations, in entrepreneur-based startup companies, in home-based businesses, in individual consulting, and in virtual corporations (mission-oriented teams of individuals and firms who come together to engage a specific project, then disband).

This book can help you acquire the skills you need to participate in today's software opportunities. It can also help hone skills that you might already have.

Supercharging your applications with graphics   As a developer, you can position your application to appeal to more users if you add images to your product, especially animated images. By supercharging your application with graphics, you can transform it into a more productive tool for your user. Remember, the competition is brisk. Anything you do to make your software more appealing, more effective, more entertaining, or more productive will assure your application its rightful place in the existing base of 6,000 Windows products.

Using applied animation

Using applied animation in your applications is an effective way to broaden your software's appeal. More than 90% of what we experience is visual. More than 90% of what we learn is through sight. More than 90% of our interaction with the world is through our eyes. A Windows application that uses imagery to reinforce its functionality enjoys more powerful interaction with the user. If the imagery is moving, even better. Those moving images are called *animation*. Applied animation can push your application out ahead of the competition. Way out ahead.

Tomorrow's applications today   Tomorrow's applications will take advantage of the computer's ability to provide different forms of output. Images, especially animated 3D images, can exploit the capabilities of the graphics engine that is built into each copy of Windows, using 16 or 256 colors and more, in resolutions ranging from 640 × 480 to 1024 × 768 and higher.

Animation, simulation, visualization, virtual reality   You can put all this potential to work for you in your own applications. Animation can be used for its own sake to clarify, to entertain, to teach. Applied animation can be used to simulate anything the human mind can conceive, or to visualize anything the human mind can imagine. Even the emerging field of virtual reality relies in large part upon animated imagery.

If you are a graphics programmer or an aspiring graphics programmer, then you likely already realize that empowering your software with animation, simulation, visualization, or virtual reality is more than just important, it's imperative. Your users expect it. Your clients demand it. Your supervisor counts on it. Your success depends on it.

Where do you start?

This book is a good starting point. It offers practical solutions that can help you build graphics-based Windows applications.

1 Images from the sample application startup.c in part one, Introducing graphics programming. The demo teaches you about general programming skills for Windows and about specific techniques for graphics.

Who should use this book?

If you want to build Windows applications that use graphics, or if you are already involved in building Windows applications, then you will want to read this book. The sample applications and the text discussion are aimed at you, whether you're a casual programmer, and corporate programmer, or an independent developer. You will benefit from reading the book if one of the following categories describes you:

- You're a programmer or developer new to Windows graphics.
- You're an experienced programmer or developer of Windows graphics applications.
- You're the technical manager of a Windows programming environment.
- You're a project manager or a team leader.

- You're a programmer, developer, or technical manager who is selecting software tools for Windows application development.
- You're a software developer who plans to use animation or 3D images in your Windows applications.
- You're a contract programmer who needs a competitive edge to help you attract new clients and better serve your existing clients in the marketplace.
- You're a corporate programmer who wants to broaden the graphics features your applications offer to in-house clients and branch office locations.
- You're an independent developer who wants to maintain a competitive edge in Windows programming techniques.
- You're a part-time programmer, amateur coder, casual programmer, or graphics aficionado who wants to broaden your Windows programming skills.
- You're a manager, consultant, or researcher who needs to track current trends in Windows graphics applications.
- You're an entrepreneurial-minded programmer considering establishing your own home-based business as a contract programmer, systems consultant, or independent developer.

What do you need?

To get the most from the book, you'll need four things:

- a computer
- an operating system
- a development system
- a desire to learn more about graphics programming

The computer is the hardware. The operating system is DOS and Windows. The development system is the C or C++ compiler you're using. The final requirement, your desire to learn more about graphics programming, is why you're already reading these lines.

PC hardware

You'll need a computer system capable of running Microsoft Windows if you want to build and run the sample applications presented in the book. Some pundits say the best choice is a personal computer with at least 4 MB of memory, using a fast 386, 486, 586, or newer Intel processor. It's important to realize, however, that even a 386SX with 2Mb of memory is suitable for learning about graphics programming. Even an 80286 relic will do, if it will run Windows. You'll also need an industry-standard VGA or SVGA display adapter (graphics card) in your computer, along with a compatible display. A mouse is recommended.

Operating system

At the time this is being written, you need MS-DOS version 3.1 or higher in order to run Windows. The sample applications in the book are designed to work with Windows versions 3.0 and 3.1, and higher. If you're developing for Windows NT, a few minor changes to the source code are all that's required to merge it with your own work.

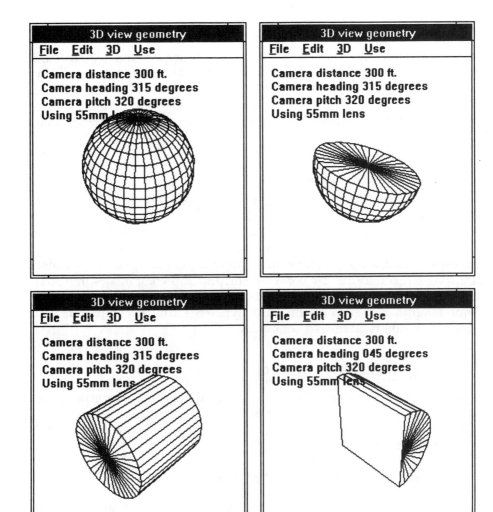

2   Images from the sample application objects.c in part two, Introducing 3D programming. The demo teaches you how to create subobjects and primitives like spheres, cylinders, and more. You can paste the 3D toolkits into your own applications. The source code is provided in the book and on the companion disk.

Development system

You can build and test the sample applications with any industry-standard C or C++ compiler package that supports Windows development. At the time this is being written, compatible compilers includes Microsoft QuickC for Windows, Borland Turbo C++ for Windows, Borland C++, Microsoft Visual C++, WATCOM C, Microsoft C/C++ and the SDK, Symantec Zortech C++, and others.

Development of the sample applications

The sample applications in the book were prototyped and tested using Microsoft QuickC for Windows on a 33 MHz 80386DX with 4Mb of memory, equipped with an SVGA running Windows in 640 × 480 × 16-color mode. During the development cycle, each application was also compiled using Borland Turbo C++ for Windows in order to ensure cross-compiler compatibility.

Testing of the sample applications

The sample applications were validated and verified by compiling them with Microsoft QuickC for Windows, Borland Turbo C++ for Windows, Borland C++, Microsoft Visual C++, Microsoft C/C++ and the SDK, WATCOM C, and Zortech C++. The demos were tested on machines with numeric coprocessors and without. The sample applications have been rigorously put through their paces in 2-color, 16-color, and 256-color modes in resolutions of 640 × 480, 800 × 600, and 1024 × 768. This exhaustive testing is your assurance of good quality, prototype code that is compatible with a variety of industry-standard compilers.

What does the book provide?

The book provides solutions. The book is crafted to promote your programming creativity, and it does so by delivering a series of easy-to-follow tutorials and hands-on, here's-how, sample applications. The book is chock-full of programming solutions, including:

- a 3D toolkit for Windows (a $199.00 value)
- an animation toolkit (a $149.00 value)
- a kinematics simulation toolkit for Windows (a $295.00 value)
- a virtual reality toolkit (a $195.00 value)

Three books in one

The book is really three books in one. First, it is an introduction to graphics programming for the Windows operating system running on today's and tomorrow's personal computers. Second, it is an ambitious tutorial guide to applied animation, knowledge-based simulation, 3D visualization, and virtual reality. Third, it is an annotated collection of sample applications that you can learn from, tinker with, and use as inspired building blocks for your own projects.

Source code

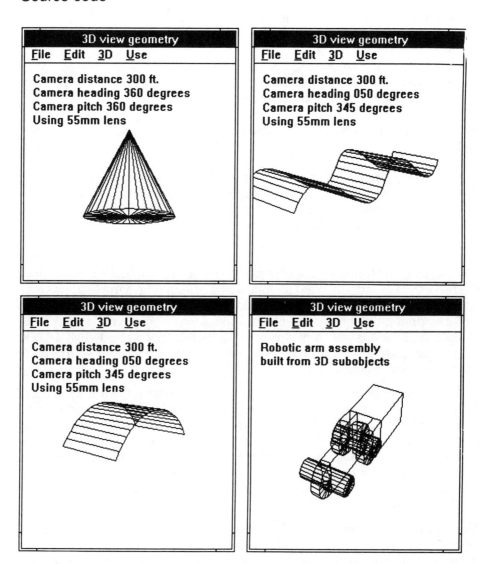

3 Images from the sample application objects.c in part two, Introducing 3D programming. The demo teaches you how to create primitives like cones, curved surfaces, and complex assemblies with articulated joints. Full source listings for the 3D toolkits are provided in the book and on the disk.

Full source code for the sample applications is provided in the book and on the companion disk. The rigorously tested source code includes a set of toolkit modules that you can paste into your own applications. Included in the book is full source code for a 3D toolkit featuring:

- Z-buffer hidden-surface removal
- facet shading
- movable light-source
- library of prebuilt 3D solid parts
- support for assemblies, moving parts, and hierarchical modeling
- animation drivers
- support for VGA and SVGA graphics
- support for 16-color and 256-color modes
- open architecture and extensible design

Also included in the book is full source code for three additional toolkits, including:

- an animation toolkit including a fully interactive playback engine with forward, reverse, freeze-frame, and singlestep capabilities
- a kinematics simulation toolkit with script-driven animation-build and playback capabilities
- a virtual reality toolkit

The full-featured functionality of these toolkits is demonstrated throughout the book by six ready-to-build sample applications. The sample apps cover graphics topics like 3D modeling and shading, animation engines and editors, kinematics physically-based animation, and virtual reality. The sample applications and their foundation toolkits are provided as 16,000 lines of program listings in the book—and as nearly 800K of source code on the companion disk.

3D toolkit for Windows   The 3D toolkit provides you with the ability to build 3D entities like boxes, spheres, cylinders, cones, wedges, and curved surfaces. The toolkit uses the Z-buffer method of hidden-surface management, ensuring that no matter how many entities you place in your 3D scene, each item will be correctly drawn. The toolkit uses back-face culling routines to ensure that only the visible portions of each 3D entity are rendered. A special module of light-source functions gives you the power to reposition the light-source almost anywhere in your 3D scene.

Animation toolkit for Windows   The animation toolkit gives you the ability to design, build, store, retrieve, and play animated sequences in the Windows environment. The toolkit implements the powerful and versatile frame-animation paradigm. Each image (frame) from the animation sequence is stored on disk during the build process. For playback, the software loads the entire animation sequence into memory, from where it can deliver animation at rates up to 18 frames per second. The software is smart enough to be able to detect low memory conditions and to reconfigure itself to run the animation from disk, if need be. Of course, the animation playback routines provide you with full interactive control, including forward, reverse, freeze-frame, single-step, and more.

Kinematics simulation toolkit for Windows   The kinematics toolkit gives you the ability to automate the build process by specifying position, velocity, acceleration, and other constraints for the entities in your 3D scene. This powerful simulation paradigm gets you started in the thrilling field of physically-based animation and the promise it holds for modeling the real world.

Virtual reality toolkit for Windows   The virtual reality toolkit uses an innovative algorithm that gives you the ability to manage an exploration-based virtual reality (VR) session on a standard personal computer. The toolkit's functionality is demonstrated by sample program that presents a 3D maze for you to explore during your VR session.

Solutions

The book's solution-centered approach rests solidly on a foundation of sample source code. Inside the book you'll find 16,000 lines of program listings. On the disk is nearly 800K of source files. All of this code is royalty-free, ready for you to paste into your own applications.

How to adapt the code for your own use   If you intend to use the source code in your own work, be sure to read the provisions of the License, which is presented in the book as FIG. 7 and which is provided on the companion disk as license.doc. Remember, however, that the license is nonexclusive. This means that every purchaser of the book enjoys the same options as you do. Also remember that the source code is not production code (what developers call *beta*), but rather it is advanced prototype code (or *alpha code*). Most of the wrinkles have been ironed out of the sample applications, but the demos have not been optimized for either speed or size. They have instead been optimized for their role in the teaching toolset.

Special features of the book

You can use this book and your favorite C or C++ compiler to create 3D and animation software that takes full advantage of personal computers running in the cooperative, multitasking operating environment of Windows. The book helps you master the skills you need to get things done in Windows.

A learning tool   The book is first and foremost a learning toolset. More important, it is a learning kit that is backed by the combined experience and reputation of the author and the publisher. Graphics programming is a

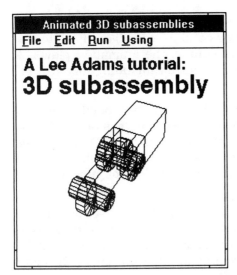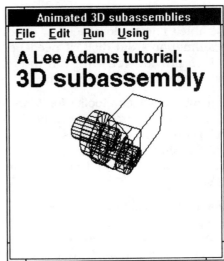

4 Images from the sample applications animate.c and assembly.c in part three, Introducing animation programming. These demos teach you how to manage frame-based animation sequences suitable for simulation, visualization, and virtual reality.

diverse, complex field, and no single book or expert has all the answers, but more than 150,000 readers worldwide are your assurance that this book can help you upgrade your competitive skills. The track record speaks for itself. Many successful retail software products contain graphics features inspired by previous books in the Windcrest graphics series from TAB/McGraw-Hill. So you're in good company. If you receive just one workable new idea from the book, or if you use just a single block of code from the book in your own application, then you'll have received full value.

Marketwise tutorials The discussion in the book and the sample applications follow a theme best described as *marketwise.* This street-savvy approach means you benefit from text and tutorials that focus on graphics topics relevant in today's world. You'll find no toy programs here, but instead real code for real coders. You get hard-working, no-nonsense code permeated with the potential to supercharge your own graphics apps. Whether you're interested in entertainment programming, physically-based simulation, knowledge-based simulation, visualization, or virtual reality, you'll find ready-to-use coding ideas that can help you get your next prototype up and running before your competition, or before your supervisor's deadline.

Hands-on learning The sample applications and toolkits in the book are designed for hands-on learning. Experienced teachers know that you learn by doing; any other approach is frivolous by comparison. The program listings in the book and the source files on the disk provide you with a set of here-is-how-it's-done demos. You can build and run these samples on your own personal computer and see for yourself how the code works in the real world.

Commitment to graphics The book practices what it preaches. As they say on the street, it talks the talk and it walks the walk. Inside the book you'll find plenty of screen prints that show how the sample applications perform their magic. You'll also find many hand-drawn line illustrations that help clarify topics being discussed in the text. All these images throughout the book's pages reflect an unshakeable belief in the power of graphics to communicate. If you've struggled through graphics-impaired books from other sources, you already realize that trying to master graphics from a text-only discussion is like a fly mastering flypaper.

Complete and unabridged The book is complete and unabridged. Nothing is missing. There are no loose ends that will torpedo your own development project. Each sample application is ready to build and test on your own personal computer. In addition, the text discussion gives you enough background information so you'll seldom need to go hunting elsewhere for answers to help you understand either the topics or their sample apps.

Document conventions The layout and typography of the book adhere to conventions that promote ease of understanding. Headings and subheadings are organized in a manner that allows you to grasp the essence of the text when you are skimming. Whenever a new word or phrase is introduced in the text, it is often displayed in italics. This indicates that a definition can be found in the glossary at the back of the book. All the program listings are grouped in the appendices so that the readability and flow of the text is not interrupted.

Device-independent philosophy The book endorses a programming philosophy of *device independence*. This means that the graphics perform equally well on different display adapters and displays.

Device-independent graphics The sample applications throughout the book provide device-independent graphics by sensing and supporting different display resolutions and different color modes.

Display resolutions The sample applications support display resolutions of 640 × 480, 800 × 600, and 1024 × 768 pixels. At program startup the code senses the display resolution and resizes the application's window to provide a standard-size viewport. The code also ensures that the application's window is centered on the desktop, no matter which resolution is in effect.

Color The sample applications provide explicit support for 1-bit 2-color modes, 4-bit 16-color modes, and 8-bit 256-color modes. If the required hardware is available, they can also support 16-bit 65,000-color modes.

Device-independent animation The sample applications throughout the book support *device-independent animation*. This means that the applica-

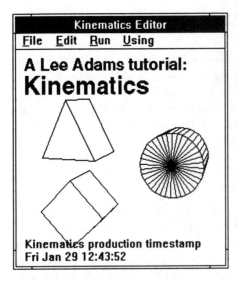
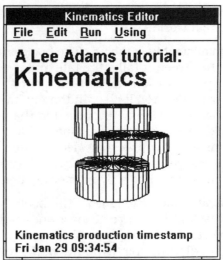

5   Images from the sample application kinematx.c in part four, Introducing simulation programming. The demo teaches you the fundamentals of physically-based animation using forward kinematics. You can adapt the kinematics toolkit and paste it into your own
applications. The source code is provided in the book and on the companion disk.

tions are flexible enough to operate on personal computers with different
amounts of memory, running at different speeds, and using different graphics adapters.

Memory-based and disk-based   The sample applications can play animation
sequence directly from memory or directly from disk. This means that your
own applications can provide frame-based animation playback from disk
on any personal computer that lacks enough memory to load the entire
animation sequence into RAM.

16 MHz to 100 MHz   The sample applications use a timer-based animation
paradigm that ensures pleasing playback on personal computers running
at clock speeds from 16 MHz to 100 MHz.

VGA and SVGA   Full support for VGA and SVGA display adapters is provided. The animation sequences in the sample applications play back correctly in 2-color, 16-color, and 256-color modes.

Images of program output   The book is generously appointed with a rich
selection of screen images that illustrate the graphics produced by the
sample applications. These images make it possible for you to use the book
when you are not at your computer—when you're commuting, for example.
They also provide a benchmark that shows how the graphics should appear
on your own personal computer system.

Illustrations, charts, and tables   A substantial collection of illustrations,
charts, and tables appears throughout the main body of the book. The hand-

drawn illustrations have been especially crafted to support the discussion in the text. The numerous tables in the book have been assembled to help you make sense of data relationships.

Ready-to-build C source listings The book contains a sizable assortment of ready-to-build sample applications. These demos introduce important features such as:

- multicompiler, cross-platform support
- open architecture
- extensible design
- royalty-free, merge-ready resources

Multicompiler, cross-platform support Each sample application offers multicompiler, cross-platform support. Multicompiler support means that you can build the sample applications using any industry-standard C or C++ compiler that supports Windows application development. Cross-platform support means that the finished executables can run on personal computers with a variety of different memory, display adapter, and processor configurations.

Open architecture The sample applications and the toolkit modules feature an open architecture that encourages understanding, modification, and maintainability. The program listings are seeded with plenty of remarks and comments. Whenever practical, the functions are implemented in a manner that encourages recycling in your own applications. The six sample applications that you'll find in the book are compelling examples of how easily the toolkit modules can be seamlessly integrated into powerful, full-featured applications for Windows.

Extensible design The sample applications feature *extensible design*. This means it is easy to extend the code by adding new features. The 3D toolkit, for example, can be expanded to support additional 3D entities and additional color rendering paradigms. The kinematics toolkit, which presently supports forward kinematics, can be extended to support inverse kinematics, forward dynamics, and inverse dynamics. The animation engine can be adapted to support animation sequences of varying lengths.

800K, royalty-free, merge-ready The program listings in the book and the source files on the convenience disk provide you with nearly 800K of royalty-free, merge-ready code. This ready-to-use inventory can save you many hours of programming. When you consider the rates currently being charged by contract programmers, if using the source code in only one of your own applications saves you an hour and a half of programming time, you'll recover the expense of acquiring your copy of the book.

The sample applications and what they do There are six sample applications in the book. Each application exercises the programming toolkits

6 The sample applications in the book teach you how to use Z-buffer hidden-surface removal to produce wire-frame and facet-shaded 3D solids. Shown here are images from the animated kinematics demo, kinematx.c, which is presented in part four, Introducing simulation programming.

already described. In order of appearance in the book, the six sample applications are:

- startup
- objects
- animate
- assembly
- kinematx
- maze

The first sample application, *startup*, is a template for graphics application development. You can use it as a starting point for your own applications. It provides a nested menu system with accelerator keys. The code demonstrates color, palettes, font, and viewport programming.

The next demo, *objects*, is a 3D geometry sampler that can generate solid, fully shaded entities like boxes, spheres, half-spheres, cylinders, half-cylinders, cones, wedges, and more.

The application named *animate* is a generic animation engine that you can use as a template to develop your own applications. In its current implementation, animate supports interactive animation of a rotating 3D entity.

The sample application *assembly* demonstrates how to animate articulated solids that have joints. The robotic arm is created by using hierarchical modeling techniques.

The next sample application, *kinematx,* is an animated forward kinematics editor that uses script files to define constraints like velocity, duration, acceleration, and so on. The tutorials include orbiting spheres and a moving camshaft simulation.

The final sample application, *maze,* is an interactive, animated, virtual reality sampler. After using the editor to build and save a series of viewpoint frames to disk, you can start a virtual reality session and immerse yourself in a 3D maze. The virtual reality manager provides an environment where you can explore the maze, but prevents any attempt to walk through the maze's walls.

How is the book organized?

The book is organized into four sections that take you on a whirlwind tour of applied animation, simulation, visualization, and virtual reality programming. The four parts are concerned with:

- graphics programming skills
- 3D programming skills
- animation programming skills
- simulation programming skills

Graphics programming skills

Part one, "Introducing graphics programming," gets you started with Windows programming in general and with Windows graphics programming in particular. A hands-on tutorial in chapter 4 provides a sample application. The background skills that you'll learn in part one can be applied to almost every graphics project you'll ever encounter.

3D programming skills

Part two, "Introducing 3D programming," provides you with a solid understanding of view geometry, rendering, and modeling. A hands-on tutorial in chapter 9 provides a sample application. The 3D programming skills that you'll learn in part two can be applied to a wide range of Windows applications, including animation, simulation, visualization, and virtual reality.

Animation programming skills

Part three, "Introducing animation programming," provides you with a working knowledge of the animation capabilities of the GDI, which is the graphics engine that is built into every copy of Windows. A hands-on tutorial in chapter 12 provides you with a powerful and versatile animation engine that you can use as a cornerstone for your own animated applications.

Another animation tutorial in chapter 13 provides here-is-how-it's-done instruction in 3D motion-control programming.

Simulation programming skills

Part four, "Introduction simulation programming," provides you with an understanding of knowledge-based simulation, physically-based animation, and virtual reality programming. A hands-on tutorial in chapter 17 illustrates the break-free potential of kinematics programming, where parameters like velocity, acceleration, and duration can be used to build animation scripts for automated simulations of 3D entities. Another tutorial in chapter 19 provides a virtual reality prototype that lets you explore the twisting and turning passageways of a 3D maze in real-time on your own personal computer.

How to build the sample applications

Appendix A provides you with the information you need to build each sample application with your own C or C++ compiler. You'll find support here for Microsoft QuickC for Windows, Visual C++, Borland Turbo C++ for Windows, Microsoft C/C++ and the SDK, Borland C++, Symantec Zortech C++, and WATCOM C. A troubleshooting guide and a tour of the companion disk ensure minimum fuss as you explore the exhilarating world of applied animation in Windows.

C source listings

The source listings for the toolkits are provided in Appendix B. The program listings for the sample applications are presented in Appendix C. As a convenience to you, all the source code is also provided on the companion disk that comes bundled with the book. A directory listing of the source files on the companion disk is presented in Appendix A.

Glossary and Index

An extensive, up-to-date glossary gives you a handy way to find out the meaning of any graphics terms you find puzzling. The index is a quick and efficient way to locate sections of the book that discuss topics of interest to you.

Where do you go from here?

Where you go next depends on your needs. The structure of the book does not force upon you any particular dogma for learning. You can read the book from start to finish or you can skip randomly from topic to topic. Either approach is the right approach if it produces results for you. Here are a few suggestions.

7 You can paste the source code from the book into your own applications as described in the License. Toolkits for animation, simulation, visualization, and virtual reality are provided, as well as six hands-on tutorial demonstration programs.

If you are a beginner. . .

If you are a beginner to Windows programming or to graphics programming, you should proceed to part 1, "Introducing graphics programming." This will give you the background you need to tackle the more advanced projects that appear later in the book.

If you are an experienced programmer. . .

If you are an experienced programmer, you can use the table of contents or the index to direct you to the section of the book that can help you most. For a discussion of 3D programming paradigms, be sure to check chapters 6, 7, and 8. You might wish to read chapter 11 for a good overview of animation programming. Chapter 15 contains an introduction of knowledge-based simulation, including reasoning, probability, game-theory, and physics-based simulation. You'll find a practical introduction to virtual reality in chapters 18 and 19.

If you have specific programming needs. . .

If you have specific programming needs, check the table of contents. The index can also help you narrow your search. You might also refer to the quick reference table provided inside the front cover of the book.

Discussion about how the source code works appears in each of the tutorial chapters. This includes chapters 4, 9, 12, 13, 17, and 19. These code-centered discussions appear under headings like "Programmer's guide to the sample application." By skimming these sections of the book, you can quickly identify chunks of code that you can paste directly into the application you're developing. This approach can save you many hours of programming time.

If you want a quick overview. . .

If you want a quick overview of the book, you can either skim or read chapters 6, 7, 8, 11, 15, and 18. These chapters provide the thematic kernel of the book. They cover topics ranging from 3D modeling to animation to simulation to virtual reality.

Where can you find more information?

No single book has all the answers. The discipline of computer graphics programming is too diverse, too complex, too evolving for a single text to monopolize the field. Here are a few additional sources of information that you might find of use to you.

Related books for C programmers For an introduction to graphics programming skills for Windows, you might enjoy *High-Performance C Graphics Programming for Windows*, published in 1992 by TAB/Windcrest (book no. 4103). For an authoritative guide to animation programming for Windows, you might wish to consider *C for Windows Animation Programming*, published in 1993 by Windcrest/McGraw-Hill (book no. 4114).

Related books for Visual Basic programmers If you're a Basic programmer, you will be pleased to learn that a Visual Basic version of this book is available. Look for it where you found this book. The title is similar, and it's published as Windcrest/McGraw-Hill book no. 4225.

For a well-rounded guide to animation programming for Windows, you might wish to consider *Visual Basic Animation Programming*, published in 1993 by Windcrest/McGraw-Hill (book no. 4224).

Windcrest is an imprint of TAB Books, a division of McGraw-Hill. You can often find these books in bookstores that have computer book sections. If not, ask your bookseller to order them for you, or else write the publisher and ask for the current TAB/McGraw-Hill catalog.

Part One

Introducing graphics programming

Your task in part one is to prepare yourself for graphics programming in Windows. You want to achieve a degree of proficiency in the fundamental skills of developing for Windows in general, and developing graphics applications for Windows in particular. You want to build a level of confidence in your fundamental programming skills that will carry you through the advanced tutorials later in the book.

In part one of the book you'll learn about the parts of a typical application for Windows, including the module definition file, the include file, the resource script file, and the C source file. In chapter 2, "Getting started with Windows programming," you'll discover how the message loop and message handler work together to provide input to your program. On the output side, you'll also learn about persistent graphics, dialog boxes, and well-behaved applications.

In chapter 3, "Getting started with graphics programming," you'll master the GDI—the graphics engine that is built into every retail copy of Windows. You'll use devices and contexts to produce images on any drawing surface. You'll see how to create and select drawing tools like pens, brushes, and color. You'll learn how to work with shapes, bitmaps, regions, and text.

In chapter 4, a hands-on tutorial shows you how to put your new skills to work. A sample application demonstrates features like display-independence, various auto-detect functions, nested menus, and a dazzling demonstration of color using palette manipulation techniques that work in both 16-color and 256-color modes.

Before you begin to delve into the fundamental skills of graphics programming for Windows, you'll need to acquaint yourself with some of the words and phrases that are used by experienced Windows developers. The first chapter, "Concepts and terms," provides you with the background knowledge you need to get started.

1
Concepts and terms

This chapter introduces some basic concepts and terms that you'll be using while you explore Part one, "Introducing Windows programming."

The task—What you want to achieve

You want to be able to understand the technical words that are used in the next few chapters. This background knowledge will make it easier for you to firmly grasp the fundamental skills required for Windows application development.

The plan—What you will learn

In this chapter you'll read about the concepts and terms that make up the world of Windows application programming in general, and graphics programming in particular. You'll become familiar with what each concept means and, more important, the role it plays in the overall system of application development for Windows.

Defining concepts and terms

Launching an application When the user selects your application's icon, Windows launches the application. This is just another way of saying Windows starts the application running. Windows first sets aside some memory for the application, then it loads the executable code from disk into memory, and sets up a local stack (working space) for the application. Then Windows loads in the application's data and resources.

Application resources *Application resources* include the menu system, accelerator keys, dialog boxes, message boxes, icons, and bitmaps that are used by the application at run-time. Sometimes Windows loads these resources into memory at the same time it launches an application; other times Windows waits until the application actually needs a resource before loading it into memory from disk. You'll need to be careful to avoid confusing application resources with system resources.

System resources *System resources* are system-wide input/output services like memory, disk access, keyboard input, mouse input, and access to the display. Windows acts like a referee in a game with many players, in order to ensure that system resources are available to all. Your application is one of the players. If more than one Windows application is running, for example, system memory might be limited. Windows uses a built-in memory manager that acts in the background to ensure that each application has the memory it requires. Sometimes this means swapping code, data, and resources out of physical memory to make room for another application.

The message loop The *message loop* is a block of code in your application. This block keeps looping while your application is running. The message loop asks Windows to check if any messages have arrived for your application.

Messages A *message* is how Windows passes input to your application. Windows continually polls the keyboard, the mouse, and the timer. When an event occurs on one of these devices, Windows builds an appropriate message and posts it in the system queue. The *system queue* is a first-in-first-out list of messages. Windows is smart enough to know if a message is intended for only your application. If so, the message is posted in a separate queue that Windows maintains explicitly for your application.

The message handler After the message loop fetches an incoming message from the system queue, it passes the message to another block of code in your application, called the *message handler.* The message handler inspects the parameters of the message. It can do so because each message is a uniform kernel of data. The message handler then calls the custom functions that you've hand-coded into your application. Another name for message handler is window procedure.

The viewport The *viewport* is what graphics programmers call the client area of the application's window. It is the blank space inside the window that your application uses to display images and text.

The GDI The GDI is the *graphics device interface.* It is a part of the Windows application programming interface (the API). The GDI provides access to the high-performance graphics engine that is built into every retail copy of Windows. By calling the functions of the GDI, your application can tap directly into the full power of Windows' graphics capabilities. The executable code for the graphics engine is in a DLL file called gdi.exe.

DLL A DLL is a *dynamic link library.* It is described as dynamic because the functions in the library are not logically linked to your application until run-time. The callable functions of the Windows API are provided in three run-time libraries. These three DLLs are kernel.exe, user.exe, and gdi.exe. The kernel.exe DLL provides functions for managing application windows and for supporting the entire Windows environment. The user.exe DLL provides system services like memory management and multitasking. The gdi.exe DLL provides a set of graphics functions that are especially well-suited for color manipulation, 3D rendering, and animation.

Devices Devices are focal points of input and output. The keyboard, the mouse, and the timer are examples of input devices. The display, the printer, and the disk drive are examples of output devices. Your application can also use simulated devices. Bitmaps and metafiles are simulated devices in memory. A bitmap is an array of bytes that can be used as a drawing surface. A bitmap stores an image. A metafile, on the other hand, is a list of GDI function calls that can be used to store the means for recreating an image, rather than storing the image itself.

Device-contexts A device-context is a description of a particular device.

Display-contexts A display-context is one type of device-context. A display-context describes a window on the display. It specifies how graphics output is to be written to the viewport of the window by the GDI. Before your application calls a GDI graphics function, it must provide device-context information to the GDI. You do so by creating a display-context, which automatically specifies parameters such as:

- the background color—the default is white
- the background mode—opaque or transparent
- the brush color—white by default
- the pen color—the default is black
- the text color—black by default
- the font
- the edges of the clipping region
- the location of the 0,0 origin in the viewport
- the location of the pen—0,0 is the default
- the location of the brush

Compatible display-contexts A compatible display-context is a device-context that refers to a simulated display. This virtual display is located in memory and possesses attributes similar to the genuine display-context of the display window. Compatible display-contexts are handy for animation, where the next image is built on a hidden page before being copied to the display window. A compatible display-context also provides a convenient method for maintaining persistent graphics. A compatible display-context is implemented as a bitmap in memory.

Persistent graphics Persistent graphics are images that are refreshed whenever they are inadvertently damaged (corrupted). If another application's window covers part of your application's window, then part of your app's viewport is corrupted. When the other application is eventually moved away, you want to quickly refresh the affected portion of the viewport so the image looks complete again. By using a compatible display-context to maintain a backup copy of the viewport image in memory, you can copy a clean image to the display whenever it's needed. The need for refreshing can also occur when the user moves your application's window past the edge of the display.

Drawing tools Drawing tools that are provided in gdi.exe include pens, brushes, bitmaps, and fonts. Pens draw lines and shapes. Brushes fill areas with color. Bitmaps provide images. Fonts provide text, captions, and titles. Before you can use a drawing tool you must create it and select it into the display-context or compatible display-context. When you are finished using a drawing tool you must delete it. You use drawing tools to perform output operations.

Output operations Drawing tools perform output operations like lines, polygons, rectangles, ellipses, text, bitblts, metafiles, and others.

Drawing tool functions You use drawing tool functions to create, select, and delete drawing tools.

Drawing attribute functions Drawing attribute functions are specialized GDI routines that modify the way that drawing tools operate. You can use drawing attribute functions to change the background color and the background mode (opaque or transparent). You can also change the drawing mode of a drawing tool. The default drawing mode is overwrite, but you can use OR, XOR, AND, NOT, and other modes to combine the color of the drawing tool with the existing color of the pixel. You can also use drawing attribute functions to change the text color and to stretch a bitmap image.

RGB color Color is an attribute of pens, brushes, and fonts. You must specify a color whenever you create a pen or a brush. A color is usually described by specifying the intensities of the red, green, and blue guns of the cathode ray tube (the display). Such a description is called RGB color. An intensity value of 0 turns off a gun. A value of 255 sets it to brightest intensity. A GDI call of RGB(0,0,0) produces black; RGB(255,255,255) produces bright white. If the color you have requested is supported by the display adapter, the GDI provides the color as a pure hue, otherwise the GDI simulates the requested color by dithering.

Dithering Dithering is the mixing of pixels of available colors to create an approximation of a color not supported by the display adapter. For example, a palette of 16 pure hues can be simultaneously displayed by an industry-standard VGA display adapter. If you request a 17th color when Windows is running on a VGA, the GDI attempts to fulfill your request by dithering.

However, if you request a 17th color when Windows is running in a 256-color mode on an SVGA, the GDI satisfies your request by providing a pure hue that conforms exactly to the RGB specifications you have provided.

Palettes   A palette is a collection of colors. The default palette is the system palette. Another name for system palette is hardware palette. When Windows starts, it resets the display adapter in order to obtain a palette of colors suitable for general windowing operations. Your application can use the system palette, but it can also use logical palettes. A logical palette is a palette that is defined by your application. Depending on whether Windows is running in 16-color or 256-color mode, the colors you request for your logical palette are provided as dithered patterns or as pure hues.

Regions   Two categories of regions are supported by the GDI. They are fill-regions and clipping-regions. A fill-region is a polygon-shaped area that can be filled with color by using a brush. A clipping-region is an invisible rectangular area that is used to clip graphics output which falls outside the rectangle.

Where do you go from here?

Now that you've familiarized yourself with some of the basic concepts and terms used in Windows application development, you're ready to start learning the fundamental skills. The next chapter, "Getting started with Windows programming," teaches you how to build a typical graphics application.

2
Getting started with Windows programming

This chapter introduces you to the fundamental techniques you'll need for developing Windows applications. It describes the parts of a typical Windows application, and discusses how to create a typical Windows application.

The task—What you want to achieve

Your task in this chapter is to prepare yourself for graphics programming. You want to achieve a degree of proficiency in the fundamental skills of developing for Windows in general. You want to know about menu systems with accelerator keys, nested menus, and more. You want to know how to associate your own code with the menu items in your application. This background knowledge will make it easier for you to understand upcoming chapters concerning graphics programming.

The plan—What you will learn

In this chapter you'll learn about the parts of a typical application for Windows, including the module definition file, the include file, the resource script file, and the C source files. You'll also delve into persistent graphics and multiple instances.

What are the parts of a typical application?

A typical Windows application consists of a collection of source files such as:

- a module definition file
- an include file
- a resource script file
- one or more C source files

Module definition file

The *module definition file* contains information about the structure of the finished executable file. This information is used by the linker. A module definition file uses the .def extension. You can use the module definition file to set the size of the application's stack (temporary working area) and to specify the name of the application's message handler function. The message handler function is the block of code in your application that performs actions or calls other functions to perform actions. These actions are usually a result of incoming messages. The messages can be from other applications or they can be from Windows itself, resulting perhaps from the user selecting an item from the menu system of your application. The message handler is named in the module definition file as a callback function because it is a part of your program that is called by Windows.

Include file

The *include file* is a header file with an .h extension. The include file provides function prototypes for functions in your C source file. A function prototype specifies the parameter lists and the return values, if any, for the C functions that you are writing into your application. The include file also defines assorted variables, including ID constants such as string identifiers and menu identifiers. The menu identifiers make it possible for you to associate your hand-coded functions with menu items in your menu system.

Resource script file

The *resource script file* describes the resources your application will use at run-time. These resources include a description of the menu system, mnemonic keys, accelerator keys, a string table, templates for dialog boxes, metafile names, and others. The resource script file uses the .rc extension. The description of the menu system relates to the menu ID constants defined in the include file. The string table and its list of strings relate to the string ID constants defined in the include file.

C source file

A *C source file* contains core functions that you've hand-coded into your application. Your application can use a number of C source files, depending on the size and complexity of your program. The primary C source file contains the mandatory WinMain() function and its message loop, as well as the message handler function.

The *message loop* is a block of code in the WinMain() function. WinMain() is the execution starting-point for your application. When Windows first launches your application it calls WinMain(), which often contains code to create and show the application's window, to determine the capabilities of the display, to check for the presence of a mouse, and to display a sign-on splash notice. The message loop is a block of code within WinMain() that is executed repeatedly while your application is running. The message loop asks Windows to check for messages waiting in the system queue. If Windows informs the message loop that there are messages waiting for your application, the message loop asks Windows to fetch a message. Windows delivers the message to a separate part of your application called the message handler.

The *message handler* is a function in your application that uses a set of nested switch() blocks to make decisions based on the attributes of the incoming message. Simply put, the message handler is a switcher for incoming messages. The message handler can make decisions based on:

- a menu item selected by the user
- a timer event
- a need to refresh the client area
- a request to resize or move the window
- various other events

Sometimes the code to carry out the necessary action is built into the switch block itself. Often, however, the switch block calls another function in your application to carry out the necessary action.

How do you create a typical application?

Whether you're a professional developer or a casual programmer, the most efficient way to build a Windows application is to take existing source code and adapt it. Many experienced programmers use a standardized simple application as a template, which becomes a starting-point for a more complex application. It serves as a framework to support the features and functions of the new application. This concept of reusing existing code has a number of important advantages.

Advantages of reusable templates

A consequence of using a template is knowing that you're building on a solid foundation. As the sample applications in this book demonstrate time and time again, starting with a reusable template makes it easy to develop high-performance, reliable, full-featured graphics applications. After you've developed a simple application to provide basic functions like menuing, display autodetect, and other housekeeping operations, you can thereafter use the code as a starting-point for advanced applications development, secure in the knowledge that you've debugged and validated the original code.

Common window and viewport   An important ingredient of a device-independent graphics program is the size and location of its window and viewport (client area). A Windows graphics application that claims to be device-independent must be able to position and display its window equally well in 2-color, 16-color, and 256-color modes, and in screen resolutions ranging from 640 × 480 to 1024 × 768 pixels. The code to enforce this protocol must detect the color mode and screen resolution at startup. The code must also be smart enough to resize the window to provide a consistent viewport across all supported resolutions. Prototyping, debugging, and testing the code on all supported displays is a nit-picking exercise in programming savvy. It makes sense to save the code as a reusable template that can you can use over and over again. The tutorial in chapter 4 provides exactly this capability, and the sample application is in fact used as a template for the sophisticated graphics demos that appear later in the book.

Common user interface   Building a menu system for your application involves carefully cross-referencing the contents of your include file, resource script file, and C source file. If you add mnemonic keys and accelerator keys it complicates the exercise even further. Features like nested menus and message boxes can be tricky to code, too. Don't reinvent the wheel—reuse the code. Adding and deleting menu elements from an existing menu system is simple and straightforward. In addition, if you use the same prototype as a template for all of your projects, you're likely to produce applications with similar user interfaces. The concept of a common user interface is one of the philosophical underpinnings of the Windows operating system.

Practical design tips for your menu system   Here are some principles you should keep in mind when creating a menu system for your application. A good menu system possesses attributes like:

- consistency
- clarity
- forgivability
- ergonomic
- proven
- standardization

Consistency   Your application is consistent when it uses familiar concepts, keystrokes, and mouse movements to implement similar functions. The user must be able to rely on common sense to find items in your application's menu system. For example, suppose your graphics application offers menu items named sphere, cylinder, and wedge. Suppose that when the user selects sphere or cylinder, a nested menu appears which allows the user to specify color. On the other hand, if the user selects wedge and your application uses instead a dialog box to prompt for color, then the application would be violating the principle of consistency.

Clarity *Clarity* means that your menu system is labelled in a manner that avoids ambiguity and redundancy. The user must be able to use context and intuition to make sense of a menu item. For example, you would want to avoid using Do, Run, and Go interchangeably as menu items indicating action. It is better to decide on one of the verbs and use it consistently throughout your menu system. Clarity also means that your application should adopt nested menus rather than a single menu stuffed with a lengthy list of menu items. Hierarchies of menus provide clarity.

Forgivability Your application possesses *forgivability* when it is ready to forgive errors the user makes. Most users learn an application by trial and error. Using this approach, it is easy to select a menu item that is inappropriate for the current context of the program. Your application should restrict the opportunities for such innocent mistakes while the user is exploring, and when an inappropriate menu item is selected your application should be smart enough to handle the situation gracefully. In other words, forgivability means that your application protects the user from the user.

Ergonomic *Ergonomic* means that your application is aware of the user's limitations. For example, your application should not use a message box to inform the user of a complicated series of commands and then expect the user to remember the commands after closing the message box. Your application should instead lead the user through the required actions step by step.

Proven The most important attribute of a good menu system is that it is *proven* in actual use. It means that your menu design has been tested by sample users. Professional developers know the insidious trap of familiarity. Idiosyncrasies and peculiarities of a menu system are quickly overlooked as they become familiar to the programmers. The sooner a new menu design is tested on real users the better.

Standardized An application that adheres to industry standards includes certain standard features and functions. It provides commonly used and expected menus like File, Edit, and Help. It displays unavailable menu items as grayed text. It indicates toggled menu items by a check-mark. Adherence to industry standards means that familiar menu items are provided, such as the File menu's New, Open..., Save, Save As..., and Exit menu items.

By following these design tips when you build a menu system for your application, you ensure that your program is easy to learn and easy to use. As the sample applications in this book demonstrate, designing and implementing practical menu systems can be quick and easy, even for advanced graphics applications.

Persistent graphics

Persistent graphics are images that are immune to unwanted side effects. Suppose, for example, that the user moves another application's window, covering part of your application's window. When the offending window is moved away, part of your application's window will be uncovered and Windows paints (refreshes) this rectangle with the default background color, usually white, unless you specify otherwise.

All of the sample applications throughout this book keep a duplicate copy of the viewport image in a hidden bitmap in memory. Whenever a portion of the application's window needs to be refreshed, the code copies the hidden image to the display window. As you'll soon learn, persistent graphics are an essential ingredient of a Windows graphics application, especially an animated application.

Running multiple copies

When the user double-clicks on your application's icon, Windows launches your program. Because Windows is a multitasking environment, the user can again select the appropriate program group and double-click again on your application's icon. Windows launches a second copy of your application. Each copy is called an *instance.*

Should you allow multiple copies to run? This is a question only you can answer. As you'll soon see, all of the sample applications in this book enforce a policy of one-instance-only. Here's how it's done. The startup code checks to see if another copy is already running. If so, the code cancels the startup process and brings the other copy's window to the top of the desktop. The code then exits, passing control to the copy that was already running.

Whether or not you permit multiple instances of your application is up to you. Keep in mind, however, that each copy is based on the same window class. A *window class* is a data structure. It tells Windows about the attributes of the window of any application based on that class. A window class is registered when the first copy of your application is launched. The window class specifies attributes such as the background color for the viewport, the name of the message handler function, the cursor style, and the menu system name. (The menu system is actually described in the resource script file.) Later, when the user starts a second copy of your application, Windows realizes that the appropriate window class is already registered. Windows uses it to create the window for the second instance of the application. So far so good. If the user resizes or moves the window of the first copy, it does not affect the second copy. However, if the user changes the background color of the first copy, the second copy's window can also be affected. In a graphics application, this can be a significant quirk, especially if the user is continually switching between the two copies during a working session.

Well-behaved applications

Well-behaved applications are applications that do not monopolize the system resources. Remember: system resources are input/output services like memory, disk access, keyboard input, mouse input, and access to the display.

Cooperative multitasking Windows is best described as a cooperative multitasking environment. (Windows NT, on the other hand, is a preemptive multitasking environment whose capabilities are not discussed in this book.) *Cooperative multitasking* means that Windows cannot seize control from an application in order to give other applications time to get their work done. Windows must wait until the application voluntarily yields control.

By cooperating and voluntarily surrendering control from time to time, each application ensures that all applications (and Windows itself) have reasonable access to system resources. Applications that cooperate are called well-behaved applications.

The message loop is a block of code in your application that repeatedly asks Windows to check for incoming messages while your application is running. On each occasion when the message loop calls Windows, control is temporarily passed to Windows. If other applications have urgent work to be done, Windows passes control to them temporarily. This is how another application can work in the background.

Many applications, however, engage in lengthy operations that tend to monopolize the system. As you'll see in later chapters, some of the 3D modeling functions demonstrated by the sample applications in this book are time-consuming. A shaded sphere, for example, can require a few minutes to render. During the rendering process, other applications are prevented from running.

Using PeekMessage( )

The Windows application programming interface (API) provides a way for your application to yield control to Windows during lengthy functions. A call to PeekMessage() checks to see if an incoming message is waiting in the queue. It does not modify the queue. More important, however, the act of calling PeekMessage() is enough to cause control to temporarily pass to Windows. This gives other applications a chance to run.

The advanced prototype code throughout this book has been kept simple and straightforward in order to increase its effectiveness as a learning tool. During a lengthy graphics operation the code does not yield control. If you intend to paste parts of the source code into your own application, you want to ensure it is a well-behaved player in the Windows cooperative multitasking environment. Here's how to do it. (Skip this section if you don't need the technical details right now.) First, place a new statement in the declarations section of your C source file:

```
MSG FAR* lpmsg;
```

Next, generously sprinkle the code with calls to PeekMessage() to make the code well-behaved. Use the following syntax:

```
PeekMessage(lpmsg,NULL,0,0,PM_NOREMOVE);
```

Each time your application calls PeekMessage(), control will be temporarily yielded to Windows.

Where do you go from here?

Now that you've familiarized yourself with the parts that make up a typical Windows application and learned some fundamental concepts of Windows programming, you're ready to take a look at graphics programming. The next chapter, "Getting started with graphics programming," teaches you how to tap directly into the power of Windows' built-in graphics engine, the GDI.

3
Getting started with graphics programming

This chapter introduces you to some concepts and skills you'll need for developing graphics applications for Windows. It discusses how to choose your drawing surface, how to select your drawing tools, and how to tell the graphics engine what to do.

The task—What you want to achieve

Your task in this chapter is to familiarize yourself with the tools and skills needed to build graphics applications for Windows. You want to know all about display-contexts and how to use them. You want to gain a thorough understanding of some of the drawing tools provided by the GDI graphics engine and how to use them. The background knowledge you acquire in this chapter gives you the skills you need to work with the advanced graphics examples later in the book.

The plan—What you will learn

In this chapter you'll learn about devices and device-contexts, and their cousin, the display-context. You'll see how a display-context lets you choose your drawing surface. You'll find out how to create, modify, use, and release a display-context. This chapter also explains how to select your drawing tools—brushes, pens, bitmaps, and fonts. Along the way, you'll learn about RGB color and palettes. You'll also become familiar with drawing functions—bitblts, regions, text, and shapes.

The GDI

The *GDI* is the graphics device interface. Stated more precisely, it is the device-independent graphics interface that is built into every retail copy of Windows. You can think of it as a Windows-hosted graphics engine. Some programmers like to think of the GDI as a graphics programming language.

The functions provided in the GDI can be called by any application running in the Windows environment. The GDI can be instructed to direct its graphics output to the display, to memory, to the printer, to a disk file, and to other devices. The tutorials in this book focus mainly on using the GDI with the display and with memory.

Although Windows is a graphical interface, your application never directly manipulates the graphics hardware (the display adapter). Instead, your code issues instructions to the GDI, which is responsible for getting the desired results from the graphics hardware. This arrangement relieves you of much of the tedium of hardware compatibility. Windows provides a significant degree of device-independence although, as you'll see later in the book, advanced graphics application development sometimes means you need an understanding of color modes, display resolutions, memory availability, and other hardware specifics.

The function prototypes, constants, data structures, and other variables used by the functions in the GDI are declared in a file named windows.h. That's why every sample application in the book contains a statement which includes windows.h. The windows.h file is bundled with your compiler package.

How to choose your drawing surface

Because the GDI is capable of doing so many different things, you must ensure that it assumes the same context you are assuming whenever you call one of its functions. A *context* is a set of attributes (assumptions) that describe the current output device.

Devices

You'll remember from previous chapters that *devices* are focal points of input and output. The keyboard, mouse, and timer are examples of input devices. The display, printer, disk drive, and modem are examples of output devices. Output devices can also mean simulated devices in memory such as bitmaps and metafiles. Before your application calls a graphics function, you must provide device-context information to the GDI.

Device-contexts A *device-context* represents an output device and its device driver. The display adapter is an example of an output device. The Windows-supplied file, vga.drv, is an example of a device-driver. Device-contexts can describe a variety of output devices. A display-context is just one type of device-context.

Display-contexts A *display-context* represents a window on the display. The display-context describes how graphics output is to be written to the viewport (client area) of a particular window. Some programmers use the acronym *DC* to mean display-context.

Using a display-context

Before you can use a display-context, you must create it. While the display-context is active, you can modify its default attributes if you wish, and you can use drawing tools to perform output operations. When you're finished drawing, it is good programming practice to release the display-context.

Creating a display-context To create a display-context, your application calls GetDC(). You pass to the GDI the handle of the window on which you intend to draw. The handle is the window's identification number.

Default attributes When the GDI creates a display-context for you, it assumes a drawing surface with:

- a white background color
- an opaque background mode
- a white brush
- a black pen
- black text
- the default proportional font
- a clipping region that equals the client area
- coordinates 0,0 at the upper-left corner
- the pen located at 0,0
- the brush located at 0,0

The meaning of these attributes will become more apparent as you delve into the tutorial in the next chapter. Your application can, of course, alter any of these default attributes to suit its own requirements.

Using drawing tools with a display-context The drawing tools provided by the GDI include pens, brushes, bitmaps, and fonts. *Pens* draw lines and shapes. *Brushes* fill areas with color. *Bitmaps* provide rectangular images and drawing surfaces. *Fonts* provide text, captions, and titles. After you've created a display-context, you can use drawing tools to perform output operations on the device described by the display-context. Output includes effects such as shape operations (lines, rectangles, polygons, and ellipses), bitmap operations like bitblts, region operations, and text operations. You'll learn more about drawing tools and output operations later in the chapter.

Releasing a display-context After you've finished drawing, your application can release the display-context by calling the GDI's ReleaseDC(). Because Windows maintains a finite number of display-contexts, you should always take care to release a display-context after you are finished with it. You can always create another one later if you again need to draw in your application's window. Most applications create a display-context at the beginning of a function that produces graphics output and release the display-context before exiting the function. Some animation programs, however, create a display-context at startup and keep it open. This is more efficient than creating and releasing a display-context each time a frame from the animation sequence is sent to the display window.

How to select your drawing tools

After you've chosen your drawing surface by obtaining a display-context, you'll want to select your drawing tools. It's important to realize that drawing tools are not the same as drawing functions, which is another name for output operations.

Drawing tools vs. output operations

Drawing tools are pens, brushes, bitmaps, and fonts. Pens draw lines and shapes. Brushes fill areas with color. Bitmaps provide rectangular images and drawing surfaces. Fonts provide text, captions, and titles.

Output operations include shape functions (lines, rectangles, polygons, and ellipses), bitmap functions (bitblts), region functions, and text functions.

Drawing tools provided by the GDI   The GDI provides four primary drawing tools. They are:

- the pen
- the brush
- the bitmap
- the font

Each of these tools can be used alone or in conjunction with other tools. The tools can be modified by your application in order to produce different types of graphic output. Each tool can create graphics on the display or in memory. If you are drawing on the display, you are usually creating images in the application's window. If you are drawing in memory, you are usually creating images on a hidden bitmap.

In order to use a tool, you must create it and select it for either the display-context of the application's window or for the compatible display-context of a hidden surface in memory. The GDI also provides a set of default tools that you do not need to create—you simply select them into the context you are using.

Creating and selecting a pen

To create a pen, your application makes a call to CreatePen(). This function takes three arguments—pen style, pen width, and pen color. The style can be solid, dash, dot, or a combination of dash and dot. The default pen width is one pixel, but you can set it wider. The pen color is always a solid color if pen width is one pixel. On a 16-color VGA, this means the GDI sets the pen color to one of the available solid colors if you request a color which would otherwise require dithering. If the pen width is greater than one pixel, the GDI uses dithering if the color you request is not a solid hue. Before you can use the pen you've created, your application must call SelectObject() to select the pen into the display-context. You'll see plenty of examples of CreatePen() and SelectObject() in the sample applications later in the book.

The appearance of any line is affected by two factors. These are the background attribute and the drawing mode.

Background attribute The *background attribute* governs how the GDI handles the empty spaces of dashed lines and dotted lines. It does not affect solid lines. If your application sets the background attribute to transparent, the GDI will not modify any pixels that fall in the empty spaces of a dashed or dotted line. If you set the background attribute to opaque, the GDI draws the empty spaces in a color equal to the current background of the drawing surface. This means that any pixels that fall in the empty spaces of a dashed or dotted line will be overwritten. To set the background attribute you call SetBkMode(). The default is opaque. As you'll see later, SetBkMode() also affects any text that your application uses.

Drawing modes The *default drawing mode* is overwrite. The drawing mode governs how the GDI applies new imagery over existing imagery. Your application can use the SetROP2() function to change the drawing mode that the GDI uses for pens and for filled objects like polygons. Supported drawing modes include OR, XOR, AND, NOT, and others. These Boolean operators are called *raster-operation codes.*

Creating and selecting a brush

To create a brush, your application usually calls CreateSolidBrush(). Before you can use the brush to fill areas of color you must select it into the display-context by calling SelectObject().

The call to CreateSolidBrush() takes one argument, the color. You indicate a color by using the GDI's RGB() macro to specify the intensities of the red, green, and blue guns. Pure medium blue, for example, is RGB(0,0,127). If the color you request is available as a solid hue, the GDI provides it exactly as you requested it. RGB(0,0,127) is an example of a solid hue that is available on a VGA. On the other hand, RGB(0,0,143) is a slightly brighter blue that is not available as one of the 16 pure hues on a VGA running Windows. If the color you request is not one of the solid colors available on the display adapter, then the GDI uses dithering to simulate the color. This dithering occurs on both a 16-color VGA and on a 256-color SVGA, even though the SVGA is capable of providing additional pure hues. Later in this chapter you'll learn how to create customized pure hues for your brushes when your application is running in 8-bit 256-color mode.

Specifying RGB color

As you learned in chapter 1, color is an attribute of pens, brushes, and fonts. You must specify a color whenever you create a pen or a brush. A color is usually described by specifying the intensities of the red, green, and blue guns of the display hardware. Such a description is called *RGB color*. An intensity value of 0 turns off a gun. A value of 255 sets it to brightest intensity. A GDI call of RGB(0,0,0) produces black. RGB(255,255,255) produces bright white. Because each gun provides a range of 64 different levels of intensity, the RGB() macro can describe $64 \times 64 \times 64 = 262,144$ different colors. Because of hardware limitations, a VGA can display only 16 of these colors at the same time. An SVGA can display any 256 of these 262,144 colors at the same time. An accelerator-based display adapter (such as the Mach 32 series from ATI Technologies, Inc.) can display up to 65,536 colors from the list of 262,144 possible colors that can be described by the RGB() macro.

Dithering is the mixing of pixels of available colors to create an approximation of a color not supported by the display adapter. If you request a 17th color when Windows is running on a 16-color VGA, the GDI attempts to fulfill your request by dithering. However, if you request a 17th color when Windows is running in a 256-color mode on an SVGA, the GDI can satisfy your request by providing a pure hue that conforms exactly to the RGB specifications you have provided. To obtain access to these extra hues, you usually must create your own palette.

As you learned in chapter 1, a *palette* is simply a collection of colors. The default palette is called the system palette. Another name for system palette is hardware palette. When Windows starts, it resets the display adapter in order to obtain a palette of colors suitable for general windowing operations. Your application can use the system palette, but it can also use logical palettes. A *logical palette* is a palette that is defined by your application. Depending on whether Windows is running in 16-color or 256-color mode, the colors you request for your logical palette will be provided as dithered patterns or as pure hues.

Creating and using a logical palette   To create a logical palette you follow four steps. First, your application sets up a data structure that contains a description of the various hues that will be contained in the palette. Second, you call CreatePalette() to create the logical palette. Third, your application calls the GDI's SelectPalette() function to select the palette into the display-context that you're using. Finally, you call RealizePalette() to ask the GDI to adjust the color registers of the display adapter. The sample application in the next chapter provides working source code to show exactly how this is done. As you'll see later in the book, all the 3D demos are smart enough to automatically support both 16-color and 256-color modes by using a logical palette.

How to tell the GDI what to do

After you've chosen a drawing surface and selected your drawing tool, you'll want to be able to tell the GDI what to do. You can use your tools to draw shapes, fill areas with color, move bitmaps, manipulate regions, display text, and more.

Shapes

Your application can use pens and brushes to create a variety of shapes. The LineTo() function draws a line from the current pen position to a point you specify as an argument when you call LineTo(). The current pen position can be moved by calling MoveTo(). Your application can use Polyline() to draw a set of connected line segments. You can call Polygon() to draw a closed, multisided polygon which the GDI automatically fills with the current brush color. Similarly, your application can create a rectangle by calling Rectangle(), which the GDI fills with the current brush color. To draw an ellipse or circle, you call Ellipse(). Again, the outline of the shape is drawn using the color, style, and thickness of the current pen, and the interior is filled by the GDI using the current brush.

Bitmaps

A *bitmap* is an array of bits in memory that represents a drawing surface or a rectangular image. Your application can draw on a bitmap in memory just like it can draw in the viewport of the application's window on the display. You can also copy bitmaps from display to memory, from memory to display, and from one location on the display to another location on the display.

Creating a bitmap   Before you can use a bitmap you must create it. Before you can create it you usually create a compatible display-context in memory. As you learned in chapter 1, a *compatible display-context* is simply a device-context that refers to a simulated display located in memory. The compatible display-context possesses attributes similar to the display-context of your application's display window. Another name for compatible display-context is memory display-context.

Your application can create a compatible display-context by calling the GDI's CreateCompatibleDC() function. To create a bitmap for this DC you call CreateCompatibleBitmap(). To select the newly created bitmap into the compatible display-context, your application calls SelectObject(). The bitmap is now ready to use as a drawing surface or as a vehicle for moving an image. You'll see plenty of hands-on examples of both later in the book.

Moving a bitmap   Your application can move a bitmap (and the image it contains) from one location to another by calling the GDI's BitBlt() function. Other names for moving a bitmap are *blitting* and *bit-blitting.* Blitting is useful for certain types of animation where individual 2D rectangles (so-called actors) are moved.

Using a hidden frame   If a bitmap's dimensions are equal to the window's viewport dimensions, the bitmap can be used as a hidden frame. Hidden frames are used for many types of animation. They are also handy for maintaining persistent graphics.

Software-controlled refresh operations   As you've already seen in chapter 1, *persistent graphics* are images that are refreshed whenever they are inadvertently damaged or corrupted. For example, when another application's window is moved away and uncovers part of your application's window, you'll want to quickly refresh the affected portion of the viewport so the image looks complete again. By using a compatible display-context to maintain a backup copy of the viewport image in memory, you can use BitBlt() to copy a clean image to the display whenever it's needed.

BitBlt() raster operators   The GDI provides a masterful selection of raster operators that you can use with the BitBlt() function. For a thorough discussion, including hands-on examples showing how to implement a transparent bitblt function capable of pasting odd-shaped, multicolored images onto multicolored backgrounds, see the author's other books on animation programming:

- *C for Windows Animation Programming,* published in 1993 by TAB/ McGraw-Hill as Windcrest book 4114;
- *Visual Basic Animation Programming,* published in 1993 by TAB/ McGraw-Hill as Windcrest book 4224.

Both books are available through your favorite bookstore, or you can write to the publisher and request the current catalog.

Regions

Regions are rectangular and polygonal areas that have special meaning to the GDI. Two categories of regions are provided by the GDI. They are fill-regions and clipping-regions.

Using a fill-region   A *fill-region* is a polygonal, elliptical, or rectangular area that can be filled with a brush. Your application can create a rectangular fill-region by calling CreateRectRgn(). To create a round-cornered rectangular region, call CreateRoundRect(). To create an ellipse-shaped region, your application can call CreateEllipticRgn(). To fill a region, you use the FillRgn() function. The 3D modeling and shading toolkit that is demonstrated later in the book uses CreatePolygonRgn() and FillRgn() to shade each facet that makes up a 3D solid. A region must be selected into the appropriate context by using SelectObject() before it can be used.

Using a clipping-region   A *clipping-region* is a rectangular region that is used to clip graphics output. To use a clipping-region, your application first calls CreateRectRgn() to create a region, then SelectClipRgn() to select it as the current clipping-region. Any subsequent graphics output will be clipped at the edges of the region.

Text

The titling, captioning, and text capabilities of the GDI fall into two categories. They are font functions and text functions. Font functions create and select fonts. A font is a style of alphanumeric characters. Text functions are used by applications to display characters on the display.

Displaying text   To display a text string using the current font, your application can call TextOut(). The location of the text is specified in the argument list when TextOut() is called. To specify the text color, you call SetTextColor(). To specify the background color for each rectangular character cel, your application can call SetBkColor(). You can call SetBkMode() if you want the background area of each character cel to be transparent.

Specifying a particular font   To choose a font, your application usually calls CreateFont(). As you'll see in the next chapter, you can specify the height, weight (thickness), style, and other attributes of a font. To select the font into the display-context, your application calls SelectObject().

Where do you go from here?

Now that you've familiarized yourself with how to choose your drawing surface, how to select your drawing tools, and how to tell the graphics engine what to draw, you're ready to delve into a hands-on session. The next chapter presents a ready-to-build sample application that demonstrates device-independent graphics, autodetect of display resolution and available colors, manipulation of palettes, a nested menu system, and titling.

4
Tutorial: Windows graphics programming

This chapter provides a hands-on tutorial that demonstrates all the fundamental skills you learned in the previous three chapters. You'll require these programming skills to develop Windows graphics applications. In this chapter you'll find a User's Guide that shows you how to operate the sample application named startup. The chapter also contains a Programmer's Guide with detailed explanations to guide you through the source code.

The task—What you want to achieve

Your task in this chapter is to familiarize yourself with how the source code works in the sample application. You want to see how persistent graphics are maintained. You want to understand how the palettes are used. You want to know how the sample application is able to automatically support 2-color, 16-color, and 256-color modes in resolutions from 640 × 480 to 1024 × 768. More important, though, you want to see how you can use the program listing as a template for your own graphics applications.

The plan—What you will learn

In this chapter you'll see how to use a bitmap in a compatible display-context to provide bungle-proof persistent images while your graphics application is running. You'll learn how to use RGB color to create a dazzling range of dithered color on a VGA running in 16-color mode—and you'll find out how to create a breathtaking palette of pure hues on any SVGA that is running Windows in 256-color mode. You'll see how to display both text and titles.

You'll become familiar with how the various parts of a Windows graphics application are put together.

User's guide to the sample application

In this section you'll learn how to use the sample application. However, before you can run the demo you must build it. The program listings for the sample application are presented as Fig. C-1 in Appendix C. The source files are also provided on the companion disk. See Appendix A if you need assistance compiling the program.

Starting the sample application

There are two quick ways to start the sample application. You can start it directly from your compiler's editor or you can start it from Windows' Program Manager.

Startup from your compiler's editor   If you're using a Windows-hosted editor you can run the sample application directly from your editor. Examples of Windows-hosted editors include QuickC for Windows, Turbo C++ for Windows, Borland C++, and others.

Startup from Windows' Program Manager   If you've previously compiled the sample application, you can start it from Windows' Program Manager. From the Windows desktop, pull down the File menu and select Run. When the dialog box appears, type the full pathname of the program. The full pathname includes the drive letter, directories, subdirectories, filename, and extension of the program you want Program Manager to run. Here is a generic example:

    c:\directory\subdirectory\startup.exe

You should substitute, insert, or delete the directory names shown in the example to accurately reflect your own system, of course. When you select the OK button of the dialog box, the sample application is launched.

Using the sample application

When the sample application starts up, a splash sign-on notice appears. Choose the OK button to continue.

Four menus are listed on the menu bar of the demo. They are File, Edit, Go, and Use. You can use the File menu to quit the program. The Edit menu contains no active features. You can use the Go menu to explore nested menus, titles and captions, and color palettes. If you select the Use menu you can investigate the run-time conditions of your system, including display resolution, available colors, memory mode, and Windows version.

You can use either a mouse or the keyboard to operate the sample application. If you're using a mouse, simply point and click. If you're using the keyboard, press Alt to move the focus to the menu bar, then press the appropriate underscored mnemonic key to pull down a menu. Strike U to pull down the Use menu, for example. Then press an item's mnemonic key to select that item from the menu. Striking R, for example, selects the Resolution of display item from the Use menu. Alternatively, you can use the up and down arrow keys to move the highlight bar to the menu item you want, then press Enter to select it.

The Use menu   The features that are provided by the Use menu are shown in Fig. 4-1. You'll want to verify the demo's mastery of its environment. You

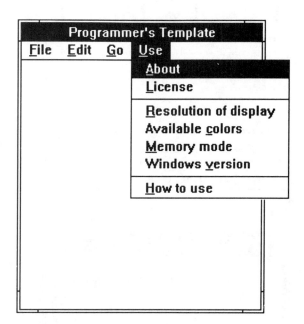

4-1   The sample application startup.c provides information about the run-time environment.

can do this by choosing any of the menu items named Resolution of display, Available colors, Memory mode, or Windows version. The message box shown in Fig. 4-2 appears when you select Resolution of display. The sample application supports resolutions ranging from 640 × 480 to 1024 × 768. The message box shown in Fig. 4-3 appears when you select Available colors. The sample application supports 2-color, 16-color, 256-color, and 65,000-color modes.

If you select Memory mode from the Use menu, a message box appears advising you whether Windows is running in real, standard, or enhanced mode. If you select Windows version from the Use menu, a message box appears indicating the version of Windows that is running. The sample application explicitly supports existing versions 3.0 and 3.1. It also anticipates the so-called vaporware versions of 3.2, 3.3, and 4.0. (That code might never have an opportunity to execute, of course).

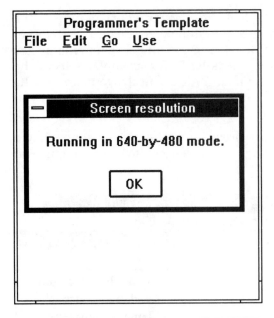

4-2 The sample application startup.c displays a message box to report the graphics mode being used by Windows.

4-3 The sample application startup.c uses a message box to report the number of available colors.

The Go menu The features that are provided by the Go menu are shown in Fig. 4-4. If you choose either of the first two menu items, you'll be able to explore nested menuing, as shown in Fig. 4-5.

If you select Color demo from the Go menu, you'll delve into the color capabilities of your display adapter, as shown in Fig. 4-6. Two sets of swatches are shown. The top set is the system palette. If your system is running Windows on a VGA in 16-color mode, the system palette shows all 16

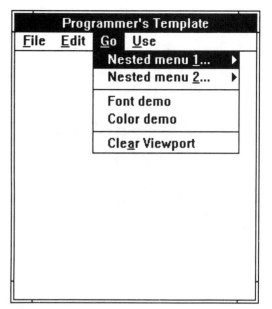

4-4 The sample application startup.c demonstrates a menu system suitable for graphics applications.

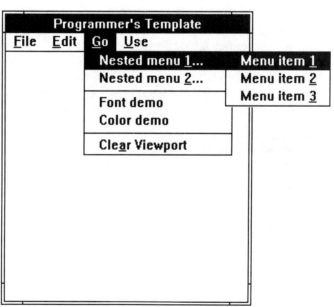

4-5 The sample application startup.c demonstrates how to use nested menus to keep your interface uncluttered.

hardware colors that are available. The bottom set of swatches shows a range of red shades, which the GDI simulates by dithering. Remember, as you learned in chapter 3, the GDI uses dithering to satisfy your application's requests for colors not available on the display adapter. On the other hand,

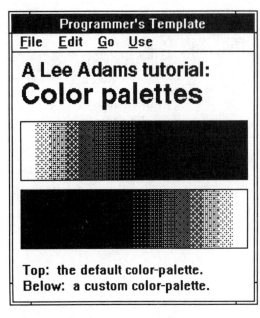

4-6 The sample application startup.c shows you how to use color-palettes. Shown here is a print from a VGA's standard 4-bit 16-color mode using dither patterns. When Windows is running in SVGA 8-bit 256-color mode the custom-color palette is displayed using pure hues instead of dithered colors.

if your system is running Windows on an SVGA in 256-color mode, the top set of swatches in Fig. 4-6 shows only the first 16-colors of 20 colors being used by Windows for general windowing operations. The bottom set of swatches shows a range of red shades, which the GDI provides as custom-defined pure hues from 0% brightness to 100% brightness.

If you select Font demo from the Go menu, you'll be presented with the image shown in Fig. 4-7. If you're using Windows 3.1 or higher, the title is

4-7 The sample application startup.c shows you how to select and use fonts for titles and captions in your applications.

displayed using the Arial font. If you're still using Windows 3.0, the Helv font is used.

Persistent graphics   You want to satisfy yourself that the sample application supports persistent graphics. First, choose Color demo from the Go menu. Then place the mouse cursor on the menu bar and drag the window until part of it is past the edge of the screen. When you move the window back to the center of the screen, you'll see how the demo refreshes the viewport image. You'll also want to start another application and use it to partially cover the window of the sample application. When you uncover the sample app, you'll see how the demo quickly refreshes the corrupted portion of its viewport.

Quitting the sample application

To quit the sample application, choose Exit from the File menu. A message box appears, as shown in Fig. 4-8, providing you with an opportunity to confirm or cancel your request. (You'll remember from chapter 2 how important it is to protect the user from inadvertent actions.)

Programmer's guide to the sample application

This section provides a description of how the source code works. The discussion occasionally refers to line numbers. These line numbers correspond to source code in the program listings presented in Fig. C-1 in Appendix C. For guidance on building the sample application, see the notes in Appendix A. The source files for the sample application are also provided as startup.* on the companion disk.

How the .h file works

The startup.h file provides function prototypes, menu ID constants, and string ID constants for the application. The code at lines 0014 through 0025 provides prototypes for functions in the startup.c file. The comments at the right margin indicate the purpose of each function. The code at lines 0032 through 0060 defines the menu ID constants. Lines 0054 through 0060, for example, define ID constants that are used in the Use menu of the application. The IDM prefix is prepended in order to make these constants easy to recognize in other parts of the application. Each menu ID constant is attached to a menu item in the application's menu system by the resource script file, which is discussed later in this chapter.

The code at lines 0066 through 0099 defines the string ID constants. The IDS prefix is prepended in order to make these constants easy to recognize in other parts of the application. Each string ID constant is assigned to a text string by the resource script file. You'll want to adopt this approach

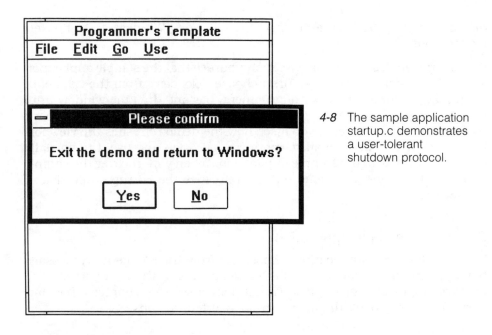

4-8 The sample application startup.c demonstrates a user-tolerant shutdown protocol.

to declaring strings for your own application development because it reduces memory requirements at run-time.

How the .rc file works

The startup.rc file contains the description of the application's menu system, a script for accelerator keys, and a list of the text strings used by the application.

The menu system   The code at lines 0018 through 0070 describes the menu system for the sample application. You'll want to carefully note how the various levels are indented. Line 0018 names the script as MENUS1. The .c file needs to refer to this script when it initializes the application's window. Line 0019 marks the start of the menu system description, which ends at line 0070. The POPUP statements at lines 0020, 0030, 0039, and 0058 each indicate a pulldown menu on the application's menu bar. Again, you'll want to note how the statements BEGIN and END are used to encapsulate a description for each of these pulldown menus. Note lines 0039 through 0057, for example, which describe the Go pulldown menu. Lines 0041 and 0047 use POPUP statements to describe nested menus. Lines 0053, 0054, and 0056 use the MENUITEM statement to describe menu items appearing in the Go menu. Note also how lines 0043 through 0045 perform this same chore for a nested menu. The MENUITEM SEPARATOR statements at lines 0052 and 0055 generate the dividers that separate some of the menu items when the application is running.

As you inspect this section of the resource script file, you want to pay particular attention to the IDM constants. Remember, these were defined in the .h file. Line 0054, for example, connects the menu ID constant IDM_ItemG with the menu item named Color demo. The .c source file also refers to IDM_ItemG whenever it needs to call a function to carry out the appropriate graphics operation.

The accelerator keys   The code at lines 0076 through 0083 provides a script for the accelerator keys. Accelerator keys are shortcut keys that the user can activate from anywhere in the menu system. They are provided here as an example only. The accelerator keys are attached to the Edit pulldown menu in the application, which does not contain any active menu items. Note how the ACCELERATORS statement at line 0076 names the script as KEYS1. The .c file needs to refer to this script when it initializes the application's window.

The string table   The code at lines 0093 through 0128 provides the text strings used by the application and attaches each one to a string ID constant. Note line 0105, for example. The string ID constant IDS_ResVGA is attached to the string "Running in 640-by-480 mode." The .c file uses IDS_ResVGA in a message box whenever the user chooses Display resolution from the Use menu, provided that the application is running on a system using a standard VGA display adapter. The maximum length for a string used in this manner is 255 characters. If you're referring to the program listing in Appendix C, you'll notice how the text has been wrapped around to the next line. If you're typing in the listing, place the entire string on a single line before striking the Enter key.

How the .c file works

The .c file contains variable declarations, the startup function, the message handler function, and the core functions for the application. You'll want to firmly grasp how this file works so you'll be prepared for the advanced sample applications later in the book.

Include files   The code at lines 0055 and 0056 includes two header files. As you learned in chapter 3, windows.h must be included in any application that calls GDI functions. The startup.h file included at line 0056 contains function prototypes, and it defines the menu ID constants and string ID constants used in the .c file.

Declarations   The code at lines 0063 through 0111 defines, declares, and sometimes initializes the constellation of constants and variables used by the code in the .c file. The comments along the right margin of the listing describe the purpose of each constant and variable. When you encounter a constant or variable later in the source code, simply refer back to this section for clarification.

The entry point   The WinMain() function at lines 0118 through 0236 marks the entry point for the sample application. This function performs a number of housekeeping chores, including:

- ensuring only one copy of the program is running
- displaying the splash sign-on notice
- determining the version of Windows
- determining the capabilities of the display
- detecting unsupported display adapters
- ensuring the application's window is centered
- determining the run-time memory mode
- enforcing the viewport dimensions
- checking for the presence of a mouse

The WinMain() function also contains the message loop, located at lines 0229 through 0234.

The code at lines 0129 through 0134 ensures that only one copy of the sample application is running in the Windows environment. You'll recall from chapter 2 that allowing multiple instances of a graphics application can sometimes produce unwanted side effects. The call to FindWindow() at line 0129 checks to see if another window from the same class is already active. Look ahead to line 0605 to see where the class is initialized for this window. If another copy of startup.exe is already running, the code at line 0132 calls BringWindowToTop() to move its window to the top of the desktop. Line 0133 cancels the startup of this second copy and exits.

The code at lines 0137 through 0140 displays the splash sign-on notice. This call to MessageBox() uses the hard-coded method of using strings. Notice how the statement at line 0140 uses the result returned by MessageBox() to determine if the user has selected either the OK button or the Cancel button of the message box.

The code at lines 0143 through 0161 determines the capabilities of the screen display. The call to GetDesktopWindow() grabs the handle to the entire desktop. Then a call to GetDC() obtains a display-context for the desktop. The code at lines 0157 through 160 calls GetDeviceCaps() to retrieve the horizontal resolution, vertical resolution, number of bits per pixel, and number of bit planes. These attributes can be used by a savvy programmer to discern the display adapter and display mode. Line 0161 releases the display-context.

The code at lines 0164 through 0181 uses the values obtained by the previous block of code to detect display adapters that are not supported by the application. If you want to adapt the application to run on any of these adapters, refer to the next section in this chapter entitled, Customizing the demo for your own needs.

The code at lines 0184 through 0187 ensures that the application's window is centered on the display, no matter what screen resolution is being used. The constants zWINDOW_WIDTH and zWINDOW_HEIGHT were defined earlier at lines 0064 and 0065. The variables DisplayWidth and DisplayHeight were initialized by the calls to GetDeviceCaps() at lines 0157 and 0158.

The code at line 0190 makes a call to GetWinFlags() to fetch a double-word whose bits contain information about the hardware on which Windows is running. This variable will be used later when the run-time memory mode is requested by the user.

The code at lines 0193 through 0199 creates and activates the application's window. Line 0194 calls a function named zInitClass() located later in the source code at lines 0592 through 0607. You'll want to familiarize yourself with zInitClass(), which initializes the attributes of the window class. The comments at the right margin tell you what each statement does. Returning back to WinMain(), you can see how line 0195 calls a function named zInitMainWindow() to initialize the application's window. You'll want to familiarize yourself with zInitMainWindow() too, which is located at lines 0613 through 0628. This function initializes a window based on the class described by zInitClass(). Again, the function is generously commented to help you understand what each statement does.

After the class has been initialized and a window has been derived from the class, the code at line 0197 calls ShowWindow() to display the application's window. Note also how the code at line 0199 activates the accelerator keys defined by the resource script file.

The code at lines 0202 through 0214 ensures that the viewport of the window is always the same size, no matter what resolution the application is running in—640 × 480 or 800 × 600 or 1024 × 768. This hands-on approach is required because of subtle differences in font sizes in different display modes. If, for example, the font used in the menu bar is one pixel higher, then the menu bar will be one pixel taller and the viewport (client area) will be one pixel shorter when Windows creates the application's window. Notice how line 0202 calls GetClientRect() to obtain the dimensions of the viewport of the window. Then lines 0203 through 0206 compare these dimensions to the desired dimensions stored in zFRAMEWIDE and zFRAMEHIGH. (These two constants were defined earlier in the source code at lines 0066 and 0067.) If an adjustment is required, the code at line 0209 calls SetWindowPos() to resize the width and height of the window appropriately.

The code at lines 0217 through 0223 checks for the presence of a mouse. If no mouse is found, a message box is used to issue a caution. The application continues to execute whether or not a mouse is detected, however. The code is included here as an example because many graphics programs are heavily dependent on the mouse in order to interact with the user.

The code at line 0226 initializes the graphics environment for the application by calling a function named zInitFrame(), located at lines 0637 through 0659. You'll want to familiarize yourself with how zInitFrame() works, because it creates the hidden bitmap that is used to refresh the viewport, thereby maintaining persistent graphics. As you learned in chapter 3, before an application can use a bitmap it must set a display-context, create a compatible display-context in memory, create a compatible bitmap, and select the bitmap into the compatible display context. That is accomplished by lines 0642 through 0654 in zInitFrame(). Note the call to GlobalCompact() at line 0641, however. This preliminary step forces Windows to maximize the amount of contiguous memory (uninterrupted, unfragmented memory) before allocating memory for the bitmap. This is a handy trick you'll want to use in your own applications to keep run-time performance high. Note also how an if() statement at lines 0645 through 0653 checks for out-of-memory conditions when the bitmap is created.

The code at lines 0229 through 0234 contains the message loop for the application. Unless you're a master programmer, it's unlikely you'll ever need to tinker with the message loop. As you learned in chapter 2, it's a standard component of every Windows application. Whenever the message loop detects an incoming message it calls DispatchMessage(). The Windows API then forwards the message to the application's message handler, which is located at line 0234 in the source code.

The message handler   The code for the message handler function for this application is located at lines 0243 through 0586. By using a set of nested switch() blocks, this block of code can respond to almost every event that might affect the application.

The switch() statement at line 0248, for example, creates a set of branches based on the incoming message. If the message denotes a menu selection by the user, then the case statement at line 0251 fires. If the message indicates that the viewport needs to be refreshed, then the case statement at line 0547 fires. If the message has been sent because the application is being shut down, then the case statement at line 0556 fires. If the message indicates that the user is attempting to resize, minimize, or maximize the application's window, then the case statement at line 0567 fires.

The switch() block at lines 0252 through 0544 is activated whenever the user makes a selection from the application's menu system. You'll want to note how the IDM menu ID constants are used here. As you learned earlier in this chapter, the .h file defines the menu ID constants and the .rc file attaches them to menu items in the script for the application's menu system. For example, note the code at lines 0301 through 0306. This case statement is fired whenever the user selects Item 2 from Nested Menu 2. Of special importance is the requirement that each case statement has its own break statement.

The case statement at line 0308 performs some general housekeeping chores and then calls the function that displays the font titling example. You'll want to walk through the code at lines 0308 through 0339. It shows how to properly set up before a function call and how to tidy up afterwards. The code that creates and displays the caption is located at lines 0314 through 0333. In particular, note how the code distinguishes between Arial and Helv when using the SYSTEM_FONT as the font.

Also of interest is the code at lines 0335 and 0336. These two lines set a token and copy the new viewport image to the hidden bitmap. The token will be used later by the software when it is decided if the viewport must be refreshed. The hidden bitmap, of course, contains a pristine image ready to refresh the viewport.

You'll also want to note lines 0309, 0310, 0337, and 0338. These four lines lock the mouse so that it cannot be hijacked by another application during this lengthy graphics operation. They also switch the style of the cursor from arrow to hourglass and back again.

The case statement at line 0341 calls the function that provides a demonstration of palette manipulation. This block adheres to the same general coding style just described.

The case statement at line 0386 fires whenever the user wants to ascertain the display resolution. You can see how the code uses nested if() statements to enforce a system of machine reasoning that deduces the correct resolution.

The case statement at line 0436 fires whenever the user wants to discover the number of available colors. Note again how machine reasoning using nested if() statements ensures that the software arrives at the correct answer.

The case statement at line 0474 fires when the user wants to know the run-time memory mode. As you'll remember from earlier in this chapter, the startup code fetches a double word by calling GetWinFlags() at line 0190 in the source code. The if() statements at lines 0475 and 0482 use the & operator to isolate bits, thereby detecting the memory mode that Windows is using.

The case statement at line 0495 fires when the user wants to know what version of Windows is running. By carefully manipulating and inspecting the high byte and low byte of the variable named Version, the code can discern the version. An earlier call to GetVersion() at line 0143 loaded Version with a double-word value.

Persistent graphics   The case statement at line 0547 is activated whenever Windows advises the application that the client area must be refreshed. This event occurs if the window is uncovered or moved. Note how line 0551 checks to ensure that a hidden bitmap was successfully created at startup before attempting to copy a clean image to the viewport by calling zCopyToDisplay() at line 0552. Note also the statement at line 0550 which determines if any graphics have been drawn. The variable named PaintImage is set by any function that draws images, as in line 0361, for example.

Graceful shutdown   The case statement at line 0556 fires if the application is about to be shut down. The if() block at lines 0557 through 0562 ensures that the hidden bitmap is deselected from the memory display-context and deleted from memory. The call to DeleteDC() at line 0561 releases the memory display-context.

Resizing The case statement at line 0567 fires whenever the user attempts to resize, minimize, or maximize the application's window. This block of code is provided as an example. It is not necessary for the successful operation of this particular application, but the animation samples later in the book rely on a standard-sized window.

The core functions The remaining lines in the .c file provide the core functions of the application. You've already learned about zInitFrame() at line 0637. The functions at lines 0665 and 0678 clear the display window and the hidden frame (the hidden bitmap used for persistent graphics). In both functions, a call to the GDI's PatBlt() function is the simplest and fastest way to set the viewport to white.

The two functions at lines 0689 and 0703 copy the bitmap from the hidden frame to the display window and vice versa. First, a call to GetDC() is used to set a display-context for the application's window. Then a call to BitBlt() copies the image. Finally, ReleaseDC() is called to release the display-context. The memory display-context used by the hidden bitmap is already in effect. It was created at startup by the function at line 0637.

Titling demo The function named zDrawItemF(), located at lines 0717 through 0775, demonstrates how to create and use a logical font. You'll want to pay special attention to the if() block at lines 0729 through 0738. This code ensures that the title will be visible on mono displays, no matter what text color is in effect. (If your application were to use yellow text on a white background, many mono displays would fail to show any text whatsoever.) Note how the code calls CreateFont() to describe the attributes of the logical font that it wants. The first argument in the call to Createfont() specifies the height of the font. The call to TextOut() causes the text to be displayed. You can use the innards of this function as a prototype whenever you need to use titles in your own graphics applications.

System palette demo The function at lines 0781 through 0892 displays the system palette (the hardware palette). The code at lines 0783 through 0797 declares the local variables for this function. The comments along the right margin explain the purpose of each variable. Before displaying the system palette, the function first initializes a data structure as a palette and loads it with data from the display adapter hardware. This occurs at lines 0800 through 0809. Next, the code creates, selects, and realizes the palette at lines 0813 through 0815. Refer back to chapter 3 to reacquaint yourself with how the GDI handles palettes. Finally, the code at lines 0818 through 0840 draws a series of swatches on the display. The for() loop at lines 0824 through 0833 is repeated for each entry in the palette. Then the code at lines 0843 through 0891 displays a title, similar to the code described previously in this chapter.

Logical palette demo The function at lines 0898 through 0999 creates and displays a logical palette. You'll remember from chapter 3 that a logical palette is a customized palette defined by your application. If Windows is running in 2-color or 16-color mode, this function creates a logical palette of 16 shades of red. The GDI provides each shade as a dithered color. If Windows is running in 256-color or 65000-color mode, this function creates a logical palette of 52 shades of red. The GDI provides each shade as a pure hue by adding new entries to the registers of the display adapter hardware.

The code at lines 0915 through 0942 uses some simple machine reasoning to determine if the palette size should be 16 or 52 (a nominal value). The code at lines 0945 through 0949 creates and initializes a data structure for the palette. Then the for() loop at lines 0953 through 0960 loads the palette with the appropriate entries. Remember, the valid range for each RGB gun is 0 to 255. Next, the code at lines 0963 through 0966 creates and activates the palette. As you learned in chapter 3, the call to RealizePalette() at line 0966 forces the GDI to write new values to the registers of the display adapter hardware. Finally, the code at lines 0969 through 0991 draws the swatches on the display.

Customizing the demo for your own needs

This sample application can serve as a prototype for more advanced graphics software you might want to build. Here are a few tips on adapting the code for your own use. (Remember to read the License, provided in FIG. 7 in the introduction, *Getting the most from this book*.)

To change the application's title as it appears on the caption bar of the window, change line 0095 in the resource script file.

To add or delete menu items, make the appropriate changes to the menu script at lines 0018 through 0070 in the resource script file. You need to define additional menu ID constants in the .h file if you're adding new menu items, of course. You should also add case statements to the switch() block at lines 0252 through 0544 in the .c file to support the new menu items. To avoid unexpected side effects, you should rename the window class at lines 0605, 0618, and 0129 in the .c file.

The sample applications throughout the book support VGA, SVGA, accelerator-based, and coprocessor-based display adapters running in resolutions from 640 × 480 to 1024 × 768 and using 2-color, 16-color, 256-color, and 65,000-color modes. However, you might want your own applications to support earlier, more primitive, display adapters. For hands-on examples of source code that supports HGA, EGA, and CGA display adapters, you might want to consider some of the author's other books:

- *C for Windows Animation Programming*, published in 1993 by TAB/McGraw-Hill as Windcrest book 4114.
- *Visual Basic Animation Programming*, published in 1993 by TAB/McGraw-Hill as Windcrest book 4224.
- *High-Performance C Graphics Programming for Windows*, published in 1992 by TAB/McGraw-Hill as Windcrest book 4103.

All three books are available through your favorite bookstore, or you can write to the publisher and request the current catalog.

Where do you go from here?

Now that you've practiced some of the fundamental programming skills required for developing graphics applications for Windows, you're ready to explore more advanced techniques. Where you go from here depends on your needs. Part 2 of the book is titled "Introducing 3D programming." It teaches you how to display a 3D scene, how to illuminate and shade surfaces, and how to create 3D entities like boxes, spheres, cylinders, wedges, cones, and others. If you prefer instead to use the book's 3D toolset as a black box, you can go right ahead and jump forward to part 3, "Introducing animation programming." You're the one in the driver's seat. The book is designed to accommodate whatever learning style you choose.

Part Two

Introducing 3D programming

Your task in part two is to prepare yourself for 3D programming in Windows. You want to acquire the fundamental skills required for 3D modeling and rendering. You want to become confident that your knowledge and understanding of 3D scenes and the entities they contain will carry you through the advanced animation and simulation tutorials later in the book.

In part two of the book you'll learn about view geometry, rendering, modeling, hidden-surface removal, and more. Chapter 5, "Concepts and terms," is your introduction to the buzzwords used by 3D programmers. In chapter 6, "Getting started with view geometry," you'll learn how to display a 3D scene in the viewport of your application's window. In chapter 7, "Getting started with rendering," you'll see how to illuminate and shade surfaces. In chapter 8, "Getting started with modeling," you'll discover how to create various 3D entities, including boxes, spheres, cylinders, cones, wedges, and others. You'll also learn how hierarchical modeling can build complex assemblies from groups of entities. In chapter 9, a hands-on tutorial shows you how to put your new 3D skills to work. A sample application demonstrates 3D entities in wire-frame and fully-shaded modes. You can use this 3D sampler to experiment with camera position, lighting, and other attributes of the modeling environment.

Before you begin to delve into the fundamental skills of 3D programming for Windows, you want to acquaint yourself with some of the words and phrases that are used by experienced 3D programmers. The next chapter, "Concepts and terms," provides you with the background knowledge you need to get started.

5

Concepts and terms: 3D programming

This chapter introduces some basic concepts and terms that you'll be using while you explore part two, "Introducing 3D programming."

The task—What you want to achieve

You want to be able to understand the technical words that are used in the next four chapters. This background knowledge will make it easier for you to grasp the fundamental skills required for using 3D graphics in your Windows applications.

The plan—What you will learn

In this chapter you'll read about the concepts and terms that describe 3D programming for Windows. You'll become familiar with what each concept means and you'll learn about the role each concept plays in the overall paradigm of 3D programming.

Defining concepts and terms

3D The term *3D* is an acronym for three-dimensional. A 3D entity possesses the three dimensions of width, height, and depth.

3D modeling   *3D modeling* refers to the creation of computer images that accurately represent the shapes of three-dimensional objects.

Rendering   *Rendering* refers to the methods used to add color, shading, brightness, texture, and other surface attributes to the entities produced by the 3D modeling process.

View geometry   *View geometry* refers to the calculations, the mathematics, and the conceptual model that are used to manipulate and display a 3D scene. View geometry is concerned with the volume of 3D space that is visible to the camera. It also pertains to the location and orientation of the camera. View geometry is distinct from modeling geometry.

Modeling geometry   *Modeling geometry* refers to the calculations and mathematics that are used to create individual 3D entities such as boxes, spheres, cylinders, cones, wedges, curved surfaces, and others. Modeling geometry is distinct from rendering geometry.

Rendering geometry   *Rendering geometry* refers to the calculations and mathematics that are used to calculate illumination values for the 3D entities in a 3D scene. Rendering geometry is also used to determine if some entities obscure other entities from view.

3D entities   A *3D entity* is a simple solid like a box (called a *parallelepiped* by 3D programmers), a sphere, a cylinder, a cone, and others. 3D entities are also called *primitives* and *subobjects*. 3D primitives are built from facets, half-edges, and vertices.

Facets, half-edges, and vertices   *Facets* are flat polygons that are used to model the exterior surface of a 3D primitive. This paradigm is called *boundary representation (b-rep) modeling*. A box, for example, can be built from six facets. Each edge of a facet is called a *half-edge*. When the half-edges of two facets abut one another, the common border that results is called an *edge*. *Vertices* are corners. A four-sided facet possesses four vertices. A 3D primitive like a box possesses eight vertices.

3D transformations   *3D transformations* are manipulations in 3D space. A 3D primitive is subjected to various transformations before it is displayed as part of a 3D scene. The aggregate of these transformations is called the *3D transformation sequence*. Some 3D programmers call it the *visualization pipeline*.

3D space   *3D space* refers to a volume of space. Any unique location (point) in 3D space can be described by its XYZ coordinates. The center of the space volume is called the *origin*. It is usually described as 0,0,0. The 3D transformation sequence contains different types of 3D space (and 2D space as well), known as *coordinate systems*. In a coordinate system, the X-coordinate refers to the left-right location of a point. The Y-coordinate refers to the up-down location. The Z-coordinate refers to the near-far location.

3D transformation sequence   The *3D transformation sequence* consists of object coordinates, structure coordinates, world coordinates, camera coordinates, image-plane coordinates, and raster coordinates. Each 3D entity must be transformed through each of these coordinate systems before it is displayed in the application's window.

Object coordinates   *Object coordinates* are 3D XYZ coordinates that define the fundamental shape and size of a 3D primitive.

Structure coordinates   *Structure coordinates* are 3D XYZ coordinates that describe a 3D primitive as part of a group of primitives that together form an assembly (a structure). A 3D representation of a robotic arm, for example, is a 3D structure that might be assembled by using primitives such as cylinders, wedges, and cones. A structure is subsequently treated as if it were a single 3D primitive during further transformations.

World coordinates   *World coordinates* are 3D XYZ coordinates that describe a 3D primitive (or structure) at a specific location and orientation in the 3D world being used by the application. When a 3D primitive is moved to a specific location, it is called *translation.* When a 3D primitive is twisted to a specific orientation, it is called *rotation.*

Camera coordinates   *Camera coordinates* are 3D XYZ coordinates that describe the location and orientation of a 3D entity relative to the camera's viewpoint. Camera coordinates describe how the entity appears to the camera.

Image-plane coordinates   *Image-plane coordinates* are 2D XY coordinates that represent how a 3D entity would appear to the camera if a two-dimensional *image-plane* (a flat viewing surface) were inserted between the camera and the entity. Image-plane coordinates are device-independent because they can fall within any range of values. Moving the image-plane farther from the camera makes the image occupy a larger area on the image-plane, and vice versa.

Raster coordinates   *Raster coordinates* are 2D XY coordinates that result when image-plane coordinates are scaled to fit the application's viewport. Some 3D programmers refer to raster coordinates as *display coordinates.* Raster coordinates are device-dependent because they fit a specific viewport.

View-volume   The *view-volume* usually means the 3D perspective view-volume. This is the volume of space that is visible to the camera. Other types of view-volumes are the canonical view-volume and the rectangular view-volume. Another name for canonical view-volume is *normalized 3D perspective view-volume,* which results when the view-volume is scaled down to the −1 to +1 range. The rectangular view-volume is a view-volume that has been especially distorted in order to simplify the calculations for hidden-surface removal in 3D scenes.

Hidden-surface removal   3D programmers often use *hidden-surface removal* as a generic concept to refer both to individual 3D primitives and to complex 3D scenes. Two types of hidden-surface removal are demonstrated by the sample applications in this book. They are back-face culling and Z-buffer depth-sorting.

Back-face culling   *Back-face culling* is a method of hidden-surface removal that is used to process individual 3D entities. Back-face culling refers to algorithms that detect and discard facets that face away from the camera. Remember, each 3D solid in a scene is built from a set of facets. Any facet that is facing backward cannot be seen from the camera's viewpoint. Imagine a sphere, for example. Backward-facing facets on the sphere's surface are located on the portion of the sphere facing away from the camera. These facets cannot be seen.

Z-buffer depth-sorting   *Z-buffer depth-sorting* is a method of hidden-surface removal that is used to process complex 3D scenes containing a number of individual 3D primitives. The Z-coordinates of each facet indicate its distance (depth) from the camera. By carefully sorting all the Z-values in a scene, the software can ensure that only the nearest facets are drawn. Because the nearest facets will obscure any facets farther from the camera, the Z-buffer method is a satisfactory approximation of how human vision works in the real world.

Shading   *Shading* refers to color that is applied to a facet as a result of the facet's *brightness* (the level of illumination exhibited by the facet). Some 3D programmers use the word *rendering* to mean shading. The location of the light-source directly affects the shading of each entity in a 3D scene.

Virtual luminance   *Virtual luminance* describes how bright a facet would appear in the real world. Virtual luminance is expressed as a percentage from 0% (cloaked in complete darkness) to 100% (the brightest possible). After a 3D rendering function has calculated the virtual luminance of a facet, the resulting value must be converted to an intensity suitable for RGB display. This conversion is necessary for most display hardware because RGB displays do not begin to produce a visible pixel until a gun's intensity reaches 35. Remember, you learned in chapter 3 that the Windows API specifies an intensity range of 0 to 255 for RGB displays. This means that the serviceable range of the guns is actually 35 to 255, and the guns are more sensitive at the higher ranges.

Hierarchical modeling   *Hierarchical modeling* refers to 3D modeling algorithms that build complex 3D objects by combining primitives. These complex objects are called *structures, assemblies, subassemblies,* or *hierarchies.* A structure can contain flexible joints and pivot-points if the XYZ coordinates of some primitives (the progeny) are described as offsets from other primitives (the parents) in the same structure. Such a pivoting structure is called an *articulated entity.*

Where do you go from here?

Now that you've familiarized yourself with some of the basic concepts and terms used in 3D programming for Windows, you're ready to start learning the fundamental skills. The next chapter, "Getting started with view geometry," teaches you how to display a 3D scene in the viewport of your application's window.

6
Getting started with view geometry

This chapter teaches you how to use view geometry to display a 3D scene in the viewport of your application's window. It discusses concepts like transformations, view-volumes, rendering methods, and hidden-surface removal.

The task—What you want to achieve

Your task in this chapter is to become familiar with view geometry. You want to know about the various coordinate systems that make up the 3D visualization pipeline. You want to gain a thorough understanding of 3D view-volumes and their importance to clipping operations and hidden-surface removal. You want to become aware of the different rendering methods that are available to 3D programmers.

The plan—What you will learn

In this chapter you'll learn about b-rep modeling. You'll find out about primitives, facets, half-edges, and Euler operations. You'll see how the 3D visualization pipeline is built from a series of coordinate systems, including object, structure, world, camera, image-plane, and raster coordinates. You'll learn about yaw, roll, and pitch—and you'll discover translation, rotation, and extrusion. You'll find out how to normalize and manipulate your camera's view-volume in order to simplify the task of hidden-surface removal in 3D scenes. You'll learn about different shading methods like flat shading, color interpolation shading, and normal-vector interpolation shading. You'll investigate two methods for hidden-surface removal, back-face culling and z-buffer depth-sorting. The 3D knowledge you'll acquire in this chapter will provide you with the background you need to proceed to the more advanced 3D material in the book.

3D primer

3D images can supercharge your Windows application development. Effective use of 3D modeling and rendering techniques can add realism and excitement to your software, especially if it's an application that supports animation, visualization, or simulation. An understanding of 3D geometry and the ability to use a 3D library are assets for any aspiring Windows programmer.

This book provides a 3D toolset that you can use with your own application development. More important, however, the 3D functions provided in Appendix B are extensible. This means you can readily adapt them to meet your own specialized requirements—and you can add more features to the existing source code. In its current implementation, the book's 3D toolkit provides you with a versatile environment for b-rep modeling. It offers advanced features such as back-face culling, z-buffer depth-sorting, a moveable light-source, and a ready-to-use library of prebuilt solids like boxes, spheres, half-spheres, cylinders, half-cylinders, cones, wedges, and curved surfaces. It is a powerful b-rep modeling tool.

B-rep modeling

B-rep is an acronym for *boundary representation.* A b-rep model portrays a 3D entity by rendering its outer surface. You can think of this outer surface as the exterior boundaries of the entity—hence the phrase *boundary representation.* Although other methods of 3D modeling are available, b-rep modeling is fast, accurate, and versatile. It's the most popular 3D paradigm in use today, and it's especially well-suited to the graphics capabilities of the Windows Graphics Device Interface (GDI). The GDI offers four tools particularly useful for 3D programming. These tools are:

- the RGB() macro
- dithering
- the CreateSolidBrush() function
- the CreatePolygonRgn() function

The RGB() macro provides precise, individual control over the RGB guns found in most display hardware. This makes it easy to specify color during the 3D illumination and rendering processes. The GDI's built-in dithering capabilities mean that almost any shade of any color can be simulated, even when Windows is running in a 16-color VGA mode. As you learned in chapter 3, the CreateSolidBrush() function provides an efficient way to apply areas of color to an image. The CreatePolygonRgn() function is especially useful for defining a region (the facet) to be filled with color by the brush.

In order to display a 3D scene using b-rep modeling, you need to become familiar with three types of calculations. These are:

- view geometry
- modeling geometry
- rendering geometry

View geometry deals with an entire 3D scene. Modeling geometry deals with individual 3D entities. Rendering geometry deals with subjective appearance.

View geometry

As you learned in the previous chapter, view geometry refers to the calculations that are used to manipulate and display an entire 3D scene. View geometry is concerned with the volume of 3D space that is visible to the camera. It deals with the location and orientation of the camera.

Modeling geometry

As you learned in chapter 5, modeling geometry is used to create individual 3D primitives.

Primitives   A *3D primitive* is a simple solid like a parallelepiped, a sphere, a cylinder, a cone, a wedge, and others. 3D primitives are also called entities and subobjects. 3D primitives are built from facets, half-edges, and vertices.

Facets, half-edges, and vertices   *Facets* are flat polygons. They are two-dimensional surfaces. Facets are used to model the exterior surface of a 3D primitive. As you've already learned, this paradigm is called boundary representation (b-rep) modeling. A box, for example, can be built from six facets. Each edge of a facet is called a *half-edge*. Half-edges, like facets, cannot exist in the real world, of course, because facets have no thickness. When the half-edges of two facets abut one another on a 3D model, the common border that results is called an edge. Unlike half-edges, edges do exist in the real world. Vertices are corners. A four-sided facet possesses four vertices. A 3D primitive like a box possesses eight vertices. In addition to facets, half-edges, and vertices, a 3D primitive can be further defined by Euler operations.

Euler operations   *Euler operations* simulate the way things work in the real world. A Euler operator transforms a 3D entity by adding or deleting facets, edges, half-edges, and vertices. Joining, intersection, and subtraction are examples of Euler operators. Joining means attaching two 3D primitives to each other. Think of it as gluing together two entities. Intersection refers to a common volume of space occupied by two primitives. Think of it as pouring two entities into a mold. Subtraction means the void occupying a common volume of space occupied by two primitives. Think of it as drilling a hole in an entity. Euler operations are named after the 18th-century mathematician Leonard Euler, who is credited with originating a formula useful for describing surfaces.

Rendering geometry

As you discovered in the previous chapter, rendering geometry manipulates the subjective appearance of a 3D scene. Rendering geometry also concerns the calculations used to infer an illumination value for each facet in a scene. Rendering geometry usually relies upon an illumination model, which provides a paradigm to explain how light and surfaces act in their 3D environment. As you'll discover later in this chapter, different illumination models (and rendering geometry) are preferred by different programmers. The choices include flat shading, color interpolation shading, normal-vector interpolation shading, ray-tracing, and others.

3D transformations: the visualization pipeline

Before a primitive can be displayed as part of a 3D scene in the viewport of your application's window, it must be transformed. 3D transformations are manipulations in 3D space. The sum of the transformations is the 3D transformation sequence. Another name for 3D transformation sequence is the visualization pipeline.

3D space is a specific volume of space. Any location in 3D space can be described by its XYZ coordinates, relative to the origin. The origin is the center of the volume, usually defined as XYZ coordinates 0,0,0. The 3D transformation sequence contains different types of 3D space. Each type of 3D space possesses its own coordinate system. In a three-dimensional coordinate system, the X-coordinate refers to left-right location. The Y-coordinate refers to up-down location. The Z-coordinate refers to near-far location. In a two-dimensional coordinate system, the X-coordinate refers to left-right location and the Y-coordinate refers to up-down location.

3D transformation sequence

As shown in Fig. 6-1, a typical 3D transformation sequence consists of:

- object coordinates
- structure coordinates
- world coordinates
- camera coordinates
- image-plane coordinates
- raster coordinates

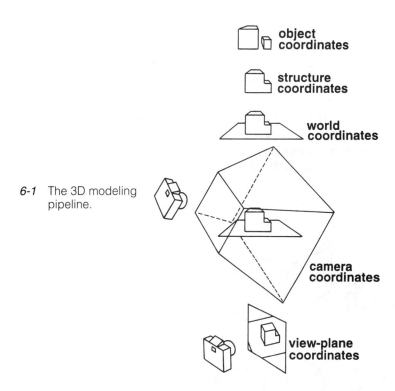

object
coordinates

structure
coordinates

world
coordinates

6-1 The 3D modeling
pipeline.

camera
coordinates

view-plane
coordinates

A 3D primitive must be transformed through each of these coordinate systems before it can be displayed in your application's window. Each coordinate system represents a different form of 3D space. Object coordinates, for example, represent object-space.

Object coordinates *Object coordinates* are XYZ coordinates that define the fundamental shape and size of a 3D primitive such as a box, sphere, cylinder, cone, wedge, and others. Object coordinates describe object-space.

Structure coordinates *Structure coordinates* are XYZ coordinates that describe a primitive in its role as part of a group of primitives that form a larger structure. Structure coordinates describe structure-space. As you learned in the previous chapter, structure coordinates are used in hierarchical operations. A structure is treated as a single 3D primitive during subsequent transformations. Hierarchical modeling can build complex 3D solids by attaching primitives to each other. These complex solids are called structures, assemblies, subassemblies, or hierarchies. A hierarchical structure can contain flexible joints. This is possible because the XYZ coordinates of some primitives (progeny) are defined as offsets relative to other primitives (parents) residing in the same structure. Structures with pivoting or jointed sections are called articulated entities.

World coordinates *World coordinates* are XYZ coordinates that describe a primitive (or a structure) at a specific location and orientation in the 3D world being used by the application. World coordinates describe world-space. When a 3D entity is moved to a specific location in world-space, it is called translation. When a primitive is twisted to a specific orientation in world-space, it is called rotation.

Camera coordinates   *Camera coordinates* are XYZ coordinates that define the location and orientation of an entity relative to the camera's viewpoint. Camera coordinates describe camera-space. Camera coordinates indicate how an entity appears to the camera. Fig. 6-2 shows the relationship between camera coordinates and world coordinates.

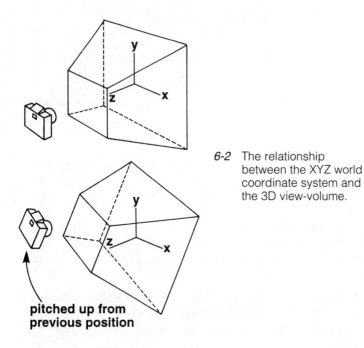

6-2 The relationship between the XYZ world coordinate system and the 3D view-volume.

Image-plane coordinates   *Image-plane coordinates* are XY coordinates that represent how a 3D entity would appear to the camera if a two-dimensional image-plane were inserted between the camera and the entity. Image-plane coordinates describe image-space. Image-plane coordinates are device-independent because they can fall within any range of values. Moving the image-plane farther from the camera makes the image occupy a larger area on the image-plane, and vice versa. As shown in Fig. 6-1, another way of saying image-plane coordinates is view-plane coordinates.

Raster coordinates   *Raster coordinates* are XY coordinates that result when image-plane coordinates are scaled to fit the application's viewport. Raster coordinates describe display-space. Some programmers refer to raster co-ordinates as display coordinates. Raster coordinates are device-dependent because they fit a specific viewport. Raster coordinates are also called screen coordinates.

Right-hand coordinate system

In most 3D modeling systems, every set of XYZ coordinates for object-space, structure-space, world-space, and camera-space is expressed using the right-hand coordinate system, which is the most widely used 3D coordinate system. It specifies +Z as nearer to the camera and −Z as farther from the camera, relative to the 0,0,0 origin. The right-hand coordinate system specifies +X as right and −X as left. It specifies +Y as up and −Y as down.

Why is it called the right-hand coordinate system? Hold your right hand up, with your flattened palm towards your face and your fingers pointing upward. Extend your thumb out to the right. Your index finger should be pointing up. Bend your middle finger so it points directly at your face. Curl the remaining two fingers in towards your palm. You've just created your own personal right-hand coordinate system. Your thumb indicates +X; your index finger indicates +Y; and your middle finger indicates +Z. The center of your palm is the 0,0,0 origin, of course.

Yaw, roll, and pitch

You can think of each coordinate system in the 3D visualization pipeline as coexisting with a spherical coordinate system. An XYZ coordinate system and its companion spherical coordinate system share the same 3D space. Whereas an XYZ coordinate system uses distance to describe a 3D entity, a spherical coordinate system uses angles. These angles are yaw, roll, and pitch. Yaw refers to compass headings. Roll means tilting left or right. Pitch means tilting forward or back. Together, an XYZ coordinate system and a spherical coordinate system can define a 3D entity's location and orientation in 3D space. The XYZ coordinate system can be used to translate (move) the entity to a particular location. The spherical coordinate system can then be used to rotate (spin) the entity into a particular orientation.

3D view-volumes

A 3D view-volume is the volume of 3D space that is visible to the camera. Three types of view-volumes are used by the 3D functions in this book. They are:

- the 3D perspective view-volume
- the normalized 3D perspective view-volume
- the rectangular view-volume

3D perspective view-volume

A 3D perspective view-volume is shown in Fig. 6-3. It is simply a truncated right-angle pyramid whose vertex is located at the camera lens. Any 3D entities located outside the view-volume cannot be seen by the camera. The

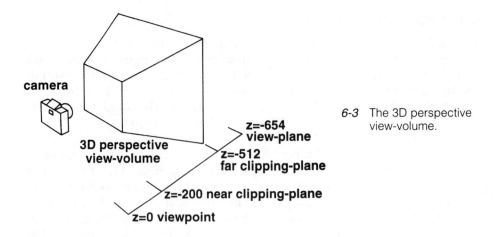

6-3 The 3D perspective view-volume.

conceptual representation in Fig. 6-3 also shows the near and far clipping-planes.

Near and far clipping-planes The near and far clipping-planes are optionally set by the programmer in order to discard 3D entities located too far from or too near to the camera. The far clipping-plane ensures that the 3D formulas do not waste time rendering entities so distant they will not occupy more than a single pixel. The near clipping-plane ensures that entities located too near the camera will be discarded. Such entities would appear distorted if rendered.

Normalized 3D perspective view-volume

A normalized 3D perspective view-volume is simply a 3D perspective view-volume that has been scaled to fit within a range of −1 to +1. A simplified conceptual representation is shown in Fig. 6-4.

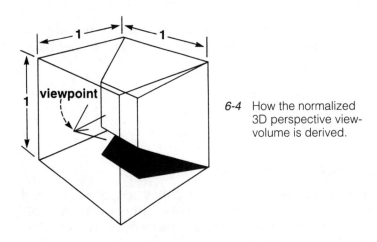

6-4 How the normalized 3D perspective view-volume is derived.

Canonical view-volume Another name for normalized 3D perspective view-volume is canonical view-volume. In a canonical view-volume, Z-values range from 0 to −1, X-values range from −1 to +1, and Y-values range from −1 to +1. Using a canonical view-volume simplifies some of the mathematics required to clip 3D facets that intersect the top, bottom, right, or left sides of the view-volume.

How to scale down to fit a normalized view-volume The illustration in Fig. 6-5 depicts a normalized 3D perspective view-volume. Compare this with the standard 3D perspective view-volume in Fig. 6-3. You'll notice, for example, how the far clipping-plane has been scaled down from −512 to −1. The distance of the near clipping-plane from the camera has been scaled from −200 to −.390625. The original scale of the 3D perspective view-volume in Fig. 6-3 was selected because it produces a 3D world convenient for the sample applications presented later in the book. As Fig. 6-6 shows, the image-plane possesses the same dimensions as the viewport used by the sample applications. This convenient side-effect simplifies the toolkit's

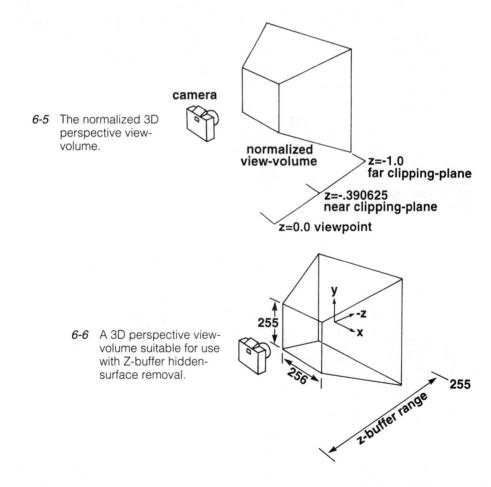

camera

6-5 The normalized 3D perspective view-volume.

normalized view-volume

z=-1.0
far clipping-plane

z=-.390625
near clipping-plane

z=0.0 viewpoint

6-6 A 3D perspective view-volume suitable for use with Z-buffer hidden-surface removal.

y

-z

x

255

256

255

z-buffer range

display functions. The mathematical formulas that scale the 3D perspective view-volume down to a canonical view-volume are discussed in chapter 9 when the 3D source code is analyzed.

Rectangular parallelepiped view-volume

A rectangular parallelepiped view-volume is a view-volume that has been especially distorted. This type of view-volume is used in order to simplify the clipping functions and, more important, to simplify the code needed to operate a z-buffer depth-sorting system (hidden-surface removal for the entire scene). As Fig. 6-7 shows, the far clipping-plane remains constant, but the near clipping-plane is deliberately deformed so that a rectangular box is created.

Why use a rectangular parallelepiped view-volume? A rectangular view-volume introduces a number of efficiencies into the 3D modeling pipeline. The mathematical formulas used to transform a canonical view-volume into a rectangular view-volume are especially designed to preserve the Z depth-values. The formulas also ensure that the contents of the rectangular view-volume can be directly mapped onto the image-plane (and the 2D viewport). This means that the Z depth-values can be used to determine whether a facet should be rendered or not. Only the nearest Z-value for any particular XY location should be drawn because it will necessarily obscure the entities located behind it.

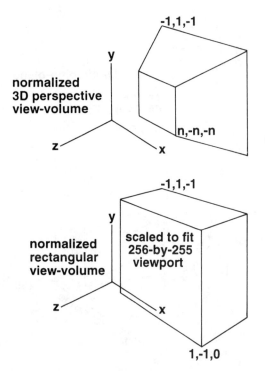

6-7 Conceptual representation of the transformation from normalized 3D perspective view-volume to a normalized rectangular view-volume that uses parallel projection.

Because the top, bottom, left, and right sides of the view-volume are right-angle planes, clipping is simplified. If the X-coordinate of a facet's vertex is greater than $+1$, for example, then it must be clipped. The value of $+1$ is a constant that always indicates the right side of the view-volume. Compare this situation with the 3D perspective view-volume shown in the top part of Fig. 6-7. Complex and onerous calculations are required to compute the clipping values at various points along the right side of a 3D perspective view-volume. Clipping solids is an exercise already fraught with intricacies, as Fig. 6-8 shows. Using a canonical view-volume keeps the math simple and reduces the time required to model and render a scene.

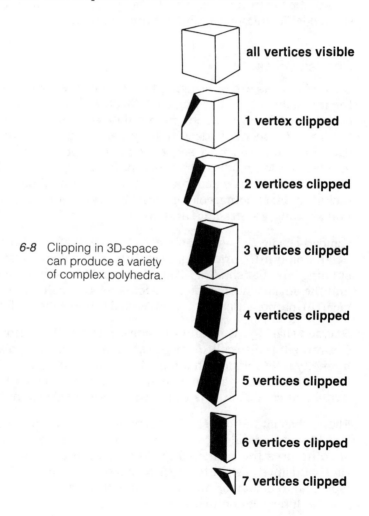

6-8 Clipping in 3D-space can produce a variety of complex polyhedra.

all vertices visible

1 vertex clipped

2 vertices clipped

3 vertices clipped

4 vertices clipped

5 vertices clipped

6 vertices clipped

7 vertices clipped

Rendering methods

The three methods of rendering are wire-frame, solid, and shaded.

Wire-frame mode

Wire-frame models are built using only edges. The software does not attempt to detect or remove hidden surfaces. If a wire-frame model is built using facets, the facets are not shaded, but are transparent.

Solid modeling mode

Solid models are built using opaque facets. Hidden surfaces are detected and removed, usually by back-face culling. A solid model appears like it would appear in the real world, except that no attempt is made to shade the model to satisfy existing lighting conditions.

Shaded solids

Shaded models are built using facets that have been shaded according to the intensity of light striking each facet. As you discovered in the previous chapter, rendering geometry manipulates the subjective appearance of entities in a 3D scene. It does this by calculating an illumination value for each facet or pixel in a scene. Rendering geometry usually relies upon an illumination model, which is a paradigm explaining how surfaces and illumination are expected to act. Different illumination models are available, including flat shading, color interpolation shading, normal-vector interpolation shading, ray-tracing, and others.

Lambert shading Lambert shading is named after 18th-century mathematician Johann Heinrich Lambert. It is also called constant shading, facet shading, and flat shading. The relationship between the incoming light ray and the surface normal of the facet is used to calculate the brightness of a facet. In mathematical terms, it is called the specific surface normal method.

Gouraud shading Gouraud shading is named after motorcar designer Henri Gouraud. It is also called smooth shading, color interpolation shading, and intensity interpolation shading. Gouraud shading uses color interpolation (averaging) along scan-lines to smooth the harsh edges between facets. In mathematical terms, it is called the average surface normal method.

Phong shading Phong shading is named after computer science researcher Bui Phong. It is also called normal-vector interpolation shading. Phong shading uses the relationships between surface normals, incoming light rays, and lines of sight to produce smooth-shaded surfaces with highlights (specular reflections). In mathematical terms, it is called the individual normal interpolation method.

Ray tracing Ray-tracing algorithms work by following individual paths of reflected light and refracted light through the 3D scene. It is a very time-consuming method, but ray-tracing makes it possible to produce subtle effects like reflections and shadows. In mathematical terms, it is called the cosine power specular reflection method.

Hidden-surface removal

As you learned in the previous chapter, hidden-surface removal is essential if you're trying to create 3D images that faithfully represent the real world. Two types of hidden-surface removal are demonstrated by the sample applications in this book. They are back-face culling and z-buffer depth-sorting. Back-face culling is applied to individual 3D primitives. The z-buffer depth-sorting method is applied to an entire 3D scene.

Between them, these two types of hidden-surface removal ensure a coherent 3D image. Here's why: first, the z-buffer depth-sorting method guarantees that entities nearer the camera will obscure entities farther from the camera—just like your visual experiences in the real world. Second, the back-face culling method ensures that portions of an entity whose facets face away from the camera are not seen by the camera—just like your visual experiences in the real world.

Back-face culling

Back-face culling is used to process individual 3D primitives like boxes, spheres, cylinders, cones, wedges, and others. Back-face culling detects and discards facets that face away from the camera (facets that face away from you, the viewer). Because each 3D solid in a scene is built using facets, any facet facing backward cannot be seen from the camera's viewpoint.

The back-face culling algorithm is founded on the standard equation for a plane. The equation is used to test the camera's XYZ location in order to determine on which side of the plane the camera is located. Remember, each facet is a plane. The test is reliable because a 3D programmer using b-rep modeling always describes a facet by the XYZ coordinates of its vertices in counterclockwise order as viewed from outside the solid on whose surface the facet resides. If the standard equation for a plane indicates that the camera is located on the inside of the plane, then the facet is facing away from the camera and is not visible. If the equation indicates that the camera is located on the outside of the plane, then the facet is facing towards the camera and is visible. The mathematical calculations for back-face culling will be discussed in more detail when the 3D source code for the sample application in chapter 9 is analyzed.

z-buffer depth-sorting

As you learned in the previous chapter, z-buffer depth-sorting is used to process complex scenes containing numerous 3D primitives. The Z-coordinates of each facet indicate its distance from the camera. This distance is called depth. By sorting the z-values in a scene, the z-buffer algorithm can ensure that only the nearest facets are drawn. Because the nearest facets will obscure any facets farther from the camera in a rectangular view-volume as shown in Fig. 6-9, the z-buffer method is a trustworthy approximation of how human vision works in the real world.

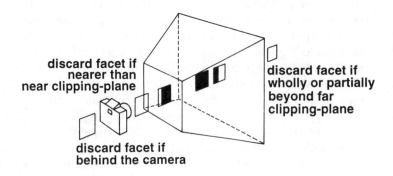

6-9 Conceptual representation of how the 3D routines clip and cull facets depending on their relationship to the 3D perspective view-volume. As shown here, only portions of facets depicted as solid color will be displayed by the modeling pipeline.

What is a z-buffer? A z-buffer is an array of bytes in memory. Each byte corresponds to a pixel on the viewport of your application's window. Each byte in the z-buffer contains the depth-value (the Z-value of the XYZ triplet) of the corresponding point in the nearest facet. As each facet is processed by the z-buffer algorithm, the value of a particular byte is changed if a smaller value (indicating a nearer facet) is discovered. When every point on every facet has been processed, as shown in Fig. 6-10, the z-buffer will contain the depth-values for only the nearest (visible) points in the scene.

At the same time the algorithm is calculating the depth-values, it is managing a frame-buffer. Like the z-buffer, the frame-buffer is an array of bytes. Each byte corresponds to a pixel on the viewport of your application's window. Whenever the algorithm writes a depth value to a byte in the z-buffer, it also writes a color value to the corresponding byte in the frame-buffer. When every point on every facet has been processed by the z-buffer algorithm, the frame-buffer will contain color values for each pixel on the viewport of your application's window.

Why use a z-buffer? The z-buffer depth-sorting algorithm is used by most b-rep modeling systems because it is foolproof. No matter how complicated the scene, the z-buffer depth-sorting method never fails to produce a visually correct image. This is because a z-buffer uses a pixel-based algorithm

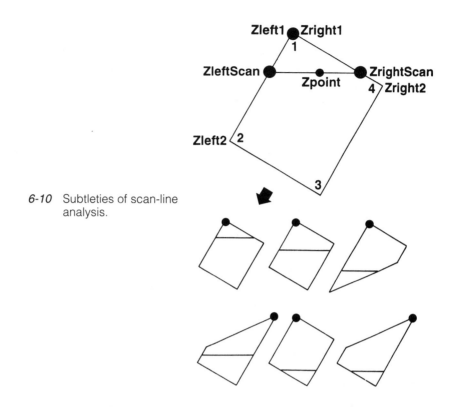

6-10 Subtleties of scan-line analysis.

where each point being processed corresponds to exactly one pixel on the display. Other hidden-surface methods sometimes use facet-based algorithms. These methods can easily become hamstrung by complicated scenes when they attempt to divide facets into ever-smaller rectangles in a bid to make sense of the scene.

Limitations of a byte-resolution z-buffer   As you'll soon learn, the 3D functions provided by the source code in the book use a z-buffer composed of bytes. One byte in the z-buffer corresponds to one byte on the viewport of the application's window. This arrangement keeps memory requirements small. Because each sample application uses a viewport 256 pixels across by 255 pixels high, a z-buffer of 65280 bytes can store the depth-values for all the pixels in the scene. However, a byte can store only 256 different values. This means the resolution of the z-buffer is limited to a range of 0 to 255. If the 3D world were 512 units deep, for example, the z-buffer could not differentiate between points differing by only one or two units of depth. In your own application development, you can overcome this limitation by using a z-buffer composed of integers or floating-point values.

Where do you go from here?

Now that you've learned how view geometry displays a 3D scene in the viewport of your application's window, you're ready to move ahead in 3D programming. The next few chapters teach you how to illuminate and shade surfaces, and how to create 3D primitives like boxes, spheres, cylinders, cones, wedges, and others.

7
Getting started with rendering

This chapter teaches you how to use rendering geometry to illuminate and shade the facets in a 3D scene. It discusses concepts like color, the light-source, and shadow maps.

The task—What you want to achieve

Your task in this chapter is to become familiar with rendering geometry. You want to know about RGB color and its cousin, descriptive color. You want to gain an understanding of light-sources and shadows, and to become aware of concepts like surface realism and transparency.

The plan—What you will learn

In this chapter you'll learn about RGB color and 8-bit, 256-color rendering. You'll delve into descriptive color and the special RGB codes for producing it. You'll also find out how to calculate the brightness of a facet in a 3D scene. You'll see how to position the light-source—and then discover how to change its location. You'll learn how shadows are rendered using a specialized buffer called a shadow-map. You'll investigate surface realism using texture mapping, reflection mapping, and detail polygons. You'll also find out how to render transparent surfaces using a looping algorithm. The rendering knowledge you'll acquire in this chapter will equip you to learn about 3D modeling in subsequent chapters.

Using RGB color

As you've already learned in the two previous chapters, *3D modeling* refers to functions that represent the shapes of three-dimensional objects. *Rendering* refers to methods that add color, shading, brightness, texture, and other surface attributes to 3D entities. Modeling and rendering rely upon three types of geometry:

- view geometry
- modeling geometry
- rendering geometry

View geometry manipulates and displays a 3D scene. *Modeling geometry* creates 3D primitives such as boxes, spheres, cylinders, cones, wedges, curved surfaces, and others. *Rendering geometry* calculates illumination values for the entities in a 3D scene. It then shades the facets of the entities, often supplementing the shading with texture, reflections, shadows, and detailing.

The b-rep modeling paradigm is the most popular 3D system used on personal computers today. That's because it is well-suited to the graphics capabilities of the Windows Graphics Device Interface (GDI). The GDI provides many functions useful for 3D programming, including:

- RGB()
- dithering
- CreateSolidBrush()
- CreatePolygonRgn()

Together, these four tools provide the following capabilities. The RGB() macro provides individual control over the RGB guns found in most VGA-compatible and SVGA-compatible display hardware. This makes it easy to specify pure hues in 256-color SVGA modes and 65,000-color accelerator-based modes, but even when Windows is running in a 16-color VGA mode the GDI's dithering engine can simulate almost any shade of any color. The CreateSolidBrush() function provides an efficient way to apply color to a region, and the CreatePolygonRgn() function can be used to define the facet-shaped region that is to be filled by the brush.

The call to CreateSolidBrush() takes one argument, the color. You indicate a color by using the GDI's RGB() macro to specify the intensities of the red, green, and blue guns. If the requested color is supported by the display adapter as a solid hue, the GDI provides it exactly as requested. RGB(0,0,127) is an example of a pure blue hue that is available on a VGA, but RGB(0,0,143) is a slightly brighter blue that is not one of 16 pure hues available on a VGA. If the requested color is not available on the display adapter, then the GDI uses dithering to simulate the color. As shown in Fig. 7-1, the 0-to-255 range of the RGB() macro is mapped by the GDI to the 0-to-63 range

255	203	151	99	47
251	199	147	95	43
247	195	143	91	39
243	191	139	87	35
239	187	135	83	31
235	183	131	79	27
231	179	127	75	23
227	175	123	71	19
223	171	119	67	15
219	167	115	63	11
215	163	111	59	7
211	159	107	55	3
207	155	103	51	0

127 produces solid normal intensity blue, green, cyan, red, magenta, brown, and gray. 191 produces solid light gray.

7-1 GDI dithering thresholds for specifying RGB colors in 4-bit 16-color modes.

available in the display hardware. This means that your application can call either RGB(127,127,127) or RGB(130,130,130) and the same medium gray will result. However, a call of RGB(131,131,131) produces a slightly brighter gray.

You must specify a color whenever you create a brush. You usually do this by specifying the intensities of the red, green, and blue guns. Because each gun provides a range of 64 different levels of intensity, the RGB() macro can describe 262,144 different colors (64 × 64 × 64 = 262,144). Because of hardware limitations, a VGA can simultaneously display only 16 of these colors as pure hues. The GDI can use dithering to approximate most of the remaining colors. Dithering is the mixing of pixels of available colors to create an approximate visual simulation of a color. If you request a 17th color on a 16-color VGA, the GDI attempts to fulfill your request by dithering. If you request a 17th color when Windows is running in a 256- color mode on an SVGA, the GDI can satisfy your request by providing a pure hue if you create your own palette.

8-bit, 256-color rendering

As you've already learned in previous chapters, a *palette* is a collection of colors. When Windows starts, it resets the display adapter in order to obtain a palette of colors suitable for general windowing operations. Your application can use this so-called *system palette*, but it can also use logical palettes defined by your application. If Windows is running in a 256-color mode, the colors you request for your logical palette will be provided as pure hues by the GDI. This is because an SVGA can simultaneously display any 256 of the 262,144 possible colors at the same time. Windows sets aside the first 20 hues for its own use, so your application define another 236 custom colors if it wants.

To create a logical palette your application must follow four steps:

1. Set up a data structure containing a description of the hues that will be contained in the palette.

2. Call CreatePalette() to create the logical palette.

3. Call SelectPalette() to select the palette into the display-context.

4. Call RealizePalette() to modify the color registers of the SVGA display adapter.

The sample application in chapter 9 shows how this is done for 3D modeling and shading. As you'll see, the sample application is smart enough to automatically support 3D modeling and rendering in both 16-color and 256-color modes. It does this by using a logical palette.

However, using 256 colors for rendering introduces two new factors which must be considered. These new factors are gamma correction and the human visual system.

As you've learned in previous chapters, *shading* means applying color to a facet corresponding to the brightness of the facet. *Brightness* is the level of illumination exhibited by the facet. The brightness of the facet is also called *virtual luminance*. Virtual luminance is expressed as a percentage from 0% (darkest) to 100% (brightest).

After a 3D rendering function has calculated the virtual luminance of a facet, the resulting value must be converted before being displayed. This conversion is necessary because most RGB displays do not produce noticeable pixel brightness until a gun's intensity reaches a level of 35. You've already learned that the Windows API specifies an intensity range of 0 to 255 for RGB displays. This means that the serviceable range of the guns is actually 35 to 255. The process that converts the virtual luminance value in order to compensate for this nonlinearity of the display hardware is called *gamma correction*. (By convention, early researchers used the gamma symbol in their mathematical equations for color correction, so the process has come to be known as gamma correction.)

The table in Fig. 7-2 shows a set of gamma-corrected intensity settings suitable for SVGA 256-color modes. You'll want to note, for example, that if the human eye is to perceive an intensity of 50%, your application must call RGB() with a value of 135, not 127, even though 127 is 50% of 255. The discrepancy is more dramatic at lower intensities. In order for the human eye to perceive 10% brightness, the RGB gun must be set to a value of 51, which is actually 21% of 255, as Fig. 7-2 illustrates. This is a significant

Virtual luminance conversions

Virtual	RGB	Virtual	RGB	Virtual	RGB	Virtual	RGB	Virtual	RGB
100%	255	80%	207	60%	159	40%	107	20%	67
99%	251	79%	203	59%	155	39%	103	19%	67
98%	251	78%	203	58%	155	38%	103	18%	63
97%	247	77%	199	57%	151	37%	99	17%	63
96%	247	76%	199	56%	151	36%	99	16%	63
95%	243	75%	195	55%	147	35%	95	15%	59
94%	239	74%	191	54%	143	34%	91	14%	59
93%	239	73%	191	53%	143	33%	91	13%	55
92%	235	72%	187	52%	139	32%	87	12%	55
91%	235	71%	187	51%	139	31%	87	11%	55
90%	231	70%	183	50%	135	30%	83	10%	51
89%	227	69%	179	49%	131	29%	83	9%	51
88%	227	68%	179	48%	131	28%	79	8%	47
87%	223	67%	175	47%	127	27%	79	7%	47
86%	223	66%	175	46%	123	26%	79	6%	47
85%	219	65%	171	45%	119	25%	75	5%	43
84%	215	64%	167	44%	115	24%	75	4%	43
83%	215	63%	167	43%	115	23%	71	3%	39
82%	211	62%	163	42%	111	22%	71	2%	39
81%	211	61%	163	41%	111	21%	71	1%	35

Valid for 8-bit, 16-bit, and 24-bit color modes
(including 256-color and 65536-color Windows modes)

7-2 Virtual luminance conversions for 8-bit 256-color modes. The luminance produced by the RGB guns is not a linear relationship and requires compensation at lower intensities.

margin of error which your application cannot afford to overlook when using a 256-color mode for 3D modeling and rendering.

Color shift is also a problem. Suppose, for example, you wish to display a virtual luminance value of (0,63,255), which is another way of saying 0% red, 25% green, and 100% blue. If you don't convert the values before you call RGB(), then the green component appears too low. The displayed color appears too blue. Without gamma correction, the displayed hue will be 0% red, 18% green, and 100% blue, as shown in Fig. 7-2. What was wanted was a green component of 25%, not 18%. If your application does not consider gamma correction, then not only is the contrast distorted, but even the hue itself might shift—introducing a reddish, greenish, or bluish tinge to your 3D entity.

The situation is further complicated by the idiosyncrasies of the human eye. It is more sensitive to comparative ratios than absolute values. Here is an example. Your eye perceives the difference between medium gray (127,127,127) and light gray (191,191,191) as much greater than the difference between light gray (191,191,191) and bright white (255,255,255), even though both use an intensity difference of 64 units (191−127=64 and 255−191=64). Medium gray is two-thirds of light gray, so your eye reacts more acutely because, in the second example, light gray is only three-quarters of bright white (127/191=.67 and 191/255=.75).

Many of these difficulties are avoided if your application is running in the 16-color VGA mode because when Windows dithers the colors it provides a coarse implementation of gamma correction.

Using descriptive color

When most people think of color, they don't visualize it as the red, green, blue, cyan, magenta, brown, and yellow of the RGB color system. Most individuals are more comfortable with descriptions like sky blue, cadmium yellow, lime green, and antique white. This is called *subjective color* or *descriptive color.*

Nominal descriptive color for 3D entities

Your application can use nominal descriptive color to render 3D primitives in a wider variety of hues. As you'll soon see, the 3D functions provided in this book can render 3D solids in shades of red, green, blue, cyan, magenta, brown, and gray. However, you can easily adapt the source code to offer hues such as navy blue, gold, olive green, and others.

RGB codes for subjective color

The table in Fig. 7-3 provides RGB intensity settings for different flavors of white, gray, and black. Note, for example, how shifting the values of the red and blue settings can produce the perception of a warm gray or a cold gray. As Fig. 7-3 shows, the same subtle manipulations can be used to produce white, ivory, titanium white, and antique white.

Subjective color			
Color	Red	Green	Blue
White	255	255	255
Ivory	255	255	243
Titanium White	255	255	247
Antique White	251	235	215
Light Gray	191	191	191
Dark Gray	127	127	127
Cold Gray	115	127	127
Warm Gray	127	127	107
Black	0	0	0
Ivory Black	23	23	15
Lamp Black	15	23	19

7-3 RGB intensity values for subjective colors in the white, gray, and black spectrum.

The table in Fig. 7-4 provides RGB intensity settings for different blends of blue, including sky blue and navy blue. The table in Fig. 7-5 shows how

7-4 RGB intensity values for
subjective colors in the
blue spectrum.

Subjective color			
Color	Red	Green	Blue
Blue	0	0	255
Navy Blue	0	0	127
Sky Blue	127	191	235
Sky Blue (light)	127	191	255
Sky Blue (dark)	63	127	235

7-5 RGB intensity values for
subjective colors in the
yellow spectrum.

Subjective color			
Color	Red	Green	Blue
Yellow	255	255	0
Light Yellow	255	255	191
Gold	255	215	11
Cadmium Yellow	255	191	15

7-6 RGB intensity values for
subjective colors in the
green spectrum.

Subjective color			
Color	Red	Green	Blue
Green	0	255	0
Dark Green	0	127	0
Olive Green	79	127	63
Lime Green	63	207	63

to produce light yellow, cadmium yellow, and gold for your 3D primitives. The table in Fig. 7-6 provides RGB intensity settings for green, dark green, olive green, and lime green.

In order to use descriptive color in your 3D modeling and rendering application, you must take into account the relative strengths of the RGB settings, not the absolute values. Suppose, for example, that your application is rendering a 3D primitive using the color orange. The conversion table in Fig. 7-7 shows the correct intensity settings for different illumination levels. If 100% orange is defined as 255,127,0, then 50% orange will be 127,63,0. You'll want to note how the ratio between the red and green guns has been preserved. In this simplified example the blue gun has no effect because it is off.

The table in Fig. 7-8 uses a more complicated example. The color salmon is described in RGB terms as 255,127,115. Notice the subtle difference between the green and blue guns. As Fig. 7-8 shows, it becomes difficult to preserve this subtlety at a brightness of 10% or 20%.

Setting the light-source location

The light-source plays a critical role in shading calculations. Its location relative to a facet determines the level of illumination falling on the facet.

Subjective color shading algorithm			
Facet shading	**Red**	**Green**	**Blue**
100% (ie Orange)	255	127	0
90%	227	111	0
80%	203	99	0
70%	175	87	0
60%	151	75	0
50%	127	63	0
40%	99	47	0
30%	75	35	0
20%	51	23	0
10%	23	11	0
0% (ie Black)	0	0	0

7-7 RGB intensity values for subjective orange at different levels of illumination.

Subjective color shading algorithm			
Facet shading	**Red**	**Green**	**Blue**
100% (ie Salmon)	255	127	115
90%	227	111	103
80%	203	99	91
70%	175	87	79
60%	151	75	67
50%	127	63	55
40%	99	47	43
30%	75	35	31
20%	51	23	23
10%	23	11	11
0% (ie Black)	0	0	0

7-8 RGB intensity values for subjective Salmon orange at different levels of illumination.

This influences the brightness of the facet, which can range from 0% to 100%.

Calculating illumination intensity

Shaded models are built using facets. Each facet is shaded according to the intensity of light striking each facet. As you discovered in previous chapters, rendering geometry calculates an illumination value for each facet or pixel in a scene. Rendering geometry relies upon an illumination model, which is a paradigm explaining how surfaces and illumination are expected to act. Different illumination models are used, including facet shading, color interpolation shading, normal-vector interpolation shading, and others. The 3D functions in this book use facet shading.

Facet shading is also called *constant shading, flat shading,* and *Lambert shading.* The relationship between the incoming light ray and the surface normal of the facet determines the brightness of a facet. This relationship is called Lambert's cosine law.

This law specifies that the cosine of the angle between an incoming light ray vector and the surface normal vector of a facet is equal to the dot product of these two vectors divided by the product of the length of these two vectors. (For a lightning course in rendering math, refer to Appendix D, "Math primer for graphics programming." The *surface normal* is a line that is perpendicular to the surface of the facet plane. A *vector* describes both magnitude and direction.)

What all this convoluted mathematical terminology means is that it's relatively straightforward for the software to calculate the angle at which light rays are striking the surface of the facet. If the angle between the light ray and the facet's surface normal is 0°, this means the light ray is perpendicular to the facet. It is producing maximum brilliance. If the angle between the light ray and the facet's surface normal is 90° or greater, this means no light is striking the facet. It is cloaked in shadow. The brightness of the facet can be altered only if your application repositions either the facet or the light-source.

Moving the light-source

Moving the light-source can be accomplished by redefining the vector that describes the incoming light ray. Because most b-rep modeling systems define the light ray as a unit vector, this redefinition is not difficult.

A *unit vector* is a vector with a magnitude (length) of one unit. In 3D geometry, a vector is comprised of X, Y, and Z components. The square of the vector's length is equal to the sum of the squares of its three components. Because the magnitude of a unit vector is always one unit, this means that the sum of the squares of the vector's components always equals one. If your application specifies a heading and an altitude for the light source, the three components of the unit vector can be calculated by four short lines of code using trigonometry. The appropriate code is analyzed when the sample 3D application in chapter 9 is discussed.

Rendering shadows

Many b-rep modeling systems can render shadows using an algorithm derived from the Z-buffer depth-sort algorithm. As you learned in previous chapters, *Z-buffer depth-sorting* is a method of hidden-surface removal that is used to process complex 3D scenes containing a number of individual 3D primitives. The Z-coordinates of each facet indicate its distance or depth from the camera. By sorting the Z-values in a scene, the software can identify the nearest facets. Because the nearest facets obscure any facets farther from the camera, the Z-buffer method is a foolproof system for hidden-surface removal.

Moving the camera to the light-source location

If the camera position is temporarily moved to the location of the light-source, a special type of Z-buffer is produced called a *shadow-map*. As Fig.

7-9 shows, a shadow-map can be used to discover the shape of shadows in a 3D scene. If the camera (repositioned at the light-source) cannot see a facet, it is because a nearer facet is obscuring the facet. The nearer facet receives the light and the farther facet falls within the shadow cast by the nearer facet.

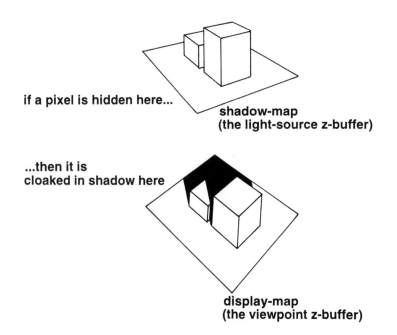

7-9 Conceptual representation of the relationship between shadow-map and display-map when rendering shadows in a Z-buffer 3D modeling pipeline.

The shadow-map

A shadow-map is, in effect, a light-source Z-buffer. Or, stated more precisely, it corresponds to the frame-buffer used by the Z-buffer depth-sort functions. The shadow-map is an array of bytes representing the pixels of an imaginary viewport that represents the scene the light-source sees.

Using the shadow-map modeling pipeline

In order to derive and display the shadows in a 3D scene, an application uses a shadow-map modeling pipeline. The steps involved are:

1. Move the camera to the light-source position.
2. Store depth-values in the shadow map.
3. For each facet being rendered. . .
   a. if the facet faces away from the light-source set a shadow-indicator to TRUE;

b. else if the facet is partly or wholly obscured by another facet, set the shadow-indicator to TRUE;

c. else set the shadow-token to FALSE.

d. Move the camera back to the observer's viewpoint.

e. If the shadow-indicator is FALSE, then render the facet, loop back to Step 3, and continue with the next facet;

f. else if the shadow-indicator is TRUE, then for each pixel in the facet. . .

    (1) use reverse-modeling and calculate world coordinates;

    (2) move the camera to the light-source position, determine if the pixel is obscured, and set a pixel shadow-indicator to TRUE or FALSE;

    (3) move the camera back to the observer's viewpoint;

    (4) if the pixel shadow-indicator is TRUE, then render the pixel in shadow;

    (5) else render the pixel in illumination.

Ray-tracing a 3D scene

Rendering geometry can also be used to ray-trace a 3D scene. As Fig. 7-10 shows, the 3D perspective view-volume can be pierced by vectors emanating from the camera position. These vectors, which correspond to lines-of-sight, can be projected onto a view-plane window. If the view-plane window is partitioned into a grid corresponding to the dimensions of the viewport of

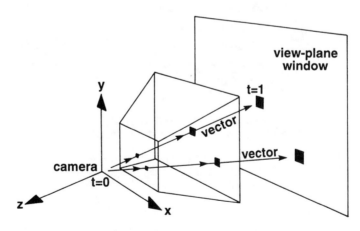

Parametric representation of a vector

$$x = x_{start} + t(x_{change})$$
$$y = y_{start} + t(y_{change})$$
$$z = z_{start} + t(z_{change})$$

7-10 Conceptual representation of ray-tracing geometry.

the application's window, then the first point struck by the line-of-sight will be rendered.

In order to calculate the intersection of a vector with a facet in 3D space, as shown in Fig. 7-11, the standard equation for a plane is used, as shown in Fig. 7-12. A typical ray-tracing algorithm follows four steps.

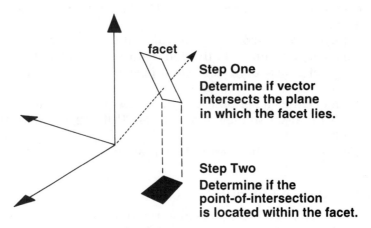

Step One
Determine if vector intersects the plane in which the facet lies.

Step Two
Determine if the point-of-intersection is located within the facet.

7-11 Conceptual representation of intersection geometry used in ray-tracing calculations.

equation of a plane: ax + by + cz = 0

parametric representation of a vector:

$$x = x_{start} + t(\, x_{change})$$
$$y = y_{start} + t(\, y_{change})$$
$$z = z_{start} + t(\, z_{change})$$

$$t = -\frac{(\, ax + by + cz + d\,)}{(\, ax + by + cz\,)}$$

if the denominator is 0, then the vector and plane do not intersect

7-12 The standard equation for a plane can be used to determine if a light-ray intersects the plane in which a facet lies.

1. Partition the view-plane window with a grid that matches the resolution of the display viewport.

2. Select a point on the view-plane window that corresponds to the pixel being tested, as shown in Fig. 7-10.

3. Establish the vector from the camera position at 0,0,0 to the selected point on the view-plane window.

4. Use the vector to find the appropriate intersections with 3D entities inside the 3D perspective view-volume, as shown in Fig. 7-11 and Fig. 7-12.

For a refresher course in vector mathematics, refer to Appendix D, Math primer for graphics programming.

Surface realism

Your application can enhance the realism of 3D entities by using three additional techniques of rendering geometry. These techniques are:

- texture mapping
- reflection mapping
- detail polygons

Texture mapping

Texture mapping uses bitmap images of textures and patterns. Texture mapping is also called *pattern mapping*. Each pixel (also called a texel) of the two-dimensional bitmap is transformed through the various coordinate systems of the 3D transformation sequence. It can thus be mapped onto the surface of the corresponding facets of the 3D entity.

Reflection mapping

Reflection mapping is a technique for adding reflections to a facet. These reflections correspond to other facets that are present in the 3D scene. The reflection mapping algorithm works in a manner similar to the shadow-map algorithm already described in this chapter. If the camera is temporarily moved to the location of the facet, then the image the camera sees will be the image that should be applied to the facet. The pattern mapping technique described in the previous paragraph can be used to map the reflected image (seen by the camera) to the facet.

Detail polygons

Detail polygons are two-dimensional polygons containing extra detail for an otherwise solid facet in a 3D scene. A 3D architectural image, for example, might make use of detail polygons for doors. The detail polygon would be a line drawing of the trim, moldings, and hardware that are found on the door. After the 3D scene has been modeled, the various line endpoints in the detail polygon are transformed through the 3D visualization pipeline and mapped onto the 3D facet that represents the door. This technique works well with the b-rep modeling system.

Rendering transparent surfaces

Even transparent surfaces can be rendered using the Z-buffer depth-sort algorithm, especially if the surfaces do not refract (bend) the light waves that pass through them.

Z-buffer-based non-refractive transparency

By using four buffers, a system can be implemented for Z-buffer-based nonrefractive transparency. One buffer each is used to store the transparency values, tokens, colors, and Z-depths for each pixel in the 3D scene. These buffers are called *transparent buffers.*

The transparency-rendering loop

A looping algorithm can be used to build the 3D scene. This is called a *transparency-rendering loop.* It operates by rendering transparent facets from farthest to nearest, gradually modifying the hue of the affected pixel.

1. Render all opaque facets using the conventional Z-buffer depth-sort method.
2. Process all transparent facets into the transparent buffers, storing a transparency value, a token, the color, and the depth-value.
3. For each pixel in the scene, if the transparent Z-buffer value is nearer than the opaque Z-buffer depth-value, then calculate and reset the transparency value, token, color, and depth-value for the various transparent buffers.
4. If the pixel's token is on, interpolate the transparent buffers with the opaque Z-buffer and frame-buffer by using the transparency value. The transparent depth-value of a pixel replaces the depth-value in the opaque Z-buffer and the token is reset to off.
5. Return to Step 3 and repeat the process to render progressively nearer transparent points at each pixel location.

Where do you go from here?

Now that you've learned how rendering geometry can display the entities in a 3D scene, you're ready to move on to modeling. The next chapter teaches you how to create 3D primitives like boxes, spheres, cylinders, cones, wedges, and others.

8
Getting started with modeling

This chapter teaches you how to use modeling geometry to create 3D entities. It describes the fundamental concepts of 3D primitive modeling and then goes on to discuss hierarchical modeling techniques.

The task—What you want to achieve

Your task in this chapter is to familiarize yourself with modeling geometry. You want to know how to model 3D primitives such as boxes, spheres, cylinders, cones, wedges, and others. You want to be aware of concepts like sweeps, extrusions, and meshes. You want to know about hierarchical modeling and how it can be used to build complex solids with features like flexible joints and rotating parts.

The plan—What you will learn

In this chapter you'll learn how to manipulate the XYZ object coordinates of 3D object-space in order to construct primitives such as boxes, deformed boxes, spheres, half-spheres, cylinders, half-cylinders, cones, wedges, curved surfaces, bulged surfaces, and others. You'll see how to use sweeps, extrusions, and meshes to extend your modeling prowess. You'll become familiar with hierarchical modeling, and you'll discover how parents and progeny can be used to build complex 3D solids with moving parts. You'll learn about different types of 3D editors, including primitive modelers, hierarchical modelers, staging editors, and articulated motion editors. You'll find out about advanced concepts like elision, pruning, and culling. The modeling knowledge you're about to acquire in this chapter will provide you with the background you need to master more advanced material later in the book.

Modeling geometry

As you learned in previous chapters, modeling geometry creates individual *3D primitives.* A 3D primitive is a simple solid like a parallelepiped, a sphere, a cylinder, a cone, a wedge, and others. 3D primitives are also called *entities* and *subobjects.*

3D primitives are built from *facets.* Facets are flat polygons used to model the exterior surface of a 3D primitive. As you've already learned, this paradigm is called *boundary representation (b-rep) modeling.* A box, for example, consists of six facets.

Before a primitive can be displayed as part of a 3D scene, it must be *transformed.* 3D transformations are manipulations in 3D space. The sum of the transformations is the *3D transformation sequence* (also called the *3D visualization pipeline).*

As you've already learned, any location in 3D space can be described by its XYZ coordinates, relative to the *origin.* The origin is the center of the 3D space, specified as XYZ coordinates 0,0,0. The 3D transformation sequence contains different types of 3D space, each with its own coordinate system. In 3D space, X refers to left or right, Y refers to up or down, and Z refers to near or far. A typical 3D transformation sequence consists of:

- object coordinates
- structure coordinates
- world coordinates
- camera coordinates
- image-plane coordinates
- raster coordinates

A 3D primitive must be transformed through each of these coordinate systems before it can be displayed. Each coordinate system represents a different form of 3D space. *Object coordinates,* the primary topic of this chapter, represent object-space. Object coordinates are XYZ coordinates that define the fundamental shape and size of a 3D primitive such as a box, sphere, cylinder, cone, wedge, and others. By manipulating the size, shape, and location of the facets that make up a primitive in 3D object-space, you can construct different types of primitive solids. By combining primitive solids in 3D structure-space, you can construct different types of complex solids.

As you've already learned in previous chapters, each coordinate system in the 3D visualization pipeline coexists with a spherical coordinate system, sharing the same 3D space. The XYZ coordinate system uses X, Y, and Z distances to describe a 3D entity. The *spherical coordinate system* uses yaw, roll, and pitch angles to describe the 3D entity. Yaw refers to compass headings, roll means tilting left or right, and pitch means tilting forward or back.

These two coordinate systems provide the tools for modeling different 3D primitives like boxes, spheres, cylinders, cones, wedges, and others. You can use the XYZ coordinate system to move (translate) a facet to a particular location. Then you can use the spherical coordinate system to spin (rotate) the facet into a particular orientation. You can thus build any primitive solid you want at any size and orientation in 3D object-space.

Parallelepipeds

A parallelepiped is a box-like primitive. Six facets are all that's needed to construct a parallelepiped, as shown in Fig. 8-1. The resulting box possesses eight vertices. The XYZ coordinates of these vertices can be inspected by different functions when the primitive is modeled, when back-face culling is implemented, and when the facets are shaded.

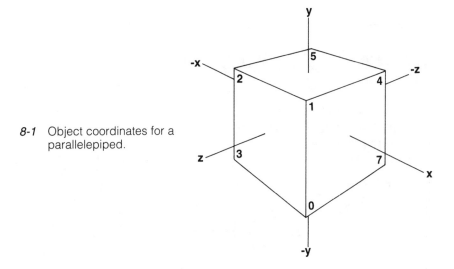

8-1 Object coordinates for a parallelepiped.

Consider, for example, the facet that is bounded by vertices 0, 1, 2, and 3 in Fig. 8-1. As you learned in previous chapters, programmers using the b-rep modeling paradigm always describe a facet using vertices ordered in a counterclockwise direction when the facet is viewed from outside the solid. The 0-1-2-3 facet lies in the XY plane of the 3D object-space coordinate system. This means that the Z-value for each vertex is identical. The 0-7-4-1 facet lies in the YZ plane. This means that the X-value for each of its vertices is identical. Only the Y and Z coordinates vary. You could, of course, define a box not positioned at right angles in the 3D coordinate system, but it would add an unnecessary extra amount of work. (Because the box passes through the 3D transformation sequence, it can always be rotated

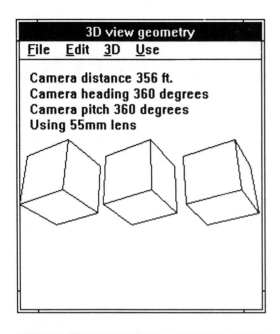

3D view geometry

File   Edit   3D   Use

Camera distance 356 ft.
Camera heading 360 degrees
Camera pitch 360 degrees
Using 55mm lens

8-2 The sample application objects.c is a 3D sampler capable of producing a variety of subobjects, including boxes (parallelepipeds), shown here running in wire-frame mode.

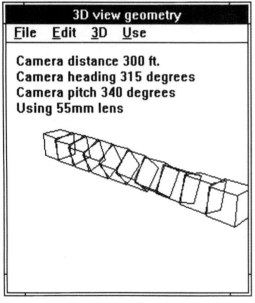

3D view geometry

File   Edit   3D   Use

Camera distance 300 ft.
Camera heading 315 degrees
Camera pitch 340 degrees
Using 55mm lens

8-3 The 3D sampler can orient a subobject to any yaw, roll, or pitch angle. The sample application objects.c is shown here running in wire-frame mode.

during later stages.) The main objective of object-space, after all, is to define the fundamental shape of the primitive.

Spheres and half-spheres

A typical sphere produced by the sample application in the next chapter is shown in Fig. 8-5. Here is how it is built. First, a function calculates 36

8-4 The sample application startup.c can create new subobjects by deforming existing primitives.

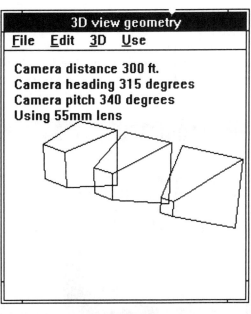

8-5 The 3D sampler can generate spheres of various sizes at different locations and orientations in 3D-space. The sample application objects.c is shown here running in wire-frame mode. See FIG. 8-6 for fully-shaded mode. See FIG. 8-7 for a half-sphere.

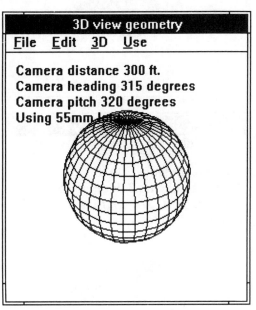

vertices evenly spaced around the girth of the sphere. Next, the same function uses sine and cosine to compute another set of corresponding vertices for a line 20° south of the first line. Together, these two sets of vertices can provide four corners for each of 36 facets forming a belt around the girth of the sphere. By using a loop, the program can read the appropriate vertices in counterclockwise order and use back-face culling as each facet is rendered. After the belt is finished, the software begins work on the next belt.

To build a half-sphere, the software uses the origin (0,0,0) as a vertex and then uses sine and cosine to calculate a set of 36 vertices around the equator of the sphere, as shown in Fig. 8-7. A series of three-sided facets are rendered in order to construct the flat surface of the halved sphere.

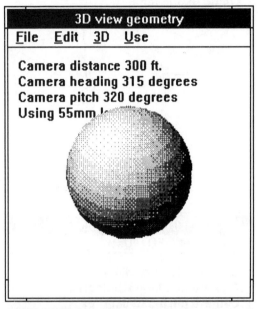

8-6 A sphere rendered in shaded mode. The sample application objects.c can generate a variety of primitives, including spheres, cylinders, cones, wedges, curved surfaces, complex assemblies, and others. See FIG. 8-5 for wire-frame mode.

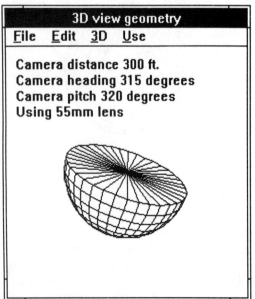

8-7 A half-sphere rendered in wire-frame mode by the sample application objects.c. See FIG. 8-5 for a full sphere.

Cylinders and half-cylinders

A typical cylinder produced by the sample application in the next chapter is shown in Fig. 8-8. You can think of this cylinder as a disk that has been extruded (stretched) along the Z-axis. A modeling function sets the XY

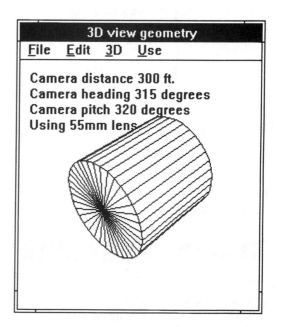

3D view geometry

File   Edit   3D   Use

Camera distance 300 ft.
Camera heading 315 degrees
Camera pitch 320 degrees
Using 55mm lens

8-8 A cylinder rendered in wire-frame mode by the sample application objects.c. See FIG. 8-9 for a half-cylinder.

coordinates to 0 and moves the Z-coordinate to the nearest end of the cylinder. The software then calculates a set of 36 vertices around the circumference of the cylinder. The code then moves the Z-coordinate to the farthest end of the cylinder and recalculates a set of 36 vertices around the circumference of the cylinder. By using a loop to select from these two sets of XYZ coordinates, the program can build the facets that make up the curved surface of the cylinder. To build the half-cylinder shown in Fig. 8-9, a single facet is used and only half of the curved surface is rendered.

Cones and wedges

A typical cone produced by the sample application in the next chapter is illustrated in Fig. 8-10. After calculating the vertices that make up the disk at the bottom of the cone, the software simply uses a single point to help it build the three-sided facets that make up the curved surface of the cone.

A set of wedges produced by the sample application in the next chapter is shown in Fig. 8-11. The program uses a simple variation of the technique for parallelepipeds, described previously.

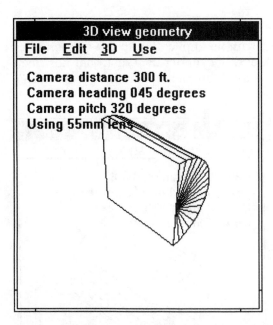

3D view geometry

File   Edit   3D   Use

Camera distance 300 ft.
Camera heading 045 degrees
Camera pitch 320 degrees
Using 55mm lens

8-9 A half-cylinder rendered in wire-frame mode by the sample application objects.c. See FIG. 8-8 for a full cylinder.

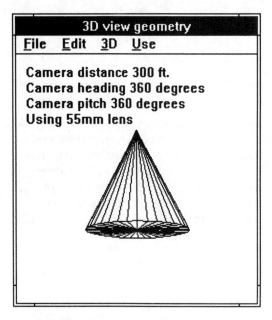

3D view geometry

File   Edit   3D   Use

Camera distance 300 ft.
Camera heading 360 degrees
Camera pitch 360 degrees
Using 55mm lens

8-10 A 3D cone rendered in wire-frame mode by the sample application objects.c.

Curved surfaces

A typical curved surface produced by the sample application in the next chapter is shown in Fig. 8-12. Here is how it's done: first, a parametric equation for a 2D curved line is used to generate a set of XY coordinates for a curve. Next, the 3D functions set the Z-value to an appropriate depth

8-11 A selection of 3D wedges rendered in wire-frame mode by the sample application objects.c.

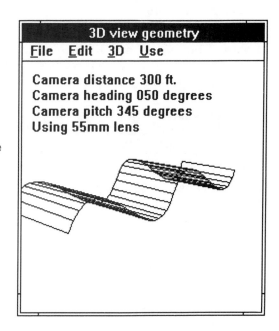

3D view geometry

File   Edit   3D   Use

Camera distance 300 ft.
Camera heading 315 degrees
Camera pitch 340 degrees
Using 55mm lens

8-12 A curved surface rendered in wire-frame mode by the sample application objects.c. See FIG. 8-13 for shaded mode.

3D view geometry

File   Edit   3D   Use

Camera distance 300 ft.
Camera heading 050 degrees
Camera pitch 345 degrees
Using 55mm lens

and calculate the XYZ object-coordinates for the near edge of the curved surface. The program then resets the Z-value to an appropriate depth for the far edge of the curved surface and calculates another set of XYZ object coordinates. The vertices along the two curves can then be used to model the facets that make up the surface. By modifying the parametric equation for a 2D curved line, the sample application can generate a bulged surface like the one shown in Fig. 8-14.

Extensible techniques

Many of the modeling techniques you've just learned are really just simplifications of advanced techniques like sweeps, extrusions, and meshes. By carefully manipulating the XYZ coordinates of the vertices that make up a facet, you can position the facet anywhere in 3D object-space. By combining facets you can construct 3D solids of different shapes. You're usually either *extruding* or *sweeping*.

Sweeps Sweeps add a third dimension to a 2D shape. As you've already learned, you can sweep a facet around successive belts to build a 3D sphere. Another way of constructing the curved surface shown in Fig. 8-13 is to build a facet and sweep it along a parametric curve. A sweep is really just a curved extrusion.

Extrusions Extrusions also add a third dimension to a 2D shape. When you extrude a shape, you pull it out from the 2D plane on which it's drawn. Consider a drawing of a 2D disk, for example. If you extrude a disk by pulling it up from its 2D plane, you can create a cylinder.

Meshes The curved surface shown in Fig. 8-13 and the bulged surface shown in Fig. 8-14 are *simplified meshes*. Only two sides of each primitive are curved. The other two sides are straight lines. If the program is retooled

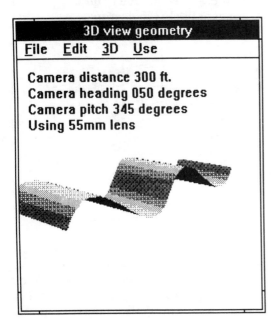

8-13 A curved surface rendered in shaded mode by the sample application objects.c. See FIG. 8-12 for wireframe mode.

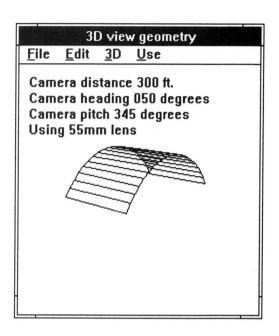

8-14 A bulged surface rendered in wire-frame mode by the sample application objects.c.

to produced a primitive possessing four curved sides, then the resulting mesh of facets can be used to model free-form curves.

Hierarchical modeling

As you've already learned, *structure coordinates* are part of the 3D transformation sequence. They are XYZ coordinates that describe a 3D primitive as part of a group of primitives forming a more complex structure.

Structure coordinates describe structure-space and they are used in so-called *hierarchical operations.* Hierarchical modeling can build complex 3D solids by attaching primitives to each other. These complex solids are called *structures, assemblies, subassemblies,* or *hierarchies.* A hierarchical structure can contain flexible joints, moving parts, rotating elements, and so on. This is possible because the XYZ coordinates of some primitives (the progeny) are defined as offsets which are relative to other primitives (their parents). Parents and progeny together form the complex 3D structure. Structures with moving parts are called *articulated entities.* B-rep modeling systems that offer hierarchical modeling capabilities must often provide a suite of different 3D editors.

Types of 3D editors

A hierarchical modeling environment typically provides a *primitives modeler,* a *hierarchical modeler,* a *staging editor,* and an *articulated motion editor.*

Primitives modeler   A primitives modeler provides interactive tools that allow the user to build 3D primitives such as boxes, spheres, cylinders, cones, wedges, and others.

Hierarchical modeler   A hierarchical modeler provides interactive tools that allow the user to combine together primitives in order to construct complex 3D solids. As you'll soon see, the sample application in the next chapter demonstrates functions suitable for both a primitives modeler and a hierarchical modeler.

Staging editor   A staging editor provides interactive tools that allow the user to specify the location (in world-space) of a stand-alone primitive or a structure. You can think of this as choreographing an animation sequence. As you'll discover, all of the animation demos in the book provide functions typically found in a staging editor. The 3D kinematics sampler described in chapter 17, "Kinematics programming," provides source code that uses physically-based animation to automate the staging process.

Articulated motion editor   An articulated motion editor provides interactive tools that allow the user to indicate the movement of a limb or component of a complex 3D solid. Such movement is called *articulated motion.* Think of it this way: the staging editor is used to specify the locations of a 3D robotic structure as it moves through the 3D world. The articulated motion editor is used to describe the sway of the robot's arms and the sweep of the robot's legs as the android (the structure) travels across the 3D world. The staging editor defines global movement while the articulated motion editor defines local movement. The animated sample application described in chapter 13, "3D motion-control programming," provides source code to implement articulated motion in hierarchical models.

Using subassemblies

A typical structure or *subassembly* produced by the sample application in the next chapter is shown in Fig. 8-15. A fully shaded version is depicted in Fig. 8-16. A *subassembly modeling pipeline* makes it easy to construct complex 3D solids.

The subassembly modeling pipeline   The table in Fig. 8-17 describes the purposes of various stages in the subassembly modeling pipeline. Structure coordinates are used in order to define the 3D subassembly by translating (moving), extruding (resizing), and rotating (spinning) the 3D primitives comprising the assembly. If a primitive (the progeny) is defined in XYZ coordinates expressed relative to another primitive (the parent), then the position of the progeny can be articulated, especially if the parent and progeny share a common interface. That interface can be a joint, an axle, a fulcrum, a hinge, and so on. Both parent and progeny abut the common interface.

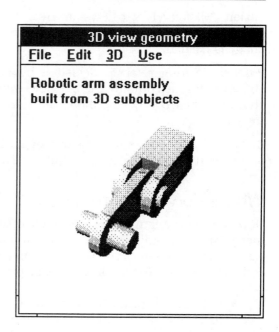

3D view geometry

File   Edit   3D   Use

**Robotic arm assembly
built from 3D subobjects**

8-15 A complex assembly
rendered in wire-frame
mode by the sample
application objects.c.
See FIG. 8-16 for
shaded mode.

3D view geometry

File   Edit   3D   Use

**Robotic arm assembly
built from 3D subobjects**

8-16 A complex assembly
rendered in shaded
mode by the sample
application objects.c.
See FIG. 8-15 for wire-
frame mode.

Complicated 3D structures often require a formal database in order to simplify the storage, manipulation, and retrieval of XYZ structure coordinates. When the 3D modeler works its way through the database, it often uses specialized operations like *elision, pruning,* and *culling.*

Subassembly modeling pipeline	
Object coordinates	The 3D definition of a subobject like a box, sphere, cylinder, wedge, cone, etc.
Structure coordinates	A 3D assembly defined as the rotation, translation, and extrusion of objects comprising the assembly.
World coordinates	The rotation and translation of the structure coordinates to position the assembly in the 3D world.
Camera coordinates	How the 3D world and its contents appears to a camera at a particular viewpoint and orientation.
View-plane coordinates	How the 3D image appears on a two-dimensional viewport placed in front of the camera.
Raster coordinates	How the image appears after being reduced or enlarged to fit the raster viewport (the display).

8-17 The subassembly hierarchical modeling pipeline.

Elision   Elision refers to decisions by a 3D modeler to refrain from rendering primitives or structures when the entity is distant or when only a simplified image is needed.

Pruning   Pruning refers to decisions by a 3D modeler to discard an entire structure if it lies outside the 3D view-volume. As you learned in previous chapters, the 3D view-volume is the volume of 3D space that is visible to the camera.

Culling   Culling refers to decisions by a 3D modeler to discard a primitive or a structure if rendering it would involve only a few pixels.

Where do you go from here?

Now that you've familiarized yourself with view geometry, rendering geometry, and modeling geometry, you're ready to delve into a hands-on tutorial. In the next chapter you'll have an opportunity to inspect working source code for a sample 3D application that provides features such as:

- built-in 3D primitives, including user-selectable boxes, spheres, half-spheres, cylinders, half-cylinders, cones, wedges, deformable parallelepipeds, curved surfaces, bulged surfaces, and others
- automatic back-face culling of 3D solids
- Z-buffer depth-sort removal of hidden-surfaces in scenes with numerous 3D entities
- a user-selectable, movable light-source

- user-selectable rendering modes, including wire-frame and fully shaded
- user-selectable shading colors, including blue, green, red, cyan, magenta, brown, and gray
- hierarchical modeling capabilities, including a complex solid with a flexible joint
- an adjustable camera focal-length
- a movable near clipping-plane
- a camera mode that is compatible with virtual reality application development

The knowledge you've acquired in this and the two previous chapters provides you with the savvy you need to understand how the sample application works—and you'll have the ability to paste its functions into your own projects if you want.

9
Tutorial: 3D programming

This chapter provides a hands-on tutorial that exercises the 3D skills you learned in the previous four chapters. You'll require these programming skills to develop animation, simulation, visualization, and virtual reality applications. In this chapter you'll find a User's Guide that shows you how to operate the sample application and a Programmer's Guide that provides detailed explanations of the source code for both the sample application and the underlying 3D toolkits.

The task—What you want to achieve

Your task in this chapter is to familiarize yourself with how the source code works in the sample application. You want to see how 3D primitives like boxes, spheres, cylinders, cones, wedges, and others are constructed and displayed. You want to understand how to toggle between wire-frame and fully shaded displays. You want to see how to manipulate the camera. Your most important task, however, is to learn how to use the functions of the 3D toolset in your own graphics applications.

The plan—What you will learn

In this chapter you'll see how to use XYZ object coordinates to build 3D primitives like boxes, deformed boxes, clipped boxes, spheres, half-spheres, cylinders, half-cylinders, cones, wedges, curved surfaces, bulged surfaces, and others. You'll find out how to move the near clipping-plane in order to clip primitives that are too near to the camera. You'll discover how to build complex structures using the techniques of hierarchical modeling. You'll learn how to adjust the camera's focal length and how to disable the camera's fixed-target mode in order to facilitate virtual reality programming. You'll become familiar with how the various parts of a 3D application are put together.

User's guide to the sample application

In this section you'll learn how to use the sample application named objects. Before you can run it you must build it. The source listings for the sample application are presented as Fig. C-2 in Appendix C. Source listings for the 3D toolkits that must be linked-in to build the finished application are presented in Appendix B. All source files are also provided on the companion disk. See Appendix A if you need assistance compiling the program.

Starting the sample application

There are two ways to start the sample application. You can start it directly from your compiler's editor or you can start it from Windows' Program Manager.

Startup from your compiler's editor   If you're using a Windows-hosted editor you can run the sample application directly from your editor. Examples of Windows-hosted editors include QuickC for Windows, Microsoft Visual C++, Turbo C++ for Windows, Borland C++, and others.

Startup from Windows' Program Manager   If you've already compiled the sample application, you can start it from Windows' Program Manager. From the Windows desktop, pull down the File menu and select Run. When the dialog box appears, type the full pathname of the program. The full pathname includes the drive letter, directories, subdirectories, filename, and extension of the program you want Program Manager to run. Here's an example.

    c:\director\ subdirectory\objects.exe

You'll want to substitute directory names that reflect your own system. When you select the OK button of the dialog box the sample application will be launched.

Using the sample application

When the sample application starts up, a splash sign-on notice appears. Choose OK to continue.

Four menus are listed on the demo's menu bar. They are File, Edit, 3D, and Use. You can use the File menu to quit the program. The Edit menu contains no active features. You can use the 3D menu to explore 3D primitives, hierarchical modeling, light-source shading, toggling the rendering mode, adjusting the camera focal length, and more. Select the Use menu to explore the run-time system, including display resolution, available colors, memory mode, and Windows version.

You can use either a mouse or the keyboard to operate this sample application. If you're using a mouse, simply point and click. If you're using the keyboard, press Alt to move the focus to the menu bar, then press the appropriate underscored mnemonic key to pull down a menu, then press a mnemonic key to select an item from the menu. You can also use the up and down arrow keys to move the highlight bar to the menu item you want. Then press Enter to select it.

The Use **Menu**   The features provided by the Use menu are cloned from the sample application in chapter 4. You can choose from menu items that report the resolution of the display, the number of available colors, the run-time memory mode, and the Windows version. The sample application supports screen resolutions from 640 × 480 to 1024 × 768, and color modes of 2, 16, 256, and 65,000 colors. Provided the required hardware and software is available, the sample application supports real, standard, and enhanced mode.

The 3D **menu**   The 3D menu provides a suite of choices that you can use to exercise the modules of the 3D toolkit, as shown in Fig. 9-1. To get started,

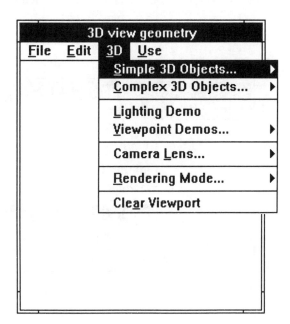

9-1 The 3D menu from the sample application objects.c.

you might first wish to select the wire-frame rendering mode, as depicted by Fig. 9-2. Using this mode results in quicker rendering, which you might find convenient while you investigate the various 3D primitives which the sample application can draw. It's recommended that you stick with the default 55mm camera lens, as shown in Fig. 9-3.

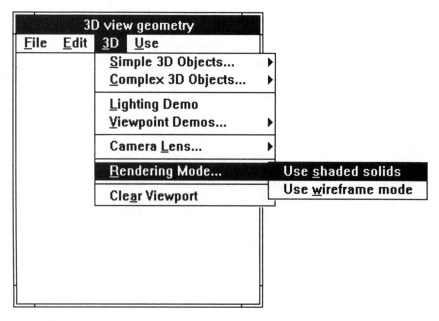

9-2 Using a nested menu to toggle between wire-frame and shaded modes in the sample application objects.c.

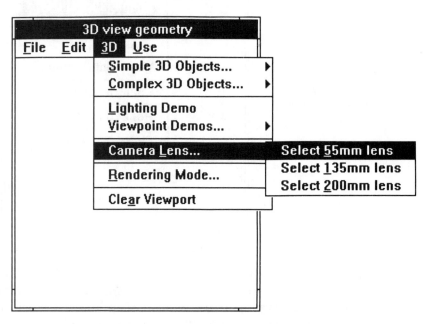

9-3 Using a nested menu to select the camera lens in the sample application objects.c.

The primitives When you select Simple 3D Objects from the 3D menu, a nested menu appears, listing the 3D primitives supported by the sample application. This menu structure is shown in Fig. 9-4.

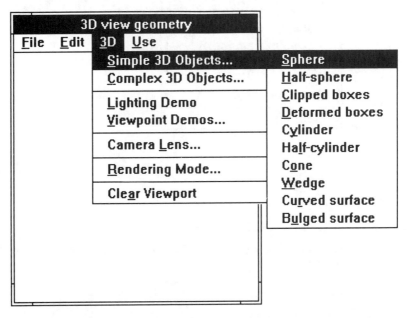

9-4 The sample application objects.c supports 10 primitives which can be rendered at various sizes in different orientations and locations.

The complex solids When you select Complex 3D Objects from the 3D menu a nested menu appears, as shown in Fig. 9-5. You can choose from two different implementations of complex solids modeling.

Investigating the 3D primitives A sampling of fully shaded primitives is provided in Fig. 9-6. The shading colors used in each primitive is hard-coded into the sample application, but you can easily alter the color schemes, as you'll find out in the programmer's guide section of this chapter. If you're running Windows in a 16-color mode, the 3D solids are rendered using dithered facets. If Windows is running in a 256-color mode, the 3D entities are rendered using 64 shades of gray.

Other demonstrations The window images shown in Fig. 9-7 illustrate the output of the Lighting Demo and the Clipped boxes. The lighting demonstration shows how the brightness of a facet changes as the facet's orientation is changed, thereby altering its relationship to the position of the light-source. The clipped boxes show how the near clipping-plane can be moved in order to clip nearer portions of a 3D primitive. In this implementation of the sample application, clipping occurs only when the boxes are rendered in fully shaded mode.

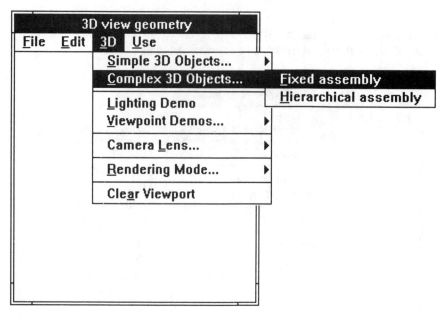

9-5 Using a nested menu to select the assembly modeling algorithm in the sample application objects.c.

Other images The window images in Fig. 9-8 show the output of the Curved surface and Bulged surface menu items. The images in Fig. 9-9 show the complex solid and the cone that the sample application can generate.

Camera manipulation Whenever the sample application renders a primitive or a complex solid, the camera direction is locked on to the entity being drawn. The camera's fixed-target mode is disabled, however, for the virtual reality viewpoint demos shown in Fig. 9-10 and Fig. 9-11. This built-in capability of the 3D toolkits makes point-of-view simulation possible, including virtual reality sessions, flight simulation, architectural walk-throughs, and so on.

Quitting the sample application

To quit the sample application, choose Exit from the File menu. A message box will appear, providing you with an opportunity to confirm or cancel your request.

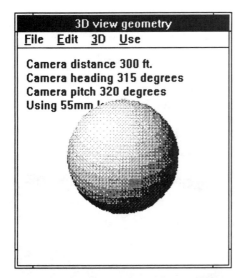

3D view geometry

File   Edit   3D   Use

Camera distance 300 ft.
Camera heading 315 degrees
Camera pitch 320 degrees
Using 55mm lens

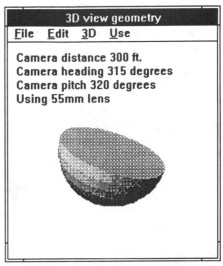

3D view geometry

File   Edit   3D   Use

Camera distance 300 ft.
Camera heading 315 degrees
Camera pitch 320 degrees
Using 55mm lens

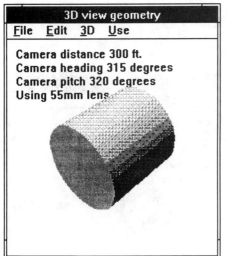

3D view geometry

File   Edit   3D   Use

Camera distance 300 ft.
Camera heading 315 degrees
Camera pitch 320 degrees
Using 55mm lens

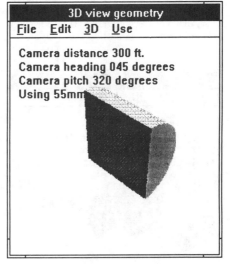

3D view geometry

File   Edit   3D   Use

Camera distance 300 ft.
Camera heading 045 degrees
Camera pitch 320 degrees
Using 55mm

9-6   Samples of shaded primitives produced by the sample application objects.c.

Programmer's guide to the sample application

This section provides a description of how the source code works. The text offers significant detail when discussing the code because many of the 3D toolkit functions that are found in this sample application are also used in more advanced demos you'll encounter later in the book. You can refer back to this chapter for an analysis of the source

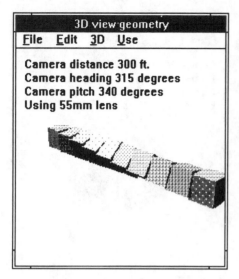

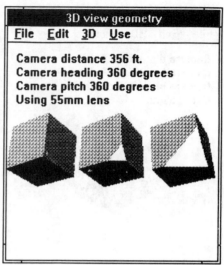

3D view geometry

File Edit 3D Use

Camera distance 300 ft.
Camera heading 315 degrees
Camera pitch 340 degrees
Using 55mm lens

3D view geometry

File Edit 3D Use

Camera distance 356 ft.
Camera heading 360 degrees
Camera pitch 360 degrees
Using 55mm lens

9-7 Samples of shaded demonstrations from the sample application objects.c. Shown at left is the illumination demonstration. Shown at right is a front clipping-plane demonstration.

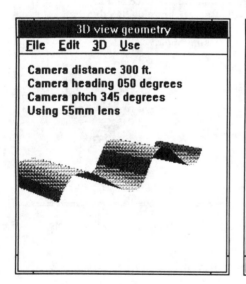

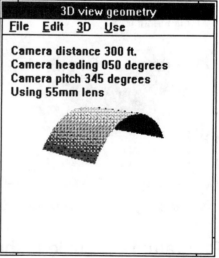

3D view geometry

File Edit 3D Use

Camera distance 300 ft.
Camera heading 050 degrees
Camera pitch 345 degrees
Using 55mm lens

3D view geometry

File Edit 3D Use

Camera distance 300 ft.
Camera heading 050 degrees
Camera pitch 345 degrees
Using 55mm lens

9-8 Samples of shaded surfaces from the sample application objects.c. Shown at left is a curved surface. Shown at right is a bulged surface.

code when you're investigating how the 3D toolkit drives the various visualization, simulation, animation, and virtual reality features of the sample applications presented in later parts of the book.

The source listings for the sample application are presented as Fig. C-

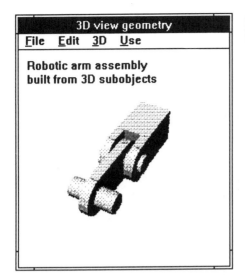
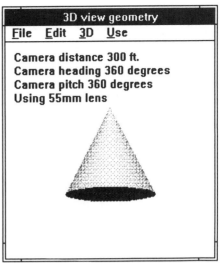

9-9 Samples of shaded displays from the sample application objects.c. Shown at left is a complex assembly of subobjects. Shown at right is a cone.

9-10 By disabling the fixed-target camera mode of the 3D toolkit, the sample application objects.c can provide a testing environment for virtual reality scenarios.

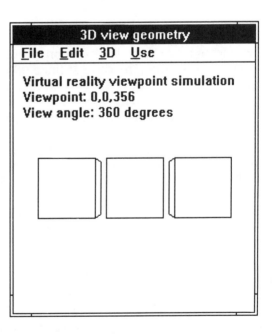

2 in Appendix C. Source listings for the linked-in 3D toolkits are provided in Appendix B. For tips on building the sample application, see Appendix A. The source files for the sample application are also provided on the companion disk as objects.*, engine3d.*, shapes3d.*, deform3d.*, lights3d.*, and assemb3d.*.

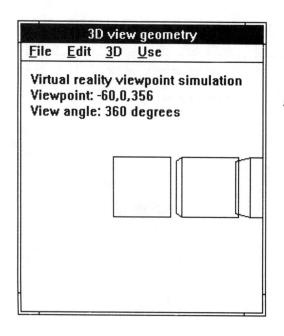

3D view geometry

File   Edit   3D   Use

Virtual reality viewpoint simulation
Viewpoint: -60,0,356
View angle: 360 degrees

9-11   The sample application objects.c can provide prototyping capabilities for virtual reality environments. Shown here is a viewpoint located west of the origin. See FIG. 9-10 for the startup position.

How the .h file works

The objects.h file provides function prototypes, menu ID constants, and string ID constants. The code at lines 0013 through 0025 declares prototypes for functions in the objects.c file. The code at lines 0031 through 0073 defines the menu ID constants. Lines 0044 through 0066, for example, define ID constants that will be used in the 3D menu and its nested menus. The IDM prefix is used in order to make the constants easy to recognize in other parts of the source code. Each menu ID constant will be attached to a menu item in the application's menu system by the resource script file.

The code at lines 0079 through 0112 defines string ID constants. The IDS prefix is prepended in order to make these constants recognizable in other parts of the application. Each string ID constant will be assigned to a text string by the resource script file.

How the .rc file works

The objects.rc file describes the application's menu system, provides a script for accelerator keys, and contains the text strings used by the application.

The menu system   The code at lines 0018 through 0095 describes the menu system. Line 0018 names the script as MENUS1. The .c file refers to this script name when it initializes the application's window. Line 0019 marks the start of the menu system description, which ends at line 0095. The POPUP statements at lines 0020, 0030, 0039, and 0084 each indicate a pulldown menu on the application's menu bar. You'll want to note how the BEGIN and END statements delineate a description for each of these pulldown menus. Note lines 0039 through 0083, for example, which describe the 3D pulldown menu. Lines 0041, 0054, 0061, and 0076 use POPUP statements to describe nested menus. Lines 0060 and 0082 use the MENU-ITEM statement to describe menu items appearing in the 3D menu. Note also how lines 000043 through 0052 do this for a nested menu. The MENUITEM SEPARATOR statements at lines 0059, 0068, 0075, and 0081 produce horizontal dividers to separate some of the menu items.

The IDM constants were defined in the .h file. Line 0060, for example, connects the menu ID constant IDM_TestLighting with the menu item named Lighting Demo. The .c source file refers to IDM_TestLighting when it needs to call an appropriate function to implement the graphics operation.

The accelerator keys   The code at lines 0101 through 0108 provides a script for the accelerator keys, which are shortcut keys the user can activate from anywhere in the menu system. The ACCELERATORS statement at line 00101 names the script as KEYS1. The .c file refers to this script name when it initializes the application's window.

The string table   The code at lines 0118 through 0153 provides the text strings used by the application and attaches each text string to a string ID constant. The maximum length for a string is 255 characters. If you're referring to the program listing in Appendix C, you'll notice how the text is wrapped to the next line. If you're typing in the listing (you should be using the companion disk instead), type the string on a single line.

How the .c file works

The .c file contains variable declarations, the startup function, the message handler function, and the core functions for the application. You'll want to understand how this code works so you'll be prepared for the animated 3D applications later in the book.

Include files   The code at lines 0077 and 0083 includes seven header files. As you learned in chapter 3, windows.h must be included in any application that calls GDI functions. The objects.h file included at line 0078 contains function prototypes, and it defines the menu ID constants and string ID constants used in the .c file. The engine3d.h, shapes3d.h, deform3d.h, lights3d.h, and assemb3d.h files included at lines 0079 through 0083 contain function prototypes and constants for the 3D toolkit that is used by this application.

Declarations   The code at lines 0090 through 0193 defines, declares, and sometimes initializes the constants and variables used throughout the .c file. The comments along the right margin describe the purpose of each constant and variable. Note the hierarchy structure declared at lines 0146 through 0174. This new variable type will hold values that describe the complex 3D solid shown in Fig. 9-9. Line 0177 declares a variable of this type.

The entry point The WinMain() function at lines 0200 through 0307 is the entry point for the sample application. This function performs a number of preparatory tasks, such as:

- ensuring that only one instance is running
- displaying the sign-on notice
- determining the capabilities of the display
- centering the application's window
- resizing the dimensions of the viewport

The WinMain() function also contains the message loop, located at lines 0300 through 0305.

The code at lines 0211 through 0216 ensures that only one copy of the sample application is running. The call to FindWindow() at line 0211 checks to see if another window from the same class is already active. If another copy of objects.exe is running, the code at line 0214 calls BringWindowToTop() to move its window to the top of the desktop. Line 0215 cancels the startup of this second copy and exits.

The code at lines 0224 through 0231 determines the capabilities of the screen display. The call to GetDesktopWindow() grabs the handle to the entire desktop. Then a call to GetDC() obtains a display-context for the desktop. The code at lines 0227 through 0230 calls GetDeviceCaps() to retrieve the horizontal resolution, vertical resolution, number of bits per pixel, and number of bit planes.

The code at lines 0253 through 0257 ensures that the application's window is centered on the display. The constants zWINDOW_WIDTH and zWINDOW_HEIGHT were defined at lines 0091 and 0092. The variables DisplayWidth and DisplayHeight were initialized by the calls to GetDeviceCaps() at lines 0227 and 0228.

The code at lines 0262 through 0269 creates and activates the application's window. The code at line 0267 calls ShowWindow() to display the application's window. Line 0269 activates the accelerator keys defined by the resource script file.

The code at lines 0271 through 0284 ensures that the viewport of the window is always the same size, no matter what resolution the application is using. The demo supports resolutions ranging from 640 × 480 to 1024 × 768. You might want to refer back to the discussion in chapter 4 to remind yourself why this hands-on approach to viewport resizing is necessary.

The code at lines 0296 and 0297 initializes the 3D toolkit and the hidden backup page for the application. The code at lines 0300 through 0305 contains the message loop for the application.

The WinMain() function that runs from line 0200 through line 0307 is cloned from the sample application described in chapter 4. A more complete discussion can be found there.

The message handler   The code for the message handler function is located at lines 0314 through 1394. A set of nested switch() blocks makes it possible for this block of code to respond to events affecting the application.

The switch() statement at line 0319 implements a set case statements depending on the identity of the incoming message. If the message indicates that a menu item has been selected by the user, then the case statement at line 0322 fires. If the message indicates that the viewport needs to be refreshed, then the case statement at line 1354 fires. If the message indicates the application is about to be shut down, then the case statement at line 1363 fires. If the message indicates that the user is attempting to resize, minimize, or maximize the application's window, then the case statement at line 1375 fires.

The switch() block at lines 0323 through 1351 becomes active when the user makes a selection from the menu system.

Calling the 3D toolkit   The case statement at lines 0360 through 0406 is a good example of how the application calls graphics functions in the 3D toolkit. This block of code is activated when the user asks the application to render a 3D sphere. The other case statements in this section of code use a similar approach. Here's how it works.

The SetCapture() call at line 0361 locks the mouse so it can't be pilfered by other applications while the sphere is being rendered by the sample application. Next, line 0362 calls SetCursor() to change the arrow cursor to an hourglass. The code at lines 0363 through 0365 clears the viewport, clears the hidden page, and resets the Z-buffer of the 3D toolkit. These are general housekeeping chores.

Next, the code at lines 0366 through 0388 displays a set of captions on the viewport. Note the if() statements at lines 0374 through 0385 and how they test the camera's focal length before writing a string of text to the display.

Before drawing the sphere, the code at lines 0390 through 0393 configures the camera and the light-source. A camera heading of 315° is similar to facing north-northeast. A camera pitch of 320° is the same as tilting 40° down from the horizontal. A light-source position of 60° elevation and 180° heading puts the light-source directly behind you, the viewer.

The application is now ready to draw the sphere. The call to zSetHierarchyMode() at line 0395 tells the 3D toolkit that only stand-alone 3D primitives are about to be rendered, not parts of a hierarchical entity. The next three statements at lines 0396 through 0398 set the size, orientation, and location of the sphere. The call to zSetShadingColor() at line 0399 asks the 3D toolkit to use green shades for the facets of the sphere. Finally, line 0400 instructs the 3D toolkit to model and render the sphere.

After the sphere is drawn, a token is set at line 0402 so the application will know that the hidden bitmap should be copied to the display window if the viewport needs to be refreshed. The statement at line 0403 copies the viewport image to the hidden bitmap. The call to the GDI's SetCursor() function at line 0404 restores the arrow cursor, and then line 0405 unlocks the mouse.

Most of the other case statements that render 3D images operate in a similar manner. The comment line that appears just before each case statement tells you the purpose of the code. After you've learned how the 3D toolkit operates, you'll be able to return to this section of code and see how each case statement gets its job done.

The case statement at line 0725 is responsible for rendering a series of rotating boxes in order to demonstrate different shades of brightness on facets. The case statements at line 0791, 0835, 0879, and 0923 demonstrate how to disable the camera's fixed-target mode.

Hierarchical modeling The case statement at line 1144 renders a complex 3D entity made up of primitives whose location and orientation is hard-coded. It calls another function located at line 1525 to help it get the job done. The case statement at line 1176 uses hierarchical modeling to render a complex 3D entity with a movable joint. This block of code calls a function located at line 1587. By comparing these two functions you can see the difference between hard-coding and variable-coding. In the zDrawRobotic-Arm() function at line 1525, each primitive's size, orientation, and location is specified by numeric constants. This means if one primitive's location is changed, for example, it is unable to affect any other primitives that might be attached to it. However, the zBuildAssembly() function at line 1587 uses variables to specify the size, orientation, and location of each primitive in the complex solid. Note lines 1621 and 1622, for example, which use variables initialized earlier at lines 1595 and 1596. This means if the parent is changed (at line 1595, for example), then the progeny is automatically affected (line 1621). The struct variable used in this section of code was declared and initialized at lines 0146 through 0177.

Although the zBuildAssembly() function is 323 lines in length, most of those statements involve specifying the primitives that make up the hierarchical solid. The complex entity is drawn by a loop at lines 1859 through 1908. The loop occupies only 49 lines of source code, and many of those lines are curly braces. The loop is commented, especially at lines 1860 through 1876, so you can see how the code builds the hierarchical assembly. Note how the switch() block at lines 1889 through 1907 determines which 3D primitive to draw on each iteration of the loop.

As you'll see, the animated sample application in chapter 13, "3D motion-control programming," shows how you can animate the moving joint of this hierarchical structure.

Persistent graphics The case statement at line 1354 is activated whenever the client area must be refreshed. This will occur if the window is uncovered or moved. Line 1358 checks to ensure that a hidden bitmap was successfully created at startup before attempting to copy a clean image to the viewport by calling zCopyToDisplay() at line 1359. Note also the statement at line 1357 which determines if any graphics have been drawn. The variable named PaintImage is set by any function that draws images.

Graceful shutdown   The case statement at line 1363 is activated when the application is about to shut down. The if() block at lines 1364 through 1369 ensures that the hidden bitmap is deselected from the memory display-context and deleted from memory.

Core functions   Core housekeeping functions for the application are found at lines 1438 through 1520. These functions are discussed in more detail in chapter 4. They are cloned from the graphics template described there.

3D functions   The 3D functions that are called by the application are provided by five additional modules. These modules are named engine3d, shapes3d, deform3d, lights3d, and assemb3d. The .h files for these modules must be included by any application that exploits their 3D features. By using the sample application as a guide, you can use the 3D modeling and shading capabilities of the 3D toolkits in your own application development.

How the engine3d toolkit works

The source listing for the engine3d toolkit is presented in Fig. B-1 in Appendix B. This module provides control over camera pitch, camera heading, and camera-to-target distance. The engine3d toolkit also provides control over the size, location, orientation, and color of each 3D primitive. It provides automatic back-face culling for all solids, and it shades each facet according to the angle between the facet and the light-source. By default, engine3d provides a light-source located above, behind, and slightly to the left of the camera position. The toolkit also provides a Z-buffer depth-sort system for ensuring the proper detection and handling of visible surfaces and hidden surfaces in scenes composed of multiple solids. The Z- buffer is hard-coded to a size of 256×255 pixels, which corresponds to the viewport dimensions of each sample application in the book. The modeling and shading functions of the engine3d toolkit explicitly support 2-color, 16-color, and 256-color images.

The basic functions and capabilities provided by the engine3d toolkit are extended by the other components of the toolset. These other components are shapes3d, deform3d, lights3d, and assemb3d. Code in each of these modules calls functions in engine3d in order to provide advanced 3D features like built-in primitives, deformed entities, a movable light-source, and hierarchical modeling.

Constants   The code at lines 0041 through 0064 defines a set of convenience values that will be used throughout the module. Each of these constants is prefaced with a z and otherwise spelled using upper-case characters. If you're using the source files on the companion disks, pay particular attention to the definition at line 0065. In order to ensure that the code compiles properly on your system, you'll want to check the discussion in Appendix

A, "Compiling the sample programs." If your development platform is a typical Windows personal computer, you'll want to read the section entitled "Preparing the toolkits for your system."

Included files   The code at lines 0071 and 0072 includes the mandatory windows.h file and another specialized header file named math.h. This second file provides function prototypes for sine, cosine, and other advanced math in the standard C run-time library that comes bundled with your compiler package.

Function prototypes   Prototypes for functions found in the engine3d module are provided at lines 0079 through 0115. Some of these functions are callable by other modules. Some are callable from only within engine3d itself.

Variable declarations   Variables that are used for 3D modeling are declared at lines 0121 through 0162. Variables for shading and back-face culling are declared at lines 0168 through 0182. Variables that are needed for viewport management and palette manipulation are declared at lines 0188 through 0198. Variables for view-volumes are declared at lines 0204 through 0220. Variables that are used for Z-buffer operations are declared at lines 0226 through 0240. Variables for a hidden bitmap that is used as a temporary image-workspace are declared at lines 0246 through 0249.

Initialization   The zInitialize3D() function at lines 0258 through 0443 prepares the 3D environment. Note line 0271, for example, which ensures that this function is called only once. The code in this function is generously commented so you'll be able to work out how it operates. The function displays a startup notice, checks the dimensions of the viewport to ensure they match the 256 × 255 Z-buffer, sets the location of the light-source, and initializes the camera. The code then defines a default 3D primitive, sets the near and far clipping-planes, initializes the hidden workspace, and sets up the Z-buffer.

The code at lines 0370 through 0439 initializes the palette for shading when Windows is running in a 256-color mode. The loop at lines 0392 through 0401 loads the color codes into the palette. Lines 0398 through 0400 specify a set of grays. If you were to disable lines 0398 and 0399, the 3D toolkit would use 64 shades of blue when running in a 256-color mode. If you were instead to disable line 0400, then facets would be rendered in shades of brown.

You want to carefully note how the GDI's MessageBox() function is used to alert the user if the application encounters any problems when it initializes the 3D toolkit. The code at lines 0296 and 0302 becomes active if an unexpected viewport dimension is encountered. The code at line 0338 guards against inadvertent division-by-zero conditions. The MessageBox() call at line 0358 is used if a memory shortage prevents the 3D toolkit from setting up the Z-buffer. Finally, the code at lines 0382, 0406, 0417, and

0429 kicks in if the code encounters difficulties setting up the palette for 256-color modes.

Rendering mode   The zUseWireframeMode() function at line 0449 sets a run-time token that indicates whether wire-frame or fully shaded rendering is wanted. The shading functions later in the module check this token before they render each facet.

Fixed-target camera functions   The functions at lines 0462 through 0577 adjust the camera when it is in fixed-target mode. A camera using this mode always points at the center of the world-space, no matter where you position the camera. The functions in this section set the camera heading, camera pitch, and camera-to-target distance. The heading and pitch automatically infer and set the location of the camera, of course, because it always points at the target. What you're really describing is the view angle.

Virtual reality camera functions   The functions at lines 0585 through 0677 adjust the camera when it is in virtual reality mode. A camera using this mode can be pointed in any direction. The functions in this section toggle between fixed-target and virtual reality mode, set the camera heading, the camera pitch, and the camera location.

Instancing   The functions at lines 0685 through 0765 are used to manipulate the translation (location), orientation (attitude), size (extrusion), and shading color of 3D primitives.

Clipping-planes   The functions at lines 0773 through 0801 set the near and far clipping-planes (see Fig. 6-3 in chapter 6). Review the code in objects.c to see how these functions are used to clip the 3D boxes at various distances from the camera.

3D view geometry   The functions at lines 0809 through 0953 provide the view geometry for this 3D toolkit. This section of code is foundation of the 3D transformation sequence (see Fig. 6-1 in chapter 6). The zSetObjAngle() function at line 0821 sets the orientation of the 3D primitive in world-space. The zSetCamAngle() function at line 0835 sets the orientation of the 3D world in camera-space (see Fig. 6-2 in chapter 6). The zGetworldCoords() function at line 0848 transforms object coordinates to world coordinates. The zGetCameraCoords() function at line 0863 transforms world-coordinates to camera coordinates. As you've already learned in previous chapters, camera coordinates make up the view seen by the camera. This is the 3D perspective view-volume (see Fig. 6-3 in chapter 6). The zNormalizeView() function at line 0880 scales this 3D perspective view-volume to a normalized view-volume (see Fig. 6-5 in chapter 6). Then the zRectangularView() function at line 0902 deforms the normalized view-volume into a rectangular view-volume suitable for Z-buffer depth-sorting. Finally, the zScaleToRaster() function at line 0925 scales the rectangular view-volume to match the dimensions of the application's viewport (see Fig. 6-7 in chapter 6).

Facet functions The zDrawFacet() function at lines 0961 through 1152 draws a generic 3D facet. This function is called whenever a 3D primitive or a 3D complex solid is rendered. The code calls the functions described in the previous paragraph to transform each vertex of the facet through the 3D transformation sequence. This is done at lines 0969 through 1019. Then the code at lines 1022 through 1050 identifies the topmost vertex and sorts the remaining vertices into counterclockwise rotation so they can be processed later by the Z-buffer functions (see Fig. 6-10 in chapter 6). Next, the code at lines 1053 through 1055 calls another function in order to clip the facet to the view-volume (see Fig. 6-9 in chapter 6).

If the facet is being rendering in wire-frame mode, the code at lines 1052 through 1095 is processed. Otherwise, the facet is being rendered in fully shaded mode and the section at lines 1097 through 1151 is processed. As you can see, a series of calls to the GDI's LineTo() function are used in order to draw a wire-frame facet. The GDI's CreateSolidBrush(), CreatePolygonRgn(), and PaintRgn() functions are used in order to render a fully shaded facet.

All graphics output is sent to the hidden workspace. Line 1146 calls the Z-buffer depth-sorting function, which decides whether to copy some of the pixels from the hidden workspace to the display viewport. This approach makes it possible to take advantage of the GDI's dithering capabilities, yet still use a Z-buffer to calculate depths on a pixel-by-pixel basis.

View-volume clipping The zClipToViewVolume() function at lines 1160 through 1232 clips facets to the normalized 3D perspective view-volume. This function is called by line 1053 in zDrawFacet() for each facet that is rendered. The zClipToViewVolume() implements the clipping regimen illustrated in Fig. 6-9 in chapter 6. Facets behind the camera are discarded. Facets entirely between the camera and the near clipping-plane are discarded. The offending portion of a facet is clipped (by the Z-buffer functions) if the facet intersects the near clipping-plane. Facets that intersect the far clipping-plane are discarded. Finally, any facet wholly beyond the far clipping-plane is discarded.

Back-face culling The zVisibilityTest() function at line 1240 uses the standard equation for a plane to determine on which side of the facet the camera viewpoint is located. It sets a variable to denote whether the facet is visible (facing towards the camera) or hidden (facing away from the camera). The variable is checked by functions in the shapes3d and deform3d modules when they create 3D primitives.

Facet shading The zGetBrightness() function at line 1254 calculates the brightness level of a facet. It works by comparing the facet's surface normal with the incoming light-ray. Maximum intensity is achieved with there is no difference between the two vectors.

Hidden workspace The functions at lines 1302 through 4121 manage the hidden bitmap that provides a temporary workspace for the images produced by the 3D toolkit. Functions are provided to create the hidden bitmap, clear it, delete it, and copy a pixel from the hidden bitmap to the viewport. The zCopyPixelToViewPort() function at line 1398 is called by the Z-buffer routines whenever they determine that a facet's pixel is nearer to the camera than the existing entry in the Z-buffer.

The Z-buffer The functions at lines 1429 through 1683 manage the Z-buffer depth-sorting operations. The zFindDepth() function at line 1429 calculates the Z-depth of a specified pixel inside a facet. This function is called repeatedly by the zDoZBufferTest() function located at line 1576, which processes the entire facet. The loop in zDoZBufferTest() tests each pixel in each scan-line in the facet. You'll want to carefully note line 1594, which will render a pixel only if it falls between the near clipping-plane and the far clipping-plane. If a facet intersects the near clipping-plane, for example, only the portion of the facet beyond the near clipping-plane will be drawn.

The zWriteZBuffer() function at line 1610 writes a Z-value to the Z-buffer. The zReadZBuffer() function at line 1635 reads a Z-value from the Z-buffer. The zResetZBuffer() at line 1660 resets every entry in the Z-buffer to the maximum distance. This function should always be called before a new scene is rendered.

How the shapes3d toolkit works

The source listing for the shapes3d toolkit is provided in Fig. B-2 in Appendix B. This module provides additional drivers for the engine3d toolkit. The code in the shapes3d module makes calls to engine3d functions in order to draw boxes, spheres, half-spheres, cylinders, cones, wedges, and curved surfaces. The functions in shapes3d have access to some of the variables used by engine3d. This means the shapes3d functions can determine if a facet is backward-facing, and whether it has been clipped or discarded by the view-volume clipping function in engine3d. Each function in shapes3d can also make a call to a function named zGetAssemblyCoords() in the assemb3d module. If the primitive being rendered is part of a hierarchical solid, then the code in assemb3d will ensure that the proper set of XYZ coordinates are used. If the primitive being rendered is a stand-alone solid, then the code in assemb3d is not called.

Boxes The zDrawCube() function at line 0149 models and renders a box. You can see how the code manipulates the eight facets that comprise the box. The code from lines 0163 through 0246 is actually executed twice. During the first pass, no facets are drawn, but they are checked to determine if they are discarded or clipped by the view-volume clipping function. If so, the entire box is discarded. If not, then the second pass renders the facets. You might want to refer again to the zDrawFacet() function in the engine3d module to see how these two functions work together. The zDrawCube() function repeatedly calls the zGetCubeCoords() function located at line 0258 to calculate and store the various XYZ coordinates used during modeling.

Spheres   The zDrawSphere() function at line 0284 renders a 3D sphere. You'll want to note lines 0301 through 0321, which makes the function smart enough to vary the size of the facets, depending on the size of the sphere and whether the program is executing in 16-color mode or 256-color mode. The function repeatedly calls the zGetSphereShape() function located at line 0444 to compute the location of vertices around the surface of the sphere.

Cylinders   The zDrawCylinder() function at line 0461 renders a 3D cylinder. The comments alongside the code show how the body and ends of the cylinder are calculated and modeled. The code repeatedly calls the zGetCylinderShape() function located at line 0586 to compute the location of XYZ coordinates on the surface of the cylinder.

Curved surfaces   The zDrawCurve() function at line 0603 renders a 3D curved surface. The parametric curve calculations are at lines 0637 through 0640. You'll want to pay particular attention to the code at lines 0667 through 0676, which draws the obverse side of the facet if the facet faces away from the camera. As Fig. 8-12 and Fig. 8-13 show in chapter 8, this produces a more informative image. The zDrawCurve() function repeatedly calls the zGetCurveShape() function located at line 0686, which calculates the xy coordinates of a parametric curve in 2D space.

Cones and wedges   The zDrawCone() function at line 0705 renders a 3D cone. It calls the zGetConeShape() function at line 0804 to compute the XYZ coordinates of points on the surface of the cone. The zDrawWedge() function at line 0820 renders a 3D wedge. This code is an adaptation of the code in zDrawCube() that renders a 3D box. The code repeatedly calls the zGetWedgeCoords() function located at line 0920 to calculate XYZ coordinates for the vertices of the wedge.

Half-spheres   The zDrawHemisphere() function at line 0947 renders a 3D half-sphere. This code is cloned from the sphere code and the cylinder code. Half of a sphere is rendered using technology from zDrawSphere(), then the flat surface at the equator is rendered using technology from zDrawCylinder().

How the deform3d toolkit works

The source listing for the deform3d toolkit is provided in Fig. B-4 in Appendix B. This module provides additional drivers for the engine3d toolkit. The code in the deform3d module makes calls to engine3d functions in order to draw deformed boxes, bulged surfaces, and half-cylinders. This module is similar in form and functionality to the shapes3d module. The zDrawDeformBox() function at line 0133 deforms the south-facing facet of a box, making the end of the box either smaller or larger, as shown by Fig. 8-4 in chapter 8. Compare the code in this function with the code in zDrawCube() in shapes3d. The zDrawHalfCylinder() function at line 0298 renders a half-cylinder, using code cloned from zDrawCylinder() in shapes3d. The zDraw-Bulge() function at line 0471 is a modification of zDrawCurve() in engine3d.

How the lights3d toolkit works

The source listing for the lights3d toolkit is provided in Fig. B-3 in Appendix B. This module provides code that can reposition the light-source used by the engine3d toolkit. The zSetLightPosition() function at line 0058 resets the elevation angle and heading angle of the light-source. Note how lines 0072 and 0073 limit the possible positions. The heading can be set to any value from 0° to 360°, but the elevation can only range from horizontal (0°) to vertical (90°).

How the assemb3d toolkit works

The source listing for the assemb3d toolkit is provided in Fig. B-5 in Appendix B. This module provides hierarchical modeling drivers for the engine3d toolkit. The code in the assemb3d module configures 3D primitives to be part of a complex 3D solid. Unless a 3D primitive is processed by assemb3d, the primitive will be rendered as a stand-alone entity.

Parents and progeny This hierarchical modeling module works by inserting another set of 3D coordinates into the 3D transformation sequence. The XYZ coordinates of the structure-space it creates (see Fig. 8-17 in chapter 8) are used to reposition and reorient primitives in their role as part of a larger complex 3D solid (see Fig. 8-16 in chapter 8). The zGetAssemblyCoords() function at line 0096 calculates these structure coordinates. Note how lines 0115 through 0123 calculate the rotation and translation for a parent in structure-space. Line 0127 calls another function named zGetSubAssy-Coords() to calculate a nested set of coordinates if the primitive is a progeny. Remember, as you've already learned in previous chapters, progeny can be positioned and moved relative to their parents in order to produce articulated motion.

Hierarchical mode The zSetHierarchyMode() function at line 0142 toggles the hierarchical modeling mode. It sets a variable in the engine3d module. Neither shapes3d nor deform3d will call assemb3d if hierarchical modeling is toggled off. The zSetHierarchyLevel() function at line 0160 specifies whether a primitive is a parent or a progeny. Note how enough levels are provided so that the progeny can be the parent of another set of progeny.

Instancing The functions at lines 0186 through 0239 set the orientation and position of the entire assembly in 3D structure-space. The functions at lines 0247 through 0337 set the orientation and position of progeny relative to the position of the parent, which is itself relative to structure-space, of course.

Customizing the demo for your own needs

This sample application can serve as a prototype for more advanced 3D software you might want to build. Here are a few tips on adapting the code for your own use. Before you begin, though, remember to read the License, provided as FIG. 7 in the introduction to the book.

To change the application's title as it appears on the caption bar of the window, change line 0120 in the resource script file.

To add or delete menu items, make changes to the menu script at lines 0018 through 0095 in the resource script file. You'll also need to define additional menu ID constants in the .h file if you're adding new menu items. You'll also want to add case statements to the switch() block at lines 0323 through 1351 in the .c file to support the new menu items. To avoid unexpected side effects, you should consider renaming the window class at lines 1413, 1426, and 0211 in the .c file.

The sample application supports VGA, SVGA, accelerator-based, and coprocessor-based display adapters running in resolutions from 640 × 480 to 1024 × 768 and using 2-color, 16-color, 256-color, and 65,000-color modes. Earlier display adapters are not explicitly supported. Here's why: more than 90% of Windows-based personal computers are VGA systems or better. However, for examples of source code to support HGA, EGA, and CGA display adapters, you can consult other books by the author:

- C for Windows Animation Programming, published in 1993 by Windcrest/McGraw-Hill (#4114);
- Visual Basic Animation Programming, published in 1993 by Windcrest/McGraw-Hill (#4224).
- High-Performance C Graphics Programming for Windows, published in 1992 by Windcrest/McGraw-Hill (#4103).

These three books are available through your favorite bookstore. You can also write to the publisher and request the current catalog.

Where do you go from here?

Now that you've practiced some of the fundamental skills required for developing 3D applications for Windows, you're ready to explore the techniques of animation. However, you're the best judge of where you go from here. The next section in the book is part 3, "Introducing animation programming." It teaches you how to implement a frame-based, interactive animation system on a personal computer running Windows. If you choose instead to use the animation toolset as a black box, you can jump forward to part 4, "Introducing simulation programming." Whichever approach you take, the decision is yours. As you've already learned, the book is organized to be helpful to you no matter what learning style you use.

Part Three

Introducing
animation
programming

Your task in part three is to prepare yourself for animation programming in Windows. You want to familiarize yourself with the fundamental skills required for 3D animation authoring, building, and playback. You also want the self-assurance that your understanding of PC-based animation will carry you through the advanced simulation and virtual reality tutorials that appear later in the book.

In part three of the book you'll learn about animation engines, animation control paradigms, 4D space-time, and more. Chapter 10, "Concepts and terms," is your introduction to the specialized language used by 3D animation programmers. In chapter 11, "Getting started with animation," you'll learn how to implement high-performance, frame-based animation sequences on personal computers running Windows. You'll discover the various paradigms that are used to control an animation sequence. In chapter 12 a hands-on tutorial shows you how to put your new animation knowledge to work. A sample application demonstrates 3D animation functions that can be used to prototype your own application development. You'll see how to rotate and move the 3D entities in a scene, and how to reposition the camera. In chapter 13 another hands-on tutorial demonstrates 3D motion-control programming. As you explore the sample application, you'll find out about articulated motion when you animate a complex 3D solid with independent moving parts.

Before you begin to delve into the fundamental skills of 3D animation programming for Windows, you'll want to acquaint yourself with some of the words and phrases used by experienced animators. The next chapter, "Concepts and terms," provides you with the background knowledge you need to get started.

10

Concepts and terms:
Animation programming

This chapter introduces some basic concepts and terms that you'll be using while you explore Part 3, "Introducing animation programming."

The task—What you want to achieve

You want to be able to understand the technical language that is used in the next three chapters. This background knowledge will make it easier for you to grasp the fundamental skills required for using animated 3D graphics in your own Windows applications.

The plan—What you will learn

In this chapter you'll read about the concepts and terms that describe animation programming for Windows. Not only will you become familiar with what each term means, but you'll also learn how each concept fits into the broader practice of 3D animation programming as a whole.

Defining concepts and terms

Authoring platform   An *authoring platform* is the development system used by a programmer to develop animated applications. It includes the software (the so-called *authoring tools*) that the programmer uses to design, build, and store an animation sequence. At a broader level, an authoring platform also includes the computer hardware configuration used by the programmer—processor type and speed, amount of memory, hard disk size and access time, display adapter, and monitor.

Delivery platform   A *delivery platform* is the software that is used to play the animation sequence on the user's computer. Delivery platforms are also called *playback engines, animation engines*, and *players*. Again, at a broader level, a delivery platform also includes the computer hardware configuration of the user.

Implementation and control   Together, *implementation* and *control* provide the means for producing animation sequences on personal computers under Windows. Implementation refers to the mechanics of creating the illusion of movement on the display. You can think of implementation as the interface between the software and the hardware. Control is concerned with managing the entities and events that are being animated. You can think of control as the interface between the subject matter and the software.

Animation engine   An *animation engine* is the software that manages the playback of an animation sequence. Animation engines are also called *playback engines* and *players*. Some engines are interactive, allowing the user to adjust the direction and rate of playback at run-time.

Computer-assisted traditional animation   *Computer-assisted traditional animation (CATA)* refers to the use of computers to automate the process of traditional animation, which includes techniques like cel animation and film animation. An example of traditional animation is the typical Saturday morning TV cartoon program. Computer-assisted traditional animation is 2D animation.

Procedural animation   *Procedural animation* is object-oriented animation. It can be 2D or 3D. Each entity in the scene is treated as an object. The software uses programmer-defined rules to calculate the next position of each *entity* (actor) during playback. The rules can describe not only the actor's behavior in the scene *(staging)*, but also the actor's behavior in relation to other actors present in the scene *(procedural interaction)*.

Physically-based animation   *Physically-based animation* is 3D animation that uses the laws of physics to regulate the motion of entities during playback. Physically-based animation is also called *constraint-based animation* because the motion is governed by so-called *constraints*. Four types of physically-based animation are available:

- forward kinematics
- forward dynamics
- inverse kinematics
- inverse dynamics

Forward kinematics concerns the process of calculating the result of the application of velocity or acceleration to an entity. *Forward dynamics* concerns the process of calculating the result of the application of force, loads, and constraints to an entity. *Inverse kinematics* is the process of calculating the velocity or acceleration required to move an entity from one position to another during a specified period of time. *Inverse dynamics* is the process of calculating the forces, loads, or constraints required to move an entity from one position to another during a proscribed period of time.

Interactive animation   *Interactive animation* refers to any animation playback that provides a means for the user to control the animation. Interactive animation can be 2D or 3D. A typical interactive animation engine provides forward/reverse, start/stop, single-step, and freeze-frame capabilities.

Virtual reality-based animation   *Virtual reality-based animation* is interactive 3D animation that is used to *model* (simulate) a 3D environment which the user can explore.

4D space-time   Computer animation is the visual display of *4D space-time.* The 4D paradigm is derived from the concept of 3D. Entities in the real-world possess the three dimensions of width, height, and depth. This is 3D, or three-dimensional modeling. When such an entity is displayed by a computer, the image is presented in 3D-space using XYZ coordinates. When the image is animated the fourth dimension of time is added. Animation is, after all, movement across space over time. An animated 3D entity is a representation of 4D space-time using XYZT coordinates.

How is animation implemented under Windows?

As you've already learned, *implementation* refers to the mechanics of creating the illusion of movement on the display. It is the interface between the software and the hardware. Four types of implementation are available under Windows:

- fixed-loop animation
- idle-loop animation
- timer-based message-handler animation
- timer-based direct-call animation

Each of these four types of implementation can be effected as either *real-time animation* or as *frame animation.*

Real-time animation   *Real-time animation* refers to animated sequences where each image element is drawn by the software at the same time the animation is being presented. Real-time animation is called *cast-based animation* by multimedia programmers.

Frame animation   *Frame animation* refers to animated sequences that fetch and display previously drawn images *(frames)*. Frame animation uses static images, whereas real-time animation uses dynamic images. The frames used by a frame-based animation sequence can be stored in memory or on hard disk.

Staging   *Staging* refers to the process of choreographing an animation sequence. Staging means specifying the location of entities (actors) as they move about the scene.

Articulated motion   *Articulated motion* refers to the process of animating hierarchical entities. Articulated motion specifies things like rotating joints, swinging arms, moving parts, and so on. Consider, for example, the animation of a 3D android. Staging would used to specify the location of the android as it walks across the scene; articulated motion would be used to specify how its arms swing while it walks.

Where do you go from here?

Now that you've familiarized yourself with some of the basic concepts and terms used in animation programming, you're ready to start learning the fundamental skills. The next chapter, "Getting started with animation," teaches you about animation authoring, building, and playback on personal computers running Windows.

11

Getting started with animation

This chapter teaches you how to use Windows-compliant animation to display moving 3D scenes in the viewport of your application's window. It discusses concepts like implementation, control, 4D space-time, frame animation, physically-based animation, and others.

The task—What you want to achieve

Your task in this chapter is to become familiar with animation. You want to know about implementation and control—and how these two concepts provide the underpinnings for animation programming. You want to gain a thorough understanding of 4D space- time, and to grasp the various low-level tools at your disposal, including blitting and page copying.

The plan—What you will learn

In this chapter you'll learn how animation can be implemented in a Windows application using different types of animation engines and paradigms. You'll discover why timer-based message-handler animation is the best medium for producing Windows-compliant animation sequences. You'll see why the process of control is so important, and you'll investigate different forms of control, including computer-assisted traditional animation, procedural animation, and physically-based animation. You'll also delve into interactive animation and virtual reality-based animation. In this chapter you'll explore the concept of 4D space-time and the three principles it embodies: motion dynamics, update dynamics, and viewing dynamics. You'll learn about low-level tools in the GDI that you can exploit to implement animation on any personal computer running Windows.

Implementation vs. control

Animation programming is founded on the concepts of *implementation* and *control.* Implementation involves the mechanics of creating the illusion of movement on the display. Control is concerned with managing the image-content of the animation itself.

Implementation

Implementation is the interface between the software and the hardware. Implementation refers to the hardware-dependent algorithms and the code that produce the illusion of movement on the display. Implementation is facilitated through two different types of animation engines. Either form of engine can use any one of four different types of animation paradigms.

Animation engines   As an application developer, you can create, build, and store your animation sequences using two types of animation engines: *real-time animation* and *frame animation.*

Real-time animation   Real-time animation refers to animated sequences in which each image element is drawn by the software while the animation is being presented. Each frame is usually built on a hidden bitmap and copied to the display when it has been completed. Real-time animation is called *cast-based animation* by multimedia programmers.

Frame animation   Frame animation refers to animated sequences that fetch and display previously drawn frames. The frames used by a frame-based animation sequence can be stored in memory or on hard disk.

Animation paradigms   Whether you're using a real-time animation engine or a frame-based animation engine, you can implement it using any one of four different paradigms, including:

- fixed-loop animation
- idle-loop animation
- timer-based message-handler animation
- timer-based direct-call animation

Fixed-loop animation   A *fixed loop* is a block of code that executes repeatedly for a preset number of iterations. While the loop is executing, other applications in the Windows environment are prevented from running. The fixed loop monopolizes all the system resources. Fixed-loop code is useful for brief splashes of animation (so-called *spot animation*), provided that the animation sequence is brief enough to avoid adversely affecting other applications that might be running.

Idle-loop animation   If you're a responsible application developer you'll modify your fixed loop and make it an idle loop. Instead of monopolizing the entire computer system, your application makes calls to the GDI's GetMessage() and DispatchMessage() functions in order to check for user input while the loop is executing. This provides Windows with opportunities to service other applications. This paradigm is called *idle-loop animation* because your animation sequence runs only if the rest of the system is idle—that is, if no other application needs processor time.

Timer-based message-handler animation   Timer-based algorithms offer the most effective means of controlling animation playback under Windows. After your application has specified a timing interval by a call to SetTimer(), Windows sends regular timer events to your application. This timer input can take two forms. In the first form, Windows posts a timer message in the queue, from where it can be fetched by your application. This paradigm is called *timer-based message-handler animation*. In the second form, Windows can directly call a function in your application. This paradigm is called *timer-based direct-call animation*.

The timer-based message-handler paradigm is the better choice, for several reasons. It provides good run-time performance. It allows you to accurately control the playback speed by adjusting timing intervals by calls to the SetTimer() function. More important, however, the timer-based message-handler paradigm is Windows-compliant. It is well-behaved. The logic flow is passing through your the switch() block of your application's message-handler, which in turn calls a function that you provide to display the next frame.

The message-handler approach is also noteworthy for its versatility. It provides two different ways to display the next frame. First, whenever a timer message is received, your message-handler can call the function you provide to display the next frame. Second, routines anywhere in your application can directly call the function you provide to display the next frame. This makes it easy to implement freeze-frame and single-step features for the user of your application.

Timer-based direct-call animation   The timer-based direct-call paradigm is an optimized variation of the timer-based message-handler approach. As you learned in chapter 2, "Getting started with Windows programming," your module definition file can declare functions as call-backs. This means Windows can directly call the function you provide to display the next frame whenever Windows detects a timer event. Although this approach can produce well-behaved, high-performance animation sequences, it is sometimes difficult to debug a rogue prototype. Further, unlike the timer-based message-handler paradigm, the timer-based direct-call approach does not permit other routines in your application to directly call the function. For sample source code in C see chapter 6, page 188, in the author's previous book about Windows animation, *C for Windows Animation Pro-*

gramming, published in 1993 by TAB/Windcrest (book no. 4114). It's available through your local bookstore, or you can write to the publisher and request the current catalog.

Control

As you've just learned, implementation is the interface between the software and the hardware. Control, on the other hand, is the interface between the subject matter and the software. Three types of control are available for your real-time and frame-based animation sequences. They are:

- computer-assisted traditional animation
- procedural animation
- physically-based animation

Computer-assisted traditional animation   Traditional animation is a mature technology that evolved from the so-called "magic lantern" parlor games of the 1820s. Traditional animation uses single-frame photography of individual celluloid sheets stacked on top of each other and illuminated from below. On each cel is a hand-drawn image of a cartoon character, a prop, or a background. Saturday-morning TV cartoon programs are examples of traditional film animation. When computers are recruited to assist in the production of traditional animation, the process is called *computer-assisted traditional animation (CATA)*. It is sometimes called *scripted animation* by computer programmers.

Scripted animation is managed by a script. Individual *entities* (actors) move in front of a background. Actors can include characters, props, and scenery elements. Multimedia developers refer to these entities as *cast-members*. The paradigm is called *cast-based animation* (especially if it is being produced using real-time animation). This type of animation control is called *explicit control.*

Scripted animation goes by many names. It is also called *character animation, cel animation, conventional animation, traditional animation,* and *film animation.* You're entering a milieu where the tricks of the trade are already well-documented and well-established. Probably the most productive trick used by traditional animators is *inbetweening* (or *tweening*).

Tweening means creating intermediate drawings from a set of key drawings prepared by a senior animator. Each key drawing represents an important moment in the animation sequence. Junior animators draw all the intermediate frames that must appear between two *key drawings* (or *key frames*). Tweening is time-consuming, laborious work. It is the type of chore for which computers are well-suited. When a personal computer is used to generate intermediate images from two key frames, the process is called *interpolation.* The interpolations can follow a straight line (*linear interpolation*) or a curve (*spline interpolation* or *curved interpolation*).

A number of "rules of animation" have been discovered (or invented) during the 70-year history of film animation. The three most important rules are *deformation, camera mechanics,* and *staging.*

Deformation refers to the squashing and stretching of an entity. A bouncing ball should be squashed (compressed) each time it strikes the floor. It should be stretched (extended) when it bounces away. Subtle deformations like these add a lifelike quality to an animation sequence.

Camera mechanics are concerned with camera movement. The slow-in/slow-out principle states that any camera movement must start very slowly. It should build up gradually to full speed. It should then reduce speed gradually before stopping gently. This carefully choreographed slow-in/slow-out camera movement is the only way to avoid jerky camera pans and zooms.

Staging is concerned with directing the animation. Choreography, timing, plot development, dramatic lighting, actor entrances and exits, props, scenery, costume, and other elements fall under the purview of staging.

Procedural animation *Procedural animation* is object-oriented animation. During animation playback, the software prepares the next frame by calculating the next position for each entity in the scene. These calculations are based on programmer-defined rules of behavior. The rules describe an entity's behavior in the scene itself and its behavior relative to other entities in the scene. In the latter case, the process is called *procedural interaction.* The actors, props, and scenery elements that make up a scene are the cast of players for the animation sequence. Procedural animation is similar to cast-based animation, a technique used by multimedia programmers.

Physically based animation *Physically based animation* uses the laws of physics to manage the motion of 3D entities during animation playback. Physically based animation is also called *constraint-based animation.* Motion in a constraint-based system is modeled using *constraints,* which are limiting conditions or forces.

Consider the animation of a bouncing baseball, for example. Gravity is one force among many acting on the ball. The baseball is not being pushed up by gravity, it is being pushed down. The force of gravity is called a constraint. The motion of the baseball is being constrained (limited) by the force of gravity. When the ball hits the rolled surface of the infield, it does not penetrate the surface, but instead bounces back. The baseball cannot pass through the surface. It is constrained to one side of the surface.

Physically based animation is concerned with positions, velocities, forces, mass, and constraints. This method of animation control embodies:

- forward kinematics
- forward dynamics
- inverse kinematics
- inverse dynamics

Kinematics means the positions and velocities of 3D entities. *Dynamics* means laws of physics such as force, mass, and others that govern those positions and velocities.

Forward kinematics   *Forward kinematics* is the process of calculating what happens when velocity or acceleration is applied to an entity. Forward kinematics does not concern itself with forces or mass, but considers only the motion itself. Your application can use forward kinematics to check if two entities collide during an animation sequence.

Forward dynamics   *Forward dynamics* is the process of calculating what happens when force, loads, or constraints are applied to an entity. In general, dynamics concerns itself with the laws of physics that govern kinematics. Your application can use dynamics to calculate the motion (the kinematics) of an entity that results from forces acting on the entity. You can also use dynamics to calculate forces resulting from the motion of the entity. Like its cousin, forward kinematics, forward dynamics can check if two entities collide, but it can also calculate the forces resulting from the impact.

Inverse kinematics   *Inverse kinematics* is the process of calculating the velocity or acceleration required to move an entity from one location to another location during a specified period of time. Inverse kinematics uses a programmer-supplied target location and calculates the amount of velocity or acceleration required to move the entity to that location.

Inverse dynamics   *Inverse dynamics* is the process of calculating the forces or constraints required to move an entity of specified mass from one location to another location during a specified period of time. Inverse dynamics uses a programmer-supplied target location and calculates the forces required to move the entity to that location.

Interactive animation   As you learned in the previous chapter, *interactive animation* refers to an animation playback environment that provides a means for the user to influence the animation. Typical interactive controls include forward/reverse, start/stop, single-step, and freeze-frame capabilities. Interactive animation can be implemented using either a real-time engine or a frame-based engine. Interactive animation can provide the functionality of computer-assisted traditional animation, procedural animation, and physically based animation.

Virtual reality-based animation   As you've already learned, *virtual reality-based animation* is interactive 3D animation that is used to simulate a 3D environment, which the user can explore. Virtual reality can be designed to operate in three modes:

- passive virtual reality
- exploratory virtual reality
- interactive virtual reality

A *passive virtual reality* session is not interactive. An automated tour through the 3D environment is provided while the user simply observes. Architectural walk-throughs and fly-pasts are examples of passive virtual reality.

An *exploratory virtual reality* session allows the user to roam through the 3D environment. The user interacts with the virtual reality engine, but cannot interact with any entities residing inside the virtual space. A simulated museum exhibit is an example of exploratory virtual reality.

An *interactive virtual reality* session allows the user to interact with entities within the virtual environment. The user can push, pull, grab, throw, and influence entities residing in virtual space. A motor vehicle training simulator is an example of interactive virtual reality.

4D space-time

Computer animation is the visual display of 4D space-time. The 4D paradigm is derived from the concept of 3D. Entities in the real world possess the three dimensions of width, height, and depth. This is 3D (three-dimensional) modeling. When a 3D entity is portrayed by a computer the image is presented in 3D-space using XYZ coordinates. When the entity is animated, the fourth dimension of time is added. Animation is movement across space over time. An animated 3D entity is a display of 4D space-time using XYZT coordinates.

In order to manage 4D space-time, your application must monitor and update three sets of animation dynamics at run-time. These dynamics are:

- motion dynamics
- update dynamics
- viewing dynamics

Taken together, these dynamic attributes describe all aspects of an animation sequence.

Motion dynamics

Motion dynamics refers to the location, orientation, and juxtaposition of individual entities. Motion dynamics is also called *time-varying position*. If the scene is rendered in 3D, motion dynamics are described by the rotation and translation of an entity.

Update dynamics

Update dynamics is concerned with changes in shape, color, and texture. During a bouncing ball sequence, for example, update dynamics ensures that the ball is suitably deformed (squashed) each time it strikes the floor.

Viewing dynamics

Viewing dynamics is concerned with changes in lighting, camera, and view-point. During an animation sequence the camera can zoom in or zoom out, pan left or right, tilt up or down, truck in or truck out, or track alongside a moving object. Viewing dynamics manages these camera movements, as well as changes in lighting and illumination.

Animation implementation

The Windows GDI provides a set of low-level tools useful for animation. The most effective of these tools are *graphic arrays* and the GDI functions that manipulate them. A graphic array is a block of memory containing a rectangular image. This image is called a *bitmap* (or a *bitblt*, pronounced *bit-blit*). Larger images (full-screen or full-window) are usually called *bitmaps*. Smaller images are called either bitmaps or bitblts.

Blitting

Pasting a bitblt at a new location is called *blitting*. Your application can call the GDI's BitBlt() function to copy a bitmap from a source location and paste it at a target location. You can copy from:

- a memory location to the screen
- the screen to a memory location
- one memory location to another
- one screen position to another screen position

Page copying

Copying a window-sized bitmap is called *page copying*. A *page* is a buffer in memory. Animators call it a *hidden frame*. Your application can call BitBlt() to copy the contents of the display window to a hidden frame. BitBlt() can also copy the contents of the hidden frame (the bitmap) back to the screen (the viewport of your application's window). This is the basis of frame animation.

Mattes and friskets

In addition to simply pasting bitmaps, the GDI provides *raster operators* that can produce different visual effects when writing the bitmap at the new location. Raster operators use boolean logic. A transparent put can be implemented by combining the XOR and OR operators. This makes it possible to cleanly paste odd-shaped, multicolored images onto multicolored backgrounds. The transparent put operation uses a white matte to prepare the area where the image will be pasted. The code uses a frisket metaphor to protect the existing scene from being overwritten by the background portion of the bitmap rectangle. Because the background portion of the rectangle does not show, it is called transparent. Mattes and friskets mean you can animate multicolored objects against a multicolored background.

For hands-on examples showing how to implement a transparent put function see the author's other books on animation programming: *C for Windows Animation Programming*, published in 1993 by TAB/Windcrest (book no. 4114); and *Visual Basic Animation Programming*, published in 1993 by TAB/Windcrest (book no. 4224). Both books are available through your favorite bookstore, or you can write to the publisher and request the current catalog.

Frame animation

As you've already learned, frame animation uses static images. During a frame animation sequence, the animation engine fetches and displays previously completed full-window images that have been stored on disk. A typical engine is smart enough to load the entire animation sequence into memory, if space permits, for better playback performance.

During development, many programmers paste small bitmap images onto the viewport of the application's window in order to assemble each completed frame. The software then saves the image from the display to the hard disk. If your application must build frames at run-time, you can make the entire process invisible to the user by building each completed image on a hidden page and saving each frame to the hard disk. If bitmap images are impractical, some programmers draw each frame from scratch. The software then saves each completed frame to the hard disk. Again, if your application needs to build new frames at run-time, the entire process can be concealed from the user by building each frame on a hidden page and saving to hard disk.

Playback of a frame animation sequence is usually disk-to-display or memory-to-display. The frames of the animation sequence are usually stored on hard disk. If memory permits, a typical playback engine attempts to load all necessary frames into memory, from where they can be quickly displayed by copying them in sequence to the viewport of the application's window. If insufficient memory is available, the engine loads individual frames from disk during playback. In such cases, animation performance is directly related to hard disk performance. In all cases, animation performance is affected by viewport size.

Figure 11-1 lists arguments for the SetTimer() function, and shows the resulting frames per second. Figure 11-2 shows the elapsed time for individual frames for SetTimer(1) (18.2 fps).

Frame storage of 256 × 255 viewport As you've already learned, the sample applications in the book use a viewport whose dimensions are 256 pixels across and 255 pixels high. If Windows is running in a 2-color mode, each frame requires 8,160 bytes of storage space:

$$(256 \times 255 \times 1bpp) / 8bpb = 8,160$$

SetTimer( ) arguments		
Clock ticks	ms	Events per second
1	55	1000/55 = 18.2 fps
2	110	1000/110 = 9.1 fps
3	165	1000/165 = 6.1 fps
4	220	1000/220 = 4.5 fps
5	275	1000/275 = 3.6 fps
6	330	1000/330 = 3.0 fps

11-1 Arguments for the GDI's SetTimer() function.

Animation timing	
Frame Number	Elapsed time
1	.0555
2	.1111
3	.1667
4	.2222
5	.2778
6	.3333
7	.3889
8	.4444
9	.5000
10	.5555
11	.6111
12	.6667
13	.7222
14	.7778
15	.8333
16	.8889
17	.9444
18	1.0000

11-2 Time cues for animation running at 18 fps.

where *bpp* is bits-per-pixel and *bpb* is bits-per-byte). If the animation is running in a VGA 16-color mode, then 32,640 bytes are needed for each frame:

$$(256 \times 255 \times 4\text{bpp}) / 8\text{bpb} = 32,640$$

If Windows is using an SVGA 256-color mode, then 65,280 bytes are needed to store each frame:

$$(256 \times 255 \times 8\text{bpp}) / 8\text{bpb} = 65,280$$

If the application is running on a system using an accelerator-based 65,000-color mode, then 130,560 bytes are required for each frame:

$$(256 \times 255 \times 16\text{bpp}) / 8\text{bpb} = 130,560$$

These file storage requirements are summarized in Fig. 11-3.

Uncompressed file storage		
256-by-255 viewport		
Bits per pixel	Color	Storage required
1	2	8160 bytes
4	16	32,640 bytes
8	256	65,280 bytes
16	65536	130,560 bytes

11-3 Storage requirements for uncompressed images.

Where do you go from here?

Now that you've familiarized yourself with the implementation and control of frame-based animation sequences on personal computers running Windows, you're ready to delve into a hands-on tutorial. In the next chapter you'll be invited to inspect the source code for a sample application that provides 3D animation features such as:

- interactive control over playback, including forward/reverse, start/stop, freeze-frame, and single-step modes
- animation support for 2-color, 16-color, and 256-color modes
- playback in VGA and SVGA display resolutions, including 640 × 480, 800 × 600, and 1024 × 768
- well-behaved animation algorithms that permit other applications to continue running in the Windows environment
- Windows-compliant code that ensures the sample application continues animating even when its window is partially covered

The knowledge you've acquired in this chapter provides you with the background you need to grasp how the animated sample application works. You'll have the ability to merge its functions into your own applications.

12

Tutorial: 3D animation programming

This chapter provides a hands-on tutorial that demonstrates the animation fundamentals you learned in the previous two chapters. You'll delve into important programming skills that you'll use to develop animation, simulation, visualization, and virtual reality applications. A User's Guide shows you how to run the sample application and a Programmer's Guide provides explanations of how the source code for the animation engine works.

The task—What you want to achieve

Your task in this chapter is to familiarize yourself with how the source code works in the sample application. You want to see how the animation engine builds the animation sequence and saves each frame to disk. You want to know how the code can switch to disk-based animation playback if it can't find enough memory to store the entire animation sequence. You want to learn how the keyboard is used to provide interactive controls like start/stop, forward/reverse, freeze-frame, and single- step. But your most important task is to learn how to use the functions of the animation engine in your own graphics applications.

The plan—What you will learn

In this chapter you'll see how to use an array of pointers to filenames in order to manage animation sequences. You'll find out how to use the pointers to select sequential filenames while the code saves each frame to disk during the build process. Later, during playback, you'll discover how to allocate memory when the animation engine attempts to load the entire animation sequence into RAM—and you'll discover how to cancel the load if memory is insufficient—and run the animation directly from disk instead. Overall, you'll become familiar with how to put together the various parts of an animated application for Windows.

User's guide to the sample application

In this section you'll learn how to use the sample application named animate. Before you can run animate you must build it. The source listings for the sample application are presented as Fig. C-3 in Appendix C. Source listings for toolkits that must be linked in to build the finished application are presented in Appendix B. All source files are also provided on the companion disk. See Appendix A if you need assistance compiling the program.

Starting the sample application

There are two ways to start the sample application. You can start it directly from your compiler's editor or you can start it from Windows' Program Manager.

Startup from your compiler's editor   If you're using a Windows-hosted editor, you can run the sample application directly from your editor. This includes QuickC for Windows, Microsoft Visual C++, Turbo C++ for Windows, Borland C++, and others.

Startup from Windows' Program Manager   If you've already compiled the sample application, you can start it from Windows' Program Manager. From the Windows desktop, pull down the File menu and select Run. When the dialog box appears, type the full pathname of the program. Here's an example.

        c:\directory\subdirectory\animate.exe

You should substitute directory names that reflect your own system. When you select the OK button of the dialog box, the sample application starts.

Using the sample application

When the sample application starts up, a splash sign-on notice appears. Choose OK to continue.

Four menu names are displayed on the menu bar. They are File, Edit, Run, and Using. You can use the File menu to quit the program. The Edit menu contains no active features. You can use the Run menu to explore the animation build process, saving to disk, loading from disk, and animation playback. The Using menu contains a brief run-time help message.

You can use either a mouse or the keyboard to operate this sample application. If you're using a mouse, simply point and click. If you're using the keyboard, press Alt to move the focus to the menu bar, then press the appropriate underscored mnemonic key to pull down a menu and select a mnemonic key to choose an item from the menu. Alternatively, you can use the up and down arrow keys to move the highlight bar to the menu item you want and then press Enter.

The Run **menu** The Run menu controls the animation engine. The features provided in the menu are shown in Fig. 12-1. If you select the Production menu item, the nested menu depicted in Fig. 12-2 appears. If you're experi-

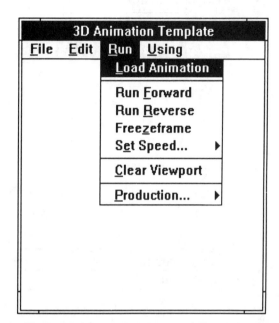

12-1 The Run menu from the sample application animate.c.

menting with the sample application for the first time, you might wish to select wire-frame mode. This speeds up the animation-build process, allowing you to play the finished animation sequence sooner than if had you selected the fully shaded mode.

Building an animation When you select Build Animation from the Production menu, the message box shown in Fig. 12-3 appears. This tip message reminds you that a build process can be interrupted at any time by clicking the right mouse button. This trapdoor allows you to cancel a build that is in progress if it is consuming more time that you can accommodate. The software technology that drives the animation engine in this chapter is also used for other demos later in the book, and some animation sequences can require 3 hours to build in fully shaded mode. However, the sample application that you're investigating here requires less time. For example, an 80386DX running at 33MHz without a numeric coprocessor needs only 35 seconds to build all 36 frames for this 3D animation sequence if you've selected wire-frame mode—and only 21 minutes if you selected fully shaded

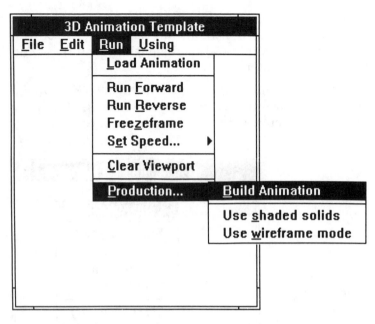

12-2 Using a nested menu to toggle between wire-frame and shaded modes in the sample application animate.c.

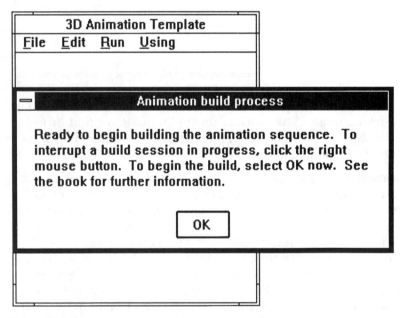

12-3 The sample application animate.c uses a message box to guide the user through the animation build process.

mode. A sample image from the build process is shown in Fig. 12-4. The difference in time is caused by the operation of the Z-buffer depth-sort routines when the fully shaded mode is selected.

12-4 A sample image from the sample application animate.c during an animation build session.

Loading an animation   To load an animation sequence from disk, select Load Animation from the Run menu, as shown in Fig. 12-1. If enough extended memory is available, the animation engine loads all 36 frames into memory. When it's finished, the message box shown in Fig. 12-5 will be displayed. If insufficient physical memory is available and Windows is running in real mode, then the sample application advises you that it intends to load each frame from disk as needed during playback of the animation sequence.

The default playback speed is 18 frames per second. Personal computers running at 25MHz or faster (and using the VGA's 640 $\times$ 480 $\times$ 16-color mode) can sustain this rate. You can reset the animation playback rate to any of the settings in the Set Speed menu as shown in Fig. 12-6. The rate can be set either before, during, or after playback.

Windows-compliant   A typical frame from a playback session provided by the sample application is shown in Fig. 12-7. During playback, you can use the mouse to drag the application's window partially off-screen—and the animation continues to run. If you start another program and it partially covers the sample application's window, the animation will still continue to run.

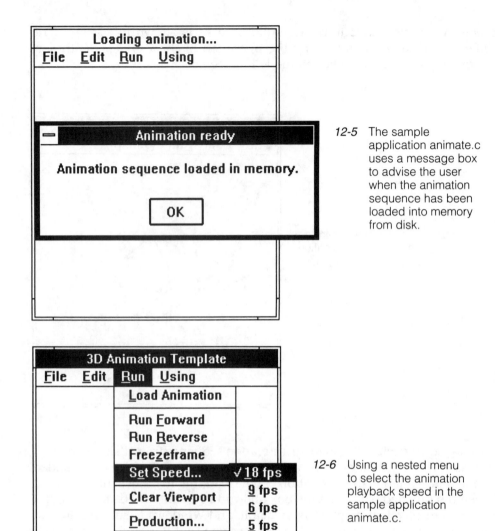

12-5 The sample application animate.c uses a message box to advise the user when the animation sequence has been loaded into memory from disk.

12-6 Using a nested menu to select the animation playback speed in the sample application animate.c.

Robust menuing If you attempt to load an animation sequence for disk after it has already been loaded, the software is robust enough to recognize the redundancy and to gracefully avoid the duplication of work, as shown in Fig. 12-8. Likewise, if you attempt to build an animation sequence that

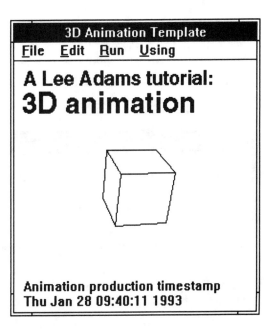

12-7 A typical image generated during animation playback by the sample application animate.c.

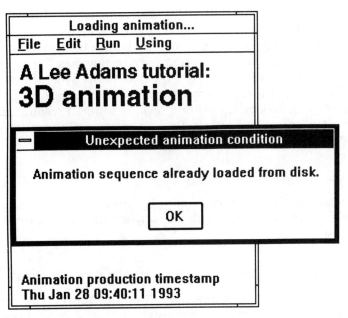

12-8 The sample application animate.c uses message boxes to provide a user-tolerant environment at run-time.

already exists on disk, the software is intelligent enough to realize that the added work is not necessary, as shown in Fig. 12-9.

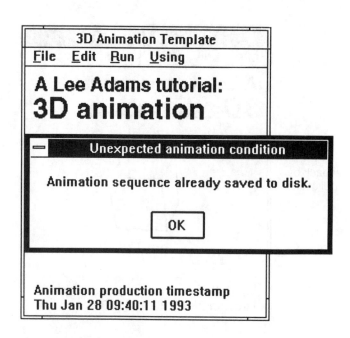

12-9 The sample application animate.c can detect the current status of the animation environment. Message boxes are used to provide a working session that is tolerant of user oversights and errors.

Running an animation   To start an animation sequence that you've loaded in from disk, simply select Run Forward from the Run menu, as shown in Fig. 12-1. The playback begins. You can then pull down the Run menu and select Run Reverse to run the animation sequence backwards. To explore single-step control, select Freezeframe from the Run menu while the animation is running. Then press the right arrow key to advance to the next frame. Strike the left arrow key to back up to the previous frame. Pressing and holding down the right arrow key causes the animation sequence to play at the fastest rate supported by your hardware.

Quitting the sample application

To quit the sample application, choose Exit from the File menu. A message box appears, providing you with an opportunity to confirm or cancel your request.

Programmer's guide to the sample application

This section describes how the source code works. The discussion emphasizes the primary .c file because many of the 3D toolkit functions that are found in this sample application have already been discussed in chapter 9.

The source listings for the sample application are presented as Fig. C-3 in Appendix C. Source listings for the linked-in toolkits are provided in Appendix B. For tips on building the sample application, see Appendix A. The source files for the sample application are also provided on the companion disk as animate.*, engine3d.*, shapes3d.*, deform3d.*, assemb3d.*, lights3d.*, and disk3d.*.

How the .h file works

The animate.h file provides function prototypes, menu ID constants, and string ID constants. The code at lines 0013 through 0027 declares prototypes for functions in the objects.c file. The code at lines 0034 through 0064 defines the menu ID constants. Lines 0046 through 0053, for example, define ID constants that are used in the Run menu and its nested menus. The IDM prefix makes the constants easy to recognize in other parts of the source code. Each menu ID constant is attached to a menu item in the application's menu system by the resource script file. The code at lines 0070 through 00129 defines string ID constants. The IDS prefix makes these constants recognizable in other parts of the application. Each string ID constant is assigned to a text string by the resource script file.

How the .rc file works

The animate.rc file describes the menu system, provides a script for accelerator keys, and contains text strings used by the application.

Menu system   The code at lines 0018 through 0072 defines the menu system. Line 0018 names the script as ANIMENUS. The .c file refers to this script name when it initializes the application's window. Line 0019 marks the start of the menu system description, which ends at line 0072. The POPUP statements at lines 0020, 0029, 0038, and 0065 each indicate a pulldown menu on the application's menu bar. The BEGIN and END statements mark off a description for each of these pulldown menus. Note lines 0038 through 0064, for example, which describe the Run pulldown menu. Lines 0045 and 0057 use POPUP statements to describe nested menus. Lines 0040, 0042, 0043, 0044, and 0055 use the MENUITEM statement to describe menu items appearing in the Run menu. Note also how lines 000047 through 0052 do this for a nested menu. The MENUITEM SEPARATOR statements produce horizontal dividers to separate the menu items.

The IDM constants were defined in the .h file. Line 0043, for example, connects the menu ID constant IDM_RunReverse with the menu item named Run Reverse. The .c source file refers to IDM_RunReverse whenever it needs to call the appropriate function to implement animation playback in reverse.

Accelerator keys   The code at lines 0078 through 0085 provides a script for the accelerator keys, which are shortcut keys the user can activate from anywhere in the menu system. The ACCELERATORS statement at line 0078 names the script as ANIMKEYS. The .c file refers to this script name when it initializes the application's window.

The string table   The code at lines 0095 through 0154 provides the text strings used by the application and attaches each text string to a string ID constant. The maximum allowable length for a string is 255 characters. In the program listing in Appendix C the text is wrapped to the next line for book-publishing purposes. If you're typing the listing, place the string on a single line.

How the .c file works

The .c file contains variable declarations, the startup function, the message handler function, and the core functions for the application. You want to gain an understanding of how this code works so you'll be prepared for the animated visualization, simulation, and virtual reality applications later in the book.

Include files   The code at lines 0069 and 0077 includes seven header files. As you've already learned in previous chapters, windows.h must be included in any application that calls GDI functions. The animate.h file included at line 0070 contains function prototypes, and it also defines menu ID constants and string ID constants. The engine3d.h, shapes3d.h, deform3d.h, lights3d.h, assemb3d.h, and disk3d.h files included at lines 0071 through 0076 contain function prototypes and constants for the toolkits that are used by this application.

Declarations   The code at lines 0085 through 0235 defines, declares, and initializes constants and variables that are used throughout the .c file. The comments describe the purpose of each constant and variable.

The entry point   The WinMain() function at lines 0242 through 0360 is the entry point for the sample application. This function performs a number of preparatory tasks, such as:

- ensuring that only one copy is running
- displaying the splash sign-on notice
- determining the capabilities of the display
- centering the application's window
- resizing the dimensions of the viewport

The WinMain() function also contains the message loop, which is located at lines 0353 through 0358.

The code at lines 0253 through 0258 ensures that only one copy of the sample application is running. The call to FindWindow() at line 0253 checks to see if another window from the same class is already active. If another instance of animate.exe is running, the code at line 0256 calls BringWindow-ToTop() to move its window to the top of the desktop. Line 0257 cancels the startup of this copy and exits.

The code at lines 0279 through 0285 determines the capabilities of the screen display. The call to GetDesktopWindow() grabs the handle to the entire desktop. Then a call to GetDC() obtains a display-context for the desktop.

The code at lines 0281 through 0284 calls GetDeviceCaps() to retrieve the horizontal resolution, vertical resolution, number of bits per pixel, and number of bit planes.

The code at lines 0308 through 0311 ensures that the application's window is centered on the display. The constants zWINDOW_WIDTH and zWINDOW_HEIGHT were defined at lines 0085 and 0086. The variables DisplayWidth and DisplayHeight were initialized by the calls to GetDeviceCaps() at lines 0281 and 0282.

The code at lines 0317 through 0323 creates and activates the application's window. The code at line 0321 calls ShowWindow() to display the application's window. Line 0323 activates the accelerator keys defined by the resource script file.

The code at lines 0326 through 0338 ensures that the viewport of the window is always the same size, no matter what resolution the application is using. The demo supports resolutions ranging from 640 × 480 to 1024 × 768. The discussion in chapter 4 explains why this hands-on approach to viewport resizing is necessary.

The code at lines 0350 initializes the hidden backup page for the application. The code at lines 0353 through 0358 contains the message loop for the application.

The message handler   The code for the message handler function is located at lines 0367 through 0656. A set of nested switch() blocks makes it possible for this block of code to respond to events affecting the application.

The switch() statement at line 0372 enables a set of case statements depending on the nature of the incoming message. If the message indicates that a menu item has been selected, then the case statement at line 0383 fires. If the message indicates that the viewport needs to be refreshed, then the case statement at line 0561 fires. If the message indicates the application is about to be shut down, then the case statement at line 0615 fires. If the message indicates that the user is attempting to resize, minimize, or maximize the application's window, then the case statement at line 0637 fires. If the message indicates an incoming keystroke, then the case statement at line 0581 fires.

Some of the general housekeeping code in this section has been modified to allow the code to coexist with a running animation sequence.

Persistent graphics   The case statement at line 0561 is activated whenever the client area must be refreshed. This event occurs if the window is uncovered or moved, and can happen when the animation is running. Line 0570 checks to determine if the animation playback is paused. If so, a run-time token named Redisplay is toggled before calling the animation engine. This ensures that the current frame number is simply redisplayed. If the animation sequence is playing, then none of the if() statements at lines 0564, 0565, or 0570 will fire and the code at line 0577 calls the animation engine to display the next frame.

Graceful shutdown The case statement at line 0615 is activated when the application is about to shut down. The if() block at lines 0616 through 0622 ensures that the hidden bitmap is deselected from the memory display-context and deleted from memory. It also releases the timer resource that was used to manage the animation playback. The if() block at lines 0623 through 0631 checks to see if an animation sequence was loaded into RAM. If so, the loop at lines 0626 through 0629 deletes the 36 bitmaps from memory. Finally, line 0632 shuts down the 3D toolkit and line 0633 shuts down the application itself.

Managing the timer The case statement at line 0375 is activated when an incoming timer event is detected. Because the Windows operating system gives a higher priority to timer events than to menuing functions, it is necessary to insert special code here to accommodate slower processors. If a 16MHz 80386SX is attempting to run the animation sequence at 18 frames per second, for example, the user will not be able to pull down any menus from the menu bar. The selected menu will simply never appear because the next timer event occurs before Windows has an opportunity to display the requested menu. The two lines of code at 0376 and 0377 decrement a variable named TimerCounter and test its value. Its normal state is zero, but if a menu has been selected then the code at line 0555 sets it to a higher value, thereby allowing the if() statement at line 0377 to fire. This causes a delay of enough duration to give Windows time to display the menu on slower processors. If no menu has been chosen by the user, then line 0379 executes whenever an incoming timer event occurs, and a function named zShowNextFrame() is called to display the next frame in the animation sequence.

Managing the animation engine The case statements from line 0403 through line 0527 manage the animation engine. The case statement at line 0446 calls a function named zSaveAnimation() in order to build the images and save each frame to disk. The layout of this function is similar to previous sample applications. First, the 3D toolkit is initialized, then the cursor is locked and changed, then the core routine is called, and upon return the cursor is unlocked and restored. You should note that most case statement blocks set the value of the TimerCounter variable to implement the timing delay discussed previously.

The case statement at line 0403 fires whenever the user selects Forward Playback from the Run menu. The if() statement at line 0404 checks to ensure that the animation is in fact ready for playback. After setting a few run-time tokens, the code at line 0416 calls a function named zShowNextFrame() to display the next frame.

The case statement at line 0418 is activated whenever the user selects Reverse Playback from the Run menu. The code in this block is similar to the code described in the previous paragraph.

The case statement at line 0433 fires whenever the user pauses the playback. Line 0443 sets a run-time token named Pause to TRUE, then line

0444 calls zShowNextFrame(), which checks the value of Pause and merely redisplays the current frame. When the animation is paused, the case statement at line 0581 allows the arrow keys to control the display of frames. If the user presses the right arrow key, for example, then line 0597 carefully ensures that the animation direction is correctly set and calls zShowNextFrame(). Note how the code at lines 0597 through 0609 masterfully toggles and juggles some run-time values before and after calling the animation engine.

How the core functions work

The core functions in the remainder of the .c source file fall into two categories. The first category of routines provides animation authoring functions that create the frames and save them to disk. The second category consists of routines that provide animation playback functions to display the next frame, to reset the animation rate, and to load the animation sequence from disk into memory.

Animation authoring functions Three authoring functions are provided as core routines. The first authoring function, at line 0812, looks after creating all 36 frames and saving them to disk. It does so by calling the second authoring function, at line 0906, which creates one frame and saves it to disk. This second function works by calling a third authoring function, at line 1016, which draws the appropriate image on the frame being built.

The zSaveAnimation() function at line 0812 supervises the animation-build process. Lines 0843 through 0852 initializes the camera starting position and path it will follow during the animation. The struct that holds these parameters was declared at the beginning of the program listing. Next, lines 0854 through 0861 initializes the light-source starting position and the path it will follow during the animation. Then, lines 0863 through 0883 initializes the actor (in this instance, a box), its starting position, and the path it will follow during the animation. Finally, the loop at lines 0886 through 0891 repeatedly calls zBuildFrame() to build each frame in the animation sequence.

The zBuildFrame() function at line 0906 builds one frame and saves it to disk. You'll want to carefully note the code at lines 0919 through 0921, which produces an ongoing progress report message on the application's caption bar during the build process. Then the code resets all toolkit buffers (lines 0924 through 0927), calls zDrawCel() to draw the image (lines 0930 through 0936), checks to see if the user wants to cancel the build (lines 0939 through 0945), displays the titles and timestamp (lines 0948 through 0994), checks again for a user-requested cancel, and then finally calls zSaveFrame() in the disk3d toolkit to save the bitmap to disk. You might find the code at lines 0987 through 0991 instructive. Line 0989, for example, calls the C run-time library function time() to help it build a string which it uses as a timestamp on the image being drawn.

The zDrawCel() function at line 1016 draws the appropriate image on the frame currently being assembled by zBuildFrame(). Note how the variable Number is used to update the camera, light-source, and actor before the code at lines 1073 through 1075 draws the box being animated. The code at lines 1050 through 1065 manipulates the actor. Refer back to lines 0178 through 0235, where the struct was initialized, to see how this code works.

Animation playback functions Three playback functions are provided as core routines in the .c source file. The first function, at line 1086, is the animation engine itself. It displays the next frame in the animation sequence. It is intelligent enough to understand if the animation is running in forward or reverse mode. If the animation is paused, the animation engine merely redisplays the current frame. The second playback function, at line 1156, loads the entire animation sequence from disk into memory. If insufficient memory is available (in real mode), the function is smart enough to cancel the load and set a token that advises the animation engine to load each frame as needed from disk during playback. The third playback function, at line 1254, resets the animation playback rate by calling the GDI's SetTimer() function.

The zShowNextFrame() function at line 1086 displays the next frame of the animation sequence. If all frames have been loaded into memory, the code at lines 1092 through 1115 executes. Lines 1093 through 1096 check various run-time tokens. The if() statements at lines 1097 and 1103 adjust the frame ID number, depending on whether the animation in running in forward or reverse mode. The call to the GDI's BitBlt() function at line 1112 copies the appropriate frame bitmap to the display. If the animation is running from disk, then the code at lines 1118 through 1149 executes. This block of code is structured similar to the code just described, except for the file-loading statements at lines 1134 through 1145.

The zLoadAnimation() function at line 1156 loads the entire animation sequence from disk. First, it creates the bitmaps that store the frames. The for() loop at lines 1193 through 1199 increments pointers that point to elements in an array of handles in order to sequentially load all 36 frames. You'll want to check back at lines 0165 through 0176, where an array of pointers to filenames was declared and initialized. Notice also line 0164, where an array of bitmap handles is declared.

If an error occurs during the bitmap-load process, the block of code at lines 1203 through 1214 uses another for() statement to delete all the bitmap objects that were created before the error occurred. The most likely cause of an error, of course, is insufficient physical memory when Windows (prior to version 3.1) is running in real mode.

The for() loop at lines 1219 through 1225 loads the bitmaps from disk into memory. It does this by calling a function named zLoadFrame() in the disk3d toolkit. The program listing for this toolkit is provided in Appendix B.

The zSetFrameRate() function at line 1254 resets the animation frame rate. First, the if() statement at line 1256 ensures that a valid timer is already in existence. Next, the code at lines 1267 through 1275 removes the check-mark from the menu. It can do this because a variable was saved by the software when it detected that a menu was selected by the user. (See line 0557.) Next, the call to KillTimer() at line 1278 releases the existing timer. The call to Settimer() at line 1279 creates a new timer with a new rate. Finally, the code at lines 1290 through 1298 adds a check-mark to the appropriate menu item.

Where do you go from here?

Now that you've practiced some of the fundamental skills required for developing 3D animation software for Windows, you're ready to explore more advanced techniques. The next chapter, "3D motion-control programming," provides a hands-on tutorial that demonstrates articulated motion. You'll see how to use hierarchical modeling to create animated displays of complex 3D solids with moving parts.

13
Tutorial: 3D motion-control programming

This chapter provides a hands-on tutorial that demonstrates the motion-control fundamentals you learned in previous chapters. A User's Guide shows you how to run the sample application, and a Programmer's Guide provides explanations of how hierarchical modeling techniques are integrated with the animation engine.

The task—What you want to achieve

Your task in this chapter is to familiarize yourself with how the source code works in the sample application. You want to see how the animation engine uses hierarchical modeling to build each frame in the animation sequence and then saves it to disk. You also want to learn how to use hierarchical modeling functions in your own animated graphics applications.

The plan—What you will learn

In this chapter you'll see how to use a hierarchical structure to create a complex 3D solid that can be animated using articulated motion. You'll see how to position the progeny relative to the parent. You'll see how to adapt the animation engine discussed in the previous chapter to support complex 3D entities with moving parts.

User's guide to the sample application

In this section you'll learn how to use the sample application named assembly. Before you can run assembly, you must build the executable. The program listings for the sample application are presented as Fig. C-4 in Appendix C. Source listings for toolkits that must be linked-in to build the finished executable are presented in Appendix B. All source files are also provided on the companion disk. See Appendix A for tips on compiling the program.

Starting the sample application

There are two ways you can start the sample application. You can start it directly from your compiler's editor or you can launch it from Windows' Program Manager.

Startup from your compiler's editor   You can run the sample application directly from your Windows-hosted editor. This includes QuickC for Windows, Microsoft Visual C++, Turbo C++ for Windows, Borland C++, and others.

Startup from Windows' Program Manager   From the Windows desktop, pull down the File menu and select Run. When the dialog box appears, type the full pathname of the program, such as:

    c:\directory\subdirectory\ assembly.exe

You will use directory names that reflect your own system, of course. When you select the OK button of the dialog box the sample application starts.

Using the sample application

When the sample application starts up, the sign-on notice appears. Choose OK to continue.

Four menu names are displayed on the menu bar. They are File, Edit, Run, and Using. You can use the File menu to quit the program. You can use the Run menu to build the animation, save it to disk, load it from disk, and play the animation sequence.

You can use a mouse or the keyboard to operate this sample application. If you're using a mouse, just point and click. If you're using the keyboard, press Alt to move the focus to the menu bar, then press the appropriate mnemonic key to pull down a menu and select a an item from the menu.

The Run menu   The Run menu controls the animation engine. Refer back to the previous chapter for a detailed discussion of how to build an animation and save it to disk. Be sure to select wire-frame mode before starting the build process for the first time.

Loading an animation   To load an animation sequence from disk, select Load Animation from the Run menu. The animation engine loads all 36 frames into memory.

Running an animation   To start an animation sequence that you've loaded in from disk, select Run Forward from the Run menu. The animation begins to play. You can select Run Reverse from the Run menu to play the animation

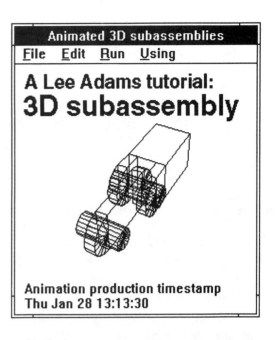

13-1 The first frame from the animation sequence generated by the sample application assembly.c. See FIG. 13-2 for the final frame of the sequence.

13-2 The final frame of the animation sequence produced by the sample application assembly.c. See FIG. 13-1 for the first frame of the sequence.

sequence backwards. To use single-step control, select Freezeframe from the Run menu while the animation is running. The keyboard controls become active. Press the right arrow key to advance to the next frame. Press the left arrow key to back up to the previous frame. Press and hold the right arrow key to play the animation sequence at the fastest rate possible on your hardware.

Quitting the sample application

To quit the sample application, choose Exit from the File menu. A message box appears, providing you with an opportunity to confirm or cancel your request.

Programmer's guide to the sample application

 This section describes how the source code works. The source listings for the sample application are presented as Fig. C-4 in Appendix C. Source listings for the linked-in toolkits are provided in Appendix B. For tips on building the sample application, see Appendix A. The source files for the sample application are also provided on the companion disk as assembly.*, engine3d.*, shapes3d.*, deform3d.*, assemb3d.*, lights3d.*, and disk3d.*.

How the .h file works

The animate.h file provides function prototypes, menu ID constants, and string ID constants. This listing is similar to the .h file described in the previous chapter. Refer back to chapter 12 if you require further discussion.

How the .rc file works

The animate.rc file describes the menu system, provides a script for accelerator keys, and contains text strings used by the application. Again, refer back to the previous chapter for a more detailed discussion.

How the .c file works

The .c file contains variable declarations, the startup function, the message handler function, and the core functions for the application. You want to understand how the hierarchical modeling component of this code works so you can add articulated motion to your own applications. The discussion in this chapter focuses on hierarchical modeling for animation. Other sections of the source code were discussed in the previous chapter. Refer back to chapter 12 if you want a more detailed analysis of portions not discussed here.

Data types Declaration of data types for the hierarchical modeling features of this application are provided at lines 0180 through 0294. First, a set of struct types are declared that define paths and movement. Lines 0181 through 0188 declare a struct type that specifies camera movement during the animation sequence. Lines 0189 through 0195 declare a struct type that specifies movement of the light-source during the animation. Lines 0196 through 0206 declare a struct type that specifies movement of an entity (actor) during the animation sequence. Lines 0208 through 0215 declare

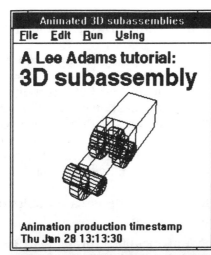

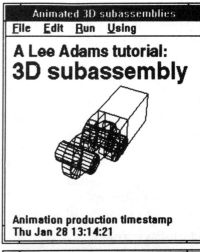

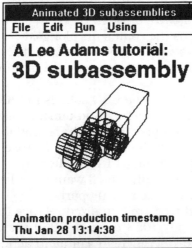

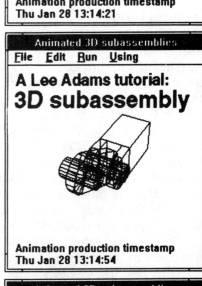

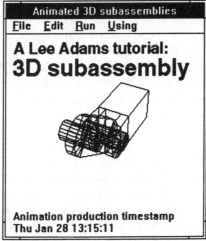

13-3   A sampling of frames from the animation sequence produced by the sample application assembly.c.

a struct type that specifies movement of an entire 3D complex solid during the animation.

Next, a set of struct types are declared that specify starting parameters. The code at lines 0217 through 0222 declares a struct type that specifies the starting location of the camera. The code at lines 0223 through 0227 declares a struct type that specifies the starting location of the light-source. The code at lines 0229 through 0237 declares a struct type that specifies the location and orientation of a 3D primitive in world-space. This primitive represents the entire 3D complex solid. The code at lines 0239 through 0266 declares a struct type that specifies a 3D primitive in its role as a part of the complex 3D solid.

Finally, the code at lines 0269 through 0277 declares variables of the struct types declared at lines 0180 through 0266.

Initializing the hierarchy   The source code at lines 0901 through 1219 initializes the variables that comprise the hierarchical solid. The camera's startup position and path is initialized at lines 0901 through 0911. You'll want to experiment with lines 0909 and 0910, as the comments alongside suggest, in order to get a feel for how the camera's path can be manipulated during the animation. The light-source's starting position and path is initialized at lines 0913 through 0920.

The starting position and path of the complex 3D solid is initialized at lines 0922 through 0932. The location, orientation, and dimensions of the various primitives that comprise the complex 3D solid are initialized at lines 0944 through 1212. The articulated motion of the level 2 progeny (the moving part) is initialized at lines 1214 through 1219. After you've built and tested the sample application successfully, you'll want to tinker with line 1219 in order to adjust the motion of the moving part.

Note in particular how some primitives are initialized relative to other primitives in the complex 3D solid. Lines 1058 through 1060 are a good example. Line 1066 shows a backward-referencing formula in action.

Building the hierarchy   The code that builds the complex 3D solid is located at lines 1377 through 1464. This section of code is an enhancement of the corresponding code from the previous chapter's animation engine—and it is cloned from the sample application discussed in chapter 9. You'll want to pay special attention to lines 1406 and 1410, which differentiate between parent and progeny (called level 1 and level 2 components in the source listing).

Where do you go from here?

Now that you've practiced hierarchical modeling for 3D animation software, you're ready to explore simulation, visualization, and virtual reality techniques. Part 4, "Introducing simulation programming," gives you the background knowledge you need to delve into the physically-based kinematics animation demo and the virtual reality sampler later in the book.

Part Four

Introducing simulation programming

Your task in part four is to prepare yourself for knowledge-based 3D simulation programming for Windows. You want to familiarize yourself with the fundamental skills required for physically-based animation and virtual reality. You also want to be confident that your understanding of 3D simulation will prepare you for the advanced kinematics demo and the virtual reality sampler that appear later in this part of the book.

In part four of the book you'll learn how to apply what you've already learned about 3D functions and animation engines to the diverse field of knowledge-based simulation. Chapter 14, "Concepts and terms," is your introduction to the words and phrases used by simulation programmers. In chapter 15, "Getting started with knowledge-based simulation," you'll learn about game-theory-based simulation, reasoning-based simulation, and physics-based simulation. When you explore game theory, you'll delve into zero-sum and nonzero-sum games, decision tables, max-min strategies, evolutionary stable strategies, and unwinnable games. When you investigate machine reasoning, you'll find out about Boolean logic, Bayesian logic, heuristic logic, fuzzy logic, connectionism, and genetic algorithms. You'll also learn about probability calculations. When you investigate physics-based simulation, you'll review fundamental principles of physics like velocity, speed, mass, elastic collisions, and others.

In chapter 16, "Getting started with kinematics and dynamics," you'll see how constraint-based animation can produce a realistic model of movement in the real-world. In chapter 17 a hands-on tutorial shows you how to put your new kinematics knowledge to work. A sample application demonstrates functions that use velocity and time to automatically manage the movement of entities in an computer-controlled animation sequence. In chapter 18, "Getting started with virtual reality," you'll learn about universes, entities, degrees-of-freedom, viewpoint nodes, and more. In chapter 19 a hands-on tutorial gives you an opportunity to experiment with a virtual reality sampler. The sample application provides a 3D maze from which there is only one exit.

Before you begin to investigate knowledge-based simulation for Windows, you want to familiarize yourself with some of the words and phrases used by experienced developers. The next chapter, "Concepts and terms," provides you with the background information you need to get started.

14

Concepts and terms: simulation programming

This chapter introduces some basic concepts and terms that you'll be using while you explore part four, "Introducing simulation programming."

The task—What you want to achieve

You'll want to be able to understand the technical language that is used in the next five chapters. This background knowledge will make it easier for you to learn the fundamental skills required for using knowledge-based 3D simulations in your own animated Windows applications.

The plan—What you will learn

In this chapter you'll read about the concepts and terms that describe knowledge-based simulation programming for Windows. You'll also learn how each term and each concept fits into the diverse field of knowledge-based simulation programming.

Defining concepts and terms

Simulation   *Simulation* is the use of computer software to model and analyze the behavior of systems occurring in the real world. The systems being modeled can be natural systems or they can be manufactured systems. A flight simulator, for example, models and simulates a manufactured system (an aircraft). A biotech simulator, on the other hand, models and simulates a natural system (a chromosome string). Here's a good way to think of it:

a computer model describes what the thing is, a computer simulation shows what the thing does. In other words, the model describes the system's appearance, the simulation shows the system's behavior.

Knowledge-based simulation *Knowledge-based simulation* uses knowledge-based methods of science to enhance the accuracy and usefulness of the simulation. Knowledge-based methods can include game theory and decision tables, reasoning and logic, probability and certainty, the laws of physics and chemistry, and others.

The simulation pipeline The *simulation pipeline* is the chain of software functions that produces the run-time simulation. A simulation pipeline relies mainly on 3D functions and animation engines. These capabilities can be enhanced with methods of visualization, simulation, and virtual reality. Visualization adds measurements, color, quantification, and attributes to the 3D pipeline that you learned about in part two of the book. Simulation adds spatial and temporal controls to the animation pipeline that you explored in part three of the book. Virtual reality adds interactive controls to the software chain.

Game-theory-based simulation *Game-theory-based simulation* relies on the science of game theory. A game is any activity, enterprise, situation, or endeavor between or amongst humans. The game can be serious or it can be trivial, it can be competitive or it can be cooperative, it can be a single occurrence or a repeated event, but the strategy adopted by each player determines the player's gain or loss each time the game is played. Game-theory-based simulations often use matrices called *decision tables* to compute the best strategy for zero-sum and nonzero-sum games. Game theory can be used to develop efficient strategies for single games and for iterated games—against the same opponent and against random opponents.

Zero-sum and nonzero-sum games In a *zero-sum game*, a gain for one player is always a loss for the other player. In a *nonzero-sum game*, a gain for one player is not necessarily at the expense of the other player. Both players can win.

Prisoner's dilemma A *prisoner's dilemma* is a special type of game in which a player has only two options—either cooperate or cheat. Cooperating usually means acting in the interest of the common good. Cheating usually means acting in selfish interest. A cheater grabs, whereas a cooperator shares. The outcome of a prisoner's dilemma game depends not just on what the player does, but on what the opponent does. The player has no way of knowing the opponent's strategy beforehand.

Here's the crux of the dilemma. If player A cheats (grabs) and player B cooperates (shares), then player A grabs the maximum gain at B's expense. Player B is awarded a so-called *sucker's payoff* in this case. However, if player B cheats too, then neither wins. In fact, both players experience a loss when both cheat. If they both cooperate (share), they are rewarded with a moderate gain (that is not nearly as large as the gain they could achieve by cheating, of course).

So what strategy should player A adopt? Thinking it through, player A realizes that player B will also want the maximum gain and will likely cheat. But if they both cheat they both lose. So it makes sense for both to cooperate and settle for a less-than-optimum gain, but a gain nonetheless. But if player B is likely to act rationally and cooperate, isn't this a good opportunity for player A to take advantage of B by cheating and grabbing the maximum gain? So there's the dilemma. Should player A cooperate or cheat?

Max-min strategy A *max-min strategy* is a strategy that attempts to maximum the potential for gain while minimizing the potential for loss.

Evolutionary-stable strategy An *evolutionary-stable strategy (ESS)* is one that makes sense over a large number of games. It ensures the survival of the player in the long run.

Unwinnable game An *unwinnable game* is a special type of game in which the best outcome a player can hope for is to minimize the loss. The player can never win (gain). Consider, for example, that you've placed a long-distance telephone call to a software support facility. You are greeted by an automated answering device that informs you your call is being queued until a technical support person becomes available. Then the elevator music begins.

How long should you wait before hanging up? It might take two minutes or it might take twenty minutes before your call is handled—and every minute is costing you long-distance charges. If you hang up after two minutes, then you'll have to call back another day and perhaps wait another two or three minutes anyway before being connected. In that case, you would have wasted two minutes in toll charges on today's call. But if you keep hanging on for two, three, five, ten minutes, there's still no guarantee your call will ever be answered before the end of the business day. You're playing an unwinnable game. The best you can hope for is to keep your long-distance costs as low as possible.

Reasoning *Reasoning* is the thinking process that draws conclusions or makes inferences. Reasoning is problem-solving thinking. *Machine reasoning* is the process of using computer software to model and simulate a thinking process or a problem-solving process. It often relies upon different forms of logic, including Boolean logic, Bayesian logic, heuristic logic, fuzzy logic, connectionism, genetic algorithms, and others.

Boolean logic *Boolean logic* uses if/then reasoning. It is based upon predicate calculus (calculations using special symbols). Boolean logic is suited for cognitive simulation software.

Bayesian logic *Bayesian logic* uses permutations and combinations. It is based upon probability calculus. Bayesian logic is suited for cognitive simulation software.

Heuristic logic *Heuristic logic* uses best-guess reasoning. It is based upon common-sense. Heuristic logic is suited for expert-system software.

Fuzzy logic *Fuzzy logic* uses approximate reasoning or best-fit reasoning. It is based upon possibility calculus. Fuzzy logic is suited for process control.

Connectionism *Connectionism* uses connection-based algorithms. It is based upon the physical brain. Neural networks are a form of connectionism. Connectionism is suited for pattern matching.

Genetic algorithms *Genetic algorithms* use processes of selection and mutation. Genetic programming is based upon the evolution of organisms. Genetic algorithms are suited for exploration control.

Deductive reasoning Deductive reasoning uses a knowledge base to infer an effect from observed causes. Here's an example of deductive reasoning using the typical given-if-then paradigm. *Given* that squirrels are usually quicker than cats, *if* you see a cat chasing a squirrel, *then* the squirrel is likely to get away safely.

Inductive reasoning *Inductive reasoning* uses empirical observations. For example, suppose you've just moved to a new part of the country and you observe the neighbor's cat chasing a squirrel who seems to always elude the cat. If you see this happening time and time again, you might infer that squirrels are generally quicker than cats. You've just used inductive reasoning.

What you've really done, of course, is add to your mind's knowledge base the fact that squirrels are usually quicker than cats. That information is now available for deductive reasoning in future situations. Suppose, for example, you see the other neighbor's cat chasing a different squirrel. Using deductive reasoning (and the new information you've just acquired through inductive reasoning) your thinking might run like this. *Given* that squirrels are usually quicker than cats, *if* you see a cat chasing a squirrel, *then* the squirrel is likely to get away safely.

Abductive reasoning *Abductive reasoning* infers a probable cause from observed effects. It is the reverse of deductive reasoning, which infers an effect from observed causes. Here's how abductive reasoning works. Suppose, for example, you glance out the window and spot a squirrel frantically scrambling up your oak tree. Using abductive reasoning, you might infer that the probable cause of the squirrel's behavior is the neighbor's cat in hot pursuit of the squirrel. Of course, the cat might not have been involved, but in the absence of contradictory observations or knowledge, it's reasonable for you to draw that conclusion. You might, for example, say that you're 90% certain that the cat was involved. Abductive reasoning is useful even if you've never seen your neighbor's cat chasing a squirrel. You might observe the squirrel's frenetic behavior and use abductive reasoning to infer that it was being pursued by another animal of unknown type. You've perhaps seen dogs, cats, and raccoons in the neighborhood, so you might be only 25% certain your neighbor's cat was involved.

Cognitive computing *Cognitive computing* means using software to simulate the thinking process of the human mind.

Probability *Probability* is a branch of mathematics concerned with the likelihood of events happening. The probability of an event occurring is obtained by dividing the number of favorable events by the number of possible results. For example, the probability of drawing a deuce from a deck of 52 randomly shuffled cards is 4 divided by 52, or .076923. Probability calculations use permutations, combinations, and binomial coefficients.

Permutations *Permutations* are lineups of members selected from a general population. For example, the total number of lineups of 4 colors chosen from a palette of 10 colors is 5,040. The permutation calculation is $10 \times 9 \times 8 \times 7 = 5,040$. It is the order of the members in the lineup that matters, not the content. That's why the number 5,040 seems so high. When you're using permutations, you consider a lineup of red-green-blue-cyan to be different from a lineup of red-green- cyan-blue, even though the same four colors are involved.

Combinations *Combinations* are committees of members chosen from a general population. For example, the total number of committees of 4 persons chosen from a group of 10 people is 210. (The binomial calculations that produce this result are discussed in the next chapter.) It is the content of the committee that matters, not the order of the members. When you're using combinations, you consider a committee of Kim, Ken, Karen, and Kevin to be the same as a committee of Kevin, Karen, Ken, and Kim, because the same four people are involved, only in different order.

Conditional probability *Conditional probability* can be used to calculate the likelihood of an event occurring after a prerequisite event has occurred. For example, suppose that two cards are drawn from a randomly shuffled deck of cards. The probability of drawing a spade on the second draw after a spade was drawn on the first draw is .2353. To arrive at this figure, the number of spades remaining after the first draw is divided by the number of cards remaining after the first draw. If a spade was drawn first, this formula is 12 divided by 51. Remember, as you've already learned, the probability of an event occurring is the number of favorable events divided by the number of possible events.

Physics-based simulation *Physics-based simulation* uses principles of physics to manage the events being modeled and simulated. The software considers factors such as velocity, speed, displacement, acceleration, deceleration, mass, density, linear momentum, kinetic energy, inelastic collisions, elastic collisions, and others.

Velocity   *Velocity* is the rate of change of displacement over time. It is speed in a specified direction. Velocity is a vector quantity.

Speed   *Speed* is displacement over time. It is a scalar quantity, such as 65 mph or 100 kph. No direction is provided.

Displacement   *Displacement* is distance measured from a fixed reference point. It is a vector quantity that uses a specified direction.

Acceleration   *Acceleration* is the rate of increase of velocity over time. It is a vector quantity, such as 12 meters per second per second.

Deceleration   *Deceleration* is the rate of decrease of velocity over time.

Mass   *Mass* is the quantity of matter in an entity. It is an indication of the entity's inertia.

Density   *Density* is mass per unit of volume. It reflects how much matter is present per unit of volume.

Linear momentum   *Linear momentum* is the product of mass and velocity.

Kinetic energy   *Kinetic energy* is the energy possessed by an entity because of its motion. It is the potential to do work.

Inelastic collision   In an *inelastic collision,* linear momentum is conserved but kinetic energy is not conserved. Some kinetic energy is lost as heat, work done, or physical damage. The entities involved in an inelastic collision are rigid or semi-rigid bodies.

Elastic collision   In an *elastic collision,* linear momentum and kinetic energy are conserved.

Physically-based animation   *Physically-based animation* is 3D animation that uses physics to manage an entity's motion. Because the motion is regulated by constraints, physically-based animation is also called *constraint-based animation.*

Constraints   *Constraints* are forces, loads, and matter that affect the motion of an entity in a physically-based animation sequence.

How physically-based animation is implemented

Physically-based animation can be implemented as forward kinematics, forward dynamics, inverse kinematics, and inverse dynamics. *Forward kinematics* concerns what happens when velocity or acceleration is applied to an entity. *Forward dynamics* concerns what happens when force, loads, and other constraints are applied to an entity. *Inverse kinematics* calculates the velocity or acceleration that is required to move an entity from one location to another location during a specified period of time. *Inverse dynamics* calculates the forces, loads, or other constraints required to move an entity from one location to another location during a specified period of time.

Virtual reality *Virtual reality* is a real-time simulation of 4D space-time. It provides a means for humans to interact with a simulated 3D environment. Simply put, virtual reality is a human-computer interface. It is a way for a user to visualize, manipulate, and interact with a database. The database is the virtual environment, the virtual entities it contains, and the script that defines how the environment and the entities interact with the user. *VR* is an acronym for virtual reality.

Universe A *universe* is a particular 3D environment, including the entities it contains and the script for managing the simulation. Some VR software can load different universes from disk in order to provide different virtual experiences.

Entity An *entity* is an actor, entity, prop, or scenery element that exists in the virtual environment.

Sensor From the user's point of view, a *sensor* is a point in 3D space in the virtual environment that responds to certain actions by the user. From the programmer's point of view, a sensor is a section of code that polls the input devices to determine if the user has triggered an event. For example, a 3D box (an entity) in the virtual environment might be scripted to change color from blue to red if the box is touched by the VR user (or by the software's representation of the user in virtual space).

The simulation manager A simulation manager is an enhanced animation engine that manages a virtual reality session. It performs four functions:

- update
- enforce
- sense
- move

First, the simulation manager updates the display image each time the user changes location or shifts the direction of gaze. For example, it generates an appropriate 3D image if the user turns to observe a doorway leading to a virtual room. Second, the simulation manager enforces the VR rules. For example, it prevents the user from walking through a closed door. Third, the simulation manager's sensors detect when portions of the virtual environment must respond to actions of the user. For example, it might illuminate the virtual room when the user enters. Fourth, the simulation manager implements the scripted motion of moving entities in the virtual environment. For example, it might automatically update the face of a clock in the virtual room.

VR rules *VR rules* are the laws that govern a virtual reality session. A VR rule, for example, might dictate that a user cannot pass through a closed door. However, another VR rule might allow a user to pass through a window, even if it's closed. Different universes can possess different sets of VR rules.

Degrees-of-freedom   *Degrees-of-freedom* refers to the axis of rotation and translation provided by an input device. A mouse, for example, provides two degrees-of-freedom.

Bat   A *bat* is a floating, mouselike input device that provides three degrees-of-freedom. The user can usually select from XYZ translation or yaw-roll-pitch rotation, but cannot use both simultaneously.

Bird   A *bird* is a floating, mouselike input device that provides six degrees of freedom. The user can simultaneously select from XYZ translation and yaw-roll-pitch rotation.

Where do you go from here?

Now that you've familiarized yourself with some of the basic concepts and terms used in simulation programming, you're ready to start learning the fundamental skills. The next chapter, "Getting started with knowledge-based simulation," teaches you about game theory, machine reasoning, probability, and physics.

15
Getting started with knowledge-based simulation

This chapter teaches you how to use knowledge-based simulation to manage and display moving 3D scenes in the viewport of your application's window. It discusses concepts like game theory, logic, reasoning, probability, and physics.

The task—What you want to achieve

Your task in this chapter is to become familiar with the underlying principles of knowledge-based simulation. You want to know about game theory, including zero-sum and nonzero-sum games, max-min strategies, and unwinnable games. You want to gain a thorough understanding of machine reasoning, including the six different forms of logic and the three different types of reasoning. You want to grasp the concept of probability and to learn about simulations based on the laws of physics.

The plan—What you will learn

In this chapter you'll learn how knowledge-based simulation can be implemented in a Windows application using different disciplines and paradigms. You'll discover why game theory is so important to simulation programming, and you'll learn about zero-sum and nonzero-sum games, max-min strategies, ESS strategies, traders and raiders, unforgiving retaliators, and unwinnable games. You'll delve into machine reasoning and the six forms of logic it can use, including Boolean logic, Bayesian logic, heuristic logic, fuzzy logic, connectionism, and genetic algorithms. You'll see why the science of formal reasoning is important to cognitive computing, and you'll investigate deductive reasoning, inductive reasoning, and abductive reasoning. You'll discover how to calculate probability by using permutations and combinations as you delve into sampling, complementary events, biased probability space, and conditional probability. You'll explore physics-based simulation, including velocity, acceleration, collisions, and more. The information you'll learn in this chapter will prepare you for the high-performance tutorials that are coming up.

The simulation pipeline

As you've already learned in the previous chapter, *simulation* means using computer software to model and analyze the behavior of real systems. The systems being simulated can be natural systems or they can be manufactured systems. For example, a spaceflight simulation might model and simulate a manufactured system (the NASA space shuttle). A wildlife management simulation might model and simulate a natural system (an ecosystem embodying the interplay between predators, food supply, weather patterns, and species populations).

These two examples highlight the differences between modeling and simulation. Modeling can describe what the system is, but only simulation can show what the system does. Modeling describes the system's appearance and technical specifications. Simulation demonstrates (or predicts) the system's behavior and performance characteristics. Knowledge-based simulations are implemented using a *simulation pipeline*.

A simulation pipeline is any collection of software algorithms and functions that can produce an animated simulation sequence in the viewport of your application's window. A minimum configuration is an animation engine and a 3D toolkit. The animation engine is for motion. The 3D toolkit is for modeling and rendering. These minimal components can be upgraded by using additional programming techniques such as visualization, simulation, and virtual reality. Each adds something new to the pipeline:

- Visualization adds quantification
- Simulation adds spatial and temporal controls
- Virtual reality adds interactive controls

Visualization   *Visualization* adds measurement, color, quantification, qualification, and other attributes to the 3D functions that you studied in part 2 of the book. Visualization provides a sense of purpose. Fidelity is the goal. Visualization makes concrete what otherwise exists only in our imaginations. Visualization is the process that transforms the contents of the human imagination to the computer display. Whatever can be imagined by the mind can be modeled, rendered, and displayed by the computer—and the process is called visualization. All that's needed are parameters—the programmer's decision about which variables, measurements, and other parameters will be used by the 3D functions. Think of it this way: a 3D entity's XYZ dimensions are usually provided as units of displacement (distance, length, and so on). But it need not be that way. Visualization means unshackling our minds and using other measurements as input for the XYZ components. For example, X might be speed, Y might be temperature, and Z might be time. Even complex mathematical theories can be visualized using this approach.

Visualization is a thinking tool. It extends the breadth and power of human imagination. It amplifies and multiplies our intelligence and our creativity. It is an important element in the knowledge-based simulation pipeline, because only after you've visualized something can you can use simulation to investigate its behavior.

Simulation   *Simulation* adds spatial and temporal controls to the animation functions that you explored in Part 3 of the book. *Spatial* refers to space; *temporal* refers to time. Simulation is 4D space-time, expressed as XYZT coordinates. It is animation with a sense of purpose. Simulation is animation that purports to represent a system (a thing or a process) from the real world. If the system has been modeled accurately and with fidelity, then the simulation will be able to visually demonstrate the performance of the system over time. It might even be able to predict the behavior of the system. When special knowledge is used to manage a simulation, the result is knowledge-based simulation. The consummate knowledge-based simulation is virtual reality.

Virtual reality   *Virtual reality* is a simulation of 4D space-time presented in an interactive, real-time context. VR provides a means for interacting with a simulated 3D environment. In its role as a human-computer interface, virtual reality provides a way for the user to manipulate and interact with a database. The database is visual. It is comprised of the 4D space-time (the artificial reality) and the entities (artificial objects) it contains, as well as a script specifying how the system and its universe interacts with the user.

A *universe* is a particular configuration of a virtual reality. The universe includes the virtual environment, the entities it contains, and a script for managing the simulation, as well as its sensors and entities. *Entities* are actors, props, or scenery elements in the virtual environment. *Sensors* are objects in the virtual environment that can interact with the user by responding to the user's actions or location. As you've already learned, a programmer considers a sensor as any block of code that polls the input devices to determine if the user has done something to trigger an event in the virtual environment. Sensors are integrated into the simulation manager of the virtual reality engine.

The *simulation manager* is an animation engine that has been modified to manage a virtual reality session. It performs various functions, including updating the display image, enforcing the VR rules, sensing when interaction occurs, and moving virtual entities.

Together and individually, the programming techniques of visualization, simulation, and virtual reality can be used to enhance a minimal configuration of animation engine and 3D toolkit in order to create an infrastructure for knowledge-based simulation.

Knowledge-based simulation

Knowledge-based simulation is simulation that uses special knowledge to boost the run-time performance and fidelity of a simulation. Knowledge-based simulations often rely upon disciplines like game theory, logic, reasoning, probability theory, and physics.

Each of these disciplines brings a different perspective to the simulation. *Game theory* is the science of calculating appropriate strategies for dealing with competitive or adversarial situations, events, and endeavors. *Logic* is the science that provides the formal principles for reasoning. *Reasoning* is the thinking process that draws conclusions and makes inferences. It is problem-solving thinking. Probability theory provides a mechanism for predicting the likelihood of an event's occurrence. The laws of physics describe behavior in the real world.

As you learned in the previous chapter, knowledge-based simulation often relies upon different forms of logic, including Boolean logic, Bayesian logic, heuristic logic, as well as different forms of cognitive computing, including fuzzy logic, connectionism, and genetic algorithms, as shown in Fig. 15-1.

Boolean logic uses if/then reasoning based upon *predicate calculus*. (A calculus is simply a set of calculations that uses operators and operands especially suited to the subject matter.) Boolean logic is used in cognitive simulation software that imitates the thinking process of the human mind. A related form of logic called *Bayesian logic* uses permutations and combi-

Knowledge-based simulation	
Boolean logic	Based upon predicate calculus. Uses *if...then* reasoning. Suited for cognitive simulation.
Bayesian logic	Based upon probability calculus. Uses permutations, combinations. Suited for cognitive simulation.
Heuristic logic	Based upon common-sense. Uses best-guess reasoning. Suited for expert-systems.
Fuzzy logic	Based upon possibility calculus. Uses approximate reasoning. Suited for process-control.
Neural networks	Based upon the physical brain. Uses connection-based algorithms. Suited for pattern-matching.
Genetic algorithms	Based upon evolution of organisms. Uses selection/mutation algorithms. Suited for exploration-control.

15-1 Programming algorithms for knowledge-based simulation.

nations. It is based upon probability calculus. Bayesian logic is also often used in cognitive simulation software.

Heuristic logic is best described as best-guess reasoning based upon common sense. Heuristic logic is used in expert-system software. Its cousin, *fuzzy logic*, on the other hand, uses approximate reasoning or best-fit reasoning. It is based upon possibility calculus. Fuzzy logic is used in process-control applications.

Connectionism uses connection-based algorithms based upon the physical brain. Neural networks are an implementation of connectionism. Connectionism is used for pattern detection, pattern recognition, and pattern matching. Another nature-based discipline, *genetic programming*, uses selection and mutation based upon the principles of evolution. Genetic algorithms are suited for exploration, discovery, and search applications.

Whether Boolean, Bayesian, heuristic, fuzzy, connectionist, or genetic, the science of logic casts its influence over most simulation software. However, only game-theory-based simulation has the ability to make logic sometimes seem illogical.

Game-theory-based simulation

Game-theory-based simulation is named for the science of game theory. A *game* is any activity, enterprise, situation, or endeavor between or amongst humans. A so-called game can be serious or trivial. It can be competitive, adversarial, or cooperative. It can be a single occurrence or repeated many times. It can be played against the same opponent or against randomly selected opponents.

The strategy used by each player determines the player's *payoff*, which is the gain or loss experienced by the player each time the game is played. As shown in Fig. 15-2, game theory-based simulations often use a matrix called a decision-table to analyze the available strategies for a particular game.

Zero-sum and nonzero-sum games

Games can be categorized as either *zero-sum* or *nonzero-sum*. In a zero-sum game a gain for one player is always a loss for the other player. In a nonzero-sum game, a gain for one player is not necessarily at the expense of the other player. Both players can win.

Here's an example of a nonzero-sum game. Suppose two retailers are competing in the same neighborhood. Each retailer could aggressively reduce prices in order to compete, and one of them will eventually dominate the market, perhaps driving the other out of business. This strategy offers maximum gain but threatens maximum loss. However, if both retailers are willing to settle for less than total market domination, each might decide to refrain from competing on the basis of price. Retailer A, who normally charges $1.00, might observe that Retailer B is charging $1.25. Rather than

Game-theory decision-table

	Player X COOPERATE	Player X CHEAT
Player Y **COOPERATE**	X+3, Y+3 Moderate GAIN for X Moderate GAIN for Y	X+5, Y+0 Maximum GAIN for X Maximum LOSS for Y
Player Y **CHEAT**	X+0, Y+5 Maximum LOSS for X Maximum GAIN for Y	X+1, Y+1 Moderate LOSS for X Moderate LOSS for Y

Prisoner's dilemma game-tables

The ranking of the rewards always adheres to two preconditions if the game is a so-called prisoner's dilemma.

Precondition 1 $A > B > C > D$ where A represents Maximum GAIN for the player, B represents Moderate GAIN, C represents Moderate LOSS, and D represents Maximum LOSS.

Precondition 2 $\dfrac{A+D}{2} \leq B$

Zero-sum and nonzero-sum games

Any game-theory decision-table can be considered as either a Zero-sum game or a Nonzero-sum game. In a zero-sum game, a win for one player is always a loss for the other player (ie X+5, Y-5). In a nonzero-sum game, both players can win (ie X+3, Y+3). Each player's perception of the game is influenced by personality type, access to outside information affecting the size of the rewards, communication with the other player, and so on.

15-2 Fundamentals of game-theory.

use this price advantage to attract new customers and extra profit, Retailer A instead simply raises the price from $1.00 to $1.25 and pockets the extra profit from existing customers. The retailers are discreetly engaging in what amounts to informal price-fixing. Both retailers survive in the marketplace. Both players win in this nonzero-sum game, because the loser is a third party. In this instance the losers are the consumers, who must pay the artificially inflated prices of the conniving retailers (at least until a nationwide chain notices the profit potential and decides to establish a retail outlet in the neighborhood). Notice that game theory does not consider morals, ethics, or laws—only strategies and their results.

On the other hand, here's an example of a zero-sum game. Suppose two competing antique dealers have decided to submit written bids for an antique being offered at private auction. A floor bid has been established by the auction house, so each dealer knows the minimum price the seller will accept. The dealers also know the maximum price each can expect to receive when they resell the antique in their retail shop. Each dealer could adopt either a cautious strategy or a bold strategy. A cautious strategy means bidding low. This is less likely to be the winning bid but offers larger profit in the end. A bold strategy means bidding high, near the maximum retail price. This is much more likely to be the winning bid but offers smaller profit potential. No matter which strategy prevails, though, only one of the dealers is going to win—and it's going to be at the expense of the other dealer. Only one of the dealers will enjoy the privilege of buying the antique at auction, marking up the wholesale price, and making a profit at retail. The other dealer will not have an antique to sell. This is a zero-sum game.

Decision tables   Both of the examples just mentioned can be simplified through the use of *decision-tables.* The example in Fig. 15-2 provides a decision-table suitable for zero-sum games. If each gain and loss is assigned a numeric value, then algorithmic formulas can be developed. This means that software functions can be used to calculate the advantages and disadvantages of each strategy. This type of analysis is particularly important in *prisoner's dilemma* games.

Prisoner's dilemma   A *prisoner's dilemma* is a special type of game in which each player possesses only two options: either cooperate or cheat. Cooperating is usually deemed to mean acting in the interest of the common good. Cheating is usually deemed to mean acting in the player's selfish interest. A cheater grabs and a cooperator shares; it's as simple as that. The outcome of a prisoner's dilemma game depends not only on the player's behavior, but also on the opponent's behavior. A player has no advance knowledge of the opponent's strategy.

Suppose, for example, that player A and player B are environmentalists who protest by throwing a cream pie in the face of a pro-development local politician during a news conference. The two players are arrested and detained in separate cells, unable to communicate with each other. The authorities don't know who actually threw the pie (in fact both players simultaneously tossed the ballistic), so the most serious indictment that can be registered against both players is mischief. But if one of the players were to testify against the other, then the thrower could be charged with assault, a more serious offense. So each player is presented with an ultimatum by the investigating officer: "Testify against your partner and we'll drop the charges against you."

So far so good. Player A begins to consider the situation. The prisoner's dilemma rapidly becomes evident. Suppose that player A cooperates (with fellow-environmentalist player B) and says nothing. Provided that player B also cooperates and keeps mum, then player A will be charged with the lesser offense of mischief. The result is likely to be a $250 fine for each player. But what's stopping player B from squealing on player A? Player A would be charged with assault while player B goes free. Player A might end up with the humiliation of a suspended sentence, mandatory probation, plus a heftier $1000 fine.

It gets worse, though. Player A speculates that if player B is thinking this situation through the same way player A is thinking it through, then B will realize A is likely to cooperate, so B will be tempted to cheat and take advantage of A's naive and trusting nature. So perhaps player A should cheat. But if both cheat, then both face the risk of the more serious assault charge.

As the decision-table in Fig. 15-2 shows, if player A cheats and player B cooperates, then player A grabs the maximum gain at player B's expense. However, if player B cheats too, then neither player wins. Both players experience a loss when both cheat. If both players cooperate they are rewarded with a moderate gain. In order for a game to be a prisoner's dilemma, the moderate gain must be a value not nearly as large as the maximum gain achieved by cheating.

What strategy does player A use? Thinking it through, player A realizes that player B also wants the maximum gain and is likely to cheat. But there's the dilemma. If they both cheat they both lose. So it makes sense for both to cooperate and settle for only a moderate gain, rather than the maximum gain. But that raises yet another dilemma. If player B is likely to act rationally and cooperate, this presents a tempting opportunity for player A to take advantage of B by cheating and grabbing the maximum gain. So, should player A cooperate or cheat?

Single-game vs. iterative games

A player can perceive a game as a single event or as a series of repeated games. This perception has a significant effect on the strategy that a clear-headed, rational player is likely to adopt.

Max-min strategy for single-game In a game played once only, a rational player can minimize potential loss by playing cheat. This is because there is simply no way to predict or to enforce the cooperation of the other player. That doesn't necessarily mean that a player will always play cheat. The player's perception of the opponent's personality, playing style, past performance, and even the availability of outside information might influence the player to adopt a different strategy. No matter what the outcome of the game, each player might have no regrets, feeling that their strategy was the best choice at the time. This situation is called an *equilibrium* by game theorists. Equilibriums are often cited as proof of rational strategies by the players, because (even with the benefit of hindsight) the players would not change their strategies.

Max-min strategies for iterative games When developing a strategy for repeated games, two types of scenarios need to be considered. First, the repeated games might be played against the same opponent. Second, the repeated games might be played against different opponents randomly selected from a large population of strangers.

Against the same opponent   In repeated games against the same opponent, a rational player can maximize gain by playing cooperate on the first move, and thereafter only playing cheat in direct retaliation to cheating by the opponent.

Against random opponents   In repeated games against random opponents from a large population, a rational player will play cooperate against an unfamiliar opponent, and against familiar opponents who have cooperated in previous games. The rational player will play cheat against a familiar player who cheated in previous games.

What constitutes a good strategy sometimes depends on your point of view. What is beneficial for an individual player might not be good for the whole population of players, as Fig. 15-3 shows. What if everyone cheated? Or what if no one cheated?

Evolutionary-stable strategies

An *evolutionary-stable strategy (ESS)* is a strategy that ensures survival over the long term if most players in the population are using it.

Consider, for example, a population of players who trade pieces of food amongst each other in order to ensure a balanced diet. Players who attempt to exist only on foodstuffs that they've gathered or grown will suffer from malnutrition and disease. Each player specializes in producing just one type of food.

A cooperator accepts a morsel of food from another player and in exchange gives a piece of food to the other player. This strategy is called *always cooperate*. Players using this strategy are called *traders*.

A cheater takes a morsel of food from the other player and then simply runs away. Clearly, the temptation to cheat is significant because a cheater gets twice the amount of food. This strategy is called *always cheat*. Players using this strategy are called *raiders*.

A grudge will cooperate in new encounters and in encounters with known cooperators, but will always cheat against players who have previously cheated. This strategy is called *unforgiving grudge*. Players using this strategy are called *unforgiving retaliators*.

But what are the long-term consequences of these various strategies for the population as a whole? Will the population thrive or will it become extinct?

Always cooperate   This strategy is stable over the long term in a population consisting mainly of other cooperators. However, if the population contains significant numbers of cheaters the cooperators will eventually be driven to extinction. Cooperators can coexist with grudges, however, because the grudges will never be provoked into cheating.

Always cheat   This strategy can be stable in a population consisting mainly of cooperators. In some ratios, however, the cheaters might initially thrive

Game-theory strategies

Type of game	Best strategy	Reasoning
Single game against unfamiliar opponent	**ALWAYS CHEAT**	In a single game, logic dictates that a rational player can minimize potential loss by always playing CHEAT, because there is simply no way to predict or to enforce cooperation of the other player.
Many games against the same opponent	**FORGIVING GRUDGE (TIT-FOR-TAT)**	In repeated games against the same opponent, a rational player can maximize gain by playing COOPERATE on the first move, and only playing CHEAT in direct retaliation to cheating by the opponent.
Many games against random opponents	**UNFORGIVING GRUDGE**	In repeated games against random opponents from a large population, a rational player will play COOPERATE against an unfamiliar opponent and familiar opponents who cooperated in previous games. A rational player plays CHEAT against a familiar player who cheated in previous games.

ESS strategies

Evolutionary-stable strategies (ESS) guarantee survival in a large population. Many strategies are available. Three are described here. The size of rewards is a critical factor in determing which strategies are stable over the long-term.

ALWAYS COOPERATE -- This strategy is stable in a Cooperator population. The Cooperators will be driven to extinction if the population contains significant numbers of Cheaters. Cooperators can coexist with Grudges.

ALWAYS CHEAT -- This strategy can be stable in a population comprised mainly of Cooperators or comprised mainly of other Cheaters. Cheaters will be driven to extinction if the population contains a significant number of Grudges. In a population comprised mainly of Cooperators, Cheaters may initially thrive but will sometimes drive themselves to extinction after victimizing and eliminating all the Cooperators.

UNFORGIVING GRUDGE -- This stragegy is stable and will survive in a population comprised mainly of Cooperators. Grudges will survive and will drive Cheaters to extinction in a population of Cheaters containing a significant minority of Grudges.

15-3 Fundamentals of game-theory strategies.

by taking advantage of the cooperators, but will often drive themselves to extinction after victimizing and eliminating all of the cooperators. The cheaters will also be driven to extinction if the population contains a significant number of grudges.

Unforgiving grudge Players using this strategy will survive in a population consisting mainly of cooperators, provided not too many grudges are present. In a population consisting mainly of cheaters, grudges will eventually drive the cheaters to extinction if there is a significant minority of grudges (so they can enjoy the advantages of occasionally bumping into each other).

Other strategies   Other strategies are available, of course, Grudges can be flexible, forgiving past transgressions of their opponents. A grudge, for example, might punish a former cheater by cheating during the next confrontation, but thereafter might cooperate. Players using this strategy are called *forgiving retaliators.* It is also feasible that some players will use arbitrarily shifting strategies.

Unwinnable games

An *unwinnable game* is a special type of game in which the best outcome a player can hope for is to minimize the potential loss. The player cannot win. You've already encountered an example of an unwinnable game in the previous chapter. Suppose that you've placed a long-distance telephone call to a software support facility. An automated answering device informs you that your call is being put on hold until a technical support person becomes available. It might be fifteen minutes before your call is answered. Every minute means long-distance toll charges, but if you hang up after two minutes, then you'll just have to call back another day, and perhaps be confronted by the same problem. In that case, you'll have wasted two minutes worth of toll charges on today's futile call. But no matter how long you keep hanging on, there's no guarantee your call will ever be answered. You are a player in an unwinnable game. The best you can hope for is to keep your long-distance costs to a minimum.

Dollar auction   The *dollar auction* is another example of an unwinnable game. Consider the following situation. You and a group of acquaintances are gathered at a reception. In order to liven up the affair, someone stands up and offers to sell a $100 bill to the highest bidder, no matter how low the bid is. The rules are simple for this dollar auction. The player making the highest bid earns the right to buy the $100 bill from the auctioneer for the amount of the bid. Here's the catch, though. The player making the second-highest bid must pay that amount to the auctioneer, and receives nothing in return.

Sooner or later someone will bid $1. After all, that means a $99 profit. Of course, someone else will bid $2, and so on. But what happens when the bid is $99? Suppose the previous bid was $98. The second-place player stands to lose a whopping $98, while the player with the winning $99 bid makes a $1 dollar profit.

The game has become unwinnable. After thinking it through, the second-place player decides to bid $100. This is a break-even strategy, of course. But now the $99 bidder stands to lose $99. This player will likely decide that losing $1 is better than losing $99, so the player will bid $101 for the right to purchase a one-hundred dollar bill. Now the other player must bid $102, and so on, throwing good money after bad. Game theory researchers call this the *invested equity syndrome.* During informal experiments among unsuspecting individuals, $10 bills have been sold for as much as $30 and belligerent shouting matches have spoiled otherwise amicable gatherings. Could the situation have been avoided by better reasoning?

Reasoning-based simulation

Reasoning-based simulation is based on software algorithms that mimic human thinking processes. As you've already learned, reasoning is founded on different forms of logic, including Boolean logic, Bayesian logic, and heuristic logic, as well as different forms of cognitive computing such as fuzzy logic, connectionism, and genetic programming.

Boolean logic uses if/then predicate calculus. Bayesian logic uses the permutations and combinations of probability calculus. Heuristic logic uses best-guess reasoning. Fuzzy logic uses best-fit reasoning. Connectionism uses connection-based algorithms such as neural networks Genetic programming uses selection and mutation based upon evolution.

The set of logic symbols is shown in Fig. 15-4. Examples of logic calculus are shown in Figs. 15-5 and 15-6. The types of cognitive computing techniques are shown in Fig. 15-7.

Logic symbols	
→	implies
¬	not
∨	or
∧	and
∀	for all
∃	there exists

15-4   Logic symbols.

Propositional logic	
Normal-language statement	**Logic calculus**
It is stormy.	STORMY
It is sunny.	SUNNY
If it is stormy, then it is not sunny.	STORMY → ¬ SUNNY
Propositional logic can represent facts from the real world as logical propositions written as wffs (well-formed formulas).	

15-5   Fundamentals of propositional logic.

Reasoning

If logic provides the formal foundation for reasoning, then reasoning is the thinking process that makes inferences. Reasoning is problem-solving. The three categories of reasoning are:

- deductive reasoning
- inductive reasoning
- abductive reasoning

Deductive reasoning   *Deductive reasoning* can infer an effect from observed causes by relying on lessons learned from previous experience. Using deductive reasoning, you would conclude the following: *given* that squirrels are quicker than cats, *if* you observe a cat chasing a squirrel, *then* the squirrel is likely to escape. In other words, *given* your previous experience, *if* a known cause is observed, *then* a specific effect is expected.

Predicate logic	
Normal-language statement	**Logic calculus**
The knight is a chess piece.	ChessPiece(knight)
The knight belongs to the white side.	WhiteSide(knight)
The white pieces are in play on the chess board.	$\forall$x: WhiteSide(x)$\rightarrow$InPlay(x)
Alekhine is a chess player.	ChessPlayer(Alekhine)
All chess pieces are controlled by either Alekhine or by his opponent.	$\forall$x: InPlay(x)$\rightarrow$ ControlledBy(x,Alekhine) $\lor$ NotControlledBy(x,Alekhine)
A chess piece is controlled by someone.	$\forall$x: $\exists$y: ControlledBy(x,y)
Predicate logic can represent facts from the real world as statements written as wffs (well-formed formulas).	

15-6   Fundamentals of predicate logic.

COGNITIVE COMPUTING		
TYPE	**PURPOSE**	**ALGORITHM**
Neural	Prediction, classification, and pattern recognition	Uses recognition, learning, and planning processes based on the behavior of the brain.
Fuzzy	Process control	Uses heuristic reasoning processes based on the behavior of the mind. Provides rule-of-thumb and best-guess approximations.
Genetic	Selection, mutation, and innovation	Uses processes based on the principles of natural selection.
Cognitive computing techniques cannot be proven or validated using the traditional analytic proofs. They rely instead on empirical evidence and field observations.		

15-7   Programming paradigms for cognitive computing.

Inductive reasoning *Inductive reasoning* uses empirical observations to learn lessons from experience. Suppose you're new to the area and you repeatedly observe the neighbor's cat chasing a squirrel who always escapes. You're likely to use inductive reasoning to generalize from these observations. You infer that squirrels are generally quicker than cats. You add to your mind's database the lesson that squirrels are usually quicker than cats.

Abductive reasoning *Abductive reasoning* infers a probable cause from observed effects. Abductive reasoning is the reverse of deductive reasoning. Here's how abductive reasoning works. Suppose you observe a squirrel scrambling up a tree. That's an effect, not a cause. Using abductive reasoning, you might infer that a possible or probable cause for the squirrel's behavior is the neighbor's cat. In the absence of contradictory information it's reasonable for you to draw that conclusion. But it's only a probability. You might attach a *truth factor* by saying you're 90% certain that the cat was involved.

Abductive reasoning is useful even if you've never seen a cat chasing a squirrel. You might observe the squirrel's behavior and infer it was being pursued by another animal of unknown type. If you've seen dogs, cats, skunks, porcupines, and raccoons in the neighborhood, you might be less certain that a cat was involved, perhaps only 25% certain.

The truth factor is the degree of confidence that you have in the inference produced by abductive reasoning. Software functions often use truth maintenance systems to store and revise the truth factors for various inferences. If you later observe, for example, that skunks, porcupines, and raccoons never seem to pursue squirrels, then you might become more confident in your inference, concluding with 50% certainty that a cat was involved. When you go back and revise your certainty factor you're using backward reasoning. When you use that knowledge in your deductive reasoning, you're using *forward reasoning.* In other words, you reason forward from what is known (deductive reasoning), and you reason backward to revise what is known (inductive reasoning and abductive reasoning). This chain of thinking is called *diagnostic reasoning.*

Diagnostic reasoning

Diagnostic reasoning using deductive, inductive, and abductive reasoning, as shown in Fig. 15-8. Diagnostic software uses mathematical set-theory to build a set of logical connections between disorders and their manifestations. (Disorders are also called *causes* or *antecedents.* Manifestations are called *effects* or *consequents.*)

The connections between antecedents and consequents are called AND/OR logic connections, as Fig. 15-8 illustrates. Diagnostic software is usually based on so-called *parsimonious covering theory.* The software seeks the simplest solution that fully explains the problem. There might be, after

Diagnostic software reasoning		
Antecedents The set of all known possible disorders	**Logic** The set of all known possible connections	**Consequents** The set of all known possible manifestations
Power supply failure	A1 ———— C1	Other appliances in the office are not operating.
Power conditioner failure	A2 ⟩⟩⟩ C2	Computer, display, and keyboard not operating.
Computer malfunction	A3 ⟩⟩ C3	Computer fan not running.
Display malfunction	A4 ⟩ C4	Computer status light is off.
Keyboard malfunction	A5 ⟩ C5	Display not operating.
	C6	Snow appears on the display.
	C7	Boot error message appears on the display.
	C8	Keyboard status light is off.

This table illustrates the AND/OR logic connections for software-controlled troubleshooting of a computer power-up failure using cognitive simulation.
Deductive reasoning -- For example, GIVEN A4 THEN C5, C6, C7.
Abductive reasoning -- For example, GIVEN C5 THEN A4, A2, A1.
Inductive reasoning -- Use statistical analysis of previous diagnoses to add new elements to the sets of antecedents, consequents and logic connections.

Mathematical set-theory for programmers

$A = \{A1, A2, A3, A4, A5\}$ The set of all possible disorders.

$B = \{C1, C2, C3, C4, C5, C6, C7, C8\}$ The set of all possible manifestations.

$D = \{C2, C3, C4, C5, C8\}$ The set of observed manifestations.

Active sets

$connections(A1) = \{C1, C2, C3, C4, C5, C8\}$

$connections(A2) = \{C2, C3, C4, C5, C8\}$

$connections(A3) = \{C3, C4, C7, C8\}$

$connections(A4) = \{C5, C6, C7\}$

$connections(A5) = \{C7, C8\}$

15-8   Fundamentals of diagnostic software reasoning.

all, more than one solution but only one best solution. *Parsimony* means frugality, thriftiness, and economy of explanation. *Covering* means completeness.

Diagnostic software uses all three forms of reasoning that you've learned about—deductive, inductive, and abductive. It relies on fuzzy logic and probabilistic calculus to explain its findings. For example, the software performance implicit in Fig. 15-8 will not diagnose a general power supply failure if other appliances in the office are operating. This is because the

AND/OR logic connection between A1 and C1 specifies that a manifestation of C1 must be present before a disorder of A1 can be inferred. But the software might make a diagnosis of power conditioner failure (30% certainty) and/or general power failure (70% certainty).

Probability

Probability is a branch of mathematics concerned with the likelihood of events happening. The probability of an event occurring is calculated by dividing the number of favorable events by the number of possible results:

$$P(event) = \frac{results^{favorable}}{results^{possible}}$$

Using this method, the probability of drawing the deuce of spades from a deck of 52 randomly shuffled cards is calculated as:

$$P(deuce) = \frac{1}{52} = .0192307$$

13 divided by 52, or .25. The probability of throwing two matching dice is:

$$P(matching) = \frac{6}{6 \times 6} = \frac{6}{36} = \frac{1}{6} = .166668$$

Probability calculations use permutations, combinations, and binomial coefficients.

Permutations *Permutations* are lineups of members selected from a general population. Here's an example. The total number of lineups of 4 members chosen from a population of 10 items is 5,040. The permutation calculation is $10 \times 9 \times 8 \times 7 = 5,040$. It is the order of the members in the lineup that matters, not the content. That's why the number 5,040 seems so high. When you're using permutations, you consider a lineup of *a-b-c-d* to be different from a lineup of *d-c-b-a*, even though the same four members are involved.

Combinations *Combinations* are committees of members chosen from a general population. The total number of committees that can be made up from a given population is determined by calculating the *binomial coefficient*. The formula for the binomial coefficient is:

$$\text{Binomial coefficient} = \binom{P}{M} = \frac{P!}{M!(P-M)!}$$

For example, the total number of committees of 4 members chosen from a population of 10 items is 210. The binomial calculations that produce this result are shown here:

$$\frac{10!}{4!6!} = \frac{10 \times 9 \times 8 \times 7 \times 6 \times 5 \times 4 \times 3 \times 2 \times 1}{4 \times 3 \times 2 \times 1 \times 6 \times 5 \times 4 \times 3 \times 2 \times 1} = \frac{10 \times 9 \times 8 \times 7}{4 \times 3 \times 2 \times 1} = \frac{5040}{24} = 210$$

where P is the population and M is the number of different committees that can be chosen from the population. Note that it is the content of the committee that matters, not the order of the members. When you're using combinations, you consider a committee of a-b-c-d to be the same as a committee of d-c-b-a because the same four members are involved, only in different sequence.

Two types of lineups and committees are used in probability calculations. They are *sampling with replacement* and *sampling without replacement*. For example, the total number of three-character words that can be formed from the alphabet is $26 \times 26 \times 26 = 17{,}576$ words, because each character in a word can be any one of 26 available characters. This is sampling with replacement. After a character has been selected it is immediately returned to the population where it is available for the next draw. On the other hand, the total number of three-character words that can be formed from a physical alphabet comprised of 26 different Scrabble™ tiles is $26 \times 25 \times 24 = 15{,}600$ words. The first character in a word can be selected from 26 different tiles, but the second character can be chosen from only the remaining 25 tiles, and so on. This example shows sampling without replacement.

Conditional probability   Conditional probability can be used to calculate the likelihood of an event occurring after a prerequisite event has occurred. The probability of event B occurring if event A has already occurred is expressed as:

$$P(B|A).$$

For example, if two cards are drawn from a randomly shuffled deck of cards, the probability of drawing a spade on the second draw after a spade was drawn on the first draw is:

$$P(spade^{second\text{-}draw}|spade^{first\text{-}draw}) = \frac{12^{spades\text{-}remaining}}{51^{cards\text{-}remaining}} = .2353$$

To arrive at this figure, the number of spades remaining after the first draw is divided by the number of cards remaining after the first draw. However, if a heart was drawn on the first draw, the probability of drawing a spade on the second draw is:

$$P(spade^{second\text{-}draw}|heart^{first\text{-}draw}) = \frac{13^{spades\text{-}remaining}}{51^{cards\text{-}remaining}} = .2549$$

Sample space and probability space

When discussing probabilities, sample space contains all possible results. Probability space contains a set of probable results.

Fair probability space   Each card in a deck of 52 playing cards has an equal chance of being drawn. The probability of a face-card being drawn is:

$$P(facecard) = \frac{16}{52} = .3076923$$

Taking into account that each face-card has a 1/52 probability of being drawn, the preceding formula can also be expressed as:

$$P(facecard) = 16 \times \frac{1}{52} = \frac{16}{52} = .3076923$$

Biased probability space   Suppose the face-cards have been doctored by a professional magician to make them more likely to be selected by an unwitting volunteer from the audience. If each face card now has ⅟32 probability instead of ⅟52, then each number card now has ⅟72 probability because the sum of all probabilities must equal 100%, expressed as:

$$\left(16 \times \frac{1}{32}\right) + \left(36 \times \frac{1}{72}\right) = .5 + .5 = 1$$

The probability that a doctored face-card will be drawn from this biased deck of playing cards is:

$$P(facecard) = 16 \times \frac{1}{32} = .5$$

The probability that a card valued ten or higher will be drawn from this biased deck is:

$$P(card) = \left(16 \times \frac{1}{32}\right) + \left(4 \times \frac{1}{72}\right) = .5 + .0555 = .5555$$

Binomial coefficients and probability space

A poker hand is combination of 5 members chosen from a population of 52 items. This is expressed as *52 choose 5*, or;

$$\binom{52}{5}.$$

Here is how to calculate the probability of receiving the ace of spades in a poker hand. A favorable result is a hand that contains the ace of spades and four other cards. So a favorable hand is just a committee of 4 members (the rest of the hand) drawn from a population of 51 items (the rest of the deck). The number of favorable hands is 51 choose 4, and the formula for calculating the probability is:

$$\binom{51}{4}.\ \therefore P(acespades) = \frac{\binom{51}{4}}{\binom{52}{5}} = \frac{\frac{51!}{4!47!}}{\frac{52!}{5!47!}} = \frac{51!}{4!47!} \times \frac{5!47!}{52!} = \frac{5}{52} = .0961538$$

Probability and game theory

When game theory and probability theory are combined, speculative scenarios can be analyzed. These analyses are also called *what-if scenarios*. The competitive situation described in Fig. 15-9, for example, shows how probability estimates can be integrated with a typical decision-table. The user can investigate various strategies and situations by adjusting the values of the variables in the equations.

Game-theory and probability-theory

15-9 Assignment of probabilities in a game-theory analysis.

		Player X HAWK	Player X DOVE
Player Y	**HAWK**	$\dfrac{V-C}{2}, \dfrac{V-C}{2}$ Moderate LOSS for X Moderate LOSS for Y	θ, V Maximum LOSS for X Maximum GAIN for Y
Player Y	**DOVE**	V, θ Maximum GAIN for X Maximum LOSS for Y	$\dfrac{V}{2}, \dfrac{V}{2}$ Moderate GAIN for X Moderate GAIN for Y

where V is the value of the GAIN and $-C$ is the cost of taking part in a physical confrontation.

Consider, for example, a situation where player X and player Y are in direct competition for a specific objective. Each player can adopt either an bold strategy or a cautious strategy, although both strategies begin with a period of posturing and bluffing intended to intimidate the opponent. A player using a bold strategy is called a *hawk*. A player using a cautious strategy is called a *dove*. A dove will retreat at the first indication of physical danger, but a hawk is willing to escalate the confrontation into violence. It is important to keep in mind that even for the player who wins the game, there will be a cost involved. In a best-case scenario this cost might only be stress. In a worst-case scenario the cost of winning might be physical injury.

If both players are evenly matched, then player X's probability of winning is 1 in 2 (or .5) and player Y's probability of winning is also .5, expressed as:

$$P(Xwins) = \frac{1}{2} = .5$$

$$P(Ywins) = \frac{1}{2} = .5$$

But suppose player X were larger, more experienced, or more skilled. You might give player X a .6 probability of winning and you might reduce player Y's probability of winning to .4.

If you inspect the decision-table in Fig. 15-9, you can see how the probability factors affect the size of the payoff to each player if both adopt a cautious strategy. In the event both adopt a bold strategy, the cost of winning is also affected by the probability calculations. In the next set of formulas, the reward for winning is represented by V; the reward for losing is represented by -C. Given that both players adopt a hawk strategy and are evenly matched, the reward that player X can realistically expect is:

$$(V \times P(Xwins)) + ((-C) \times P(Ywins))$$

$$= \left(V \times \frac{1}{2}\right) + \left((-C) \times \frac{1}{2}\right) = \frac{V - C}{2}$$

Physics-based simulation

Physics-based simulation software uses principles of physics. The software considers factors such as velocity, speed, displacement, acceleration, deceleration, mass, density, linear momentum, and kinetic energy. Figure 15-10 shows some typical principals of physics that can be modeled by knowledge-based simulation software. Figure 15-11 summarizes the fundamentals of physics that are useful in simulation programming.

Velocity   *Velocity* is the rate of change of displacement over time. It is speed in a specified direction. It is a vector quantity.

Speed   *Speed* is displacement over time. It is a scalar quantity, such as 65 mph or 100 kph. No direction is indicated.

Displacement   *Displacement* is distance measured from a fixed reference point. It is a vector quantity that uses a specified direction.

Acceleration and deceleration   *Acceleration* is the rate of increase of velocity over time. It is a vector quantity, such as 12 meters per second per second. *Deceleration* is the rate of decrease of velocity over time.

Mass and linear momentum   *Mass* is the quantity of matter in an entity. It is an indication of the entity's inertia. *Density* is mass per unit of volume. It reflects how much matter is present per unit of volume. *Linear momentum* is the product of mass and velocity.

Kinetic energy   *Kinetic energy* is the energy possessed by an entity because of its motion. It is the potential to do work.

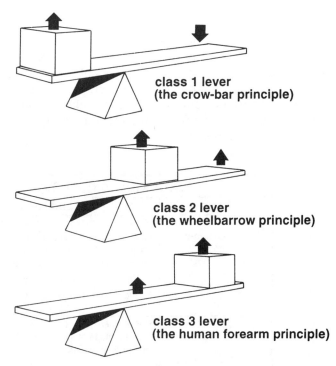

15-10 Typical principles of physics which can be modeled by knowledge-based simulation software.

Physics primer for programmers	
Term	**Description**
Velocity	Velocity is the rate of change of displacement over time, or speed in a specified direction. It is a vector quanity such as 15 inches per second in a northwest direction..
Speed	Speed is displacement over time. It is a scalar quantity, such as km/hr or mph.
Displacement	Displacement is distance measured from a fixed reference point. It is a vector quantity that uses a specified direction.
Acceleration	Acceleration is the rate of increase of velocity over time. It is a vector quantity, such as 2 meters per second squared.
Deceleration	Deceleration is the rate of decrease of velocity over time. It is a vector quantity.
Mass	Mass is the quantity of matter in a body. Mass is an indication of the body's inertia.
Density	Density is mass per unit of volume, or how much matter is present per unit of volume.

15-11 Fundamentals of physics useful for programmers developing knowledge-based simulation software.

Collisions

Collision detection and response are important components of physics-based simulations. Bounding-boxes are often used to help simplify the collision-detection process. Principles of kinematics and dynamics, which you'll investigate in the next chapter, are used to determine a collision response to either elastic collisions or inelastic collisions. Figure 15-12 presents a summary of the fundamental collision principles that are commonly used in simulation programming.

Collision simulation	
Term	**Description and sample formula**
Linear momentum	Linear momentum is the product of mass and velocity. Mass is the quantity of matter in a body, an indication of intertia. Velocity is the speed and direction of the body. Linear momentum is measured in kg m/sec. $LinearMomentum = Mass \times Velocity$
Kinetic energy	Kinetic energy is the energy possessed by a body because of its motion. Kinetic energy is measured in joules. $KineticEnergy = \dfrac{1}{2} Mass \times Velocity^2$
Inelastic collision	In an inelastic collision, linear momentum is conserved but kinetic energy is not conserved, because some energy is lost as heat or work done or physical damage. $FinalVelocity = \dfrac{Mass1 \times Velocity1}{Mass1 + Mass2}$
Elastic collision	Linear momentum and kinetic energy are conserved. $FinalVelocity1 = \dfrac{(M1 \times V1) - (M2 \times FV2)}{M1}$

The activity in an inelastic collision can be described by
$$Mass1 \times Velocity1 = (Mass1 + Mass2) \times FinalVelocity$$

The activity in an elastic collision can be described by
$$Mass1 \times Velocity1 = (Mass1 \times FinalVel1) + (Mass2 \times FinalVel2)$$

15-12 Fundamentals of collisions useful for programmers developing knowledge-based simulation software.

Elastic collisions   In an *elastic collision*, linear momentum and kinetic energy are conserved, as shown in Fig. 15-12. The solid entities involved in an elastic collision are flexible (elastic), thereby avoiding any damage or any loss of energy. Simply stated, they bounce.

Inelastic collisions   In an *inelastic collision,* linear momentum is conserved but kinetic energy is not. Some kinetic energy is lost as heat, as work done, or as physical damage. The entities involved in an inelastic collision are rigid. Simply stated, they do not bounce—they break.

Physically-based animation

Physically-based animation is a subset of physics-based simulation. It is 3D animation that uses constraints to manage an entity's motion. Physically-based animation is also called constraint-based animation. Constraints are forces, loads, and matter. A constraint affects the motion of an entity in a physically-based animation sequence. Physically-based animation can be implemented as forward kinematics, forward dynamics, inverse kinematics, and inverse dynamics.

Forward kinematics calculates what happens when velocity or acceleration is applied to an entity. *Forward dynamics* calculates what happens when force, loads, and other constraints are applied to an entity. *Inverse kinematics* calculates the amount of velocity or acceleration required to move an entity from one location to another location during a specified period of time. *Inverse dynamics* calculates the forces, loads, or other constraints required to move an entity from one location to another location during a specified period of time.

Where do you go from here?

Now that you've familiarized yourself with some of the fundamentals of implementing knowledge-based simulation on personal computers running Windows, you're ready to delve into more advanced discussions. The next chapter investigates kinematics and dynamics. You'll learn how your applications can automatically manage the motion of 3D entities by considering their velocity, starting location, and other attributes.

16
Getting started with kinematics and dynamics

This chapter teaches you about kinematics and dynamics. It describes how these paradigms can be used to automatically manage the movement and motion of 3D entities in animated scenes. The chapter discusses concepts like forward kinematics, inverse dynamics, constraints, collision detection, and the simulation-modeling pipeline.

The task—What you want to achieve

Your task in this chapter is to become familiar with the fundamentals of kinematics and dynamics. You want to understand the difference between the forward and inverse variations. You want to acquaint yourself with the simulation-modeling pipeline, and how the dynamics and kinematics engines can be used to drive the animation engine.

The plan—What you will learn

In this chapter you'll learn about constraint-based animation. You'll see how forward kinematics, inverse kinematics, forward dynamics, and inverse dynamics can be used to manage the movement and motion of 3D entities in an animated sequence. You'll see how the dynamics engine and the kinematics engine provide the staring point for the simulation-modeling pipeline, and how they provide input for the animation engine and its underpinnings, the 3D toolkit. You'll also find out about multiple constraints and collision detection. In this chapter you'll acquire knowledge that will prepare you for the hands-on tutorial presented in the next chapter.

Constraint-based animation

As you've learned in previous chapters, *physics-based simulation* uses principles of physics to manage the events being modeled and simulated. The software considers factors such as velocity, speed, displacement, acceleration, deceleration, mass, density, linear momentum, kinetic energy, inelastic collisions, elastic collisions, and others. The output of a physics-based simulation is displayed as *physically-based animation.* Because the motion in the resulting animation sequence is affected by so-called constraints, physically-based animation is also called *constraint-based animation.*

Constraint-based animation uses three modeling components. These three components are:

- primitives
- constraints
- external applied-forces

Primitives *Primitives* are 3D entities such as boxes, spheres, cylinders, cones, wedges, and complex 3D hierarchical solids. You've already learned about these in chapter 8 and experimented with a hands-on tutorial in chapter 9. Each 3D primitive is assigned attributes such as density, dimension, velocity, rotational inertia, and other attributes depending on the nature of the simulation.

Constraints *Constraints* are limiting factors that regulate the behavior of a primitive. Constraints can include forces, loads, matter, and design attributes that affect the primitive's movement, motion, deformation, evolution. For example, gravity constrains the motion of a tennis ball. The net is a constraint that affects the tennis ball's potential trajectory. The clay surface of the court is yet another constraint. The resilience and elasticity of the tennis ball itself constrain the magnitude and the direction of the ball's bounce. The roughness and coarseness of the ball's covering acts as a constraint on its propensity to spin during flight, because those attributes affect wind resistance. You've already tentatively explored constraints in chapter 13, when you investigated source code that animated a complex 3D solid with a moving part rotating around a joint.

External applied-forces *External applied-forces* are used to initiate and to motivate the simulation. For example, a brisk cross-wind over the tennis court is an external applied-force influencing the path of the tennis ball. The stroke of the racket on the tennis ball is also an external applied-force.

Methods of control

As you've already learned, physically-based animation can be implemented as forward kinematics, forward dynamics, inverse kinematics, and inverse dynamics. *Forward kinematics* concerns what happens when velocity or acceleration is applied to an entity. *Forward dynamics* concerns what happens when force, loads, and other constraints are applied to an entity. *Inverse kinematics* calculates the velocity or acceleration that is required to move an entity from one location to another location during a specified period of time. *Inverse dynamics* calculates the forces, loads, or other constraints required to move an entity from one location to another location during a specified period of time.

Implementation of constraints   Before any kinematics or dynamics simulation is started, the programmer must select and apply constraints that will affect the entity's behavior. Typical examples of constraints include:

- point-to-nail constraints
- point-on-line constraints
- point-to-point constraints
- point-to-path constraints
- point-on-skin constraints

Point constraints   *Point-to-nail constraints* are used to attach a point located on an entity to a point located in 3D-space. The entity can rotate and swivel about the point. *Point-on-line constraints* are used to attach a point located on an entity to a line in 3D-space. The entity can rotate and swivel about the point, which can slide along the line. *Point-to-point constraints* attach a point located on one entity to a point located on another entity. *Point-to-path constraints* are used to attach a point located on an entity to a path in 3D-space. The path can be arbitrarily curved, bent, or jointed, or it can be the result of a trajectory calculation. The entity can rotate and swivel about the point, which can slide along the path. *Point-on-skin constraints* are used to attach a point located on an entity to a point located on the surface of another entity. The first entity can rotate and swivel about the point, while the point can slide anywhere over the surface of the second entity.

Other, more advanced, forms of constraints include:

- point-in-volume constraints
- volume-in-volume constraints
- point-outside-volume constraints
- volume-outside-volume constraints

Volume constraints   *Point-in-volume constraints* are used to limit a point located on an entity to the interior of a specified volume located in 3D-space. The entity can rotate and swivel about the point, which itself cannot leave the volume. *Volume-in-volume constraints* are used to limit a volume (usually an entity) to the interior of another specified volume in 3D-space. This limitation can affect either the location and orientation of the constrained entity, or its dimensions, or both. *Point-outside-volume constraints* are used to limit a point located on an entity to the exterior of a specified volume located in 3D-space. *Volume-outside-volume constraints* are used to restrict a volume (usually an entity) to the exterior of another volume (usually another entity). Consider, for example, the tennis ball and the clay court mentioned previously. A volume-outside-volume constraint is used to prevent the tennis ball from passing through the surface of the clay court. Volume-outside-volume constraints are based upon collision detection.

Collision detection

Two issues are involved in collision detection. First, the simulation software must be able to detect the occurrence of a collision between two entities. Second, an appropriate post-collision response must be simulated.

Detecting a collision   The most efficient algorithms for collision detection are based on 3D entities constructed from three-sided facets or four-side facets. Suppose, for example, that two solid cubes have collided during an animated simulation. This means that one of the cubes has penetrated the other cube. Stated more precisely, one or more vertices of the striking cube is now located behind one or more facets of the struck cube.

As you've already learned, b-rep programmers always describe the vertices of a facet in counterclockwise direction as viewed from outside the solid on whose surface the facet is located. This convention means that the equation for a plane can be used to determine whether the viewpoint is located on the outside or inside of the facet in question. If the viewpoint is located inside (behind) the facet, it means the facet faces away from the viewpoint. Because it is a backward-facing facet, it cannot be seen. On the other hand, if the viewpoint is located outside the facet, it can be seen. By using the same formulas and substituting the XYZ coordinates of the suspect vertex for the XYZ coordinates of the viewpoint, your application can use the standard equation for a plane to test the vertex of the penetrating cube against the penetrated facet. Thus your application can determine whether the vertex is located inside or outside the plane of the facet in question. If the vertex is located inside (behind) all of the visible facets, then you know that the vertex is either behind or inside the struck cube. If the vertex is also located inside all of the backward-facing facets, then you can safely infer that the vertex is inside the struck cube. The equation for a plane can also detect if the vertex is located on the surface of the facet (which is, of course, the moment of collision).

Bounding-boxes   *Parallelepipeds* are six-sided, right-angled primitives. A *cube* is simply a parallelepiped with equal dimensions of width, height, and depth. These types of primitives provide the most straightforward cases for collision detection. Many kinematics applications temporarily build a box around a complex 3D hierarchical solid that is being tested for collision. This parallelepiped box is called a *bounding-box,* and it is used in order to simplify the collision detection calculations. It does so by reducing the number of vertices and facets that require testing. If the offending vertex does not penetrate the bounding-box, then no collision has occurred and no further calculations are necessary. However, if the offending vertex has penetrated the bounding-box, then the software can conclude that there might have been a collision between the two entities. It is important to realize, though, that a collision might not have occurred. This is because the complex 3D entity does not completely fill the volume of the bounding-box, and the offending vertex might be located in an unoccupied portion of the bounding-box. The vertex must now be tested against most (and perhaps all) of the facets of the complex 3D entity. Some software builds a bounding-box around each primitive in the complex 3D assembly in order to further optimize the search for a collision. You can think of it as searching through a relational database of 3D primitives and points.

Responding to a collision   After a collision has been detected, a kinematics application must provide a response. The nature of the response depends on whether the collision is elastic or inelastic. In an elastic collision, linear momentum and kinetic energy are conserved. The solid entities involved in an elastic collision are flexible (elastic), thereby avoiding any damage or any loss of energy. Simply stated, they bounce, rebound, and ricochet. The application must recalculate the velocities of each entity involved in the collision. However, in an inelastic collision, linear momentum is conserved but kinetic energy is not. Some kinetic energy is lost as heat, as work done, or as physical damage. The entities involved in an inelastic collision are rigid. They do not simply bounce, rebound, or ricochet, but instead they break. The application must calculate the deformation and destruction of each entity, recalculate the kinetic energy of the deformed participants, and then recalculate the velocities of each entity involved in the collision. You can refer back to Fig. 15-12 in the previous chapter for examples of formulas for linear momentum, kinetic energy, and final velocity in elastic and inelastic collisions. Consider again the example of the clay tennis court. The tennis ball striking the clay court is an elastic collision. There is a rebound. A beanbag striking the clay is an inelastic collision. There is no rebound.

The collision plane   In a constraint-based animation, whenever an elastic collision is detected, the software temporarily inserts a stiff spring constraint between the colliding points. The standard engineering equations for spring performance can then be used to regulate the motion of the colliding entities. This approach to collision response depends on using only a single point of collision on a so-called *collision plane*. The point of collision is usually at the location of the offending vertex. The collision plane is the plane containing the penetrated facet. The collision plane determines the angle of incidence and all subsequently-calculated post-collision paths and trajectories.

The simulation-modeling pipeline

The chain of calculations that an application uses to manage a physics-based simulation is called the *simulation-modeling pipeline.* If both dynamics and kinematics are being calculated, the sequence is called the *dynamics-kinematics pipeline.*

The dynamics-kinematics pipeline

Kinematics means the positions and velocities of 3D entities. *Dynamics* means laws of physics such as force, mass, momentum, and others that govern those positions and velocities.

Forward kinematics   Forward kinematics is the process of calculating what happens when velocity or acceleration is applied to an entity. Forward kinematics does not concern itself with forces or mass. It considers only the motion itself. Your application can use forward kinematics to check if two entities collide during an animation sequence. Kinematics can be inverted, in which case the paradigm is called inverse kinematics.

Inverse kinematics   Inverse kinematics is the process of calculating the velocity or acceleration required to move an entity from one location to another location during a specified period of time. Inverse kinematics uses a user-supplied target location and calculates the amount of velocity or acceleration required to move the entity to that location.

Forward dynamics   Forward dynamics is the process of calculating what happens when force, loads, or other constraints are applied to an entity. In general, dynamics concerns itself with the laws of physics that govern kinematics. Your application can use dynamics to calculate the motion (the kinematics) of an entity that results from forces acting on the entity. You can also use dynamics to calculate forces resulting from the motion of the entity. Forward dynamics can calculate the forces resulting from the impact of a collision. Dynamics can be inverted, in which case the paradigm is called inverse dynamics.

Inverse dynamics   Inverse dynamics is the process of calculating the forces or constraints required to move an entity of specified mass from one location to another location during a specified period of time. Inverse dynamics uses a user-supplied target location and calculates the forces required to move the entity to that location.

The pipeline components   The dynamics-kinematics pipeline consists of a dynamics engine, kinematics engine, animation engine, 3D engine, and a resulting display image. You'll recall how each entity must pass through the 3D transformation sequence before being displayed. Likewise, each entity in a physics-based simulation must pass through the dynamics-kinematics pipeline before being displayed.

Dynamics engine The *dynamics engine* calculates the velocity or acceleration that results from forces being applied to an entity. These results are passed to the kinematics engine. If a simulator does not contain a dynamics engine, then the programmer provides the velocity or acceleration values.

Kinematics engine The *kinematics engine* calculates the displacement that results from the application of velocity or acceleration to the entity. These results are passed to the animation engine.

Animation engine The *animation engine* processes and implements the motion dynamics, update dynamics, and viewing dynamics that are used in physically-based animation. You'll want to take care to note that these three forms of animation dynamics have a meaning different from forward dynamics and inverse dynamics. As you already learned in chapter 11, animation is movement across space over time. An animated 3D entity is a display of 4D space-time using XYZT coordinates. In order to manage 4D space-time, your application must monitor and update three sets of animation dynamics at run-time. These dynamics are motion dynamics, update dynamics, and viewing dynamics. Taken together, these attributes describe an animation sequence. *Motion dynamics* refers to the location, orientation, and juxtaposition of individual entities. *Update dynamics* is concerned with changes in shape, color, and texture. During a bouncing ball sequence, for example, update dynamics ensures that the ball is suitably deformed whenever it strikes the floor. *Viewing dynamics* is concerned with changes in lighting, camera, and viewpoint.

The animation engine acts as an interface between the time-based calculations of the simulation and the frame-based calculations of the animation implementation, as shown in Fig. 16-1. The results produced by the

Animation timing	
Frame Number	**Elapsed time**
1	.0555
2	.1111
3	.1667
4	.2222
5	.2778
6	.3333
7	.3889
8	.4444
9	.5000
10	.5555
11	.6111
12	.6667
13	.7222
14	.7778
15	.8333
16	.8889
17	.9444
18	1.0000

16-1 Correlation between frame count and elapsed time useful for animated kinematics simulation software.

animation engine are passed to the 3D engine, which models and renders a 3D scene for each frame in the animation sequence.

Where do you go from here?

Now that you've familiarized yourself with some of the fundamentals of kinematics and dynamics, you're ready for a hands-on tutorial. The sample application in the next chapter is an interactive kinematics editor. You'll be invited to explore the capabilities of the demo program. You'll do this by loading scripts and using the scripts to build, store, and play kinematics animation sequences. The first script rotates a set of 3D entities. The second script simulates two satellites orbiting a planet. The third script provides a moving camshaft simulation. Finally, you'll be taken on a personal guided tour through the source code so you'll acquire the knowledge you need to use kinematics functions in your own project development.

17

Tutorial: kinematics programming

This chapter provides a hands-on tutorial that demonstrates some of the kinematics fundamentals you learned in the previous chapter. A User's Guide shows you how to run the sample application, and a Programmer's Guide provides explanations of how the kinematics module is integrated with the animation engine.

The task—What you want to achieve

Your task in this chapter is to familiarize yourself with how the source code works. You want to see how the animation engine uses functions in the kinematics module in order to build each frame in the animation sequence. You also want to learn how to use kinematics in your own animated graphics applications.

The plan—What you will learn

In this chapter you'll see how to use kinematics functions to automate the production of an animation sequence. You'll discover how to provide to the kinematics module the initial attributes of a 3D entity. Then you'll learn how to use velocity and acceleration parameters to tell the kinematics module all it needs to know in order to plot the movement of the 3D entity. You'll see how to use animation preview functions so you can validate the first and final frame of an animation sequence before beginning a time-consuming build. You'll find out how to use scripts to store the instructions for a kinematics animation sequence.

User's guide to the sample application

In this section you'll learn how to use the sample application named kinematx. Before you can run kinematx you must build the executable. The program listings for the sample application are presented as Fig. C-5 in Appendix C. Source listings for toolkits that must be linked in to build the finished executable are presented in Appendix B. All source files are also provided on the companion disk. See Appendix A for tips on compiling the program.

Starting the sample application

There are two ways you can start the sample application. You can start it directly from your compiler's editor or you can launch it from Windows' Program Manager.

Startup from your compiler's editor   You can run the sample application directly from your editor if it is Windows-hosted. This includes editors provided with QuickC for Windows, Microsoft Visual C++, Turbo C++ for Windows, Borland C++, and others.

Startup from Windows' Program Manager   From the Windows desktop, pull down the File menu and select Run. When the dialog box appears, type the full pathname of the program, such as

        c:\directory\subdirectory\kinematx.exe

You'll want to take care to use directory names that reflect your own system, of course. When you select the OK button of the dialog box the sample application starts.

Using the sample application

When the sample application starts up, the sign-on notice appears. Choose OK to continue.

Four menu names are displayed on the menu bar. They are File, Edit, Run, and Using. You can use the File menu to quit the program. You can use the Run menu, shown in Fig. 17-1, to load a script file from disk, to preview the first and final frames, to build the animation sequence and save it to disk, to load an animation sequence or script from disk, and to play an animation sequence.

You can use a mouse or the keyboard to operate this sample application. To use your mouse, just point and click. To use your keyboard, press Alt to move the focus to the menu bar, then press the appropriate mnemonic keys to pull down a menu and select an item from the menu.

The Run menu   The Run menu controls the kinematics module and the animation engine. To build the default kinematics simulation, select Build Animation from the Production menu item in the Run menu, as shown in Fig. 17-

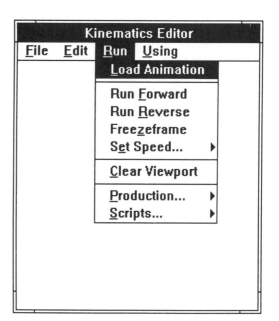

17-1 The Run menu from the sample application kinematx.c.

2. Be sure to select wire-frame mode before starting the build process for the first time. The software will build the default kinematics animation and save it to disk.

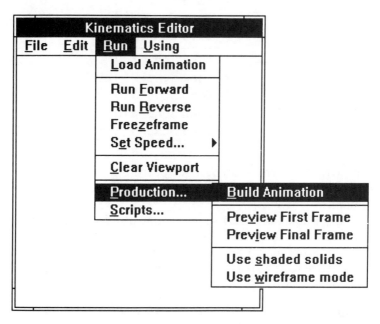

17-2 Using a nested menu to adjust animation-built parameters in the sample application kinematx.c.

Selecting a different script If you're using the companion disk, three pre-written script files are already provided. If you're working with just the book, you'll find instructions later in this chapter covering how to prepare these scripts. To load in a script, choose Scripts from the Run menu, as shown in Fig. 17-3. The default script is Script 1, which manages the independent rotation of three primitives, as shown in Fig. 17-4. This default script is hard-coded into the demo at startup. Sample frames from the resulting animation sequence are shown in Fig. 17-5. The software overwrites this hard-coded

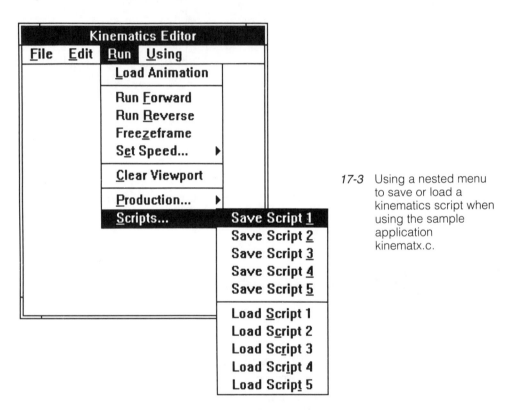

17-3 Using a nested menu to save or load a kinematics script when using the sample application kinematx.c.

block of data whenever you load in a script from disk. Script 2 manages a simulation of two satellites orbiting a planet. Script 3 is a simulation of a moving camshaft.

Whenever you load in a script, you must build the animation, save it to disk, and then load it in from disk before you can run it.

You can also save scripts. Whenever you select Save Script from the Run menu, the software saves to disk the current script under whichever name you've selected.

Loading an animation To load an animation sequence from disk, select Load Animation from the Run menu. The animation engine loads all 36 frames into memory. Remember, loading an animation is not the same as loading a

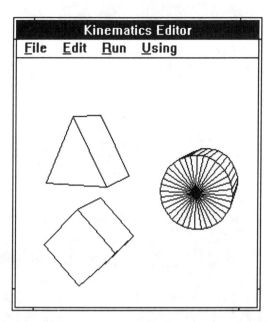

17-4 A sample image from the default script used by the sample application kinematx.c. Shown here is wire-frame mode. The demo also supports shaded entities.

script. An animation consists of bitmap images. A script is a set of instructions describing the motion of 3D entities.

Running an animation   To start an animation sequence that you've loaded in from disk, select Run Forward from the Run menu. The animation begins to play. You can select Run Reverse from the Run menu to play the animation sequence backwards. To use single-step control, select Freezeframe from the Run menu while the animation is running. The keyboard controls become active. Press the right arrow key to advance to the next frame. Press the left arrow key to back up to the previous frame. Press and hold the right arrow key to play the animation sequence at the fastest rate possible on your hardware.

Programmer's guide to the sample application

This section describes how the source code works. The source listings for the sample application are presented as Fig. C-5 in Appendix C. Source listings for the linked-in toolkits are provided in Appendix B. For tips on building the sample application, see Appendix A. The source files for the sample application are also provided on the companion disk as kinematx.*, engine3d.*, shapes3d.*, deform3d.*, assemb3d.*, lights3d.*, disk3d.*, and knmatx3d.*.

The kinematx.h program listing adheres to the form established in previous sample applications. So does the kinematx.rc program listing. Refer to chapter 12 or chapter 13 if you need a line-by-line tour of these two listings.

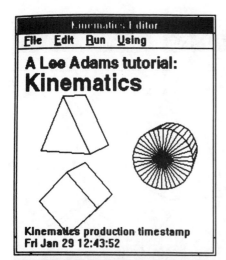

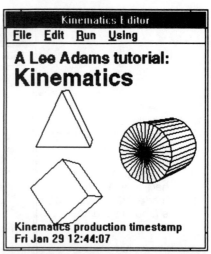

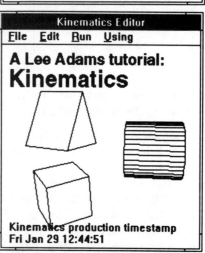

17-5 Sample frames from the kinematics animation sequence produced by the sample application kinematx.c using script01.scr. You can use the menu system to toggle to shaded mode if desired.

How the .c file works

The .c file contains variable declarations, the startup function, the message handler function, and the core functions for the application. You want to understand how the kinematics functions are called by this code so you can add kinematics to your own applications. The discussion in this chapter limits itself to the use of kinematics in 3D animation sequences. You'll find chapter 12 helpful if you need a more detailed analysis of sections that are not discussed here.

The script database   You want to note the code at lines 0191 through 0271, which declares data types for the kinematics script. The Header struct at lines 0194 through 0200 contains parameters governing the entire script, such as the animation frame rate, the number of 3D entities being animated, the first frame number, and the final frame number. Specifying the frame rate is required because the kinematics module must be able to translate elapsed time into frame numbers (as shown in Fig. 16-1 in chapter 16).

You'll also want to pay careful attention to the ActorParams struct at lines 0232 through 0261. Each 3D entity in the kinematics simulation will be described by a variable of the ActorParams struct type. Note how attributes such as velocity and acceleration are stored in the struct.

The code at lines 0263 through 0271 declares a ScriptDatabase struct. This is a database of 25 entities, each described by parameters of the ActorParams struct at lines 0232 through 0261. The members of the Script-Database struct are declared at lines 0265 through 0270. They include a header, startup camera specifications, camera movement specifications, startup light-source specifications, light-source movement specifications, and 25 entities (at line 0270).

Variables for manipulating and saving the script are declared at lines 0274 through 0282. Memory for the database is allocated by lines 0400 through 0409.

The message handler   The message handler contains some new features not seen in previous sample applications. The case statement at lines 0525 through 0536 provides a preview of the first frame in the animation sequence. It calls a function named zPreviewFirstFrame() which resets all the animation-based variables and draws the first image. The case statement at lines 0537 through 0548 provides a preview for the final frame.

The case statements that appear in lines 0581 through 0625 save and load the scripts to and from disk. They call two functions named zSaveScript() and zLoadScript(). You'll want to note how a pointer to the array of filenames is passed to the functions. The array was declared at lines 0276 through 0280.

Building the animation frames   The animation-build process adheres to the format established by the prototype applications discussed in chapter 12 and chapter 13. You'll want to note, however, how line 0977 in zSaveAnimation() calls a function named zInitializeModel() to initialize the kinematics parameters. The zDrawCel() function at lines 1110 through 1152 has also been slightly modified. Take care to note how the code uses -> notation to access variables in the script database that describe the motion of the camera and the light-source. The call to kmRenderScene() at line 1151 instructs the kinematics module, knmatx3d.c, to draw the current configuration of the 3D scene.

Initializing the kinematics The zInitializeModel() function at lines 1159 through 1355 initializes (or reinitializes) the kinematics parameters for the simulation. Because the variable named Script is a pointer to the kinematics database block, the -> notation is used to address members in the database. The Script pointer was initialized at line 1162. After first initializing the camera and the light-source, the code specifies a set of parameters for three entities. This is where the linear velocity, rotational velocity, and acceleration are defined for each entity in the 3D scene. Finally, the code at lines 1309 through 1350 calls functions in the kinematics module in order to reset the kinematics engine. The for() block at line 1310 loops once for each 3D entity in the database. You can see how the arguments passed to each called function are fetched from the database by using -> notation.

Previewing the frames The zPreviewFirstFrame() function at line 1361 resets the 3D environment and draws the first frame in the animation sequence. This function makes it possible for you to view a single frame without going to the time and trouble of building the entire animation sequence. The zPreviewFinalFrame() function at line 1388 draws the final frame. Note how the code calls the zSelectPreviewFrame() function located at line 1417 to help it set up for the preview. A call to zDrawCel() passes the desired frame number to the toolkit modules.

Using script files

The zSaveScript() function at lines 1460 through 1539 saves a script database to disk. Most of this code is concerned with trapping errors and reporting progress to the user. The OpenFile() and _lwrite() functions perform the low-level work. The zLoadScript() function at lines 1545 through 1618 loads a script database from disk, overwriting the data buffer.

Rotating subobjects The file named script01.scr describes the motion for a set of rotating primitives. A typical image produced during the animation-build process is shown in Fig. 17-4. A sampling of frames from the animation sequence in wire-frame mode is shown in Fig. 17-5. This script is hard-coded into the sample application at lines 1217 through 1307.

Orbit simulations The file named script02.scr describes the motion for two satellites orbiting a planet. A typical image produced during the animation-build process is shown in Fig. 17-6. A sampling of frames from the animation sequence in wire-frame mode is shown in Fig. 17-7. A sampling of frames in fully-shaded mode is shown in Fig. 17-8.

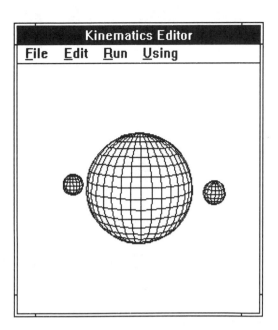

17-6 A typical image from the sample application kinematx.c.

Camshaft simulation The file named script03.scr describes the motion of a moving camshaft. A typical image produced during the animation-build process is shown in Fig. 17-9. A sampling of frames from the animation sequence in wire-frame mode is shown in Fig. 17-10.

Creating the scripts The kinematics attribute settings for the orbiting sphere simulation are shown in Fig. 17-11. The kinematics attribute settings for the camshaft simulation are shown in Fig. 17-12. Simply substitute the values shown in Fig. 17-11 or Fig. 17-12 for the default values at lines 1217 through 1307 if you want to tinker with the settings for these two simulations. After you've created your own customized simulation, you can save the script as Script 4 or Script 5 by using the Save Script menu shown in Fig. 17-3.

How the kinematics module works

The knmatx3d.c kinematics module is presented in Fig. B-7 in Appendix B. This program listing provides functions that implement a set of kinematics controls that manage the motion of entities in a 3D scene. The module calls functions in the 3D toolkit in order to draw the 3D entities whose location and orientation it has calculated from the velocities and accelerations provided by the main module. After the animation begins, the kinematics module recalculates a new location and orientation for each entity for each subsequent frame in the animation sequence.

Kinematics state The struct declared at lines 0133 through 0181 holds attributes that describe the kinematics state for each entity in the 3D scene.

Kinematics Editor

File Edit Run Using

A Lee Adams tutorial:
Kinematics

Kinematics production timestamp
Fri Jan 29 09:08:48

Kinematics Editor

File Edit Run Using

A Lee Adams tutorial:
Kinematics

Kinematics production timestamp
Fri Jan 29 09:08:56

Kinematics Editor

File Edit Run Using

A Lee Adams tutorial:
Kinematics

Kinematics production timestamp
Fri Jan 29 09:09:04

Kinematics Editor

File Edit Run Using

A Lee Adams tutorial:
Kinematics

Kinematics production timestamp
Fri Jan 29 09:09:12

Kinematics Editor

File Edit Run Using

A Lee Adams tutorial:
Kinematics

Kinematics production timestamp
Fri Jan 29 09:09:20

Kinematics Editor

File Edit Run Using

A Lee Adams tutorial:
Kinematics

Kinematics production timestamp
Fri Jan 29 09:09:28

17-7 Sample frames from the kinematics animation sequence produced by the sample application kinematx.c using script02.scr. See FIG. 17-8 for shaded version.

Kinematics Editor	Kinematics Editor
File Edit Run Using	**File Edit Run Using**

A Lee Adams tutorial:
Kinematics

**Kinematics production timestamp
Fri Jan 29 10:14:56**

A Lee Adams tutorial:
Kinematics

**Kinematics production timestamp
Fri Jan 29 10:57:00**

Kinematics Editor	Kinematics Editor
File Edit Run Using	**File Edit Run Using**

A Lee Adams tutorial:
Kinematics

**Kinematics production timestamp
Fri Jan 29 11:17:59**

A Lee Adams tutorial:
Kinematics

**Kinematics production timestamp
Fri Jan 29 11:39:00**

Kinematics Editor	Kinematics Editor
File Edit Run Using	**File Edit Run Using**

A Lee Adams tutorial:
Kinematics

**Kinematics production timestamp
Fri Jan 29 12:00:05**

A Lee Adams tutorial:
Kinematics

**Kinematics production timestamp
Fri Jan 29 12:21:08**

17-8 Sample frames from the kinematics animation sequence produced by the sample application kinematx.c using script02.scr. See FIG. 17-7 for wire-frame version.

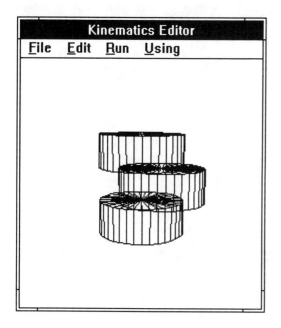

Kinematics Editor

File   Edit   Run   Using

17-9 A typical image from the sample application kinematx.c.

The code at lines 0184 through 0298 declares variables of this new data type. The module supports up to 25 entities in any one simulation. You'll want to note line 0211, which declares a pointer to a struct. This pointer is used to address the currently entity during calculations.

Initialization   The kmInitializeKinematics() callable function at line 0220 initializes the kinematics environment. You'll want to note the TimeSlice variable at line 0255, which is derived from the animation frame rate. As you'll recall, this concept was illustrated by Fig. 16-1 in chapter 16. The code at lines 0257 through 0305 is smart enough to initialize only the required number of entities. It calls a function named kmInitBody() to initialize each entity's parameters. You'll also want to note the directives at lines 0310 through 0314. This block of code ensures that you've read Appendix A, where tips are provided on configuring the toolkit for your particular system.

Reset   The kmReset() callable function at line 0322 resets the kinematics environment. It does this by setting the current frame number to 1 and by resetting the current time to 0.0.

Preview   The kmSelectPreviewFrame() callable function at line 0334 adjusts the kinematics parameters for a particular preview frame. The for() loop at line 0340 simply steps the kinematics engine up to the desired frame. The for() loop at line 0344 ensures that each entity is updated.

Setting the kinematics attributes   The callable functions at lines 0368 through 0554 can be called by the main module in order to set the linear acceleration, rotational acceleration, heading change rate, pitch change rate, location, orientation, dimensions, linear velocity, rotational velocity,

17-10 Sample frames from the kinematics animation sequence produced by the sample application kinematx.c using script03.scr. Shaded images are also supported by the demo.

Orbiting spheres			
Attribute	Entity 1	Entity 2	Entity 3
Solid	zSPHERE	zSPHERE	zSPHERE
Dimensions	50,50,50	10,10,10	10,10,10
Location	0,0,0	70,0,0	-70,0,0
Velocity heading	zWEST	zSOUTH	zNORTH
Velocity pitch	zHORIZONTAL	zHORIZONTAL	zHORIZONTAL
Velocity speed	0	220	220
Heading change/sec	0	180	180
Duration (seconds)	0	2	2

17-11 Kinematics parameters for script02.scr.

Camshaft simulation			
Attribute	Entity 1	Entity 2	Entity 3
Solid	zCYLINDER	zCYLINDER	zCYLINDER
Dimensions	40,40,15	40,40,15	40,40,15
Location	0,-30,0	20,0,0	0,30,0
Orientation pitch	90	90	90
Velocity heading		zSOUTH	
Velocity pitch		zHORIZONTAL	
Velocity speed		62.832	
Heading change/sec		180	
Duration (seconds)		2	

17-12 Kinematics parameters for script03.scr.

primitive type, color, and mass of any entity in the 3D scene. Note how each function calls kmSelectBody() to reset the pointer to the database of entities.

Rendering the scene The callable kmRenderScene() function at line 0560 draws the 3D scene in its current configuration. The for() loop at line 0565 ensures that each entity is rendered.

Internal functions The kmInitBody() function at line 0595 uses -> notation to initialize an entity in the kinematics database with default values. The kmSelectBody() function at line 0640 adjusts the BodyPointer pointer to address the selected entity in the database. The kmRenderBody() at line 0658 uses the 3D toolkit to render a 3D entity at a particular location and orientation. Note how the BodyPointer->Solid notation is used at line 0685 to determine which type of primitive to draw.

The kinematics pipeline The seven functions that make up the kinematics modeling pipeline are located at lines 0706 through 0839. They are:

1. Get the new linear speed
2. Get the new rotational speed
3. Get the new velocity heading

4. Get the new velocity pitch
5. Calculate the new location
6. Calculate the new orientation
7. Calculate the new dimensions

Note how the TimeSlice variable is used to increment these attributes by an amount appropriate to one frame change. All of these functions are internal functions which can be called only by the kinematics module itself.

Where do you go from here?

Now that you've practiced using kinematics in 3D animation sequences, you're ready to explore some advanced techniques for virtual reality. The next chapter, "Getting started with virtual reality," gives you the background information you need to grasp the virtual reality sampler presented later in the book.

18
Getting started with virtual reality

This chapter teaches you about virtual reality. It describes how VR's human-computer interface can be used to animate 3D environments and the entities they contain. The chapter discusses concepts like sensors, universes, degrees-of-freedom, and storage requirements.

The task—What you want to achieve

Your task in this chapter is to become familiar with the fundamentals of virtual reality programming for Windows. You want to understand the difference between interactive animation and interactive virtual reality. You want to acquaint yourself with practical details of implementing a virtual reality session on a personal computer running Windows.

The plan—What you will learn

In this chapter you'll learn about virtual reality programming. You'll see how interactive access to a three-dimensional database of prebuilt images can be used to manage the user's view during a virtual reality session. You'll learn about storage requirements. In this chapter you'll acquire background information to prepare you for the hands-on tutorial presented in the next chapter.

What is virtual reality?

Virtual reality is a simulation of 4D space-time. It is viewpoint animation that is displayed in an interactive, real-time context. Virtual reality provides a way for the participant to interact with a simulated 3D environment. It is a human/computer interface, providing controls for the user to manipulate and interact with a database. The database is the 4D space-time, including the artificial reality (virtual space) and the entities (virtual objects) it contains.

A *universe* is a particular virtual reality configuration. The universe includes the virtual environment, the entities it contains, and a script for managing the simulation. Loading different universes from disk can provide different virtual experiences. Each experience is called a *virtual reality session.*

Universes contain sensors and entities. *Entities* are actors, props, and scenery elements. *Sensors* are triggers in the virtual environment that can cause entities to interact with the user. Sensors respond to the actions or to the location of the user. A programmer sees a sensor in a somewhat different context. Programmers consider sensors to be sections of code that poll the computer's input devices in order to determine if the user has done something to trigger an event. Sensors are an important component of the virtual reality's simulation manager.

The *simulation manager* is an animation engine modified to run in single-step mode for use in a virtual reality session. It performs run-time functions such as updating, enforcing, sensing, and moving. This means that the simulation manager:

- updates the display image
- enforces the VR rules
- senses interactivity
- moves entities

The simulation manager updates the display image whenever the viewpoint location or the viewing direction changes. It enforces the *VR rules,* which are programmer-defined laws that govern and regulate the behavior of the virtual reality system during a session. VR rules also regulate what actions the user can undertake. The simulation manager's sensors detect when entities in the virtual environment should respond to the user's actions. The simulation manager implements the motion of entities that have been scripted to move about in the virtual environment.

Types of virtual reality

Your application can deliver a virtual reality session in three different forms:

- passive virtual reality
- exploratory virtual reality
- interactive virtual reality

Passive virtual reality A *passive virtual reality* session provides a hands-off, automated tour for the user through the 3D environment. The route and the views are explicitly and exclusively controlled by the software. The user has no control, except perhaps to exit the session.

Exploratory virtual reality An *exploratory virtual reality* session provides a user-directed tour through the 3D environment. The participant can select the route and the views, but cannot otherwise interact with entities contained in the 3D scene. The hands-on tutorial that you'll encounter in the next chapter is an example of exploratory virtual reality.

Interactive virtual reality An *interactive virtual reality* session provides a user-directed tour through the 3D environment. In addition, the virtual entities in the 3D environment respond and react to the participant's actions. For example, if the user moves the viewpoint towards a door, the door might appear to open and allow the participant to pass through. The simulation manager's sensors detect when the viewpoint node moves inside a specified volume of 3D-space. The simulation manager then calls a function to animate the door's opening in cyberspace.

Cyberspace vs. virtual reality *Cyberspace* is the simulated 4D space-time that is managed by the virtual reality interface. Cyberspace exists only within the computer, if it can be said to exist anywhere. Cyberspace is imaginary space. Virtual reality, on the other hand, is the human/computer interface that allows the user to experience cyberspace. You might find it convenient to think of cyberspace as the computer's imagination.

Input devices

One of the significant attributes that differentiates virtual reality from other human/computer interfaces is the variety of input devices and their capabilities. The versatility and usefulness of an input device is usually measured by degrees-of-freedom.

Degrees-of-freedom *Degrees-of-freedom* refers to the number of axes of rotation and translation provided by an input device. PC-based virtual reality sessions often use a mouse, a bat, or a bird as an input device. Joysticks, bodysuits, and facial sensors are also used for specialized input requirements.

A *mouse* provides two degrees-of-freedom. It can move on one plane along an X-axis and a Y-axis. The software nominally interprets these measurements as two members of the XYZ triplet in 3D space.

A *bat* is a floating, mouselike input device that provides three degrees-of-freedom. It can move along the X-axis, the Y-axis, and the Z-axis simultaneously. The user can usually select from XYZ translation or yaw-roll-pitch rotation, but cannot use both triples at the same time. A bat is usually hand-held.

A *bird* is a floating, mouselike input device that provides six degrees-of-freedom. The user can simultaneously select from XYZ translation and yaw-roll-pitch rotation. A bird can be hand-held, but a more common configuration is a group of birds attached to the joints of a human subject.

Implementing a virtual reality environment

You can implement a virtual reality session on a Windows-based personal computer if you take special steps to overcome the extreme demands that virtual reality imposes on the processor. Virtual reality sessions are image-intensive. Each time the participant moves the viewpoint node or changes the direction of view, the processor must generate and display a fresh image. This can cause an annoying delay, especially if the imagery consists of fully shaded scenes prepared with Z-buffer hidden-surface removal. However, your application can provide instant displays if the images have been prepared in advance. There are, after all, only a finite number of viewpoint positions and viewing angles in any one particular 3D environment, especially if the exploratory form of virtual reality is being implemented.

Using columns, rows, and grids for frame storage

Suppose, for example, that the user can move about in the virtual environment, which might be a maze of dividers in a closed room. The viewpoint nodes available to the user can be stored as a two-dimensional array of pointers to bitmap images.

At each viewpoint node, however, the user can theoretically gaze in any direction. If the programmer nominally restricts the number of available viewing directions to 36, for example, then the number of images that will be required at run-time is finite, and hence predictable. If four viewing directions (north, south, east, west) are supported at each viewpoint node, then the three-dimensional array of pointers shown in Fig. 18-1 is all that's required.

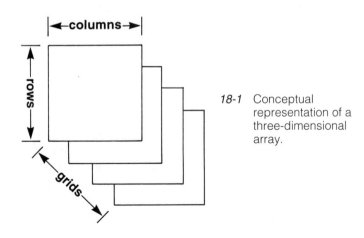

18-1 Conceptual representation of a three-dimensional array.

The first array might contain pointers to images for every viewpoint node in the maze when the user is gazing north. The next two-dimensional array might hold pointers to images for every possible viewpoint node in the maze when the user is gazing west. The third array provides southward gazes. The fourth array provides eastward gazes.

Managing a three-dimensional array   Managing this three-dimensional array of pointers to bitmap images is not unduly complicated at run-time. As Fig. 18-2 illustrates, whenever the user moves the viewpoint node, the software simply selects a neighboring pointer in the current two-dimensional array. If the user changes the viewing angle, the software simply moves up or down to a neighboring array of pointers.

18-2   Adapting a three-dimensional array to support frame-based interactive animation for virtual reality applications.

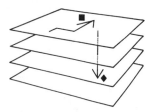

■**selecting a different viewpoint**
◆**selecting a different viewing direction**

The hands-on virtual reality sampler that is provided in the next chapter uses this approach to simulate a 3D maze. The sample application supports 16 different viewpoint locations inside a virtual room that is partitioned by dividers. At each viewpoint, 4 different viewing directions are located. This means that each viewing direction is organized into a four-by-four array of viewpoint nodes. The entire virtual reality cyberspace can be stored in 4 of these four-by-four arrays, as shown in Fig. 18-2.

From a programmer's context, the entire simulation is managed by manipulating an index into these arrays of pointers. If the animation engine you've already experimented with is running in single-step mode, then the keyboard's direction keys can be used to control movement and viewing direction. Whenever the virtual reality participant selects a new viewing direction the virtual reality engine selects a different four-by-four array of pointers, but it carefully retains the current index into the array of pointers. Whenever the VR participant selects a new viewpoint, the virtual reality engine selects a different index into the current array of pointers. In other words, when the participant changes the viewpoint location, the software changes the index, but retains the array. When the participant changes the viewing direction, the software changes the array, but retains the index.

Calculation of storage requirements   Calculating the disk storage requirements is also straightforward. If the virtual reality session is running in the VGA's standard $640 \times 480 \times 16$-color mode, then each 256×255

viewport image requires 32,640 bytes of storage on disk. You've already learned that each sample application in this book uses a standard-size window whose viewport dimensions are 256-by-255 pixels.

If a virtual reality environment similar to Fig. 18-3 is planned, then 25 different viewpoint nodes can be used to prototype the application. You'll

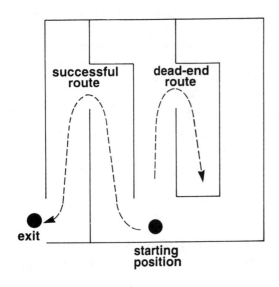

18-3 The maze design used in the virtual reality sample application presented in the next chapter.

want more nodes in your finished product, of course. A sample layout is shown in Fig. 18-4. If 4 different viewing directions are supported at each node, then 25 × 4 = 100 images are required. This means 100 images at 32,640 bytes each, resulting in 3,264,000 or slightly more than 3Mb of required disk space. This is not an unreasonable requirement. On a per-

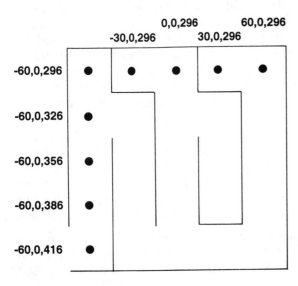

18-4 Assignment of 3D coordinates to the viewpoint nodes used in the virtual reality application presented in the next chapter.

sonal computer with 4Mb or more of memory, the entire virtual reality image-set will fit into memory, ready for instant display. Even larger image databases can be used, of course, because the animation engine you experimented with in chapter 12 can load frames from disk on-the-fly. So the size of your virtual reality environment is limited only by the availability of disk space. This means that the virtual reality sampler provided in the next chapter will run on any personal computer that can run Windows.

Where do you go from here?

Now that you've familiarized yourself with some of the fundamentals of virtual reality, you're ready for a hands-on tutorial. The sample application in the next chapter is a virtual reality sampler. You'll explore the capabilities of the demo program during your own virtual reality session as you investigate the twists and turns of a 3D maze with only one exit. You'll also delve into the source code, so you'll acquire the skills you need to use virtual reality techniques in your own applications.

19
Tutorial: virtual reality programming

This chapter provides a hands-on tutorial that demonstrates some of the principles of virtual reality that you learned in the previous chapter. A User's Guide shows you how to run the sample application. A Programmer's Guide provides explanations of how the virtual reality session is implemented by a specially modified animation engine.

The task—What you want to achieve

Your task in this chapter is to acquaint yourself with how the source code works. You want to see how the animation engine uses arrays of pointers to filenames in order to build an image for each view in the 3D environment. You also want to learn how the software maps the keyboard direction keys to the arrays of pointers in order to display the proper bitmap image at run-time.

The plan—What you will learn

In this chapter you'll see how a virtual reality session can be delivered by an application running under Windows. You'll find out how to build and store all the required images in advance. You learn how to manipulate an index into an array of pointers in order to select the next appropriate image for the virtual reality user. You'll also discover how to modify the animation engine to run in single-frame mode. In this chapter you'll see how to use sensors to prevent the VR participant from penetrating the walls of the maze.

User's guide to the sample application

In this section you'll learn how to use the sample application named maze. Before you can run this virtual reality sampler you must build the executable. The program listings for the sample application are presented as Fig. C-6 in Appendix C. Source listings for toolkits that must be linked in to build the finished executable are presented in Appendix B. All source files are also provided on the companion disk. See Appendix A for tips on compiling the program.

Starting the sample application

There are two ways you can start the sample application. You can start it directly from your compiler's editor or you can launch it from Windows' Program Manager.

Startup from your compiler's editor   You can run the sample application directly from your editor if it is Windows-hosted. This includes the editors that are provided with QuickC for Windows, Microsoft Visual C++, Turbo C++ for Windows, Borland C++, and others.

Startup from Windows' Program Manager   From the Windows desktop, pull down the File menu and select Run. When the dialog box appears, type the full pathname of the program, such as:

    c:\directory\subdirectory\maze.exe

You'll need to use directory names that reflect your own system. When you select the OK button of the dialog box the sample application starts.

Using the sample application

Four menu names are displayed on the menu bar. They are File, Edit, VR, and Using. You can use the File menu to quit the program. You can use the VR menu, shown in Fig. 19-1, to load a universe from disk, to preview the starting position and the goal position of the maze, to build the universe and save it to disk, and to run a universe.

You can use a mouse or the keyboard to operate the menu system of this sample application. To use your mouse, just point and click. To use your keyboard, press Alt to move the focus to the menu bar, then press the appropriate mnemonic keys to pull down a menu and select an item from the menu. As you'll soon discover, you also use the direction keys of the keyboard to operate the virtual reality engine.

The VR menu   The VR menu provides control over the virtual reality engine. To experience a virtual reality session you must first build a universe and save it to disk. The universe is the collection of viewpoint images that will be available when you wander through the 3D maze. After you've built a universe, you can load it from disk and run it.

Building a universe   To build a universe and save its images to disk, choose Build Universe from the VR menu, as shown in Fig. 19-1. For your first session, you might consider choosing wire-frame mode from the VR menu. This reduces the amount of time required to build the 100 images.

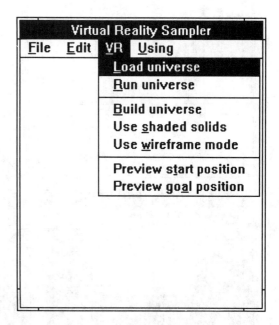

19-1   The VR menu from the virtual reality sample application maze.c.

Previewing a universe   You can preview the participant's starting position and goal position before you build the universe. This is a quick way to see the universe before you go to the time and trouble of building it. The images in Fig. 19-2 show both the wire-frame and fully shaded versions of these preview images. The image at lower left shows the participant's startup position, gazing north. You can see an open aisle partway down the right side of the pathway, as well as another open aisle on the left near the far wall of the maze. You can compare this image with the scene directly above it in Fig. 19-2 in order to get a feeling for the difference between wire-frame and fully shaded rendering.

Loading a universe   To load a universe from disk, select Load Universe from the VR menu. The virtual reality engine loads all 100 bitmap images into memory if enough space is available. Otherwise, the engine loads each image as required while the virtual reality session is in progress.

Running a universe   To start the universe that you've loaded from disk, select Run Universe from the VR menu. The virtual reality session begins, and your starting position is displayed as shown in Fig. 19-3 (depicted here in wire-frame mode).

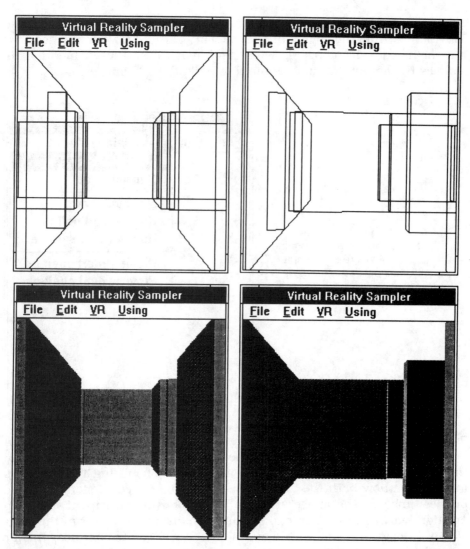

19-2 Sample images from the virtual reality sample application maze.c. Shown above wire-frame views looking north and west from the starting position. Shown below are shaded views looking north and east from the starting point.

Exploring the maze   To move ahead, press the up arrow key. To move back, press the down arrow key. The left arrow and right arrow keys send you left and right, respectively. You'll want to remember that the simulation manager prevents you from moving back when you first start, because your viewpoint is already at the maze's outside wall. You can verify this by gazing westward, as shown in Fig. 19-4. To change your angle of gaze, press Num-Lock. The movement controls are disabled and the gaze controls become active. Press the left arrow key to gaze westward. Press the right arrow key

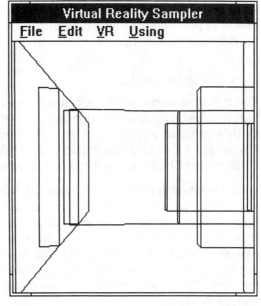

19-3 Looking north from the startup position. The doorway along the right wall of the hallway is visible.

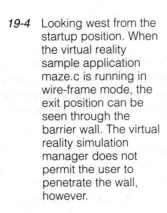

19-4 Looking west from the startup position. When the virtual reality sample application maze.c is running in wire-frame mode, the exit position can be seen through the barrier wall. The virtual reality simulation manager does not permit the user to penetrate the wall, however.

to look eastward. Press the down arrow key to gaze southward. Pressing the up arrow key shifts your gaze northward again.

Simply stated, here's how the numeric keypad controls work. When NumLock is off, the direction keys control your movement inside the maze. When NumLock is toggled on, the direction keys control the direction of your gaze.

If you attempt to move through one of the maze's partitions, the simulation manager issues an audio warning. The VR sensors prevent any penetration, except at the exit point, which is located at the southwestern corner of the maze. Refer back to Fig. 18-4 in the previous chapter for a reminder of how the maze is designed.

Leaving the maze   If you move to the maze's exit, you'll be congratulated by a special message box. At any time during the virtual reality session, you can quit the application by selecting from the File menu.

Programmer's guide to the sample application

This section describes how the source code works. The source listings for the sample application are presented as Fig. C-6 in Appendix C. Source listings for the linked-in toolkits are provided in Appendix B. For tips on building the sample application, see Appendix A. You'll need to make a few simple changes to the engine3d.c 3D toolkit, so check the discussion near the end of this chapter. The source files for the sample application are provided on the companion disk as maze.*, engine3d.*, shapes3d.*, deform3d.*, assemb3d.*, lights3d.*, and disk3d.*.

The maze.h and maze.rc program listings follow the conventions established in previous sample applications. Refer to chapter 12 and chapter 13 for discussions of these two listings.

How the .c file works

The .c file contains variable declarations, the startup function, the message handler function, and the core functions for the application. The discussion in this chapter is limited to virtual reality functions and single-step 3D animation. You'll find chapter 12 helpful if you need a more detailed analysis of sections of code that are not discussed here.

Virtual reality extensions   The code at lines 0152 through 0179 declares variables that are unique to the virtual reality engine. The constants at lines 0153 through 0171 are simply a convenient way to keep track of various arrays and the indexes pointing into them. You'll want to pay particular attention to lines 0172 and 0173, where some special pointers to arrays are declared. The array of handles is used to access the bitmap images in memory. The array of pointers is used to access the filenames of the bitmap images on disk.

Viewpoint nodes   The code at lines 0194 through 0224 declares an array of pointers to filenames. This array is carefully organized to represent four levels of images, as described in Fig. 18-1 and Fig. 18-2 in the previous chapter. By studying the organization of the filenames, you can see how it is possible to manage the image-display process by manipulating an index that points into this array.

The message handler   The message handler function is located at lines 0360 through 0696. This section of code is a subset of the animation engine presented in Chapter 12. The code emphasizes single-step displays. It does not support full forward or full reverse playback. The most important block of code is probably the case statements located at lines 0567 through 0647. This section of the message handler detects incoming keystrokes that control the virtual reality session. You should note how the code resets the vrMove or vrView variables before calling a function named vrWalkthrough() to select and display the next image.

Building the universe frames   The animation-build process adheres to the format established by the prototype applications discussed in chapter 12 and chapter 13. You should note, however, the code at lines 1006 through 1033 in the zDrawCel() function. This switch() block contains the XYZ coordinates for all 25 viewpoint nodes for northward-facing gazes. Other gazes are managed by switch() statements later in the zDrawCel() function. Note how these XYZ coordinates correspond to the layout in Fig. 18-2 in the previous chapter.

Drawing the maze   The code that draws the maze and its partitions is located at lines 1138 through 1210 in zDrawCel(). The camera's fixed-target mode is disabled by line 0998. Rather than always pointing at the center of the 3D world, the camera can now be reoriented to point in any direction.

The virtual reality engine   The vrWalkthrough() function at line 1264 is the foundation of this sample application. This function is actually a dedicated animation engine that supports only single-step playback. Most of the code in this function is concerned with ensuring that the correct bitmap image is selected for display. By using if/then deductive reasoning, the code first verifies (or updates) the direction of gaze and then marries it to the movement direction. This careful reasoning is needed because, as the switch() block at lines 1284 through 1290 illustrates, the up arrow key means move north only if the gaze is northward. If the gaze is westward, the meaning of the key changes and the up arrow key means move west. From the user's context, the up arrow key always means move ahead. From the programmer's context, the paradigm is somewhat more complex, of course.

Implementing the sensors   The code that implements the sensors is located at lines 1313 through 1372. The software uses if/then reasoning to make a decision based on the current location of the participant. At some locations, for example, a move northward is permitted. At other locations, it is prohibited because it would mean penetrating one of the maze's partitions or walls. The nested if() statements at lines 1362 through 1372 detect when the participant has successfully reached the maze's exit. The first if() statement confirms that the participant is attempting to move west, and the nested if() statement confirms that the participant is located at the node adjacent to the maze's exit.

Adapting the 3D toolkit Because this virtual reality sample application allows you to move the viewpoint very close to a 3D entity, the near clipping-plane functions in the engine3d.c 3D toolkit must be disabled. Otherwise the near clipping-plane prevents many of the maze's partitions and walls from being displayed. Before you build the application, be sure to read the tips in Appendix A. In particular, you want to ensure that you've changed every occurrence of && to ÷ ÷ in lines 1165 through 1167 in engine3d.c. And you want to be certain you've used remark tokens to disable lines 1191 through 1198, as well as lines 1594, 1595, and 1595 in engine3d.c.

Where do you go from here?

Now that you've delved into virtual reality, you can add this skill to your Windows programming toolset, which already includes 3D modeling, animation, knowledge-based simulation, and kinematics. Where you go from here is up to you. Many of the functions in the sample applications and in the toolkits are ready to paste into your own prototypes. You'll want to remind yourself, however, that the source code in the book is optimized for clarity and for teaching, not for speed or size. It is not production-quality code. Whether you're designing your own applications for the freeware, shareware, or in-house corporate markets—or perhaps for the domestic and international retail software marketplaces—you'll want to thoroughly retest the code for stability and robustness before you release your product.

In the appendices to the book, you can find the program listings for all the sample applications and toolkits modules, in addition to helpful tips on building the demos. You'll also want to skim the math primer in appendix D.

Your hands-on, guided tour through the warrens and niches of applied animation programming has reached its destination. You're ready now. Ready to begin the fun part, the challenging part, as you design, prototype, test, and build your own Windows applications using the knowledge you've gained in the book.

Like the early North American pioneers who broke the first trails through the vast wilderness, you're ready to push ahead. Your provisions are loaded, you've checked your bearings, and you've got a taste for discovery that only the restless know. Like all programmers, you'll be doing your best work mostly alone, but always among friends.

Appendices

This section of the book contains the program listings for the sample applications and the toolkits. Appendix A provides instructions on compiling the programs. It also describes hardware and software requirements, and it offers troubleshooting tips. Appendix B contains the source listings for the toolkits, including engine3d.c, shapes3d.c, lights3d.c, deform3d.c, assemb3d.c, disk3d.c, and knmatx3d.c. Appendix C contains the source listings for the sample applications, including startup.c, objects.c, animate.c, assembly.c, kinematx.c, and maze.c. Appendix D provides a math primer for graphics programmers.

Appendix A
Compiling the sample programs

This appendix provides instructions on building the sample applications. You'll also find a discussion of software and hardware requirements, as well as a troubleshooting table.

Where do you start?

As you likely already realize, the sample applications and toolkits in this book are advanced prototype code. They've been designed to be easy to understand, easy to use, and easy to build. However, as every Windows programmer knows, there is no free launch (no free lunch either). This is especially true if you're compiling projects that use multiple source files. The fastest way to make a good compile go bad is to neglect the fundamentals. What are the fundamentals? Pretesting your development platform. It's as simple as that.

Testing your system with startup.c

Before you try to build any of the advanced applications, you should verify your compiler configuration by building the sample application that was presented first in the book, startup.c. The source code for this application is discussed in chapter 4. The program listings are provided as Fig. C-1 in Appendix C. The source files are provided on the companion disk as startup.def, startup.h, startup.rc, and startup.c. After you've successfully built and run this sample application, you can proceed with confidence to the other apps in the book. You'll know that any idiosyncrasies that might arise will be unique to the application being built, rather than a consequence of your compiler or your directory structures.

What do you need?

To build and run the sample applications in the book you'll need a personal computer running Windows version 3.0 in real mode, standard mode, or enhanced mode; or a personal computer running Windows version 3.1 or newer in standard mode or enhanced mode. You'll also need a VGA display adapter and compatible monitor, or better.

Can you use your favorite C compiler?

Your favorite C compiler can successfully build the sample applications, provided it conforms to industry standards and provided it supports Windows application development. At the time this is being written, this includes Microsoft Visual C++, Microsoft C/C++ and the SDK, Microsoft C and the SDK, Microsoft QuickC for Windows, Borland Turbo C++ for Windows, Borland C++, WATCOM C, Symantec Zortech C++, and others.

Can you use a C++ compiler?

Because most C++ compilers are also C compilers, you can use your favorite C++ compiler if it supports Windows application development. You'll want to check your compiler's documentation to see if you are required to tell it to use C conventions rather than C++ conventions. The source code in this book uses C conventions.

What graphics card do you need?

The sample applications in the book require a VGA display adapter and compatible monitor. At the time this is being written, more than 92% of personal computers running Windows are equipped with VGA display adapters. You can also use SVGA display adapters, accelerator-based display adapters, and coprocessor-based display adapters, provided that they explicitly support Windows.

What type of computer do the demos require?

You'll need a personal computer running Windows version 3.0 in real mode, standard mode, or enhanced mode; or a personal computer running Windows version 3.1 or newer in standard mode or enhanced mode. This usually means a 80286 or higher if you're using Windows 3.0. It means an 80386 or higher if you're using Windows 3.1 or newer.

How much memory do you need?

As long as your computer can run Windows, you've got all the memory you need. Even the memory-intensive animation applications in the book are smart enough to load each frame from disk if not enough memory is available to store the entire animation sequence. However, 4Mb of memory is recommended, and 8 MB is even better. More memory usually means better performance.

Do you need a numeric coprocessor?

You don't require a numeric coprocessor to build and run the sample applications, but the 3D functions run significantly faster if you have a math coprocessor because the functions use floating-point math. The Z-buffer depth-sort routines benefit some, but not much, from a numeric coprocessor because the routines use integer values, not floating-point values. Animation playback is not affected at all because the animation engine uses the computer's timer chip, not the numeric coprocessor.

How have the demo programs been tested?

The demo programs have been rigorously pretested on a variety of hardware platforms and run-time modes. Each application has been built using Microsoft Visual C++ 1.00, Microsoft QuickC for Windows 1.00, Microsoft C/C++ 7.0 and SDK 3.1, Microsoft C 6.00a and SDK 3.0, Borland Turbo C++ for Windows 3.0, Borland C++ 3.1. Each application offers nominal compatibility with Zortech C++ 3.0 and WATCOM C 9.0.

Display modes

The demo programs have been tested at 640 × 480, 800 × 600, and 1024 × 768 resolution. The sample applications have been tested in 2-color, 16-color, and 256-color modes.

What type of performance can you expect on your system?

The performance that you can expect on your system from the sample applications depends on your processor speed, the display mode you're using, and the amount of memory installed.

Microprocessor speed   You'll need a processor running at 25 MHz or faster using the VGA's 640 × 480 × 16-color mode in order to play animations at 18 frames per second. You'll need 33 MHz or faster if you're using the SVGA's 640 × 480 × mode. Keep in mind, however, that the animation sequences can be played on slower machines, but they won't run as quickly.

Display resolution and color depth   The higher the display resolution, the more processor power needed to move images onto the display. The more colors the more data required to store the images, and that means more processor power is needed to move the images onto the display. Although the 640 × 480 × 2-color mode offers the quickest animation, its monochromatic color is disappointing. The 640 × 480 × mode offers good performance with a reasonable number of colors. The 1024 × 768 × 256-color mode provides the slowest performance.

Numeric coprocessor availability   If a numeric coprocessor is available, the 3D functions runs 8 times faster.

Amount of memory   If you've got 4Mb of memory or more, each animation demo in the book will play directly from memory. All 36 frames are loaded into RAM by the animation engine. On some systems, the 100 images of the virtual reality demo will load into 4Mb, but usually an 8Mb system is required for memory-based playback. Remember, however, that the virtual reality engine is smart enough to load each image directly from disk if memory is insufficient.

How to use the companion disk

The companion disk contains every file you need. Nothing is missing. The directory listing shown in Fig. A-1 is taken directly from the author's copies of the companion disk.

Installation   Simply copy the contents of the companion disk to the directory on your hard disk where you normally store your source files for your compiler. You can use either DOS or Windows' File Manager to perform this chore.

Preparing the toolkits for your system   Before you attempt to build the sample applications, you'll want to modify a line of code in some of the toolkits. In engine3d.c, use remark tokens to disable line 65. In the shapes3d.c toolkit, use remark tokens to disable line 44. In deform3d.c, use remark tokens to disable line 43. In the assemb3d.c source file, use remark tokens to disable line 36. In knmatx3d.c, use remark tokens to disable line 63. In every case, the resulting line should appear like this:

```
/* #define COMPILING 1 */
```

If you are using QuickC for Windows   Simply use the .mak project files provided on the companion disk if you're using Microsoft QuickC for Windows. You'll also want to disable the load optimization feature for the resource compiler.

If you are using Turbo C++ for Windows   Use the .prj project files provided on the companion disk if you're using Borland Turbo C++ for Windows. If you're working directly from the book and not using the companion disk,

README	TXT	1082	09-30-93	12:00p
LICENSE	TXT	6454	09-30-93	12:00p
WELCOME	TXT	5589	09-30-93	12:00p
CONTENTS	TXT	6112	09-30-93	12:00p
ENGINE3D	H	2152	09-30-93	12:00p
ENGINE3D	C	69825	09-30-93	12:00p
SHAPES3D	H	993	09-30-93	12:00p
SHAPES3D	C	52008	09-30-93	12:00p
LIGHTS3D	H	564	09-30-93	12:00p
LIGHTS3D	C	4677	09-30-93	12:00p
DEFORM3D	H	720	09-30-93	12:00p
DEFORM3D	C	26657	09-30-93	12:00p
ASSEMB3D	H	1001	09-30-93	12:00p
ASSEMB3D	C	14628	09-30-93	12:00p
KNMATX3D	H	2037	09-30-93	12:00p
KNMATX3D	C	34443	09-30-93	12:00p
DISK3D	H	1019	09-30-93	12:00p
DISK3D	C	14226	09-30-93	12:00p
STARTUP	DEF	273	09-30-93	12:00p
STARTUP	H	4030	09-30-93	12:00p
STARTUP	RC	6635	09-30-93	12:00p
STARTUP	C	45953	09-30-93	12:00p
STARTUP	PRJ	3268	09-30-93	12:00p
STARTUP	MAK	1514	09-30-93	12:00p
STARTUP	$RJ	2896	09-30-93	12:00p
OBJECTS	DEF	273	09-30-93	12:00p
OBJECTS	H	4423	09-30-93	12:00p
OBJECTS	RC	7579	09-30-93	12:00p
OBJECTS	C	79553	09-30-93	12:00p
OBJECTS	PRJ	4292	09-30-93	12:00p
OBJECTS	MAK	1879	09-30-93	12:00p
OBJECTS	$RJ	3536	09-30-93	12:00p
ANIMATE	DEF	274	09-30-93	12:00p
ANIMATE	H	4876	09-30-93	12:00p
ANIMATE	RC	8633	09-30-93	12:00p
ANIMATE	C	54156	09-30-93	12:00p
ANIMATE	PRJ	4516	09-30-93	12:00p
ANIMATE	MAK	1869	09-30-93	12:00p
ANIMATE	$RJ	4432	09-30-93	12:00p
ASSEMBLY	DEF	273	09-30-93	12:00p
ASSEMBLY	H	4877	09-30-93	12:00p
ASSEMBLY	RC	8637	09-30-93	12:00p
ASSEMBLY	C	67761	09-30-93	12:00p
ASSEMBLY	PRJ	4548	09-30-93	12:00p
ASSEMBLY	MAK	1958	09-30-93	12:00p
ASSEMBLY	$RJ	3952	09-30-93	12:00p
KINEMATX	DEF	274	09-30-93	12:00p
KINEMATX	H	5715	09-30-93	12:00p
KINEMATX	RC	9519	09-30-93	12:00p
KINEMATX	C	74928	09-30-93	12:00p
KINEMATX	PRJ	4644	09-30-93	12:00p
KINEMATX	MAK	2040	09-30-93	12:00p
KINEMATX	$RJ	4080	09-30-93	12:00p
MAZE	DEF	274	09-30-93	12:00p
MAZE	H	4844	09-30-93	12:00p
MAZE	RC	8839	09-30-93	12:00p
MAZE	C	65064	09-30-93	12:00p
MAZE	PRJ	4356	09-30-93	12:00p
MAZE	MAK	1842	09-30-93	12:00p
MAZE	$RJ	3824	09-30-93	12:00p
SCRIPT01	SCR	5142	09-30-93	12:00p
SCRIPT02	SCR	5142	09-30-93	12:00p
SCRIPT03	SCR	5142	09-30-93	12:00p

A-1   The files on the companion disk.

be sure to list all files except the .h file in the project list. For a warning-free compile session, you should disable the following error messages by selecting the appropriate Turbo C++ menu options:

- Bit fields must be signed. . .
- Constant is long
- Parameter . . . is never used

- . . . is assigned a value that is never used
- Condition is always false
- Unreachable code
- Code has no effect
- . . . declared but never used

If you are using Borland C++   If you're using Borland C++, first erase the .prj files on the companion disk, then rename the .$rj files to .prj files. If you're working directly from the book and not using the companion disk, be sure to list all files except the .h file in the project list. For a warning-free compile session, you should disable the following error-messages by selecting the appropriate Borland C++ menu options:

- Bit fields must be signed. . .
- Constant is long
- Parameter . . . is never used
- . . . is assigned a value that is never used
- Condition is always false
- Unreachable code
- Code has no effect
- . . . declared but never used
- Suspicious pointer conversion

If you are using Microsoft Visual C++   If you're using Microsoft Visual C++, first erase the .mak files on the companion disk, then rename the .$ak files to .mak files. You'll also want to be sure to select Disable Load Optimization from the Resource Compiler Options of the Projects Options menu. If you're working directly from the book and not using the companion disk, use the following steps:

1. Use DOS to create a directory on your hard disk to hold the source files.

2. Use DOS to copy the files from the companion disk to the directory you've created on your hard disk.

3. Use DOS to rename the *.mak files to *.qc or else simply erase the *.mak files.

4. Use DOS rename the *.$ak files to *.mak.

5. Start Windows and Visual C++.

6. Use Visual C++ to create a new project and add the required .c, .def, and .rc files to the project list.

7. Select Disable Load Optimization from the Resource Compiler Options dialog box in the Project Options menu.

8. Build the application.

9. Ignore any warnings concerning unreferenced labels and variables.

If you are using Microsoft C/C++ If you're using Microsoft C/C++ and the SDK, you want to check the compiler command-lines in Fig. A-2, the linker command-lines in Fig. A-3, and the resource compiler command-line in Fig. A-4.

A-2 Sample command-lines for compiling.

Compiler command-lines
Microsoft C/C++ 7.0 and SDK 3.1 cl -c -AM Os -Gsw -Zpe -W2 -Fpi filename.c <enter>
Microsoft C 6.0a and SDK 3.0 cl -c -AM -Os -Gsw -Zpe -W2 -Fpi filename.c <enter>
Zortech C++ 3.0 ztc -c -mm -v -W filename.c <enter>
Watcom C 9.0 wcc -mm -oaxt -zw -W2 -Fpi filename.c <enter>
If you are working with QuickC for Windows or Turbo C++ for Windows or Borland C++, you can use the integrated development environment (IDE) to build the sample applications.

If you are using Microsoft C If you're using Microsoft C and the SDK you'll want to refer to the compiler command-lines in Fig. A-2, the linker command-lines in Fig. A-3, and the resource compiler command-line in Fig. A-4.

If you are using Zortech C++ If you're using ZortechC++ you'll want to check the compiler command-lines in Fig. A-2, the linker command-lines in Fig. A-3, and the resource compiler command-line in Fig. A-4.

If you are using Watcom C If you're using WATCOM C++ you'll want to use the compiler command-lines in Fig. A-2, the linker command-lines in Fig. A-3, and the resource compiler command-line in Fig. A-4.

Troubleshooting guide—Software tips from the author

If you encounter difficulties compiling the sample applications, you might find a solution in the troubleshooting table provided in Fig. A-5. As you'd expect, in order to be helpful to you the troubleshooting table needs to be candid, direct, and occasionally blunt. It doesn't pull any punches. If you're looking for tactful guidance, don't look in Fig. A-5. But if you want results, you've come to the right place. As every programmer knows, sometimes the bug is to be found in the wetware, not in the software or the hardware.

Linker command-lines

Microsoft C/C++ 7.0 and SDK 3.1
Microsoft C 6.0a and SDK 3.0
link <enter>
object modules: /al:16 /NOD f1.obj+f2.obj+ <enter>
object modules: f3.obj+f4.obj <enter>
run file: <enter>
list file: <enter>
libraries: LIBW+MLIBCEW+WIN87EM <enter>
definitions file: filename.def <enter>

Zortech C++ 3.0
blink filename/al:16,file1 file2,,/NOD LIBW ZWM,
     filename.def <enter>

Watcom C 9.0
wlink form win memory font opt st=8192, heap=1024
     opt a=16 f file1.obj, file2.obj I windows
     exp zMessageHandler <enter>

**If you are working with QuickC for Windows or
Turbo C++ for Windows or Borland C++, you can
use the integrated development environment (IDE)
to build the sample applications.**

A-3 Sample command-lines for linking.

Resource compiler generic command-line

rc -K filename.rc <enter>

**If you are working with QuickC for Windows or
Turbo C++ for Windows or Borland C++, you can
use the integrated development environment (IDE)
to build the sample applications.**

A-4 Resource compiler command-line.

What warning messages might you encounter?   Different compilers provide different levels of warnings during a compilation. Depending on your configuration, you might occasionally receive a warning that some variables are declared but never used. You can safely ignore this warning. Some compilers might issue the same warning in the guise of unreferenced labels and variables. Borland's compilers can sometimes produce a bevy of warning messages, but these are usually caused by improper settings in the IDE. You can almost always avoid any warning messages whatsoever by using the project files provided on the companion disk.

Software tips from the author

The sample applications in the book have been tested with the compilers described in Appendix A. The resulting executables have been run in a variety of Windows display modes and run-time memory modes. If you experience difficulty, here's what the author suggests you do next...

Your situation...	Don't do this...	Do this...
Your supported compiler is up and running, but you can't get the samples to compile.	Don't assume the problem is in the listing. All code has been rigorously tested.	Do review the instructions in Appendix A. Use the supplied project files.
You believe you have found a minor bug in the run-time performance of a demo app.	Don't contact the publisher. Remember, the book's editors are not programmers.	Do track down the bug and fine-tune the source code to meet your own requirements.
You have an idea for a new software concept and you want to use the source code in your product development.	Don't assume that the book's editors can override the provisions of the License.	Do go ahead and use the source code, but be sure to read the License first.
Your compiler issues an error message that advises you to consult the book.	Don't contact the publisher. Remember, the books' editors are not thoroughly familiar with the source code.	Do remember that you must prepare the toolkit modules before compiling. Review Appendix A.
You're looking for a contract programmer to build a Windows app for your company.	Don't have unrealistic expectations about the service the author provides.	Do select and recruit a contract programmer through normal business channels.
You're looking for private tutoring in graphics.	Don't have unrealistic expectations of unlimited free consulting services.	Do join a special-interest group through electronic mail or investigate college courses.
You're wondering where to find more specialized books about graphics programming.	Don't have unrealistic expectations of unlimited free research or advice.	Do request the publisher's catalog. Other sources are trade journals, book clubs, and bookstores.
You've followed all the instructions in the book, but a sample application just won't compile without errors.	Don't assume the problem is with the code. Compiler configuration or subdirectory layout is often the culprit.	Do ensure that you're using clean source files from the companion disk. Review the instructions in Appendix A.
You see unintelligible characters when you view the source files with a Windows-based text-editor.	Don't assume the worst until you check the companion disk files using a different Windows-based text-editor.	Do request a replacement copy of the companion disk from the publisher.
You tinkered with the source code and now it won't compile.	Don't contact the publisher. Remember, the book's editors are not programmers.	Do remember that you must be prepared to debug your own work.
You're using a non-standard computer system and you're having trouble with the demos.	Don't expect the publisher's staff to be hardware consultants.	Do consult your dealer or contact the manufacturer of the computer hardware.

A-5 Troubleshooting guide for the sample applications.

Appendix B
Source listings for the toolkit modules

This appendix contains the listings for the toolkit modules that must be linked-in with the sample applications in order to build the executables. The 3D engine, engine3d.c, is presented in Fig. B-1. The 3D shapes toolkit, shapes3d.c, is provided in Fig. B-2. The 3D light-source toolkit, lights3d.c, appears in Fig. B-3. The 3D deformation toolkit, deform3d.c, is found in Fig. B-4. The 3D hierarchical modeling toolkit, assemb3d.c, is presented in Fig. B-5. The disk read/write toolkit for animation, disk3d.c, is provided in Fig. B-6. The 3D kinematics toolkit, knmatx3d.c, appears in Fig. B-7.

Preparing the toolkits for your system

Before you build the sample applications, you'll want to use remark tokens to disable a line in each of the following toolkit modules:

Module	Disable Line
engine3d.c	65
shapes3d.c	44
deform3d.c	43
assemb3d.c	36
knmatx3d.c	63

After you've disabled the line, it should appear like this:

```
/* define COMPILING 1 */.
```

This revision ensures that the source code compiles correctly under Windows versions 3.0 and 3.1 and newer.

You should also take care to modify the 3D engine, engine3d.c, before you build the virtual reality sampler, maze.c. The near clipping-plane must be disabled in the 3D toolkit in order for the moving-viewpoint feature of the virtual reality session to operate properly. Make the following changes to engine3d.c:

- change every occurrence of && to || in lines 1165 through 1167
- use remark tokens to disable lines 1191 through 1198
- use remark tokens to disable lines 1594, 1595, and 1597

These changes to engine3d.c are necessary only for the maze.c sample application. You'll want to use the original version of engine3d.c when building objects.c, animate.c, assembly.c, and kinematx.c.

Source listings

B-1 Source listings for the 3D modeling and shading toolkit, engine3d.c. See Appendix C for applications that use this toolkit. See Appendix A for instructions on building the demos.

```
0001   /*
0002   ------------------------------------------------------------------
0003                          ENGINE3D.H
0004   ------------------------------------------------------------------
0005                                                                  */
0006   #define zRED      1                    /* shading colors... */
0007   #define zGREEN    2
0008   #define zBROWN    3
0009   #define zBLUE     4
0010   #define zMAGENTA  5
0011   #define zCYAN     6
0012   #define zGRAY     7
0013
0014   void zInitialize3D(HWND);        /* initializes 3D configuration */
0015   void zDrawCube(void);                        /* draws 3D box */
0016   void zSetShadingColor(int);            /* sets dithering hue */
0017   void zSetCameraHeading(int);      /* sets camera heading angle */
0018   void zSetCameraPitch(int);          /* sets camera pitch angle */
0019   void zSetCameraDistance(int); /* sets camera-to-subject distance */
0020   void zSetCameraLens(int);       /* sets camera lens focal length */
0021   void zSetSubjectLocation(int,int,int);   /* instance translation */
0022   void zSetSubjectAttitude(int,int,int); /* sets instance rotation */
0023   void zSetSubjectSize(int,int,int);    /* sets instance extrusion */
0024   void zClearHidden3DPage(void);         /* clears the hidden-page */
0025   void zClose3D(void);        /* deletes hidden-page and z-buffer */
0026   void zResetZBuffer(void);              /* resets the z-buffer */
0027   void zSetNearClippingPlane(unsigned char);    /* sets near plane */
0028   void zSetFarClippingPlane(unsigned char);      /* sets far plane */
0029   void zEnableTarget(void);        /* lock camera to fixed-target */
```

```
0030   void zDisableTarget(void);     /* unlock camera from fixed-target */
0031   void zSetVRCameraHeading(int);    /* set unlocked camera heading */
0032   void zSetVRCameraPitch(int);         /* set unlocked camera pitch */
0033   void zSetVRCameraLocation(int,int,int); /* set unlocked location */
0034   void zUseWireframeMode(BOOL);          /* disables shading */
0035   /*
0036   -----------------------------------------------------------------
0037              End of header file for 3D functions.
0038   -----------------------------------------------------------------
0039                                                                  */
0001   /*
0002   -----------------------------------------------------------------
0003          Module of 3D functions for Windows applications
0004   -----------------------------------------------------------------
0005      Source file: ENGINE3D.C
0006      Release version: 2.10                Programmer: Lee Adams
0007      Type: C source file for Windows multimodule applications.
0008      Compilers: Microsoft C/C++, Borland C++, Zortech C++,
0009        QuickC for Windows, Turbo C++ for Windows, WATCOM C.
0010      Memory model: medium.
0011      Dependencies: ENGINE3D.H include file.  Compile ENGINE3D.C and
0012        link the resulting .OBJ file to your compiled main .C file.
0013        Include ENGINE3D.H in your main .C file.
0014      Output and features:  Provides control over camera pitch,
0015        camera heading, and camera-to-subject distance in both
0016        target-dependent 3D modeling mode and in target-independent
0017        virtual reality mode.  Provides precise control over the size,
0018        location, attitude, and color of each 3D object being drawn.
0019        Provides automatic backface culling.  Provides constant
0020        shading of each facet according to its illumination level
0021        resulting from a point light-source located above, behind, and
0022        to the left of the camera position.  Implements a 256-by-255
0023        z-buffer of unsigned char values in far heap.  Math division
0024        errors are trapped.  Supports 2-color, 16-color, and 256-color
0025        graphics displays.
0026      Publication: Contains material from Windcrest/McGraw-Hill book
0027        4115 published by TAB BOOKS Division of McGraw-Hill Inc.
0028      License:  As purchaser of the book you are granted a royalty-
0029        free license to distribute executable files generated using
0030        this code provided you accept the conditions of the License
0031        Agreement and Limited Warranty described in the book and on
0032        the companion disk.  Government users:  This software and
0033        documentation are subject to restrictions set forth in The
0034        Rights in Technical Data and Computer Software clause at
0035        252.227-7013 and elsewhere.
0036   -----------------------------------------------------------------
0037         (c) Copyright 1988-1993 Lee Adams.  All rights reserved.
0038            Lee Adams(tm) is a trademark of Lee Adams.
0039   -----------------------------------------------------------------
0040                                                                  */
0041   #define zRED          1                  /* shading colors... */
0042   #define zGREEN        2
0043   #define zBROWN        3
0044   #define zBLUE         4
0045   #define zMAGENTA      5
0046   #define zCYAN         6
0047   #define zGRAY         7
0048   #define zMAX_HEADING  360              /* max camera heading */
0049   #define zMIN_HEADING  0                /* min camera heading */
0050   #define zMAX_PITCH    360               /* max camera pitch */
0051   #define zMIN_PITCH    270               /* min camera pitch */
```

```
0052    #define zMAX_DISTANCE 700        /* max camera-to-target distance */
0053    #define zMIN_DISTANCE 0          /* min camera-to-target distance */
0054    #define zMAX_EXTRUDE  50               /* max size of 3D solid */
0055    #define zMIN_EXTRUDE  2                /* min size of 3D solid */
0056    #define zMAX_SHADES   64         /* num shades in logical palette */
0057    #define zVIEWPOINT    0                /* z-buffer minimum depth */
0058    #define zINFINITY     255             /* z-buffer maximum depth */
0059    #define zFAR_CLIP     200           /* virtual far clipping plane */
0060    #define zNEAR_CLIP    78           /* virtual near clipping plane */
0061    #define zHIGHLIGHT16  255     /* maximum illum for 16-color mode */
0062    #define zAMBIENT16    47      /* minimum illum for 16-color mode */
0063    #define zHIGHLIGHT256 63     /* maximum illum for 256-color mode */
0064    #define zAMBIENT256   25     /* minimum illum for 256-color mode */
0065    /* #define COMPILING 1 */
0066    /*
0067    --------------------------------------------------------------------
0068                            Include files
0069    --------------------------------------------------------------------
0070                                                                      */
0071    #include <WINDOWS.H>
0072    #include <math.h>
0073    /*
0074    --------------------------------------------------------------------
0075        Function prototypes:  low-level 3D graphics operations
0076    --------------------------------------------------------------------
0077                                                                      */
0078    /* ----- callable from both outside and inside this module ----- */
0079    void zInitialize3D(HWND);          /* initialize 3D configuration */
0080    void zSetShadingColor(int);             /* sets shading color */
0081    void zSetCameraHeading(int);        /* sets camera heading angle */
0082    void zSetCameraPitch(int);            /* sets camera pitch angle */
0083    void zSetCameraDistance(int);  /* sets camera-to-target distance */
0084    void zSetCameraLens(int);         /* sets focal length of camera */
0085    void zSetSubjectLocation(int,int,int);   /* instance translation */
0086    void zSetSubjectAttitude(int,int,int);      /* instance rotation */
0087    void zSetSubjectSize(int,int,int);         /* instance extrusion */
0088    void zClose3D(void);            /* delete hidden page and z-buffer */
0089    void zClearHidden3DPage(void);         /* clears the hidden-page */
0090    void zResetZBuffer(void);               /* clears the z-buffer */
0091    void zSetNearClippingPlane(unsigned char);      /* clipping plane */
0092    void zSetFarClippingPlane(unsigned char);       /* clipping plane */
0093    void zEnableTarget(void);          /* lock camera to fixed-target */
0094    void zDisableTarget(void);      /* unlock camera from fixed-target */
0095    void zSetVRCameraHeading(int);     /* set unlocked camera heading */
0096    void zSetVRCameraPitch(int);         /* set unlocked camera pitch */
0097    void zSetVRCameraLocation(int,int,int); /* set unlocked location */
0098    void zGetCameraCoords(void);        /* wrld coords to cam coords */
0099    void zGetWorldCoords(void);         /* obj coords to wrld coords */
0100    void zVisibilityTest(void);           /* back-plane visibility */
0101    void zDrawFacet(void);                          /* draws facet */
0102    void zUseWireframeMode(BOOL);              /* disables shading */
0103
0104    /* ----------- callable from only inside this module ----------- */
0105    static void zGetBrightness(void); /* finds brightness of a facet */
0106    static void zSetObjAngle(void); /* sine, cosine rotation factors */
0107    static void zSetCamAngle(void); /* sine, cosine rotation factors */
0108    static void zShowMessage(void);       /* shows debugging message */
0109    static void zWriteZBuffer(int,int,unsigned char);      /* write */
0110    static unsigned char zReadZBuffer(int,int);             /* read */
0111    static void zCreateHidden3DPage(HWND); /* initialize hidden page */
0112    static void zCopyPixelToViewPort(int,int);        /* write pixel */
```

```
0113    static unsigned char zFindDepth(int,int);        /* find z depth */
0114    static void zDoZBufferTest(HRGN);               /* z-buffer manager */
0115    static void zClipToViewVolume(void);     /* clip facet to view vol */
0116    /*
0117    -------------------------------------------------------------------
0118                    Declaration of variables: 3D modeling
0119    -------------------------------------------------------------------
0120                                                                      */
0121    static double far_clip_plane_dist= 512.0;
0122    static double near_clip_plane_dist= 200.0;
0123    double x=0.0,y=0.0,z=0.0;      /* wrld coords in,cam coords out */
0124    double xc1=0.0,xc2=0.0,xc3=0.0,xc4=0.0,xc5=0.0,
0125           xc6=0.0,xc7=0.0,yc1=0.0,yc2=0.0,yc3=0.0,
0126           yc4=0.0,yc5=0.0,yc6=0.0,yc7=0.0,zc1=0.0,
0127           zc2=0.0,zc3=0.0,zc4=0.0,zc5=0.0,zc6=0.0,
0128           zc7=0.0;                        /* camera coords of facet */
0129    double xw1=0,xw2=0,xw3=0,yw1=0,yw2=0,yw3=0,
0130       zw1=0,zw2=0,zw3=0;           /* raw world coords for brightness */
0131    double cursorx=10,cursory=10,
0132           cursorz=10;               /* volume of 3D bounding box */
0133    static double xa=0.0,ya=0.0,za=0.0;  /* temporary in 3D formulas */
0134    static double ObjYaw=6.28319,ObjRoll=6.28319,
0135       ObjPitch=6.28319;               /* object rotation angles */
0136    static double sOYaw=0.0,cOYaw=0.0;
0137    static double sORoll=0.0,cORoll=0.0;
0138    static double sOPitch=0.0,cOPitch=0.0;
0139    static double xObj=0.0,yObj=0.0,zObj=0.0;      /* obj trans values */
0140    static double CamYaw=6.28319,CamRoll=6.28319,
0141       CamPitch=6.28319;                             /* camera */
0142    static double sCYaw=0.0,sCRoll=0.0,sCPitch=0.0;
0143    static double cCYaw=0.0,cCRoll=0.0,cCPitch=0.0;
0144    static double xCam=0.0,yCam=0.0,
0145           zCam=-360.0;              /* world translation values */
0146    static double hcenter=0.0,vcenter=0.0;     /* center of viewport */
0147    static double viewheight=0; /* viewer's height 0 ft above ground */
0148    static double dist=360;    /* camera virtual distance from target */
0149    static double yawdist=360; /* camera actual distance from target */
0150    static int cameralens= 55;                    /* use 55mm lens */
0151    static int pitchheading=360,yawheading=0;  /* cam angle, degrees */
0152    static double yawdelta=0,pitchdelta=0;/* current absolute change */
0153    static double signmx=1,signmy=-1,
0154           signmz=-1;                     /* coord system tweaking */
0155    double cubeObj[] [3]={                   /* cube xyz object coords */
0156     {10,-10,10},     {10,10,10},     {-10,10,10},     {-10,-10,10},
0157     {10,10,-10},     {-10,10,-10},   {-10,-10,-10},   {10,-10,-10}, };
0158    double cubeWorld[8] [3];        /* xw1,yw1,zw1 vertex world coords */
0159    double camcoords[8] [3];         /* xc1,yc1,zc1 vertex cam coords */
0160    BOOL bAssembly= FALSE;      /* TRUE if using hierarchical modeling */
0161    BOOL bTarget= TRUE;        /* FALSE if using virtual reality mode */
0162    BOOL bUseWireframe= FALSE;              /* TRUE if shading disabled */
0163    /*
0164    -------------------------------------------------------------------
0165          Declaration of variables: rendering & backplane removal
0166    -------------------------------------------------------------------
0167                                                                      */
0168    double visible=0.0;                         /* visibility factor */
0169    static double sp1=0.0,sp2=0.0,sp3=0.0;        /* temp values of sp */
0170    double xLight=-.1294089,yLight=.8660256,zLight=.4829627;
0171    static double illum_range= 255;        /* Windows-dependent range */
0172    static double normalized_illum=0.0; /* illum factor 0 to 1 range */
0173    static double xu=0.0,yu=0.0,zu=0.0;       /* vector vertex 1 to 2 */
```

```
0174   static double xv=0.0,yv=0.0,zv=0.0;        /* vector vertex 1 to 3 */
0175   static double x_surf_normal=0.0,
0176                y_surf_normal=0.0,z_surf_normal=0.0;
0177   static double v1=0.0,v2=0.0;        /* length, surface perp vector */
0178   static double v3=0.0;            /* ratio, surf perp to unit vector */
0179   static double x_unit_vector=0.0,
0180                y_unit_vector=0.0,z_unit_vector=0.0;
0181   static int zDeviceIllum=0;       /* Windows-dependent brightness */
0182   static int zShadingColor= 4;                 /* dithering hue */
0183   /*
0184   ------------------------------------------------------------------
0185             Declaration of variables: pixel-based operations
0186   ------------------------------------------------------------------
0187                                                                   */
0188   static HWND hWnd;                      /* handle to active window */
0189   BOOL bInitialized= FALSE;              /* 3D system initialized? */
0190   static int clipx1=0, clipy1=0;         /* min client area coords */
0191   static int clipx2=255, clipy2=254;     /* max client area coords */
0192   static int ViewportWidth= 256;         /* width of client area */
0193   static int ViewportDepth= 255;         /* depth of client area */
0194   static POINT Points[4];              /* polygon 2D raster coords */
0195   BOOL bUsePalette= FALSE;               /* 256-color palette? */
0196   static NPLOGPALETTE lpGrayPal;         /* ptr to logical palette */
0197   static int Shade;                      /* index into palette */
0198   static HPALETTE hGrayPal;              /* handle to logical palette */
0199   /*
0200   ------------------------------------------------------------------
0201      Declaration of variables: view volume and raster viewport
0202   ------------------------------------------------------------------
0203                                                                   */
0204   static double xPersp, yPersp, zPersp; /* perspective view volume */
0205   static double xNorm, yNorm, zNorm;     /* normalized view volume */
0206   static double xRect, yRect, zRect;     /* rectangular view volume */
0207   static double xRast, yRast, zRast;     /* raster viewport */
0208   static double Znear, Zfar;          /* normalized clipping planes */
0209   BOOL Discard = FALSE;                  /* TRUE if discarded */
0210   BOOL Clipped = FALSE;                  /* TRUE if clipped */
0211   BOOL TestOnly= FALSE;               /* TRUE if facet to be drawn */
0212   static int NumEdges= 4;             /* indicates 4-sided polygon */
0213   struct VStruct
0214     {     /* declare a structure of 3D rect view volume coords... */
0215     double x;
0216     double y;
0217     double z;
0218     };
0219   struct VStruct ViewVolume[4];          /* array of 4 structs */
0220   static double TempVariable;            /* temporary variable */
0221   /*
0222   ------------------------------------------------------------------
0223             Declaration of variables: z-buffer operations
0224   ------------------------------------------------------------------
0225                                                                   */
0226   static BOOL ZBufferReady= FALSE;          /* z-buffer ready? */
0227   HANDLE hMem;                    /* handle to z-buffer memory block */
0228   LPSTR lpMem;                    /* address of z-buffer memory block */
0229   HANDLE hMemFree;                    /* to test discard of block */
0230   struct RStruct
0231     {              /* declare a structure of z-buffer coords... */
0232     int x;
0233     int y;
0234     unsigned char z;
```

```
0235    };
0236    struct RStruct Raster[4];                    /* array of 4 structs */
0237    static int FirstY;
0238    static int FirstVertex, SecondVertex, ThirdVertex, FourthVertex;
0239    static unsigned char FarClip= 200;   /* far clipping plane depth */
0240    static unsigned char NearClip= 78;  /* near clipping plane depth */
0241    /*
0242    -------------------------------------------------------------------
0243            Declaration of variables: hidden-page workspace
0244    -------------------------------------------------------------------
0245                                                                     */
0246    HDC hPageDC;            /* memory display-context for hidden-page */
0247    HBITMAP hPage;                         /* handle to hidden-page bitmap */
0248    HBITMAP hPrevPage;                          /* default bitmap */
0249    BOOL PageReady= FALSE;                    /* hidden-page created? */
0250
0251    /*
0252    -------------------------------------------------------------------
0253                    3D initialization functions
0254    -------------------------------------------------------------------
0255                    Initialize the 3D environment
0256    -------------------------------------------------------------------
0257                                                                     */
0258    void zInitialize3D(HWND hWndow)
0259                /* this function is called by main module at startup */
0260    {                       /* call with hWndow handle to active window */
0261      RECT rcClientArea;   /* data structure of 4 xy coords for rect */
0262      BYTE Red, Green, Blue;                    /* crt gun intensities */
0263      HWND hDesktopWnd;                            /* handle to desktop */
0264      HDC hDCcaps;                               /* display-context */
0265      int DisplayBits;                      /* num of bits-per-pixel */
0266      HPALETTE PrevPalette;
0267      int NumMapped;
0268      HFONT h3DFont, h3DPrevFont; /* handles to new & previous font */
0269      HDC h3DFontDC;                        /* display-context for font */
0270
0271      if (bInitialized==TRUE) return;            /* callable once only */
0272      hWnd= hWndow;   /* store global handle that all routines can use */
0273      GetClientRect(hWnd, &rcClientArea);       /* fetch bounding coords */
0274      clipx1= rcClientArea.left; clipy1= rcClientArea.top;
0275      clipx2= rcClientArea.right; clipy2= rcClientArea.bottom;
0276
0277      /* --------------------- startup notice --------------------- */
0278      h3DFontDC= GetDC(hWnd);
0279      h3DFont= GetStockObject(SYSTEM_FONT);
0280      h3DPrevFont= SelectObject(h3DFontDC,h3DFont);
0281      SetTextColor(h3DFontDC,RGB(0,0,0));
0282      SetBkMode(h3DFontDC,TRANSPARENT);
0283      TextOut(h3DFontDC,10,221,"C tutorial 3D kit version 2.10",30);
0284      TextOut(h3DFontDC,10,236,"Copyright- 1988-1993 Lee Adams",30);
0285      SetTextColor(h3DFontDC,RGB(255,255,255));
0286      SelectObject(h3DFontDC,h3DPrevFont);
0287      ReleaseDC(hWnd,h3DFontDC);
0288
0289      /* --------------------- viewport --------------------- */
0290      ViewportWidth= (clipx2 - clipx1) + 1;         /* width of viewport */
0291      ViewportDepth= (clipy2 - clipy1) + 1;         /* depth of viewport */
0292      hcenter= ViewportWidth / 2;/* calculate horiz center of viewport */
0293      vcenter= ViewportDepth / 2; /* calculate vert center of viewport */
0294      if (ViewportWidth != 256)      /* trap client area dimensions... */
0295      {
```

```
0296    MessageBox(GetFocus(),
0297    "Viewport width not 256 pixels in zInitialize3D( ) function.",
0298    "3D kit error:  line 00298",
0299    MB_OK);
0300    ViewportWidth= 256;        /* force virtual width to 256 pixels */
0301    }
0302 if (ViewportDepth != 255)
0303    {                         /* if font distorts height of client area... */
0304    MessageBox(GetFocus(),
0305    "Viewport height not 255 pixels in zInitialize3D( ) function.",
0306    "3D kit error:  line 00306",
0307    MB_OK);
0308    ViewportDepth= 255;        /* force virtual height to 255 pixels */
0309    }
0310
0311 /* -------------------- illumination ------------------------ */
0312 xLight= -.21131; yLight= .86603; zLight= .45315; /* light source */
0313 illum_range= 255;                      /* surface brightness 0 to 255 */
0314
0315 /* ------------------------ camera -------------------------- */
0316 far_clip_plane_dist= 512.0;    /* distance to far clipping plane */
0317 near_clip_plane_dist= 200.0;   /* distance to near clipping plane */
0318 viewheight= 0;   /* 0 for camera, else set to 5 or 6 for android */
0319 dist= 360;                             /* camera-to-target distance */
0320 cameralens= 55;                        /* focal length of camera lens */
0321 CamYaw= 0.0; CamRoll= 0.0; CamPitch= 6.28319;
0322 pitchheading= 360; yawheading= 0;              /* camera direction */
0323 yawdelta= 0; pitchdelta= 0;
0324 zSetCamAngle();
0325 xCam= 0.0; yCam= 0.0; zCam= -360.0;            /* camera location */
0326 bTarget= TRUE;                 /* using fixed target for camera */
0327
0328 /* ---------------------- objects -------------------------- */
0329 ObjYaw= 0.0; ObjRoll= 0.0; ObjPitch= 0.0;  /* object orientation */
0330 zSetObjAngle();
0331 xObj= 0.0; yObj= 0.0; zObj= 0.0;               /* object location */
0332 cursorx=15; cursory=15; cursorz=15;            /* size of object */
0333
0334 /* --------------- view volume transformations --------------- */
0335 Zfar= -1;          /* depth value of normalized far clipping plane */
0336 if (far_clip_plane_dist==0)
0337    {
0338    MessageBox(GetFocus(),
0339    "Attempted division by 0 in zInitialize3D( ) function.",
0340    "3D kit error:  line 00340",
0341    MB_OK);
0342    }
0343 Znear= (-1)*(near_clip_plane_dist/far_clip_plane_dist);  /* near */
0344
0345 /* --------------- initialize the hidden page ---------------- */
0346 zCreateHidden3DPage(hWnd);
0347 if (PageReady==FALSE)
0348    {
0349    bInitialized= FALSE;
0350    return;
0351    }
0352 /* ---------------- initialize the z-buffer ------------------- */
0353 GlobalCompact((DWORD)-1L);             /* maximize contiguous memory */
0354 hMem= GlobalAlloc(GMEM_MOVEABLE,65280);   /* alloc 256x255 block */
0355 if (hMem==NULL)                /* if memory allocation failed... */
0356    {
```

```
0357    MessageBeep(0);
0358    MessageBox(GetFocus(),
0359      "zInitialize3D( ) unable to allocate z-buffer memory.",
0360      "3D kit error:  line 00360", MB_OK);
0361    ZBufferReady= FALSE;
0362    bInitialized= FALSE;
0363    return;
0364    }
0365  FarClip= zFAR_CLIP;                    /* far clipping plane depth */
0366  NearClip= zNEAR_CLIP;                  /* near clipping plane depth */
0367  ZBufferReady= TRUE;                    /* set status indicators... */
0368  bAssembly= FALSE;
0369
0370  /* ----------------- initialize the palette ----------------- */
0371  hDesktopWnd= GetDesktopWindow();
0372  hDCcaps= GetDC(hDesktopWnd);
0373  DisplayBits= GetDeviceCaps(hDCcaps,BITSPIXEL);
0374  ReleaseDC(hDesktopWnd,hDCcaps);
0375  if(DisplayBits==8)                     /* if running in 256-color mode... */
0376    {                     /* create and initialize a palette structure... */
0377    lpGrayPal=(NPLOGPALETTE)LocalAlloc(LMEM_FIXED, /* allocate mem */
0378            (sizeof(LOGPALETTE) +
0379            (sizeof(PALETTEENTRY)*(zMAX_SHADES))));
0380    if (lpGrayPal==NULL)                 /* if memory allocation error... */
0381      {
0382      MessageBox(GetFocus(),
0383      "Unable to allocate memory for logical palette.",
0384      "3D kit error:  line 00384", MB_OK);
0385      bUsePalette= FALSE;
0386      bInitialized= TRUE;
0387      return;
0388      }
0389    lpGrayPal->palVersion= 0x300;                      /* version */
0390    lpGrayPal->palNumEntries= zMAX_SHADES;          /* num entries */
0391    Red= 3; Green= 3; Blue= 3;                      /* initialize */
0392    for (Shade= 0; Shade < zMAX_SHADES; Shade++)
0393      {                 /* for each entry in the palette structure... */
0394      lpGrayPal->palPalEntry[Shade].peRed= Red;   /* set values... */
0395      lpGrayPal->palPalEntry[Shade].peGreen= Green;
0396      lpGrayPal->palPalEntry[Shade].peBlue= Blue;
0397      lpGrayPal->palPalEntry[Shade].peFlags= (BYTE)0;
0398      Red= Red + (BYTE)4;                /* increment intensities... */
0399      Green= Green + (BYTE)4;
0400      Blue= Blue + (BYTE)4;
0401      }
0402
0403    hGrayPal= CreatePalette(lpGrayPal);            /* create palette */
0404    if (hGrayPal==NULL)
0405      {
0406      MessageBox(GetFocus(),
0407      "Unable to create palette for 256-color graphics.",
0408      "3D kit error:  line 00408", MB_OK);
0409      LocalFree(hGrayPal);
0410      bUsePalette= FALSE;
0411      bInitialized= TRUE;
0412      return;
0413      }
0414    PrevPalette= SelectPalette(hPageDC,hGrayPal,0);  /* select pal */
0415    if (PrevPalette==NULL)
0416      {
0417      MessageBox(GetFocus(),
```

```
0418      "Unable to select palette for 256-color graphics.",
0419      "3D kit error:  line 00419", MB_OK);
0420      LocalFree(hGrayPal);
0421      bUsePalette= FALSE;
0422      bInitialized= TRUE;
0423      return;
0424      }
0425
0426    NumMapped= RealizePalette(hPageDC);   /* remap hardware palette */
0427    if (NumMapped != zMAX_SHADES)  /* if all entries not mapped... */
0428      {
0429      MessageBox(GetFocus(),
0430      "Problem remapping system palette for 256-color graphics.",
0431      "3D kit error:  line 00431", MB_OK);
0432      LocalFree(hGrayPal);
0433      bUsePalette= FALSE;
0434      bInitialized= TRUE;
0435      return;
0436      }
0437
0438    bUsePalette= TRUE;                              /* set a token */
0439    }
0440  bInitialized= TRUE;
0441  bAssembly= FALSE;
0442  return;
0443  }
0444  /*
0445  ------------------------------------------------------------------
0446              Select shading or wireframe rendering
0447  ------------------------------------------------------------------
0448                                                       */
0449  void zUseWireframeMode(BOOL TheMode)
0450  {
0451  if (TheMode == TRUE) bUseWireframe= TRUE;
0452  if (TheMode == FALSE) bUseWireframe= FALSE;
0453  return;
0454  }
0455  /*
0456  ------------------------------------------------------------------
0457              Fixed-target camera functions
0458  ------------------------------------------------------------------
0459              Set the fixed-target camera heading.
0460  ------------------------------------------------------------------
0461                                                       */
0462  void zSetCameraHeading(int Heading)
0463  {                 /* call with Heading in degrees range 0 to 360 */
0464  if (bInitialized==FALSE)
0465    {
0466    zShowMessage(); return;
0467    }
0468  if (bTarget==FALSE) return;           /* if not using fixed target */
0469  if (Heading > zMAX_HEADING) return;
0470  if (Heading < zMIN_HEADING) return;
0471  yawheading= Heading;
0472  CamYaw= ((double)yawheading)*.0175433;
0473  if (yawheading==360) CamYaw= 6.28319;
0474  if (yawheading==0) CamYaw= 0.0;
0475  zSetCamAngle();
0476  if ((CamYaw >= 4.71239) && (CamYaw <= 6.28319))
0477    {
0478    signmx= -1; signmz= -1; yawdelta= 6.28319 - CamYaw;
```

```
0479      goto calccamyaw1;
0480      }
0481   if ((CamYaw >= 0) && (CamYaw < 1.57079))
0482      {
0483      signmx= 1; signmz= -1; yawdelta= CamYaw;
0484      goto calccamyaw1;
0485      }
0486   if ((CamYaw >= 1.57079) && (CamYaw < 3.14159))
0487      {
0488      signmx= 1; signmz= 1; yawdelta= 3.14159 - CamYaw;
0489      goto calccamyaw1;
0490      }
0491   if ((CamYaw >= 3.14159) && (CamYaw < 4.71239))
0492      {
0493      signmx= -1; signmz= 1; yawdelta= CamYaw - 3.14159;
0494      goto calccamyaw1;
0495      }
0496   calccamyaw1:
0497   xCam= sin(yawdelta) * yawdist * signmx;
0498   zCam= cos(yawdelta) * yawdist * signmz;
0499   return;
0500   }
0501   /*
0502   ------------------------------------------------------------
0503                 Set the fixed-target camera pitch.
0504   ------------------------------------------------------------
0505                                                           */
0506   void zSetCameraPitch(int Pitch)
0507   {          /* call with Pitch in range 270 to 360 (horizontal) */
0508   if (bInitialized==FALSE)
0509      {
0510      zShowMessage();
0511      return;
0512      }
0513   if (bTarget==FALSE) return;          /* if not using fixed target */
0514   if (Pitch > zMAX_PITCH) return;  /* do not penetrate groundplane */
0515   if (Pitch < zMIN_PITCH) return;          /* do not exceed vertical */
0516   pitchheading= Pitch;
0517   CamPitch= ((double)pitchheading) * .0174533;      /* make radians */
0518   if (pitchheading==360) CamPitch= 6.28319;
0519   if (pitchheading==0) CamPitch= 0.0;
0520   zSetCamAngle();
0521   pitchdelta= 6.28319 - CamPitch; /* change in pitch from start-up */
0522   yCam=sin(pitchdelta) * dist * signmy;      /* new y translation */
0523   yawdist=sqrt((dist * dist) - (yCam * yCam));      /* hypotenuse */
0524   xCam=sin(yawdelta) * yawdist * signmx;      /* new x translation */
0525   zCam=sqrt((yawdist * yawdist) - (xCam * xCam)) * signmz;   /* z */
0526   return;
0527   }
0528   /*
0529   ------------------------------------------------------------
0530                 Set the camera-to-target distance.
0531   ------------------------------------------------------------
0532                                                           */
0533   void zSetCameraDistance(int Range)
0534   {
0535   if (bInitialized==FALSE)
0536      {
0537      zShowMessage();
0538      return;
0539      }
```

```
0540  if (bTarget==FALSE) return;              /* if not using fixed target */
0541  if (Range < zMIN_DISTANCE)
0542    {
0543    Range= zMIN_DISTANCE; MessageBeep(0);
0544    MessageBox(GetFocus(),
0545    "Resetting camera-to-target distance to zMIN_DISTANCE.",
0546    "3D kit error:  line 00546", MB_OK);
0547    }
0548  if (Range > zMAX_DISTANCE)
0549    {
0550    Range= zMAX_DISTANCE; MessageBeep(0);
0551    MessageBox(GetFocus(),
0552    "Resetting camera-to-target distance to zMAX_DISTANCE.",
0553    "3D kit error:  line 00553", MB_OK);
0554    }
0555  dist= (double) Range;
0556  yCam=sin(pitchdelta) * dist * signmy;          /* new y translation */
0557  yawdist=sqrt((dist * dist) - (yCam * yCam));        /* hypotenuse */
0558  xCam=sin(yawdelta) * yawdist * signmx;       /* new x translation */
0559  zCam=sqrt((yawdist * yawdist) - (xCam * xCam)) * signmz;   /* z */
0560  return;
0561  }
0562  /*
0563  -------------------------------------------------------------------
0564                  Set the camera lens focal length
0565  -------------------------------------------------------------------
0566                                                                  */
0567  void zSetCameraLens(int iFocLength)
0568  {
0569  if (bInitialized==FALSE)
0570    {
0571    zShowMessage();
0572    return;
0573    }
0574  if ((iFocLength!=55)&&(iFocLength!=135)&&(iFocLength!=200)) return;
0575  cameralens= iFocLength;
0576  return;
0577  }
0578  /*
0579  -------------------------------------------------------------------
0580                  Virtual reality camera functions
0581  -------------------------------------------------------------------
0582                  Toggle the camera target off.
0583  -------------------------------------------------------------------
0584                                                                  */
0585  void zDisableTarget(void)
0586  { /* unlocks camera from target, permits virtual reality touring */
0587  if (bInitialized==FALSE)
0588    {
0589    zShowMessage();
0590    return;
0591    }
0592  bTarget= FALSE;
0593  return;
0594  }
0595  /*
0596  -------------------------------------------------------------------
0597                  Toggle the camera target on.
0598  -------------------------------------------------------------------
0599                                                                  */
0600  void zEnableTarget(void)
```

```
0601  {  /* locks camera to a fixed target point in the 3D environment */
0602  if (bInitialized==FALSE)
0603    {
0604    zShowMessage();
0605    return;
0606    }
0607  if (bTarget==TRUE) return;      /* if already in fixed-target mode */
0608  bTarget= TRUE;                                    /* reset the token */
0609  dist= 360;                    /* restore camera-to-target distance */
0610  cameralens= 55;            /* restore focal length of camera lens */
0611  CamYaw= 0.0; CamRoll= 0.0; CamPitch= 6.28319;
0612  pitchheading= 360; yawheading= 0;      /* restore camera direction */
0613  yawdelta= 0; pitchdelta= 0;
0614  zSetCamAngle();
0615  xCam= 0.0; yCam= 0.0; zCam= -360.0;   /* restore camera location */
0616  return;
0617  }
0618  /*
0619  -----------------------------------------------------------------
0620              Set the target-independent camera heading.
0621  -----------------------------------------------------------------
0622                                                                  */
0623  void zSetVRCameraHeading(int Heading)
0624  {                  /* call with Heading in degrees range 0 to 360 */
0625  if (bInitialized==FALSE)
0626    {
0627    zShowMessage(); return;
0628    }
0629  if (bTarget==TRUE) return;          /* cancel if using fixed target */
0630  if (Heading > zMAX_HEADING) return;
0631  if (Heading < zMIN_HEADING) return;
0632  yawheading= Heading;
0633  CamYaw= ((double)yawheading)*.0175433;
0634  if (yawheading==360) CamYaw= 6.28319;
0635  if (yawheading==0) CamYaw= 0.0;
0636  zSetCamAngle();
0637  return;
0638  }
0639  /*
0640  -----------------------------------------------------------------
0641              Set the target-independent camera pitch.
0642  -----------------------------------------------------------------
0643                                                                  */
0644  void zSetVRCameraPitch(int Pitch)
0645  {              /* call with Pitch in range 270 to 360 (horizontal) */
0646  if (bInitialized==FALSE)
0647    {
0648    zShowMessage();
0649    return;
0650    }
0651  if (bTarget==TRUE) return;        /* cancel if using fixed target */
0652  if (Pitch > zMAX_PITCH) return;  /* do not penetrate groundplane */
0653  if (Pitch < zMIN_PITCH) return;         /* do not exceed vertical */
0654  pitchheading= Pitch;
0655  CamPitch= ((double)pitchheading) * .0174533;   /* make radians */
0656  if (pitchheading==360) CamPitch= 6.28319;
0657  if (pitchheading==0) CamPitch= 0.0;
0658  zSetCamAngle();
0659  return;
0660  }
0661  /*
```

```
0662    -----------------------------------------------------------
0663              Set the target-independent camera location.
0664    -----------------------------------------------------------
0665                                                               */
0666    void zSetVRCameraLocation(int xPos, int yPos, int zPos)
0667    {                                      /* call with xyz location */
0668    if (bInitialized==FALSE)
0669      {
0670      zShowMessage(); return;
0671      }
0672    if (bTarget==TRUE) return;          /* cancel if using fixed target */
0673    xCam= (double)((-1) * xPos);
0674    yCam= (double)((-1) * yPos);
0675    zCam= (double)((-1) * zPos);
0676    return;
0677    }
0678    /*
0679    -----------------------------------------------------------
0680              Subobject instancing functions
0681    -----------------------------------------------------------
0682              Set the location of the object.
0683    -----------------------------------------------------------
0684                                                               */
0685    void zSetSubjectLocation(int SSLx, int SSLy, int SSLz)
0686    {
0687    if (bInitialized==FALSE)
0688      {
0689      zShowMessage();
0690      return;
0691      }
0692    xObj= (double) SSLx;
0693    yObj= (double) SSLy;
0694    zObj= (double) SSLz;
0695    return;
0696    }
0697    /*
0698    -----------------------------------------------------------
0699              Set the attitude of the object.
0700    -----------------------------------------------------------
0701                                                               */
0702    void zSetSubjectAttitude(int Yaw, int Roll, int Pitch)
0703    {
0704    if (bInitialized==FALSE)
0705      {
0706      zShowMessage(); return;
0707      }
0708    if (Yaw < 0) return;                        /* trap illegal values... */
0709    if (Yaw > 360) return;
0710    if (Roll < 0) return;
0711    if (Roll > 360) return;
0712    if (Pitch < 0) return;
0713    if (Pitch > 360) return;
0714    ObjYaw=    ((double)Yaw) * .0175433;     /* convert to radians... */
0715    ObjRoll=   ((double)Roll) * .0175433;
0716    ObjPitch= ((double)Pitch) * .0175433;
0717    if (Yaw==360) ObjYaw= 6.28319;       /* tidy up boundary values... */
0718    if (Yaw==0) ObjYaw= 0.0;
0719    if (Roll==360) ObjRoll= 6.28319;
0720    if (Roll==0) ObjRoll= 0.0;
0721    if (Pitch==360) ObjPitch= 6.28319;
0722    if (Pitch==0) ObjPitch= 0.0;
```

```
0723   zSetObjAngle();                        /* set sine and cosine factors */
0724   return;
0725   }
0726   /*
0727   --------------------------------------------------------------------
0728                   Set the extrusion of the object.
0729   --------------------------------------------------------------------
0730                                                                     */
0731   void zSetSubjectSize(int Width, int Height, int Depth)
0732   {
0733   if (bInitialized==FALSE)
0734     {
0735     zShowMessage();
0736     return;
0737     }
0738   if (Width < zMIN_EXTRUDE)  Width= zMIN_EXTRUDE; /* inhibit range */
0739   if (Width > zMAX_EXTRUDE)  Width= zMAX_EXTRUDE;
0740   if (Height < zMIN_EXTRUDE) Height= zMIN_EXTRUDE;
0741   if (Height > zMAX_EXTRUDE) Height= zMAX_EXTRUDE;
0742   if (Depth < zMIN_EXTRUDE)  Depth= zMIN_EXTRUDE;
0743   if (Depth > zMAX_EXTRUDE)  Depth= zMAX_EXTRUDE;
0744   cursorx= (double) Width;             /* set the extrusion factors... */
0745   cursory= (double) Height;
0746   cursorz= (double) Depth;
0747   return;
0748   }
0749   /*
0750   --------------------------------------------------------------------
0751                   Set the current shading color
0752   --------------------------------------------------------------------
0753                                                                     */
0754   void zSetShadingColor(int iHue)
0755   {
0756   if (bInitialized==FALSE)
0757     {
0758     zShowMessage();
0759     return;
0760     }
0761   if (iHue < 1) return;
0762   if (iHue > 7) return;
0763   zShadingColor= iHue;
0764   return;
0765   }
0766   /*
0767   --------------------------------------------------------------------
0768                   Clipping-plane functions
0769   --------------------------------------------------------------------
0770                   Set the near clipping-plane.
0771   --------------------------------------------------------------------
0772                                                                     */
0773   void zSetNearClippingPlane(unsigned char NearDist)
0774   {
0775   if (bInitialized==FALSE)
0776     {
0777     zShowMessage();
0778     return;
0779     }
0780   if (NearDist< zVIEWPOINT) return;     /* must be between viewpoint */
0781   if (NearDist>= FarClip) return;       /* ...and far clipping plane */
0782   NearClip= NearDist;
0783   return;
```

```
0784  }
0785  /*
0786  -----------------------------------------------------------------
0787                 Set the far clipping-plane.
0788  -----------------------------------------------------------------
0789                                                                 */
0790  void zSetFarClippingPlane(unsigned char FarDist)
0791  {
0792  if (bInitialized==FALSE)
0793     {
0794     zShowMessage();
0795     return;
0796     }
0797  if (FarDist> zINFINITY) return;     /* must be between infinity... */
0798  if (FarDist<= NearClip) return;     /* ...and near clipping plane */
0799  FarClip= FarDist;
0800  return;
0801  }
0802  /*
0803  -----------------------------------------------------------------
0804                       3D system functions
0805  -----------------------------------------------------------------
0806      Display a debugging message if 3D system not initialized.
0807  -----------------------------------------------------------------
0808                                                                 */
0809  static void zShowMessage(void)
0810  {               /* called by 3D functions if module not initialized */
0811  MessageBox(GetFocus(),
0812    "The 3D module is not initialized.",
0813    "3D kit error:  line 00813", MB_OK);
0814  return;
0815  }
0816  /*
0817  -----------------------------------------------------------------
0818       Calculate object sine and cosine rotation factors
0819  -----------------------------------------------------------------
0820                                                                 */
0821  static void zSetObjAngle(void)
0822  {         /* called by zInitialize3D() and zSetSubjectAttitude() */
0823    /* Enter with ObjYaw,ObjRoll,ObjPitch object rotation angles.
0824      Exit with sine, cosine object rotation factors.           */
0825  sOYaw=sin(ObjYaw);cOYaw=cos(ObjYaw);
0826  sORoll=sin(ObjRoll);cORoll=cos(ObjRoll);
0827  sOPitch=sin(ObjPitch);cOPitch=cos(ObjPitch);
0828  return;
0829  }
0830  /*
0831  -----------------------------------------------------------------
0832       Calculate camera sine and cosine rotation factors
0833  -----------------------------------------------------------------
0834                                                                 */
0835  static void zSetCamAngle(void)
0836  {             /* called by zInitialize3D() and zSetCameraPitch() */
0837    /* Enter with Yaw,Roll,Pitch world rotation angles.
0838      Exit with sine, cosine world rotation factors.            */
0839  sCYaw=sin(CamYaw);sCRoll=sin(CamRoll);sCPitch=sin(CamPitch);
0840  cCYaw=cos(CamYaw);cCRoll=cos(CamRoll);cCPitch=cos(CamPitch);
0841  return;
0842  }
0843  /*
0844  -----------------------------------------------------------------
```

```
0845          Calculate world coordinates from object coordinates
0846    ------------------------------------------------------------------
0847                                                                    */
0848    void zGetWorldCoords(void)
0849    {                  /* this function is called by zGetCubeCoords() */
0850      /* Enter with xyz unclipped 3D object coordinates.
0851         Exit with unclipped xyz 3D world coordinates.           */
0852    xa=cORoll*x+sORoll*y; ya=cORoll*y-sORoll*x;       /* roll rotate */
0853    x=cOYaw*xa-sOYaw*z; za=sOYaw*xa+cOYaw*z;           /* yaw rotate */
0854    z=cOPitch*za-sOPitch*ya; y=sOPitch*za+cOPitch*ya;/* pitch rotate */
0855    x=x+xObj; y=y+yObj; z=z+zObj;                /* lateral movement */
0856    return;
0857    }
0858    /*
0859    ------------------------------------------------------------------
0860          Calculate camera coordinates from world coordinates
0861    ------------------------------------------------------------------
0862                                                                    */
0863    void zGetCameraCoords(void)
0864    {                  /* this function is called by zGetCubeCoords() */
0865      /* Enter with unclipped xyz 3D world coordinates.
0866         Exit with unclipped xyz 3D camera coordinates.         */
0867    x=(-1)*x;              /* adjust for cartesian coords of 2D screen */
0868    y=y-viewheight;       /* adjust world coords to height of viewer */
0869    x=x-xCam; y=y+yCam; z=z+zCam;                /* lateral movement */
0870    xa=cCYaw*x-sCYaw*z; za=sCYaw*x+cCYaw*z;            /* yaw rotate */
0871    z=cCPitch*za-sCPitch*y; ya=sCPitch*za+cCPitch*y; /* pitch rotate */
0872    x=cCRoll*xa+sCRoll*ya; y=cCRoll*ya-sCRoll*xa;     /* roll rotate */
0873    return;
0874    }
0875    /*
0876    ------------------------------------------------------------------
0877        Scale perspective view volume to normalized view volume
0878    ------------------------------------------------------------------
0879                                                                    */
0880    static void zNormalizeView(void)
0881    {                    /* this function is called by zDrawFacet() */
0882      /* Enter with xPersp, yPersp, zPersp camera coordinates for
0883         3D perspective view volume.  Exit with xNorm, yNorm, zNorm
0884         camera coordinates normalized 3D perspective view volume.  */
0885    if (far_clip_plane_dist==0)
0886      {
0887      MessageBox(GetFocus(),
0888      "Attempted division by 0 in zNormalizeView( ) function.",
0889      "3D kit error:  line 00889",
0890      MB_OK);
0891      }
0892    xNorm= xPersp / far_clip_plane_dist;
0893    yNorm= yPersp / far_clip_plane_dist;
0894    zNorm= zPersp / far_clip_plane_dist;
0895    return;
0896    }
0897    /*
0898    ------------------------------------------------------------------
0899        Scale normalized view volume to rectangular view volume
0900    ------------------------------------------------------------------
0901                                                                    */
0902    static void zRectangularView(void)
0903    {                    /* this function is called by zDrawFacet() */
0904      /* Enter with xNorm, yNorm, zNorm camera coordinates for
0905         3D normalized view volume.  Exit with xRect, yRect, zRect
```

Source listings for the toolkit modules   261

```
0906        camera coordinates for rectangular normalized view volume.  */
0907   TempVariable= zNorm * (-Znear / (1 + Znear));
0908   if (TempVariable == 0)
0909      {
0910      MessageBox(GetFocus(),
0911      "Attempted division by 0 in zRectangularView( ) function.",
0912      "3D kit error:  line 00912",
0913      MB_OK);
0914      }
0915   xRect= xNorm / TempVariable;
0916   yRect= yNorm / TempVariable;
0917   zRect= zNorm;
0918   return;
0919   }
0920   /*
0921   --------------------------------------------------------------------
0922             Scale rectangular view volume to raster viewport
0923   --------------------------------------------------------------------
0924                                                                   */
0925   static void zScaleToRaster(void)
0926   {                        /* this function is called by zDrawFacet() */
0927      /* Enter with xRect, yRect, zRect camera coordinates for
0928         rectangular view volume.  Exit with xRast, yRast, zRast
0929         coordinates for a view volume that maps directly onto the
0930         256-by-255 raster viewport.                              */
0931   xRast= xRect * ViewportWidth;          /* scale x coord to viewport */
0932   yRast= yRect * ViewportDepth;          /* scale y coord to viewport */
0933   if (cameralens==55)                         /* if using 55mm lens... */
0934      {
0935      xRast= xRast * 1; yRast= yRast * 1;
0936      }
0937   if (cameralens==135)          /* if using 135mm telephoto lens... */
0938      {
0939      xRast= xRast * 2; yRast= yRast * 2;
0940      }
0941   if (cameralens==200)          /* if using 200mm telephoto lens... */
0942      {
0943      xRast= xRast * 3; yRast= yRast * 3;
0944      }
0945   xRast= xRast + hcenter;   /* shift x coord to center of viewport */
0946   yRast= yRast + vcenter;   /* shift y coord to center of viewport */
0947   zRast= zRect;                             /* grab the depth value */
0948   zRast= zRast * (-1); /* convert -1 to 0 range to positive values */
0949   zRast= zRast * zFAR_CLIP;    /* expand to 0 to 255 unsigned char */
0950   if (zRast < zVIEWPOINT) zRast= zVIEWPOINT;    /* if less than 0  */
0951   if (zRast > zINFINITY) zRast= zINFINITY;  /* if greater than 255 */
0952   return;
0953   }
0954   /*
0955   --------------------------------------------------------------------
0956                    Polygon and facet functions
0957   --------------------------------------------------------------------
0958                    Draw a 4-sided polygon
0959   --------------------------------------------------------------------
0960                                                                   */
0961   void zDrawFacet(void)
0962   {                        /* this function is called by zDrawCube() */
0963      HDC hDC;
0964      HBRUSH hPrevBrush, hFacetBrush;
0965      HRGN hPrevRegion, hFacetRegion;
0966      HPEN hPrevPen, hHalfEdgePen;
```

```
0967
0968    /* --------------- calculate and store coords ---------------- */
0969    xPersp= xc1; yPersp= yc1; zPersp= zc1;      /* grab camera coords */
0970    zNormalizeView();          /* convert to normalized 3D view volume */
0971    zRectangularView();        /* convert to rectangular 3D view volume */
0972    zScaleToRaster();                     /* scale to fit the 2D viewport */
0973    Points[0].x= (int)xRast;         /* store polygon-drawing coords... */
0974    Points[0].y= (int)yRast;
0975    Raster[0].x= (int)xRast;                  /* store z-buffer coords... */
0976    Raster[0].y= (int)yRast;
0977    Raster[0].z= (unsigned char)zRast;
0978    ViewVolume[0].x= xRect;              /* store clip-ready coords... */
0979    ViewVolume[0].y= yRect;
0980    ViewVolume[0].z= zRect;
0981                      /* repeat the process for other 3 vertices... */
0982    xPersp= xc2; yPersp= yc2; zPersp= zc2;
0983    zNormalizeView();
0984    zRectangularView();
0985    zScaleToRaster();
0986    Points[1].x= (int)xRast;
0987    Points[1].y= (int)yRast;
0988    Raster[1].x= (int)xRast;
0989    Raster[1].y= (int)yRast;
0990    Raster[1].z= (unsigned char)zRast;
0991    ViewVolume[1].x= xRect;
0992    ViewVolume[1].y= yRect;
0993    ViewVolume[1].z= zRect;
0994
0995    xPersp= xc3; yPersp= yc3; zPersp= zc3;
0996    zNormalizeView();
0997    zRectangularView();
0998    zScaleToRaster();
0999    Points[2].x= (int)xRast;
1000    Points[2].y= (int)yRast;
1001    Raster[2].x= (int)xRast;
1002    Raster[2].y= (int)yRast;
1003    Raster[2].z= (unsigned char)zRast;
1004    ViewVolume[2].x= xRect;
1005    ViewVolume[2].y= yRect;
1006    ViewVolume[2].z= zRect;
1007
1008    xPersp= xc4; yPersp= yc4; zPersp= zc4;
1009    zNormalizeView();
1010    zRectangularView();
1011    zScaleToRaster();
1012    Points[3].x= (int)xRast;
1013    Points[3].y= (int)yRast;
1014    Raster[3].x= (int)xRast;
1015    Raster[3].y= (int)yRast;
1016    Raster[3].z= (unsigned char)zRast;
1017    ViewVolume[3].x= xRect;
1018    ViewVolume[3].y= yRect;
1019    ViewVolume[3].z= zRect;
1020
1021    /* -------------- sort the vertices of the polygon ------------- */
1022    FirstY= Points[0].y;      /* find the top vertex of the polygon... */
1023    FirstVertex= 0;
1024    if (Points[1].y < FirstY)
1025      {
1026      FirstVertex= 1; FirstY= Points[1].y;
1027      }
```

```
1028   if (Points[2].y < FirstY)
1029     {
1030     FirstVertex= 2; FirstY= Points[2].y;
1031     }
1032   if (Points[3].y < FirstY)
1033     {
1034     FirstVertex= 3; FirstY= Points[3].y;
1035     }
1036   switch (FirstVertex)        /* assign counterclockwise ordering... */
1037     {
1038     case 0:  FirstVertex= 0; SecondVertex= 1;
1039              ThirdVertex= 2; FourthVertex= 3;
1040              break;
1041     case 1:  FirstVertex= 1; SecondVertex= 2;
1042              ThirdVertex= 3; FourthVertex= 0;
1043              break;
1044     case 2:  FirstVertex= 2; SecondVertex= 3;
1045              ThirdVertex= 0; FourthVertex= 1;
1046              break;
1047     case 3:  FirstVertex= 3; SecondVertex= 0;
1048              ThirdVertex= 1; FourthVertex= 2;
1049              break;
1050     }
1051
1052   /* ----------- clip facet to the 3D view volume -------------- */
1053   zClipToViewVolume();
1054   if (Discard==TRUE) goto FACET_DONE;      /* jump if not visible */
1055   if (TestOnly==TRUE) goto FACET_DONE;  /* jump if in testing mode */
1056
1057   /* -------------- if using wireframe rendering --------------- */
1058   if (bUseWireframe == TRUE)
1059     {
1060     switch (zShadingColor)
1061       {               /* select appropriate color for halfedges... */
1062       case zRED:
1063               hHalfEdgePen= CreatePen(PS_SOLID,1,RGB(127,0,0));
1064               break;
1065       case zGREEN:
1066               hHalfEdgePen= CreatePen(PS_SOLID,1,RGB(0,127,0));
1067               break;
1068       case zBROWN:
1069               hHalfEdgePen= CreatePen(PS_SOLID,1,RGB(127,127,0));
1070               break;
1071       case zBLUE:
1072               hHalfEdgePen= CreatePen(PS_SOLID,1,RGB(0,0,127));
1073               break;
1074       case zMAGENTA:
1075               hHalfEdgePen= CreatePen(PS_SOLID,1,RGB(127,0,127));
1076               break;
1077       case zCYAN:
1078               hHalfEdgePen= CreatePen(PS_SOLID,1,RGB(0,127,127));
1079               break;
1080       case zGRAY:
1081               hHalfEdgePen= CreatePen(PS_SOLID,1,RGB(0,0,0));
1082               break;
1083       }
1084     hDC= GetDC(hWnd);
1085     hPrevPen= SelectObject(hDC, hHalfEdgePen);
1086     MoveTo(hDC, Points[0].x, Points[0].y);
1087     LineTo(hDC, Points[1].x, Points[1].y);
1088     LineTo(hDC, Points[2].x, Points[2].y);
```

```
1089    LineTo(hDC, Points[3].x, Points[3].y);
1090    LineTo(hDC, Points[0].x, Points[0].y);
1091    SelectObject(hDC, hPrevPen);
1092    DeleteObject(hHalfEdgePen);
1093    ReleaseDC(hWnd, hDC);
1094    return;
1095    }
1096
1097    /* -------------------- set up the shading -------------------- */
1098    zGetBrightness();                    /* get brightness factor of facet */
1099    if (bUsePalette==FALSE)
1100      {      /* if using dithered shades, create a dithered brush... */
1101      switch (zShadingColor)
1102        {
1103        case zRED:
1104          hFacetBrush= CreateSolidBrush(RGB(zDeviceIllum,0,0));
1105          break;
1106        case zGREEN:
1107          hFacetBrush= CreateSolidBrush(RGB(0,zDeviceIllum,0));
1108          break;
1109        case zBROWN:
1110          hFacetBrush=
1111            CreateSolidBrush(RGB(zDeviceIllum,zDeviceIllum,0));
1112          break;
1113        case zBLUE:
1114          hFacetBrush= CreateSolidBrush(RGB(0,0,zDeviceIllum));
1115          break;
1116        case zMAGENTA:
1117          hFacetBrush=
1118            CreateSolidBrush(RGB(zDeviceIllum,0,zDeviceIllum));
1119          break;
1120        case zCYAN:
1121          hFacetBrush=
1122            CreateSolidBrush(RGB(0,zDeviceIllum,zDeviceIllum));
1123          break;
1124        case zGRAY:
1125          hFacetBrush=
1126            CreateSolidBrush(RGB(zDeviceIllum,zDeviceIllum,zDeviceIllum));
1127          break;
1128        default:
1129          hFacetBrush= CreateSolidBrush(RGB(0,0,zDeviceIllum));
1130        }
1131      }
1132
1133    /* ------------ draw facet on hidden-page workspace ------------ */
1134    hFacetRegion= CreatePolygonRgn(Points,NumEdges,WINDING);
1135    if (bUsePalette==FALSE)              /* if using dithered shades... */
1136      {                       /* ...draw facet on hidden 3D workspace */
1137      hPrevBrush= SelectObject(hPageDC,hFacetBrush); /* select brush */
1138      hPrevRegion= SelectObject(hPageDC,hFacetRegion); /* and region */
1139      PaintRgn(hPageDC,hFacetRegion);           /* fill the region */
1140      SelectObject(hPageDC,hPrevBrush);          /* deselect brush */
1141      SelectObject(hPageDC,hPrevRegion);         /* deselect region */
1142      DeleteObject(hFacetBrush);                  /* destroy brush */
1143      }
1144
1145    /* -------- do z-buffer tests and draw facet on viewport ------- */
1146    zDoZBufferTest(hFacetRegion);
1147
1148    /* -------------------- tidy up and return -------------------- */
1149    DeleteObject(hFacetRegion);                  /* destroy region */
```

```
1150   FACET_DONE:
1151   return;
1152   }
1153   /*
1154   --------------------------------------------------------------------
1155                     View volume clipping functions
1156   --------------------------------------------------------------------
1157             Clip facets to the normalized 3D view volume
1158   --------------------------------------------------------------------
1159                                                                      */
1160   static void zClipToViewVolume(void)
1161   {                        /* this function is called by zDrawFacet() */
1162   Discard= FALSE; Clipped= FALSE;                       /* reset tokens */
1163
1164   /* -------------- discard if facet behind viewpoint ------------ */
1165   if ((ViewVolume[FirstVertex].z >  0) &&
1166       (ViewVolume[SecondVertex].z > 0) &&
1167       (ViewVolume[ThirdVertex].z >  0) &&
1168       (ViewVolume[FourthVertex].z > 0))
1169      {
1170      Discard= TRUE;
1171      return;
1172      }
1173   /* ---------------- test the far clipping plane --------------- */
1174   if ((ViewVolume[FirstVertex].z <  Zfar) &&
1175       (ViewVolume[SecondVertex].z < Zfar) &&
1176       (ViewVolume[ThirdVertex].z <  Zfar) &&
1177       (ViewVolume[FourthVertex].z < Zfar))
1178      {
1179      Discard= TRUE;         /* discard if fully beyond clipping plane */
1180      return;
1181      }
1182   if ((ViewVolume[FirstVertex].z <  Zfar) ||
1183       (ViewVolume[SecondVertex].z < Zfar) ||
1184       (ViewVolume[ThirdVertex].z <  Zfar) ||
1185       (ViewVolume[FourthVertex].z < Zfar))
1186      {
1187      /* Clipped= TRUE;   discard if facet penetrates clipping plane */
1188      return;
1189      }
1190   /* ---------------- test the near clipping plane --------------- */
1191   if ((ViewVolume[FirstVertex].z > Znear) &&
1192       (ViewVolume[SecondVertex].z > Znear) &&
1193       (ViewVolume[ThirdVertex].z > Znear) &&
1194       (ViewVolume[FourthVertex].z > Znear))
1195      {
1196      Discard= TRUE;
1197      return;
1198      }
1199   /* -------- discard if facet outside left clipping plane ------- */
1200   if ((ViewVolume[FirstVertex].x <  -1) &&
1201       (ViewVolume[SecondVertex].x < -1) &&
1202       (ViewVolume[ThirdVertex].x <  -1) &&
1203       (ViewVolume[FourthVertex].x < -1))
1204      {
1205      Discard= TRUE; return;
1206      }
1207   /* ------- discard if facet outside right clipping plane ------- */
1208   if ((ViewVolume[FirstVertex].x > 1) &&
1209       (ViewVolume[SecondVertex].x > 1) &&
1210       (ViewVolume[ThirdVertex].x >  1) &&
```

```
1211      (ViewVolume[FourthVertex].x > 1))
1212    {
1213    Discard= TRUE; return;
1214    }
1215  /* ------- discard if facet outside bottom clipping plane ------ */
1216  if ((ViewVolume[FirstVertex].y <  -1) &&
1217      (ViewVolume[SecondVertex].y < -1) &&
1218      (ViewVolume[ThirdVertex].y <  -1) &&
1219      (ViewVolume[FourthVertex].y < -1))
1220    {
1221    Discard= TRUE; return;
1222    }
1223  /* -------- discard if facet outside top clipping plane -------- */
1224  if ((ViewVolume[FirstVertex].y >  1) &&
1225      (ViewVolume[SecondVertex].y > 1) &&
1226      (ViewVolume[ThirdVertex].y >  1) &&
1227      (ViewVolume[FourthVertex].y > 1))
1228    {
1229    Discard= TRUE; return;
1230    }
1231  return;
1232  }
1233  /*
1234  -----------------------------------------------------------------
1235                  Facet visibility and shading functions
1236  -----------------------------------------------------------------
1237                  Perform the backplane visibility test
1238  -----------------------------------------------------------------
1239                                                                  */
1240  void zVisibilityTest(void)
1241  {                        /* this function is called by zDrawCube() */
1242    /* Enter with 3 vertices as camera coords.
1243       Exit with visibility token.                                */
1244  sp1=xc1*(yc2*zc3-yc3*zc2);sp1=(-1)*sp1;
1245  sp2=xc2*(yc3*zc1-yc1*zc3);sp3=xc3*(yc1*zc2-yc2*zc1);
1246  visible=sp1-sp2-sp3;
1247  return;
1248  }
1249  /*
1250  -----------------------------------------------------------------
1251                  Calculate the brightness level of a facet
1252  -----------------------------------------------------------------
1253                                                                  */
1254  static void zGetBrightness(void)
1255  {                       /* this function is called by zDrawFacet() */
1256    /* Enter with facet world coordinates.  Exit with illum level. */
1257    double Factor, TempIllum;
1258  xu=xw2-xw1;yu=yw2-yw1;zu=zw2-zw1; /* vector vertex 1 to vertex 2 */
1259  xv=xw3-xw1;yv=yw3-yw1;zv=zw3-zw1; /* vector vertex 1 to vertex 3 */
1260  x_surf_normal=(yu*zv)-(zu*yv);
1261  y_surf_normal=(zu*xv)-(xu*zv);
1262  z_surf_normal=(xu*yv)-(yu*xv);
1263  y_surf_normal=y_surf_normal*(-1);
1264  z_surf_normal=z_surf_normal*(-1); /* convert to cartesian system */
1265  v1=(x_surf_normal*x_surf_normal)+(y_surf_normal*y_surf_normal)
1266    +(z_surf_normal*z_surf_normal);
1267  v2=sqrt(v1);        /* magnitude of surface perpendicular vector */
1268  if (v2 == 0)
1269    {
1270    MessageBox(GetFocus(),
1271    "Attempted division by 0 in zGetBrightness( ) function.",
```

```
1272     "3D kit error:  line 01272",
1273     MB_OK);
1274     }
1275  v3=1/v2;            /* ratio of magnitude to length of unit vector */
1276  x_unit_vector=v3*x_surf_normal;
1277  y_unit_vector=v3*y_surf_normal;
1278  z_unit_vector=v3*z_surf_normal;/* surf perpendicular unit vector */
1279  normalized_illum=(x_unit_vector*xLight)+(y_unit_vector*yLight)
1280     +(z_unit_vector*zLight);            /* illumination factor 0 to 1 */
1281  normalized_illum=normalized_illum*illum_range;/* expand 0 to 255 */
1282  zDeviceIllum= (int) normalized_illum;            /* cast to int */
1283  if (zDeviceIllum < zAMBIENT16) zDeviceIllum= zAMBIENT16;
1284  if (zDeviceIllum > zHIGHLIGHT16) zDeviceIllum= zHIGHLIGHT16;
1285  if (bUsePalette==TRUE)            /* if using 256-color mode... */
1286     {            /* ...calculate the palette index... */
1287     Factor= (double)(zMAX_SHADES / illum_range);
1288     TempIllum= normalized_illum * Factor;
1289     Shade= (int) TempIllum - 1;
1290     if (Shade < zAMBIENT256) Shade= zAMBIENT256;
1291     if (Shade > zHIGHLIGHT256) Shade= zHIGHLIGHT256;
1292     }
1293  return;
1294  }
1295  /*
1296  -----------------------------------------------------------------
1297                  Hidden 3D workspace functions
1298  -----------------------------------------------------------------
1299              Create a hidden-page for 3D workspace
1300  -----------------------------------------------------------------
1301                                                              */
1302  static void zCreateHidden3DPage(HWND hWnd)
1303  {            /* this function is called by zInitialize3D() */
1304     HDC hDisplayDC;
1305  GlobalCompact((DWORD)-1L);            /* maximize contiguous memory */
1306  hDisplayDC= GetDC(hWnd);            /* set the display-context */
1307  hPageDC= CreateCompatibleDC(hDisplayDC);            /* create page... */
1308  hPage= CreateCompatibleBitmap(hDisplayDC,
1309     ViewportWidth,ViewportDepth);
1310  if (hPage==NULL)
1311     {            /* if unable to create hidden-page... */
1312     MessageBeep(0);
1313     MessageBox(GetFocus(),
1314       "zCreateHidden3DPage( ) unable to create hidden-page.",
1315       "3D kit error:  line 01315",MB_OK);
1316     DeleteDC(hPageDC);
1317     ReleaseDC(hWnd,hDisplayDC);
1318     PageReady= FALSE;
1319     return;
1320     }
1321  hPrevPage= SelectObject(hPageDC,hPage);  /* select the bitmap */
1322  PatBlt(hPageDC,0,0,ViewportWidth,ViewportDepth,WHITENESS);
1323  ReleaseDC(hWnd,hDisplayDC);   /* release the display-context */
1324  PageReady= TRUE;
1325  return;
1326  }
1327  /*
1328  -----------------------------------------------------------------
1329                  Clear the hidden-page
1330  -----------------------------------------------------------------
1331                                                              */
1332  void zClearHidden3DPage(void)
```

```
1333  {              /* this function is called by interactive main module */
1334    HRGN hPrevRegion, hFacetRegion;
1335    POINT Points[4];
1336    /* Note:  The hPageDC display-context for the 3D hidden-page
1337        remains valid for the entire runtime session.  However,
1338        a quirk in the GDI's SelectObject() function prevents the
1339        default region from being restored by the code in
1340        zDrawFacet().  Therefore, the following code implements a
1341        workaround that establishes a full bitmap region so PatBlt()
1342        will clear the entire bitmap of the hidden-page.
1343                                          - L.A.               */
1344    if (PageReady==FALSE) return;
1345    Points[0].x= 0; Points[0].y= 0;
1346    Points[1].x= ViewportWidth; Points[1].y= 0;
1347    Points[2].x= ViewportWidth; Points[2].y= ViewportDepth;
1348    Points[3].x= 0; Points[3].y= ViewportDepth;
1349    hFacetRegion= CreatePolygonRgn(Points,4,WINDING);
1350    hPrevRegion= SelectObject(hPageDC,hFacetRegion);
1351    PatBlt(hPageDC,0,0,ViewportWidth,ViewportDepth,WHITENESS);
1352    SelectObject(hPageDC,hPrevRegion);
1353    DeleteObject(hFacetRegion);
1354    return;
1355  }
1356  /*
1357  ------------------------------------------------------------------
1358        Discard the hidden-page, the z-buffer, and the palette
1359  ------------------------------------------------------------------
1360                                                                    */
1361  void zClose3D(void)
1362  {              /* this function is called by interactive main module */
1363    if (PageReady==TRUE)            /* if a hidden-page was created... */
1364      {
1365      SelectObject(hPageDC,hPrevPage);
1366      DeleteObject(hPage);                          /* ...discard it */
1367      DeleteDC(hPageDC);
1368      }
1369    if (ZBufferReady==TRUE)   /* if memory for z-buffer allocated... */
1370      {
1371      hMemFree= GlobalFree(hMem);                     /* ...discard it */
1372      if (hMemFree!=NULL)             /* if unable to discard it... */
1373        {
1374        MessageBeep(0);
1375        MessageBox(GetFocus(),
1376          "zClose3D( ) unable to discard z-buffer memory.",
1377          "3D kit error:  line 01377", MB_OK);
1378        }
1379      }
1380    if (bUsePalette==TRUE)     /* if a logical palette was created... */
1381      {
1382      hMemFree= LocalFree(hGrayPal);  /* ...discard the memory block */
1383      if (hMemFree!=NULL)             /* if unable to discard it... */
1384        {
1385        MessageBeep(0);
1386        MessageBox(GetFocus(),
1387          "zClose3D( ) unable to discard palette memory block.",
1388          "3D kit error:  line 01388", MB_OK);
1389        }
1390      }
1391    return;
1392  }
1393  /*
```

```
1394    --------------------------------------------------------------
1395            Copy a pixel from the hidden 3D page to the viewport
1396    --------------------------------------------------------------
1397                                                                  */
1398    static void zCopyPixelToViewPort(int xCoord, int yCoord)
1399    {                 /* this function is called by zDoZBufferTest() */
1400      HDC hDC;
1401      DWORD PixelColor;
1402      HPALETTE PrevPalette;
1403    if (PageReady==FALSE) return;
1404    if ((xCoord<0)||(xCoord>(ViewportWidth-1))) return;
1405    if ((yCoord<0)||(yCoord>(ViewportDepth-1))) return;
1406
1407    hDC= GetDC(hWnd);             /* grab display-context for viewport */
1408    if (bUsePalette==FALSE)            /* if using dithered shades... */
1409      {
1410      PixelColor= GetPixel(hPageDC, xCoord, yCoord);/* get pixel clr */
1411      SetPixel(hDC, xCoord, yCoord, PixelColor);        /* write pixel */
1412      }
1413    else if(bUsePalette==TRUE)   /* else if using logical palette... */
1414      {
1415      PrevPalette= SelectPalette(hDC,hGrayPal,0);  /* select palette */
1416      SetPixel(hDC, xCoord, yCoord, PALETTEINDEX(Shade));
1417      SelectPalette(hDC,PrevPalette,0);          /* deselect palette */
1418      }
1419    ReleaseDC(hWnd,hDC);                   /* release display-context */
1420    return;
1421    }
1422    /*
1423    --------------------------------------------------------------
1424                        Z-buffer functions
1425    --------------------------------------------------------------
1426        Find the depth of a specified pixel in a 3D polygon
1427    --------------------------------------------------------------
1428                                                                  */
1429    static unsigned char zFindDepth(int Xpoint, int Ypoint)
1430    {              /* this function is called by zDoZBufferTest() */
1431      unsigned char Zpoint;
1432      double TempZpoint;
1433      double ZleftScan, ZrightScan;
1434      double XleftScan, XrightScan;
1435      double YleftScan, YrightScan;
1436      double Zleft1, Zleft2, Zright1, Zright2;
1437      double Yleft1, Yleft2, Yright1, Yright2;
1438      double Xleft1, Xleft2, Xright1, Xright2;
1439      int Index1, Index2;
1440
1441    if ((Xpoint==Raster[FirstVertex].x)&&       /* if first vertex */
1442        (Ypoint==Raster[FirstVertex].y))
1443      {
1444      Zpoint= Raster[FirstVertex].z;
1445      return Zpoint;
1446      }
1447    if ((Xpoint==Raster[SecondVertex].x)&&      /* if second vertex */
1448        (Ypoint==Raster[SecondVertex].y))
1449      {
1450      Zpoint= Raster[SecondVertex].z;
1451      return Zpoint;
1452      }
1453    if ((Xpoint==Raster[ThirdVertex].x)&&       /* if third vertex */
1454        (Ypoint==Raster[ThirdVertex].y))
```

```
1455    {
1456    Zpoint= Raster[ThirdVertex].z;
1457    return Zpoint;
1458    }
1459    if ((Xpoint==Raster[FourthVertex].x)&&        /* if fourth vertex */
1460       (Ypoint==Raster[FourthVertex].y))
1461    {
1462    Zpoint= Raster[FourthVertex].z;
1463    return Zpoint;
1464    }
1465    #ifdef COMPILING          /* if compiling for Windows 3.0 and 3.1 */
1466    #undef COMPILING
1467    #line 1 "E"
1468    #error See compile tips in companion book by Lee Adams.
1469    #endif
1470
1471    /* ------- determine appropriate line segments to be used ------ */
1472    if (Ypoint<=Raster[SecondVertex].y)     /* which left-side lines? */
1473    {
1474    Index1= FirstVertex; Index2= SecondVertex;
1475    }
1476    else if (Ypoint<=Raster[ThirdVertex].y)
1477    {
1478    Index1= SecondVertex; Index2= ThirdVertex;
1479    }
1480    else
1481    {
1482    Index1= ThirdVertex; Index2= FourthVertex;
1483    }
1484    Zleft1= (double)Raster[Index1].z;
1485    Yleft1= (double)Raster[Index1].y;
1486    Xleft1= (double)Raster[Index1].x;
1487    Zleft2= (double)Raster[Index2].z;
1488    Yleft2= (double)Raster[Index2].y;
1489    Xleft2= (double)Raster[Index2].x;
1490    if (Ypoint<=Raster[FourthVertex].y)     /* which right-side lines? */
1491    {
1492    Index1= FirstVertex; Index2= FourthVertex;
1493    }
1494    else if (Ypoint<=Raster[ThirdVertex].y)
1495    {
1496    Index1= FourthVertex; Index2= ThirdVertex;
1497    }
1498    else
1499    {
1500    Index1= ThirdVertex; Index2= SecondVertex;
1501    }
1502    Zright1= (double)Raster[Index1].z;
1503    Yright1= (double)Raster[Index1].y;
1504    Xright1= (double)Raster[Index1].x;
1505    Zright2= (double)Raster[Index2].z;
1506    Yright2= (double)Raster[Index2].y;
1507    Xright2= (double)Raster[Index2].x;
1508    YleftScan= (double)Ypoint;
1509    YrightScan= (double)Ypoint;
1510
1511    /* use facet edges to interpolate the depth of the target point */
1512                /* STEP ONE: calculate scan-line end-point y values */
1513    if (Yleft1-Yleft2==0)
1514    {
1515    ZleftScan= Zleft2;
```

```
1516    }
1517    else
1518    {
1519    ZleftScan= Zleft1-(Zleft1-Zleft2) *
1520              ((Yleft1-YleftScan)/(Yleft1-Yleft2));
1521    }
1522    if (Yright1-Yright2==0)
1523    {
1524    ZrightScan= Zright2;
1525    }
1526    else
1527    {
1528    ZrightScan= Zright1-(Zright1-Zright2) *
1529              ((Yright1-YrightScan)/(Yright1-Yright2));
1530    }
1531            /* STEP TWO:  calculate scan-line end-point x values */
1532    if (Yleft1-Yleft2==0)
1533    {
1534    XleftScan= Xleft2;
1535    }
1536    else
1537    {
1538    XleftScan= Xleft1-(Xleft1-Xleft2) *
1539              ((Yleft1-YleftScan)/(Yleft1-Yleft2));
1540    }
1541    if (Yright1-Yright2==0)
1542    {
1543    XrightScan= Xright2;
1544    }
1545    else
1546    {
1547    XrightScan= Xright1-(Xright1-Xright2) *
1548              ((Yright1-YrightScan)/(Yright1-Yright2));
1549    }
1550    /* STEP THREE:  use scan line to calculate depth of target point */
1551    if (XrightScan-XleftScan==0)
1552    {
1553    TempZpoint= ZrightScan;
1554    }
1555    else
1556    {
1557    TempZpoint= ZrightScan-(ZrightScan-ZleftScan) *
1558              ((XrightScan-Xpoint)/(XrightScan-XleftScan));
1559    }
1560    if (TempZpoint < 0)     /* floating-point math idiosyncracies... */
1561    {       /* ...can cause values to slip outside the 0 to 255... */
1562    TempZpoint == 0; MessageBeep(0);   /* ...range when a facet... */
1563    }                       /* ...is displayed at an oblique angle so... */
1564    if (TempZpoint > 255)   /* ...the facet's edge is towards the... */
1565    {                   /* ...viewpoint and only a few pixels are seen; */
1566    TempZpoint == 255; MessageBeep(0);       /* this behavior is... */
1567    }   /* ...present whether or not a numeric coprocessor is used */
1568    Zpoint= (unsigned char)TempZpoint;
1569    return Zpoint;
1570    }
1571    /*
1572    ----------------------------------------------------------------
1573            Process a 3D facet using the z-buffer algorithm
1574    ----------------------------------------------------------------
1575                                                                    */
1576    static void zDoZBufferTest(HRGN hPolyRegion)
```

```
1577 {                        /* this function is called by zDrawFacet() */
1578   BOOL bValidPt= FALSE;                   /* point inside region? */
1579   unsigned char zPrevDepth;       /* existing depth in z-buffer */
1580   unsigned char zDepth;               /* depth of pt being tested */
1581   int CurrentX, CurrentY;                 /* pt being tested */
1582 for (CurrentY= 0; CurrentY< ViewportDepth; CurrentY++)
1583   {                        /* for each y position scan line... */
1584   bValidPt= FALSE;
1585   for (CurrentX= 0; CurrentX< ViewportWidth; CurrentX++)
1586     {                 /* for each x position on the scan line... */
1587     bValidPt= PtInRegion(hPolyRegion, CurrentX, CurrentY);
1588     if (bValidPt!=FALSE)    /* if point is inside the polygon... */
1589       {
1590       zDepth= zFindDepth(CurrentX, CurrentY);     /* check depth */
1591       zPrevDepth= zReadZBuffer(CurrentX, CurrentY);  /* z-buffer */
1592       if (zDepth< zPrevDepth)          /* compare the two depths */
1593         {               /* if depth is nearer than z-buffer value... */
1594       if ((zDepth<= FarClip)&&(zDepth>= NearClip))
1595         {          /* ...and it is between the clipping planes... */
1596         zWriteZBuffer(CurrentX, CurrentY, zDepth); /* store it */
1597         zCopyPixelToViewPort(CurrentX, CurrentY); /* write it */
1598         }               /* end of clipping plane if() block */
1599       }               /* end of depth comparison if() block */
1600     }          /*logical end of bValidPt if() block */
1601   }               /* logical end of CurrentX for() loop */
1602   }               /* logical end of CurrentY for() loop */
1603 return;
1604 }
1605 /*
1606 ----------------------------------------------------------------
1607               Write a depth value to the z-buffer
1608 ----------------------------------------------------------------
1609                                                              */
1610 static void zWriteZBuffer(int xCoord, int yCoord,
1611                           unsigned char zDepth1)
1612 {               /* this function is called by zDoZBufferTest() */
1613   int Address;
1614 if ((xCoord<0)||(xCoord>(ViewportWidth-1))) return;
1615 if ((yCoord<0)||(yCoord>(ViewportDepth-1))) return;
1616 if (ZBufferReady==FALSE) return;
1617 lpMem= GlobalLock(hMem);   /* grab address and lock memory block */
1618 if (lpMem==(LPSTR)NULL)           /* if unable to grab address... */
1619   {
1620   MessageBeep(0);
1621   MessageBox(GetFocus(),
1622     "zWriteZBuffer( ) unable to grab z-buffer address.",
1623     "3D kit error:  line 01622", MB_OK);
1624   }
1625 Address= (yCoord * ViewportWidth) + xCoord;      /* data address */
1626 lpMem[Address]= zDepth1;              /* write to memory block */
1627 GlobalUnlock(hMem);   /* unlock memory block, discard address */
1628 return;
1629 }
1630 /*
1631 ----------------------------------------------------------------
1632               Read a depth value from the z-buffer
1633 ----------------------------------------------------------------
1634                                                              */
1635 static unsigned char zReadZBuffer(int xCoord, int yCoord)
1636 {               /* this function is called by zDoZBufferTest() */
1637   unsigned char zDepth1;
```

```
1638     int Address;
1639   if ((xCoord<0)||(xCoord>(ViewportWidth-1))) return 255;
1640   if ((yCoord<0)||(yCoord>(ViewportDepth-1))) return 255;
1641   if (ZBufferReady==FALSE) return 255;
1642   lpMem= GlobalLock(hMem);    /* grab address and lock memory block */
1643   if (lpMem==(LPSTR)NULL)            /* if unable to grab address... */
1644     {
1645     MessageBeep(0);
1646     MessageBox(GetFocus(),
1647       "zReadZBuffer( ) unable to grab z-buffer address.",
1648       "3D kit error:  line 01647", MB_OK);
1649     }
1650   Address= (yCoord * ViewportWidth) + xCoord;       /* data address */
1651   zDepth1= lpMem[Address];                 /* read from memory block */
1652   GlobalUnlock(hMem);      /* unlock memory block, discard address */
1653   return zDepth1;
1654   }
1655   /*
1656   ------------------------------------------------------------------
1657                       Reset the z-buffer
1658   ------------------------------------------------------------------
1659                                                                   */
1660   void zResetZBuffer(void)
1661   {            /* this function is called by interactive main module */
1662     int xCoord, yCoord;
1663     int Address;
1664   if (ZBufferReady==FALSE) return;
1665   lpMem= GlobalLock(hMem);    /* grab address and lock memory block */
1666   if (lpMem==(LPSTR)NULL)            /* if unable to grab address... */
1667     {
1668     MessageBeep(0);
1669     MessageBox(GetFocus(),
1670       "zResetZBuffer( ) unable to grab z-buffer address.",
1671       "3D kit error:  line 01670", MB_OK);
1672     }
1673   for (yCoord=0; yCoord<=(ViewportDepth-1); yCoord++)
1674     {          /* for each scan line represented in the z-buffer... */
1675     for (xCoord=0; xCoord<=(ViewportWidth-1); xCoord++)
1676       {             /* for each x coordinate on each scan line... */
1677       Address= (yCoord * ViewportWidth) + xCoord;  /* data address */
1678       lpMem[Address]= (unsigned char)255; /* write to memory block */
1679       }
1680     }
1681   GlobalUnlock(hMem);        /* unlock memory block, discard address */
1682   return;
1683   }
1684   /*
1685   ------------------------------------------------------------------
1686       End of module of 3D functions for Windows applications.
1687   ------------------------------------------------------------------
1688                                                                   */
```

B-2 Source listings for the 3D shapes toolkit, shapes3d.c. See Appendix C for applications that use this toolkit. See Appendix A for instructions on building the demos.

```
0001   /*
0002   ------------------------------------------------------------------
0003                       SHAPES3D.H
0004   ------------------------------------------------------------------
0005                                                                   */
0006   void zDrawCube(void);                       /* renders 3D box */
```

```
0007   void zDrawSphere(void);                         /* renders 3D sphere */
0008   void zDrawCylinder(void);                     /* renders 3D cylinder */
0009   void zDrawCurve(void);                   /* renders 3D curved surface */
0010   void zDrawCone(void);                           /* renders 3D cone */
0011   void zDrawHemisphere(void);               /* renders 3D half-sphere */
0012   void zDrawWedge(void);                          /* renders 3D wedge */
0013   /*
0014   ----------------------------------------------------------------------
0015                   End of header file for 3D shapes.
0016   ----------------------------------------------------------------------
0017                                                                        */
0001   /*
0002   ----------------------------------------------------------------------
0003         Module of 3D shape drivers for Windows applications
0004   ----------------------------------------------------------------------
0005      Source file: SHAPES3D.C
0006      Release version: 1.00                 Programmer: Lee Adams
0007      Type:  C source file for Windows multimodule applications.
0008      Compilers:  Microsoft C/C++, Borland C++, Zortech C++,
0009        QuickC for Windows, Turbo C++ for Windows, WATCOM C.
0010      Memory model: medium.
0011      Dependencies:  ENGINE3D.C 3D functions.  Compile ENGINE3D.C and
0012        SHAPES3D.C and link the resulting .OBJ files to your compiled
0013        primary .C file.  Include SHAPES3D.H and ENGINE3D.H in your
0014        primary .C file.
0015      Output and features:  Provides drivers for the ENGINE3D.C
0016        3D routines in order to render spheres, boxes, cylinders,
0017        curved surfaces, cones, wedges, etc.
0018      Publication: Contains material from Windcrest/McGraw-Hill book
0019        4115 published by TAB BOOKS Division of McGraw-Hill Inc.
0020      License:  As purchaser of the book you are granted a royalty-
0021        free license to distribute executable files generated using
0022        this code provided you accept the conditions of the License
0023        Agreement and Limited Warranty described in the book and on
0024        the companion disk.  Government users:  This software and
0025        documentation are subject to restrictions set forth in The
0026        Rights in Technical Data and Computer Software clause at
0027        252.227-7013 and elsewhere.
0028   ----------------------------------------------------------------------
0029        (c) Copyright 1988-1993 Lee Adams.  All rights reserved.
0030             Lee Adams(tm) is a trademark of Lee Adams.
0031   ----------------------------------------------------------------------
0032                                                                        */
0033
0034   #include <WINDOWS.H>              /* for GDI MessageBox() function */
0035   #include <math.h>                 /* for sine and cosine functions */
0036
0037   #define z00_DEGREES      .0                       /* radian angles... */
0038   #define z05_DEGREES      .08727
0039   #define z10_DEGREES      .17453
0040   #define z20_DEGREES      .34907
0041   #define z90_DEGREES      1.57079
0042   #define zMIN_RADIUS      10                       /* minimum radius */
0043   #define zMIN_DIMENSION   10         /* min curved surface extrusion */
0044   /* #define COMPILING 1 */
0045   /*
0046   ----------------------------------------------------------------------
0047        Function prototypes for functions found in this module
0048   ----------------------------------------------------------------------
0049                                                                        */
0050   /* ----- callable from both outside and inside this module ----- */
```

```
0051    void zDrawCube(void);                          /* draw 3D cube */
0052    void zDrawSphere(void);                        /* draw 3D sphere */
0053    void zDrawCylinder(void);                      /* draw 3D cylinder */
0054    void zDrawCurve(void);                  /* draw 3D curved surface */
0055    void zDrawCone(void);                          /* draw 3D cone */
0056    void zDrawHemisphere(void);               /* draw 3D half-sphere */
0057    void zDrawWedge(void);                         /* draw 3D wedge */
0058
0059    /* ----------- callable from only inside this module ---------- */
0060    static void zGetCubeCoords(void); /* cam coords & display coords */
0061    static void zGetSphereShape(void);     /* pt on surface of sphere */
0062    static void zGetCylinderShape(void);   /* pt on cylinder surface */
0063    static void zGetCurveShape(void);       /* pt on curved surface */
0064    static void zGetConeShape(void);          /* pt on cone surface */
0065    static void zGetWedgeCoords(void); /* cam coords, display coords */
0066    /*
0067    ------------------------------------------------------------------
0068                Declare functions found in ENGINE3D.C
0069    ------------------------------------------------------------------
0070                                                                    */
0071    void zGetCameraCoords(void);     /* world coords to camera coords */
0072    void zGetWorldCoords(void);      /* object coords to world coords */
0073    void zVisibilityTest(void);            /* back-plane visibility */
0074    void zDrawFacet(void);                          /* draws facet */
0075    /*
0076    ------------------------------------------------------------------
0077                Declare functions found in ASSEMB3D.C
0078    ------------------------------------------------------------------
0079                                                                    */
0080    void zGetAssemblyCoords(void);    /* subobject to assembly coords */
0081    /*
0082    ------------------------------------------------------------------
0083            Static variables visible throughout this file
0084    ------------------------------------------------------------------
0085                                                                    */
0086    static double SphereX, SphereY, SphereZ;    /* sphere obj coords */
0087    static double SphereRadius;                  /* radius of sphere */
0088    static double VertAngle, HorizAngle;      /* angular description */
0089    static double PrevVert, PrevHoriz;         /* scratchpad values */
0090    static double TempX;                        /* scratchpad value */
0091    static double SinVert, CosVert,           /* sin, cos factors... */
0092              SinHoriz, CosHoriz;
0093    static int NumStrips, NumFacets;      /* num of strips and facets */
0094    static int Strip;                          /* strip loop counter */
0095    static int Facet;                          /* facet loop counter */
0096    static double StripHeight, FacetWidth;    /* angular ht & width */
0097    static double CapHeight;                 /* angular height of cap */
0098
0099    static double CylinderX, CylinderY, CylinderZ;    /* obj coords */
0100    static double CylinderRadius, CylinderExtrude;     /* dimensions */
0101    static double FacetDimension;        /* angular dimension of facet */
0102
0103    static double T= 0.0, T2= 0.0, T3= 0.0; /* primary, square, cube */
0104    static double PrevT;                             /* scratchpad */
0105    static double Pull1= 0.0, Pull2= 0.0,  /* effect of curve points */
0106              Pull3= 0.0, Pull4= 0.0;
0107    static double CurveX1= 0.0, CurveY1= 0.0;     /* curve startpoint */
0108    static double CurveX4= 0.0, CurveY4= 0.0;       /* curve endpoint */
0109    static double CurveX2= -10.0, CurveY2= 0.0;    /* first control */
0110    static double CurveX3= 10.0, CurveY3= 0.0;    /* second control */
0111    static double SurfaceX, SurfaceY;                 /* obj coords */
```

```
0112    static double SurfaceEdge1, SurfaceEdge2;      /* extruded edges */
0113    static double ParamChange, ParamMax, ParamMin;      /* parameters */
0114    static double ControlStrength;      /* effect of control points */
0115    static double SwapStorage;                /* scratchpad for swaps */
0116
0117    static double ConeRadius, ConeExtrude;            /* dimensions */
0118    static double ConeX, ConeY, ConeZ;               /* obj coords */
0119    /*
0120    -------------------------------------------------------------------
0121            Declare extern variables defined in ENGINE3D.C
0122    -------------------------------------------------------------------
0123                                                                     */
0124    extern BOOL bUsePalette;                  /* using 256-color mode? */
0125    extern BOOL bAssembly;            /* using hierarchical modeling? */
0126    extern double cursorx, cursory, cursorz;      /* volumetric cursor */
0127    extern double x, y, z;                         /* initial coords */
0128    extern double cubeObj[8][3];            /* array of object coords */
0129    extern double cubeWorld[8][3];           /* array of world coords */
0130    extern double camcoords[8][3];          /* array of camera coords */
0131    extern double visible;         /* result of backplane removal test */
0132    extern BOOL Discard, Clipped; /* view volume attributes of facet */
0133    extern BOOL bInitialized;       /* TRUE if 3D library initialized */
0134    extern BOOL TestOnly;                 /* pretests parallelepiped */
0135    extern double xc1, yc1, zc1,          /* camera coords of facet... */
0136                  xc2, yc2, zc2,
0137                  xc3, yc3, zc3,
0138                  xc4, yc4, zc4;
0139    extern double xw1, yw1, zw1,             /* world coords of facet... */
0140                  xw2, yw2, zw2,
0141                  xw3, yw3, zw3;
0142    /*
0143    -------------------------------------------------------------------
0144                        3D solids drivers
0145    -------------------------------------------------------------------
0146                    Draw a solid parallelepiped
0147    -------------------------------------------------------------------
0148                                                                     */
0149    void zDrawCube(void)
0150    {        /* this function is called by interactive main module */
0151    if (bInitialized==FALSE)
0152      {
0153      MessageBox(GetFocus(),
0154        "zDrawCube( ) reports that the 3D library is not initialized.",
0155        "shapes3D.c error:  line 00155", MB_OK);
0156      return;
0157      }
0158    zGetCubeCoords();           /* get camera coords and display coords */
0159
0160    TestOnly= TRUE;                    /* reset token for first pass */
0161    SECOND_PASS:             /* will loop back to here for second pass */
0162
0163    surface0:
0164      xc1=camcoords[7][0];yc1=camcoords[7][1];zc1=camcoords[7][2];
0165      xc2=camcoords[0][0];yc2=camcoords[0][1];zc2=camcoords[0][2];
0166      xc3=camcoords[3][0];yc3=camcoords[3][1];zc3=camcoords[3][2];
0167      xc4=camcoords[6][0];yc4=camcoords[6][1];zc4=camcoords[6][2];
0168      zVisibilityTest();
0169      if (visible > 0) goto surface1;
0170      xw3=cubeWorld[7][0];yw3=cubeWorld[7][1];zw3=cubeWorld[7][2];
0171      xw2=cubeWorld[0][0];yw2=cubeWorld[0][1];zw2=cubeWorld[0][2];
0172      xw1=cubeWorld[3][0];yw1=cubeWorld[3][1];zw1=cubeWorld[3][2];
```

```
0173    zDrawFacet();
0174  if ((Discard==TRUE) || (Clipped==TRUE)) goto DISCARD_SOLID;
0175
0176    surface1:
0177    xc1=camcoords[6][0];yc1=camcoords[6][1];zc1=camcoords[6][2];
0178    xc2=camcoords[5][0];yc2=camcoords[5][1];zc2=camcoords[5][2];
0179    xc3=camcoords[4][0];yc3=camcoords[4][1];zc3=camcoords[4][2];
0180    xc4=camcoords[7][0];yc4=camcoords[7][1];zc4=camcoords[7][2];
0181    zVisibilityTest();
0182    if (visible > 0) goto surface2;
0183    xw3=cubeWorld[6][0];yw3=cubeWorld[6][1];zw3=cubeWorld[6][2];
0184    xw2=cubeWorld[5][0];yw2=cubeWorld[5][1];zw2=cubeWorld[5][2];
0185    xw1=cubeWorld[4][0];yw1=cubeWorld[4][1];zw1=cubeWorld[4][2];
0186    zDrawFacet();
0187  if ((Discard==TRUE) || (Clipped==TRUE)) goto DISCARD_SOLID;
0188
0189    surface2:
0190    xc1=camcoords[3][0];yc1=camcoords[3][1];zc1=camcoords[3][2];
0191    xc2=camcoords[2][0];yc2=camcoords[2][1];zc2=camcoords[2][2];
0192    xc3=camcoords[5][0];yc3=camcoords[5][1];zc3=camcoords[5][2];
0193    xc4=camcoords[6][0];yc4=camcoords[6][1];zc4=camcoords[6][2];
0194    zVisibilityTest();
0195    if (visible > 0) goto surface3;
0196    xw3=cubeWorld[3][0];yw3=cubeWorld[3][1];zw3=cubeWorld[3][2];
0197    xw2=cubeWorld[2][0];yw2=cubeWorld[2][1];zw2=cubeWorld[2][2];
0198    xw1=cubeWorld[5][0];yw1=cubeWorld[5][1];zw1=cubeWorld[5][2];
0199    zDrawFacet();
0200  if ((Discard==TRUE) || (Clipped==TRUE)) goto DISCARD_SOLID;
0201
0202    surface3:
0203    xc1=camcoords[0][0];yc1=camcoords[0][1];zc1=camcoords[0][2];
0204    xc2=camcoords[1][0];yc2=camcoords[1][1];zc2=camcoords[1][2];
0205    xc3=camcoords[2][0];yc3=camcoords[2][1];zc3=camcoords[2][2];
0206    xc4=camcoords[3][0];yc4=camcoords[3][1];zc4=camcoords[3][2];
0207    zVisibilityTest();
0208    if (visible > 0) goto surface4;
0209    xw3=cubeWorld[0][0];yw3=cubeWorld[0][1];zw3=cubeWorld[0][2];
0210    xw2=cubeWorld[1][0];yw2=cubeWorld[1][1];zw2=cubeWorld[1][2];
0211    xw1=cubeWorld[2][0];yw1=cubeWorld[2][1];zw1=cubeWorld[2][2];
0212    zDrawFacet();
0213  if ((Discard==TRUE) || (Clipped==TRUE)) goto DISCARD_SOLID;
0214
0215    surface4:
0216    xc1=camcoords[7][0];yc1=camcoords[7][1];zc1=camcoords[7][2];
0217    xc2=camcoords[4][0];yc2=camcoords[4][1];zc2=camcoords[4][2];
0218    xc3=camcoords[1][0];yc3=camcoords[1][1];zc3=camcoords[1][2];
0219    xc4=camcoords[0][0];yc4=camcoords[0][1];zc4=camcoords[0][2];
0220    zVisibilityTest();
0221    if (visible > 0) goto surface5;
0222    xw3=cubeWorld[7][0];yw3=cubeWorld[7][1];zw3=cubeWorld[7][2];
0223    xw2=cubeWorld[4][0];yw2=cubeWorld[4][1];zw2=cubeWorld[4][2];
0224    xw1=cubeWorld[1][0];yw1=cubeWorld[1][1];zw1=cubeWorld[1][2];
0225    zDrawFacet();
0226  if ((Discard==TRUE) || (Clipped==TRUE)) goto DISCARD_SOLID;
0227
0228    surface5:
0229    xc1=camcoords[1][0];yc1=camcoords[1][1];zc1=camcoords[1][2];
0230    xc2=camcoords[4][0];yc2=camcoords[4][1];zc2=camcoords[4][2];
0231    xc3=camcoords[5][0];yc3=camcoords[5][1];zc3=camcoords[5][2];
0232    xc4=camcoords[2][0];yc4=camcoords[2][1];zc4=camcoords[2][2];
0233    zVisibilityTest();
```

```
0234    if (visible > 0) goto surfaces_done;
0235    xw3=cubeWorld[1][0];yw3=cubeWorld[1][1];zw3=cubeWorld[1][2];
0236    xw2=cubeWorld[4][0];yw2=cubeWorld[4][1];zw2=cubeWorld[4][2];
0237    xw1=cubeWorld[5][0];yw1=cubeWorld[5][1];zw1=cubeWorld[5][2];
0238    zDrawFacet();
0239 if ((Discard==TRUE) || (Clipped==TRUE)) goto DISCARD_SOLID;
0240
0241 surfaces_done:
0242 if (TestOnly==TRUE)
0243    {                               /* if just finished first pass... */
0244    TestOnly= FALSE;                        /* reset token and... */
0245    goto SECOND_PASS;                /* loop back for second pass */
0246    }
0247 return;                     /* fall through to here after second pass */
0248
0249 DISCARD_SOLID:  /* jump to here if facet discarded on first pass */
0250 MessageBeep(0);    /* issue audio cue if solid has been discarded */
0251 return;
0252 }
0253 /*
0254 ------------------------------------------------------------------
0255                 Calculate coords for parallelepiped
0256 ------------------------------------------------------------------
0257                                                                  */
0258 static void zGetCubeCoords(void)
0259 {                       /* this function is called by zDrawCube() */
0260    int t= 0;
0261    double negx,negy,negz;
0262 negx=(-1)*(cursorx);negy=(-1)*(cursory);negz=(-1)*(cursorz);
0263 cubeObj[0][0]=cursorx;cubeObj[0][1]=negy;cubeObj[0][2]=cursorz;
0264 cubeObj[1][0]=cursorx;cubeObj[1][1]=cursory;cubeObj[1][2]=cursorz;
0265 cubeObj[2][0]=negx;cubeObj[2][1]=cursory;cubeObj[2][2]=cursorz;
0266 cubeObj[3][0]=negx;cubeObj[3][1]=negy;cubeObj[3][2]=cursorz;
0267 cubeObj[4][0]=cursorx;cubeObj[4][1]=cursory;cubeObj[4][2]=negz;
0268 cubeObj[5][0]=negx;cubeObj[5][1]=cursory;cubeObj[5][2]=negz;
0269 cubeObj[6][0]=negx;cubeObj[6][1]=negy;cubeObj[6][2]=negz;
0270 cubeObj[7][0]=cursorx;cubeObj[7][1]=negy;cubeObj[7][2]=negz;
0271 for (t=0;t<=7;t++)
0272    {
0273    x=cubeObj[t][0];y=cubeObj[t][1];z=cubeObj[t][2];
0274    if (bAssembly == TRUE) zGetAssemblyCoords();
0275    zGetWorldCoords();
0276    cubeWorld[t][0]=x;cubeWorld[t][1]=y;cubeWorld[t][2]=z;
0277    zGetCameraCoords();
0278    camcoords[t][0]=x;camcoords[t][1]=y;camcoords[t][2]=z;
0279    }
0280 return;
0281 }
0282 /*
0283 ------------------------------------------------------------------
0284                         Draw a 3D sphere
0285 ------------------------------------------------------------------
0286                                                                  */
0287 void zDrawSphere(void)
0288 {       /* this function uses extern cursorx as radius of sphere */
0289 if (bInitialized==FALSE)
0290    {
0291    MessageBox(GetFocus(),
0292     "zDrawSphere( ) reports that 3D library is not initialized.",
0293      "shapes3D.c error:  line 00293", MB_OK);
0294    return;
```

```
0295    }
0296    TestOnly= FALSE;                        /* do not discard entire solid */
0297    SphereRadius= cursorx;                    /* grab radius of sphere */
0298    if (SphereRadius < zMIN_RADIUS) return;   /* if radius too small */
0299    CapHeight= z10_DEGREES;              /* set height of facets for cap */
0300
0301    if (SphereRadius >= 25)
0302        {                    /* if a large radius, use smaller facets... */
0303        NumStrips= 16;                            /* num of strips */
0304        NumFacets= 36;                      /* num of facets per strip */
0305        FacetWidth= z10_DEGREES;                 /* width of facets */
0306        StripHeight= z10_DEGREES;                /* height of facets */
0307        if (bUsePalette == TRUE)        /* if using 256-color mode... */
0308            {              /* ...increase the resolution of the rendering */
0309            NumStrips= 32;
0310            NumFacets= 36;
0311            FacetWidth= z10_DEGREES;
0312            StripHeight= z05_DEGREES;
0313            }
0314        }
0315    else if (SphereRadius < 25)
0316        {                    /* if a smaller radius, use larger facets... */
0317        NumStrips= 8;                            /* num of strips */
0318        NumFacets= 18;                      /* num of facets per strip */
0319        FacetWidth= z20_DEGREES;                 /* width of facets */
0320        StripHeight= z20_DEGREES;                /* height of facets */
0321        }
0322
0323    /* ---------------- draw north cap of sphere ---------------- */
0324    VertAngle= z00_DEGREES;                  /* set vertical angle */
0325    HorizAngle= z00_DEGREES;                 /* set horiz angle */
0326    for (Facet= 1; Facet <= NumFacets; Facet++)
0327        {                              /* for each facet on the cap... */
0328        /* -------------- calculate first vertex -------------- */
0329        zGetSphereShape();                     /* calculate obj coords */
0330        x= SphereX; y= SphereY; z= SphereZ;    /* grab object coords */
0331        if (bAssembly == TRUE) zGetAssemblyCoords();
0332        zGetWorldCoords();                   /* calculate world coords */
0333        zGetCameraCoords();                /* calculate camera coords */
0334        xc1= x; yc1= y; zc1= z;              /* grab camera coords */
0335        /* -------------- calculate second vertex -------------- */
0336        PrevHoriz= HorizAngle; HorizAngle= HorizAngle + FacetWidth;
0337        zGetSphereShape(); x= SphereX; y= SphereY; z= SphereZ;
0338        if (bAssembly == TRUE) zGetAssemblyCoords();
0339        zGetWorldCoords(); xw3= x; yw3= y; zw3= z;
0340        zGetCameraCoords(); xc2= x; yc2= y; zc2= z;
0341        /* -------------- calculate third vertex -------------- */
0342        PrevVert= VertAngle; VertAngle= VertAngle + CapHeight;
0343        zGetSphereShape(); x= SphereX; y= SphereY; z= SphereZ;
0344        if (bAssembly == TRUE) zGetAssemblyCoords();
0345        zGetWorldCoords(); xw2= x; yw2= y; zw2= z;
0346        zGetCameraCoords(); xc3= x; yc3= y; zc3= z;
0347        /* -------------- calculate fourth vertex -------------- */
0348        HorizAngle= PrevHoriz;
0349        zGetSphereShape(); x= SphereX; y= SphereY; z= SphereZ;
0350        if (bAssembly == TRUE) zGetAssemblyCoords();
0351        zGetWorldCoords(); xw1= x; yw1= y; zw1= z;
0352        zGetCameraCoords(); xc4= x; yc4= y; zc4= z;
0353        /* --------- test visibility and render the facet ---------- */
0354        zVisibilityTest();                   /* backface culling test */
0355        if (visible <= 0) zDrawFacet();      /* render z-buffered facet */
```

```
0356    /* ------------- reset to start of next facet --------------- */
0357    HorizAngle= HorizAngle + FacetWidth;
0358    VertAngle= PrevVert;
0359    }                                    /* loop back to do next facet */
0360
0361    /* ------------------- draw body of sphere -------------------- */
0362    VertAngle= z10_DEGREES;                      /* reset vertical angle */
0363    HorizAngle= z00_DEGREES;                        /* reset horiz angle */
0364    for (Strip= 1; Strip <= NumStrips; Strip++)
0365      {                    /* for each strip on surface of sphere... */
0366      for (Facet= 1; Facet <= NumFacets; Facet++)
0367        {                         /* for each facet on the strip... */
0368        /* ------------- calculate first vertex ------------------ */
0369        zGetSphereShape(); x= SphereX; y= SphereY; z= SphereZ;
0370        if (bAssembly == TRUE) zGetAssemblyCoords();
0371        zGetWorldCoords(); xw3= x; yw3= y; zw3= z;
0372        zGetCameraCoords(); xc1= x; yc1= y; zc1= z;
0373        /* ------------- calculate second vertex ---------------- */
0374        PrevHoriz= HorizAngle; HorizAngle= HorizAngle + FacetWidth;
0375        zGetSphereShape(); x= SphereX; y= SphereY; z= SphereZ;
0376        if (bAssembly == TRUE) zGetAssemblyCoords();
0377        zGetWorldCoords(); xw2= x; yw2= y; zw2= z;
0378        zGetCameraCoords(); xc2= x; yc2= y; zc2= z;
0379        /* ------------- calculate third vertex ----------------- */
0380        PrevVert= VertAngle; VertAngle= VertAngle + StripHeight;
0381        zGetSphereShape(); x= SphereX; y= SphereY; z= SphereZ;
0382        if (bAssembly == TRUE) zGetAssemblyCoords();
0383        zGetWorldCoords(); xw1= x; yw1= y; zw1= z;
0384        zGetCameraCoords(); xc3= x; yc3= y; zc3= z;
0385        /* ------------- calculate fourth vertex ---------------- */
0386        HorizAngle= PrevHoriz;
0387        zGetSphereShape(); x= SphereX; y= SphereY; z= SphereZ;
0388        if (bAssembly == TRUE) zGetAssemblyCoords();
0389        zGetWorldCoords();
0390        zGetCameraCoords(); xc4= x; yc4= y; zc4= z;
0391        /* -------- test visibility and render the facet ---------- */
0392        zVisibilityTest();
0393        if (visible <= 0) zDrawFacet();
0394        /* ----------- reset to start of next facet -------------- */
0395        HorizAngle= HorizAngle + FacetWidth;
0396        VertAngle= PrevVert;
0397        }                               /* loop back to do next facet */
0398      VertAngle= VertAngle + StripHeight;       /* select next strip */
0399      HorizAngle= z00_DEGREES;                  /* reset to first facet */
0400      }                                 /* loop back to do next strip */
0401
0402    /* ----------------- draw south cap of sphere ----------------- */
0403    HorizAngle= z00_DEGREES;                        /* reset horiz angle */
0404    for (Facet= 1; Facet <= NumFacets; Facet++)
0405      {                                /* for each facet on the cap... */
0406      /* ------------- calculate first vertex ------------------ */
0407      zGetSphereShape(); x= SphereX; y= SphereY; z= SphereZ;
0408      if (bAssembly == TRUE) zGetAssemblyCoords();
0409      zGetWorldCoords(); xw3= x; yw3= y; zw3= z;
0410      zGetCameraCoords(); xc1= x; yc1= y; zc1= z;
0411      /* ------------- calculate second vertex ------------------ */
0412      PrevHoriz= HorizAngle; HorizAngle= HorizAngle + FacetWidth;
0413      zGetSphereShape(); x= SphereX; y= SphereY; z= SphereZ;
0414      if (bAssembly == TRUE) zGetAssemblyCoords();
0415      zGetWorldCoords(); xw2= x; yw2= y; zw2= z;
0416      zGetCameraCoords(); xc2= x; yc2= y; zc2= z;
```

```
0417        /* --------------- calculate third vertex -------------------- */
0418        PrevVert= VertAngle; VertAngle= VertAngle + CapHeight;
0419        zGetSphereShape(); x= SphereX; y= SphereY; z= SphereZ;
0420        if (bAssembly == TRUE) zGetAssemblyCoords();
0421        zGetWorldCoords(); xw1= x; yw1= y; zw1= z;
0422        zGetCameraCoords(); xc3= x; yc3= y; zc3= z;
0423        /* --------------- calculate fourth vertex ------------------ */
0424        HorizAngle= PrevHoriz;
0425        zGetSphereShape(); x= SphereX; y= SphereY; z= SphereZ;
0426        if (bAssembly == TRUE) zGetAssemblyCoords();
0427        zGetWorldCoords();
0428        zGetCameraCoords(); xc4= x; yc4= y; zc4= z;
0429        /* --------- test visibility and render the facet ----------- */
0430        zVisibilityTest();
0431        if (visible <= 0) zDrawFacet();
0432        /* ------------- reset to start of next facet --------------- */
0433        HorizAngle= HorizAngle + FacetWidth;
0434        VertAngle= PrevVert;
0435        }
0436
0437    return;
0438    }
0439    /*
0440    --------------------------------------------------------------------
0441             Calculate obj coords for pt on surface of sphere
0442    --------------------------------------------------------------------
0443                                                                    */
0444    static void zGetSphereShape(void)
0445    {                    /* uses VertAngle, HorizAngle, and SphereRadius */
0446    SinHoriz= sin(HorizAngle);
0447    CosHoriz= cos(HorizAngle);
0448    SinVert= sin(VertAngle);
0449    CosVert= cos(VertAngle);
0450    TempX= SinVert * SphereRadius;
0451    SphereY= CosVert * SphereRadius;
0452    SphereX= CosHoriz * TempX;
0453    SphereZ= SinHoriz * TempX;
0454    return;
0455    }
0456    /*
0457    --------------------------------------------------------------------
0458                          Draw a 3D cylinder
0459    --------------------------------------------------------------------
0460                                                         •      */
0461    void zDrawCylinder(void)
0462    {       /* uses extern cursorx and cursorz to configure cylinder */
0463    if (bInitialized==FALSE)
0464      {
0465      MessageBox(GetFocus(),
0466        "zDrawCylinder( ) reports that 3D library is not initialized.",
0467        "shapes3D.c error:  line 00467", MB_OK);
0468      return;
0469      }
0470    TestOnly= FALSE;                        /* do not discard entire solid */
0471    CylinderRadius= cursorx;                             /* grab radius */
0472    CylinderExtrude= cursorz;                         /* grab extrusion */
0473    if (CylinderRadius < zMIN_RADIUS) return; /* if radius too small */
0474    VertAngle= z00_DEGREES;                         /* vertical angle */
0475    HorizAngle= z00_DEGREES;                        /* horiz angle */
0476
0477    if (CylinderRadius >= 25)
```

```
0478     {                        /* if a large radius, use smaller facets... */
0479     NumFacets= 36;                                      /* num of facets */
0480     FacetDimension= z10_DEGREES;                     /* width of facets */
0481     }
0482  else if (CylinderRadius < 25)
0483     {                        /* if a smaller radius, use larger facets... */
0484     NumFacets= 18;
0485     FacetDimension= z20_DEGREES;
0486     }
0487
0488  /* ----------------- draw body of cylinder ------------------- */
0489  for (Facet= 1; Facet <= NumFacets; Facet++)
0490     {                                             /* for each facet... */
0491     /* --------------- calculate first vertex ----------------- */
0492     zGetCylinderShape(); x= CylinderX; y= CylinderY; z= CylinderZ;
0493     if (bAssembly == TRUE) zGetAssemblyCoords();
0494     zGetWorldCoords(); xw3= x; yw3= y; zw3= z;
0495     zGetCameraCoords(); xc1= x; yc1= y; zc1= z;
0496     /* --------------- calculate second vertex ----------------- */
0497     PrevVert= VertAngle; VertAngle= VertAngle + FacetDimension;
0498     zGetCylinderShape(); x= CylinderX; y= CylinderY; z= CylinderZ;
0499     if (bAssembly == TRUE) zGetAssemblyCoords();
0500     zGetWorldCoords(); xw2= x; yw2= y; zw2= z;
0501     zGetCameraCoords(); xc2= x; yc2= y; zc2= z;
0502     /* --------------- calculate third vertex ----------------- */
0503     zGetCylinderShape(); x= CylinderX; y= CylinderY; z= -CylinderZ;
0504     if (bAssembly == TRUE) zGetAssemblyCoords();
0505     zGetWorldCoords(); xw1= x; yw1= y; zw1= z;
0506     zGetCameraCoords(); xc3= x; yc3= y; zc3= z;
0507     /* --------------- calculate fourth vertex ----------------- */
0508     VertAngle= PrevVert;
0509     zGetCylinderShape(); x= CylinderX; y= CylinderY; z= -CylinderZ;
0510     if (bAssembly == TRUE) zGetAssemblyCoords();
0511     zGetWorldCoords();
0512     zGetCameraCoords(); xc4= x; yc4= y; zc4= z;
0513     /* ---------- test visibility and render the facet ---------- */
0514     zVisibilityTest();
0515     if (visible <= 0) zDrawFacet();
0516     VertAngle= VertAngle + FacetDimension;
0517     }
0518
0519  /* ----------------- draw ends of cylinder ------------------- */
0520  VertAngle= z00_DEGREES;                      /* reset vertical angle */
0521  for (Facet= 1; Facet <= NumFacets; Facet++)
0522     {                                  /* for each facet of near end... */
0523     /* --------------- calculate first vertex ----------------- */
0524     x= 0; y= 0; z= CylinderZ;
0525     if (bAssembly == TRUE) zGetAssemblyCoords();
0526     zGetWorldCoords(); xw3= x; yw3= y; zw3= z;
0527     zGetCameraCoords(); xc1= x; yc1= y; zc1= z;
0528     /* --------------- calculate second vertex ----------------- */
0529     PrevVert= VertAngle; VertAngle= VertAngle + FacetDimension;
0530     zGetCylinderShape(); x= CylinderX; y= CylinderY; z= CylinderZ;
0531     if (bAssembly == TRUE) zGetAssemblyCoords();
0532     zGetWorldCoords(); xw2= x; yw2= y; zw2= z;
0533     zGetCameraCoords(); xc2= x; yc2= y; zc2= z;
0534     /* --------------- calculate third vertex ----------------- */
0535     VertAngle= PrevVert;
0536     zGetCylinderShape(); x= CylinderX; y= CylinderY; z= CylinderZ;
0537     if (bAssembly == TRUE) zGetAssemblyCoords();
0538     zGetWorldCoords(); xw1= x; yw1= y; zw1= z;
```

```
0539   zGetCameraCoords(); xc3= x; yc3= y; zc3= z;
0540   /* ------------- calculate fourth vertex ----------------- */
0541   x= 0; y= 0; z= CylinderZ;
0542   if (bAssembly == TRUE) zGetAssemblyCoords();
0543   zGetWorldCoords();
0544   zGetCameraCoords(); xc4= x; yc4= y; zc4= z;
0545   /* -------- test visibility and render the facet ----------- */
0546   zVisibilityTest();
0547   if (visible <= 0) zDrawFacet();
0548   VertAngle= VertAngle + FacetDimension;
0549   }
0550 VertAngle= z00_DEGREES;                    /* reset vertical angle */
0551 for (Facet= 1; Facet <= NumFacets; Facet++)
0552   {                              /* for each facet of far end... */
0553   /* --------------- calculate first vertex ------------------ */
0554   x= 0; y= 0; z= -CylinderZ;
0555   if (bAssembly == TRUE) zGetAssemblyCoords();
0556   zGetWorldCoords(); xw3= x; yw3= y; zw3= z;
0557   zGetCameraCoords(); xc1= x; yc1= y; zc1= z;
0558   /* --------------- calculate second vertex ----------------- */
0559   zGetCylinderShape(); x= CylinderX; y= CylinderY; z= -CylinderZ;
0560   if (bAssembly == TRUE) zGetAssemblyCoords();
0561   zGetWorldCoords(); xw2= x; yw2= y; zw2= z;
0562   zGetCameraCoords(); xc2= x; yc2= y; zc2= z;
0563   /* --------------- calculate third vertex ------------------ */
0564   VertAngle= VertAngle + FacetDimension;
0565   zGetCylinderShape(); x= CylinderX; y= CylinderY; z= -CylinderZ;
0566   if (bAssembly == TRUE) zGetAssemblyCoords();
0567   zGetWorldCoords(); xw1= x; yw1= y; zw1= z;
0568   zGetCameraCoords(); xc3= x; yc3= y; zc3= z;
0569   /* ------------- calculate fourth vertex ----------------- */
0570   x= 0; y= 0; z= -CylinderZ;
0571   if (bAssembly == TRUE) zGetAssemblyCoords();
0572   zGetWorldCoords();
0573   zGetCameraCoords(); xc4= x; yc4= y; zc4= z;
0574   /* -------- test visibility and render the facet ----------- */
0575   zVisibilityTest();
0576   if (visible <= 0) zDrawFacet();
0577   }
0578
0579 return;
0580 }
0581 /*
0582 -------------------------------------------------------------------
0583        Calculate obj coords for pt on surface of cylinder
0584 -------------------------------------------------------------------
0585                                                                   */
0586 static void zGetCylinderShape(void)
0587 { /* uses VertAngle, HorizAngle, CylinderRadius, CylinderExtrude */
0588 SinHoriz= sin(HorizAngle);
0589 CosHoriz= cos(HorizAngle);
0590 SinVert= sin(VertAngle);
0591 CosVert= cos(VertAngle);
0592 TempX= SinVert * CylinderRadius;
0593 CylinderY= CosVert * CylinderRadius;
0594 CylinderX= CosHoriz * TempX;
0595 CylinderZ= CylinderExtrude;
0596 return;
0597 }
0598 /*
0599 -------------------------------------------------------------------
```

```
0600                          Draw a 3D curved surface
0601   ------------------------------------------------------------------
0602                                                                   */
0603   void zDrawCurve(void)
0604   {               /* this funtion uses cursorx, cursory, and cursorz */
0605   if (bInitialized==FALSE)
0606     {
0607     MessageBox(GetFocus(),
0608       "zDrawCurve( ) reports that 3D library is not initialized.",
0609       "shapes3D.c error:  line 00609", MB_OK);
0610     return;
0611     }
0612   ParamChange= .05;                           /* parametric increment */
0613   ParamMax= 1.00;                        /* maximum parametric value */
0614   ParamMin= 0.0;                         /* minimum parametric value */
0615   ControlStrength= .50;               /* influence of control points */
0616   if (bUsePalette == TRUE)            /* if using 256-color mode... */
0617     {                    /* ...increase the resolution of the rendering */
0618     ParamChange= .025;
0619     }
0620
0621   /* --------- configure the curved edge of the surface ---------- */
0622   CurveX1= (-1) * cursorx;
0623   CurveX4= cursorx;
0624   CurveY1= 0.0; CurveY4= 0.0;
0625
0626   /* ------------ configure the width of the surface ------------- */
0627   SurfaceEdge1= (-1) * cursorz;
0628   SurfaceEdge2= cursorz;
0629
0630   /* ----------- configure the magnitude of the curve ----------- */
0631   CurveY2= cursory;
0632   CurveY3= (-1) * cursory;
0633   CurveX2= ControlStrength * CurveX1;
0634   CurveX3= ControlStrength * CurveX4;
0635
0636   /* ----------------- render the curved surface ----------------- */
0637   for (T= ParamMin; T <= ParamMax; T+= ParamChange)
0638     {                    /* for each lamina in the curved surface... */
0639     T2= T * T;
0640     T3= T * T * T;
0641     /* ---------------- calculate first vertex ---------------- */
0642     zGetCurveShape(); x= SurfaceX; y= SurfaceY; z= SurfaceEdge1;
0643     if (bAssembly == TRUE) zGetAssemblyCoords();
0644     zGetWorldCoords(); xw3= x; yw3= y; zw3= z;
0645     zGetCameraCoords(); xc1= x; yc1= y; zc1= z;
0646     /* ---------------- calculate second vertex ---------------- */
0647     x= SurfaceX; y= SurfaceY; z= SurfaceEdge2;
0648     if (bAssembly == TRUE) zGetAssemblyCoords();
0649     zGetWorldCoords(); xw2= x; yw2= y; zw2= z;
0650     zGetCameraCoords(); xc2= x; yc2= y; zc2= z;
0651     /* ---------------- calculate third vertex ----------------- */
0652     PrevT= T;                           /* remember position on curve */
0653     T+= ParamChange;            /* move to next position on curve... */
0654     T2= T * T;
0655     T3= T * T * T;
0656     zGetCurveShape(); x= SurfaceX; y= SurfaceY; z= SurfaceEdge2;
0657     if (bAssembly == TRUE) zGetAssemblyCoords();
0658     zGetWorldCoords(); xw1= x; yw1= y; zw1= z;
0659     zGetCameraCoords(); xc3= x; yc3= y; zc3= z;
0660     /* ---------------- calculate fourth vertex ---------------- */
```

```
0661    x= SurfaceX; y= SurfaceY; z= SurfaceEdge1;
0662    if (bAssembly == TRUE) zGetAssemblyCoords();
0663    zGetWorldCoords();
0664    zGetCameraCoords(); xc4= x; yc4= y; zc4= z;
0665    /* ---------- test visibility and render the lamina ---------- */
0666    zVisibilityTest();
0667    if (visible <= 0) zDrawFacet();        /* if visible, draw lamina */
0668    else {                    /* else draw obverse side of lamina... */
0669        SwapStorage= xw1; xw1= xw3; xw3= SwapStorage;
0670        SwapStorage= yw1; yw1= yw3; yw3= SwapStorage;
0671        SwapStorage= zw1; zw1= zw3; zw3= SwapStorage;
0672        SwapStorage= xc1; xc1= xc3; xc3= SwapStorage;
0673        SwapStorage= yc1; yc1= yc3; yc3= SwapStorage;
0674        SwapStorage= zc1; zc1= zc3; zc3= SwapStorage;
0675        zDrawFacet();
0676        }
0677    T= PrevT;                    /* restore current position on curve */
0678    }                            /* loop back and render next facet */
0679    return;
0680    }
0681    /*
0682    --------------------------------------------------------------------
0683                    Calculate obj coords for pt on curved surface
0684    --------------------------------------------------------------------
0685                                                                      */
0686    static void zGetCurveShape(void)
0687    {
0688    Pull1= CurveX1 * (-T3 + 3 * T2 - 3 * T + 1);
0689    Pull2= CurveX2 * (3 * T3 - 6 * T2 + 3 * T);
0690    Pull3= CurveX3 * (-3 * T3 + 3 * T2);
0691    Pull4= CurveX4 * T3;
0692    SurfaceX= Pull1 + Pull2 + Pull3 + Pull4;
0693    Pull1= CurveY1 * (-T3 + 3 * T2 - 3 * T + 1);
0694    Pull2= CurveY2 * (3 * T3 - 6 * T2 + 3 * T);
0695    Pull3= CurveY3 * (-3 * T3 + 3 * T2);
0696    Pull4= CurveY4 * T3;
0697    SurfaceY= Pull1 + Pull2 + Pull3 + Pull4;
0698    return;
0699    }
0700    /*
0701    --------------------------------------------------------------------
0702                             Draw a 3D cone
0703    --------------------------------------------------------------------
0704                                                                      */
0705    void zDrawCone(void)
0706    {              /* uses extern cursorx and cursorz to configure cone */
0707    if (bInitialized==FALSE)
0708      {
0709      MessageBox(GetFocus(),
0710        "zDrawCone( ) reports that the 3D library is not initialized.",
0711        "shapes3D.c error:  line 00711", MB_OK);
0712      return;
0713      }
0714    TestOnly= FALSE;                  /* do not discard entire solid */
0715    ConeRadius= cursorx;                          /* grab radius */
0716    ConeExtrude= cursorz;                      /* grab extrusion */
0717    if (ConeRadius < zMIN_RADIUS) return;   /* if radius too small */
0718    VertAngle= z00_DEGREES;                   /* vertical angle */
0719    HorizAngle= z00_DEGREES;                    /* horiz angle */
0720    ConeZ= ConeExtrude;               /* grab 3D extrusion point */
0721
```

```
0722   if (ConeRadius >= 25)
0723     {                        /* if a large radius, use smaller facets... */
0724     NumFacets= 36;                                       /* num of facets */
0725     FacetDimension= z10_DEGREES;                /* width of facets */
0726     }
0727   else if (ConeRadius < 25)
0728     {                        /* if a smaller radius, use larger facets... */
0729     NumFacets= 18;
0730     FacetDimension= z20_DEGREES;
0731     }
0732
0733   /* -------------------- draw end of cone -------------------- */
0734   VertAngle= z00_DEGREES;                         /* reset vertical angle */
0735   for (Facet= 1; Facet <= NumFacets; Facet++)
0736     {                                           /* for each facet... */
0737     /* --------------- calculate first vertex ------------------ */
0738     x= 0; y= 0; z= ConeZ;
0739     if (bAssembly == TRUE) zGetAssemblyCoords();
0740     zGetWorldCoords(); xw3= x; yw3= y; zw3= z;
0741     zGetCameraCoords(); xc1= x; yc1= y; zc1= z;
0742     /* --------------- calculate second vertex ------------------ */
0743     PrevVert= VertAngle; VertAngle= VertAngle + FacetDimension;
0744     zGetConeShape(); x= ConeX; y= ConeY; z= ConeZ;
0745     if (bAssembly == TRUE) zGetAssemblyCoords();
0746     zGetWorldCoords(); xw2= x; yw2= y; zw2= z;
0747     zGetCameraCoords(); xc2= x; yc2= y; zc2= z;
0748     /* --------------- calculate third vertex ------------------ */
0749     VertAngle= PrevVert;
0750     zGetConeShape(); x= ConeX; y= ConeY; z= ConeZ;
0751     if (bAssembly == TRUE) zGetAssemblyCoords();
0752     zGetWorldCoords(); xw1= x; yw1= y; zw1= z;
0753     zGetCameraCoords(); xc3= x; yc3= y; zc3= z;
0754     /* ------------- calculate fourth vertex ---------------- */
0755     x= 0; y= 0; z= ConeZ;
0756     if (bAssembly == TRUE) zGetAssemblyCoords();
0757     zGetWorldCoords();
0758     zGetCameraCoords(); xc4= x; yc4= y; zc4= z;
0759     /* -------- test visibility and render the facet ---------- */
0760     zVisibilityTest();
0761     if (visible <= 0) zDrawFacet();
0762     VertAngle= VertAngle + FacetDimension;
0763     }
0764
0765   /* -------------------- draw body of cone -------------------- */
0766   VertAngle= z00_DEGREES;                         /* reset vertical angle */
0767   for (Facet= 1; Facet <= NumFacets; Facet++)
0768     {                                           /* for each facet... */
0769     /* --------------- calculate first vertex ------------------ */
0770     x= 0; y= 0; z= -ConeZ;
0771     if (bAssembly == TRUE) zGetAssemblyCoords();
0772     zGetWorldCoords(); xw3= x; yw3= y; zw3= z;
0773     zGetCameraCoords(); xc1= x; yc1= y; zc1= z;
0774     /* --------------- calculate second vertex ------------------ */
0775     zGetConeShape(); x= ConeX; y= ConeY; z= ConeZ;
0776     if (bAssembly == TRUE) zGetAssemblyCoords();
0777     zGetWorldCoords(); xw2= x; yw2= y; zw2= z;
0778     zGetCameraCoords(); xc2= x; yc2= y; zc2= z;
0779     /* --------------- calculate third vertex ------------------ */
0780     PrevVert= VertAngle; VertAngle= VertAngle + FacetDimension;
0781     zGetConeShape(); x= ConeX; y= ConeY; z= ConeZ;
0782     if (bAssembly == TRUE) zGetAssemblyCoords();
```

```
0783    zGetWorldCoords(); xw1= x; yw1= y; zw1= z;
0784    zGetCameraCoords(); xc3= x; yc3= y; zc3= z;
0785    /* -------------- calculate fourth vertex ----------------- */
0786    VertAngle= PrevVert;
0787    x= 0; y= 0; z= -ConeZ;
0788    if (bAssembly == TRUE) zGetAssemblyCoords();
0789    zGetWorldCoords();
0790    zGetCameraCoords(); xc4= x; yc4= y; zc4= z;
0791    /* -------- test visibility and render the facet ----------- */
0792    zVisibilityTest();
0793    if (visible <= 0) zDrawFacet();
0794    VertAngle= VertAngle + FacetDimension;
0795    }
0796
0797    return;
0798    }
0799    /*
0800    --------------------------------------------------------------
0801            Calculate obj coords for pt on surface of cone
0802    --------------------------------------------------------------
0803                                                              */
0804    static void zGetConeShape(void)
0805    {
0806    SinHoriz= sin(HorizAngle);
0807    CosHoriz= cos(HorizAngle);
0808    SinVert= sin(VertAngle);
0809    CosVert= cos(VertAngle);
0810    TempX= SinVert * ConeRadius;
0811    ConeY= CosVert * ConeRadius;
0812    ConeX= CosHoriz * TempX;
0813    return;
0814    }
0815    /*
0816    --------------------------------------------------------------
0817                          Draw a 3D wedge
0818    --------------------------------------------------------------
0819                                                              */
0820    void zDrawWedge(void)
0821    {
0822    if (bInitialized==FALSE)
0823      {
0824      MessageBox(GetFocus(),
0825        "zDrawWedge( ) reports that 3D library is not initialized.",
0826        "shapes3D.c error:  line 00826", MB_OK);
0827      return;
0828      }
0829    zGetWedgeCoords();        /* get camera coords and display coords */
0830    #ifdef COMPILING         /* if compiling for Windows 3.0 and 3.1 */
0831    #undef COMPILING
0832    #line 1 "E"
0833    #error See compile tips in companion book by Lee Adams.
0834    #endif
0835    TestOnly= TRUE;                        /* reset token for first pass */
0836    WEDGE_SECOND_PASS:    /* will loop back to here for second pass */
0837
0838    wedge_surface0:
0839      xc1=camcoords[5][0];yc1=camcoords[5][1];zc1=camcoords[5][2];
0840      xc2=camcoords[0][0];yc2=camcoords[0][1];zc2=camcoords[0][2];
0841      xc3=camcoords[2][0];yc3=camcoords[2][1];zc3=camcoords[2][2];
0842      xc4=camcoords[4][0];yc4=camcoords[4][1];zc4=camcoords[4][2];
0843      zVisibilityTest();
```

```
0844    if (visible > 0) goto wedge_surface1;
0845    xw3=cubeWorld[5][0];yw3=cubeWorld[5][1];zw3=cubeWorld[5][2];
0846    xw2=cubeWorld[0][0];yw2=cubeWorld[0][1];zw2=cubeWorld[0][2];
0847    xw1=cubeWorld[2][0];yw1=cubeWorld[2][1];zw1=cubeWorld[2][2];
0848    zDrawFacet();
0849    if ((Discard==TRUE) || (Clipped==TRUE)) goto WDISCARD_SOLID;
0850
0851    wedge_surface1:
0852      xc1=camcoords[3][0];yc1=camcoords[3][1];zc1=camcoords[3][2];
0853      xc2=camcoords[5][0];yc2=camcoords[5][1];zc2=camcoords[5][2];
0854      xc3=camcoords[4][0];yc3=camcoords[4][1];zc3=camcoords[4][2];
0855      xc4=camcoords[3][0];yc4=camcoords[3][1];zc4=camcoords[3][2];
0856      zVisibilityTest();
0857      if (visible > 0) goto wedge_surface2;
0858      xw3=cubeWorld[3][0];yw3=cubeWorld[3][1];zw3=cubeWorld[3][2];
0859      xw2=cubeWorld[5][0];yw2=cubeWorld[5][1];zw2=cubeWorld[5][2];
0860      xw1=cubeWorld[4][0];yw1=cubeWorld[4][1];zw1=cubeWorld[4][2];
0861      zDrawFacet();
0862    if ((Discard==TRUE) || (Clipped==TRUE)) goto WDISCARD_SOLID;
0863
0864    wedge_surface2:
0865      xc1=camcoords[1][0];yc1=camcoords[1][1];zc1=camcoords[1][2];
0866      xc2=camcoords[3][0];yc2=camcoords[3][1];zc2=camcoords[3][2];
0867      xc3=camcoords[4][0];yc3=camcoords[4][1];zc3=camcoords[4][2];
0868      xc4=camcoords[2][0];yc4=camcoords[2][1];zc4=camcoords[2][2];
0869      zVisibilityTest();
0870      if (visible > 0) goto wedge_surface3;
0871      xw3=cubeWorld[1][0];yw3=cubeWorld[1][1];zw3=cubeWorld[1][2];
0872      xw2=cubeWorld[3][0];yw2=cubeWorld[3][1];zw2=cubeWorld[3][2];
0873      xw1=cubeWorld[4][0];yw1=cubeWorld[4][1];zw1=cubeWorld[4][2];
0874      zDrawFacet();
0875    if ((Discard==TRUE) || (Clipped==TRUE)) goto WDISCARD_SOLID;
0876
0877    wedge_surface3:
0878      xc1=camcoords[1][0];yc1=camcoords[1][1];zc1=camcoords[1][2];
0879      xc2=camcoords[2][0];yc2=camcoords[2][1];zc2=camcoords[2][2];
0880      xc3=camcoords[0][0];yc3=camcoords[0][1];zc3=camcoords[0][2];
0881      xc4=camcoords[1][0];yc4=camcoords[1][1];zc4=camcoords[1][2];
0882      zVisibilityTest();
0883      if (visible > 0) goto wedge_surface4;
0884      xw3=cubeWorld[1][0];yw3=cubeWorld[1][1];zw3=cubeWorld[1][2];
0885      xw2=cubeWorld[2][0];yw2=cubeWorld[2][1];zw2=cubeWorld[2][2];
0886      xw1=cubeWorld[0][0];yw1=cubeWorld[0][1];zw1=cubeWorld[0][2];
0887      zDrawFacet();
0888    if ((Discard==TRUE) || (Clipped==TRUE)) goto WDISCARD_SOLID;
0889
0890    wedge_surface4:
0891      xc1=camcoords[3][0];yc1=camcoords[3][1];zc1=camcoords[3][2];
0892      xc2=camcoords[1][0];yc2=camcoords[1][1];zc2=camcoords[1][2];
0893      xc3=camcoords[0][0];yc3=camcoords[0][1];zc3=camcoords[0][2];
0894      xc4=camcoords[5][0];yc4=camcoords[5][1];zc4=camcoords[5][2];
0895      zVisibilityTest();
0896      if (visible > 0) goto wedge_surfaces_done;
0897      xw3=cubeWorld[3][0];yw3=cubeWorld[3][1];zw3=cubeWorld[3][2];
0898      xw2=cubeWorld[1][0];yw2=cubeWorld[1][1];zw2=cubeWorld[1][2];
0899      xw1=cubeWorld[0][0];yw1=cubeWorld[0][1];zw1=cubeWorld[0][2];
0900      zDrawFacet();
0901    if ((Discard==TRUE) || (Clipped==TRUE)) goto WDISCARD_SOLID;
0902
0903    wedge_surfaces_done:
0904    if (TestOnly==TRUE)
```

```
0905     {                              /* if just finished first pass... */
0906       TestOnly= FALSE;                       /* reset token and... */
0907       goto WEDGE_SECOND_PASS;            /* loop back for second pass */
0908     }
0909   return;                    /* fall through to here after second pass */
0910
0911   WDISCARD_SOLID: /* jump to here if facet discarded on first pass
               */
0912   MessageBeep(0);    /* issue audio cue if solid has been discarded */
0913   return;
0914   }
0915   /*
0916   ------------------------------------------------------------------
0917                      Calculate coords for wedge
0918   ------------------------------------------------------------------
0919                                                                    */
0920   static void zGetWedgeCoords(void)
0921   {                      /* this function is called by zDrawWedge() */
0922     int t= 0;
0923     double negx,negy,negz;
0924   negx=(-1)*(cursorx);negy=(-1)*(cursory);negz=(-1)*(cursorz);
0925   cubeObj[0][0]=cursorx; cubeObj[0][1]=negy; cubeObj[0][2]=cursorz;
0926   cubeObj[1][0]= 0; cubeObj[1][1]= cursory; cubeObj[1][2]= cursorz;
0927   cubeObj[2][0]= negx; cubeObj[2][1]= negy; cubeObj[2][2]= cursorz;
0928   cubeObj[3][0]= 0; cubeObj[3][1]= cursory; cubeObj[3][2]= negz;
0929   cubeObj[4][0]= negx; cubeObj[4][1]= negy; cubeObj[4][2]= negz;
0930   cubeObj[5][0]= cursorx; cubeObj[5][1]= negy; cubeObj[5][2]= negz;
0931   for (t=0; t<=5; t++)
0932     {
0933     x= cubeObj[t][0]; y= cubeObj[t][1]; z= cubeObj[t][2];
0934     if (bAssembly == TRUE) zGetAssemblyCoords();
0935     zGetWorldCoords();
0936     cubeWorld[t][0]= x; cubeWorld[t][1]= y; cubeWorld[t][2]= z;
0937     zGetCameraCoords();
0938     camcoords[t][0]= x; camcoords[t][1]= y; camcoords[t][2]= z;
0939     }
0940   return;
0941   }
0942   /*
0943   ------------------------------------------------------------------
0944                        Draw a 3D hemisphere
0945   ------------------------------------------------------------------
0946                                                                    */
0947   void zDrawHemisphere(void)
0948   {         /* this function uses extern cursorx as radius of sphere */
0949   if (bInitialized==FALSE)
0950     {
0951     MessageBox(GetFocus(),
0952       "zDrawHemisphere( ) reports 3D library is not initialized.",
0953       "shapes3D.c error:  line 00953", MB_OK);
0954     return;
0955     }
0956   TestOnly= FALSE;                     /* do not discard entire solid */
0957   SphereRadius= cursorx;                   /* grab radius of sphere */
0958   if (SphereRadius < zMIN_RADIUS) return;   /* if radius too small */
0959   CapHeight= z10_DEGREES;            /* set height of facets for cap */
0960
0961   if (SphereRadius >= 25)
0962     {                  /* if a large radius, use smaller facets... */
0963     NumStrips= 8;                            /* num of strips */
0964     NumFacets= 36;                  /* num of facets per strip */
```

```
0965    FacetWidth= z10_DEGREES;                            /* width of facets */
0966    StripHeight= z10_DEGREES;                           /* height of facets */
0967    if (bUsePalette == TRUE)           /* if using 256-color mode... */
0968        {                   /* ...increase the resolution of the rendering */
0969      NumStrips= 16;
0970      NumFacets= 36;
0971      FacetWidth= z10_DEGREES;
0972      StripHeight= z05_DEGREES;
0973        }
0974    }
0975  else if (SphereRadius < 25)
0976      {                       /* if a smaller radius, use larger facets... */
0977      NumStrips= 4;                                      /* num of strips */
0978      NumFacets= 18;                            /* num of facets per strip */
0979      FacetWidth= z20_DEGREES;                           /* width of facets */
0980      StripHeight= z20_DEGREES;                          /* height of facets */
0981      }
0982
0983  /* ---------------- draw flat cap of hemisphere --------------- */
0984  VertAngle= z90_DEGREES;                          /* set vertical angle */
0985  HorizAngle= z00_DEGREES;                         /* set horiz angle */
0986  for (Facet= 1; Facet <= NumFacets; Facet++)
0987      {                                            /* for each facet... */
0988      /* -------------- calculate first vertex ------------------- */
0989      x= 0; y= 0; z= 0;                          /* grab object coords */
0990      if (bAssembly == TRUE) zGetAssemblyCoords();
0991      zGetWorldCoords();                       /* calculate world coords */
0992      zGetCameraCoords();                      /* calculate camera coords */
0993      xc1= x; yc1= y; zc1= z;                  /* grab camera coords */
0994      /* -------------- calculate second vertex ------------------ */
0995      PrevHoriz= HorizAngle; HorizAngle= HorizAngle + FacetWidth;
0996      zGetSphereShape(); x= SphereX; y= SphereY; z= SphereZ;
0997      if (bAssembly == TRUE) zGetAssemblyCoords();
0998      zGetWorldCoords(); xw3= x; yw3= y; zw3= z;
0999      zGetCameraCoords(); xc2= x; yc2= y; zc2= z;
1000      /* -------------- calculate third vertex ------------------- */
1001      HorizAngle= PrevHoriz;
1002      zGetSphereShape(); x= SphereX; y= SphereY; z= SphereZ;
1003      if (bAssembly == TRUE) zGetAssemblyCoords();
1004      zGetWorldCoords(); xw2= x; yw2= y; zw2= z;
1005      zGetCameraCoords(); xc3= x; yc3= y; zc3= z;
1006      /* -------------- calculate fourth vertex ------------------ */
1007      x= 0; y= 0; z= 0;
1008      if (bAssembly == TRUE) zGetAssemblyCoords();
1009      zGetWorldCoords(); xw1= x; yw1= y; zw1= z;
1010      zGetCameraCoords(); xc4= x; yc4= y; zc4= z;
1011      /* --------- test visibility and render the facet ----------- */
1012      zVisibilityTest();                       /* backface culling test */
1013      if (visible <= 0) zDrawFacet();          /* render z-buffered facet */
1014      /* ------------- reset to start of next facet --------------- */
1015      HorizAngle= HorizAngle + FacetWidth;
1016      }                                       /* loop back to do next facet */
1017
1018  /* ----------------- draw body of hemisphere ------------------- */
1019  VertAngle= z90_DEGREES;                          /* reset vertical angle */
1020  HorizAngle= z00_DEGREES;                         /* reset horiz angle */
1021  for (Strip= 1; Strip <= NumStrips; Strip++)
1022      {                 /* for each strip on surface of hemisphere... */
1023      for (Facet= 1; Facet <= NumFacets; Facet++)
1024          {                             /* for each facet on the strip... */
1025          /* -------------- calculate first vertex ------------------- */
```

```
1026      zGetSphereShape(); x= SphereX; y= SphereY; z= SphereZ;
1027      if (bAssembly == TRUE) zGetAssemblyCoords();
1028      zGetWorldCoords(); xw3= x; yw3= y; zw3= z;
1029      zGetCameraCoords(); xc1= x; yc1= y; zc1= z;
1030      /* -------------- calculate second vertex ------------------ */
1031      PrevHoriz= HorizAngle; HorizAngle= HorizAngle + FacetWidth;
1032      zGetSphereShape(); x= SphereX; y= SphereY; z= SphereZ;
1033      if (bAssembly == TRUE) zGetAssemblyCoords();
1034      zGetWorldCoords(); xw2= x; yw2= y; zw2= z;
1035      zGetCameraCoords(); xc2= x; yc2= y; zc2= z;
1036      /* -------------- calculate third vertex ------------------ */
1037      PrevVert= VertAngle; VertAngle= VertAngle + StripHeight;
1038      zGetSphereShape(); x= SphereX; y= SphereY; z= SphereZ;
1039      if (bAssembly == TRUE) zGetAssemblyCoords();
1040      zGetWorldCoords(); xw1= x; yw1= y; zw1= z;
1041      zGetCameraCoords(); xc3= x; yc3= y; zc3= z;
1042      /* -------------- calculate fourth vertex ------------------ */
1043      HorizAngle= PrevHoriz;
1044      zGetSphereShape(); x= SphereX; y= SphereY; z= SphereZ;
1045      if (bAssembly == TRUE) zGetAssemblyCoords();
1046      zGetWorldCoords();
1047      zGetCameraCoords(); xc4= x; yc4= y; zc4= z;
1048      /* -------- test visibility and render the facet ----------- */
1049      zVisibilityTest();
1050      if (visible <= 0) zDrawFacet();
1051      /* ------------ reset to start of next facet -------------- */
1052      HorizAngle= HorizAngle + FacetWidth;
1053      VertAngle= PrevVert;
1054      }                              /* loop back to do next facet */
1055    VertAngle= VertAngle + StripHeight;      /* select next strip */
1056    HorizAngle= z00_DEGREES;               /* reset to first facet */
1057    }                              /* loop back to do next strip */
1058
1059  /* -------------- draw south cap of hemisphere --------------- */
1060  HorizAngle= z00_DEGREES;                    /* reset horiz angle */
1061  for (Facet= 1; Facet <= NumFacets; Facet++)
1062  {                                  /* for each facet on the cap... */
1063    /* -------------- calculate first vertex ------------------ */
1064    zGetSphereShape(); x= SphereX; y= SphereY; z= SphereZ;
1065    if (bAssembly == TRUE) zGetAssemblyCoords();
1066    zGetWorldCoords(); xw3= x; yw3= y; zw3= z;
1067    zGetCameraCoords(); xc1= x; yc1= y; zc1= z;
1068    /* -------------- calculate second vertex ------------------ */
1069    PrevHoriz= HorizAngle; HorizAngle= HorizAngle + FacetWidth;
1070    zGetSphereShape(); x= SphereX; y= SphereY; z= SphereZ;
1071    if (bAssembly == TRUE) zGetAssemblyCoords();
1072    zGetWorldCoords(); xw2= x; yw2= y; zw2= z;
1073    zGetCameraCoords(); xc2= x; yc2= y; zc2= z;
1074    /* -------------- calculate third vertex ------------------ */
1075    PrevVert= VertAngle; VertAngle= VertAngle + CapHeight;
1076    zGetSphereShape(); x= SphereX; y= SphereY; z= SphereZ;
1077    if (bAssembly == TRUE) zGetAssemblyCoords();
1078    zGetWorldCoords(); xw1= x; yw1= y; zw1= z;
1079    zGetCameraCoords(); xc3= x; yc3= y; zc3= z;
1080    /* -------------- calculate fourth vertex ------------------ */
1081    HorizAngle= PrevHoriz;
1082    zGetSphereShape(); x= SphereX; y= SphereY; z= SphereZ;
1083    if (bAssembly == TRUE) zGetAssemblyCoords();
1084    zGetWorldCoords();
1085    zGetCameraCoords(); xc4= x; yc4= y; zc4= z;
1086    /* --------- test visibility and render the facet ----------- */
```

B-2 Continued.

```
1087    zVisibilityTest();
1088    if (visible <= 0) zDrawFacet();
1089    /* ------------- reset to start of next facet --------------- */
1090    HorizAngle= HorizAngle + FacetWidth;
1091    VertAngle= PrevVert;
1092    }
1093 return;
1094 }
1095 /*
1096 ------------------------------------------------------------------
1097        End of module of 3D shapes for Windows applications.
1098 ------------------------------------------------------------------
1099                                                                 */
```

B-3 Source listings for the 3D light-source toolkit, lights3d.c. See Appendix C for applications that use this toolkit. See Appendix A for instructions on building the demos.

```
0001 /*
0002 ------------------------------------------------------------------
0003                          LIGHTS3D.H
0004 ------------------------------------------------------------------
0005                                                                 */
0006 void zSetLightPosition(int Elevation, int Heading);
0007 /*
0008 ------------------------------------------------------------------
0009             End of header file for 3D lighting.
0010 ------------------------------------------------------------------
0011                                                                 */
0001 /*
0002 ------------------------------------------------------------------
0003       Module of 3D lighting drivers for Windows applications
0004 ------------------------------------------------------------------
0005    Source file:  LIGHTS3D.C
0006    Release version: 1.00              Programmer:  Lee Adams
0007    Type:  C source file for Windows multimodule applications.
0008    Compilers:  Microsoft C/C++, Borland C++, Zortech C++,
0009      QuickC for Windows, Turbo C++ for Windows, WATCOM C.
0010    Memory model:  medium.
0011    Dependencies:  ENGINE3D.C and SHAPES3D.C functions.
0012      Compile ENGINE3D.C, SHAPES3D.C, and LIGHTS.C and link the
0013      resulting .OBJ files to your compiled primary .C file.
0014      Include SHAPES3D.H, ENGINE3D.H, and LIGHTS3D.H in your
0015      primary .C file.
0016    Output and features:  Provides drivers for the ENGINE3D.C and
0017      SHAPES3D.C routines in order to reposition the light-source.
0018    Publication: Contains material from Windcrest/McGraw-Hill book
0019      4115 published by TAB BOOKS Division of McGraw-Hill Inc.
0020    License:  As purchaser of the book you are granted a royalty-
0021      free license to distribute executable files generated using
0022      this code provided you accept the conditions of the License
0023      Agreement and Limited Warranty described in the book and on
0024      the companion disk.  Government users:  This software and
0025      documentation are subject to restrictions set forth in The
0026      Rights in Technical Data and Computer Software clause at
0027      252.227-7013 and elsewhere.
0028 ------------------------------------------------------------------
0029      (c) Copyright 1991-1993 Lee Adams.  All rights reserved.
0030           Lee Adams(tm) is a trademark of Lee Adams.
0031 ------------------------------------------------------------------
0032                                                                 */
0033
```

```
0034    #include <windows.h>                    /* for BOOL and MessageBox() */
0035    #include <math.h>            /* for sine, cosine, and sqrt functions */
0036    #define zRADIAN .017453              /* convert degrees to radians */
0037    /*
0038    -----------------------------------------------------------------
0039         Function prototypes for functions found in this module
0040    -----------------------------------------------------------------
0041                                                                  */
0042    /* ----- callable from both outside and inside this module ----- */
0043    void zSetLightPosition(int Elevation, int Heading);
0044    /*
0045    -----------------------------------------------------------------
0046            Declare extern variables defined in ENGINE3D.C
0047    -----------------------------------------------------------------
0048                                                                  */
0049    extern BOOL bInitialized;      /* TRUE if 3D routines initialized */
0050    extern double xLight, yLight, zLight;    /* light-source position */
0051    /*
0052    -----------------------------------------------------------------
0053                         3D lighting drivers
0054    -----------------------------------------------------------------
0055                         Reposition the light-source
0056    -----------------------------------------------------------------
0057                                                                  */
0058    void zSetLightPosition(int Elevation, int Heading)
0059    {           /* this function is called by interactive main module */
0060      double ElevationRads, HeadingRads;
0061      double MaxRemainder;
0062
0063    /* ------------ ensure the 3D library is initialized ---------- */
0064    if (bInitialized==FALSE)
0065      {
0066      MessageBox(GetFocus(),
0067        "zSetLightPosition( ) reports 3D library is not initialized.",
0068        "lights3D.c error:  line 00068", MB_OK);
0069      return;
0070      }
0071    /* ------------ trap illegal light-source parameters ---------- */
0072    if ((Elevation > 90) || (Elevation < 0)) return;
0073    if ((Heading > 360) || (Heading < 0)) return;
0074
0075    /* ---------- calculate new components of unit vector ---------
0076        NOTE: This algorithm is from my Visualization Graphics in C,
0077        (Windcrest/McGraw-Hill book #3487) page 236, published in 1991,
0078        ISBN 0-8306-3487-8.                           - L.A.     */
0079    ElevationRads= Elevation * zRADIAN;
0080    HeadingRads= Heading * zRADIAN;
0081    yLight= sin(ElevationRads);
0082    MaxRemainder= sqrt(1- (yLight * yLight));
0083    xLight= (sin(HeadingRads)) * MaxRemainder * (-1);
0084    zLight= (cos(HeadingRads)) * MaxRemainder * (-1);
0085    return;
0086    }
0087    /*
0088    -----------------------------------------------------------------
0089        End of module of 3D lighting drivers for Windows applications.
0090    -----------------------------------------------------------------
0091                                                                  */
```

B-4 Source listings for the 3D deformation toolkit, deform3d.c. See Appendix C for applications that use this toolkit. See Appendix A for instructions on building the demos.

```
0001  /*
0002  ----------------------------------------------------------------
0003                          DEFORM3D.H
0004  ----------------------------------------------------------------
0005                                                                */
0006  void zDrawDeformBox(int,int,int,int);     /* 3D box deformation*/
0007  void zDrawHalfCylinder(void);             /* 3D half-cylinder */
0008  void zDrawBulge(void);                    /* 3D bulged surface */
0009  /*
0010  ----------------------------------------------------------------
0011            End of header file for 3D deformations.
0012  ----------------------------------------------------------------
0013                                                                */
0001  /*
0002  ----------------------------------------------------------------
0003       Module of 3D deformation drivers for Windows applications
0004  ----------------------------------------------------------------
0005     Source file: DEFORM3D.C
0006     Release version: 1.00              Programmer:  Lee Adams
0007     Type:  C source file for Windows multimodule applications.
0008     Compilers:  Microsoft C/C++, Borland C++, Zortech C++,
0009       QuickC for Windows, Turbo C++ for Windows, WATCOM C.
0010     Memory model:  medium.
0011     Dependencies:  ENGINE3D.C 3D functions.  Compile ENGINE3D.C and
0012       SHAPES3D.C and link the resulting .OBJ files to your compiled
0013       primary .C file.  Include DEFORM3D.H and ENGINE3D.H in your
0014       primary .C file.
0015     Output and features:  Provides drivers for the ENGINE3D.C
0016       3D routines in order to render half-cylinders, deformed
0017       parallelepipeds, etc.
0018     Publication: Contains material from Windcrest/McGraw-Hill book
0019       4115 published by TAB BOOKS Division of McGraw-Hill Inc.
0020     License:  As purchaser of the book you are granted a royalty-
0021       free license to distribute executable files generated using
0022       this code provided you accept the conditions of the License
0023       Agreement and Limited Warranty described in the book and on
0024       the companion disk.  Government users:  This software and
0025       documentation are subject to restrictions set forth in The
0026       Rights in Technical Data and Computer Software clause at
0027       252.227-7013 and elsewhere.
0028  ----------------------------------------------------------------
0029       (c) Copyright 1988-1993 Lee Adams.  All rights reserved.
0030            Lee Adams(tm) is a trademark of Lee Adams.
0031  ----------------------------------------------------------------
0032                                                                */
0033
0034  #include <WINDOWS.H>            /* for GDI MessageBox() function */
0035  #include <math.h>               /* for sine and cosine functions */
0036
0037  #define z00_DEGREES     .0                   /* radian angles... */
0038  #define z10_DEGREES     .17453
0039  #define z20_DEGREES     .34907
0040  #define z180_DEGREES    3.14159
0041  #define zMIN_RADIUS     10                   /* minimum radius */
0042  #define zMIN_DEFORM     2           /* min deformed thickness */
0043  /* #define COMPILING 1 */
0044  /*
0045  ----------------------------------------------------------------
0046       Function prototypes for functions found in this module
0047  ----------------------------------------------------------------
```

```
0048                                                                      */
0049    /* ----- callable from both outside and inside this module ----- */
0050    void zDrawDeformBox(int,int,int,int);      /* draw 3D deformed box */
0051    void zDrawHalfCylinder(void);                   /* draw 3D cylinder */
0052    void zDrawBulge(void);                    /* draw 3D curved surface */
0053
0054    /* ------------ callable from only inside this module ---------- */
0055    static void zGetDeformBoxCoords(void);   /* cam & display coords */
0056    static void zGetHalfCylShape(void);      /* pt on cylinder surface */
0057    static void zGetBulgeShape(void);          /* pt on bulged surface */
0058    /*
0059    -----------------------------------------------------------------
0060                  Declare functions found in ENGINE3D.C
0061    -----------------------------------------------------------------
0062                                                                      */
0063    void zGetCameraCoords(void);    /* world coords to camera coords */
0064    void zGetWorldCoords(void);     /* object coords to world coords */
0065    void zVisibilityTest(void);             /* back-plane visibility */
0066    void zDrawFacet(void);                            /* draws facet */
0067    /*
0068    -----------------------------------------------------------------
0069                  Declare functions found in ASSEMB3D.C
0070    -----------------------------------------------------------------
0071                                                                      */
0072    void zGetAssemblyCoords(void);   /* subobject to assembly coords */
0073    /*
0074    -----------------------------------------------------------------
0075              Static variables visible throughout this file
0076    -----------------------------------------------------------------
0077                                                                      */
0078    static int xExtrudeRight, xExtrudeLeft; /* deformation of box... */
0079    static int yExtrudeUp, yExtrudeDown;
0080    static double VertAngle, HorizAngle;      /* angular description */
0081    static double PrevVert;                     /* scratchpad values */
0082    static double TempX;                         /* scratchpad value */
0083    static double SinVert, CosVert,           /* sin, cos factors... */
0084                  SinHoriz, CosHoriz;
0085    static int NumFacets;                         /* num of facets */
0086    static int Facet;                          /* facet loop counter */
0087    static double CylinderX, CylinderY, CylinderZ;    /* obj coords */
0088    static double CylinderRadius, CylinderExtrude;    /* dimensions */
0089    static double FacetDimension;       /* angular dimension of facet */
0090    static double T= 0.0, T2= 0.0, T3= 0.0; /* primary, square, cube */
0091    static double PrevT;                             /* scratchpad */
0092    static double Pull1= 0.0, Pull2= 0.0,  /* effect of curve points */
0093                  Pull3= 0.0, Pull4= 0.0;
0094    static double CurveX1= 0.0, CurveY1= 0.0;     /* curve startpoint */
0095    static double CurveX4= 0.0, CurveY4= 0.0;       /* curve endpoint */
0096    static double CurveX2= -10.0, CurveY2= 0.0;     /* first control */
0097    static double CurveX3= 10.0, CurveY3= 0.0;     /* second control */
0098    static double SurfaceX, SurfaceY;                 /* obj coords */
0099    static double SurfaceEdge1, SurfaceEdge2;      /* extruded edges */
0100    static double ParamChange, ParamMax, ParamMin;     /* parameters */
0101    static double ControlStrength;         /* effect of control points */
0102    static double SwapStorage;               /* scratchpad for swaps */
0103    /*
0104    -----------------------------------------------------------------
0105             Declare extern variables defined in ENGINE3D.C
0106    -----------------------------------------------------------------
0107                                                                      */
0108    extern BOOL bUsePalette;              /* using 256-color mode? */
```

```
0109  extern BOOL bAssembly;              /* using hierarchical modeling? */
0110  extern double cursorx, cursory, cursorz;    /* volumetric cursor */
0111  extern double x, y, z;                       /* initial coords */
0112  extern double cubeObj[8][3];          /* array of object coords */
0113  extern double cubeWorld[8][3];         /* array of world coords */
0114  extern double camcoords[8][3];         /* array of camera coords */
0115  extern double visible;        /* result of backplane removal test */
0116  extern BOOL Discard, Clipped; /* view volume attributes of facet */
0117  extern BOOL bInitialized;        /* TRUE if 3D library initialized */
0118  extern BOOL TestOnly;                  /* pretests parallelepiped */
0119  extern double xc1, yc1, zc1,         /* camera coords of facet... */
0120               xc2, yc2, zc2,
0121               xc3, yc3, zc3,
0122               xc4, yc4, zc4;
0123  extern double xw1, yw1, zw1,          /* world coords of facet... */
0124               xw2, yw2, zw2,
0125               xw3, yw3, zw3;
0126  /*
0127  ------------------------------------------------------------------
0128                        3D deformation drivers
0129  ------------------------------------------------------------------
0130                    Draw a deformed parallelepiped
0131  ------------------------------------------------------------------
0132                                                                   */
0133  void zDrawDeformBox(int xRight, int xLeft, int yUp, int yDown)
0134  {            /* deforms the south-facing facet of a parallelepiped */
0135  if (bInitialized==FALSE)
0136    {
0137    MessageBox(GetFocus(),
0138      "zDrawDeformBox( ) reports 3D library is not initialized.",
0139      "deform3D.c error:  line 00139", MB_OK);
0140    return;
0141    }
0142  if ((double)xRight > cursorx) return;       /* inhibit ranges... */
0143  if ((double)xLeft < (-1)*cursorx) return;
0144  if (xRight < xLeft + zMIN_DEFORM) return;
0145  if ((double)yUp > cursory) return;
0146  if ((double)yDown < (-1)*cursory) return;
0147  if (yUp < yDown + zMIN_DEFORM) return;
0148
0149  xExtrudeRight= xRight;            /* grab deformation parameters... */
0150  xExtrudeLeft= xLeft;
0151  yExtrudeUp= yUp;
0152  yExtrudeDown= yDown;
0153  zGetDeformBoxCoords();   /* get camera coords and display coords */
0154
0155  TestOnly= TRUE;                    /* reset token for first pass */
0156  SECOND_PASS:              /* will loop back to here for second pass */
0157
0158  surface0:
0159    xc1=camcoords[7][0];yc1=camcoords[7][1];zc1=camcoords[7][2];
0160    xc2=camcoords[0][0];yc2=camcoords[0][1];zc2=camcoords[0][2];
0161    xc3=camcoords[3][0];yc3=camcoords[3][1];zc3=camcoords[3][2];
0162    xc4=camcoords[6][0];yc4=camcoords[6][1];zc4=camcoords[6][2];
0163    zVisibilityTest();
0164    if (visible > 0) goto surface1;
0165    xw3=cubeWorld[7][0];yw3=cubeWorld[7][1];zw3=cubeWorld[7][2];
0166    xw2=cubeWorld[0][0];yw2=cubeWorld[0][1];zw2=cubeWorld[0][2];
0167    xw1=cubeWorld[3][0];yw1=cubeWorld[3][1];zw1=cubeWorld[3][2];
0168    zDrawFacet();
0169  if ((Discard==TRUE) || (Clipped==TRUE)) goto DISCARD_SOLID;
```

```
0170
0171    surface1:
0172        xc1=camcoords[6][0];yc1=camcoords[6][1];zc1=camcoords[6][2];
0173        xc2=camcoords[5][0];yc2=camcoords[5][1];zc2=camcoords[5][2];
0174        xc3=camcoords[4][0];yc3=camcoords[4][1];zc3=camcoords[4][2];
0175        xc4=camcoords[7][0];yc4=camcoords[7][1];zc4=camcoords[7][2];
0176        zVisibilityTest();
0177        if (visible > 0) goto surface2;
0178        xw3=cubeWorld[6][0];yw3=cubeWorld[6][1];zw3=cubeWorld[6][2];
0179        xw2=cubeWorld[5][0];yw2=cubeWorld[5][1];zw2=cubeWorld[5][2];
0180        xw1=cubeWorld[4][0];yw1=cubeWorld[4][1];zw1=cubeWorld[4][2];
0181        zDrawFacet();
0182    if ((Discard==TRUE) || (Clipped==TRUE)) goto DISCARD_SOLID;
0183
0184    surface2:
0185        xc1=camcoords[3][0];yc1=camcoords[3][1];zc1=camcoords[3][2];
0186        xc2=camcoords[2][0];yc2=camcoords[2][1];zc2=camcoords[2][2];
0187        xc3=camcoords[5][0];yc3=camcoords[5][1];zc3=camcoords[5][2];
0188        xc4=camcoords[6][0];yc4=camcoords[6][1];zc4=camcoords[6][2];
0189        zVisibilityTest();
0190        if (visible > 0) goto surface3;
0191        xw3=cubeWorld[3][0];yw3=cubeWorld[3][1];zw3=cubeWorld[3][2];
0192        xw2=cubeWorld[2][0];yw2=cubeWorld[2][1];zw2=cubeWorld[2][2];
0193        xw1=cubeWorld[5][0];yw1=cubeWorld[5][1];zw1=cubeWorld[5][2];
0194        zDrawFacet();
0195    if ((Discard==TRUE) || (Clipped==TRUE)) goto DISCARD_SOLID;
0196
0197    surface3:
0198        xc1=camcoords[0][0];yc1=camcoords[0][1];zc1=camcoords[0][2];
0199        xc2=camcoords[1][0];yc2=camcoords[1][1];zc2=camcoords[1][2];
0200        xc3=camcoords[2][0];yc3=camcoords[2][1];zc3=camcoords[2][2];
0201        xc4=camcoords[3][0];yc4=camcoords[3][1];zc4=camcoords[3][2];
0202        zVisibilityTest();
0203        if (visible > 0) goto surface4;
0204        xw3=cubeWorld[0][0];yw3=cubeWorld[0][1];zw3=cubeWorld[0][2];
0205        xw2=cubeWorld[1][0];yw2=cubeWorld[1][1];zw2=cubeWorld[1][2];
0206        xw1=cubeWorld[2][0];yw1=cubeWorld[2][1];zw1=cubeWorld[2][2];
0207        zDrawFacet();
0208    if ((Discard==TRUE) || (Clipped==TRUE)) goto DISCARD_SOLID;
0209
0210    surface4:
0211        xc1=camcoords[7][0];yc1=camcoords[7][1];zc1=camcoords[7][2];
0212        xc2=camcoords[4][0];yc2=camcoords[4][1];zc2=camcoords[4][2];
0213        xc3=camcoords[1][0];yc3=camcoords[1][1];zc3=camcoords[1][2];
0214        xc4=camcoords[0][0];yc4=camcoords[0][1];zc4=camcoords[0][2];
0215        zVisibilityTest();
0216        if (visible > 0) goto surface5;
0217        xw3=cubeWorld[7][0];yw3=cubeWorld[7][1];zw3=cubeWorld[7][2];
0218        xw2=cubeWorld[4][0];yw2=cubeWorld[4][1];zw2=cubeWorld[4][2];
0219        xw1=cubeWorld[1][0];yw1=cubeWorld[1][1];zw1=cubeWorld[1][2];
0220        zDrawFacet();
0221    if ((Discard==TRUE) || (Clipped==TRUE)) goto DISCARD_SOLID;
0222
0223    surface5:
0224        xc1=camcoords[1][0];yc1=camcoords[1][1];zc1=camcoords[1][2];
0225        xc2=camcoords[4][0];yc2=camcoords[4][1];zc2=camcoords[4][2];
0226        xc3=camcoords[5][0];yc3=camcoords[5][1];zc3=camcoords[5][2];
0227        xc4=camcoords[2][0];yc4=camcoords[2][1];zc4=camcoords[2][2];
0228        zVisibilityTest();
0229        if (visible > 0) goto surfaces_done;
0230        xw3=cubeWorld[1][0];yw3=cubeWorld[1][1];zw3=cubeWorld[1][2];
```

```
0231    xw2=cubeWorld[4][0];yw2=cubeWorld[4][1];zw2=cubeWorld[4][2];
0232    xw1=cubeWorld[5][0];yw1=cubeWorld[5][1];zw1=cubeWorld[5][2];
0233    zDrawFacet();
0234  if ((Discard==TRUE) || (Clipped==TRUE)) goto DISCARD_SOLID;
0235
0236  surfaces_done:
0237  if (TestOnly==TRUE)
0238    {                               /* if just finished first pass... */
0239    TestOnly= FALSE;                          /* reset token and... */
0240    goto SECOND_PASS;                   /* loop back for second pass */
0241    }
0242  return;                   /* fall through to here after second pass */
0243
0244  DISCARD_SOLID:  /* jump to here if facet discarded on first pass */
0245  MessageBeep(0);    /* issue audio cue if solid has been discarded */
0246  return;
0247  }
0248  /*
0249  -------------------------------------------------------------------
0250            Calculate coords for deformed parallelepiped
0251  -------------------------------------------------------------------
0252                                                                     */
0253  static void zGetDeformBoxCoords(void)
0254  {                   /* this function is called by zDrawDeformBox() */
0255    int t= 0;
0256    double negx,negy,negz;
0257  negx=(-1)*(cursorx);negy=(-1)*(cursory);negz=(-1)*(cursorz);
0258    cubeObj[0][0]= (double) xExtrudeRight;
0259    cubeObj[0][1]= (double) yExtrudeDown;
0260    cubeObj[0][2]= cursorz;
0261    cubeObj[1][0]= (double) xExtrudeRight;
0262    cubeObj[1][1]= (double) yExtrudeUp;
0263    cubeObj[1][2]= cursorz;
0264    cubeObj[2][0]= (double) xExtrudeLeft;
0265    cubeObj[2][1]= (double) yExtrudeUp;
0266    cubeObj[2][2]= cursorz;
0267    cubeObj[3][0]= (double) xExtrudeLeft;
0268    cubeObj[3][1]= (double) yExtrudeDown;
0269    cubeObj[3][2]= cursorz;
0270    cubeObj[4][0]= cursorx;
0271    cubeObj[4][1]= cursory;
0272    cubeObj[4][2]= negz;
0273    cubeObj[5][0]= negx;
0274    cubeObj[5][1]= cursory;
0275    cubeObj[5][2]= negz;
0276    cubeObj[6][0]= negx;
0277    cubeObj[6][1]= negy;
0278    cubeObj[6][2]= negz;
0279    cubeObj[7][0]= cursorx;
0280    cubeObj[7][1]= negy;
0281    cubeObj[7][2]= negz;
0282    for (t=0;t<=7;t++)
0283      {
0284      x=cubeObj[t][0];y=cubeObj[t][1];z=cubeObj[t][2];
0285      if (bAssembly == TRUE) zGetAssemblyCoords();
0286      zGetWorldCoords();
0287      cubeWorld[t][0]=x;cubeWorld[t][1]=y;cubeWorld[t][2]=z;
0288      zGetCameraCoords();
0289      camcoords[t][0]=x;camcoords[t][1]=y;camcoords[t][2]=z;
0290      }
0291    return;
```

```
0292   }
0293   /*
0294   ----------------------------------------------------------------
0295                        Draw a 3D half-cylinder
0296   ----------------------------------------------------------------
0297                                                                  */
0298   void zDrawHalfCylinder(void)
0299   {          /* uses extern cursorx and cursorz to configure cylinder */
0300   if (bInitialized==FALSE)
0301     {
0302     MessageBox(GetFocus(),
0303       "zDrawHalfCylinder( ) reports 3D library is not initialized.",
0304       "deform3D.c error:  line 00304", MB_OK);
0305     return;
0306     }
0307   TestOnly= FALSE;                   /* do not discard entire solid */
0308   CylinderRadius= cursorx;                         /* grab radius */
0309   CylinderExtrude= cursorz;                      /* grab extrusion */
0310   if (CylinderRadius < zMIN_RADIUS) return; /* if radius too small */
0311   VertAngle= z00_DEGREES;                      /* vertical angle */
0312   HorizAngle= z00_DEGREES;                     /* horiz angle */
0313
0314   if (CylinderRadius >= 25)
0315     {                /* if a large radius, use smaller facets... */
0316     NumFacets= 18;                          /* num of facets */
0317     FacetDimension= z10_DEGREES;          /* width of facets */
0318     }
0319   else if (CylinderRadius < 25)
0320     {                /* if a smaller radius, use larger facets... */
0321     NumFacets= 9;
0322     FacetDimension= z20_DEGREES;
0323     }
0324
0325   /* --------------- draw body of half-cylinder ----------------- */
0326   for (Facet= 1; Facet <= NumFacets; Facet++)
0327     {                                      /* for each facet... */
0328     /* --------------- calculate first vertex ------------------ */
0329     zGetHalfCylShape(); x= CylinderX; y= CylinderY; z= CylinderZ;
0330     if (bAssembly == TRUE) zGetAssemblyCoords();
0331     zGetWorldCoords(); xw3= x; yw3= y; zw3= z;
0332     zGetCameraCoords(); xc1= x; yc1= y; zc1= z;
0333     /* --------------- calculate second vertex ----------------- */
0334     PrevVert= VertAngle; VertAngle= VertAngle + FacetDimension;
0335     zGetHalfCylShape(); x= CylinderX; y= CylinderY; z= CylinderZ;
0336     if (bAssembly == TRUE) zGetAssemblyCoords();
0337     zGetWorldCoords(); xw2= x; yw2= y; zw2= z;
0338     zGetCameraCoords(); xc2= x; yc2= y; zc2= z;
0339     /* --------------- calculate third vertex ------------------ */
0340     zGetHalfCylShape(); x= CylinderX; y= CylinderY; z= -CylinderZ;
0341     if (bAssembly == TRUE) zGetAssemblyCoords();
0342     zGetWorldCoords(); xw1= x; yw1= y; zw1= z;
0343     zGetCameraCoords(); xc3= x; yc3= y; zc3= z;
0344     /* --------------- calculate fourth vertex ----------------- */
0345     VertAngle= PrevVert;
0346     zGetHalfCylShape(); x= CylinderX; y= CylinderY; z= -CylinderZ;
0347     if (bAssembly == TRUE) zGetAssemblyCoords();
0348     zGetWorldCoords();
0349     zGetCameraCoords(); xc4= x; yc4= y; zc4= z;
0350     /* ---------- test visibility and render the facet ---------- */
0351     zVisibilityTest();
0352     if (visible <= 0) zDrawFacet();
```

```
0353    VertAngle= VertAngle + FacetDimension;
0354    }
0355
0356    /* --------------- draw ends of half-cylinder ------------------ */
0357    VertAngle= z00_DEGREES;                    /* reset vertical angle */
0358    for (Facet= 1; Facet <= NumFacets; Facet++)
0359    {                                    /* for each facet of near end... */
0360    /* --------------- calculate first vertex ------------------ */
0361    x= 0; y= 0; z= CylinderZ;
0362    if (bAssembly == TRUE) zGetAssemblyCoords();
0363    zGetWorldCoords(); xw3= x; yw3= y; zw3= z;
0364    zGetCameraCoords(); xc1= x; yc1= y; zc1= z;
0365    /* --------------- calculate second vertex ------------------ */
0366    PrevVert= VertAngle; VertAngle= VertAngle + FacetDimension;
0367    zGetHalfCylShape(); x= CylinderX; y= CylinderY; z= CylinderZ;
0368    if (bAssembly == TRUE) zGetAssemblyCoords();
0369    zGetWorldCoords(); xw2= x; yw2= y; zw2= z;
0370    zGetCameraCoords(); xc2= x; yc2= y; zc2= z;
0371    /* --------------- calculate third vertex ------------------ */
0372    VertAngle= PrevVert;
0373    zGetHalfCylShape(); x= CylinderX; y= CylinderY; z= CylinderZ;
0374    if (bAssembly == TRUE) zGetAssemblyCoords();
0375    zGetWorldCoords(); xw1= x; yw1= y; zw1= z;
0376    zGetCameraCoords(); xc3= x; yc3= y; zc3= z;
0377    /* --------------- calculate fourth vertex ------------------ */
0378    x= 0; y= 0; z= CylinderZ;
0379    if (bAssembly == TRUE) zGetAssemblyCoords();
0380    zGetWorldCoords();
0381    zGetCameraCoords(); xc4= x; yc4= y; zc4= z;
0382    /* --------- test visibility and render the facet ----------- */
0383    zVisibilityTest();
0384    if (visible <= 0) zDrawFacet();
0385    VertAngle= VertAngle + FacetDimension;
0386    }
0387    VertAngle= z00_DEGREES;                    /* reset vertical angle */
0388    for (Facet= 1; Facet <= NumFacets; Facet++)
0389    {                                    /* for each facet of far end... */
0390    /* --------------- calculate first vertex ------------------ */
0391    x= 0; y= 0; z= -CylinderZ;
0392    if (bAssembly == TRUE) zGetAssemblyCoords();
0393    zGetWorldCoords(); xw3= x; yw3= y; zw3= z;
0394    zGetCameraCoords(); xc1= x; yc1= y; zc1= z;
0395    /* --------------- calculate second vertex ------------------ */
0396    zGetHalfCylShape(); x= CylinderX; y= CylinderY; z= -CylinderZ;
0397    if (bAssembly == TRUE) zGetAssemblyCoords();
0398    zGetWorldCoords(); xw2= x; yw2= y; zw2= z;
0399    zGetCameraCoords(); xc2= x; yc2= y; zc2= z;
0400    /* --------------- calculate third vertex ------------------ */
0401    VertAngle= VertAngle + FacetDimension;
0402    zGetHalfCylShape(); x= CylinderX; y= CylinderY; z= -CylinderZ;
0403    if (bAssembly == TRUE) zGetAssemblyCoords();
0404    zGetWorldCoords(); xw1= x; yw1= y; zw1= z;
0405    zGetCameraCoords(); xc3= x; yc3= y; zc3= z;
0406    /* --------------- calculate fourth vertex ------------------ */
0407    x= 0; y= 0; z= -CylinderZ;
0408    if (bAssembly == TRUE) zGetAssemblyCoords();
0409    zGetWorldCoords();
0410    zGetCameraCoords(); xc4= x; yc4= y; zc4= z;
0411    /* --------- test visibility and render the facet ----------- */
0412    zVisibilityTest();
0413    if (visible <= 0) zDrawFacet();
```

```
0414    }
0415    #ifdef COMPILING         /* if compiling for Windows 3.0 and 3.1 */
0416    #undef COMPILING
0417    #line 1 "E"
0418    #error See compile tips in companion book by Lee Adams.
0419    #endif
0420    /* ------------- draw flat side of half-cylinder -------------- */
0421    VertAngle= z00_DEGREES;                    /* reset angle */
0422    /* ---------------- calculate first vertex -------------------- */
0423    zGetHalfCylShape(); x= CylinderX; y= CylinderY; z= CylinderZ;
0424    if (bAssembly == TRUE) zGetAssemblyCoords();
0425    zGetWorldCoords(); xw3= x; yw3= y; zw3= z;
0426    zGetCameraCoords(); xc1= x; yc1= y; zc1= z;
0427    /* ----------------- calculate second vertex ------------------ */
0428    x= CylinderX; y= CylinderY; z= -CylinderZ;
0429    if (bAssembly == TRUE) zGetAssemblyCoords();
0430    zGetWorldCoords(); xw2= x; yw2= y; zw2= z;
0431    zGetCameraCoords(); xc2= x; yc2= y; zc2= z;
0432    /* ----------------- calculate third vertex ------------------- */
0433    VertAngle= z180_DEGREES;                    /* reset angle */
0434    zGetHalfCylShape(); x= CylinderX; y= CylinderY; z= -CylinderZ;
0435    if (bAssembly == TRUE) zGetAssemblyCoords();
0436    zGetWorldCoords(); xw1= x; yw1= y; zw1= z;
0437    zGetCameraCoords(); xc3= x; yc3= y; zc3= z;
0438    /* ----------------- calculate fourth vertex ------------------ */
0439    x= CylinderX; y= CylinderY; z= CylinderZ;
0440    if (bAssembly == TRUE) zGetAssemblyCoords();
0441    zGetWorldCoords();
0442    zGetCameraCoords(); xc4= x; yc4= y; zc4= z;
0443    /* ----------- test visibility and render the facet ----------- */
0444    zVisibilityTest();
0445    if (visible <= 0) zDrawFacet();
0446
0447    return;
0448    }
0449    /*
0450    -------------------------------------------------------------
0451        Calculate obj coords for pt on surface of half-cylinder
0452    -------------------------------------------------------------
0453                                                              */
0454    static void zGetHalfCylShape(void)
0455    {              /* this function is called by zDrawHalfCylinder() */
0456    SinHoriz= sin(HorizAngle);
0457    CosHoriz= cos(HorizAngle);
0458    SinVert= sin(VertAngle);
0459    CosVert= cos(VertAngle);
0460    TempX= SinVert * CylinderRadius;
0461    CylinderY= CosVert * CylinderRadius;
0462    CylinderX= CosHoriz * TempX;
0463    CylinderZ= CylinderExtrude;
0464    return;
0465    }
0466    /*
0467    -------------------------------------------------------------
0468                        Draw a 3D bulged surface
0469    -------------------------------------------------------------
0470                                                              */
0471    void zDrawBulge(void)
0472    {              /* this funtion uses cursorx, cursory, and cursorz */
0473    if (bInitialized==FALSE)
0474        {
```

```
0475    MessageBox(GetFocus(),
0476      "zDrawBulge( ) reports that 3D library is not initialized.",
0477      "deform3D.c error:  line 00477", MB_OK);
0478    return;
0479    }
0480  ParamChange= .05;                         /* parametric increment */
0481  ParamMax= 1.00;                       /* maximum parametric value */
0482  ParamMin= 0.0;                        /* minimum parametric value */
0483  ControlStrength= .50;              /* influence of control points */
0484  if (bUsePalette == TRUE)             /* if using 256-color mode... */
0485    {             /* ...increase the resolution of the rendering */
0486    ParamChange= .025;
0487    }
0488
0489  /* --------- configure the curved edge of the surface ---------- */
0490  CurveX1= (-1) * cursorx;
0491  CurveX4= cursorx;
0492  CurveY1= 0.0; CurveY4= 0.0;
0493
0494  /* ------------ configure the width of the surface ------------- */
0495  SurfaceEdge1= (-1) * cursorz;
0496  SurfaceEdge2= cursorz;
0497
0498  /* ----------- configure the magnitude of the curve ----------- */
0499  CurveY2= cursory;
0500  CurveY3= cursory;
0501  CurveX2= ControlStrength * CurveX1;
0502  CurveX3= ControlStrength * CurveX4;
0503
0504  /* ---------------- render the curved surface ----------------- */
0505  for (T= ParamMin; T <= ParamMax; T+= ParamChange)
0506    {                 /* for each lamina in the curved surface... */
0507    T2= T * T;
0508    T3= T * T * T;
0509    /* ---------------- calculate first vertex ----------------- */
0510    zGetBulgeShape(); x= SurfaceX; y= SurfaceY; z= SurfaceEdge1;
0511    if (bAssembly == TRUE) zGetAssemblyCoords();
0512    zGetWorldCoords(); xw3= x; yw3= y; zw3= z;
0513    zGetCameraCoords(); xc1= x; yc1= y; zc1= z;
0514    /* ---------------- calculate second vertex ---------------- */
0515    x= SurfaceX; y= SurfaceY; z= SurfaceEdge2;
0516    if (bAssembly == TRUE) zGetAssemblyCoords();
0517    zGetWorldCoords(); xw2= x; yw2= y; zw2= z;
0518    zGetCameraCoords(); xc2= x; yc2= y; zc2= z;
0519    /* ---------------- calculate third vertex ----------------- */
0520    PrevT= T;                          /* remember position on curve */
0521    T+= ParamChange;          /* move to next position on curve... */
0522    T2= T * T;
0523    T3= T * T * T;
0524    zGetBulgeShape(); x= SurfaceX; y= SurfaceY; z= SurfaceEdge2;
0525    if (bAssembly == TRUE) zGetAssemblyCoords();
0526    zGetWorldCoords(); xw1= x; yw1= y; zw1= z;
0527    zGetCameraCoords(); xc3= x; yc3= y; zc3= z;
0528    /* ---------------- calculate fourth vertex ---------------- */
0529    x= SurfaceX; y= SurfaceY; z= SurfaceEdge1;
0530    if (bAssembly == TRUE) zGetAssemblyCoords();
0531    zGetWorldCoords();
0532    zGetCameraCoords(); xc4= x; yc4= y; zc4= z;
0533    /* ---------- test visibility and render the lamina ---------- */
0534    zVisibilityTest();
0535    if (visible <= 0) zDrawFacet();       /* if visible, draw lamina */
```

```
0536    else {                        /* else draw obverse side of lamina... */
0537        SwapStorage= xw1; xw1= xw3; xw3= SwapStorage;
0538        SwapStorage= yw1; yw1= yw3; yw3= SwapStorage;
0539        SwapStorage= zw1; zw1= zw3; zw3= SwapStorage;
0540        SwapStorage= xc1; xc1= xc3; xc3= SwapStorage;
0541        SwapStorage= yc1; yc1= yc3; yc3= SwapStorage;
0542        SwapStorage= zc1; zc1= zc3; zc3= SwapStorage;
0543        zDrawFacet();
0544        }
0545    T= PrevT;                     /* restore current position on curve */
0546    }                                 /* loop back and render next facet */
0547  return;
0548  }
0549  /*
0550  -----------------------------------------------------------------
0551            Calculate obj coords for pt on bulged surface
0552  -----------------------------------------------------------------
0553                                                                  */
0554  static void zGetBulgeShape(void)
0555  {                     /* this function is called by zDrawBulge() */
0556  Pull1= CurveX1 * (-T3 + 3 * T2 - 3 * T + 1);
0557  Pull2= CurveX2 * (3 * T3 - 6 * T2 + 3 * T);
0558  Pull3= CurveX3 * (-3 * T3 + 3 * T2);
0559  Pull4= CurveX4 * T3;
0560  SurfaceX= Pull1 + Pull2 + Pull3 + Pull4;
0561  Pull1= CurveY1 * (-T3 + 3 * T2 - 3 * T + 1);
0562  Pull2= CurveY2 * (3 * T3 - 6 * T2 + 3 * T);
0563  Pull3= CurveY3 * (-3 * T3 + 3 * T2);
0564  Pull4= CurveY4 * T3;
0565  SurfaceY= Pull1 + Pull2 + Pull3 + Pull4;
0566  return;
0567  }
0568  /*
0569  -----------------------------------------------------------------
0570      End of module of 3D deformations for Windows applications.
0571  -----------------------------------------------------------------
0572                                                                  */
```

B-5 Source listings for the 3D hierarchical modeling toolkit, assemb3d.c. See Appendix
C for applications that use this toolkit. See Appendix A for instructions on building
the demos.

```
0001  /*
0002  -----------------------------------------------------------------
0003                        ASSEMB3D.H
0004  -----------------------------------------------------------------
0005                                                                  */
0006  void zSetHierarchyMode(BOOL);          /* toggles hierarchy on|off */
0007  void zSetSubobjectAttitude(int,int,int);  /* reorients subobject */
0008  void zSetSubobjectLocation(int,int,int);   /* repositions subobj */
0009  void zSetHierarchyLevel(int);          /* sets subobject in subassy */
0010  void zSetSubAssyPivot(int,int,int);    /* sets subassy pivot-point */
0011  void zSetSubAssyRotation(int,int,int); /* sets subassy rotation */
0012  void zSetSubAssyPosition(int,int,int); /* sets subassy position */
0013  /*
0014  -----------------------------------------------------------------
0015            End of header file for 3D hierarchical modeling.
0016  -----------------------------------------------------------------
0017                                                                  */
0001  /*
```

```
0002   -----------------------------------------------------------
0003         Module of 3D hierarchy drivers for Windows applications
0004   -----------------------------------------------------------
0005      Source file: ASSEMB3D.C
0006      Release version: 1.00              Programmer: Lee Adams
0007      Type:  C source file for Windows multimodule applications.
0008      Compilers:  Microsoft C/C++, Borland C++, Zortech C++,
0009         QuickC for Windows, Turbo C++ for Windows, WATCOM C.
0010      Memory model:  medium.
0011      Dependencies:  ENGINE3D.C 3D functions.  Compile ENGINE3D.C and
0012         ASSEMB3D.C and link the resulting .OBJ files to your compiled
0013         primary .C file.  Include ASSEMB3D.H and ENGINE3D.H in your
0014         primary .C file.
0015      Output and features:  Provides drivers for the ENGINE3D.C
0016         3D routines in order to render complex assemblies built
0017         from 3D subobjects like cylinders, parallelepipeds, etc.
0018      Publication: Contains material from Windcrest/McGraw-Hill book
0019         4115 published by TAB BOOKS Division of McGraw-Hill Inc.
0020      License:  As purchaser of the book you are granted a royalty-
0021         free license to distribute executable files generated using
0022         this code provided you accept the conditions of the License
0023         Agreement and Limited Warranty described in the book and on
0024         the companion disk.  Government users:  This software and
0025         documentation are subject to restrictions set forth in The
0026         Rights in Technical Data and Computer Software clause at
0027         252.227-7013 and elsewhere.
0028   -----------------------------------------------------------
0029         (c) Copyright 1993 Lee Adams.  All rights reserved.
0030            Lee Adams(tm) is a trademark of Lee Adams.
0031   -----------------------------------------------------------
0032                                                              */
0033
0034   #include <WINDOWS.H>                    /* for BOOL declaration */
0035   #include <math.h>                  /* for sine and cosine functions */
0036   /* #define COMPILING 1 */
0037   /*
0038   -----------------------------------------------------------
0039         Function prototypes for functions found in this module
0040   -----------------------------------------------------------
0041                                                              */
0042   /* ----- callable from both outside and inside this module ----- */
0043   void zSetHierarchyMode(BOOL);        /* toggles hierarchy modeling */
0044   void zGetAssemblyCoords(void);       /* calculates assembly coords */
0045   void zSetSubobjectAttitude(int,int,int);    /* subobj orientation */
0046   void zSetSubobjectLocation(int,int,int);       /* subobj position */
0047   void zSetHierarchyLevel(int);        /* sets subobject in subassy */
0048   void zSetSubAssyPivot(int,int,int);  /* sets subassy pivot-point */
0049   void zSetSubAssyRotation(int,int,int);  /* sets subassy rotation */
0050   void zSetSubAssyPosition(int,int,int);  /* sets subassy position */
0051
0052   /* ------------ callable from only inside this module ---------- */
0053   static void zSetSubobjectAngle(void);       /* convert to radians */
0054   static void zSetSubAssyAngle(void);         /* convert to radians */
0055   static void zGetSubAssyCoords(void);/* calculates subassy coords */
0056   /*
0057   -----------------------------------------------------------
0058         Static variables visible throughout this file
0059   -----------------------------------------------------------
0060                                                              */
0061   /* ----------------- variables for assemblies ---------------- */
0062   static double xAssy= 0.0, yAssy= 0.0, zAssy= 0.0;
```

```
0063    static double sAYaw, cAYaw, sARoll, cARoll, sAPitch, cAPitch;
0064    static double AssyYaw= 0.0, AssyRoll= 0.0, AssyPitch= 0.0;
0065    static double xa, ya, za;
0066    static BOOL bAssembInit= FALSE;          /* this module initialized? */
0067
0068    /* --------------- variables for subassemblies ---------------- */
0069    #define zLEVEL1      1       /* level of subobject in hierarchy... */
0070    #define zLEVEL2      2
0071    #define zLEVEL3      3
0072    static int HierarchyLevel= 1;                /* remembers the level */
0073    static double xSubAssy= 0.0,                /* subassembly position */
0074                  ySubAssy=0.0, zSubAssy= 0.0;
0075    static double SubAssyYaw= 0.0,           /* subassembly orientation */
0076                  SubAssyRoll= 0.0, SubAssyPitch= 0.0;
0077    static double sAAYaw, cAAYaw,     /* subassy sine, cosine factors */
0078                  sAARoll, cAARoll, sAAPitch, cAAPitch;
0079    static double xSubAssyPivot= 0.0,        /* subassembly pivot-point */
0080                  ySubAssyPivot=0.0, zSubAssyPivot= 0.0;
0081    /*
0082    ------------------------------------------------------------------
0083                 Declare extern variables defined in ENGINE3D.C
0084    ------------------------------------------------------------------
0085                                                                     */
0086    extern BOOL bInitialized;       /* TRUE if 3D library initialized */
0087    extern double x, y, z;       /* coords for 3D modeling pipeline */
0088    extern BOOL bAssembly;       /* TRUE if using hierarchy modeling */
0089    /*
0090    ------------------------------------------------------------------
0091                           3D hierarchy drivers
0092    ------------------------------------------------------------------
0093                      Calculate assembly-space coords
0094    ------------------------------------------------------------------
0095                                                                     */
0096    void zGetAssemblyCoords(void)
0097    {                    /* the function is called by other 3D modules */
0098    /* Enter with unclipped xyz 3D subobject coordinates.
0099        Exit with unclipped xyz 3D assembly coordinates.             */
0100    if (bInitialized==FALSE)
0101      {
0102      MessageBox(GetFocus(),
0103        "zGetAssemblyCoords( ) reports 3D library is not initialized.",
0104        "assemb3D.c internal error:  line 00104", MB_OK);
0105      return;
0106      }
0107    if (bAssembInit==FALSE)
0108      {
0109      MessageBox(GetFocus(),
0110        "zGetAssemblyCoords( ) reports 3D hierarchy not initialized.",
0111        "assemb3D.c error:  line 00111", MB_OK);
0112      return;
0113      }
0114
0115    xa= cARoll * x + sARoll * y;                      /* roll rotation... */
0116    ya= cARoll * y - sARoll * x;
0117    x= cAYaw * xa - sAYaw * z;                         /* yaw rotation... */
0118    za= sAYaw * xa + cAYaw * z;
0119    z= cAPitch * za - sAPitch * ya;                /* pitch rotation... */
0120    y= sAPitch * za + cAPitch * ya;
0121    x= x + xAssy;    /* reposition subobject in 3D assembly-space... */
0122    y= y + yAssy;
0123    z= z + zAssy;
```

```
0124
0125    if (HierarchyLevel == zLEVEL2)                 /* if a subassembly... */
0126      {
0127      zGetSubAssyCoords();
0128      }
0129
0130    #ifdef COMPILING           /* if compiling for Windows 3.0 and 3.1 */
0131    #undef COMPILING
0132    #line 1 "E"
0133    #error See compile tips in companion book by Lee Adams.
0134    #endif
0135    return;
0136    }
0137    /*
0138    --------------------------------------------------------------------
0139                     Toggle the hierarchy mode.
0140    --------------------------------------------------------------------
0141                                                                      */
0142    void zSetHierarchyMode(BOOL Mode)
0143      {     /* this function is called by the interactive main module */
0144    if (bInitialized==FALSE)
0145      {
0146      MessageBox(GetFocus(),
0147        "zSetHierarchyMode( ) reports 3D library is not initialized.",
0148        "assemb3D.c error:  line 00148", MB_OK);
0149      return;
0150      }
0151    if (Mode == TRUE) bAssembly=  TRUE;
0152    if (Mode == FALSE) bAssembly= FALSE;
0153    return;
0154    }
0155    /*
0156    --------------------------------------------------------------------
0157                     Set the hierarchy level.
0158    --------------------------------------------------------------------
0159                                                                      */
0160    void zSetHierarchyLevel(int WhichLevel)
0161      {     /* this function is called by the interactive main module */
0162    if (WhichLevel == zLEVEL1)
0163      {
0164      HierarchyLevel= zLEVEL1;
0165      return;
0166      }
0167    if (WhichLevel == zLEVEL2)
0168      {
0169      HierarchyLevel= zLEVEL2;
0170      return;
0171      }
0172    if (WhichLevel == zLEVEL3)
0173      {
0174      HierarchyLevel= zLEVEL3;
0175      return;
0176      }
0177    return;
0178    }
0179    /*
0180    --------------------------------------------------------------------
0181                     Assembly functions
0182    --------------------------------------------------------------------
0183          Calculate subobject sine and cosine rotation factors
0184    --------------------------------------------------------------------
```

```
0185                                                               */
0186    static void zSetSubobjectAngle(void)
0187    {              /* this function is called by zSetSubobjectAttitude() */
0188    /* Enter with AssyYaw,AssyRoll,AssyPitch subobject rotation angles.
0189       Exit with sine, cosine object rotation factors for subobject. */
0190
0191    sAYaw= sin(AssyYaw);
0192    cAYaw= cos(AssyYaw);
0193    sARoll= sin(AssyRoll);
0194    cARoll= cos(AssyRoll);
0195    sAPitch= sin(AssyPitch);
0196    cAPitch= cos(AssyPitch);
0197    bAssembInit= TRUE;                          /* set runtime token */
0198    return;
0199    }
0200    /*
0201    -----------------------------------------------------------------
0202                   Set the attitude of the subobject.
0203    -----------------------------------------------------------------
0204                                                               */
0205    void zSetSubobjectAttitude(int Yaw, int Roll, int Pitch)
0206    {        /* this function is called by the interactive main module */
0207    if (Yaw < 0)      return;                 /* trap illegal values... */
0208    if (Yaw > 360)    return;
0209    if (Roll < 0)     return;
0210    if (Roll > 360)   return;
0211    if (Pitch < 0)    return;
0212    if (Pitch > 360) return;
0213
0214    AssyYaw= ((double)Yaw) * .0175433;        /* convert to radians... */
0215    AssyRoll= ((double)Roll) * .0175433;
0216    AssyPitch= ((double)Pitch) * .0175433;
0217
0218    if (Yaw==360)    AssyYaw= 6.28319;  /* tidy up boundary values... */
0219    if (Yaw==0)      AssyYaw= 0.0;
0220    if (Roll==360)   AssyRoll= 6.28319;
0221    if (Roll==0)     AssyRoll= 0.0;
0222    if (Pitch==360) AssyPitch= 6.28319;
0223    if (Pitch==0)    AssyPitch= 0.0;
0224
0225    zSetSubobjectAngle();                  /* set sine and cosine factors */
0226    return;
0227    }
0228    /*
0229    -----------------------------------------------------------------
0230              Reposition the subobject in 3D assembly-space.
0231    -----------------------------------------------------------------
0232                                                               */
0233    void zSetSubobjectLocation(int ReposX, int ReposY, int ReposZ)
0234    {        /* this function is called by the interactive main module */
0235    xAssy= (double) ReposX;
0236    yAssy= (double) ReposY;
0237    zAssy= (double) ReposZ;
0238    return;
0239    }
0240    /*
0241    -----------------------------------------------------------------
0242                       Subassembly functions
0243    -----------------------------------------------------------------
0244          Calculate subobject sine and cosine rotation factors
0245    -----------------------------------------------------------------
```

```
0246                                                              */
0247  static void zSetSubAssyAngle(void)
0248  {               /* this function is called by zSetSubAssyRotation() */
0249  /* Enter with SubAssyYaw,SubAssyRoll,SubAssyPitch subassembly
0250     rotation angles.  Exit with sine, cosine object rotation
0251     factors for subassembly. */
0252
0253  sAAYaw= sin(SubAssyYaw);
0254  cAAYaw= cos(SubAssyYaw);
0255  sAARoll= sin(SubAssyRoll);
0256  cAARoll= cos(SubAssyRoll);
0257  sAAPitch= sin(SubAssyPitch);
0258  cAAPitch= cos(SubAssyPitch);
0259  return;
0260  }
0261  /*
0262  ------------------------------------------------------------------
0263              Set the orientation of the subassembly.
0264  ------------------------------------------------------------------
0265                                                              */
0266  void zSetSubAssyRotation(int Yaw, int Roll, int Pitch)
0267  {      /* this function is called by the interactive main module */
0268  if (Yaw < 0)     return;                /* trap illegal values... */
0269  if (Yaw > 360)   return;
0270  if (Roll < 0)    return;
0271  if (Roll > 360)  return;
0272  if (Pitch < 0)   return;
0273  if (Pitch > 360) return;
0274
0275  SubAssyYaw= ((double)Yaw) * .0175433;   /* convert to radians... */
0276  SubAssyRoll= ((double)Roll) * .0175433;
0277  SubAssyPitch= ((double)Pitch) * .0175433;
0278
0279  if (Yaw==360) SubAssyYaw= 6.28319; /* tidy up boundary values... */
0280  if (Yaw==0) SubAssyYaw= 0.0;
0281  if (Roll==360) SubAssyRoll= 6.28319;
0282  if (Roll==0) SubAssyRoll= 0.0;
0283  if (Pitch==360) SubAssyPitch= 6.28319;
0284  if (Pitch==0) SubAssyPitch= 0.0;
0285  zSetSubAssyAngle();                     /* set sine and cosine factors */
0286  return;
0287  }
0288  /*
0289  ------------------------------------------------------------------
0290          Reposition the subassembly in 3D assembly-space.
0291  ------------------------------------------------------------------
0292                                                              */
0293  void zSetSubAssyPosition(int ReposX, int ReposY, int ReposZ)
0294  {      /* this function is called by the interactive main module */
0295  xSubAssy= (double) ReposX;
0296  ySubAssy= (double) ReposY;
0297  zSubAssy= (double) ReposZ;
0298  return;
0299  }
0300  /*
0301  ------------------------------------------------------------------
0302          Reposition the subassembly pivot-point.
0303  ------------------------------------------------------------------
0304                                                              */
0305  void zSetSubAssyPivot(int ReposX, int ReposY, int ReposZ)
0306  {      /* this function is called by the interactive main module */
```

B-5 Continued.

```
0307   xSubAssyPivot= (double) ReposX;
0308   ySubAssyPivot= (double) ReposY;
0309   zSubAssyPivot= (double) ReposZ;
0310   return;
0311   }
0312   /*
0313   ------------------------------------------------------------
0314            Calculate subassembly coords in assembly-space.
0315   ------------------------------------------------------------
0316                                                            */
0317   void zGetSubAssyCoords(void)
0318   {                   /* the function is called zGetAssemblyCoords() */
0319     /* Enter with unclipped xyz 3D subobject coordinates.
0320         Exit with unclipped xyz 3D subassembly coordinates.      */
0321
0322   x= x + xSubAssyPivot;   /* reposition subassembly pivot-point... */
0323   y= y + ySubAssyPivot;
0324   z= z + zSubAssyPivot;
0325
0326   xa= cAARoll * x + sAARoll * y;              /* roll rotation... */
0327   ya= cAARoll * y - sAARoll * x;
0328   x= cAAYaw * xa - sAAYaw * z;                 /* yaw rotation... */
0329   za= sAAYaw * xa + cAAYaw * z;
0330   z= cAAPitch * za - sAAPitch * ya;         /* pitch rotation... */
0331   y= sAAPitch * za + cAAPitch * ya;
0332
0333   x= x + xSubAssy;  /* reposition subassembly in assembly-space... */
0334   y= y + ySubAssy;
0335   z= z + zSubAssy;
0336   return;
0337   }
0338   /*
0339   ------------------------------------------------------------
0340     End of module of 3D hierarchy drivers for Windows applications.
0341   ------------------------------------------------------------
0342                                                            */
```

B-6 Source listings for the disk read/write toolkit, disk3d.c. See Appendix C for applications that use this toolkit. See Appendix A for instructions on building the demos.

```
0001   /*
0002   ------------------------------------------------------------
0003                     Include file DISK3D.H
0004            Copyright 1993 Lee Adams.  All rights reserved.
0005     Include this file in the .C source file.  It contains function
0006        prototypes, menu ID constants, and string ID constants.
0007   ------------------------------------------------------------
0008   ------------------------------------------------------------
0009                       Function prototypes
0010   ------------------------------------------------------------
0011                                                            */
0012   BOOL zSaveFrame(HBITMAP, LPSTR);        /* saves a frame to disk */
0013   BOOL zLoadFrame(HBITMAP, LPSTR);        /* loads a frame from disk*/
0014   /*
0015   ------------------------------------------------------------
0016                       End of include file
0017   ------------------------------------------------------------
0018                                                            */
0001   /*
0002   ------------------------------------------------------------
0003     Disk routines for Windows applications that use image files
```

```
0004        for disk-based frame animation.
0005    ------------------------------------------------------------------
0006        Source file:  DISK3D.C
0007        Release version:  2.00                    Programmer:  Lee Adams
0008        Type:  C file for multimodule Windows application development.
0009        Compilers:  Microsoft C/C++, Borland C++, Zortech C++,
0010          QuickC for Windows, Turbo C++ for Windows, Watcom C.
0011        Memory model:  medium.
0012        Dependencies:  include DISK3D.H in your main C source file.
0013          Compile DISK3D.C and link in DISK3D.OBJ to create your
0014          finished executable.
0015        Output and features:  Saves the bits of a given bitmap as a
0016          disk file.  Loads the image bits from a previously-saved
0017          disk file.  Supports 2-color, 16-color, and 256-color images.
0018          Detects attempt to run animation sequence in a color mode
0019          other than the mode in which it was saved.
0020        Publication: Contains material from Windcrest/McGraw-Hill book
0021          4115 published by TAB BOOKS Division of McGraw-Hill Inc.
0022        License:  As purchaser of the book you are granted a royalty-
0023          free license to distribute executable files generated using
0024          this code provided you accept the conditions of the License
0025          Agreement and Limited Warranty described in the book and on
0026          the companion disk.  Government users:  This software and
0027          documentation are subject to restrictions set forth in The
0028          Rights in Technical Data and Computer Software clause at
0029          252.227-7013 and elsewhere.
0030    ------------------------------------------------------------------
0031        (c) Copyright 1991-1993 Lee Adams.  All rights reserved.
0032            Lee Adams(tm) is a trademark of Lee Adams.
0033    ------------------------------------------------------------------
0034
0035    ------------------------------------------------------------------
0036                              Include files
0037    ------------------------------------------------------------------
0038                                                                  */
0039    #include <WINDOWS.H>
0040    #include <SYS\TYPES.H>
0041    #include <SYS\STAT.H>
0042    /*
0043    ------------------------------------------------------------------
0044        Function prototypes (callable from outside this module).
0045    ------------------------------------------------------------------
0046                                                                  */
0047    BOOL zSaveFrame(HBITMAP, LPSTR);        /* saves a frame to disk */
0048    BOOL zLoadFrame(HBITMAP, LPSTR);        /* loads a frame from disk*/
0049    /*
0050    ------------------------------------------------------------------
0051                      Define necessary constants.
0052    ------------------------------------------------------------------
0053                                                                  */
0054    #define IDS_Unexpected  44
0055    #define IDS_Disk9       54
0056    #define IDS_Disk10      55
0057    #define IDS_Disk11      56
0058    #define IDS_Disk12      57
0059    #define IDS_Disk13      58
0060    #define IDS_Disk14      59
0061    #define IDS_Disk15      60
0062    #define IDS_Disk16      61
0063    #define IDS_Disk17      62
0064    #define IDS_Disk18      63
```

Source listings for the toolkit modules **311**

```
0065   #define IDS_Disk19      64
0066   #define IDS_Disk20      65
0067   #define IDS_Disk21      66
0068   #define IDS_Disk22      67
0069   #define IDS_Disk23      68
0070   #define IDS_Disk24      69
0071   #define IDS_Disk25      70
0072   /*
0073   -------------------------------------------------------------------
0074                     Declare external variables.
0075   -------------------------------------------------------------------
0076                                                                   */
0077   extern BOOL FrameReady;
0078   extern HANDLE hInst;
0079   extern char lpCaption[];
0080   extern char lpMessage[];
0081   extern int Max;
0082   extern int MaxText;
0083   extern int RetVal;
0084   /*
0085   -------------------------------------------------------------------
0086                     Save a frame file to disk.
0087   -------------------------------------------------------------------
0088                                                                   */
0089   BOOL zSaveFrame(HBITMAP hBitmap, LPSTR lpFileName)
0090   {
0091     BITMAP bmImage;                        /* bitmap data structure */
0092     short BytesPerLine;                         /* width of bitmap */
0093     short RasterLines;                          /* height of bitmap */
0094     BYTE NumPlanes;                          /* number of bitplanes */
0095     LPSTR lpImageData;  /* pointer to buffer that holds bit array */
0096     GLOBALHANDLE hMem;    /* handle to buffer that holds bit array */
0097     WORD NumBytes;                     /* length of array, in bytes */
0098     LONG TestLength;                                /* hash value */
0099     DWORD BytesCopied;       /* value returned by GetBitmapBits() */
0100     int hFile;                              /* DOS file handle */
0101     OFSTRUCT FileStruct;              /* data structure for file */
0102
0103     HWND hDesktopWnd;                /* handle to desktop display */
0104     HDC hDCcaps;                            /* a display-context */
0105     int DisplayBits;                  /* number of bits-per-pixel */
0106
0107   hDesktopWnd= GetDesktopWindow();                    /* grab handle */
0108   hDCcaps= GetDC(hDesktopWnd);           /* grab a display-context */
0109   DisplayBits= GetDeviceCaps(hDCcaps,12);    /* get bits-per-pixel */
0110   ReleaseDC(hDesktopWnd,hDCcaps);     /* release display-context */
0111
0112   if (FrameReady==FALSE)              /* if no hidden-frame exists... */
0113     {
0114     MessageBeep(0);
0115     LoadString(hInst,IDS_Unexpected,lpCaption,Max);
0116     LoadString(hInst,IDS_Disk9,lpMessage,MaxText);
0117     MessageBox(GetFocus(),lpMessage,lpCaption,MB_OK);
0118     return FALSE;
0119     }
0120
0121   RetVal= GetObject(hBitmap,          /* grab bitmap data structure */
0122           sizeof(BITMAP),(LPSTR)&bmImage);
0123   if (RetVal==0)
0124     {
0125     MessageBeep(0);
```

```
0126    LoadString(hInst,IDS_Unexpected,lpCaption,Max);
0127    LoadString(hInst,IDS_Disk10,lpMessage,MaxText);
0128    MessageBox(GetFocus(),lpMessage,lpCaption,MB_OK);
0129    return FALSE;
0130    }
0131 BytesPerLine= bmImage.bmWidthBytes;              /* width of bitmap */
0132 RasterLines= bmImage.bmHeight;                   /* height of bitmap */
0133 NumPlanes= bmImage.bmPlanes;                     /* number of bitplanes */
0134 TestLength=                            /* calculate length of data */
0135            (LONG)(BytesPerLine * RasterLines * NumPlanes);
0136 if (TestLength > 65534) /* if too large for single-pass write... */
0137    {
0138    MessageBeep(0);
0139    LoadString(hInst,IDS_Unexpected,lpCaption,Max);
0140    LoadString(hInst,IDS_Disk11,lpMessage,MaxText);
0141    MessageBox(GetFocus(),lpMessage,lpCaption,MB_OK);
0142    return FALSE;
0143    }
0144 NumBytes= (WORD) TestLength;      /* initialize arg for _lwrite() */
0145
0146 hMem= GlobalAlloc(GMEM_MOVEABLE, NumBytes);   /* create a buffer */
0147 if (hMem==0)
0148    {
0149    MessageBeep(0);
0150    LoadString(hInst,IDS_Unexpected,lpCaption,Max);
0151    LoadString(hInst,IDS_Disk12,lpMessage,MaxText);
0152    MessageBox(GetFocus(),lpMessage,lpCaption,MB_OK);
0153    return FALSE;
0154    }
0155 lpImageData= GlobalLock(hMem);   /* lock buffer and grab pointer */
0156 BytesCopied= GetBitmapBits(hBitmap,NumBytes,lpImageData);
0157 if (BytesCopied==0)          /* if unable to copy bits to buffer... */
0158    {
0159    MessageBeep(0);
0160    LoadString(hInst,IDS_Unexpected,lpCaption,Max);
0161    LoadString(hInst,IDS_Disk13,lpMessage,MaxText);
0162    MessageBox(GetFocus(),lpMessage,lpCaption,MB_OK);
0163    GlobalUnlock(hMem); GlobalFree(hMem); return FALSE;
0164    }
0165
0166 hFile= OpenFile(lpFileName,&FileStruct,OF_EXIST);      /* exists? */
0167 if (hFile >= 0)
0168    {
0169    MessageBeep(0);
0170    LoadString(hInst,IDS_Unexpected,lpCaption,Max);
0171    LoadString(hInst,IDS_Disk14,lpMessage,MaxText);
0172    RetVal= MessageBox(GetFocus(),lpMessage,lpCaption,MB_YESNO);
0173    if (RetVal==IDNO)      /* if user does not want to overwrite... */
0174       {
0175       GlobalUnlock(hMem); GlobalFree(hMem); return FALSE;
0176       }
0177    }
0178 hFile= OpenFile(lpFileName,&FileStruct,OF_CREATE|OF_WRITE);
0179 if (hFile==-1)
0180    {
0181    MessageBeep(0);
0182    LoadString(hInst,IDS_Unexpected,lpCaption,Max);
0183    LoadString(hInst,IDS_Disk15,lpMessage,MaxText);
0184    MessageBox(GetFocus(),lpMessage,lpCaption,MB_OK);
0185    GlobalUnlock(hMem); GlobalFree(hMem); return FALSE;
0186    }
```

```
0187
0188   RetVal= _lwrite(hFile,lpImageData,NumBytes);      /* write to disk */
0189   if (RetVal==-1)
0190     {
0191     MessageBeep(0);
0192     LoadString(hInst,IDS_Unexpected,lpCaption,Max);
0193     LoadString(hInst,IDS_Disk16,lpMessage,MaxText);
0194
0195     MessageBox(GetFocus(),lpMessage,lpCaption,MB_OK);
0196     _lclose(hFile);
0197     GlobalUnlock(hMem); GlobalFree(hMem); return FALSE;
0198     }
0199
0200   RetVal= _lclose(hFile);                          /* close the file */
0201   if (RetVal==-1)                      /* if unable to close file... */
0202     {
0203     MessageBeep(0);
0204     LoadString(hInst,IDS_Unexpected,lpCaption,Max);
0205     LoadString(hInst,IDS_Disk17,lpMessage,MaxText);
0206     MessageBox(GetFocus(),lpMessage,lpCaption,MB_OK);
0207     GlobalUnlock(hMem); GlobalFree(hMem); return FALSE;
0208     }
0209
0210   GlobalUnlock(hMem);            /* discard the pointer to the buffer */
0211   GlobalFree(hMem);                        /* discard the buffer */
0212   return TRUE;
0213   }
0214   /*
0215   ------------------------------------------------------------------
0216                      Load one frame file from disk.
0217   ------------------------------------------------------------------
0218                                                                   */
0219   BOOL zLoadFrame(HBITMAP hBitmap, LPSTR lpFileName)
0220   {
0221     BITMAP bmImage;                       /* bitmap data structure */
0222     short BytesPerLine;                       /* width of bitmap */
0223     short RasterLines;                        /* height of bitmap */
0224     BYTE NumPlanes;                        /* number of bitplanes */
0225     LPSTR lpImageData;    /* pointer to buffer that holds bit array */
0226     GLOBALHANDLE hMem;    /* handle to buffer that holds bit array */
0227     WORD NumBytes;                     /* length of array, in bytes */
0228     LONG TestLength;                              /* hash value */
0229     DWORD BytesCopied;        /* value returned by GetBitmapBits() */
0230     int hFile;                                /* DOS file handle */
0231     OFSTRUCT FileStruct;             /* data structure for file */
0232
0233     HWND hDesktopWnd;                  /* handle to desktop display */
0234     HDC hDCcaps;                         /* a display-context */
0235     int DisplayBits;                 /* number of bits-per-pixel */
0236
0237   hDesktopWnd= GetDesktopWindow();                   /* grab handle */
0238   hDCcaps= GetDC(hDesktopWnd);           /* grab a display-context */
0239   DisplayBits= GetDeviceCaps(hDCcaps,12);   /* get bits-per-pixel */
0240   ReleaseDC(hDesktopWnd,hDCcaps);        /* release display-context */
0241
0242   if (FrameReady==FALSE)            /* if no hidden-frame exists... */
0243     {
0244     MessageBeep(0);
0245     LoadString(hInst,IDS_Unexpected,lpCaption,Max);
0246     LoadString(hInst,IDS_Disk18,lpMessage,MaxText);
0247     MessageBox(GetFocus(),lpMessage,lpCaption,MB_OK);
```

```
0248    return FALSE;
0249    }
0250
0251  RetVal= GetObject(hBitmap,              /* grab bitmap data structure */
0252          sizeof(BITMAP),(LPSTR)&bmImage);
0253  if (RetVal==0)
0254    {
0255    MessageBeep(0);
0256    LoadString(hInst,IDS_Unexpected,lpCaption,Max);
0257    LoadString(hInst,IDS_Disk10,lpMessage,MaxText);
0258    MessageBox(GetFocus(),lpMessage,lpCaption,MB_OK);
0259    return FALSE;
0260    }
0261
0262  BytesPerLine= bmImage.bmWidthBytes;           /* width of bitmap */
0263  RasterLines= bmImage.bmHeight;               /* height of bitmap */
0264  NumPlanes= bmImage.bmPlanes;             /* number of bitplanes */
0265  TestLength=                         /* calculate length of data */
0266             (LONG)(BytesPerLine * RasterLines * NumPlanes);
0267  NumBytes= (WORD) 65280;         /* initialize max arg for _lread() */
0268
0269  hMem= GlobalAlloc(GMEM_MOVEABLE, NumBytes);    /* create a buffer */
0270  if (hMem==0)
0271    {
0272    MessageBeep(0);
0273    LoadString(hInst,IDS_Unexpected,lpCaption,Max);
0274    LoadString(hInst,IDS_Disk20,lpMessage,MaxText);
0275    MessageBox(GetFocus(),lpMessage,lpCaption,MB_OK);
0276    return FALSE;
0277    }
0278  lpImageData= GlobalLock(hMem);    /* lock buffer and grab pointer */
0279
0280  hFile= OpenFile(lpFileName,&FileStruct,OF_READ);
0281  if (hFile==-1)
0282    {
0283    MessageBeep(0);
0284    LoadString(hInst,IDS_Unexpected,lpCaption,Max);
0285    LoadString(hInst,IDS_Disk21,lpMessage,MaxText);
0286    MessageBox(GetFocus(),lpMessage,lpCaption,MB_OK);
0287    GlobalUnlock(hMem); GlobalFree(hMem); return FALSE;
0288    }
0289
0290  RetVal= _lread(hFile,lpImageData,NumBytes);     /* read from disk */
0291  if (RetVal==-1)
0292    {
0293    MessageBeep(0);
0294    LoadString(hInst,IDS_Unexpected,lpCaption,Max);
0295    LoadString(hInst,IDS_Disk22,lpMessage,MaxText);
0296    MessageBox(GetFocus(),lpMessage,lpCaption,MB_OK);
0297    _lclose(hFile);
0298    GlobalUnlock(hMem); GlobalFree(hMem); return FALSE;
0299    }
0300
0301  /* ----- trap attempt to run animation in wrong color mode ----- */
0302  if (RetVal != (int) TestLength)          /* if wrong file length */
0303    {     /* ...then animation was saved in a different color mode */
0304    MessageBeep(0);
0305    LoadString(hInst,IDS_Unexpected,lpCaption,Max);
0306    LoadString(hInst,IDS_Disk23,lpMessage,MaxText);
0307    MessageBox(GetFocus(),lpMessage,lpCaption,MB_OK);
0308    _lclose(hFile);
```

```
0309    GlobalUnlock(hMem); GlobalFree(hMem); return FALSE;
0310    }
0311
0312  RetVal= _lclose(hFile);                          /* close the file */
0313  if (RetVal==-1)                    /* if unable to close file... */
0314    {
0315    MessageBeep(0);
0316    LoadString(hInst,IDS_Unexpected,lpCaption,Max);
0317    LoadString(hInst,IDS_Disk24,lpMessage,MaxText);
0318    MessageBox(GetFocus(),lpMessage,lpCaption,MB_OK);
0319    GlobalUnlock(hMem); GlobalFree(hMem); return FALSE;
0320    }
0321
0322  BytesCopied= SetBitmapBits(hBitmap,NumBytes,lpImageData);
0323  if (BytesCopied==0)        /* if unable to copy bits to bitmap... */
0324    {
0325    MessageBeep(0);
0326    LoadString(hInst,IDS_Unexpected,lpCaption,Max);
0327    LoadString(hInst,IDS_Disk25,lpMessage,MaxText);
0328    MessageBox(GetFocus(),lpMessage,lpCaption,MB_OK);
0329    GlobalUnlock(hMem); GlobalFree(hMem); return FALSE;
0330    }
0331
0332  GlobalUnlock(hMem);        /* discard the pointer to the buffer */
0333  GlobalFree(hMem);                        /* discard the buffer */
0334  return TRUE;
0335  }
0336  /*
0337  ------------------------------------------------------------------
0338                  End of disk routines C source file
0339  ------------------------------------------------------------------
0340                                                              */
```

B-7 Source listings for the 3D kinematics toolkit, knmatx3d.c. See Appendix C for applications that use this toolkit. See Appendix A for instructions on building the demos.

```
0001  /*
0002  ------------------------------------------------------------------
0003                          KNMATX3D.H
0004  ------------------------------------------------------------------
0005                                                              */
0006  void kmInitializeKinematics(double,int,int,int);
0007  void kmReset(void);
0008  void kmSelectPreviewFrame(int);
0009  void kmSetSolid(int,int);
0010  void kmSetColor(int,int);
0011  void kmSetLinearAcceleration(int,double,double);
0012  void kmSetRotationalAcceleration(int,double,double,double,double);
0013  void kmSetHeadingChange(int,double,double);
0014  void kmSetPitchChange(int,double,double);
0015  void kmSetAxisHdgChg(int,double,double);
0016  void kmSetAxisPtchChg(int,double,double);
0017  void kmDetectCollision(int,int);
0018  void kmSetLocation(int,double,double,double);
0019  void kmSetOrientation(int,double,double,double);
0020  void kmSetDimensions(int,double,double,double);
0021  void kmSetLinearVelocity(int,double,double,double);
0022  void kmSetRotationalVelocity(int,double,double,double);
0023  void kmSetMass(int,double);
0024  void kmRenderScene(void);
0025
```

B-7 Continued.

```
0026   #define zBOX           1                      /* available solids... */
0027   #define zSPHERE        2
0028   #define zCYLINDER      3
0029   #define zCONE          4
0030   #define zWEDGE         5
0031   #define zCURVE         6
0032   #define zHEMISPHERE    7
0033   #define zDEFORMBOX     8
0034   #define zHALFCYL       9
0035   #define zBULGE         10
0036   #define zNULL          11
0037
0038   #define zVERTICAL      0                  /* useful pitch values... */
0039   #define zHORIZONTAL    90
0040
0041   #define zNORTH         0                /* useful heading values... */
0042   #define zEAST          90
0043   #define zSOUTH         180
0044   #define zWEST          270
0045
0046   #define zBODY1         1                      /* useful body IDs... */
0047   #define zBODY2         2
0048   #define zBODY3         3
0049   #define zBODY4         4
0050   #define zBODY5         5
0051
0052   /*
0053   -------------------------------------------------------------------
0054            End of header file for 3D kinematics driver.
0055   -------------------------------------------------------------------
0056                                                                    */
0001   /*
0002   -------------------------------------------------------------------
0003        Module of 3D kinematics drivers for Windows applications
0004   -------------------------------------------------------------------
0005      Source file: KNMATX3D.C
0006      Release version: 1.00              Programmer: Lee Adams
0007      Type: C source file for Windows multimodule applications.
0008      Compilers: Microsoft C/C++, Borland C++, Zortech C++,
0009        QuickC for Windows, Turbo C++ for Windows, WATCOM C.
0010      Memory model: medium.
0011      Dependencies: ENGINE3D.C, SHAPES3D.C, DEFORM3D.C, and
0012        ASSEMB3D.C functions.  Compile ENGINE3D.C, SHAPES3D.C,
0013        DEFORM3D.C, ASSEMB3D.C, and KNMATX3D.C and link the resulting
0014        .OBJ files to your compiled primary .C file.  Include
0015        ENGINE3D.H, SHAPES3D.H, DEFORM3D.H, ASSEMB3D.H, and
0016        KNMATX3D.H in your primary .C file.
0017      Output and features:  Provides kinematics drivers for the
0018        ENGINE3D.C 3D routines in order to use acceleration,
0019        decleration, linear velocity, angular velocity,
0020        solids deformation, and collision detection to control
0021        movement of 3D bodies in animation sequences.
0022      Publication: Contains material from Windcrest/McGraw-Hill book
0023        4115 published by TAB BOOKS Division of McGraw-Hill Inc.
0024      License: As purchaser of the book you are granted a royalty-
0025        free license to distribute executable files generated using
0026        this code provided you accept the conditions of the License
0027        Agreement and Limited Warranty described in the book and on
0028        the companion disk.  Government users:  This software and
0029        documentation are subject to restrictions set forth in The
0030        Rights in Technical Data and Computer Software clause at
```

```
0031        252.227-7013 and elsewhere.
0032     ------------------------------------------------------------------
0033           (c) Copyright 1993 Lee Adams.  All rights reserved.
0034              Lee Adams(tm) is a trademark of Lee Adams.
0035     ------------------------------------------------------------------
0036                                                                      */
0037
0038     #include <WINDOWS.H>    /* for GDI MessageBox() function and BOOL */
0039     #include <math.h>              /* for sine, cosine, sqrt functions */
0040
0041     #define zMAX_BODIES   25      /* max available number of 3D bodies */
0042     #define zMAX_FPS      18.2        /* max supported animation rate */
0043
0044     #define zBOX          1              /* available solid subobjects... */
0045     #define zSPHERE       2
0046     #define zCYLINDER     3
0047     #define zCONE         4
0048     #define zWEDGE        5
0049     #define zCURVE        6
0050     #define zHEMISPHERE   7
0051     #define zDEFORMBOX    8
0052     #define zHALFCYL      9
0053     #define zBULGE        10
0054     #define zNULL         11
0055
0056     #define zRED          1                   /* available shading hues... */
0057     #define zGREEN        2
0058     #define zBROWN        3
0059     #define zBLUE         4
0060     #define zMAGENTA      5
0061     #define zCYAN         6
0062     #define zGRAY         7
0063     /* #define COMPILING 1 */
0064
0065     /*
0066     ------------------------------------------------------------------
0067          Function prototypes for functions found in this module
0068     ------------------------------------------------------------------
0069                                                                      */
0070     /* ----- callable from both outside and inside this module ----- */
0071     void kmInitializeKinematics(double,int,int,int);
0072     void kmReset(void);
0073     void kmSelectPreviewFrame(int);
0074     void kmSetSolid(int,int);
0075     void kmSetColor(int,int);
0076     void kmSetLinearAcceleration(int,double,double);
0077     void kmSetRotationalAcceleration(int,double,double,double,double);
0078     void kmSetHeadingChange(int,double,double);
0079     void kmSetPitchChange(int,double,double);
0080     void kmDetectCollision(int,int);
0081     void kmSetLocation(int,double,double,double);
0082     void kmSetOrientation(int,double,double,double);
0083     void kmSetDimensions(int,double,double,double);
0084     void kmSetLinearVelocity(int,double,double,double);
0085     void kmSetRotationalVelocity(int,double,double,double);
0086     void kmSetMass(int,double);
0087     void kmRenderScene(void);
0088
0089     /* ------------ callable from only inside this module ---------- */
0090     static void kmInitBody(void);
0091     static void kmSelectBody(int);
```

```
0092   static void kmGetNewLinearSpeed(void);
0093   static void kmGetNewRotationalSpeed(void);
0094   static void kmGetNewHeading(void);
0095   static void kmGetNewPitch(void);
0096   static void kmGetNewLocation(void);
0097   static void kmGetNewOrientation(void);
0098   static void kmGetNewSize(void);
0099   static void kmRenderBody(int);
0100   /*
0101   ----------------------------------------------------------------
0102            Declare called functions of other modules
0103   ----------------------------------------------------------------
0104                                                                   */
0105   void zSetShadingColor(int);              /* sets shading color */
0106   void zSetSubjectLocation(int,int,int);   /* instance translation */
0107   void zSetSubjectAttitude(int,int,int);   /* sets instance rotation */
0108   void zSetSubjectSize(int,int,int);       /* sets instance extrusion */
0109   void zDrawCube(void);                    /* renders 3D box */
0110   void zDrawSphere(void);                  /* renders 3D sphere */
0111   void zDrawCylinder(void);                /* renders 3D cylinder */
0112   void zDrawCurve(void);                   /* renders 3D curved surface */
0113   void zDrawCone(void);                    /* renders 3D cone */
0114   void zDrawHemisphere(void);              /* renders 3D half-sphere */
0115   void zDrawWedge(void);                   /* renders 3D wedge */
0116   void zDrawDeformBox(int,int,int,int);    /* 3D box deformation */
0117   void zDrawHalfCylinder(void);            /* 3D half-cylinder */
0118   void zDrawBulge(void);                   /* 3D bulged surface */
0119   void zSetHierarchyMode(BOOL);            /* toggles hierarchy modeling */
0120   /*
0121   ----------------------------------------------------------------
0122            Static variables visible throughout only this file
0123   ----------------------------------------------------------------
0124                                                                   */
0125   static BOOL bKinematicsReady= FALSE;     /* TRUE if initialized */
0126   static double fps= 18.2;                 /* animation rate */
0127   static double TimeSlice= .054945;        /* time resolution */
0128   static int FinalFrame= 36;               /* final frame of sequence */
0129   static int CurrentFrame= 1;              /* current frame */
0130   static double CurrentTime= 0.0;          /* current time */
0131   static int ActiveBodies= 1;              /* number of active 3D bodies */
0132
0133   /* ----------- the current kinematic state of a body ----------- */
0134   static struct KinematicState
0135       {
0136       /* --------------------- attributes --------------------- */
0137       int Solid;                           /* box, sphere, cone, etc. */
0138       int Color;                           /* shading color */
0139       /* --------------------- location --------------------- */
0140       double LocationX;                    /* current translation in units... */
0141       double LocationY;
0142       double LocationZ;
0143       /* --------------------- orientation --------------------- */
0144       double Yaw;            /* current rotation in degrees 0 to 360... */
0145       double Roll;
0146       double Pitch;
0147       /* --------------------- size --------------------- */
0148       double DimensionX;                   /* current extrusion in units... */
0149       double DimensionY;
0150       double DimensionZ;
0151       /* ------------------ linear velocity -------------------- */
0152       double LinearHeading;    /* current heading in degrees 0 to 360 */
```

```
0153     double LinearPitch;          /* current pitch in degrees 0 to 360 */
0154     double LinearSpeed;          /* current speed in units per second */
0155     /* ----------------- rotational velocity ------------------- */
0156     double YawSpeed;             /* yaw rotation in degrees per second */
0157     double RollSpeed;            /* roll rotation in degrees per second */
0158     double PitchSpeed;           /* pitch rotation in degrees per second */
0159     /* ----------------- acceleration factors ------------------- */
0160     double LinearAcceleration;           /* units per second squared */
0161     double LinearAccelerationDuration;     /* duration in seconds */
0162     double YawAcceleration;           /* degrees per second squared */
0163     double RollAcceleration;          /* degrees per second squared */
0164     double PitchAcceleration;         /* degrees per second squared */
0165     double RotationAccelerationDuration;   /* duration in seconds */
0166     /* ----------------- redirection factors ------------------- */
0167     double HeadingChange;                   /* degrees per second */
0168     double HeadingChangeDuration;                   /* seconds */
0169     double PitchChange;                     /* degrees per second */
0170     double PitchChangeDuration;                     /* seconds */
0171     /* ----------------- forward dynamics ------------------- */
0172     double Mass;                         /* measured in kg or g */
0173     double Volume;                     /* measured in units cubed */
0174     double Density;                       /* = mass/volume */
0175     double Elasticity;           /* range 0 inelastic to 1 elastic */
0176     double LinearMomentum;               /* = mass * linear velocity */
0177     double AngularMomentum;     /* = moment of inertia * rot velocity */
0178     double MomentOfInertia;     /* a function of mass, size, shape */
0179     double LinearEnergy;        /* = .5 * mass * velocity * velocity */
0180     double RotationEnergy;      /* = .5 * moment * rotvel * rotvel */
0181     };
0182
0183 /* ----------------- declare some 3D bodies ------------------- */
0184 static struct KinematicState Body1;
0185 static struct KinematicState Body2;
0186 static struct KinematicState Body3;
0187 static struct KinematicState Body4;
0188 static struct KinematicState Body5;
0189 static struct KinematicState Body6;
0190 static struct KinematicState Body7;
0191 static struct KinematicState Body8;
0192 static struct KinematicState Body9;
0193 static struct KinematicState Body10;
0194 static struct KinematicState Body11;
0195 static struct KinematicState Body12;
0196 static struct KinematicState Body13;
0197 static struct KinematicState Body14;
0198 static struct KinematicState Body15;
0199 static struct KinematicState Body16;
0200 static struct KinematicState Body17;
0201 static struct KinematicState Body18;
0202 static struct KinematicState Body19;
0203 static struct KinematicState Body20;
0204 static struct KinematicState Body21;
0205 static struct KinematicState Body22;
0206 static struct KinematicState Body23;
0207 static struct KinematicState Body24;
0208 static struct KinematicState Body25;
0209
0210 /* ------ declare a pointer to the currently-selected body ----- */
0211 static struct KinematicState *BodyPointer;
0212
0213 /*
```

```
0214    ----------------------------------------------------------------
0215                    Callable 3D kinematics functions
0216    ----------------------------------------------------------------
0217                    Initialize the kinematics module
0218    ----------------------------------------------------------------
0219                                                                    */
0220    void kmInitializeKinematics(double FramesPerSec,
0221                                int NumBodies,
0222                                int StartFrame,
0223                                int EndFrame)
0224    {
0225    if (bKinematicsReady == TRUE) return;              /* use once only */
0226    if ((NumBodies < 1)||(NumBodies > zMAX_BODIES)) return;
0227    if ((FramesPerSec < 3.0)||(FramesPerSec > zMAX_FPS)) return;
0228
0229    ActiveBodies= NumBodies;  /* remember number of active 3D bodies */
0230    FinalFrame= EndFrame;                /* remember length of animation */
0231
0232    if (FramesPerSec < 3.6)          /* remember the animation rate... */
0233      {
0234      fps= 3.0; goto DONE_FPS;
0235      }
0236    if (FramesPerSec < 4.5)
0237      {
0238      fps= 3.6; goto DONE_FPS;
0239      }
0240    if (FramesPerSec < 6.1)
0241      {
0242      fps= 4.5; goto DONE_FPS;
0243      }
0244    if (FramesPerSec < 9.1)
0245      {
0246      fps= 6.1; goto DONE_FPS;
0247      }
0248    if (FramesPerSec < 18.2)
0249      {
0250      fps= 9.1; goto DONE_FPS;
0251      }
0252    fps= 18.2;
0253
0254    DONE_FPS:
0255    TimeSlice= 1 / fps;                /* calculate the timing resolution */
0256
0257    BodyPointer= &Body1; kmInitBody();
0258    if (ActiveBodies < 2) goto DONE_INITIALIZATION;
0259    BodyPointer= &Body2; kmInitBody();
0260    if (ActiveBodies < 3) goto DONE_INITIALIZATION;
0261    BodyPointer= &Body3; kmInitBody();
0262    if (ActiveBodies < 4) goto DONE_INITIALIZATION;
0263    BodyPointer= &Body4; kmInitBody();
0264    if (ActiveBodies < 5) goto DONE_INITIALIZATION;
0265    BodyPointer= &Body5; kmInitBody();
0266    if (ActiveBodies < 6) goto DONE_INITIALIZATION;
0267    BodyPointer= &Body6; kmInitBody();
0268    if (ActiveBodies < 7) goto DONE_INITIALIZATION;
0269    BodyPointer= &Body7; kmInitBody();
0270    if (ActiveBodies < 8) goto DONE_INITIALIZATION;
0271    BodyPointer= &Body8; kmInitBody();
0272    if (ActiveBodies < 9) goto DONE_INITIALIZATION;
0273    BodyPointer= &Body9; kmInitBody();
0274    if (ActiveBodies < 10) goto DONE_INITIALIZATION;
```

```
0275  BodyPointer= &Body10; kmInitBody();
0276  if (ActiveBodies < 11) goto DONE_INITIALIZATION;
0277  BodyPointer= &Body11; kmInitBody();
0278  if (ActiveBodies < 12) goto DONE_INITIALIZATION;
0279  BodyPointer= &Body12; kmInitBody();
0280  if (ActiveBodies < 13) goto DONE_INITIALIZATION;
0281  BodyPointer= &Body13; kmInitBody();
0282  if (ActiveBodies < 14) goto DONE_INITIALIZATION;
0283  BodyPointer= &Body14; kmInitBody();
0284  if (ActiveBodies < 15) goto DONE_INITIALIZATION;
0285  BodyPointer= &Body15; kmInitBody();
0286  if (ActiveBodies < 16) goto DONE_INITIALIZATION;
0287  BodyPointer= &Body16; kmInitBody();
0288  if (ActiveBodies < 17) goto DONE_INITIALIZATION;
0289  BodyPointer= &Body17; kmInitBody();
0290  if (ActiveBodies < 18) goto DONE_INITIALIZATION;
0291  BodyPointer= &Body18; kmInitBody();
0292  if (ActiveBodies < 19) goto DONE_INITIALIZATION;
0293  BodyPointer= &Body19; kmInitBody();
0294  if (ActiveBodies < 20) goto DONE_INITIALIZATION;
0295  BodyPointer= &Body20; kmInitBody();
0296  if (ActiveBodies < 21) goto DONE_INITIALIZATION;
0297  BodyPointer= &Body21; kmInitBody();
0298  if (ActiveBodies < 22) goto DONE_INITIALIZATION;
0299  BodyPointer= &Body22; kmInitBody();
0300  if (ActiveBodies < 23) goto DONE_INITIALIZATION;
0301  BodyPointer= &Body23; kmInitBody();
0302  if (ActiveBodies < 24) goto DONE_INITIALIZATION;
0303  BodyPointer= &Body24; kmInitBody();
0304  if (ActiveBodies < 25) goto DONE_INITIALIZATION;
0305  BodyPointer= &Body25; kmInitBody();
0306
0307  DONE_INITIALIZATION:
0308  BodyPointer= &Body1;              /* restore pointer to default body */
0309  bKinematicsReady= TRUE;                     /* set the status token */
0310  #ifdef COMPILING          /* if compiling for Windows 3.0 and 3.1 */
0311  #undef COMPILING
0312  #line 1 "E"
0313  #error See compile tips in companion book by Lee Adams.
0314  #endif
0315  return;
0316  }
0317  /*
0318  --------------------------------------------------------------------
0319                    Re-initialize the kinematics module
0320  --------------------------------------------------------------------
0321                                                                    */
0322  void kmReset(void)
0323  {
0324  if (bKinematicsReady == FALSE) return;
0325  CurrentFrame= 1;
0326  CurrentTime= 0.0;
0327  return;
0328  }
0329  /*
0330  --------------------------------------------------------------------
0331      Adjust kinematic parameters for a particular preview frame
0332  --------------------------------------------------------------------
0333                                                                    */
0334  void kmSelectPreviewFrame(int WhichFrame)
0335  {
```

```
0336     int PreviewCount;
0337     int BodyCount;
0338  if (bKinematicsReady == FALSE) return;
0339
0340  for (PreviewCount= 1; PreviewCount< WhichFrame; PreviewCount++)
0341     {                    /* for each frame preceding the preview frame... */
0342     CurrentFrame= PreviewCount;               /* update the frame ID */
0343     CurrentTime= CurrentTime + TimeSlice;        /* update the time */
0344     for (BodyCount= 1; BodyCount<= ActiveBodies; BodyCount++)
0345       {                              /* for each body in the scene... */
0346       kmSelectBody(BodyCount);                   /* select the body... */
0347       if (CurrentFrame > 1) /* ...and update the body's kinematics */
0348         {
0349         kmGetNewLinearSpeed();
0350         kmGetNewRotationalSpeed();
0351         kmGetNewHeading();
0352         kmGetNewPitch();
0353         kmGetNewLocation();
0354         kmGetNewOrientation();
0355         kmGetNewSize();
0356         }
0357       }                              /* do next body in the scene */
0358     }                                /* do next preview frame */
0359  CurrentFrame++;                               /* set to preview frame */
0360  CurrentTime= CurrentTime + TimeSlice;     /* set to preview frame */
0361  return;
0362  }
0363  /*
0364  ----------------------------------------------------------------
0365                       Set new linear acceleration
0366  ----------------------------------------------------------------
0367                                                                  */
0368  void kmSetLinearAcceleration(int Body,
0369                              double UnitsPerSecSqd,
0370                              double Seconds)
0371  {
0372  if (bKinematicsReady == FALSE) return;
0373  if ((Body < 1)||(Body > ActiveBodies)) return;
0374  kmSelectBody(Body);
0375  BodyPointer->LinearAcceleration= UnitsPerSecSqd;
0376  BodyPointer->LinearAccelerationDuration= Seconds;
0377  return;
0378  }
0379  /*
0380  ----------------------------------------------------------------
0381                       Set new rotational acceleration
0382  ----------------------------------------------------------------
0383                                                                  */
0384  void kmSetRotationalAcceleration(int Body,
0385         double AYaw, double ARoll, double APitch, double Seconds)
0386  {
0387  if (bKinematicsReady == FALSE) return;
0388  if ((Body < 1)||(Body > ActiveBodies)) return;
0389  kmSelectBody(Body);
0390  BodyPointer->YawAcceleration= AYaw;
0391  BodyPointer->RollAcceleration= ARoll;
0392  BodyPointer->PitchAcceleration= APitch;
0393  BodyPointer->RotationAccelerationDuration= Seconds;
0394  return;
0395  }
0396  /*
```

```
0397    --------------------------------------------------------------
0398                     Set new heading change rate
0399    --------------------------------------------------------------
0400                                                                */
0401    void kmSetHeadingChange(int Body,
0402                               double DegreesPerSec,
0403                               double Seconds)
0404    {
0405    if (bKinematicsReady == FALSE) return;
0406    if ((Body < 1)||(Body > ActiveBodies)) return;
0407    kmSelectBody(Body);
0408    BodyPointer->HeadingChange= DegreesPerSec;
0409    BodyPointer->HeadingChangeDuration= Seconds;
0410    return;
0411    }
0412    /*
0413    --------------------------------------------------------------
0414                      Set new pitch change rate
0415    --------------------------------------------------------------
0416                                                                */
0417    void kmSetPitchChange(int Body,
0418                              double DegreesPerSec,
0419                              double Seconds)
0420    {
0421    if (bKinematicsReady == FALSE) return;
0422    if ((Body < 1)||(Body > ActiveBodies)) return;
0423    kmSelectBody(Body);
0424    BodyPointer->PitchChange= DegreesPerSec;
0425    BodyPointer->PitchChangeDuration= Seconds;
0426    return;
0427    }
0428    /*
0429    --------------------------------------------------------------
0430                        Reset the location
0431    --------------------------------------------------------------
0432                                                                */
0433    void kmSetLocation(int Body,
0434                         double X, double Y, double Z)
0435    {
0436    if (bKinematicsReady == FALSE) return;
0437    if ((Body < 1)||(Body > ActiveBodies)) return;
0438    kmSelectBody(Body);
0439    BodyPointer->LocationX= X;
0440    BodyPointer->LocationY= Y;
0441    BodyPointer->LocationZ= Z;
0442    return;
0443    }
0444    /*
0445    --------------------------------------------------------------
0446                       Reset the orientation
0447    --------------------------------------------------------------
0448                                                                */
0449    void kmSetOrientation(int Body,
0450                            double dYaw, double dRoll, double dPitch)
0451    {
0452    if (bKinematicsReady == FALSE) return;
0453    if ((Body < 1)||(Body > ActiveBodies)) return;
0454    if (dYaw < 0) dYaw= dYaw + 360;
0455    if (dYaw > 360) dYaw= dYaw - 360;
0456    if (dRoll < 0) dRoll= dRoll + 360;
0457    if (dRoll > 360) dRoll= dRoll - 360;
```

```
0458   if (dPitch < 0) dPitch= dPitch + 360;
0459   if (dPitch > 360) dPitch= dPitch - 360;
0460   kmSelectBody(Body);
0461   BodyPointer->Yaw= dYaw;
0462   BodyPointer->Roll= dRoll;
0463   BodyPointer->Pitch= dPitch;
0464   return;
0465   }
0466   /*
0467   -----------------------------------------------------------------
0468                         Reset the dimensions
0469   -----------------------------------------------------------------
0470                                                                 */
0471   void kmSetDimensions(int Body,
0472                         double X, double Y, double Z)
0473   {
0474   if (bKinematicsReady == FALSE) return;
0475   if ((Body < 1)||(Body > ActiveBodies)) return;
0476   kmSelectBody(Body);
0477   BodyPointer->DimensionX= X;
0478   BodyPointer->DimensionY= Y;
0479   BodyPointer->DimensionZ= Z;
0480   return;
0481   }
0482   /*
0483   -----------------------------------------------------------------
0484                      Reset the linear velocity
0485   -----------------------------------------------------------------
0486                                                                 */
0487   void kmSetLinearVelocity(int Body,
0488                         double Heading, double Pitch, double Speed)
0489   {
0490   if (bKinematicsReady == FALSE) return;
0491   if ((Body < 1)||(Body > ActiveBodies)) return;
0492   kmSelectBody(Body);
0493   BodyPointer->LinearHeading= Heading;
0494   BodyPointer->LinearPitch= Pitch;
0495   BodyPointer->LinearSpeed= Speed;
0496   return;
0497   }
0498   /*
0499   -----------------------------------------------------------------
0500                    Reset the rotational velocity
0501   -----------------------------------------------------------------
0502                                                                 */
0503   void kmSetRotationalVelocity(int Body,
0504          double RYawSpeed, double RRollSpeed, double RPitchSpeed)
0505   {
0506   if (bKinematicsReady == FALSE) return;
0507   if ((Body < 1)||(Body > ActiveBodies)) return;
0508   kmSelectBody(Body);
0509   BodyPointer->YawSpeed= RYawSpeed;
0510   BodyPointer->RollSpeed= RRollSpeed;
0511   BodyPointer->PitchSpeed= RPitchSpeed;
0512   return;
0513   }
0514   /*
0515   -----------------------------------------------------------------
0516                     Specify the subobject type
0517   -----------------------------------------------------------------
0518                                                                 */
```

```
0519    void kmSetSolid(int Body, int Subobject)
0520    {
0521    if (bKinematicsReady == FALSE) return;
0522    if ((Body < 1)||(Body > ActiveBodies)) return;
0523    if ((Subobject < zBOX)||(Subobject > zNULL)) return;
0524    kmSelectBody(Body);
0525    BodyPointer->Solid= Subobject;
0526    return;
0527    }
0528    /*
0529    ----------------------------------------------------------------
0530                        Specify the subobject color
0531    ----------------------------------------------------------------
0532                                                                 */
0533    void kmSetColor(int Body, int Hue)
0534    {
0535    if (bKinematicsReady == FALSE) return;
0536    if ((Body < 1)||(Body > ActiveBodies)) return;
0537    if ((Hue < zRED)||(Hue > zGRAY)) return;
0538    kmSelectBody(Body);
0539    BodyPointer->Color= Hue;
0540    return;
0541    }
0542    /*
0543    ----------------------------------------------------------------
0544                              Set the mass
0545    ----------------------------------------------------------------
0546                                                                 */
0547    void kmSetMass(int Body, double dMass)
0548    {
0549    if (bKinematicsReady == FALSE) return;
0550    if ((Body < 1)||(Body > ActiveBodies)) return;
0551    kmSelectBody(Body);
0552    BodyPointer->Mass= dMass;
0553    return;
0554    }
0555    /*
0556    ----------------------------------------------------------------
0557              Render all the bodies in the 3D scene
0558    ----------------------------------------------------------------
0559                                                                 */
0560    void kmRenderScene(void)
0561    {
0562      int Count;
0563    if (bKinematicsReady == FALSE) return;
0564    if (CurrentFrame > FinalFrame) return;
0565    for (Count= 1; Count<= ActiveBodies; Count++)
0566      {                             /* for each body in the scene... */
0567      kmRenderBody(Count);                    /* ...render the body */
0568      }
0569    CurrentFrame++;                  /* increment the frame counter */
0570    CurrentTime= CurrentTime + TimeSlice;    /* increment the time */
0571    return;
0572    }
0573    /*
0574    ----------------------------------------------------------------
0575              Detect a collision between two bodies
0576    ----------------------------------------------------------------
0577                                                                 */
0578    void kmDetectCollision(int Body1, int Body2)
0579    {                        /* call with the two bodies to be tested */
```

```
0580   if (bKinematicsReady == FALSE) return;
0581   if ((Body1 < 1)||(Body1 > ActiveBodies)) return;
0582   if ((Body2 < 1)||(Body2 > ActiveBodies)) return;
0583
0584   /* add future code here */
0585
0586   return;
0587   }
0588   /*
0589   --------------------------------------------------------------
0590                     Internal 3D kinematics drivers
0591   --------------------------------------------------------------
0592              Initialize the currently-selected body
0593   --------------------------------------------------------------
0594                                                            */
0595   static void kmInitBody(void)
0596   {
0597   BodyPointer->Solid= zBOX;
0598   BodyPointer->Color= zGREEN;
0599   BodyPointer->LocationX= 0;
0600   BodyPointer->LocationY= 0;
0601   BodyPointer->LocationZ= 0;
0602   BodyPointer->Yaw= 0;
0603   BodyPointer->Roll= 0;
0604   BodyPointer->Pitch= 0;
0605   BodyPointer->DimensionX= 25;
0606   BodyPointer->DimensionY= 25;
0607   BodyPointer->DimensionZ= 25;
0608   BodyPointer->LinearHeading= 0;
0609   BodyPointer->LinearPitch= 0;
0610   BodyPointer->LinearSpeed= 0;
0611   BodyPointer->YawSpeed= 0;
0612   BodyPointer->RollSpeed= 0;
0613   BodyPointer->PitchSpeed= 0;
0614   BodyPointer->LinearAcceleration= 0;
0615   BodyPointer->LinearAccelerationDuration= 0;
0616   BodyPointer->YawAcceleration= 0;
0617   BodyPointer->RollAcceleration= 0;
0618   BodyPointer->PitchAcceleration= 0;
0619   BodyPointer->RotationAccelerationDuration= 0;
0620   BodyPointer->HeadingChange= 0;
0621   BodyPointer->HeadingChangeDuration= 0;
0622   BodyPointer->PitchChange= 0;
0623   BodyPointer->PitchChangeDuration= 0;
0624   BodyPointer->Mass= 1.0;
0625   BodyPointer->Volume= 15625;
0626   BodyPointer->Density= 1.0;
0627   BodyPointer->Elasticity= 1.0;
0628   BodyPointer->LinearMomentum= 0;
0629   BodyPointer->AngularMomentum= 0;
0630   BodyPointer->MomentOfInertia= 0;
0631   BodyPointer->LinearEnergy= 0;
0632   BodyPointer->RotationEnergy= 0;
0633   return;
0634   }
0635   /*
0636   --------------------------------------------------------------
0637                       Select the current body
0638   --------------------------------------------------------------
0639                                                            */
0640   static void kmSelectBody(int WhichBody)
```

```
0641  {
0642  switch (WhichBody)
0643      {            /* point to the currently-selected body struct... */
0644      case 1:  BodyPointer= &Body1; break;
0645      case 2:  BodyPointer= &Body2; break;
0646      case 3:  BodyPointer= &Body3; break;
0647      case 4:  BodyPointer= &Body4; break;
0648      case 5:  BodyPointer= &Body5; break;
0649          /* add additional cases here if required by your simulation */
0650      }
0651  return;
0652  }
0653  /*
0654  -----------------------------------------------------------------
0655                   Render the currently-selected body
0656  -----------------------------------------------------------------
0657                                                                  */
0658  static void kmRenderBody(int Body)
0659  {        /* this function is called repeatedly by kmRenderScene() */
0660  kmSelectBody(Body);   /* grab pointer to currently-selected body */
0661
0662  /* ------- Step One:  update the body's kinematic state -------- */
0663  if (CurrentFrame > 1)
0664      {                    /* if first frame, do not move body yet... */
0665      kmGetNewLinearSpeed();
0666      kmGetNewRotationalSpeed();
0667      kmGetNewHeading();
0668      kmGetNewPitch();
0669      kmGetNewLocation();
0670      kmGetNewOrientation();
0671      kmGetNewSize();
0672      }
0673  /* --------------- Step Two:  render the body ---------------- */
0674  zSetHierarchyMode(FALSE);          /* specify hierarchy mode */
0675  zSetShadingColor(BodyPointer->Color);   /* specify shading color */
0676  zSetSubjectSize((int)BodyPointer->DimensionX,    /* set extrusion */
0677                  (int)BodyPointer->DimensionY,
0678                  (int)BodyPointer->DimensionZ);
0679  zSetSubjectAttitude((int)BodyPointer->Yaw,     /* set orientation */
0680                  (int)BodyPointer->Roll,
0681                  (int)BodyPointer->Pitch);
0682  zSetSubjectLocation((int)BodyPointer->LocationX, /* set location */
0683                  (int)BodyPointer->LocationY,
0684                  (int)BodyPointer->LocationZ);
0685  switch (BodyPointer->Solid)            /* render the subobject... */
0686      {
0687      case zBOX: zDrawCube(); break;
0688      case zSPHERE: zDrawSphere(); break;
0689      case zCYLINDER: zDrawCylinder(); break;
0690      case zCONE: zDrawCone(); break;
0691      case zWEDGE: zDrawWedge(); break;
0692      case zCURVE: zDrawCurve(); break;
0693      case zHEMISPHERE: zDrawHemisphere(); break;
0694      case zDEFORMBOX: zDrawCube(); break;    /* for prototyping only */
0695      case zHALFCYL: zDrawHalfCylinder(); break;
0696      case zBULGE: zDrawBulge(); break;
0697      case zNULL: break;
0698      }
0699  zSetHierarchyMode(FALSE);       /* restore default hierarchy mode */
0700  return;
0701  }
```

```
0702  /*
0703  -----------------------------------------------------------------
0704              The nine-step kinematics animation pipeline
0705  -----------------------------------------------------------------
0706  Step 1                    Get new linear speed
0707  -----------------------------------------------------------------
0708                                                                  */
0709  static void kmGetNewLinearSpeed(void)
0710  {
0711  BodyPointer->LinearSpeed= BodyPointer->LinearSpeed +
0712                    (BodyPointer->LinearAcceleration * TimeSlice);
0713  return;
0714  }
0715  /*
0716  -----------------------------------------------------------------
0717  Step2                    Get new rotational speed
0718  -----------------------------------------------------------------
0719                                                                  */
0720  static void kmGetNewRotationalSpeed(void)
0721  {
0722  BodyPointer->YawSpeed= BodyPointer->YawSpeed +
0723            (BodyPointer->YawAcceleration * TimeSlice);
0724  BodyPointer->RollSpeed= BodyPointer->RollSpeed +
0725            (BodyPointer->RollAcceleration * TimeSlice);
0726  BodyPointer->PitchSpeed= BodyPointer->PitchSpeed +
0727            (BodyPointer->PitchAcceleration * TimeSlice);
0728  return;
0729  }
0730  /*
0731  -----------------------------------------------------------------
0732  Step 3                    Get new velocity heading
0733  -----------------------------------------------------------------
0734                                                                  */
0735  static void kmGetNewHeading(void)
0736  {
0737  BodyPointer->LinearHeading= BodyPointer->LinearHeading +
0738                    (BodyPointer->HeadingChange * TimeSlice);
0739  if (BodyPointer->LinearHeading < 0)
0740    {
0741    BodyPointer->LinearHeading= BodyPointer->LinearHeading + 360;
0742    }
0743  if (BodyPointer->LinearHeading > 360)
0744    {
0745    BodyPointer->LinearHeading= BodyPointer->LinearHeading - 360;
0746    }
0747  return;
0748  }
0749  /*
0750  -----------------------------------------------------------------
0751  Step 4                    Get new velocity pitch
0752  -----------------------------------------------------------------
0753                                                                  */
0754  static void kmGetNewPitch(void)
0755  {
0756  BodyPointer->LinearPitch= BodyPointer->LinearPitch +
0757                    (BodyPointer->PitchChange * TimeSlice);
0758  if (BodyPointer->LinearPitch < 0)
0759    {
0760    BodyPointer->LinearPitch= BodyPointer->LinearPitch + 360;
0761    }
0762  if (BodyPointer->LinearPitch > 360)
```

```
0763      {
0764        BodyPointer->LinearPitch= BodyPointer->LinearPitch - 360;
0765      }
0766    return;
0767    }
0768    /*
0769    -------------------------------------------------------------------
0770    Step 5                     Calculate new location
0771    -------------------------------------------------------------------
0772                                                                   */
0773    static void kmGetNewLocation(void)
0774    {
0775      double xFactor, yFactor, zFactor;              /* unit vector */
0776      double PitchRads, HeadingRads;                 /* radian angles */
0777      double MaxRemainder;                        /* temporary variable */
0778
0779    /* ---------- Step One:  convert degrees to radians ----------- */
0780    PitchRads= BodyPointer->LinearPitch * .017453;
0781    HeadingRads= BodyPointer->LinearHeading * .017453;
0782
0783    /* ------- Step Two:  calculate components of unit vector ------ */
0784    yFactor= cos(PitchRads);    /* 1 at 0 degrees, -1 at 180 degrees */
0785    MaxRemainder= sqrt(1 - (yFactor * yFactor));
0786    xFactor= (sin(HeadingRads)) * MaxRemainder;
0787    zFactor= (cos(HeadingRads)) * MaxRemainder * (-1);
0788
0789    /* ------- Step Three:  calculate the time-sliced vector ------- */
0790    xFactor= xFactor * TimeSlice;
0791    yFactor= yFactor * TimeSlice;
0792    zFactor= zFactor * TimeSlice;
0793
0794    /* --------- Step Four:  calculate the new translation --------- */
0795    BodyPointer->LocationX=
0796         BodyPointer->LocationX + (xFactor * BodyPointer->LinearSpeed);
0797    BodyPointer->LocationY=
0798         BodyPointer->LocationY + (yFactor * BodyPointer->LinearSpeed);
0799    BodyPointer->LocationZ=
0800         BodyPointer->LocationZ + (zFactor * BodyPointer->LinearSpeed);
0801    return;
0802    }
0803    /*
0804    -------------------------------------------------------------------
0805    Step 6                     Calculate new orientation
0806    -------------------------------------------------------------------
0807                                                                   */
0808    static void kmGetNewOrientation(void)
0809    {
0810    BodyPointer->Yaw=
0811      BodyPointer->Yaw + (BodyPointer->YawSpeed * TimeSlice);
0812    BodyPointer->Roll=
0813      BodyPointer->Roll + (BodyPointer->RollSpeed * TimeSlice);
0814    BodyPointer->Pitch=
0815      BodyPointer->Pitch + (BodyPointer->PitchSpeed * TimeSlice);
0816    if (BodyPointer->Yaw < 0)
0817      BodyPointer->Yaw= BodyPointer->Yaw + 360;
0818    if (BodyPointer->Yaw > 360)
0819      BodyPointer->Yaw= BodyPointer->Yaw - 360;
0820    if (BodyPointer->Roll < 0)
0821      BodyPointer->Roll= BodyPointer->Roll + 360;
0822    if (BodyPointer->Roll > 360)
0823      BodyPointer->Roll= BodyPointer->Roll - 360;
```

```
0824   if (BodyPointer->Pitch < 0)
0825     BodyPointer->Pitch= BodyPointer->Pitch + 360;
0826   if (BodyPointer->Pitch > 360)
0827     BodyPointer->Pitch= BodyPointer->Pitch - 360;
0828   return;
0829   }
0830   /*
0831   ----------------------------------------------------------------
0832   Step 7                    Calculate new size
0833   ----------------------------------------------------------------
0834                                                                */
0835   static void kmGetNewSize(void)
0836   {
0837                       /* This is a stub routine not yet implemented. */
0838   return;
0839   }
0840   /*
0841   ----------------------------------------------------------------
0842     End of module of 3D kinematics drivers for Windows applications.
0843   ----------------------------------------------------------------
0844                                                                */
```

Appendix C
Source listings for the sample applications

This appendix contains the listings for the sample applications. These listings must be linked with the toolkit modules presented in the previous appendix in order to build the executables. Read Appendix A for tips on building the application.

The template for graphics application development, startup.c, is presented in Fig. C-1. The 3D geometry sampler, objects.c, is provided in Fig. C-2. The template for interactive 3D animation, animate.c, appears in Fig. C-3. The hierarchical modeling animation sampler, assembly.c, is found in Fig. C-4. The animated forward kinematics editor, kinematx.c, is presented in Fig. C-5. The interactive, animated, virtual reality sampler, maze.c, appears in Fig. C-6.

Source listings

C-1 Source listings for the sample application, startup, consisting of .def, .h, .rc, and .c files. See Appendix B for the toolkits which must be linked in to build this application. See Appendix A for instructions on building the demo.

```
0001   NAME          DEFDEMO
0002   DESCRIPTION   'Copyright 1993 Lee Adams.  All rights reserved.'
```

```
0003   EXETYPE        WINDOWS
0004   STUB           'WINSTUB.EXE'
0005   CODE           PRELOAD MOVEABLE
0006   DATA           PRELOAD MOVEABLE MULTIPLE
0007   HEAPSIZE       1024
0008   STACKSIZE      8192
0009   EXPORTS        zMessageHandler
0001   /*
0002   ----------------------------------------------------------------
0003                      Include file startup.h
0004          Copyright 1993 Lee Adams.  All rights reserved.
0005      Include this file in the .RC resource script file and in the
0006      .C source file.  It contains function prototypes, menu ID
0007      constants, and string ID constants.
0008   ----------------------------------------------------------------
0009   ----------------------------------------------------------------
0010                         Function prototypes
0011   ----------------------------------------------------------------
0012                                                                 */
0013   #if !defined(zRCFILE)                    /* if not an .RC file... */
0014     LONG FAR PASCAL zMessageHandler(HWND, unsigned, WORD, LONG);
0015     int PASCAL WinMain(HANDLE,HANDLE,LPSTR,int);
0016     HWND zInitMainWindow(HANDLE);
0017     BOOL zInitClass(HANDLE);
0018   static void zClear(HWND);               /* blank the display window */
0019   static void zInitFrame(HWND);               /* creates hidden frame */
0020   static void zCopyToDisplay(HWND);      /* copies frame to display */
0021   static void zCopyToFrame(HWND);        /* copies display to frame */
0022   static void zClearHiddenFrame(void);      /* clears hidden frame */
0023   static void zDrawItemF(HWND);          /* sample drawing function */
0024   static void zDrawItemG(HWND);          /* sample drawing function */
0025   static void zBuildPalette(HWND);       /* sample drawing function */
0026   #endif
0027   /*
0028   ----------------------------------------------------------------
0029                         Menu ID constants
0030   ----------------------------------------------------------------
0031                                                                 */
0032   #define IDM_New            1
0033   #define IDM_Open           2
0034   #define IDM_Save           3
0035   #define IDM_SaveAs         4
0036   #define IDM_Exit           5
0037   #define IDM_Restart        6
0038
0039   #define IDM_Undo           7
0040   #define IDM_Cut            8
0041   #define IDM_Copy           90
0042   #define IDM_Paste          10
0043   #define IDM_Delete         11
0044
0045   #define IDM_ItemA          12
0046   #define IDM_ItemB          13
0047   #define IDM_ItemC          14
0048   #define IDM_ItemD          15
0049   #define IDM_ItemE          16
0050   #define IDM_ItemF          17
0051   #define IDM_ItemG          18
0052   #define IDM_Clear          19
0053
0054   #define IDM_About          20
```

C-1 Continued.

```
0055  #define IDM_License         21
0056  #define IDM_Display         22
0057  #define IDM_Colors          23
0058  #define IDM_Mode            24
0059  #define IDM_Version         25
0060  #define IDM_GeneralHelp     26
0061  /*
0062  ---------------------------------------------------------------
0063                              String ID constants
0064  ---------------------------------------------------------------
0065                                                              */
0066  #define IDS_Caption         1
0067  #define IDS_Warning         2
0068  #define IDS_NoMouse         3
0069  #define IDS_About           4
0070  #define IDS_AboutText       5
0071  #define IDS_License         6
0072  #define IDS_LicenseText     7
0073  #define IDS_Help            8
0074  #define IDS_HelpText        9
0075  #define IDS_Completed       10
0076  #define IDS_Resolution      11
0077  #define IDS_ResVGA          12
0078  #define IDS_ResEGA          13
0079  #define IDS_ResCGA          14
0080  #define IDS_ResSVGA         15
0081  #define IDS_Res8514         16
0082  #define IDS_ResHerc         17
0083  #define IDS_ResCustom       18
0084  #define IDS_Color           19
0085  #define IDS_Color16         20
0086  #define IDS_Color256        21
0087  #define IDS_Color65000      22
0088  #define IDS_Color2          23
0089  #define IDS_ColorCustom     24
0090  #define IDS_Machine         25
0091  #define IDS_Enhanced        26
0092  #define IDS_Standard        27
0093  #define IDS_Real            28
0094  #define IDS_Ready           29
0095  #define IDS_NotReady        30
0096  #define IDS_NoMem           31
0097  #define IDS_FrameOK         32
0098  #define IDS_ReqdHdwr1       33
0099  #define IDS_ReqdHdwr2       34
0100  /*
0101  ---------------------------------------------------------------
0102                              End of include file
0103  ---------------------------------------------------------------
0104                                                              */
0001  /*
0002  ---------------------------------------------------------------
0003                      Resource script file startup.rc
0004                  Copyright 1993 Lee Adams.  All rights reserved.
0005    This file defines the menu resources, the accelerator key
0006    resources, and the string resources that will be used by the
0007    demonstration application at runtime.
0008  ---------------------------------------------------------------
0009                                                              */
0010  #define zRCFILE
0011  #include <WINDOWS.H>
```

C-1 Continued.

```
0012    #include "STARTUP.H"
0013    /*
0014    --------------------------------------------------------------------
0015                            Script for menus
0016    --------------------------------------------------------------------
0017                                                                     */
0018    MENUS1 MENU
0019      BEGIN
0020      POPUP "&File"
0021        BEGIN
0022          MENUITEM  "&New", IDM_New, GRAYED
0023          MENUITEM  "&Open...", IDM_Open, GRAYED
0024          MENUITEM  "&Save", IDM_Save, GRAYED
0025          MENUITEM  "Save &As...", IDM_SaveAs, GRAYED
0026          MENUITEM SEPARATOR
0027          MENUITEM  "E&xit...", IDM_Exit
0028          MENUITEM  "&Restart Windows...", IDM_Restart
0029        END
0030      POPUP "&Edit"
0031        BEGIN
0032          MENUITEM  "&Undo\tAlt+BkSp", IDM_Undo, GRAYED
0033          MENUITEM SEPARATOR
0034          MENUITEM  "Cu&t\tShift+Del", IDM_Cut, GRAYED
0035          MENUITEM  "&Copy\tCtrl+Ins", IDM_Copy, GRAYED
0036          MENUITEM  "&Paste\tShift+Ins", IDM_Paste, GRAYED
0037          MENUITEM  "&Delete\tDel", IDM_Delete, GRAYED
0038        END
0039      POPUP "&Go"
0040        BEGIN
0041          POPUP "Nested menu &1..."
0042            BEGIN
0043            MENUITEM  "Menu item &1", IDM_ItemA
0044            MENUITEM  "Menu item &2", IDM_ItemB
0045            MENUITEM  "Menu item &3", IDM_ItemC
0046            END
0047          POPUP "Nested menu &2..."
0048            BEGIN
0049            MENUITEM  "Menu item &1", IDM_ItemD
0050            MENUITEM  "Menu item &2", IDM_ItemE
0051            END
0052          MENUITEM SEPARATOR
0053          MENUITEM  "Font demo", IDM_ItemF
0054          MENUITEM  "Color demo", IDM_ItemG
0055          MENUITEM SEPARATOR
0056          MENUITEM  "Cle&ar Viewport", IDM_Clear
0057        END
0058      POPUP "&Use"
0059        BEGIN
0060          MENUITEM "&About", IDM_About
0061          MENUITEM "&License", IDM_License
0062          MENUITEM SEPARATOR
0063          MENUITEM "&Resolution of display", IDM_Display
0064          MENUITEM "Available &colors", IDM_Colors
0065          MENUITEM "&Memory mode", IDM_Mode
0066          MENUITEM "Windows &version", IDM_Version
0067          MENUITEM SEPARATOR
0068          MENUITEM "&How to use", IDM_GeneralHelp
0069        END
0070      END
0071    /*
0072    --------------------------------------------------------------------
```

```
0073                    Script for accelerator keys
0074   ---------------------------------------------------------------
0075                                                               */
0076   KEYS1 ACCELERATORS
0077     BEGIN
0078     VK_BACK, IDM_Undo, VIRTKEY, ALT
0079     VK_DELETE, IDM_Cut, VIRTKEY, SHIFT
0080     VK_INSERT, IDM_Copy, VIRTKEY, CONTROL
0081     VK_INSERT, IDM_Paste, VIRTKEY, SHIFT
0082     VK_DELETE, IDM_Delete, VIRTKEY
0083     END
0084   /*
0085   ---------------------------------------------------------------
0086                       Script for strings
0087     If you are typing this listing, set your right margin to 255
0088     characters so you can create lengthy strings without embedded
0089     carriage returns.  The line wraparounds in the following
0090     STRINGTABLE script are used only for readability.
0091   ---------------------------------------------------------------
0092                                                               */
0093   STRINGTABLE
0094     BEGIN
0095       IDS_Caption      "Programmer's Template"
0096       IDS_Warning      "Graphics system warning"
0097       IDS_NoMouse      "No mouse found.  Some features of this
                 demonstration program may require a mouse."
0098       IDS_About        "About this program"
0099       IDS_AboutText    "This is a demo from Windcrest McGraw-Hill
                 book 4115.  Copyright- 1993 Lee Adams.  All rights reserved."
0100       IDS_License      "License Agreement"
0101       IDS_LicenseText "You can use this code as part of your own
                 software product subject to the License Agreement and
                 Limited Warranty in Windcrest McGraw-Hill book 4115 and on
                 its companion disk."
0102       IDS_Help         "How to use this demo"
0103       IDS_HelpText     "Select from the Go menu to explore menuing.
                 Select from the Use menu to determine display resolution,
                 available colors, runtime memory mode, and more.  Also see
                 the discussion in Windcrest/McGraw-Hill book 4115."
0104       IDS_Resolution   "Screen resolution"
0105       IDS_ResVGA       "Running in 640-by-480 mode."
0106       IDS_ResEGA       "Running in 640-by-350 mode."
0107       IDS_ResCGA       "Running in 640-by-200 mode."
0108       IDS_ResSVGA      "Running in 800-by-600 mode."
0109       IDS_Res8514      "Running in 1024-by-768 mode."
0110       IDS_ResHerc      "Running in 720-by-348 mode."
0111       IDS_ResCustom    "Running in a custom-resolution mode."
0112       IDS_Color        "Available colors"
0113       IDS_Color16      "Running in 4-bit, 16-color mode."
0114       IDS_Color256     "Running in 8-bit, 256-color mode."
0115       IDS_Color2       "Running in 1-bit, 2-color mode."
0116       IDS_Color65000   "Running in 16-bit, 65000-color mode."
0117       IDS_ColorCustom "Running in 24-bit, 16.7 million-color mode."
0118       IDS_Machine      "Memory mode"
0119       IDS_Enhanced     "Running in enhanced mode.  Can allocate up to
                 16 MB extended physical memory (XMS) if available.  Virtual
                 memory up to 4 times physical memory (maximum 64 MB) is also
                 available via automatic disk swapping of 4K pages."
0120       IDS_Standard     "Running in standard mode.  Can allocate up to
                 16 MB extended physical memory (XMS) if available."
0121       IDS_Real         "Running in real mode.  Can allocate blocks of
```

```
                        memory from the first 640K of RAM.  Can also allocate blocks
                        from expanded memory (EMS) if available."
0122      IDS_Ready          "Graphics system ready"
0123      IDS_NotReady       "Graphics system not ready"
0124      IDS_NoMem          "Insufficient memory.  Hidden frame not
                        created.  Any images you create will not be preserved if the
                        window is covered or clipped.  Close other applications to
                        free memory and restart this demo."
0125      IDS_FrameOK        "The hidden frame has been successfully
                        created and ready for use in refreshing the viewport."
0126      IDS_ReqdHdwr1   "Graphics hardware"
0127      IDS_ReqdHdwr2   "CGA, HGA, or EGA graphics card has been
                        detected.  This demo requires an industry-standard VGA or a
                        VESA-standard SuperVGA and compatible display -- or a
                        graphics accelerator card (16-bit or 24-bit) and appropriate
                        display."
0128      END
0129      /*
0130      ----------------------------------------------------------------
0131                        End of resource script file
0132      ----------------------------------------------------------------
0133                                                                    */
0001      /*
0002      ----------------------------------------------------------------
0003                   Programmer's template and compiler tester
0004      ----------------------------------------------------------------
0005      Source file: startup.c
0006      Release version: 2.00               Programmer: Lee Adams
0007      Type:  C source file for Windows application development.
0008      Supported compilers:  Explicit compatibility with Microsoft
0009        QuickC for Windows v1.00 and Borland Turbo C++ for Windows
0010        v3.0.  Nominal compatibility with all Windows-compatible C
0011        and C++ compilers such as Borland C++, Zortech C++, Watcom C,
0012        and Microsoft C/C++.
0013      Memory model:  medium.
0014      Build notes:  Use this sample application to test your compiler
0015        before you build the other demos.  For trouble-free compiling
0016        follow the tips in the book.
0017      Project notes:  Load the objects.mak project file if you are
0018        using QuickC for Windows.  Load the objects.prj file if you
0019        are using Turbo C++ for Windows.  Refer to the book if you
0020        are using another compiler.  The following files are needed
0021        to build the executable.
0022          startup.def      module definition file
0023          startup.h        include file
0024          startup.rc       resource script file
0025          startup.c        C source file
0026      Output and features:  Demonstrates a display-independent,
0027        extensible application that can be used as a template to
0028        build graphics software for Windows.  This template will
0029        produce a consistent display in the following display
0030        resolutions:  640x480, 800x600, and 1024x768.  The palette
0031        demo operates correctly in the following color modes:
0032        1-bit (2-color), 4-bit (16-color), 8-bit (256-color),
0033        16-bit (65000-color), and 24-bit (16.7 million colors).
0034        The results achieved on your system depend on the graphics
0035        card and display monitor.
0036      Publication: Contains material from Windcrest/McGraw-Hill book
0037        4115 published by TAB BOOKS Division of McGraw-Hill Inc.
0038      License:  As purchaser of the book you are granted a royalty-
0039        free license to distribute executable files generated using
```

```
0040        this code provided you accept the conditions of the License
0041        Agreement and Limited Warranty described in the book and on
0042        the companion disk.  Government users:  This software and
0043        documentation are subject to restrictions set forth in The
0044        Rights in Technical Data and Computer Software clause at
0045        252.227-7013 and elsewhere.
0046   -----------------------------------------------------------------
0047        (c) Copyright 1991-1993 Lee Adams.  All rights reserved.
0048             Lee Adams(tm) is a trademark of Lee Adams.
0049   -----------------------------------------------------------------
0050
0051   -----------------------------------------------------------------
0052                           Include files
0053   -----------------------------------------------------------------
0054                                                                  */
0055   #include <WINDOWS.H>                /* declarations for Windows API */
0056   #include "STARTUP.H"            /* declares function prototypes, etc. */
0057
0058   /*
0059   -----------------------------------------------------------------
0060              Static variables visible throughout this file
0061   -----------------------------------------------------------------
0062                                                                  */
0063   /* ----------------- window specifications ------------------ */
0064   #define zWINDOW_WIDTH 263                        /* width of window */
0065   #define zWINDOW_HEIGHT 300                       /* depth of window */
0066   #define zFRAMEWIDE 256                          /* width of viewport */
0067   #define zFRAMEHIGH 255                         /* depth of viewporta */
0068   int WindowX, WindowY;                         /* location of window */
0069
0070   /* ----------------- instance operations ------------------- */
0071   HANDLE hInst;                      /* handle to this copy of the app */
0072   HWND MainhWnd;                         /* handle to the app's window */
0073   HANDLE hAccel;                        /* handle to the accelerator keys */
0074   HMENU hMenu;                   /* handle to an active menu at runtime */
0075   PAINTSTRUCT ps;                /* used for Windows-generated refreshes */
0076   int MessageRet;               /* will receive value returned by system */
0077
0078   /* ----------------- mouse and cursor -------------------- */
0079   HCURSOR hPrevCursor;                     /* handle to arrow cursor */
0080   HCURSOR hHourGlass;                  /* handle to hourglass cursor */
0081   int MousePresent;                       /* indicates if mouse found */
0082
0083   /* ----------------- runtime conditions -------------------- */
0084   int DisplayWidth, DisplayHeight;       /* resolution of display */
0085   int DisplayBits;                      /* number of bits per pixel */
0086   int DisplayPlanes;                        /* number of bitplanes */
0087   DWORD MemoryMode;                       /* runtime memory mode */
0088   static DWORD Version;                      /* version of Windows */
0089   static BOOL bUseArial= TRUE;      /* FALSE, use Helv if Windows 3.0 */
0090
0091   /* ----------------- message box operations ----------------- */
0092   char lpCaption[51];               /* stores caption for message box */
0093   int Max= 50;                        /* max length of caption */
0094   char lpMessage[250];              /* stores text for message box */
0095   int MaxText= 249;                      /* max length of text */
0096   int MessageBoxChoice= 0;            /* user's selection, if any */
0097
0098   /* ----------------- font operations -------------------- */
0099   HFONT hFont, hPrevFont;           /* handles to new, previous font */
0100   HDC hFontDC;                         /* display-context for font */
```

```
0101
0102   /* -------------- persistent image operations ----------------- */
0103   #define zBLANK 0
0104   #define zIMAGE 1
0105   int PaintImage= zBLANK;              /* indicates viewport status */
0106
0107   /* -----------------hidden frame operations ------------------- */
0108   HDC hFrameDC;                   /* display-context of hidden-frame */
0109   HBITMAP hFrame;                      /* bitmap of hidden-frame */
0110   HBITMAP hPrevFrame;                       /* default bitmap */
0111   BOOL FrameReady= FALSE;              /* hidden-frame ready? */
0112
0113   /*
0114   -------------------------------------------------------------------
0115                    Entry point for the application
0116   -------------------------------------------------------------------
0117                                                                  */
0118   int PASCAL WinMain(HANDLE hInstance, HANDLE hPrevInstance,
0119                      LPSTR lpCmdLine, int nCmdShow)
0120   {
0121     MSG msg;                             /* holds incoming messages */
0122     HWND hWndPrev;                  /* handle to previous copy of app */
0123     HWND hDesktopWnd;                /* handle to the entire display */
0124     HDC hDCcaps;          /* display-context for the entire display */
0125     RECT rcClientReqd;        /* size of viewport before adjustment */
0126     int AdjustX, AdjustY; /* amount to adjust to ensure 256-by-255 */
0127
0128   /* -------------- ensure only one copy is running -------------- */
0129   hWndPrev = FindWindow("DEMOCLASS", NULL);
0130   if (hWndPrev != NULL)
0131     {          /* if another app of class DEMOCLASS is running... */
0132     BringWindowToTop(hWndPrev);              /* use it instead... */
0133     return FALSE;                   /* ...and cancel this launch */
0134     }
0135
0136   /* ------------- display the splash signon notice ------------- */
0137   MessageBoxChoice= MessageBox(GetFocus(),
0138   "Graphics demo from Windcrest McGraw-Hill book 4115",
0139   "Copyright- 1993 Lee Adams", MB_OKCANCEL);
0140   if (MessageBoxChoice == IDCANCEL) return FALSE;
0141
0142   /* --------------- determine version of Windows --------------- */
0143   Version= (DWORD)GetVersion();
0144   if ((LOBYTE(LOWORD(Version))==3) &&
0145      (HIBYTE(LOWORD(Version))==0))
0146     {                         /* if running Windows version 3.0... */
0147     bUseArial= FALSE;           /* ...use Helv font in client area */
0148     }
0149   else
0150     {               /* ...else if running Windows 3.1 or newer... */
0151     bUseArial= TRUE;          /* ...use Arial font in client area */
0152     }
0153
0154   /* --------- determine capabilities of screen display --------- */
0155   hDesktopWnd= GetDesktopWindow();
0156   hDCcaps= GetDC(hDesktopWnd);
0157   DisplayWidth= GetDeviceCaps(hDCcaps,HORZRES);
0158   DisplayHeight= GetDeviceCaps(hDCcaps,VERTRES);
0159   DisplayBits= GetDeviceCaps(hDCcaps,BITSPIXEL);
0160   DisplayPlanes= GetDeviceCaps(hDCcaps,PLANES);
0161   ReleaseDC(hDesktopWnd,hDCcaps);
```

```
0162
0163   /* ------------- trap unsupported graphics adapters ------------ */
0164   if (DisplayWidth==720)
0165       {                                        /* if HGA detected... */
0166       LoadString(hInstance,IDS_ReqdHdwr1,lpCaption,Max);
0167       LoadString(hInstance,IDS_ReqdHdwr2,lpMessage,MaxText);
0168       MessageBeep(0); MessageBox(GetFocus(),lpMessage,lpCaption,MB_OK);
0169       return FALSE;
0170       }
0171   if (DisplayWidth==640)
0172       {
0173       if ((DisplayHeight==350)||(DisplayHeight==200))
0174           {                                    /* if EGA or CGA detected... */
0175           LoadString(hInstance,IDS_ReqdHdwr1,lpCaption,Max);
0176           LoadString(hInstance,IDS_ReqdHdwr2,lpMessage,MaxText);
0177           MessageBeep(0);
0178           MessageBox(GetFocus(),lpMessage,lpCaption,MB_OK);
0179           return FALSE;
0180           }
0181       }
0182
0183   /* ------- calculate screen position to center the window ------ */
0184   WindowX= (DisplayWidth - zWINDOW_WIDTH) / 2;        /* horizontal */
0185   WindowY= (DisplayHeight - zWINDOW_HEIGHT) /2;         /* vertical */
0186   if (WindowX < 0) WindowX= 0;                          /* failsafe */
0187   if (WindowY < 0) WindowY= 0;                          /* failsafe */
0188
0189   /* ---- determine memory mode (enhanced, standard, or real) ---- */
0190   MemoryMode= GetWinFlags(); /* software will use this value later */
0191
0192   /* --------------- create and show the window --------------- */
0193   hInst= hInstance;             /* store handle to this copy of the app */
0194   if (!zInitClass(hInstance)) return FALSE;      /* initialize class */
0195   MainhWnd= zInitMainWindow(hInstance);          /* initialize window */
0196   if (!MainhWnd) return FALSE;         /* if error, cancel startup */
0197   ShowWindow(MainhWnd, nCmdShow);                 /* show the window */
0198   UpdateWindow(MainhWnd);                          /* force a refresh */
0199   hAccel= LoadAccelerators(hInstance,"KEYS1");      /* activate keys */
0200
0201   /* ------------- enforce a 256-by-255 client area ------------- */
0202   GetClientRect(MainhWnd, &rcClientReqd);          /* get dimensions */
0203   AdjustX=              /* compare actual width to desired width... */
0204           zFRAMEWIDE - (rcClientReqd.right + 1);
0205   AdjustY=              /* compare actual height to desired height... */
0206           zFRAMEHIGH - (rcClientReqd.bottom + 1);
0207   if ((AdjustX != 0)||(AdjustY != 0)) /* if adjustment required... */
0208       {
0209       SetWindowPos(MainhWnd, (HWND)NULL,
0210                   WindowX, WindowY,         /* retain same location */
0211                   zWINDOW_WIDTH + AdjustX,      /* resize the width */
0212                   zWINDOW_HEIGHT + AdjustY,     /* resize the height */
0213                   SWP_NOZORDER);               /* retain same order */
0214       }
0215
0216   /* --------------------- check for mouse --------------------- */
0217   MousePresent= GetSystemMetrics(SM_MOUSEPRESENT);
0218   if (!MousePresent)                        /* if no mouse found... */
0219       {
0220       LoadString(hInst,IDS_Warning,lpCaption,Max);   /* load caption */
0221       LoadString(hInst,IDS_NoMouse,lpMessage,MaxText); /* load text */
0222       MessageBox(GetFocus(),lpMessage,lpCaption,MB_OK);   /* message */
```

```
0223    }
0224
0225    /* ------------ initialize the drawing environment ----------- */
0226    zInitFrame(MainhWnd);   /* initialize hidden frame for refreshes */
0227
0228    /* ---------- begin retrieving messages for the window --------- */
0229    while (GetMessage(&msg,0,0,0))
0230      {
0231      if(TranslateAccelerator(MainhWnd, hAccel, &msg)) continue;
0232      TranslateMessage(&msg);
0233      DispatchMessage(&msg);
0234      }
0235    return(msg.wParam);
0236    }
0237
0238    /*
0239    -------------------------------------------------------------------
0240                        Switcher for incoming messages
0241    -------------------------------------------------------------------
0242                                                                      */
0243    LONG FAR PASCAL zMessageHandler(HWND hWnd, unsigned message,
0244                                    WORD wParam, LONG lParam)
0245    {
0246      HDC hDCpaint;         /* display-context for persistent graphics */
0247
0248    switch (message)
0249      {
0250      /* ------------------ menu system commands ----------------- */
0251      case WM_COMMAND:
0252        switch(wParam)
0253          {
0254          case IDM_New:      break;
0255          case IDM_Open:     break;
0256          case IDM_Save:     break;
0257          case IDM_SaveAs:   break;
0258          case IDM_Exit:
0259              MessageBoxChoice= MessageBox(GetFocus(),
0260                "Exit the demo and return to Windows?",
0261                "Please confirm", MB_YESNO);
0262              if (MessageBoxChoice == IDYES) PostQuitMessage(0);
0263              break;
0264          case IDM_Restart:
0265              MessageBoxChoice= MessageBox(GetFocus(),
0266                "Exit the demo and restart Windows?",
0267                "Please confirm", MB_YESNO);
0268              if (MessageBoxChoice == IDYES) ExitWindows(0x42L,0);
0269              break;
0270          case IDM_Undo:     break;
0271          case IDM_Cut:      break;
0272          case IDM_Copy:     break;
0273          case IDM_Paste:    break;
0274          case IDM_Delete:   break;
0275
0276          case IDM_ItemA:                             /* a stub... */
0277              MessageBeep(0);
0278              MessageBox(GetFocus(),
0279                "You selected Item 1 from Nested Menu 1.",
0280                "Menu selection report", MB_OK);
0281              break;
0282          case IDM_ItemB:                             /* a stub... */
0283              MessageBeep(0);
```

```
0284            MessageBox(GetFocus(),
0285              "You selected Item 2 from Nested Menu 1.",
0286              "Menu selection report", MB_OK);
0287            break;
0288          case IDM_ItemC:                            /* a stub... */
0289            MessageBeep(0);
0290            MessageBox(GetFocus(),
0291              "You selected Item 3 from Nested Menu 1.",
0292              "Menu selection report", MB_OK);
0293            break;
0294
0295          case IDM_ItemD:                            /* a stub... */
0296            MessageBeep(0);
0297            MessageBox(GetFocus(),
0298              "You selected Item 1 from Nested Menu 2.",
0299              "Menu selection report", MB_OK);
0300            break;
0301          case IDM_ItemE:                            /* a stub... */
0302            MessageBeep(0);
0303            MessageBox(GetFocus(),
0304              "You selected Item 2 from Nested Menu 2.",
0305              "Menu selection report", MB_OK);
0306            break;
0307
0308          case IDM_ItemF:              /* some sample graphics... */
0309            SetCapture(hWnd);                       /* lock the mouse */
0310            hPrevCursor= SetCursor(hHourGlass); /* hourglass cursor */
0311            zClear(hWnd);                       /* clear the viewport */
0312            /* ----------- perform drawing operations ----------- */
0313            zDrawItemF(hWnd);
0314            hFontDC= GetDC(MainhWnd);    /* display the captions... */
0315            hFont= GetStockObject(SYSTEM_FONT);
0316            hPrevFont= SelectObject(hFontDC,hFont);
0317            SetTextColor(hFontDC,RGB(0,0,0));
0318            SetBkMode(hFontDC,TRANSPARENT);
0319            if (bUseArial == FALSE)
0320              {                        /* if using Helv for titling... */
0321              TextOut(hFontDC,10,214,
0322                "The titles use the Helv font.",29);
0323              }
0324            if (bUseArial == TRUE)
0325              {                        /* if using Arial for titling... */
0326              TextOut(hFontDC,10,214,
0327                "The titles use the Arial font.",30);
0328              }
0329            TextOut(hFontDC,10,230,
0330              "This caption uses the system font.",34);
0331            SetTextColor(hFontDC,RGB(255,255,255));
0332            SelectObject(hFontDC,hPrevFont);
0333            ReleaseDC(MainhWnd,hFontDC);
0334            /* ----------- perform system maintenance ----------- */
0335            PaintImage= zIMAGE;
0336            if (FrameReady==TRUE) zCopyToFrame(hWnd);
0337            SetCursor(hPrevCursor);      /* restore previous cursor */
0338            ReleaseCapture();                       /* unlock mouse */
0339            break;
0340
0341          case IDM_ItemG:              /* some sample graphics... */
0342            SetCapture(hWnd);                       /* lock the mouse */
0343            hPrevCursor= SetCursor(hHourGlass); /* hourglass cursor */
0344            zClear(hWnd);                       /* clear the viewport */
```

```
0345                /* ------------ perform drawing operations ------------ */
0346                zDrawItemG(hWnd);              /* call a drawing function */
0347                zBuildPalette(hWnd);           /* call a drawing function */
0348                hFontDC= GetDC(MainhWnd);      /* display the captions... */
0349                hFont= GetStockObject(SYSTEM_FONT);
0350                hPrevFont= SelectObject(hFontDC,hFont);
0351                SetTextColor(hFontDC,RGB(0,0,0));
0352                SetBkMode(hFontDC,TRANSPARENT);
0353                TextOut(hFontDC,10,214,
0354                  "Top:  the default color-palette.",32);
0355                TextOut(hFontDC,10,230,
0356                  "Below:  a custom color-palette.",31);
0357                SetTextColor(hFontDC,RGB(255,255,255));
0358                SelectObject(hFontDC,hPrevFont);
0359                ReleaseDC(MainhWnd,hFontDC);
0360                /* ----------- perform system maintenance ------------ */
0361                PaintImage= zIMAGE;
0362                if (FrameReady==TRUE) zCopyToFrame(hWnd);
0363                SetCursor(hPrevCursor);        /* restore previous cursor */
0364                ReleaseCapture();                       /* unlock mouse */
0365                break;
0366
0367            case IDM_Clear:                        /* clear the viewport */
0368                zClear(hWnd);
0369                PaintImage= zBLANK;
0370                if (FrameReady == TRUE) zCopyToFrame(hWnd);
0371                break;
0372
0373            /* ----- display the About and License message boxes ----- */
0374            case IDM_About:
0375              LoadString(hInst,IDS_About,lpCaption,Max);
0376              LoadString(hInst,IDS_AboutText,lpMessage,MaxText);
0377              MessageBox(GetFocus(),lpMessage,lpCaption,MB_OK);
0378              break;
0379            case IDM_License:
0380              LoadString(hInst,IDS_License,lpCaption,Max);
0381              LoadString(hInst,IDS_LicenseText,lpMessage,MaxText);
0382              MessageBox(GetFocus(),lpMessage,lpCaption,MB_OK);
0383              break;
0384
0385            /* ------------- report the display resolution ----------- */
0386            case IDM_Display:
0387              if (DisplayWidth==640)
0388                {
0389                if (DisplayHeight==480)
0390                  {                        /* 640-by-480 VGA mode detected */
0391                  LoadString(hInst,IDS_Resolution,lpCaption,Max);
0392                  LoadString(hInst,IDS_ResVGA,lpMessage,MaxText);
0393                  MessageBox(GetFocus(),lpMessage,lpCaption,MB_OK);
0394                  }
0395                if (DisplayHeight==350)      /* (not used in this demo) */
0396                  {                        /* 640-by-350 EGA mode detected */
0397                  LoadString(hInst,IDS_Resolution,lpCaption,Max);
0398                  LoadString(hInst,IDS_ResEGA,lpMessage,MaxText);
0399                  MessageBox(GetFocus(),lpMessage,lpCaption,MB_OK);
0400                  }
0401                if (DisplayHeight==200)      /* (not used in this demo) */
0402                  {                        /* 640-by-200 CGA mode detected */
0403                  LoadString(hInst,IDS_Resolution,lpCaption,Max);
0404                  LoadString(hInst,IDS_ResCGA,lpMessage,MaxText);
0405                  MessageBox(GetFocus(),lpMessage,lpCaption,MB_OK);
```

```
0406                    }
0407                  break;
0408                  }
0409            if (DisplayWidth==800)
0410                  {                    /* 800-by-600 SVGA mode detected */
0411              LoadString(hInst,IDS_Resolution,lpCaption,Max);
0412              LoadString(hInst,IDS_ResSVGA,lpMessage,MaxText);
0413              MessageBox(GetFocus(),lpMessage,lpCaption,MB_OK);
0414              break;
0415                  }
0416            if (DisplayWidth==1024)
0417                  {                    /* 1024-by-768 SVGA mode detected */
0418              LoadString(hInst,IDS_Resolution,lpCaption,Max);
0419              LoadString(hInst,IDS_Res8514,lpMessage,MaxText);
0420              MessageBox(GetFocus(),lpMessage,lpCaption,MB_OK);
0421              break;
0422                  }
0423            if (DisplayWidth==720)           /* (not used in this demo) */
0424                  {                    /* 720-by-348 HGA mode detected */
0425              LoadString(hInst,IDS_Resolution,lpCaption,Max);
0426              LoadString(hInst,IDS_ResHerc,lpMessage,MaxText);
0427              MessageBox(GetFocus(),lpMessage,lpCaption,MB_OK);
0428              break;
0429                  }
0430            LoadString(hInst,IDS_Resolution,lpCaption,Max);
0431            LoadString(hInst,IDS_ResCustom,lpMessage,MaxText);
0432            MessageBox(GetFocus(),lpMessage,lpCaption,MB_OK);
0433            break;
0434
0435            /* -------- report the display color capabilities -------- */
0436            case IDM_Colors:
0437              if (DisplayBits==1)
0438                  {
0439                if (DisplayPlanes==4)
0440                    {                    /* 4-bit, 16-color mode detected */
0441                  LoadString(hInst,IDS_Color,lpCaption,Max);
0442                  LoadString(hInst,IDS_Color16,lpMessage,MaxText);
0443                  MessageBox(GetFocus(),lpMessage,lpCaption,MB_OK);
0444                  break;
0445                    }
0446                if (DisplayPlanes==1)
0447                    {                    /* 1-bit, 2-color mode detected */
0448                  LoadString(hInst,IDS_Color,lpCaption,Max);
0449                  LoadString(hInst,IDS_Color2,lpMessage,MaxText);
0450                  MessageBox(GetFocus(),lpMessage,lpCaption,MB_OK);
0451                  break;
0452                    }
0453                  }
0454              if (DisplayBits==8)
0455                  {                    /* 8-bit, 256-color mode detected */
0456                LoadString(hInst,IDS_Color,lpCaption,Max);
0457                LoadString(hInst,IDS_Color256,lpMessage,MaxText);
0458                MessageBox(GetFocus(),lpMessage,lpCaption,MB_OK);
0459                break;
0460                  }
0461              if (DisplayBits==16)
0462                  {                    /* 16-bit, 65000-color mode detected */
0463                LoadString(hInst,IDS_Color,lpCaption,Max);
0464                LoadString(hInst,IDS_Color65000,lpMessage,MaxText);
0465                MessageBox(GetFocus(),lpMessage,lpCaption,MB_OK);
0466                break;
```

```
0467                }
0468                LoadString(hInst,IDS_Color,lpCaption,Max);
0469                LoadString(hInst,IDS_ColorCustom,lpMessage,MaxText);
0470                MessageBox(GetFocus(),lpMessage,lpCaption,MB_OK);
0471                break;
0472
0473            /* ------------ report the runtime memory mode ----------- */
0474            case IDM_Mode:
0475                if (MemoryMode & WF_ENHANCED)
0476                  {                             /* enhanced mode detected */
0477                  LoadString(hInst,IDS_Machine,lpCaption,Max);
0478                  LoadString(hInst,IDS_Enhanced,lpMessage,MaxText);
0479                  MessageBox(GetFocus(),lpMessage,lpCaption,MB_OK);
0480                  break;
0481                  }
0482                if (MemoryMode & WF_STANDARD)
0483                  {                             /* standard mode detected */
0484                  LoadString(hInst,IDS_Machine,lpCaption,Max);
0485                  LoadString(hInst,IDS_Standard,lpMessage,MaxText);
0486                  MessageBox(GetFocus(),lpMessage,lpCaption,MB_OK);
0487                  break;
0488                  }
0489                LoadString(hInst,IDS_Machine,lpCaption,Max);
0490                LoadString(hInst,IDS_Real,lpMessage,MaxText);
0491                MessageBox(GetFocus(),lpMessage,lpCaption,MB_OK);
0492                break;
0493
0494            /* ----------- report the version of Windows ----------- */
0495            case IDM_Version:
0496                if ((LOBYTE(LOWORD(Version))==3) &&
0497                  (HIBYTE(LOWORD(Version))==0))
0498                  {                      /* if running Windows version 3.0... */
0499                  MessageBox(GetFocus(),
0500                    "Running under Windows version 3.0.",
0501                    "Version report", MB_OK);
0502                  }
0503                else if ((LOBYTE(LOWORD(Version))==3) &&
0504                       (HIBYTE(LOWORD(Version))==10))
0505                  {                      /* if running Windows version 3.1... */
0506                  MessageBox(GetFocus(),
0507                    "Running under Windows version 3.1.",
0508                    "Version report", MB_OK);
0509                  }
0510                else if ((LOBYTE(LOWORD(Version))==3) &&
0511                       (HIBYTE(LOWORD(Version))==20))
0512                  {                      /* if running Windows version 3.2... */
0513                  MessageBox(GetFocus(),
0514                    "Running under Windows version 3.2.",
0515                    "Version report", MB_OK);
0516                  }
0517                else if ((LOBYTE(LOWORD(Version))==3) &&
0518                       (HIBYTE(LOWORD(Version)) >= 30))
0519                  {        /* if running Windows version 3.3 or newer... */
0520                  MessageBox(GetFocus(),
0521                    "Running under Windows version 3.3 or newer.",
0522                    "Version report", MB_OK);
0523                  }
0524                else if (LOBYTE(LOWORD(Version))==4)
0525                  {                  /* if running Windows major version 4... */
0526                  MessageBox(GetFocus(),
0527                    "Running under Windows version 4.0 or newer.",
```

C-1 Continued.

```
0528                    "Version report", MB_OK);
0529               }
0530           else MessageBox(GetFocus(),
0531                   "Unable to report Windows version number.",
0532                   "Version report", MB_OK);
0533           break;
0534
0535       /* -------- display the runtime help message box --------- */
0536       case IDM_GeneralHelp:
0537         LoadString(hInst,IDS_Help,lpCaption,Max);
0538         LoadString(hInst,IDS_HelpText,lpMessage,MaxText);
0539         MessageBox(GetFocus(),lpMessage,lpCaption,MB_OK);
0540         break;
0541       default:
0542         return(DefWindowProc(hWnd, message, wParam, lParam));
0543     }
0544     break;
0545
0546   /* -------- oversee Windows-generated refresh requests ------- */
0547   case WM_PAINT:          /* if viewport needs to be refreshed... */
0548     hDCpaint= BeginPaint(hWnd,&ps);      /* load structure and... */
0549     EndPaint(hWnd, &ps);             /* ...validate the client area */
0550     if (PaintImage==zBLANK) break;      /* if blank do nothing */
0551     if (FrameReady==FALSE) break;    /* if no hidden frame, break */
0552     zCopyToDisplay(hWnd);    /* else copy hidden frame to display */
0553     break;
0554
0555   /* --------------- ensure a graceful shutdown --------------- */
0556   case WM_DESTROY:  /* if user is terminating the application... */
0557     if (FrameReady==TRUE)
0558       {                          /* remove the hidden frame bitmap */
0559       SelectObject(hFrameDC,hPrevFrame);
0560       DeleteObject(hFrame);
0561       DeleteDC(hFrameDC);
0562       }
0563     PostQuitMessage(0);
0564     break;
0565
0566   /* ---- trap attempts to resize, minimize, maximize window --- */
0567   case WM_SYSCOMMAND:
0568     if ((wParam & 0xfff0)== SC_SIZE)
0569       {
0570       MessageBeep(0); break;
0571       }
0572     if ((wParam & 0xfff0)== SC_MINIMIZE)
0573       {
0574       MessageBeep(0); break;
0575       }
0576     if ((wParam & 0xfff0)== SC_MAXIMIZE)
0577       {
0578       MessageBeep(0); break;
0579       }
0580
0581   /* ------- pass any unprocessed messages to the system ------- */
0582   default:
0583     return(DefWindowProc(hWnd, message, wParam, lParam));
0584   }
0585 return FALSE;
0586 }
0587 /*
0588 -------------------------------------------------------------------
```

```
0589                  Initialize the attributes of the window class
0590    -------------------------------------------------------------------
0591                                                                     */
0592    BOOL zInitClass(HANDLE hInstance)
0593    {
0594      WNDCLASS WndClass;
0595    WndClass.style= 0;                                     /* class style */
0596    WndClass.lpfnWndProc= zMessageHandler;  /* app's message handler */
0597    WndClass.cbClsExtra= 0;              /* unused, no customized data */
0598    WndClass.cbWndExtra= 0;              /* unused, no customized data */
0599    WndClass.hInstance= hInstance;           /* this copy of the app */
0600    WndClass.hIcon= LoadIcon(NULL,IDI_EXCLAMATION);     /* app's icon */
0601    WndClass.hCursor= LoadCursor(NULL,IDC_ARROW);     /* app's cursor */
0602    WndClass.hbrBackground=      /* background color for the viewport */
0603                     CreateSolidBrush(RGB(255,255,255));
0604    WndClass.lpszMenuName= "MENUS1";      /* menu script in .rc file */
0605    WndClass.lpszClassName= "DEMOCLASS";    /* nominal name of class */
0606    return RegisterClass(&WndClass); /* tell Windows about the class */
0607    }
0608    /*
0609    -------------------------------------------------------------------
0610                          Create the main window
0611    -------------------------------------------------------------------
0612                                                                     */
0613    HWND zInitMainWindow(HANDLE hInstance)
0614    {
0615      HWND hWnd;
0616    LoadString(hInstance,IDS_Caption,lpCaption,Max); /* load caption */
0617    hHourGlass= LoadCursor(NULL,IDC_WAIT);  /* load hourglass cursor */
0618    hWnd= CreateWindow("DEMOCLASS",                      /* class name */
0619         lpCaption,                            /* window caption */
0620         WS_OVERLAPPED | WS_THICKFRAME | WS_CLIPCHILDREN, /* style */
0621         WindowX,WindowY,                     /* location of window */
0622         zWINDOW_WIDTH,zWINDOW_HEIGHT,        /* dimensions of window */
0623         0,                               /* parent window, if any */
0624         0,                               /* special menu, if any */
0625         hInstance,                       /* this copy of the app */
0626         (LPSTR)NULL);    /* for multiple-document interface, if any */
0627    return hWnd;    /* return the newly-created handle to the caller */
0628    }
0629    /*
0630    -------------------------------------------------------------------
0631               THE CORE FUNCTIONS OF THE APPLICATION
0632    -------------------------------------------------------------------
0633    -------------------------------------------------------------------
0634                        Create the hidden frame.
0635    -------------------------------------------------------------------
0636                                                                     */
0637    static void zInitFrame(HWND hWnd)
0638    {
0639      HDC hDisplayDC;                           /* display-context */
0640
0641    GlobalCompact((DWORD)-1L);         /* maximize contiguous memory */
0642    hDisplayDC= GetDC(hWnd);               /* set the display-context */
0643    hFrameDC= CreateCompatibleDC(hDisplayDC);    /* create frame... */
0644    hFrame= CreateCompatibleBitmap(hDisplayDC,zFRAMEWIDE,zFRAMEHIGH);
0645    if (hFrame==NULL)
0646      {
0647      LoadString(hInst,IDS_NotReady,lpCaption,Max);
0648      LoadString(hInst,IDS_NoMem,lpMessage,MaxText);
0649      MessageBox(GetFocus(),lpMessage,lpCaption,MB_OK);
```

```
0650    DeleteDC(hFrameDC);
0651    FrameReady= FALSE;
0652    return;
0653    }
0654 hPrevFrame= SelectObject(hFrameDC,hFrame);  /* select the bitmap */
0655 zClearHiddenFrame();                        /* clear the hidden frame */
0656 ReleaseDC(hWnd,hDisplayDC);         /* release the display-context */
0657 FrameReady= TRUE;                           /* set a global token */
0658 return;
0659 }
0660 /*
0661 ------------------------------------------------------------------
0662                   Clear the display window.
0663 ------------------------------------------------------------------
0664                                                                  */
0665 static void zClear(HWND hWnd)
0666 {
0667    HDC hDC;
0668 hDC= GetDC(hWnd);
0669 PatBlt(hDC,0,0,zFRAMEWIDE,zFRAMEHIGH,WHITENESS);
0670 ReleaseDC(hWnd,hDC);
0671 return;
0672 }
0673 /*
0674 ------------------------------------------------------------------
0675                   Clear the hidden frame.
0676 ------------------------------------------------------------------
0677                                                                  */
0678 static void zClearHiddenFrame(void)
0679 {
0680 if (FrameReady==FALSE) return;
0681 PatBlt(hFrameDC,0,0,zFRAMEWIDE,zFRAMEHIGH,WHITENESS);
0682 return;
0683 }
0684 /*
0685 ------------------------------------------------------------------
0686           Copy the hidden frame to the display window.
0687 ------------------------------------------------------------------
0688                                                                  */
0689 static void zCopyToDisplay(HWND hWnd)
0690 {
0691    HDC hDC;
0692 if (FrameReady==FALSE) return;
0693 hDC= GetDC(hWnd);
0694 BitBlt(hDC,0,0,zFRAMEWIDE,zFRAMEHIGH,hFrameDC,0,0,SRCCOPY);
0695 ReleaseDC(hWnd,hDC);
0696 return;
0697 }
0698 /*
0699 ------------------------------------------------------------------
0700           Copy the display window to the hidden frame.
0701 ------------------------------------------------------------------
0702                                                                  */
0703 static void zCopyToFrame(HWND hWnd)
0704 {
0705    HDC hDC;
0706 if (FrameReady==FALSE) return;
0707 hDC= GetDC(hWnd);
0708 BitBlt(hFrameDC,0,0,zFRAMEWIDE,zFRAMEHIGH,hDC,0,0,SRCCOPY);
0709 ReleaseDC(hWnd,hDC);
0710 return;
```

```
0711  }
0712  /*
0713  -----------------------------------------------------------------
0714                    Sample drawing function.
0715  -----------------------------------------------------------------
0716                                                                */
0717  static void zDrawItemF(HWND HandleWnd)
0718  {
0719    HFONT Font;                              /* handle to new font */
0720    HFONT PrevFont;                 /* handle to existing default font */
0721    DWORD PrevFontColor;              /* existing default font color */
0722    DWORD PrevBkColor;                        /* new font color */
0723    HDC hDC;                 /* handle to display-context for viewport */
0724
0725  /* ------------------ grab display-context -------------------- */
0726  hDC= GetDC(HandleWnd); /* uses handle to window received in call */
0727
0728  /* -------------------- display the titles -------------------- */
0729  if ((DisplayBits==1)&&(DisplayPlanes==1))
0730    {                    /* if a mono display use black typeface... */
0731    PrevFontColor= SetTextColor(hDC,RGB(0,0,0));        /* use black */
0732    PrevBkColor=  SetBkColor(hDC,RGB(255,255,255));    /* white bg */
0733    }
0734  else
0735    {   /* else if a color display use any solid color typeface... */
0736    PrevFontColor= SetTextColor(hDC,RGB(0,0,0)); /* use any color */
0737    PrevBkColor=  SetBkColor(hDC,RGB(255,255,255));    /* white bg */
0738    }
0739  SetBkMode(hDC,TRANSPARENT);    /* use transparent font background */
0740
0741  if (bUseArial == FALSE)
0742    {                     /* if running Windows 3.0 use Helv font... */
0743    Font= CreateFont(24, 0, 0, 0, FW_BOLD, FALSE, FALSE, FALSE,
0744         ANSI_CHARSET, OUT_DEFAULT_PRECIS, CLIP_DEFAULT_PRECIS,
0745         DRAFT_QUALITY, VARIABLE_PITCH | FF_SWISS, "Helv");
0746    PrevFont= SelectObject(hDC,Font);
0747    TextOut(hDC,10,6,"A Lee Adams tutorial:",21);
0748    Font= CreateFont(36, 0, 0, 0, FW_BOLD, FALSE, FALSE, FALSE,
0749         ANSI_CHARSET, OUT_DEFAULT_PRECIS, CLIP_DEFAULT_PRECIS,
0750         DRAFT_QUALITY, VARIABLE_PITCH | FF_SWISS, "Helv");
0751    SelectObject(hDC,Font);
0752    TextOut(hDC,8,24,"Font captions",13);
0753    }
0754  else   /* else if running Windows 3.1 or newer use Arial font... */
0755    {
0756    Font= CreateFont(24, 0, 0, 0, FW_BOLD, FALSE, FALSE, FALSE,
0757         ANSI_CHARSET, OUT_DEFAULT_PRECIS, CLIP_DEFAULT_PRECIS,
0758         DRAFT_QUALITY, VARIABLE_PITCH | FF_SWISS, "Arial");
0759    PrevFont= SelectObject(hDC,Font);
0760    TextOut(hDC,10,6,"A Lee Adams tutorial:",21);
0761    Font= CreateFont(36, 0, 0, 0, FW_BOLD, FALSE, FALSE, FALSE,
0762         ANSI_CHARSET, OUT_DEFAULT_PRECIS, CLIP_DEFAULT_PRECIS,
0763         DRAFT_QUALITY, VARIABLE_PITCH | FF_SWISS, "Arial");
0764    SelectObject(hDC,Font);
0765    TextOut(hDC,8,24,"Font captions",13);
0766    }
0767
0768  /* -------------------- tidy up and return -------------------- */
0769  SelectObject(hDC,PrevFont);                /* restore default font */
0770  SetBkMode(hDC,OPAQUE);             /* restore opaque font background */
0771  SetBkColor(hDC,PrevBkColor);              /* restore default bg color */
```

```
0772    SetTextColor(hDC,PrevFontColor);    /* restore default font color */
0773    ReleaseDC(HandleWnd,hDC);           /* release the display-context */
0774    return;                             /* return control to caller */
0775    }
0776    /*
0777    -------------------------------------------------------------------
0778                        Sample drawing function.
0779    -------------------------------------------------------------------
0780                                                                      */
0781    static void zDrawItemG(HWND HandleWnd)
0782    {
0783      HDC hDC;                  /* handle to display-context for viewport */
0784      HBRUSH hPrevBrush, hSwatchBrush;                     /* brushes */
0785      RECT rcSwatch;         /* data structure of 4 xy coords for rect */
0786      HPEN hPrevPen, hBorderPen;                              /* pens */
0787      int iWidth= 15, iDepth= 60;      /* width and depth of swatch */
0788      int iSwatchX= 8, iSwatchY= 70;   /* starting coords for swatch */
0789      int PaletteSize= 16;    /* number of colors in desired palette */
0790      NPLOGPALETTE pPalette;                /* ptr to logical palette */
0791      WORD iIndex;                  /* palette index and loop counter */
0792      HANDLE hPal;                        /* handle to logical palette */
0793      int iX1, iY1, iX2, iY2;          /* bounding coords for border */
0794      HFONT Font;                            /* handle to new font */
0795      HFONT PrevFont;                /* handle to existing default font */
0796      DWORD PrevFontColor;           /* existing default font color */
0797      DWORD PrevBkColor;                        /* new font color */
0798
0799    /* -------- create and initialize a palette data struct -------- */
0800    pPalette= (NPLOGPALETTE) LocalAlloc(LMEM_FIXED, /* allocate mem */
0801          (sizeof(LOGPALETTE)+(sizeof(PALETTEENTRY)*(PaletteSize))));
0802    pPalette->palVersion= 0x300;                /* specify version */
0803    pPalette->palNumEntries= PaletteSize;   /* specify palette size */
0804    for (iIndex= 0; iIndex< (WORD)PaletteSize; iIndex++)  /* init... */
0805      {      /* ...with low order word as index into hardware palette */
0806      *((WORD *)(&pPalette->palPalEntry[iIndex].peRed))= iIndex;
0807      pPalette->palPalEntry[iIndex].peBlue= 0;
0808      pPalette->palPalEntry[iIndex].peFlags= PC_EXPLICIT;
0809      }
0810
0811    /* ------------- create and activate the palette --------------- */
0812    hDC= GetDC(HandleWnd);                     /* get the display-context */
0813    hPal= CreatePalette((LPLOGPALETTE)pPalette);   /* create palette */
0814    SelectPalette(hDC,hPal,0);/* select palette into display-context */
0815    RealizePalette(hDC); /* activate palette entries in the hardware */
0816
0817    /* ---------------- perform graphics operations ---------------- */
0818    rcSwatch.left= iSwatchX;         /* initialize the swatch coords... */
0819    rcSwatch.top= iSwatchY;
0820    rcSwatch.right= rcSwatch.left + iWidth;
0821    rcSwatch.bottom= rcSwatch.top + iDepth;
0822    iX1= rcSwatch.left; iY1= rcSwatch.top;     /* calculate border... */
0823    iX2= iX1 + (iWidth * 16); iY2= rcSwatch.bottom;
0824    for (iIndex= 0; iIndex< (WORD)PaletteSize; iIndex++)
0825      {   /* this loop draws a swatch for each hue in the palette... */
0826      hSwatchBrush= CreateSolidBrush(PALETTEINDEX(iIndex));
0827      hPrevBrush= SelectObject(hDC,hSwatchBrush);
0828      FillRect(hDC,&rcSwatch,hSwatchBrush);
0829      SelectObject(hDC,hPrevBrush);
0830      DeleteObject(hSwatchBrush);
0831      rcSwatch.left= rcSwatch.left + iWidth;
0832      rcSwatch.right= rcSwatch.left + iWidth;
```

```
0833   }                        /* loop back until all hues are drawn */
0834   hBorderPen= CreatePen(PS_SOLID,1,PALETTEINDEX(0)); /* create pen */
0835   hPrevPen= SelectObject(hDC,hBorderPen);      /* select the pen... */
0836   MoveTo(hDC,iX1,iY1);                    /* ...and draw the border */
0837   LineTo(hDC,iX2,iY1);
0838   LineTo(hDC,iX2,iY2);
0839   LineTo(hDC,iX1,iY2);
0840   LineTo(hDC,iX1,iY1);
0841
0842   /* -------------------- display the titles -------------------- */
0843   if ((DisplayBits==1)&&(DisplayPlanes==1))
0844   {                    /* if a mono display use black typeface... */
0845     PrevFontColor= SetTextColor(hDC,RGB(0,0,0));       /* use black */
0846     PrevBkColor=  SetBkColor(hDC,RGB(255,255,255));    /* white bg */
0847   }
0848   else
0849   {   /* else if a color display use any solid color typeface... */
0850     PrevFontColor= SetTextColor(hDC,RGB(0,0,0));  /* use any color */
0851     PrevBkColor=  SetBkColor(hDC,RGB(255,255,255));    /* white bg */
0852   }
0853   SetBkMode(hDC,TRANSPARENT);   /* use transparent font background */
0854
0855   if (bUseArial == FALSE)
0856   {                    /* if running Windows 3.0 use Helv font... */
0857     Font= CreateFont(24, 0, 0, 0, FW_BOLD, FALSE, FALSE, FALSE,
0858          ANSI_CHARSET, OUT_DEFAULT_PRECIS, CLIP_DEFAULT_PRECIS,
0859          DRAFT_QUALITY, VARIABLE_PITCH | FF_SWISS, "Helv");
0860     PrevFont= SelectObject(hDC,Font);
0861     TextOut(hDC,10,6,"A Lee Adams tutorial:",21);
0862     Font= CreateFont(36, 0, 0, 0, FW_BOLD, FALSE, FALSE, FALSE,
0863          ANSI_CHARSET, OUT_DEFAULT_PRECIS, CLIP_DEFAULT_PRECIS,
0864          DRAFT_QUALITY, VARIABLE_PITCH | FF_SWISS, "Helv");
0865     SelectObject(hDC,Font);
0866     TextOut(hDC,8,24,"Color palettes",14);
0867   }
0868   else   /* else if running Windows 3.1 or newer use Arial font... */
0869   {
0870     Font= CreateFont(24, 0, 0, 0, FW_BOLD, FALSE, FALSE, FALSE,
0871          ANSI_CHARSET, OUT_DEFAULT_PRECIS, CLIP_DEFAULT_PRECIS,
0872          DRAFT_QUALITY, VARIABLE_PITCH | FF_SWISS, "Arial");
0873     PrevFont= SelectObject(hDC,Font);
0874     TextOut(hDC,10,6,"A Lee Adams tutorial:",21);
0875     Font= CreateFont(36, 0, 0, 0, FW_BOLD, FALSE, FALSE, FALSE,
0876          ANSI_CHARSET, OUT_DEFAULT_PRECIS, CLIP_DEFAULT_PRECIS,
0877          DRAFT_QUALITY, VARIABLE_PITCH | FF_SWISS, "Arial");
0878     SelectObject(hDC,Font);
0879     TextOut(hDC,8,24,"Color Palettes",14);
0880   }
0881
0882   /* -------------------- tidy up and return -------------------- */
0883   SelectObject(hDC,PrevFont);              /* restore default font */
0884   SetBkMode(hDC,OPAQUE);         /* restore opaque font background */
0885   SetBkColor(hDC,PrevBkColor);          /* restore default bg color */
0886   SetTextColor(hDC,PrevFontColor);   /* restore default font color */
0887   SelectObject(hDC,hPrevPen);         /* restore the default pen */
0888   DeleteObject(hPal);                 /* delete the new palette */
0889   DeleteObject(hBorderPen);               /* delete the new pen */
0890   ReleaseDC(HandleWnd,hDC);      /* release the display-context */
0891   return;
0892   }
0893   /*
```

```
0894   ------------------------------------------------------------------
0895                        Sample drawing function.
0896   ------------------------------------------------------------------
0897                                                                   */
0898   static void zBuildPalette(HWND HandleWnd)
0899   {
0900     HDC hDC;                   /* handle to display-context for viewport */
0901     HBRUSH hPrevBrush, hSwatchBrush;                      /* brushes */
0902     RECT rcSwatch;            /* data structure of 4 xy coords for rect */
0903     HPEN hPrevPen, hBorderPen;                               /* pens */
0904     int Width= 15, Depth= 60;          /* width and depth of swatch */
0905     int SwatchX= 8, SwatchY= 140;    /* starting coords for swatch */
0906     int PaletteSize= 16;     /* number of colors in desired palette */
0907     NPLOGPALETTE Palette;                     /* pointer to palette */
0908     WORD Index= 0;                          /* index into palette */
0909     BYTE Intensity= 0;                    /* intensity of RGB gun */
0910     BYTE Increment= 17;                  /* increment for RGB gun */
0911     HANDLE hPal;                            /* handle to palette */
0912     int iX1, iY1, iX2, iY2;          /* bounding coords for border */
0913
0914   /* ---------- reconfigure code for current color mode ---------- */
0915   if ((DisplayBits==1) && (DisplayPlanes==4))
0916      {                               /* if using 4-bit, 16-color mode */
0917      PaletteSize= 16;
0918      Increment= 17;
0919      Width= 15;
0920      SwatchX= 8;
0921      }
0922   else if ((DisplayBits==1) && (DisplayPlanes==1))
0923      {                               /* if using 1-bit, 2-color mode */
0924      PaletteSize= 16;
0925      Increment= 17;
0926      Width= 15;
0927      SwatchX= 8;
0928      }
0929   else if (DisplayBits==8)
0930      {                               /* if using 8-bit, 256-color mode */
0931      PaletteSize= 52;
0932      Increment= 5;
0933      Width= 4;
0934      SwatchX= 24;
0935      }
0936   else if (DisplayBits==16)
0937      {                               /* if using 16-bit, 65000-color mode */
0938      PaletteSize= 52;
0939      Increment= 5;
0940      Width= 4;
0941      SwatchX= 24;
0942      }
0943
0944   /* -------- create and initialize a palette data struct -------- */
0945   Palette=                    /* allocate memory to store the palette... */
0946         (NPLOGPALETTE) LocalAlloc(LMEM_FIXED,
0947         (sizeof(LOGPALETTE)+(sizeof(PALETTEENTRY)*(PaletteSize))));
0948   Palette->palVersion= 0x300;                    /* store version ID */
0949   Palette->palNumEntries= PaletteSize;        /* store palette size */
0950
0951   /* -------------- initialize the palette colors -------------- */
0952   Intensity= 0;                      /* initialize the intensity to 0 */
0953   for (Index= 0; Index< (WORD)PaletteSize; Index++)
0954      {                             /* for each entry in the palette... */
```

```
0955    Palette->palPalEntry[Index].peRed= Intensity;     /* store it... */
0956    Palette->palPalEntry[Index].peGreen= 0;
0957    Palette->palPalEntry[Index].peBlue= 0;
0958    Palette->palPalEntry[Index].peFlags= (BYTE) 0;
0959    if (Intensity<= (BYTE)(255-Increment)) Intensity+= Increment;
0960    }
0961
0962    /* ------------- create and activate the palette --------------- */
0963    hDC= GetDC(HandleWnd);                    /* set the display-context */
0964    hPal= CreatePalette((LPLOGPALETTE)Palette);   /* create palette */
0965    SelectPalette(hDC,hPal,0);/* select palette into display-context */
0966    RealizePalette(hDC);                     /* map the palette entries */
0967
0968    /* -------------------- draw the swatches --------------------- */
0969    rcSwatch.left= SwatchX;          /* initialize the swatch coords... */
0970    rcSwatch.top= SwatchY;
0971    rcSwatch.right= rcSwatch.left + Width;
0972    rcSwatch.bottom= rcSwatch.top + Depth;
0973    iX1= rcSwatch.left; iY1= rcSwatch.top;      /* calculate border... */
0974    iX2= iX1 + (Width * (int)PaletteSize); iY2= rcSwatch.bottom;
0975    for (Index= 0; Index< (WORD)PaletteSize; Index++)
0976    {                               /* for each color in the palette... */
0977      hSwatchBrush= CreateSolidBrush(PALETTEINDEX(Index));
0978      hPrevBrush= SelectObject(hDC,hSwatchBrush);
0979      FillRect(hDC,&rcSwatch,hSwatchBrush);      /* ...draw a swatch */
0980      SelectObject(hDC,hPrevBrush);
0981      DeleteObject(hSwatchBrush);
0982      rcSwatch.left= rcSwatch.left + Width;
0983      rcSwatch.right= rcSwatch.left + Width;
0984    }                        /* loop back until all swatches are drawn */
0985    hBorderPen= CreatePen(PS_SOLID,1,PALETTEINDEX(0)); /* create pen */
0986    hPrevPen= SelectObject(hDC,hBorderPen);             /* select pen */
0987    MoveTo(hDC,iX1,iY1);             /* draw border around swatches... */
0988    LineTo(hDC,iX2,iY1);
0989    LineTo(hDC,iX2,iY2);
0990    LineTo(hDC,iX1,iY2);
0991    LineTo(hDC,iX1,iY1);
0992
0993    /* -------------------- tidy up and return -------------------- */
0994    SelectObject(hDC,hPrevPen);                 /* restore default pen */
0995    ReleaseDC(HandleWnd,hDC);         /* release the display-context */
0996    DeleteObject(hPal);                       /* delete the new palette */
0997    DeleteObject(hBorderPen);                     /* delete the new pen */
0998    return;
0999    }
1000    /*
1001    --------------------------------------------------------------------
1002                         End of the C source file
1003    --------------------------------------------------------------------
1004                                                                      */
```

C-2 Source listings for the 3D geometry sampler, objects.c, consisting of .def, .h, .rc, and .c files. See Appendix B for the toolkits which must be linked in to build this application. See Appendix A for instructions on building the demo.

```
0001    NAME            DEFDEMO
0002    DESCRIPTION     'Copyright 1993 Lee Adams.  All rights reserved.'
0003    EXETYPE         WINDOWS
0004    STUB            'WINSTUB.EXE'
0005    CODE            PRELOAD MOVEABLE
0006    DATA            PRELOAD MOVEABLE MULTIPLE
```

C-2 Continued.

```
0007   HEAPSIZE      1024
0008   STACKSIZE     8192
0009   EXPORTS       zMessageHandler
0001   /*
0002   ------------------------------------------------------------
0003                    Include file objects.h
0004        Copyright 1993 Lee Adams.  All rights reserved.
0005     Include this file in the .RC resource script file and in the
0006     .C source file.  It contains function prototypes, menu ID
0007     constants, and string ID constants.
0008   ------------------------------------------------------------
0009   ------------------------------------------------------------
0010                    Function prototypes
0011   ------------------------------------------------------------
0012                                                             */
0013   #if !defined(zRCFILE)                  /* if not an .RC file... */
0014     LONG FAR PASCAL zMessageHandler(HWND, unsigned, WORD, LONG);
0015     int PASCAL WinMain(HANDLE,HANDLE,LPSTR,int);
0016     HWND zInitMainWindow(HANDLE);
0017     BOOL zInitClass(HANDLE);
0018   static void zClear(HWND);                /* blank the display window */
0019   static void zInitFrame(HWND);              /* creates hidden frame */
0020   static void zCopyToDisplay(HWND);     /* copies frame to display */
0021   static void zCopyToFrame(HWND);       /* copies display to frame */
0022   static void zClearHiddenFrame(void);      /* clears hidden frame */
0023   static void zDrawRoboticArm(void);   /* builds hardcoded assembly */
0024   static void zBuildAssembly(void);    /* builds hierarchy assembly */
0025   #endif
0026   /*
0027   ------------------------------------------------------------
0028                    Menu ID constants
0029   ------------------------------------------------------------
0030                                                             */
0031   #define IDM_New               1
0032   #define IDM_Open              2
0033   #define IDM_Save              3
0034   #define IDM_SaveAs            4
0035   #define IDM_Exit              5
0036   #define IDM_Restart           6
0037
0038   #define IDM_Undo              7
0039   #define IDM_Cut               8
0040   #define IDM_Copy              90
0041   #define IDM_Paste             10
0042   #define IDM_Delete            11
0043
0044   #define IDM_DrawSphere        12
0045   #define IDM_DrawBox           13
0046   #define IDM_DrawCylinder      14
0047   #define IDM_DrawCurve         15
0048   #define IDM_DrawCone          16
0049   #define IDM_DrawHemisphere    17
0050   #define IDM_DrawWedge         18
0051   #define IDM_TestLighting      19
0052   #define IDM_VRtestA           20
0053   #define IDM_VRtestB           21
0054   #define IDM_VRtestC           22
0055   #define IDM_VRtestD           23
0056   #define IDM_Lens1             24
0057   #define IDM_Lens2             25
0058   #define IDM_Lens3             26
```

```
0059    #define IDM_UseShaded          27
0060    #define IDM_UseWireframe       28
0061    #define IDM_DrawDeformBox      29
0062    #define IDM_DrawHalfCylinder   30
0063    #define IDM_DrawBulge          31
0064    #define IDM_DrawRobotArm       32
0065    #define IDM_BuildAssembly      33
0066    #define IDM_Clear              34
0067
0068    #define IDM_About              35
0069    #define IDM_License            36
0070    #define IDM_Display            37
0071    #define IDM_Colors             38
0072    #define IDM_Mode               39
0073    #define IDM_GeneralHelp        40
0074    /*
0075    -----------------------------------------------------------------
0076                        String ID constants
0077    -----------------------------------------------------------------
0078                                                                   */
0079    #define IDS_Caption        1
0080    #define IDS_Warning        2
0081    #define IDS_NoMouse        3
0082    #define IDS_About          4
0083    #define IDS_AboutText      5
0084    #define IDS_License        6
0085    #define IDS_LicenseText    7
0086    #define IDS_Help           8
0087    #define IDS_HelpText       9
0088    #define IDS_Completed      10
0089    #define IDS_Resolution     11
0090    #define IDS_ResVGA         12
0091    #define IDS_ResEGA         13
0092    #define IDS_ResCGA         14
0093    #define IDS_ResSVGA        15
0094    #define IDS_Res8514        16
0095    #define IDS_ResHerc        17
0096    #define IDS_ResCustom      18
0097    #define IDS_Color          19
0098    #define IDS_Color16        20
0099    #define IDS_Color256       21
0100    #define IDS_Color65000     22
0101    #define IDS_Color2         23
0102    #define IDS_ColorCustom    24
0103    #define IDS_Machine        25
0104    #define IDS_Enhanced       26
0105    #define IDS_Standard       27
0106    #define IDS_Real           28
0107    #define IDS_Ready          29
0108    #define IDS_NotReady       30
0109    #define IDS_NoMem          31
0110    #define IDS_FrameOK        32
0111    #define IDS_ReqdHdwr1      33
0112    #define IDS_ReqdHdwr2      34
0113    /*
0114    -----------------------------------------------------------------
0115                        End of include file
0116    -----------------------------------------------------------------
0117                                                                   */
0001    /*
0002    -----------------------------------------------------------------
```

```
0003                     Resource script file objects.rc
0004           Copyright 1993 Lee Adams.  All rights reserved.
0005       This file defines the menu resources, the accelerator key
0006       resources, and the string resources that will be used by the
0007       demonstration application at runtime.
0008       -----------------------------------------------------------------
0009                                                                       */
0010    #define zRCFILE
0011    #include <WINDOWS.H>
0012    #include "OBJECTS.H"
0013    /*
0014       -----------------------------------------------------------------
0015                             Script for menus
0016       -----------------------------------------------------------------
0017                                                                       */
0018    MENUS1 MENU
0019      BEGIN
0020      POPUP "&File"
0021        BEGIN
0022          MENUITEM  "&New", IDM_New, GRAYED
0023          MENUITEM  "&Open...", IDM_Open, GRAYED
0024          MENUITEM  "&Save", IDM_Save, GRAYED
0025          MENUITEM  "Save &As...", IDM_SaveAs, GRAYED
0026          MENUITEM SEPARATOR
0027          MENUITEM  "E&xit...", IDM_Exit
0028          MENUITEM  "&Restart Windows...", IDM_Restart
0029        END
0030      POPUP "&Edit"
0031        BEGIN
0032          MENUITEM  "&Undo\tAlt+BkSp", IDM_Undo, GRAYED
0033          MENUITEM SEPARATOR
0034          MENUITEM  "Cu&t\tShift+Del", IDM_Cut, GRAYED
0035          MENUITEM  "&Copy\tCtrl+Ins", IDM_Copy, GRAYED
0036          MENUITEM  "&Paste\tShift+Ins", IDM_Paste, GRAYED
0037          MENUITEM  "&Delete\tDel", IDM_Delete, GRAYED
0038        END
0039      POPUP "&3D"
0040        BEGIN
0041          POPUP "&Simple 3D Objects..."
0042            BEGIN
0043            MENUITEM  "&Sphere", IDM_DrawSphere
0044            MENUITEM  "&Half-sphere", IDM_DrawHemisphere
0045            MENUITEM  "&Clipped boxes", IDM_DrawBox
0046            MENUITEM  "&Deformed boxes", IDM_DrawDeformBox
0047            MENUITEM  "C&ylinder", IDM_DrawCylinder
0048            MENUITEM  "Ha&lf-cylinder", IDM_DrawHalfCylinder
0049            MENUITEM  "C&one", IDM_DrawCone
0050            MENUITEM  "&Wedge", IDM_DrawWedge
0051            MENUITEM  "Cu&rved surface", IDM_DrawCurve
0052            MENUITEM  "B&ulged surface", IDM_DrawBulge
0053            END
0054          POPUP "&Complex 3D Objects..."
0055            BEGIN
0056            MENUITEM  "&Fixed assembly", IDM_DrawRobotArm
0057            MENUITEM  "&Hierarchical assembly", IDM_BuildAssembly
0058            END
0059          MENUITEM SEPARATOR
0060          MENUITEM  "&Lighting Demo", IDM_TestLighting
0061          POPUP "&Viewpoint Demos..."
0062            BEGIN
0063            MENUITEM  "View &A", IDM_VRtestA
```

```
0064            MENUITEM  "View &B", IDM_VRtestB
0065            MENUITEM  "View &C", IDM_VRtestC
0066            MENUITEM  "View &D", IDM_VRtestD
0067            END
0068         MENUITEM SEPARATOR
0069         POPUP "Camera &Lens..."
0070           BEGIN
0071           MENUITEM  "Select &55mm lens", IDM_Lens1
0072           MENUITEM  "Select &135mm lens", IDM_Lens2
0073           MENUITEM  "Select &200mm lens", IDM_Lens3
0074           END
0075         MENUITEM SEPARATOR
0076         POPUP "&Rendering Mode..."
0077           BEGIN
0078           MENUITEM "Use &shaded solids", IDM_UseShaded
0079           MENUITEM "Use &wireframe mode", IDM_UseWireframe
0080           END
0081         MENUITEM SEPARATOR
0082         MENUITEM "Cle&ar Viewport", IDM_Clear
0083      END
0084   POPUP "&Use"
0085      BEGIN
0086        MENUITEM "&About", IDM_About
0087        MENUITEM "&License", IDM_License
0088        MENUITEM SEPARATOR
0089        MENUITEM "&Resolution of display", IDM_Display
0090        MENUITEM "Available &colors", IDM_Colors
0091        MENUITEM "&Memory mode", IDM_Mode
0092        MENUITEM SEPARATOR
0093        MENUITEM "&How to use", IDM_GeneralHelp
0094      END
0095   END
0096   /*
0097   -----------------------------------------------------------------
0098                    Script for accelerator keys
0099   -----------------------------------------------------------------
0100                                                                 */
0101   KEYS1 ACCELERATORS
0102     BEGIN
0103     VK_BACK, IDM_Undo, VIRTKEY, ALT
0104     VK_DELETE, IDM_Cut, VIRTKEY, SHIFT
0105     VK_INSERT, IDM_Copy, VIRTKEY, CONTROL
0106     VK_INSERT, IDM_Paste, VIRTKEY, SHIFT
0107     VK_DELETE, IDM_Delete, VIRTKEY
0108     END
0109   /*
0110   -----------------------------------------------------------------
0111                       Script for strings
0112    If you are typing this listing, set your right margin to 255
0113    characters so you can create lengthy strings without embedded
0114    carriage returns.  The line wraparounds in the following
0115    STRINGTABLE script are used only for readability.
0116   -----------------------------------------------------------------
0117                                                                 */
0118   STRINGTABLE
0119     BEGIN
0120       IDS_Caption      "3D view geometry"
0121       IDS_Warning      "Graphics system warning"
0122       IDS_NoMouse      "No mouse found.  Some features of this
             demonstration program may require a mouse."
0123       IDS_About        "About this program"
```

```
0124    IDS_AboutText   "This is a demo from Windcrest McGraw-Hill
            book 4115. Copyright⁻ 1993 Lee Adams. All rights reserved."
0125    IDS_License     "License Agreement"
0126    IDS_LicenseText "You can use this code as part of your own
            software product subject to the License Agreement and
            Limited Warranty in Windcrest McGraw-Hill book 4115 and on
            its companion disk."
0127    IDS_Help        "How to use this 3D demo"
0128    IDS_HelpText    "Select from the 3D menu to render various 3D
            solids using the 3D shapes engine. See the discussion in
            Windcrest/McGraw-Hill book 4115 for further help."
0129    IDS_Resolution  "Screen resolution"
0130    IDS_ResVGA      "Running in 640-by-480 mode."
0131    IDS_ResEGA      "Running in 640-by-350 mode."
0132    IDS_ResCGA      "Running in 640-by-200 mode."
0133    IDS_ResSVGA     "Running in 800-by-600 mode."
0134    IDS_Res8514     "Running in 1024-by-768 mode."
0135    IDS_ResHerc     "Running in 720-by-348 mode."
0136    IDS_ResCustom   "Running in a custom-resolution mode."
0137    IDS_Color       "Available colors"
0138    IDS_Color16     "Running in 4-bit, 16-color mode."
0139    IDS_Color256    "Running in 8-bit, 256-color mode."
0140    IDS_Color2      "Running in 1-bit, 2-color mode."
0141    IDS_Color65000  "Running in 16-bit, 65000-color mode."
0142    IDS_ColorCustom "Running in 24-bit, 16.7 million-color mode."
0143    IDS_Machine     "Memory mode"
0144    IDS_Enhanced    "Running in enhanced mode. Can allocate up to
            16 MB extended physical memory (XMS) if available. Virtual
            memory up to 4 times physical memory (maximum 64 MB) is also
            available via automatic disk swapping of 4K pages."
0145    IDS_Standard    "Running in standard mode. Can allocate up to
            16 MB extended physical memory (XMS) if available."
0146    IDS_Real        "Running in real mode. Can allocate blocks of
            memory from the first 640K of RAM. Can also allocate blocks
            from expanded memory (EMS) if available."
0147    IDS_Ready       "3D graphics system ready"
0148    IDS_NotReady    "3D graphics system not ready"
0149    IDS_NoMem       "Insufficient memory. Hidden frame not
            created. Any 3D images you create will not be preserved if
            the window is covered or clipped. Close other applications
            to free memory and restart this demo."
0150    IDS_FrameOK     "The 3D library has been successfully
            initialized. The hidden frame has been successfully
            created."
0151    IDS_ReqdHdwr1   "Graphics hardware"
0152    IDS_ReqdHdwr2   "CGA, HGA, or EGA graphics card has been
            detected. This demo requires an industry-standard VGA or a
            VESA-standard SuperVGA and compatible display -- or a
            graphics accelerator card (16-bit or 24-bit) and appropriate
            display."
0153    END
0154    /*
0155    -------------------------------------------------------------------
0156                      End of resource script file
0157    -------------------------------------------------------------------
0158                                                                    */
0001    /*
0002    -------------------------------------------------------------------
0003                      3D geometry sampler
0004    -------------------------------------------------------------------
0005      Source file: objects.c
```

```
0006      Release version: 2.00              Programmer: Lee Adams
0007      Type: C source file for Windows application development.
0008      Supported compilers: Explicit compatibility with Microsoft
0009        QuickC for Windows v1.00 and Borland Turbo C++ for Windows
0010        v3.0. Nominal compatibility with all Windows-compatible C
0011        and C++ compilers such as Borland C++, Zortech C++, Watcom C,
0012        and Microsoft C/C++.
0013      Memory model: medium.
0014      Build notes: Do not use the load optimization feature of the
0015        Resource Compiler (or use the command-line -K switch).
0016        For trouble-free compiling follow the tips in the book.
0017      Project notes: Load the objects.mak project file if you are
0018        using QuickC for Windows. Load the objects.prj file if you
0019        are using Turbo C++ for Windows. Refer to the book if you
0020        are using another compiler. The following files are needed
0021        to build the executable.
0022          objects.def      module definition file
0023          objects.h        include file
0024          objects.rc       resource script file
0025          objects.c        C source file
0026          engine3d.h       include file for 3D functions
0027          engine3d.c       3D toolkit
0028          shapes3d.h       include file for 3D solids
0029          shapes3d.c       3D shapes toolkit
0030          deform3d.h       include file for 3D deformations
0031          deform3d.c       3D deformations toolkit
0032          lights3d.h       include file for light-source functions
0033          lights3d.c       light-source toolkit
0034          assemb3d.h       include file for hierarchy functions
0035          assemb3d.c       hierarchical modeling toolkit
0036      Output and features: Demonstrates a display-independent
0037        3D modeling and shading toolkit named engine3d.c that can be
0038        used to build scenes. Demonstrates a 3D shapes driver named
0039        shapes3d.c that can be used to configure the functions in
0040        engine3d.c to render spheres, boxes, cylinders, curves, etc.
0041        Demonstrates a 3D lighting driver named lights3d.c that can
0042        be used to reposition the light-source. Demonstrates
0043        functions to manipulate the near and far clipping planes.
0044        Demonstrates functions to reposition the camera for
0045        target-based 3D modeling and to reposition the viewpoint for
0046        3D virtual reality scenes.
0047          Uses a 256-by-255 raster viewport. Uses camera coords to
0048        perform backface culling and world coords to calculate
0049        shading levels. Then transforms camera coords of the 3D view
0050        volume to a normalized 3D perspective view volume, then to a
0051        normalized rectangular view volume, scaled to fit a 256-by-255
0052        raster viewport. Visible surface detection for the scene is
0053        implemented by a 256-by-255 z-buffer of unsigned char
0054        depth-values.
0055          Also demonstrates user interface functions such as nested
0056        menus, accelerator keys, interactive message boxes, display
0057        capabilities status reports, and code to restart Windows.
0058      Publication: Contains material from Windcrest/McGraw-Hill book
0059        4115 published by TAB BOOKS Division of McGraw-Hill Inc.
0060      License: As purchaser of the book you are granted a royalty-
0061        free license to distribute executable files generated using
0062        this code provided you accept the conditions of the License
0063        Agreement and Limited Warranty described in the book and on
0064        the companion disk. Government users: This software and
0065        documentation are subject to restrictions set forth in The
0066        Rights in Technical Data and Computer Software clause at
```

```
0067        252.227-7013 and elsewhere.
0068   --------------------------------------------------------------
0069        (c) Copyright 1991-1993 Lee Adams.  All rights reserved.
0070            Lee Adams(tm) is a trademark of Lee Adams.
0071   --------------------------------------------------------------
0072
0073   --------------------------------------------------------------
0074                          Include files
0075   --------------------------------------------------------------
0076                                                                */
0077   #include <WINDOWS.H>              /* declarations for Windows API */
0078   #include "OBJECTS.H"        /* declares function prototypes, etc. */
0079   #include "ENGINE3D.H"          /* declares functions in 3D engine */
0080   #include "SHAPES3D.H"   /* declares functions in 3D shapes module */
0081   #include "DEFORM3D.H"/* declares functions in deformation module */
0082   #include "LIGHTS3D.H"    /* declares functions in lighting module */
0083   #include "ASSEMB3D.H"  /* declares functions in hierarchy module */
0084
0085   /*
0086   --------------------------------------------------------------
0087           Static variables visible throughout this file
0088   --------------------------------------------------------------
0089                                                                */
0090   /* ----------------- window specifications ----------------- */
0091   #define zWINDOW_WIDTH 263                   /* width of window */
0092   #define zWINDOW_HEIGHT 300                  /* depth of window */
0093   #define zFRAMEWIDE 256                    /* width of viewport */
0094   #define zFRAMEHIGH 255                   /* depth of viewporta */
0095   int WindowX, WindowY;                    /* location of window */
0096
0097   /* ------------------ instance operations ------------------- */
0098   HANDLE hInst;                 /* handle to this copy of the app */
0099   HWND MainhWnd;                     /* handle to the app's window */
0100   HANDLE hAccel;                /* handle to the accelerator keys */
0101   HMENU hMenu;             /* handle to an active menu at runtime */
0102   PAINTSTRUCT ps;          /* used for Windows-generated refreshes */
0103   int MessageRet;       /* will receive value returned by system */
0104
0105   /* -------------------- mouse and cursor -------------------- */
0106   HCURSOR hPrevCursor;              /* handle to arrow cursor */
0107   HCURSOR hHourGlass;           /* handle to hourglass cursor */
0108   int MousePresent;               /* indicates if mouse found */
0109
0110   /* ------------------- runtime conditions ------------------- */
0111   int DisplayWidth, DisplayHeight;      /* resolution of display */
0112   int DisplayBits;               /* number of bits per pixel */
0113   int DisplayPlanes;                /* number of bitplanes */
0114   DWORD MemoryMode;                 /* runtime memory mode */
0115
0116   /* ----------------- message box operations ---------------- */
0117   char lpCaption[51];        /* stores caption for message box */
0118   int Max= 50;                      /* max length of caption */
0119   char lpMessage[250];          /* stores text for message box */
0120   int MaxText= 249;                    /* max length of text */
0121   int MessageBoxChoice= 0;          /* user's selection, if any */
0122
0123   /* --------------------- font operations -------------------- */
0124   HFONT hFont, hPrevFont;       /* handles to new, previous font */
0125   HDC hFontDC;                  /* display-context for font */
0126
0127   /* ------------- persistent image operations ---------------- */
```

```
0128   #define zBLANK 0
0129   #define zIMAGE 1
0130   int PaintImage= zBLANK;              /* indicates viewport status */
0131
0132   /* -----------------hidden frame operations ------------------ */
0133   HDC hFrameDC;                  /* display-context of hidden-frame */
0134   HBITMAP hFrame;                        /* bitmap of hidden-frame */
0135   HBITMAP hPrevFrame;                          /* default bitmap */
0136   BOOL FrameReady= FALSE;                   /* hidden-frame ready? */
0137
0138   /* ---------------------- runtime tokens ---------------------- */
0139   static int CamLens= 55;          /* focal length of camera lens */
0140   static int SubjZ= 0;                     /* z-value of 3D object */
0141   static int SubjX= 0;                     /* x-value of 3D object */
0142   static int RowCount= 0;                          /* loop counter */
0143   static int ColCount= 0;                          /* loop counter */
0144   static int SubjClr= 0;                   /* color of 3D object */
0145
0146   /* --------------- object hierarchy structure --------------- */
0147   static struct SubobjectStruct
0148     {                  /* declare a struct type for each subobject */
0149     unsigned char Solid;               /* type of 3D solid */
0150     int Level;                              /* hierarchy level */
0151     int Color;                              /* rendering color */
0152     int SizeX;                              /* width of subobject */
0153     int SizeY;                              /* height of subobject */
0154     int SizeZ;                              /* depth of subobject */
0155     int PositionX;   /* position of subobject in assembly-space... */
0156     int PositionY;
0157     int PositionZ;
0158     int Yaw;        /* orientation of subobject in assembly-space... */
0159     int Roll;
0160     int Pitch;
0161     int DeformRightX;     /* extrusion deformation of subobject... */
0162     int DeformLeftX;
0163     int DeformUpY;
0164     int DeformDownY;
0165     int PivotX;                      /* subassembly pivot-point... */
0166     int PivotY;
0167     int PivotZ;
0168     int SubAssyYaw;/* subassembly orientation in assembly-space... */
0169     int SubAssyRoll;
0170     int SubAssyPitch;
0171     int SubAssyX;      /* subassembly position in assembly-space... */
0172     int SubAssyY;
0173     int SubAssyZ;
0174     };
0175
0176   /* ---------- declarations for a specific assembly ----------- */
0177   static struct SubobjectStruct RobotArm[10];     /* 10 subobjects */
0178   #define zROBOT_START  0      /* parameters for rendering loop... */
0179   #define zROBOT_FINISH 9
0180   #define zBOX          1                   /* available solids... */
0181   #define zSPHERE       2
0182   #define zCYLINDER     3
0183   #define zCONE         4
0184   #define zWEDGE        5
0185   #define zCURVE        6
0186   #define zHEMISPHERE   7
0187   #define zDEFORMBOX    8
0188   #define zHALFCYL      9
```

```
0189   #define zBULGE        10
0190   #define zNULL         11
0191   #define zLEVEL1        1                     /* progeny in 3D hierarchy... */
0192   #define zLEVEL2        2
0193   #define zLEVEL3        3
0194
0195   /*
0196   -----------------------------------------------------------------
0197                      Entry point for the application
0198   -----------------------------------------------------------------
0199                                                                   */
0200   int PASCAL WinMain(HANDLE hInstance, HANDLE hPrevInstance,
0201                      LPSTR lpCmdLine, int nCmdShow)
0202   {
0203     MSG msg;                               /* holds incoming messages */
0204     HWND hWndPrev;                 /* handle to previous copy of app */
0205     HWND hDesktopWnd;              /* handle to the entire display */
0206     HDC hDCcaps;           /* display-context for the entire display */
0207     RECT rcClientReqd;        /* size of viewport before adjustment */
0208     int AdjustX, AdjustY; /* amount to adjust to ensure 256-by-255 */
0209
0210   /* -------------- ensure only one copy is running -------------- */
0211   hWndPrev = FindWindow("DEMOCLASS", NULL);
0212   if (hWndPrev != NULL)
0213     {            /* if another app of class DEMOCLASS is running... */
0214     BringWindowToTop(hWndPrev);                  /* use it instead... */
0215     return FALSE;                         /* ...and cancel this launch */
0216     }
0217
0218   /* ------------- display the splash signon notice ------------- */
0219   MessageBoxChoice= MessageBox(GetFocus(),
0220   "3D sampler from Windcrest McGraw-Hill book 4115",
0221   "Copyright- 1993 Lee Adams", MB_OKCANCEL);
0222   if (MessageBoxChoice == IDCANCEL) return FALSE;
0223
0224   /* --------- determine capabilities of screen display ---------- */
0225   hDesktopWnd= GetDesktopWindow();
0226   hDCcaps= GetDC(hDesktopWnd);
0227   DisplayWidth= GetDeviceCaps(hDCcaps,HORZRES);
0228   DisplayHeight= GetDeviceCaps(hDCcaps,VERTRES);
0229   DisplayBits= GetDeviceCaps(hDCcaps,BITSPIXEL);
0230   DisplayPlanes= GetDeviceCaps(hDCcaps,PLANES);
0231   ReleaseDC(hDesktopWnd,hDCcaps);
0232
0233   /* ------------- trap unsupported graphics adapters ----------- */
0234   if (DisplayWidth==720)
0235     {                                    /* if HGA detected... */
0236     LoadString(hInstance,IDS_ReqdHdwr1,lpCaption,Max);
0237     LoadString(hInstance,IDS_ReqdHdwr2,lpMessage,MaxText);
0238     MessageBeep(0); MessageBox(GetFocus(),lpMessage,lpCaption,MB_OK);
0239     return FALSE;
0240     }
0241   if (DisplayWidth==640)
0242     {
0243     if ((DisplayHeight==350)||(DisplayHeight==200))
0244       {                                  /* if EGA or CGA detected... */
0245       LoadString(hInstance,IDS_ReqdHdwr1,lpCaption,Max);
0246       LoadString(hInstance,IDS_ReqdHdwr2,lpMessage,MaxText);
0247       MessageBeep(0);
0248       MessageBox(GetFocus(),lpMessage,lpCaption,MB_OK);
0249       return FALSE;
```

```
0250      }
0251    }
0252
0253    /* ------- calculate screen position to center the window ------ */
0254    WindowX= (DisplayWidth - zWINDOW_WIDTH) / 2;        /* horizontal */
0255    WindowY= (DisplayHeight - zWINDOW_HEIGHT) /2;         /* vertical */
0256    if (WindowX < 0) WindowX= 0;                         /* failsafe */
0257    if (WindowY < 0) WindowY= 0;                         /* failsafe */
0258
0259    /* ---- determine memory mode (enhanced, standard, or real) ---- */
0260    MemoryMode= GetWinFlags(); /* software will use this value later */
0261
0262    /* ---------------- create and show the window ---------------- */
0263    hInst= hInstance;        /* store handle to this copy of the app */
0264    if (!zInitClass(hInstance)) return FALSE;    /* initialize class */
0265    MainhWnd= zInitMainWindow(hInstance);       /* initialize window */
0266    if (!MainhWnd) return FALSE;        /* if error, cancel startup */
0267    ShowWindow(MainhWnd, nCmdShow);             /* show the window */
0268    UpdateWindow(MainhWnd);                      /* force a refresh */
0269    hAccel= LoadAccelerators(hInstance,"KEYS1");    /* activate keys */
0270
0271    /* ------------- enforce a 256-by-255 client area ------------- */
0272    GetClientRect(MainhWnd, &rcClientReqd);      /* get dimensions */
0273    AdjustX=              /* compare actual width to desired width... */
0274            zFRAMEWIDE - (rcClientReqd.right + 1);
0275    AdjustY=       /* compare actual height to desired height... */
0276            zFRAMEHIGH - (rcClientReqd.bottom + 1);
0277    if ((AdjustX != 0)||(AdjustY != 0)) /* if adjustment required... */
0278      {
0279      SetWindowPos(MainhWnd, (HWND)NULL,
0280                   WindowX, WindowY,        /* retain same location */
0281                   zWINDOW_WIDTH + AdjustX,    /* resize the width */
0282                   zWINDOW_HEIGHT + AdjustY,   /* resize the height */
0283                   SWP_NOZORDER);             /* retain same order */
0284      }
0285
0286    /* --------------------- check for mouse --------------------- */
0287    MousePresent= GetSystemMetrics(SM_MOUSEPRESENT);
0288    if (!MousePresent)                    /* if no mouse found... */
0289      {
0290      LoadString(hInst,IDS_Warning,lpCaption,Max);   /* load caption */
0291      LoadString(hInst,IDS_NoMouse,lpMessage,MaxText);  /* load text */
0292      MessageBox(GetFocus(),lpMessage,lpCaption,MB_OK);  /* message */
0293      }
0294
0295    /* --------------- initialize the 3D environment --------------- */
0296    zInitialize3D(MainhWnd);           /* initialize the 3D toolkit */
0297    zInitFrame(MainhWnd);   /* initialize hidden frame for refreshes */
0298
0299    /* ---------- begin retrieving messages for the window --------- */
0300    while (GetMessage(&msg,0,0,0))
0301      {
0302      if(TranslateAccelerator(MainhWnd, hAccel, &msg)) continue;
0303      TranslateMessage(&msg);
0304      DispatchMessage(&msg);
0305      }
0306    return(msg.wParam);
0307    }
0308
0309    /*
0310    -------------------------------------------------------------------
```

```
0311                        Switcher for incoming messages
0312    --------------------------------------------------------------------
0313                                                                       */
0314    LONG FAR PASCAL zMessageHandler(HWND hWnd, unsigned message,
0315                                    WORD wParam, LONG lParam)
0316    {
0317      HDC hDCpaint;          /* display-context for persistent graphics */
0318
0319    switch (message)
0320      {
0321      /* ----------------- menu system commands ----------------- */
0322      case WM_COMMAND:
0323        switch(wParam)
0324          {
0325          case IDM_New:      break;
0326          case IDM_Open:     break;
0327          case IDM_Save:     break;
0328          case IDM_SaveAs:   break;
0329          case IDM_Exit:
0330               MessageBoxChoice= MessageBox(GetFocus(),
0331                 "Exit the 3D sampler and return to Windows?",
0332                 "Please confirm", MB_YESNO);
0333               if (MessageBoxChoice == IDYES) PostQuitMessage(0);
0334               break;
0335          case IDM_Restart:
0336               MessageBoxChoice= MessageBox(GetFocus(),
0337                 "Exit the 3D sampler and restart Windows?",
0338                 "Please confirm", MB_YESNO);
0339               if (MessageBoxChoice == IDYES) ExitWindows(0x42L,0);
0340               break;
0341          case IDM_Undo:     break;
0342          case IDM_Cut:      break;
0343          case IDM_Copy:     break;
0344          case IDM_Paste:    break;
0345          case IDM_Delete:   break;
0346
0347          case IDM_UseShaded:     /* use fully-shaded 3D objects... */
0348               zUseWireframeMode(FALSE);
0349               MessageBox(GetFocus(),
0350                 "Using shaded solids mode.","3D status report", MB_OK);
0351               break;
0352          case IDM_UseWireframe:      /* use wireframe 3D objects... */
0353               zUseWireframeMode(TRUE);
0354               MessageBox(GetFocus(),
0355                 "Using wireframe modeling mode.",
0356                 "3D status report", MB_OK);
0357               break;
0358
0359          /* ----------------- render a 3D sphere ----------------- */
0360          case IDM_DrawSphere:
0361               SetCapture(hWnd);                        /* lock the mouse */
0362               hPrevCursor= SetCursor(hHourGlass); /* hourglass cursor */
0363               zClear(hWnd);                        /* clear the viewport */
0364               zClearHidden3DPage();        /* clear the 3D hidden-page */
0365               zResetZBuffer();                     /* reset the z-buffer */
0366               hFontDC= GetDC(MainhWnd);    /* display the captions... */
0367               hFont= GetStockObject(SYSTEM_FONT);
0368               hPrevFont= SelectObject(hFontDC,hFont);
0369               SetTextColor(hFontDC,RGB(0,0,0));
0370               SetBkMode(hFontDC,TRANSPARENT);
0371               TextOut(hFontDC,10,10,"Camera distance 300 ft.",23);
```

```
0372            TextOut(hFontDC,10,26,"Camera heading 315 degrees",26);
0373            TextOut(hFontDC,10,42,"Camera pitch 320 degrees",24);
0374            if (CamLens==55)
0375              {
0376              TextOut(hFontDC,10,58,"Using 55mm lens",15);
0377              }
0378            if (CamLens==135)
0379              {
0380              TextOut(hFontDC,10,58, "Using 135mm lens",16);
0381              }
0382            if (CamLens==200)
0383              {
0384              TextOut(hFontDC,10,58, "Using 200mm lens",16);
0385              }
0386            SetTextColor(hFontDC,RGB(255,255,255));
0387            SelectObject(hFontDC,hPrevFont);
0388            ReleaseDC(MainhWnd,hFontDC);
0389            /* -------------- configure the camera -------------- */
0390            zSetCameraDistance(300);     /* camera-to-target distance */
0391            zSetCameraHeading(315);             /* camera heading */
0392            zSetCameraPitch(320);                /* camera pitch */
0393            zSetLightPosition(60,180);  /* light elevation, heading */
0394            /* ---------- configure and render one sphere --------- */
0395            zSetHierarchyMode(FALSE);       /* top-level objects only */
0396            zSetSubjectSize(50,50,50);          /* radius of sphere */
0397            zSetSubjectAttitude(0,0,0);     /* orientation of sphere */
0398            zSetSubjectLocation(0,0,0);       /* location of sphere */
0399            zSetShadingColor(zGREEN);            /* color of sphere */
0400            zDrawSphere();                      /* render sphere */
0401            /* ----------- perform system maintenance ----------- */
0402            PaintImage= zIMAGE;
0403            if (FrameReady==TRUE) zCopyToFrame(hWnd);
0404            SetCursor(hPrevCursor);        /* restore previous cursor */
0405            ReleaseCapture();                  /* unlock mouse */
0406            break;
0407
0408        /* ------ render 3D boxes using near clipping plane ------ */
0409        case IDM_DrawBox:
0410            SetCapture(hWnd);
0411            hPrevCursor= SetCursor(hHourGlass);
0412            zClear(hWnd);
0413            zClearHidden3DPage();
0414            zResetZBuffer();
0415            hFontDC= GetDC(MainhWnd);
0416            hFont= GetStockObject(SYSTEM_FONT);
0417            hPrevFont= SelectObject(hFontDC,hFont);
0418            SetTextColor(hFontDC,RGB(0,0,0));
0419            SetBkMode(hFontDC,TRANSPARENT);
0420            TextOut(hFontDC,10,10,"Camera distance 356 ft.",23);
0421            TextOut(hFontDC,10,26,"Camera heading 360 degrees",26);
0422            TextOut(hFontDC,10,42,"Camera pitch 360 degrees",24);
0423            if (CamLens==55)
0424              {
0425              TextOut(hFontDC,10,58,"Using 55mm lens",15);
0426              }
0427            if (CamLens==135)
0428              {
0429              TextOut(hFontDC,10,58, "Using 135mm lens",16);
0430              }
0431            if (CamLens==200)
0432              {
```

```
0433                    TextOut(hFontDC,10,58, "Using 200mm lens",16);
0434                    }
0435                SetTextColor(hFontDC,RGB(255,255,255));
0436                SelectObject(hFontDC,hPrevFont);
0437                ReleaseDC(MainhWnd,hFontDC);
0438                /* -------------- configure the camera -------------- */
0439                zSetCameraDistance(356);
0440                zSetCameraHeading(360);
0441                zSetCameraPitch(360);
0442                zSetLightPosition(60,180);
0443                /* ------- render 3 boxes using clipping planes ------- */
0444                zSetHierarchyMode(FALSE);      /* top-level objects only */
0445                zSetSubjectSize(25,25,25);           /* dimensions of box */
0446                zSetSubjectAttitude(30,0,30);       /* orientation of box */
0447                zSetSubjectLocation(-75,0,0);          /* location of box */
0448                zSetShadingColor(zRED);                   /* color of box */
0449                zDrawCube();                 /* render the first box, etc. */
0450                zSetShadingColor(zBROWN);
0451                zSetSubjectLocation(0,0,0);
0452                zSetNearClippingPlane(125); /* reset the clipping plane */
0453                zDrawCube();
0454                zSetShadingColor(zGREEN);
0455                zSetSubjectLocation(75,0,0);
0456                zSetNearClippingPlane(129); /* reset the clipping plane */
0457                zDrawCube();
0458                zSetNearClippingPlane(78);     /* default clipping plane */
0459                /* ----------- perform system maintenance ----------- */
0460                PaintImage= zIMAGE;
0461                if (FrameReady==TRUE) zCopyToFrame(hWnd);
0462                SetCursor(hPrevCursor);
0463                ReleaseCapture();
0464                break;
0465
0466            /* ---------------- render a 3D cylinder ---------------- */
0467            case IDM_DrawCylinder:
0468                SetCapture(hWnd);
0469                hPrevCursor= SetCursor(hHourGlass);
0470                zClear(hWnd);
0471                zClearHidden3DPage();
0472                zResetZBuffer();
0473                hFontDC= GetDC(MainhWnd);
0474                hFont= GetStockObject(SYSTEM_FONT);
0475                hPrevFont= SelectObject(hFontDC,hFont);
0476                SetTextColor(hFontDC,RGB(0,0,0));
0477                SetBkMode(hFontDC,TRANSPARENT);
0478                TextOut(hFontDC,10,10,"Camera distance 300 ft.",23);
0479                TextOut(hFontDC,10,26,"Camera heading 315 degrees",26);
0480                TextOut(hFontDC,10,42,"Camera pitch 320 degrees",24);
0481                if (CamLens==55)
0482                    {
0483                    TextOut(hFontDC,10,58,"Using 55mm lens",15);
0484                    }
0485                if (CamLens==135)
0486                    {
0487                    TextOut(hFontDC,10,58, "Using 135mm lens",16);
0488                    }
0489                if (CamLens==200)
0490                    {
0491                    TextOut(hFontDC,10,58, "Using 200mm lens",16);
0492                    }
0493                SetTextColor(hFontDC,RGB(255,255,255));
```

```
0494          SelectObject(hFontDC,hPrevFont);
0495          ReleaseDC(MainhWnd,hFontDC);
0496          /* --------------- configure the camera --------------- */
0497          zSetCameraDistance(300);
0498          zSetCameraHeading(315);
0499          zSetCameraPitch(320);
0500          zSetLightPosition(60,180);
0501          /* -------- configure and render one cylinder --------- */
0502          zSetHierarchyMode(FALSE);
0503          zSetSubjectSize(40,40,40);           /* radius and length */
0504          zSetSubjectAttitude(0,0,0);              /* orientation */
0505          zSetSubjectLocation(0,0,0);                 /* location */
0506          zSetShadingColor(zCYAN);                       /* color */
0507          zDrawCylinder();                              /* render */
0508          /* ----------- perform system maintenance ----------- */
0509          PaintImage= zIMAGE;
0510          if (FrameReady==TRUE) zCopyToFrame(hWnd);
0511          SetCursor(hPrevCursor);
0512          ReleaseCapture();
0513          break;
0514
0515      /* ------------- render a 3D curved surface ------------- */
0516      case IDM_DrawCurve:
0517        SetCapture(hWnd);
0518        hPrevCursor= SetCursor(hHourGlass);
0519        zClear(hWnd);
0520        zClearHidden3DPage();
0521        zResetZBuffer();
0522        hFontDC= GetDC(MainhWnd);
0523        hFont= GetStockObject(SYSTEM_FONT);
0524        hPrevFont= SelectObject(hFontDC,hFont);
0525        SetTextColor(hFontDC,RGB(0,0,0));
0526        SetBkMode(hFontDC,TRANSPARENT);
0527        TextOut(hFontDC,10,10,"Camera distance 300 ft.",23);
0528        TextOut(hFontDC,10,26,"Camera heading 050 degrees",26);
0529        TextOut(hFontDC,10,42,"Camera pitch 345 degrees",24);
0530        if (CamLens==55)
0531          {
0532          TextOut(hFontDC,10,58,"Using 55mm lens",15);
0533          }
0534        if (CamLens==135)
0535          {
0536          TextOut(hFontDC,10,58, "Using 135mm lens",16);
0537          }
0538        if (CamLens==200)
0539          {
0540          TextOut(hFontDC,10,58, "Using 200mm lens",16);
0541          }
0542        SetTextColor(hFontDC,RGB(255,255,255));
0543        SelectObject(hFontDC,hPrevFont);
0544        ReleaseDC(MainhWnd,hFontDC);
0545        /* --------------- configure the camera --------------- */
0546        zSetCameraDistance(300);
0547        zSetCameraHeading(50);
0548        zSetCameraPitch(345);
0549        zSetLightPosition(60,180);
0550        /* ------ configure and render a curved surface ------- */
0551        zSetHierarchyMode(FALSE);
0552        zSetSubjectSize(50,           /* x-length of surface edge */
0553                        50,      /* y-magnitude of control-points */
0554                        30);        /* z-depth of curved surface */
```

```
0555            zSetSubjectAttitude(0,0,0);                    /* orientation */
0556            zSetSubjectLocation(-50,0,0);                     /* location */
0557            zSetShadingColor(zRED);                             /* color */
0558            zDrawCurve();                                      /* render */
0559            zSetSubjectLocation(50,0,0);             /* set new location */
0560            zSetShadingColor(zMAGENTA);                 /* set new color */
0561            zDrawCurve();                         /* render another section */
0562            /* ----------- perform system maintenance ------------ */
0563            PaintImage= zIMAGE;
0564            if (FrameReady==TRUE) zCopyToFrame(hWnd);
0565            SetCursor(hPrevCursor);
0566            ReleaseCapture();
0567            break;
0568
0569         /* ------------------- render a 3D cone ----------------- */
0570         case IDM_DrawCone:
0571            SetCapture(hWnd);
0572            hPrevCursor= SetCursor(hHourGlass);
0573            zClear(hWnd);
0574            zClearHidden3DPage();
0575            zResetZBuffer();
0576            hFontDC= GetDC(MainhWnd);
0577            hFont= GetStockObject(SYSTEM_FONT);
0578            hPrevFont= SelectObject(hFontDC,hFont);
0579            SetTextColor(hFontDC,RGB(0,0,0));
0580            SetBkMode(hFontDC,TRANSPARENT);
0581            TextOut(hFontDC,10,10,"Camera distance 300 ft.",23);
0582            TextOut(hFontDC,10,26,"Camera heading 360 degrees",26);
0583            TextOut(hFontDC,10,42,"Camera pitch 360 degrees",24);
0584            if (CamLens==55)
0585              {
0586              TextOut(hFontDC,10,58,"Using 55mm lens",15);
0587              }
0588            if (CamLens==135)
0589              {
0590              TextOut(hFontDC,10,58, "Using 135mm lens",16);
0591              }
0592            if (CamLens==200)
0593              {
0594              TextOut(hFontDC,10,58, "Using 200mm lens",16);
0595              }
0596            SetTextColor(hFontDC,RGB(255,255,255));
0597            SelectObject(hFontDC,hPrevFont);
0598            ReleaseDC(MainhWnd,hFontDC);
0599            /* -------------- configure the camera -------------- */
0600            zSetCameraDistance(300);
0601            zSetCameraHeading(360);
0602            zSetCameraPitch(360);
0603            zSetLightPosition(60,180);
0604            /* -------- configure and render one cylinder --------- */
0605            zSetHierarchyMode(FALSE);
0606            zSetSubjectSize(40,40,40);             /* radius and length */
0607            zSetSubjectAttitude(0,0,285);              /* orientation */
0608            zSetSubjectLocation(0,0,0);                   /* location */
0609            zSetShadingColor(zGREEN);                        /* color */
0610            zDrawCone();                                    /* render */
0611            /* ----------- perform system maintenance ------------ */
0612            PaintImage= zIMAGE;
0613            if (FrameReady==TRUE) zCopyToFrame(hWnd);
0614            SetCursor(hPrevCursor);
0615            ReleaseCapture();
```

```
0616            break;
0617
0618        /* -------------- render a 3D half-sphere -------------- */
0619        case IDM_DrawHemisphere:
0620            SetCapture(hWnd);
0621            hPrevCursor= SetCursor(hHourGlass);
0622            zClear(hWnd);
0623            zClearHidden3DPage();
0624            zResetZBuffer();
0625            hFontDC= GetDC(MainhWnd);
0626            hFont= GetStockObject(SYSTEM_FONT);
0627            hPrevFont= SelectObject(hFontDC,hFont);
0628            SetTextColor(hFontDC,RGB(0,0,0));
0629            SetBkMode(hFontDC,TRANSPARENT);
0630            TextOut(hFontDC,10,10,"Camera distance 300 ft.",23);
0631            TextOut(hFontDC,10,26,"Camera heading 315 degrees",26);
0632            TextOut(hFontDC,10,42,"Camera pitch 320 degrees",24);
0633            if (CamLens==55)
0634              {
0635              TextOut(hFontDC,10,58,"Using 55mm lens",15);
0636              }
0637            if (CamLens==135)
0638              {
0639              TextOut(hFontDC,10,58, "Using 135mm lens",16);
0640              }
0641            if (CamLens==200)
0642              {
0643              TextOut(hFontDC,10,58, "Using 200mm lens",16);
0644              }
0645            SetTextColor(hFontDC,RGB(255,255,255));
0646            SelectObject(hFontDC,hPrevFont);
0647            ReleaseDC(MainhWnd,hFontDC);
0648            /* -------------- configure the camera -------------- */
0649            zSetCameraDistance(300);
0650            zSetCameraHeading(315);
0651            zSetCameraPitch(320);
0652            zSetLightPosition(60,180);
0653            /* -------- configure and render one hemisphere ------- */
0654            zSetHierarchyMode(FALSE);
0655            zSetSubjectSize(50,50,50);      /* radius of half-sphere */
0656            zSetSubjectAttitude(0,0,25);                /* orientation */
0657            zSetSubjectLocation(0,0,0);                 /* location */
0658            zSetShadingColor(zMAGENTA);                 /* color */
0659            zDrawHemisphere();                          /* render */
0660            /* ----------- perform system maintenance ----------- */
0661            PaintImage= zIMAGE;
0662            if (FrameReady==TRUE) zCopyToFrame(hWnd);
0663            SetCursor(hPrevCursor);
0664            ReleaseCapture();
0665            break;
0666
0667        /* ---------------- render a 3D wedge ----------------- */
0668        case IDM_DrawWedge:
0669            SetCapture(hWnd);
0670            hPrevCursor= SetCursor(hHourGlass);
0671            zClear(hWnd);
0672            zClearHidden3DPage();
0673            zResetZBuffer();
0674            hFontDC= GetDC(MainhWnd);
0675            hFont= GetStockObject(SYSTEM_FONT);
0676            hPrevFont= SelectObject(hFontDC,hFont);
```

```
0677                SetTextColor(hFontDC,RGB(0,0,0));
0678                SetBkMode(hFontDC,TRANSPARENT);
0679                TextOut(hFontDC,10,10,"Camera distance 300 ft.",23);
0680                TextOut(hFontDC,10,26,"Camera heading 315 degrees",26);
0681                TextOut(hFontDC,10,42,"Camera pitch 340 degrees",24);
0682                if (CamLens==55)
0683                  {
0684                  TextOut(hFontDC,10,58,"Using 55mm lens",15);
0685                  }
0686                if (CamLens==135)
0687                  {
0688                  TextOut(hFontDC,10,58, "Using 135mm lens",16);
0689                  }
0690                if (CamLens==200)
0691                  {
0692                  TextOut(hFontDC,10,58, "Using 200mm lens",16);
0693                  }
0694                SetTextColor(hFontDC,RGB(255,255,255));
0695                SelectObject(hFontDC,hPrevFont);
0696                ReleaseDC(MainhWnd,hFontDC);
0697                /* -------------- configure the camera -------------- */
0698                zSetCameraDistance(300);
0699                zSetCameraHeading(315);
0700                zSetCameraPitch(340);
0701                zSetLightPosition(60,180);
0702                /* ----------- configure and render 3 wedges ---------- */
0703                zSetHierarchyMode(FALSE);
0704                zSetSubjectSize(25,25,25);
0705                zSetSubjectAttitude(0,0,0);
0706                zSetSubjectLocation(-50,0,0);
0707                zSetShadingColor(zRED);
0708                zDrawWedge();
0709                zSetSubjectLocation(0,0,0);
0710                zSetSubjectAttitude(90,0,0);
0711                zSetShadingColor(zBROWN);
0712                zDrawWedge();
0713                zSetSubjectLocation(50,0,0);
0714                zSetSubjectAttitude(0,0,0);
0715                zSetShadingColor(zGREEN);
0716                zDrawWedge();
0717                /* ----------- perform system maintenance ----------- */
0718                PaintImage= zIMAGE;
0719                if (FrameReady==TRUE) zCopyToFrame(hWnd);
0720                SetCursor(hPrevCursor);
0721                ReleaseCapture();
0722                break;
0723
0724          /* ----------- test the moveable light-source ---------- */
0725          case IDM_TestLighting:
0726                SetCapture(hWnd);
0727                hPrevCursor= SetCursor(hHourGlass);
0728                zClear(hWnd);
0729                zClearHidden3DPage();
0730                zResetZBuffer();
0731                hFontDC= GetDC(MainhWnd);
0732                hFont= GetStockObject(SYSTEM_FONT);
0733                hPrevFont= SelectObject(hFontDC,hFont);
0734                SetTextColor(hFontDC,RGB(0,0,0));
0735                SetBkMode(hFontDC,TRANSPARENT);
0736                TextOut(hFontDC,10,10,"Camera distance 300 ft.",23);
0737                TextOut(hFontDC,10,26,"Camera heading 315 degrees",26);
```

```
0738            TextOut(hFontDC,10,42,"Camera pitch 340 degrees",24);
0739            if (CamLens==55)
0740              {
0741              TextOut(hFontDC,10,58,"Using 55mm lens",15);
0742              }
0743            if (CamLens==135)
0744              {
0745              TextOut(hFontDC,10,58, "Using 135mm lens",16);
0746              }
0747            if (CamLens==200)
0748              {
0749              TextOut(hFontDC,10,58, "Using 200mm lens",16);
0750              }
0751            SetTextColor(hFontDC,RGB(255,255,255));
0752            SelectObject(hFontDC,hPrevFont);
0753            ReleaseDC(MainhWnd,hFontDC);
0754            /* -------------- configure the camera -------------- */
0755            zSetCameraDistance(300);
0756            zSetCameraHeading(315);
0757            zSetCameraPitch(340);
0758            zSetLightPosition(60,180);  /* light elevation, heading */
0759            /* ------ configure and render a series of boxes ------ */
0760            zSetHierarchyMode(FALSE);
0761            zSetShadingColor(zGREEN);
0762            zSetSubjectSize(10,10,10);
0763            zSetSubjectLocation(-90,0,0);
0764            zSetSubjectAttitude(0,0,0);    zDrawCube();
0765            zSetSubjectLocation(-70,0,0);
0766            zSetSubjectAttitude(0,0,350); zDrawCube();
0767            zSetSubjectLocation(-50,0,0);
0768            zSetSubjectAttitude(0,0,340); zDrawCube();
0769            zSetSubjectLocation(-30,0,0);
0770            zSetSubjectAttitude(0,0,330); zDrawCube();
0771            zSetSubjectLocation(-10,0,0);
0772            zSetSubjectAttitude(0,0,320); zDrawCube();
0773            zSetSubjectLocation(10,0,0);
0774            zSetSubjectAttitude(0,0,310); zDrawCube();
0775            zSetSubjectLocation(30,0,0);
0776            zSetSubjectAttitude(0,0,300); zDrawCube();
0777            zSetSubjectLocation(50,0,0);
0778            zSetSubjectAttitude(0,0,290); zDrawCube();
0779            zSetSubjectLocation(70,0,0);
0780            zSetSubjectAttitude(0,0,280); zDrawCube();
0781            zSetSubjectLocation(90,0,0);
0782            zSetSubjectAttitude(0,0,270); zDrawCube();
0783            /* ----------- perform system maintenance ----------- */
0784            PaintImage= zIMAGE;
0785            if (FrameReady==TRUE) zCopyToFrame(hWnd);
0786            SetCursor(hPrevCursor);
0787            ReleaseCapture();
0788            break;
0789
0790        /* --------- test the virtual reality functions --------- */
0791        case IDM_VRtestA:
0792            SetCapture(hWnd);
0793            hPrevCursor= SetCursor(hHourGlass);
0794            zClear(hWnd);
0795            zClearHidden3DPage();
0796            zResetZBuffer();
0797            hFontDC= GetDC(MainhWnd);
0798            hFont= GetStockObject(SYSTEM_FONT);
```

```
0799            hPrevFont= SelectObject(hFontDC,hFont);
0800            SetTextColor(hFontDC,RGB(0,0,0));
0801            SetBkMode(hFontDC,TRANSPARENT);
0802            TextOut(hFontDC,10,10,
0803              "Virtual reality viewpoint simulation",36);
0804            TextOut(hFontDC,10,26,"Viewpoint: 0,0,356",18);
0805            TextOut(hFontDC,10,42,"View angle: 360 degrees",23);
0806            SetTextColor(hFontDC,RGB(255,255,255));
0807            SelectObject(hFontDC,hPrevFont);
0808            ReleaseDC(MainhWnd,hFontDC);
0809            /* -------------- configure the camera -------------- */
0810            zDisableTarget();              /* unlock from fixed-target */
0811            zSetVRCameraLocation(0,0,356);          /* set location */
0812            zSetVRCameraHeading(360);         /* set viewing heading */
0813            zSetVRCameraPitch(360);            /* set viewing pitch */
0814            zSetLightPosition(60,180);         /* set light position */
0815            /* ----------------- render 3 boxes ----------------- */
0816            zSetHierarchyMode(FALSE);
0817            zSetSubjectSize(25,25,25);
0818            zSetSubjectAttitude(0,0,0);
0819            zSetSubjectLocation(-60,0,0);
0820            zSetShadingColor(zRED);
0821            zDrawCube();
0822            zSetShadingColor(zBROWN);
0823            zSetSubjectLocation(0,0,0);
0824            zDrawCube();
0825            zSetShadingColor(zGREEN);
0826            zSetSubjectLocation(60,0,0);
0827            zDrawCube();
0828            zEnableTarget();           /* restore fixed-target mode */
0829            /* ----------- perform system maintenance ----------- */
0830            PaintImage= zIMAGE;
0831            if (FrameReady==TRUE) zCopyToFrame(hWnd);
0832            SetCursor(hPrevCursor);
0833            ReleaseCapture();
0834            break;
0835          case IDM_VRtestB:
0836            SetCapture(hWnd);
0837            hPrevCursor= SetCursor(hHourGlass);
0838            zClear(hWnd);
0839            zClearHidden3DPage();
0840            zResetZBuffer();
0841            hFontDC= GetDC(MainhWnd);
0842            hFont= GetStockObject(SYSTEM_FONT);
0843            hPrevFont= SelectObject(hFontDC,hFont);
0844            SetTextColor(hFontDC,RGB(0,0,0));
0845            SetBkMode(hFontDC,TRANSPARENT);
0846            TextOut(hFontDC,10,10,
0847              "Virtual reality viewpoint simulation",36);
0848            TextOut(hFontDC,10,26,"Viewpoint: -60,0,356",20);
0849            TextOut(hFontDC,10,42,"View angle: 360 degrees",23);
0850            SetTextColor(hFontDC,RGB(255,255,255));
0851            SelectObject(hFontDC,hPrevFont);
0852            ReleaseDC(MainhWnd,hFontDC);
0853            /* -------------- configure the camera -------------- */
0854            zDisableTarget();
0855            zSetVRCameraLocation(-60,0,356);
0856            zSetVRCameraHeading(360);
0857            zSetVRCameraPitch(360);
0858            zSetLightPosition(60,180);
0859            /* ----------------- render 3 boxes ----------------- */
```

```
0860          zSetHierarchyMode(FALSE);
0861          zSetSubjectSize(25,25,25);
0862          zSetSubjectAttitude(0,0,0);
0863          zSetSubjectLocation(-60,0,0);
0864          zSetShadingColor(zRED);
0865          zDrawCube();
0866          zSetShadingColor(zBROWN);
0867          zSetSubjectLocation(0,0,0);
0868          zDrawCube();
0869          zSetShadingColor(zGREEN);
0870          zSetSubjectLocation(60,0,0);
0871          zDrawCube();
0872          zEnableTarget();
0873          /* ------------ perform system maintenance ------------ */
0874          PaintImage= zIMAGE;
0875          if (FrameReady==TRUE) zCopyToFrame(hWnd);
0876          SetCursor(hPrevCursor);
0877          ReleaseCapture();
0878          break;
0879        case IDM_VRtestC:
0880          SetCapture(hWnd);
0881          hPrevCursor= SetCursor(hHourGlass);
0882          zClear(hWnd);
0883          zClearHidden3DPage();
0884          zResetZBuffer();
0885          hFontDC= GetDC(MainhWnd);
0886          hFont= GetStockObject(SYSTEM_FONT);
0887          hPrevFont= SelectObject(hFontDC,hFont);
0888          SetTextColor(hFontDC,RGB(0,0,0));
0889          SetBkMode(hFontDC,TRANSPARENT);
0890          TextOut(hFontDC,10,10,
0891            "Virtual reality viewpoint simulation",36);
0892          TextOut(hFontDC,10,26,"Viewpoint: 60,0,356",19);
0893          TextOut(hFontDC,10,42,"View angle: 360 degrees",23);
0894          SetTextColor(hFontDC,RGB(255,255,255));
0895          SelectObject(hFontDC,hPrevFont);
0896          ReleaseDC(MainhWnd,hFontDC);
0897          /* -------------- configure the camera -------------- */
0898          zDisableTarget();
0899          zSetVRCameraLocation(60,0,356);
0900          zSetVRCameraHeading(360);
0901          zSetVRCameraPitch(360);            /* set viewing pitch */
0902          zSetLightPosition(60,180);
0903          /* ----------------- render 3 boxes ----------------- */
0904          zSetHierarchyMode(FALSE);
0905          zSetSubjectSize(25,25,25);
0906          zSetSubjectAttitude(0,0,0);
0907          zSetSubjectLocation(-60,0,0);
0908          zSetShadingColor(zRED);
0909          zDrawCube();
0910          zSetShadingColor(zBROWN);
0911          zSetSubjectLocation(0,0,0);
0912          zDrawCube();
0913          zSetShadingColor(zGREEN);
0914          zSetSubjectLocation(60,0,0);
0915          zDrawCube();
0916          zEnableTarget();              /* restore fixed-target mode */
0917          /* ------------ perform system maintenance ------------ */
0918          PaintImage= zIMAGE;
0919          if (FrameReady==TRUE) zCopyToFrame(hWnd);
0920          SetCursor(hPrevCursor);
```

```
0921            ReleaseCapture();
0922            break;
0923          case IDM_VRtestD:
0924            SetCapture(hWnd);
0925            hPrevCursor= SetCursor(hHourGlass);
0926            zClear(hWnd);
0927            zClearHidden3DPage();
0928            zResetZBuffer();
0929            hFontDC= GetDC(MainhWnd);
0930            hFont= GetStockObject(SYSTEM_FONT);
0931            hPrevFont= SelectObject(hFontDC,hFont);
0932            SetTextColor(hFontDC,RGB(0,0,0));
0933            SetBkMode(hFontDC,TRANSPARENT);
0934            TextOut(hFontDC,10,10,
0935              "Virtual reality viewpoint simulation",36);
0936            TextOut(hFontDC,10,26,"Viewpoint: 0,0,356",18);
0937            TextOut(hFontDC,10,42,"View angle: 090 degrees",23);
0938            SetTextColor(hFontDC,RGB(255,255,255));
0939            SelectObject(hFontDC,hPrevFont);
0940            ReleaseDC(MainhWnd,hFontDC);
0941            /* -------------- configure the camera -------------- */
0942            zDisableTarget();          /* unlock from fixed-target */
0943            zSetVRCameraLocation(0,0,356);          /* set location */
0944            zSetVRCameraHeading(90);           /* set viewing heading */
0945            zSetVRCameraPitch(360);            /* set viewing pitch */
0946            zSetLightPosition(60,180);
0947            /* ----------------- render 3 boxes ----------------- */
0948            zSetHierarchyMode(FALSE);
0949            zSetSubjectSize(25,25,25);
0950            zSetSubjectAttitude(0,0,0);
0951            zSetSubjectLocation(356,0,296);
0952            zSetShadingColor(zRED);
0953            zDrawCube();
0954            zSetShadingColor(zGRAY);
0955            zSetSubjectLocation(356,0,356);
0956            zDrawCube();
0957            zSetShadingColor(zBLUE);
0958            zSetSubjectLocation(356,0,416);
0959            zDrawCube();
0960            zEnableTarget();           /* restore fixed-target mode */
0961            /* ------------ perform system maintenance ------------ */
0962            PaintImage= zIMAGE;
0963            if (FrameReady==TRUE) zCopyToFrame(hWnd);
0964            SetCursor(hPrevCursor);
0965            ReleaseCapture();
0966            break;
0967
0968          /* ------------ select different camera lens ------------ */
0969          case IDM_Lens1:
0970            zSetCameraLens(55); CamLens= 55;
0971            MessageBox(GetFocus(),
0972              "55mm standard lens has been selected.",
0973              "3D camera", MB_OK);
0974            break;
0975          case IDM_Lens2:
0976            zSetCameraLens(135); CamLens= 135;
0977            MessageBox(GetFocus(),
0978              "135mm telephoto lens has been selected.",
0979              "3D camera", MB_OK);
0980            break;
0981          case IDM_Lens3:
```

```
0982            zSetCameraLens(200); CamLens= 200;
0983            MessageBox(GetFocus(),
0984              "200mm telephoto lens has been selected.",
0985              "3D camera", MB_OK);
0986            break;
0987
0988        /* ---------------- render deformed boxes -------------- */
0989        case IDM_DrawDeformBox:
0990            SetCapture(hWnd);
0991            hPrevCursor= SetCursor(hHourGlass);
0992            zClear(hWnd);
0993            zClearHidden3DPage();
0994            zResetZBuffer();
0995            hFontDC= GetDC(MainhWnd);
0996            hFont= GetStockObject(SYSTEM_FONT);
0997            hPrevFont= SelectObject(hFontDC,hFont);
0998            SetTextColor(hFontDC,RGB(0,0,0));
0999            SetBkMode(hFontDC,TRANSPARENT);
1000            TextOut(hFontDC,10,10,"Camera distance 300 ft.",23);
1001            TextOut(hFontDC,10,26,"Camera heading 315 degrees",26);
1002            TextOut(hFontDC,10,42,"Camera pitch 340 degrees",24);
1003            if (CamLens==55)
1004              {
1005              TextOut(hFontDC,10,58,"Using 55mm lens",15);
1006              }
1007            if (CamLens==135)
1008              {
1009              TextOut(hFontDC,10,58, "Using 135mm lens",16);
1010              }
1011            if (CamLens==200)
1012              {
1013              TextOut(hFontDC,10,58, "Using 200mm lens",16);
1014              }
1015            SetTextColor(hFontDC,RGB(255,255,255));
1016            SelectObject(hFontDC,hPrevFont);
1017            ReleaseDC(MainhWnd,hFontDC);
1018            /* -------------- configure the camera -------------- */
1019            zSetCameraDistance(300);
1020            zSetCameraHeading(315);
1021            zSetCameraPitch(340);
1022            zSetLightPosition(60,180);
1023            /* ------ configure and render 3 deformed boxes ------- */
1024            zSetHierarchyMode(FALSE);
1025            zSetSubjectAttitude(0,0,0);
1026            zSetSubjectSize(25,25,25);
1027            zSetSubjectLocation(-60,0,0);
1028            zSetShadingColor(zRED);
1029            zDrawDeformBox(15,-15,15,-15);
1030            zSetSubjectLocation(0,0,0);
1031            zSetShadingColor(zBROWN);
1032            zDrawDeformBox(10,-10,10,-10);
1033            zSetSubjectLocation(60,0,0);
1034            zSetShadingColor(zGREEN);
1035            zDrawDeformBox(5,-5,5,-5);
1036            /* ----------- perform system maintenance ----------- */
1037            PaintImage= zIMAGE;
1038            if (FrameReady==TRUE) zCopyToFrame(hWnd);
1039            SetCursor(hPrevCursor);
1040            ReleaseCapture();
1041            break;
1042
```

```
1043        /* -------------- render a half-cylinder -------------- */
1044        case IDM_DrawHalfCylinder:
1045          SetCapture(hWnd);
1046          hPrevCursor= SetCursor(hHourGlass);
1047          zClear(hWnd);
1048          zClearHidden3DPage();
1049          zResetZBuffer();
1050          hFontDC= GetDC(MainhWnd);
1051          hFont= GetStockObject(SYSTEM_FONT);
1052          hPrevFont= SelectObject(hFontDC,hFont);
1053          SetTextColor(hFontDC,RGB(0,0,0));
1054          SetBkMode(hFontDC,TRANSPARENT);
1055          TextOut(hFontDC,10,10,"Camera distance 300 ft.",23);
1056          TextOut(hFontDC,10,26,"Camera heading 045 degrees",26);
1057          TextOut(hFontDC,10,42,"Camera pitch 320 degrees",24);
1058          if (CamLens==55)
1059            {
1060            TextOut(hFontDC,10,58,"Using 55mm lens",15);
1061            }
1062          if (CamLens==135)
1063            {
1064            TextOut(hFontDC,10,58, "Using 135mm lens",16);
1065            }
1066          if (CamLens==200)
1067            {
1068            TextOut(hFontDC,10,58, "Using 200mm lens",16);
1069            }
1070          SetTextColor(hFontDC,RGB(255,255,255));
1071          SelectObject(hFontDC,hPrevFont);
1072          ReleaseDC(MainhWnd,hFontDC);
1073          /* --------------- configure the camera -------------- */
1074          zSetCameraDistance(300);
1075          zSetCameraHeading(45);
1076          zSetCameraPitch(320);
1077          zSetLightPosition(60,180);
1078          /* ------ configure and render one half-cylinder ------ */
1079          zSetHierarchyMode(FALSE);
1080          zSetSubjectSize(40,40,40);      /* set radius and length */
1081          zSetSubjectAttitude(0,0,0);             /* orientation */
1082          zSetSubjectLocation(0,0,0);                /* location */
1083          zSetShadingColor(zCYAN);                      /* color */
1084          zDrawHalfCylinder();                         /* render */
1085          /* ----------- perform system maintenance ----------- */
1086          PaintImage= zIMAGE;
1087          if (FrameReady==TRUE) zCopyToFrame(hWnd);
1088          SetCursor(hPrevCursor);
1089          ReleaseCapture();
1090          break;
1091
1092        /* --------------- render a bulged surface -------------- */
1093        case IDM_DrawBulge:
1094          SetCapture(hWnd);
1095          hPrevCursor= SetCursor(hHourGlass);
1096          zClear(hWnd);
1097          zClearHidden3DPage();
1098          zResetZBuffer();
1099          hFontDC= GetDC(MainhWnd);
1100          hFont= GetStockObject(SYSTEM_FONT);
1101          hPrevFont= SelectObject(hFontDC,hFont);
1102          SetTextColor(hFontDC,RGB(0,0,0));
1103          SetBkMode(hFontDC,TRANSPARENT);
```

```
1104            TextOut(hFontDC,10,10,"Camera distance 300 ft.",23);
1105            TextOut(hFontDC,10,26,"Camera heading 050 degrees",26);
1106            TextOut(hFontDC,10,42,"Camera pitch 345 degrees",24);
1107            if (CamLens==55)
1108              {
1109              TextOut(hFontDC,10,58,"Using 55mm lens",15);
1110              }
1111            if (CamLens==135)
1112              {
1113              TextOut(hFontDC,10,58, "Using 135mm lens",16);
1114              }
1115            if (CamLens==200)
1116              {
1117              TextOut(hFontDC,10,58, "Using 200mm lens",16);
1118              }
1119            SetTextColor(hFontDC,RGB(255,255,255));
1120            SelectObject(hFontDC,hPrevFont);
1121            ReleaseDC(MainhWnd,hFontDC);
1122            /* -------------- configure the camera -------------- */
1123            zSetCameraDistance(300);
1124            zSetCameraHeading(50);
1125            zSetCameraPitch(345);
1126            zSetLightPosition(60,180);
1127            /* ------ configure and render a curved surface ------- */
1128            zSetHierarchyMode(FALSE);
1129            zSetSubjectSize(50,            /* x-length of surface edge */
1130                            40,     /* y-magnitude of control-points */
1131                            30);        /* z-depth of curved surface */
1132            zSetSubjectAttitude(0,0,0);              /* orientation */
1133            zSetSubjectLocation(0,0,0);                 /* location */
1134            zSetShadingColor(zMAGENTA);                    /* color */
1135            zDrawBulge();                                 /* render */
1136            /* ----------- perform system maintenance ----------- */
1137            PaintImage= zIMAGE;
1138            if (FrameReady==TRUE) zCopyToFrame(hWnd);
1139            SetCursor(hPrevCursor);
1140            ReleaseCapture();
1141            break;
1142
1143        /* ---------------- render a fixed assembly -------------- */
1144        case IDM_DrawRobotArm:
1145            SetCapture(hWnd);
1146            hPrevCursor= SetCursor(hHourGlass);
1147            zClear(hWnd);
1148            zClearHidden3DPage();
1149            zResetZBuffer();
1150            hFontDC= GetDC(MainhWnd);
1151            hFont= GetStockObject(SYSTEM_FONT);
1152            hPrevFont= SelectObject(hFontDC,hFont);
1153            SetTextColor(hFontDC,RGB(0,0,0));
1154            SetBkMode(hFontDC,TRANSPARENT);
1155            TextOut(hFontDC,10,10,"Robotic arm assembly",20);
1156            TextOut(hFontDC,10,26,"built from 3D subobjects",24);
1157            SetTextColor(hFontDC,RGB(255,255,255));
1158            SelectObject(hFontDC,hPrevFont);
1159            ReleaseDC(MainhWnd,hFontDC);
1160            /* -------------- configure the camera -------------- */
1161            zSetCameraDistance(356);
1162            zSetCameraHeading(330);
1163            zSetCameraPitch(320);
1164            zSetLightPosition(60,180);
```

```
1165              /* ---------------- draw the assembly --------------- */
1166              zSetHierarchyMode(FALSE);
1167              zDrawRoboticArm();
1168              /* ----------- perform system maintenance ----------- */
1169              PaintImage= zIMAGE;
1170              if (FrameReady==TRUE) zCopyToFrame(hWnd);
1171              SetCursor(hPrevCursor);
1172              ReleaseCapture();
1173              break;
1174
1175          /* ----------- render a hierarchical assembly ---------- */
1176          case IDM_BuildAssembly:
1177              SetCapture(hWnd);
1178              hPrevCursor= SetCursor(hHourGlass);
1179              zClear(hWnd);
1180              zClearHidden3DPage();
1181              zResetZBuffer();
1182              hFontDC= GetDC(MainhWnd);
1183              hFont= GetStockObject(SYSTEM_FONT);
1184              hPrevFont= SelectObject(hFontDC,hFont);
1185              SetTextColor(hFontDC,RGB(0,0,0));
1186              SetBkMode(hFontDC,TRANSPARENT);
1187              TextOut(hFontDC,10,10,"Robotic arm structures",22);
1188              TextOut(hFontDC,10,26,"built from hierarchy",20);
1189              TextOut(hFontDC,10,42,"of 3D subobjects.",17);
1190              SetTextColor(hFontDC,RGB(255,255,255));
1191              SelectObject(hFontDC,hPrevFont);
1192              ReleaseDC(MainhWnd,hFontDC);
1193              /* -------------- configure the camera -------------- */
1194              zSetCameraDistance(356);
1195              zSetCameraHeading(330);
1196              zSetCameraPitch(320);
1197              zSetLightPosition(60,180);
1198              /* ---------------- draw the assembly --------------- */
1199              zSetHierarchyMode(TRUE);   /* enable hierarchy modeling */
1200              zSetSubjectAttitude(0,0,0);        /* orient assembly... */
1201              zSetSubjectLocation(-35,0,0);   /* position assembly... */
1202              zBuildAssembly();          /* ...and build first instance */
1203              zSetSubjectAttitude(0,0,30);     /* reorient assembly... */
1204              zSetSubjectLocation(35,0,0);  /* reposition assembly... */
1205              zBuildAssembly();          /* ...and build second instance */
1206              zSetHierarchyMode(FALSE); /* disable hierarchy modeling */
1207              /* ----------- perform system maintenance ----------- */
1208              PaintImage= zIMAGE;
1209              if (FrameReady==TRUE) zCopyToFrame(hWnd);
1210              SetCursor(hPrevCursor);
1211              ReleaseCapture();
1212              break;
1213
1214          /* ----------------- clear the viewport --------------- */
1215          case IDM_Clear:
1216              zClear(hWnd); zClearHidden3DPage();
1217              PaintImage= zBLANK;
1218              if (FrameReady==TRUE) zCopyToFrame(hWnd);
1219              break;
1220
1221          /* ----- display the About and License message boxes ----- */
1222          case IDM_About:
1223            LoadString(hInst,IDS_About,lpCaption,Max);
1224            LoadString(hInst,IDS_AboutText,lpMessage,MaxText);
1225            MessageBox(GetFocus(),lpMessage,lpCaption,MB_OK);
```

```
1226          break;
1227        case IDM_License:
1228          LoadString(hInst,IDS_License,lpCaption,Max);
1229          LoadString(hInst,IDS_LicenseText,lpMessage,MaxText);
1230          MessageBox(GetFocus(),lpMessage,lpCaption,MB_OK);
1231          break;
1232
1233        /* ------------- report the display resolution ----------- */
1234        case IDM_Display:
1235          if (DisplayWidth==640)
1236            {
1237            if (DisplayHeight==480)
1238              {                        /* 640-by-480 VGA mode detected */
1239              LoadString(hInst,IDS_Resolution,lpCaption,Max);
1240              LoadString(hInst,IDS_ResVGA,lpMessage,MaxText);
1241              MessageBox(GetFocus(),lpMessage,lpCaption,MB_OK);
1242              }
1243            if (DisplayHeight==350)      /* (not used in this demo) */
1244              {                        /* 640-by-350 EGA mode detected */
1245              LoadString(hInst,IDS_Resolution,lpCaption,Max);
1246              LoadString(hInst,IDS_ResEGA,lpMessage,MaxText);
1247              MessageBox(GetFocus(),lpMessage,lpCaption,MB_OK);
1248              }
1249            if (DisplayHeight==200)      /* (not used in this demo) */
1250              {                        /* 640-by-200 CGA mode detected */
1251              LoadString(hInst,IDS_Resolution,lpCaption,Max);
1252              LoadString(hInst,IDS_ResCGA,lpMessage,MaxText);
1253              MessageBox(GetFocus(),lpMessage,lpCaption,MB_OK);
1254              }
1255            break;
1256            }
1257          if (DisplayWidth==800)
1258            {                          /* 800-by-600 SVGA mode detected */
1259            LoadString(hInst,IDS_Resolution,lpCaption,Max);
1260            LoadString(hInst,IDS_ResSVGA,lpMessage,MaxText);
1261            MessageBox(GetFocus(),lpMessage,lpCaption,MB_OK);
1262            break;
1263            }
1264          if (DisplayWidth==1024)
1265            {                          /* 1024-by-768 SVGA mode detected */
1266            LoadString(hInst,IDS_Resolution,lpCaption,Max);
1267            LoadString(hInst,IDS_Res8514,lpMessage,MaxText);
1268            MessageBox(GetFocus(),lpMessage,lpCaption,MB_OK);
1269            break;
1270            }
1271          if (DisplayWidth==720)              /* (not used in this demo) */
1272            {                          /* 720-by-348 HGA mode detected */
1273            LoadString(hInst,IDS_Resolution,lpCaption,Max);
1274            LoadString(hInst,IDS_ResHerc,lpMessage,MaxText);
1275            MessageBox(GetFocus(),lpMessage,lpCaption,MB_OK);
1276            break;
1277            }
1278          LoadString(hInst,IDS_Resolution,lpCaption,Max);
1279          LoadString(hInst,IDS_ResCustom,lpMessage,MaxText);
1280          MessageBox(GetFocus(),lpMessage,lpCaption,MB_OK);
1281          break;
1282
1283        /* -------- report the display color capabilities -------- */
1284        case IDM_Colors:
1285          if (DisplayBits==1)
1286            {
```

```
1287              if (DisplayPlanes==4)
1288                  {                  /* 4-bit, 16-color mode detected */
1289                LoadString(hInst,IDS_Color,lpCaption,Max);
1290                LoadString(hInst,IDS_Color16,lpMessage,MaxText);
1291                MessageBox(GetFocus(),lpMessage,lpCaption,MB_OK);
1292                break;
1293                  }
1294              if (DisplayPlanes==1)
1295                  {                  /* 1-bit, 2-color mode detected */
1296                LoadString(hInst,IDS_Color,lpCaption,Max);
1297                LoadString(hInst,IDS_Color2,lpMessage,MaxText);
1298                MessageBox(GetFocus(),lpMessage,lpCaption,MB_OK);
1299                break;
1300                  }
1301              }
1302            if (DisplayBits==8)
1303                {                    /* 8-bit, 256-color mode detected */
1304              LoadString(hInst,IDS_Color,lpCaption,Max);
1305              LoadString(hInst,IDS_Color256,lpMessage,MaxText);
1306              MessageBox(GetFocus(),lpMessage,lpCaption,MB_OK);
1307              break;
1308                }
1309            if (DisplayBits==16)
1310                {                    /* 16-bit, 65000-color mode detected */
1311              LoadString(hInst,IDS_Color,lpCaption,Max);
1312              LoadString(hInst,IDS_Color65000,lpMessage,MaxText);
1313              MessageBox(GetFocus(),lpMessage,lpCaption,MB_OK);
1314              break;
1315                }
1316            LoadString(hInst,IDS_Color,lpCaption,Max);
1317            LoadString(hInst,IDS_ColorCustom,lpMessage,MaxText);
1318            MessageBox(GetFocus(),lpMessage,lpCaption,MB_OK);
1319            break;
1320
1321            /* ----------- report the runtime memory mode ----------- */
1322            case IDM_Mode:
1323              if (MemoryMode & WF_ENHANCED)
1324                  {                              /* enhanced mode detected */
1325                LoadString(hInst,IDS_Machine,lpCaption,Max);
1326                LoadString(hInst,IDS_Enhanced,lpMessage,MaxText);
1327                MessageBox(GetFocus(),lpMessage,lpCaption,MB_OK);
1328                break;
1329                  }
1330              if (MemoryMode & WF_STANDARD)
1331                  {                              /* standard mode detected */
1332                LoadString(hInst,IDS_Machine,lpCaption,Max);
1333                LoadString(hInst,IDS_Standard,lpMessage,MaxText);
1334                MessageBox(GetFocus(),lpMessage,lpCaption,MB_OK);
1335                break;
1336                  }
1337            LoadString(hInst,IDS_Machine,lpCaption,Max);
1338            LoadString(hInst,IDS_Real,lpMessage,MaxText);
1339            MessageBox(GetFocus(),lpMessage,lpCaption,MB_OK);
1340            break;
1341
1342            /* -------- display the runtime help message box --------- */
1343            case IDM_GeneralHelp:
1344              LoadString(hInst,IDS_Help,lpCaption,Max);
1345              LoadString(hInst,IDS_HelpText,lpMessage,MaxText);
1346              MessageBox(GetFocus(),lpMessage,lpCaption,MB_OK);
1347              break;
```

```
1348       default:
1349          return(DefWindowProc(hWnd, message, wParam, lParam));
1350       }
1351     break;
1352
1353   /* -------- oversee Windows-generated refresh requests ------- */
1354   case WM_PAINT:            /* if viewport needs to be refreshed... */
1355     hDCpaint= BeginPaint(hWnd,&ps);      /* load structure and... */
1356     EndPaint(hWnd, &ps);          /* ...validate the client area */
1357     if (PaintImage==zBLANK) break;        /* if blank do nothing */
1358     if (FrameReady==FALSE) break;   /* if no hidden frame, break */
1359     zCopyToDisplay(hWnd);   /* else copy hidden frame to display */
1360     break;
1361
1362   /* -------------- ensure a graceful shutdown --------------- */
1363   case WM_DESTROY:  /* if user is terminating the application... */
1364     if (FrameReady==TRUE)
1365       {                       /* remove the hidden frame bitmap */
1366       SelectObject(hFrameDC,hPrevFrame);
1367       DeleteObject(hFrame);
1368       DeleteDC(hFrameDC);
1369       }
1370     zClose3D();             /* remove 3D hidden page and z-buffer */
1371     PostQuitMessage(0);
1372     break;
1373
1374   /* ---- trap attempts to resize, minimize, maximize window --- */
1375   case WM_SYSCOMMAND:
1376     if ((wParam & 0xfff0)== SC_SIZE)
1377       {
1378       MessageBeep(0); break;
1379       }
1380     if ((wParam & 0xfff0)== SC_MINIMIZE)
1381       {
1382       MessageBeep(0); break;
1383       }
1384     if ((wParam & 0xfff0)== SC_MAXIMIZE)
1385       {
1386       MessageBeep(0); break;
1387       }
1388
1389   /* ------- pass any unprocessed messages to the system ------- */
1390   default:
1391     return(DefWindowProc(hWnd, message, wParam, lParam));
1392   }
1393 return FALSE;
1394 }
1395 /*
1396 --------------------------------------------------------------------
1397            Initialize the attributes of the window class
1398 --------------------------------------------------------------------
1399                                                                    */
1400 BOOL zInitClass(HANDLE hInstance)
1401 {
1402   WNDCLASS WndClass;
1403 WndClass.style= 0;                                   /* class style */
1404 WndClass.lpfnWndProc= zMessageHandler; /* app's message handler */
1405 WndClass.cbClsExtra= 0;              /* unused, no customized data */
1406 WndClass.cbWndExtra= 0;              /* unused, no customized data */
1407 WndClass.hInstance= hInstance;          /* this copy of the app */
1408 WndClass.hIcon= LoadIcon(NULL,IDI_EXCLAMATION);   /* app's icon */
```

```
1409   WndClass.hCursor= LoadCursor(NULL,IDC_ARROW);     /* app's cursor */
1410   WndClass.hbrBackground=      /* background color for the viewport */
1411                      CreateSolidBrush(RGB(255,255,255));
1412   WndClass.lpszMenuName= "MENUS1";       /* menu script in .rc file */
1413   WndClass.lpszClassName= "DEMOCLASS";    /* nominal name of class */
1414   return RegisterClass(&WndClass); /* tell Windows about the class */
1415   }
1416   /*
1417   --------------------------------------------------------------------
1418                      Create the main window
1419   --------------------------------------------------------------------
1420                                                                      */
1421   HWND zInitMainWindow(HANDLE hInstance)
1422   {
1423     HWND hWnd;
1424   LoadString(hInstance,IDS_Caption,lpCaption,Max); /* load caption */
1425   hHourGlass= LoadCursor(NULL,IDC_WAIT);  /* load hourglass cursor */
1426   hWnd= CreateWindow("DEMOCLASS",                    /* class name */
1427       lpCaption,                          /* window caption */
1428       WS_OVERLAPPED | WS_THICKFRAME | WS_CLIPCHILDREN,  /* style */
1429       WindowX,WindowY,                     /* location of window */
1430       zWINDOW_WIDTH,zWINDOW_HEIGHT,       /* dimensions of window */
1431       0,                                  /* parent window, if any */
1432       0,                                  /* special menu, if any */
1433       hInstance,                          /* this copy of the app */
1434       (LPSTR)NULL);   /* for multiple-document interface, if any */
1435   return hWnd;    /* return the newly-created handle to the caller */
1436   }
1437   /*
1438   --------------------------------------------------------------------
1439                  THE CORE FUNCTIONS OF THE APPLICATION
1440   --------------------------------------------------------------------
1441   --------------------------------------------------------------------
1442                      Create the hidden frame.
1443   --------------------------------------------------------------------
1444                                                                      */
1445   static void zInitFrame(HWND hWnd)
1446   {
1447     HDC hDisplayDC;                            /* display-context */
1448
1449   GlobalCompact((DWORD)-1L);         /* maximize contiguous memory */
1450   hDisplayDC= GetDC(hWnd);               /* set the display-context */
1451   hFrameDC= CreateCompatibleDC(hDisplayDC);     /* create frame... */
1452   hFrame= CreateCompatibleBitmap(hDisplayDC,zFRAMEWIDE,zFRAMEHIGH);
1453   if (hFrame==NULL)
1454     {
1455     LoadString(hInst,IDS_NotReady,lpCaption,Max);
1456     LoadString(hInst,IDS_NoMem,lpMessage,MaxText);
1457     MessageBox(GetFocus(),lpMessage,lpCaption,MB_OK);
1458     DeleteDC(hFrameDC);
1459     FrameReady= FALSE;
1460     return;
1461     }
1462   hPrevFrame= SelectObject(hFrameDC,hFrame);  /* select the bitmap */
1463   zClearHiddenFrame();                     /* clear the hidden frame */
1464   ReleaseDC(hWnd,hDisplayDC);        /* release the display-context */
1465   FrameReady= TRUE;                         /* set a global token */
1466   return;
1467   }
1468   /*
1469   --------------------------------------------------------------------
```

```
1470                          Clear the display window.
1471   --------------------------------------------------------------------
1472                                                                       */
1473   static void zClear(HWND hWnd)
1474   {
1475      HDC hDC;
1476   hDC= GetDC(hWnd);
1477   PatBlt(hDC,0,0,zFRAMEWIDE,zFRAMEHIGH,WHITENESS);
1478   ReleaseDC(hWnd,hDC);
1479   return;
1480   }
1481   /*
1482   --------------------------------------------------------------------
1483                          Clear the hidden frame.
1484   --------------------------------------------------------------------
1485                                                                       */
1486   static void zClearHiddenFrame(void)
1487   {
1488   if (FrameReady==FALSE) return;
1489   PatBlt(hFrameDC,0,0,zFRAMEWIDE,zFRAMEHIGH,WHITENESS);
1490   return;
1491   }
1492   /*
1493   --------------------------------------------------------------------
1494              Copy the hidden frame to the display window.
1495   --------------------------------------------------------------------
1496                                                                       */
1497   static void zCopyToDisplay(HWND hWnd)
1498   {
1499      HDC hDC;
1500   if (FrameReady==FALSE) return;
1501   hDC= GetDC(hWnd);
1502   BitBlt(hDC,0,0,zFRAMEWIDE,zFRAMEHIGH,hFrameDC,0,0,SRCCOPY);
1503   ReleaseDC(hWnd,hDC);
1504   return;
1505   }
1506   /*
1507   --------------------------------------------------------------------
1508              Copy the display window to the hidden frame.
1509   --------------------------------------------------------------------
1510                                                                       */
1511   static void zCopyToFrame(HWND hWnd)
1512   {
1513      HDC hDC;
1514   if (FrameReady==FALSE) return;
1515   hDC= GetDC(hWnd);
1516   BitBlt(hFrameDC,0,0,zFRAMEWIDE,zFRAMEHIGH,hDC,0,0,SRCCOPY);
1517   ReleaseDC(hWnd,hDC);
1518   return;
1519   }
1520   /*
1521   --------------------------------------------------------------------
1522         Build a 3D assembly of subobjects:   hardcoded technique.
1523   --------------------------------------------------------------------
1524                                                                       */
1525   static void zDrawRoboticArm(void)
1526   {
1527   /* ---------- configure and render the component parts --------- */
1528   zSetShadingColor(zGREEN);
1529   zSetSubjectSize(20,20,30);                    /* arm extensor (1) */
1530   zSetSubjectAttitude(0,0,0);
```

```
1531    zSetSubjectLocation(0,0,-50);
1532    zDrawCube();
1533
1534    zSetShadingColor(zGREEN);
1535    zSetSubjectSize(5,20,10);              /* arm swivel extensors (2) */
1536    zSetSubjectAttitude(0,0,0);
1537    zSetSubjectLocation(15,0,-10);
1538    zDrawCube();
1539    zSetSubjectLocation(-15,0,-10);
1540    zDrawCube();
1541
1542    zSetShadingColor(zGREEN);
1543    zSetSubjectSize(20,20,5);              /* arm swivel brackets (2) */
1544    zSetSubjectAttitude(90,0,0);
1545    zSetSubjectLocation(15,0,0);
1546    zDrawHalfCylinder();
1547    zSetSubjectLocation(-15,0,0);
1548    zDrawHalfCylinder();
1549
1550    zSetShadingColor(zRED);
1551    zSetSubjectSize(10,10,25);                    /* swivel pin (1) */
1552    zSetSubjectAttitude(90,0,0);
1553    zSetSubjectLocation(0,0,0);
1554    zDrawCylinder();
1555
1556    zSetShadingColor(zBROWN);
1557    zSetSubjectSize(20,20,5);              /* wrist swivel bracket (1) */
1558    zSetSubjectAttitude(270,0,0);
1559    zSetSubjectLocation(0,0,0);
1560    zDrawHalfCylinder();
1561
1562    zSetShadingColor(zBROWN);
1563    zSetSubjectSize(5,20,30);                   /* wrist extensor (1) */
1564    zSetSubjectAttitude(0,0,0);
1565    zSetSubjectLocation(0,0,30);
1566    zDrawCube();
1567
1568    zSetShadingColor(zBROWN);
1569    zSetSubjectSize(20,20,5);              /* wrist swivel bracket (1) */
1570    zSetSubjectAttitude(90,0,0);
1571    zSetSubjectLocation(0,0,60);
1572    zDrawHalfCylinder();
1573
1574    zSetShadingColor(zRED);
1575    zSetSubjectSize(10,10,25);                    /* swivel pin (1) */
1576    zSetSubjectAttitude(90,0,0);
1577    zSetSubjectLocation(0,0,60);
1578    zDrawCylinder();
1579
1580    return;
1581    }
1582    /*
1583    --------------------------------------------------------------------
1584         Build a 3D assembly of subobjects:  hierarchical technique.
1585    --------------------------------------------------------------------
1586                                                                       */
1587    static void zBuildAssembly(void)
1588    {
1589      int PartID;                /* counter is used in the drawing loop */
1590
1591    /* -------------- STEP ONE:  define the assembly -------------- */
```

```
1592    RobotArm[0].Solid= zBOX;                    /* define the arm extensor */
1593    RobotArm[0].Level= zLEVEL1;
1594    RobotArm[0].Color= zGREEN;
1595    RobotArm[0].SizeX= 20;
1596    RobotArm[0].SizeY= 20;
1597    RobotArm[0].SizeZ= 30;
1598    RobotArm[0].Yaw= 0;
1599    RobotArm[0].Roll= 0;
1600    RobotArm[0].Pitch= 0;
1601    RobotArm[0].PositionX= 0;
1602    RobotArm[0].PositionY= 0;
1603    RobotArm[0].PositionZ= -50;
1604    RobotArm[0].DeformRightX= 0;
1605    RobotArm[0].DeformLeftX= 0;
1606    RobotArm[0].DeformUpY= 0;
1607    RobotArm[0].DeformDownY= 0;
1608    RobotArm[0].PivotX= 0;
1609    RobotArm[0].PivotY= 0;
1610    RobotArm[0].PivotZ= 0;
1611    RobotArm[0].SubAssyYaw= 0;
1612    RobotArm[0].SubAssyRoll= 0;
1613    RobotArm[0].SubAssyPitch= 0;
1614    RobotArm[0].SubAssyX= 0;
1615    RobotArm[0].SubAssyY= 0;
1616    RobotArm[0].SubAssyZ= 0;
1617
1618    RobotArm[1].Solid= zBOX;             /* arm swivel extensor (1 of 2) */
1619    RobotArm[1].Level= zLEVEL1;
1620    RobotArm[1].Color= zGREEN;
1621    RobotArm[1].SizeX= RobotArm[0].SizeX / 4;
1622    RobotArm[1].SizeY= RobotArm[0].SizeY;
1623    RobotArm[1].SizeZ= 10;
1624    RobotArm[1].Yaw= 0;
1625    RobotArm[1].Roll= 0;
1626    RobotArm[1].Pitch= 0;
1627    RobotArm[1].PositionX= RobotArm[0].SizeX - RobotArm[1].SizeX;
1628    RobotArm[1].PositionY= RobotArm[0].PositionY;
1629    RobotArm[1].PositionZ= (RobotArm[0].PositionZ+RobotArm[0].SizeZ) +
1630                           RobotArm[1].SizeZ;
1631    RobotArm[1].DeformRightX= 0;
1632    RobotArm[1].DeformLeftX= 0;
1633    RobotArm[1].DeformUpY= 0;
1634    RobotArm[1].DeformDownY= 0;
1635    RobotArm[1].PivotX= 0;
1636    RobotArm[1].PivotY= 0;
1637    RobotArm[1].PivotZ= 0;
1638    RobotArm[1].SubAssyYaw= 0;
1639    RobotArm[1].SubAssyRoll= 0;
1640    RobotArm[1].SubAssyPitch= 0;
1641    RobotArm[1].SubAssyX= 0;
1642    RobotArm[1].SubAssyY= 0;
1643    RobotArm[1].SubAssyZ= 0;
1644
1645    RobotArm[2].Solid= zBOX;             /* arm swivel extensor (2 of 2) */
1646    RobotArm[2].Level= zLEVEL1;
1647    RobotArm[2].Color= zGREEN;
1648    RobotArm[2].SizeX= RobotArm[0].SizeX / 4;
1649    RobotArm[2].SizeY= RobotArm[0].SizeY;
1650    RobotArm[2].SizeZ= 10;
1651    RobotArm[2].Yaw= 0;
1652    RobotArm[2].Roll= 0;
```

```
1653    RobotArm[2].Pitch= 0;
1654    RobotArm[2].PositionX= ((-1)*RobotArm[0].SizeX)+RobotArm[2].SizeX;
1655    RobotArm[2].PositionY= RobotArm[0].PositionY;
1656    RobotArm[2].PositionZ= (RobotArm[0].PositionZ+RobotArm[0].SizeZ) +
1657                            RobotArm[2].SizeZ;;
1658    RobotArm[2].DeformRightX= 0;
1659    RobotArm[2].DeformLeftX= 0;
1660    RobotArm[2].DeformUpY= 0;
1661    RobotArm[2].DeformDownY= 0;
1662    RobotArm[2].PivotX= 0;
1663    RobotArm[2].PivotY= 0;
1664    RobotArm[2].PivotZ= 0;
1665    RobotArm[2].SubAssyYaw= 0;
1666    RobotArm[2].SubAssyRoll= 0;
1667    RobotArm[2].SubAssyPitch= 0;
1668    RobotArm[2].SubAssyX= 0;
1669    RobotArm[2].SubAssyY= 0;
1670    RobotArm[2].SubAssyZ= 0;
1671
1672    RobotArm[3].Solid= zHALFCYL;        /* arm swivel bracket (1 of 2) */
1673    RobotArm[3].Level= zLEVEL1;
1674    RobotArm[3].Color= zGREEN;
1675    RobotArm[3].SizeX= RobotArm[0].SizeX;
1676    RobotArm[3].SizeY= RobotArm[0].SizeY;
1677    RobotArm[3].SizeZ= RobotArm[1].SizeX;
1678    RobotArm[3].Yaw= 90;
1679    RobotArm[3].Roll= 0;
1680    RobotArm[3].Pitch= 0;
1681    RobotArm[3].PositionX= RobotArm[1].PositionX;
1682    RobotArm[3].PositionY= RobotArm[1].PositionY;
1683    RobotArm[3].PositionZ= RobotArm[1].PositionZ + RobotArm[1].SizeZ;
1684    RobotArm[3].DeformRightX= 0;
1685    RobotArm[3].DeformLeftX= 0;
1686    RobotArm[3].DeformUpY= 0;
1687    RobotArm[3].DeformDownY= 0;
1688    RobotArm[3].PivotX= 0;
1689    RobotArm[3].PivotY= 0;
1690    RobotArm[3].PivotZ= 0;
1691    RobotArm[3].SubAssyYaw= 0;
1692    RobotArm[3].SubAssyRoll= 0;
1693    RobotArm[3].SubAssyPitch= 0;
1694    RobotArm[3].SubAssyX= 0;
1695    RobotArm[3].SubAssyY= 0;
1696    RobotArm[3].SubAssyZ= 0;
1697
1698    RobotArm[4].Solid= zHALFCYL;        /* arm swivel bracket (2 of 2) */
1699    RobotArm[4].Level= zLEVEL1;
1700    RobotArm[4].Color= zGREEN;
1701    RobotArm[4].SizeX= RobotArm[0].SizeX;
1702    RobotArm[4].SizeY= RobotArm[0].SizeY;
1703    RobotArm[4].SizeZ= RobotArm[2].SizeX;
1704    RobotArm[4].Yaw= 90;
1705    RobotArm[4].Roll= 0;
1706    RobotArm[4].Pitch= 0;
1707    RobotArm[4].PositionX= RobotArm[2].PositionX;
1708    RobotArm[4].PositionY= RobotArm[2].PositionY;
1709    RobotArm[4].PositionZ= RobotArm[2].PositionZ + RobotArm[2].SizeZ;
1710    RobotArm[4].DeformRightX= 0;
1711    RobotArm[4].DeformLeftX= 0;
1712    RobotArm[4].DeformUpY= 0;
1713    RobotArm[4].DeformDownY= 0;
```

```
1714    RobotArm[4].PivotX= 0;
1715    RobotArm[4].PivotY= 0;
1716    RobotArm[4].PivotZ= 0;
1717    RobotArm[4].SubAssyYaw= 0;
1718    RobotArm[4].SubAssyRoll= 0;
1719    RobotArm[4].SubAssyPitch= 0;
1720    RobotArm[4].SubAssyX= 0;
1721    RobotArm[4].SubAssyY= 0;
1722    RobotArm[4].SubAssyZ= 0;
1723
1724    RobotArm[5].Solid= zCYLINDER;                    /* swivel pin (1) */
1725    RobotArm[5].Level= zLEVEL1;
1726    RobotArm[5].Color= zRED;
1727    RobotArm[5].SizeX= 10;
1728    RobotArm[5].SizeY= 10;
1729    RobotArm[5].SizeZ= RobotArm[0].SizeX + 5;
1730    RobotArm[5].Yaw= 90;
1731    RobotArm[5].Roll= 0;
1732    RobotArm[5].Pitch= 0;
1733    RobotArm[5].PositionX= RobotArm[0].PositionX;
1734    RobotArm[5].PositionY= RobotArm[3].PositionY;
1735    RobotArm[5].PositionZ= RobotArm[3].PositionZ;
1736    RobotArm[5].DeformRightX= 0;
1737    RobotArm[5].DeformLeftX= 0;
1738    RobotArm[5].DeformUpY= 0;
1739    RobotArm[5].DeformDownY= 0;
1740    RobotArm[5].PivotX= 0;
1741    RobotArm[5].PivotY= 0;
1742    RobotArm[5].PivotZ= 0;
1743    RobotArm[5].SubAssyYaw= 0;
1744    RobotArm[5].SubAssyRoll= 0;
1745    RobotArm[5].SubAssyPitch= 0;
1746    RobotArm[5].SubAssyX= 0;
1747    RobotArm[5].SubAssyY= 0;
1748    RobotArm[5].SubAssyZ= 0;
1749
1750    /* ------------- STEP ONE:  define the subassembly ------------- */
1751         /* This particular subassembly is already located at an
1752             appropriate pivot-point, from where it will rotated
1753             30 degrees in the pitch plane.                       */
1754    RobotArm[6].Solid= zHALFCYL;          /* wrist swivel bracket (1) */
1755    RobotArm[6].Level= zLEVEL2;
1756    RobotArm[6].Color= zBROWN;
1757    RobotArm[6].SizeX= RobotArm[4].SizeX;
1758    RobotArm[6].SizeY= RobotArm[4].SizeY;
1759    RobotArm[6].SizeZ= RobotArm[4].SizeZ;
1760    RobotArm[6].Yaw= 270;                      /* reorient half-cylinder */
1761    RobotArm[6].Roll= 0;
1762    RobotArm[6].Pitch= 0;
1763    RobotArm[6].PositionX= RobotArm[5].PositionX;
1764    RobotArm[6].PositionY= RobotArm[5].PositionY;
1765    RobotArm[6].PositionZ= RobotArm[5].PositionZ;
1766    RobotArm[6].DeformRightX= 0;
1767    RobotArm[6].DeformLeftX= 0;
1768    RobotArm[6].DeformUpY= 0;
1769    RobotArm[6].DeformDownY= 0;
1770    RobotArm[6].PivotX= 0;
1771    RobotArm[6].PivotY= 0;
1772    RobotArm[6].PivotZ= 0;
1773    RobotArm[6].SubAssyYaw= 0;
1774    RobotArm[6].SubAssyRoll= 0;
```

```
1775    RobotArm[6].SubAssyPitch= 30;
1776    RobotArm[6].SubAssyX= 0;
1777    RobotArm[6].SubAssyY= 0;
1778    RobotArm[6].SubAssyZ= 0;
1779
1780    RobotArm[7].Solid= zBOX;                       /* wrist extensor (1) */
1781    RobotArm[7].Level= zLEVEL2;
1782    RobotArm[7].Color= zBROWN;
1783    RobotArm[7].SizeX= RobotArm[6].SizeZ;
1784    RobotArm[7].SizeY= RobotArm[6].SizeX;
1785    RobotArm[7].SizeZ= 30;
1786    RobotArm[7].Yaw= 0;
1787    RobotArm[7].Roll= 0;
1788    RobotArm[7].Pitch= 0;
1789    RobotArm[7].PositionX= RobotArm[6].PositionX;
1790    RobotArm[7].PositionY= RobotArm[6].PositionY;
1791    RobotArm[7].PositionZ= RobotArm[6].PositionX + RobotArm[7].SizeZ;
1792    RobotArm[7].DeformRightX= 0;
1793    RobotArm[7].DeformLeftX= 0;
1794    RobotArm[7].DeformUpY= 0;
1795    RobotArm[7].DeformDownY= 0;
1796    RobotArm[7].PivotX= 0;
1797    RobotArm[7].PivotY= 0;
1798    RobotArm[7].PivotZ= 0;
1799    RobotArm[7].SubAssyYaw= 0;
1800    RobotArm[7].SubAssyRoll= 0;
1801    RobotArm[7].SubAssyPitch= 30;
1802    RobotArm[7].SubAssyX= 0;
1803    RobotArm[7].SubAssyY= 0;
1804    RobotArm[7].SubAssyZ= 0;
1805
1806    RobotArm[8].Solid= zHALFCYL;            /* wrist swivel bracket (1) */
1807    RobotArm[8].Level= zLEVEL2;
1808    RobotArm[8].Color= zBROWN;
1809    RobotArm[8].SizeX= RobotArm[6].SizeX;
1810    RobotArm[8].SizeY= RobotArm[6].SizeY;
1811    RobotArm[8].SizeZ= RobotArm[6].SizeZ;
1812    RobotArm[8].Yaw= 90;
1813    RobotArm[8].Roll= 0;
1814    RobotArm[8].Pitch= 0;
1815    RobotArm[8].PositionX= RobotArm[7].PositionX;
1816    RobotArm[8].PositionY= RobotArm[7].PositionY;
1817    RobotArm[8].PositionZ= RobotArm[7].PositionZ + RobotArm[7].SizeZ;
1818    RobotArm[8].DeformRightX= 0;
1819    RobotArm[8].DeformLeftX= 0;
1820    RobotArm[8].DeformUpY= 0;
1821    RobotArm[8].DeformDownY= 0;
1822    RobotArm[8].PivotX= 0;
1823    RobotArm[8].PivotY= 0;
1824    RobotArm[8].PivotZ= 0;
1825    RobotArm[8].SubAssyYaw= 0;
1826    RobotArm[8].SubAssyRoll= 0;
1827    RobotArm[8].SubAssyPitch= 30;
1828    RobotArm[8].SubAssyX= 0;
1829    RobotArm[8].SubAssyY= 0;
1830    RobotArm[8].SubAssyZ= 0;
1831
1832    RobotArm[9].Solid= zCYLINDER;                     /* swivel pin (1) */
1833    RobotArm[9].Level= zLEVEL2;
1834    RobotArm[9].Color= zCYAN;
1835    RobotArm[9].SizeX= RobotArm[5].SizeX;
```

```
1836    RobotArm[9].SizeY= RobotArm[5].SizeY;
1837    RobotArm[9].SizeZ= RobotArm[8].SizeZ + 15;
1838    RobotArm[9].Yaw= 90;
1839    RobotArm[9].Roll= 0;
1840    RobotArm[9].Pitch= 0;
1841    RobotArm[9].PositionX= RobotArm[8].PositionX;
1842    RobotArm[9].PositionY= RobotArm[8].PositionY;
1843    RobotArm[9].PositionZ= RobotArm[8].PositionZ;
1844    RobotArm[9].DeformRightX= 0;
1845    RobotArm[9].DeformLeftX= 0;
1846    RobotArm[9].DeformUpY= 0;
1847    RobotArm[9].DeformDownY= 0;
1848    RobotArm[9].PivotX= 0;
1849    RobotArm[9].PivotY= 0;
1850    RobotArm[9].PivotZ= 0;
1851    RobotArm[9].SubAssyYaw= 0;
1852    RobotArm[9].SubAssyRoll= 0;
1853    RobotArm[9].SubAssyPitch= 30;
1854    RobotArm[9].SubAssyX= 0;
1855    RobotArm[9].SubAssyY= 0;
1856    RobotArm[9].SubAssyZ= 0;
1857
1858    /* ------------- STEP THREE:  render the assembly ------------- */
1859    for (PartID= zROBOT_START; PartID<= zROBOT_FINISH; PartID++)
1860        {                       /* for each subobject in the assembly... */
1861        zSetShadingColor(RobotArm[PartID].Color);          /* set color */
1862        zSetSubjectSize(RobotArm[PartID].SizeX,              /* resize */
1863                        RobotArm[PartID].SizeY,
1864                        RobotArm[PartID].SizeZ);
1865        zSetSubobjectAttitude(RobotArm[PartID].Yaw,        /* reorient */
1866                        RobotArm[PartID].Roll,
1867                        RobotArm[PartID].Pitch);
1868        zSetSubobjectLocation(RobotArm[PartID].PositionX,/* reposition */
1869                        RobotArm[PartID].PositionY,
1870                        RobotArm[PartID].PositionZ);
1871        if (RobotArm[PartID].Level == zLEVEL1)
1872            {       /* if subobject is part of top-level assembly... */
1873            zSetHierarchyLevel(zLEVEL1);
1874            }
1875        else if (RobotArm[PartID].Level == zLEVEL2)
1876            {              /* if subobject is part of a subassembly... */
1877            zSetSubAssyPivot(RobotArm[PartID].PivotX,
1878                        RobotArm[PartID].PivotY,
1879                        RobotArm[PartID].PivotZ);
1880            zSetSubAssyRotation(RobotArm[PartID].SubAssyYaw,
1881                        RobotArm[PartID].SubAssyRoll,
1882                        RobotArm[PartID].SubAssyPitch);
1883            zSetSubAssyPosition(RobotArm[PartID].SubAssyX,
1884                        RobotArm[PartID].SubAssyY,
1885                        RobotArm[PartID].SubAssyZ);
1886            zSetHierarchyLevel(zLEVEL2);
1887            }
1888
1889        switch (RobotArm[PartID].Solid)           /* render the subobject */
1890            {
1891            case zBOX:          zDrawCube();        break;
1892            case zSPHERE:       zDrawSphere();      break;
1893            case zCYLINDER:     zDrawCylinder();    break;
1894            case zCONE:         zDrawCone();        break;
1895            case zWEDGE:        zDrawWedge();       break;
1896            case zCURVE:        zDrawCurve();       break;
```

```
1897        case zHEMISPHERE: zDrawHemisphere(); break;
1898        case zDEFORMBOX:  zDrawDeformBox(RobotArm[PartID].DeformRightX,
1899                                         RobotArm[PartID].DeformLeftX,
1900                                         RobotArm[PartID].DeformUpY,
1901                                         RobotArm[PartID].DeformDownY);
1902                                         break;
1903        case zHALFCYL:    zDrawHalfCylinder(); break;
1904        case zBULGE:      zDrawBulge();        break;
1905        case zNULL: break;
1906        default:    break;
1907        }                                      /* end of switch() block */
1908     }                               /* end of subobject rendering loop */
1909  return;                                        /* return to caller */
1910  }                                              /* end of function */
1911  /*
1912  ------------------------------------------------------------------
1913                       End of the C source file
1914  ------------------------------------------------------------------
1915                                                                   */
```

C-3 Source listings for the interactive 3D animation template, animate.c, consisting of .def, .h, .rc, and .c files. See Appendix B for the toolkits which must be linked in to build this application. See Appendix A for instructions on building the demo.

```
0001  NAME          ANIM4115
0002  DESCRIPTION   'Copyright 1993 Lee Adams.  All rights reserved.'
0003  EXETYPE       WINDOWS
0004  STUB          'WINSTUB.EXE'
0005  CODE          PRELOAD MOVEABLE
0006  DATA          PRELOAD MOVEABLE MULTIPLE
0007  HEAPSIZE      1024
0008  STACKSIZE     8192
0009  EXPORTS       zMessageHandler
0001  /*
0002  ------------------------------------------------------------------
0003                       Include file animate.h
0004          Copyright 1993 Lee Adams.  All rights reserved.
0005     Include this file in the .RC resource script file and in the
0006     .C source file.  It contains function prototypes, menu ID
0007     constants, and string ID constants.
0008  ------------------------------------------------------------------
0009  ------------------------------------------------------------------
0010                       Function prototypes
0011  ------------------------------------------------------------------
0012                                                                   */
0013  #if !defined(zRCFILE)                   /* if not an .rc file... */
0014    LONG FAR PASCAL zMessageHandler(HWND, unsigned, WORD, LONG);
0015    int PASCAL WinMain(HANDLE,HANDLE,LPSTR,int);
0016    HWND zInitMainWindow(HANDLE);
0017    BOOL zInitClass(HANDLE);
0018  static void zClear(HWND);                /* blank the display window */
0019  static void zInitFrame(HWND);              /* creates hidden frame */
0020  static void zShowNextFrame(HWND);           /* the playback engine */
0021  static void zSetFrameRate(HWND,WORD);         /* resets the timer */
0022  static void zSaveAnimation(HWND);     /* saves animation sequence */
0023  static BOOL zBuildFrame(int,HWND,LPSTR);       /* builds a frame */
0024  static void zDrawCel(int);                       /* draws a cel */
0025  static void zLoadAnimation(HWND);     /* loads animation sequence */
0026  static void zCopyToDisplay(HWND);      /* copies frame to display */
0027  static void zClearHiddenFrame(void);       /* clears hidden frame */
0028  #endif
```

```
0029   /*
0030   ------------------------------------------------------------------
0031                            Menu ID constants
0032   ------------------------------------------------------------------
0033                                                                  */
0034   #define IDM_New              1
0035   #define IDM_Open             2
0036   #define IDM_Save             3
0037   #define IDM_SaveAs           4
0038   #define IDM_Exit             5
0039
0040   #define IDM_Undo             6
0041   #define IDM_Cut              7
0042   #define IDM_Copy             8
0043   #define IDM_Paste            9
0044   #define IDM_Delete           10
0045
0046   #define IDM_LoadAnimation    11
0047   #define IDM_RunForward       12
0048   #define IDM_RunReverse       13
0049   #define IDM_Clear            14
0050   #define IDM_StopAnimation    15
0051   #define IDM_SaveAnimation    16
0052   #define IDM_UseShaded        17
0053   #define IDM_UseWireframe     18
0054
0055   #define IDM_FPS182           19
0056   #define IDM_FPS91            20
0057   #define IDM_FPS61            21
0058   #define IDM_FPS45            22
0059   #define IDM_FPS36            23
0060   #define IDM_FPS30            24
0061
0062   #define IDM_About            25
0063   #define IDM_License          26
0064   #define IDM_GeneralHelp      27
0065   /*
0066   ------------------------------------------------------------------
0067                           String ID constants
0068   ------------------------------------------------------------------
0069                                                                  */
0070   #define IDS_Caption       1
0071   #define IDS_Warning       2
0072   #define IDS_NoMouse       3
0073   #define IDS_About         4
0074   #define IDS_AboutText     5
0075   #define IDS_License       6
0076   #define IDS_LicenseText   7
0077   #define IDS_Help          8
0078   #define IDS_HelpText      9
0079   #define IDS_Completed     10
0080   #define IDS_Error         11
0081   #define IDS_NotReady      12
0082   #define IDS_Ready         13
0083   #define IDS_BuildBefore   14
0084   #define IDS_Already       15
0085   #define IDS_InsufMem1     16
0086
0087   #define IDS_InsufMem2     17
0088   #define IDS_NoTimer       18
0089   #define IDS_NoReset       19
```

C-3 Continued.

```
0090    #define IDS_CannotReset 20
0091    #define IDS_NoFrame     21
0092    #define IDS_AnimReady    22
0093
0094    #define IDS_Unexpected  44
0095    #define IDS_Status      45
0096    #define IDS_Disk1       46
0097    #define IDS_Disk2       47
0098    #define IDS_Disk3       48
0099    #define IDS_Disk4       49
0100    #define IDS_Disk5       50
0101    #define IDS_Disk6       51
0102    #define IDS_Disk7       52
0103    #define IDS_Disk8       53
0104    #define IDS_Disk9       54
0105    #define IDS_Disk10      55
0106    #define IDS_Disk11      56
0107    #define IDS_Disk12      57
0108    #define IDS_Disk13      58
0109    #define IDS_Disk14      59
0110    #define IDS_Disk15      60
0111    #define IDS_Disk16      61
0112    #define IDS_Disk17      62
0113    #define IDS_Disk18      63
0114    #define IDS_Disk19      64
0115    #define IDS_Disk20      65
0116    #define IDS_Disk21      66
0117    #define IDS_Disk22      67
0118    #define IDS_Disk23      68
0119    #define IDS_Disk24      69
0120    #define IDS_Disk25      70
0121    #define IDS_Disk26      71
0122    #define IDS_NoBg        72
0123    #define IDS_BgAlready   73
0124    #define IDS_InsufMemBg  74
0125    #define IDS_ReqdHdwr1   75
0126    #define IDS_ReqdHdwr2   76
0127    #define IDS_Build       77
0128    #define IDS_ToCancel    78
0129    #define IDS_Loading     79
0130    /*
0131    ----------------------------------------------------------------
0132                         End of include file
0133    ----------------------------------------------------------------
0134                                                                  */
0001    /*
0002    ----------------------------------------------------------------
0003                 Resource script file animate.rc
0004          Copyright 1993 Lee Adams.  All rights reserved.
0005      This file defines the menu resources, the accelerator key
0006      resources, and the string resources that will be used by the
0007      demonstration application at runtime.
0008    ----------------------------------------------------------------
0009                                                                  */
0010    #define zRCFILE
0011    #include <WINDOWS.H>
0012    #include "ANIMATE.H"
0013    /*
0014    ----------------------------------------------------------------
0015                         Script for menus
0016    ----------------------------------------------------------------
```

```
0017                                                                    */
0018    ANIMENUS MENU
0019       BEGIN
0020       POPUP "&File"
0021         BEGIN
0022           MENUITEM  "&New", IDM_New, GRAYED
0023           MENUITEM  "&Open...", IDM_Open, GRAYED
0024           MENUITEM  "&Save", IDM_Save, GRAYED
0025           MENUITEM  "Save &As...", IDM_SaveAs, GRAYED
0026           MENUITEM SEPARATOR
0027           MENUITEM  "E&xit", IDM_Exit
0028         END
0029       POPUP "&Edit"
0030         BEGIN
0031           MENUITEM  "&Undo\tAlt+BkSp", IDM_Undo, GRAYED
0032           MENUITEM SEPARATOR
0033           MENUITEM  "Cu&t\tShift+Del", IDM_Cut, GRAYED
0034           MENUITEM  "&Copy\tCtrl+Ins", IDM_Copy, GRAYED
0035           MENUITEM  "&Paste\tShift+Ins", IDM_Paste, GRAYED
0036           MENUITEM  "&Delete\tDel", IDM_Delete, GRAYED
0037         END
0038       POPUP "&Run"
0039         BEGIN
0040           MENUITEM "&Load Animation", IDM_LoadAnimation
0041           MENUITEM SEPARATOR
0042           MENUITEM "Run &Forward", IDM_RunForward
0043           MENUITEM "Run &Reverse", IDM_RunReverse
0044           MENUITEM "Free&zeframe", IDM_StopAnimation
0045           POPUP "S&et Speed..."
0046             BEGIN
0047               MENUITEM "&18 fps", IDM_FPS182, CHECKED
0048               MENUITEM " &9 fps", IDM_FPS91
0049               MENUITEM " &6 fps", IDM_FPS61
0050               MENUITEM " &5 fps", IDM_FPS45
0051               MENUITEM " &4 fps", IDM_FPS36
0052               MENUITEM " &3 fps", IDM_FPS30
0053             END
0054           MENUITEM SEPARATOR
0055           MENUITEM "&Clear Viewport", IDM_Clear
0056           MENUITEM SEPARATOR
0057           POPUP "&Production..."
0058             BEGIN
0059               MENUITEM "&Build Animation", IDM_SaveAnimation
0060               MENUITEM SEPARATOR
0061               MENUITEM "Use &shaded solids", IDM_UseShaded
0062               MENUITEM "Use &wireframe mode", IDM_UseWireframe
0063             END
0064         END
0065       POPUP "&Using"
0066         BEGIN
0067         MENUITEM "&About", IDM_About
0068         MENUITEM "&License", IDM_License
0069         MENUITEM SEPARATOR
0070         MENUITEM "&How to Use", IDM_GeneralHelp
0071         END
0072       END
0073     /*
0074     ----------------------------------------------------------------
0075                        Script for accelerator keys
0076     ----------------------------------------------------------------
0077                                                                    */
```

```
0078   ANIMKEYS ACCELERATORS
0079     BEGIN
0080     VK_BACK, IDM_Undo, VIRTKEY, ALT
0081     VK_DELETE, IDM_Cut, VIRTKEY, SHIFT
0082     VK_INSERT, IDM_Copy, VIRTKEY, CONTROL
0083     VK_INSERT, IDM_Paste, VIRTKEY, SHIFT
0084     VK_DELETE, IDM_Delete,VIRTKEY
0085     END
0086   /*
0087   --------------------------------------------------------------------
0088                       Script for strings
0089     If you are typing this listing, set your right margin to 255
0090     characters so you can create lengthy strings without embedded
0091     carriage returns.  The line wraparounds in the following
0092     STRINGTABLE listing are used only for readability.
0093   --------------------------------------------------------------------
0094                                                                     */
0095   STRINGTABLE
0096     BEGIN
0097     IDS_Caption      "3D Animation Template"
0098     IDS_Warning      "Warning"
0099     IDS_NoMouse      "No mouse found.  Some features of this
                demonstration program may require a mouse."
0100     IDS_About        "About this program"
0101     IDS_AboutText    "This is a demo from Windcrest McGraw-Hill
                book 4115.  Copyright- 1993 Lee Adams.  All rights reserved."
0102     IDS_License      "License Agreement"
0103     IDS_LicenseText "You can use this code as part of your own
                software product subject to the License Agreement and
                Limited Warranty in Windcrest McGraw-Hill book 4115 and on
                its companion disk."
0104     IDS_Help         "How to use this 3D animation demo"
0105     IDS_HelpText     "For animation playback pick Load Animation
                then Run Forward from the Run menu.  To build and save an
                animation, choose the Production submenu.  Also see the
                book."
0106     IDS_Completed    "Task completed OK"
0107     IDS_Error        "Runtime error"
0108     IDS_NotReady     "Animation not ready"
0109     IDS_Ready        "Animation ready"
0110     IDS_BuildBefore "Animation frames not ready for playback."
0111     IDS_Already      "The hidden frame has already been created."
0112     IDS_InsufMem1    "Unable to create hidden-frame because
                insufficient global memory.  Animation functions
                unavailable.  Close other applications before restarting
                this demo."
0113     IDS_NoTimer      "Unable to create a timer.  Animation
                functions unavailable.  Restart this demo after closing
                other applications that may be using timers."
0114     IDS_NoReset      "Create hidden frame before attempting to
                reset timer."
0115     IDS_CannotReset "Unable to reset the timer."
0116     IDS_NoFrame      "Hidden frame not yet created."
0117     IDS_AnimReady    "Animation ready"
0118     IDS_Unexpected   "Unexpected animation condition"
0119     IDS_Status       "Animation status"
0120     IDS_Disk1        "Animation sequence already saved to disk."
0121     IDS_Disk2        "Animation sequence saved to disk."
0122     IDS_Disk3        "Unable to load next frame from disk.
                Animation halted."
0123     IDS_Disk4        "Animation sequence already loaded from disk."
```

```
0124      IDS_Disk5        "Previous load failed.  Cancelling this
             attempt."
0125      IDS_Disk6        "Not enough memory available to store
          animation sequence in memory.  Each frame will be loaded as
          needed from disk during playback."
0126      IDS_Disk7        "Animation sequence loaded in memory."
0127      IDS_Disk8        "Previous save failed.  Cancelling this
             attempt."
0128      IDS_Disk9        "No hidden-frame exists.  No frame saved to
          disk."
0129      IDS_Disk10       "Unable to retrieve bitmap data structure."
0130      IDS_Disk11       "Bit array is too long to save to disk in a
          single pass."
0131      IDS_Disk12       "Cannot create memory buffer for disk write."
0132      IDS_Disk13       "Unable to copy bits from bitmap to buffer."
0133      IDS_Disk14       "File already exists.  Overwrite existing
          file?"
0134      IDS_Disk15       "Unable to open the file for writing."
0135      IDS_Disk16       "Unable to write to the opened file."
0136      IDS_Disk17       "Unable to close the file after writing."
0137      IDS_Disk18       "No memory bitmap exists.  Unable to load from
          disk."
0138      IDS_Disk19       "Image file is larger than animation frame.
          No file loaded."
0139      IDS_Disk20       "Cannot create memory buffer for file read."
0140      IDS_Disk21       "Unable to open the file for reading.  Be sure
          you have saved an animation sequence to disk before
          attempting to load it."
0141      IDS_Disk22       "An error occurred while reading the file."
0142      IDS_Disk23       "Windows must be using same color mode as when
          this animation was saved, either 2, 16, or 256 colors.  To
          run the existing animation, use Windows Setup to switch
          color modes.  Otherwise rebuild the animation in the current
          mode."
0143      IDS_Disk24       "Unable to close the file after reading."
0144      IDS_Disk25       "Unable to copy bits from buffer to bitmap."
0145      IDS_Disk26       "Not all frames saved to disk because
          insufficient space available on disk or because the frames
          have already been saved to disk or because you interrupted
          the build process."
0146      IDS_NoBg         "Hidden background image not yet created."
0147      IDS_BgAlready    "The hidden background bitmap has already been
          created."
0148      IDS_InsufMemBg   "Insufficient global memory for background
          bitmap."
0149      IDS_ReqdHdwr1    "Graphics hardware not supported"
0150      IDS_ReqdHdwr2    "CGA, HGA, or EGA graphics adapter detected.
          This application requires either an industry-standard VGA, a
          VESA-standard SuperVGA, an 8514/a, or an XGA graphics
          adapter and compatible display."
0151      IDS_Build        "Animation build process"
0152      IDS_ToCancel     "Ready to begin building the animation
          sequence.  To interrupt a build session in progress, click
          the right mouse button.  To begin the build, select OK now.
          See the book for further information."
0153      IDS_Loading      "Loading animation..."
0154   END
0155   /*
0156   ----------------------------------------------------------------
0157                   End of resource script file
0158   ----------------------------------------------------------------
```

C-3 Continued.

```
0159                                                                    */
0001    /*
0002    ------------------------------------------------------------------
0003                    3D interactive animation template
0004    ------------------------------------------------------------------
0005      Source file:  animate.c
0006      Release version:  1.2                     Programmer:  Lee Adams
0007      Type:  C source file for Windows application development.
0008      Supported compilers:  Explicit compatibility with Microsoft
0009        QuickC for Windows v1.00 and Borland Turbo C++ for Windows
0010        v3.0.  Nominal compatibility with all Windows-compatible C
0011        and C++ compilers such as Borland C++, Zortech C++, Watcom C,
0012        and Microsoft C/C++.
0013      Memory model:  medium.
0014      Build notes:  Do not use the load optimization feature of the
0015        Resource Compiler (or use the command-line -K switch).
0016        For trouble-free compiling follow the tips in the book.
0017      Project notes:  Load the assembly.mak project file if you are
0018        using QuickC for Windows.  Load the assembly.prj project file
0019        if you are using Turbo C++ for Windows.  Refer to the book if
0020        you are using another compiler.  The following files are
0021        needed to build the executable:
0022          animate.def      module definition file
0023          animate.h        include file
0024          animate.rc       resource script file
0025          animate.c        C source file
0026          engine3d.h       include file for 3D functions
0027          engine3d.c       3D toolkit
0028          shapes3d.h       include file for 3D solids
0029          shapes3d.c       3D shapes toolkit
0030          assemb3d.h       include file for hierarchical modeling
0031          assemb3d.c       3D hierarchical modeling toolkit
0032          lights3d.h       include file for light-source functions
0033          lights3d.c       light-source toolkit
0034          disk3d.h         include file for disk functions
0035          disk3d.c         image save/load toolkit
0036      Output and features:  Demonstrates 3D modeling and shading for
0037        animation sequences and storage of frames on disk as binary
0038        image files.  Demonstrates loading of frames from disk and
0039        interactive playback of animation sequence from RAM or from
0040        disk if insufficient memory available.  The startup code
0041        automatically sizes the window to yield a client area with
0042        dimensions of 256-by-255 pixels in any graphics mode.  You
0043        can use the menu system to toggle between wireframe and
0044        shaded modes.
0045        NUMBER OF FRAMES:  In its current implementation, the
0046        application produces an animation sequence of 36 frames.
0047        To create a sequence that uses fewer frames or more frames,
0048        you can edit lines 00148 and 00149, and then remove or add
0049        filenames as required at lines 00167 to 00175.
0050      Publication: Contains material from Windcrest/McGraw-Hill book
0051        4115 published by TAB BOOKS Division of McGraw-Hill Inc.
0052      License:  As purchaser of the book you are granted a royalty-
0053        free license to distribute executable files generated using
0054        this code provided you accept the conditions of the License
0055        Agreement and Limited Warranty described in the book and on
0056        the companion disk.  Government users:  This software and
0057        documentation are subject to restrictions set forth in The
0058        Rights in Technical Data and Computer Software clause at
0059        252.227-7013 and elsewhere.
0060    ------------------------------------------------------------------
```

```
0061          (c) Copyright 1991-1993 Lee Adams.  All rights reserved.
0062               Lee Adams(tm) is a trademark of Lee Adams.
0063     ------------------------------------------------------------
0064
0065     ------------------------------------------------------------
0066                          Include files
0067     ------------------------------------------------------------
0068                                                              */
0069     #include <WINDOWS.H>              /* declarations for Windows API */
0070     #include "ANIMATE.H"          /* declares function prototypes, etc. */
0071     #include "DISK3D.H"        /* declares functions in disk engine */
0072     #include "ENGINE3D.H"         /* declares functions in 3D engine */
0073     #include "SHAPES3D.H"  /* declares functions in 3D shapes module */
0074     #include "DEFORM3D.H"        /* functions in deformation module */
0075     #include "LIGHTS3D.H"   /* declares functions in lighting module */
0076     #include "ASSEMB3D.H"  /* declares functions in hierarchy module */
0077     #include <time.h>                 /* supports date and time */
0078
0079     /*
0080     ------------------------------------------------------------
0081           Static variables visible throughout this file
0082     ------------------------------------------------------------
0083                                                              */
0084     /* ------------------ window specifications ---------------- */
0085     #define zWINDOW_WIDTH 263                 /* width of window */
0086     #define zWINDOW_HEIGHT 300               /* depth of window */
0087     #define zFRAMEWIDE 256               /* width of viewport */
0088     #define zFRAMEHIGH 255               /* depth of viewport */
0089     static int WindowX, WindowY;            /* location of window */
0090
0091     /* ---------------- instance operations -------------------- */
0092     HANDLE hInst;                 /* handle to this copy of the app */
0093     static HWND MainhWnd;              /* handle to the app's window */
0094     static HANDLE hAccel;        /* handle to the accelerator keys */
0095     static HMENU hMenu;      /* handle to an active menu at runtime */
0096     static PAINTSTRUCT ps;   /* used for Windows-generated refreshes */
0097
0098     /* ------------------- mouse and cursor -------------------- */
0099     static HCURSOR hPrevCursor;             /* handle to arrow cursor */
0100     static HCURSOR hHourGlass;          /* handle to hourglass cursor */
0101     static int MousePresent;          /* indicates if mouse found */
0102
0103     /* ------------------- runtime conditions ------------------ */
0104     static int DisplayWidth, DisplayHeight; /* resolution of display */
0105     static int DisplayBits;            /* number of bits per pixel */
0106     static int DisplayPlanes;              /* number of bitplanes */
0107     static DWORD MemoryMode;             /* runtime memory mode */
0108     static DWORD Version;                 /* version of Windows */
0109     static BOOL bUseArial= TRUE;   /* FALSE, use Helv if Windows 3.0 */
0110
0111     /* ------------------ message box operations ---------------- */
0112     char lpCaption[51];           /* stores caption for message box */
0113     int Max= 50;                     /* max length of caption */
0114     char lpMessage[250];            /* stores text for message box */
0115     int MaxText= 249;                    /* max length of text */
0116     static short TextLength= 0;         /* stores wsprintf() string */
0117     static int MessageBoxChoice= 0;      /* user's selection, if any */
0118
0119     /* ----------------- persistent image operations -------------- */
0120     #define zBLANK 0
0121     #define zANIMATING  1
```

```
0122   #define zPREVIEW  2
0123   static int PaintImage= zBLANK;        /* indicates viewport status */
0124
0125   /* -------------------- timer operations -------------------- */
0126   #define zTIMER_PAUSE 3
0127   static int TimerCounter= zTIMER_PAUSE; /* timing delay mechanism */
0128   static BOOL TimerExists= FALSE;                   /* timer active? */
0129   static WORD TimerID1;                                  /* timer ID */
0130
0131   /* ----------------- hidden-frame operations ----------------- */
0132   static HDC hFrameDC;          /* display-context of hidden-frame */
0133   static HBITMAP hFrame;                 /* bitmap of hidden-frame */
0134   static HBITMAP hPrevFrame;                   /* default bitmap */
0135   BOOL FrameReady= FALSE;                   /* hidden-frame ready? */
0136
0137   /* -------------------- animation engine -------------------- */
0138   static BOOL Pause= TRUE;                   /* animation paused? */
0139   static WORD wFrameRate= 55;                   /* animation rate */
0140   static WORD wPrevRate= 55;           /* remembers previous rate */
0141   #define zFORWARD 1
0142   #define zREVERSE 0
0143   static int FrameDirection= zFORWARD;     /* animation direction */
0144   static BOOL Redisplay= FALSE;          /* for refresh when paused */
0145   static BOOL AnimationReady= FALSE;  /* animation sequence ready? */
0146   static int FrameNum= 1;                          /* current frame */
0147   #define zFIRSTFRAME 1      /* first frame of animation sequence */
0148   #define zFINALFRAME 36      /* final frame of animation sequence */
0149   #define zNUMCELS 36      /* number of cels in animation sequence */
0150   static int LoopCount;                          /* loop counter */
0151
0152   /* ---------------- disk save/load operations ---------------- */
0153   int RetVal;                      /* value returned by functions */
0154   static BOOL bFrameSaved= FALSE;                   /* frame saved? */
0155   static BOOL bFrameLoaded= FALSE;                 /* frame loaded? */
0156   static BOOL bAnimationSaved= FALSE;          /* animation saved? */
0157   static BOOL bAnimationLoaded= FALSE;         /* animation loaded? */
0158   static BOOL bPrevSaveAttempt= FALSE; /* previous save attempted? */
0159   static BOOL bPrevLoadAttempt= FALSE; /* previous load attempted? */
0160   static BOOL bUseDisk= FALSE;     /* use RAM or disk for playback? */
0161   static BOOL bAnimationHalted= FALSE;         /* playback paused? */
0162   static HDC hFDC;     /* memory display-context for hidden bitmaps */
0163   static HBITMAP hPrevF;                         /* default bitmap */
0164   static HBITMAP BitmapHandles[zNUMCELS];      /* array of bitmaps */
0165   static char *FrameFiles[zNUMCELS]=
0166       {    /* array of pointers to filenames for animation frames... */
0167       "ANIM01.BIT", "ANIM02.BIT", "ANIM03.BIT", "ANIM04.BIT",
0168       "ANIM05.BIT", "ANIM06.BIT", "ANIM07.BIT", "ANIM08.BIT",
0169       "ANIM09.BIT", "ANIM10.BIT", "ANIM11.BIT", "ANIM12.BIT",
0170       "ANIM13.BIT", "ANIM14.BIT", "ANIM15.BIT", "ANIM16.BIT",
0171       "ANIM17.BIT", "ANIM18.BIT", "ANIM19.BIT", "ANIM20.BIT",
0172       "ANIM21.BIT", "ANIM22.BIT", "ANIM23.BIT", "ANIM24.BIT",
0173       "ANIM25.BIT", "ANIM26.BIT", "ANIM27.BIT", "ANIM28.BIT",
0174       "ANIM29.BIT", "ANIM30.BIT", "ANIM31.BIT", "ANIM32.BIT",
0175       "ANIM33.BIT", "ANIM34.BIT", "ANIM35.BIT", "ANIM36.BIT",
0176       };
0177
0178   /* ---------- declare data types for animation script ---------- */
0179   static struct CameraPath
0180       {                /* camera movement during specified frames... */
0181       int StartFrame;
0182       int EndFrame;
```

```
0183      int ChgHeading;
0184      int ChgPitch;
0185      int ChgDistance;
0186      };
0187   static struct LightPath
0188      {             /* light-source movement during specified frames... */
0189      int StartFrame;
0190      int EndFrame;
0191      int ChgHeading;
0192      int ChgElevation;
0193      };
0194   static struct ActorPath
0195      {   /* actor movement & deformation during specified frames... */
0196      int StartFrame;
0197      int EndFrame;
0198      int ChgYaw;
0199      int ChgRoll;
0200      int ChgPitch;
0201      int ChgPosX;
0202      int ChgPosY;
0203      int ChgPosZ;
0204      };
0205
0206   static struct CameraDefine
0207      {                           /* camera startup parameters... */
0208      int Heading;
0209      int Pitch;
0210      int Distance;
0211      };
0212   static struct LightDefine
0213      {                       /* light-source startup parameters... */
0214      int Heading;
0215      int Elevation;
0216      };
0217
0218   static struct ActorDefine
0219      {                           /* actor startup parameters... */
0220      int PositionX;            /* position of actor in 3D world... */
0221      int PositionY;
0222      int PositionZ;
0223      int Yaw;                  /* orientation of actor in 3D world... */
0224      int Roll;
0225      int Pitch;
0226      };
0227
0228   /* --------- camera, light, actor, subassembly structs --------- */
0229   static struct CameraDefine    Cam1;                    /* camera */
0230   static struct CameraPath      Cam1Path1;          /* camera path */
0231   static struct LightDefine     Lt1;               /* light-source */
0232   static struct LightPath       Lt1Path1;     /* light-source path */
0233
0234   static struct ActorDefine     Actor1;            /* an actor... */
0235   static struct ActorPath       Actor1Path1;   /* ...and its path */
0236
0237   /*
0238   -----------------------------------------------------------------
0239                    Entry point for the application
0240   -----------------------------------------------------------------
0241                                                                   */
0242   int PASCAL WinMain(HANDLE hInstance, HANDLE hPrevInstance,
0243                   LPSTR lpCmdLine, int nCmdShow)
```

```
0244   {
0245     MSG msg;                              /* holds incoming messages */
0246     HWND hWndPrev;                   /* handle to previous copy of app */
0247     HWND hDesktopWnd;                   /* handle to the entire display */
0248     HDC hDCcaps;            /* display-context for the entire display */
0249     RECT rcClientReqd;        /* size of viewport before adjustment */
0250     int AdjustX, AdjustY; /* amount to adjust to ensure 256-by-255 */
0251
0252   /* ------------- ensure only one copy is running ------------- */
0253   hWndPrev = FindWindow("ANIMDEMO", "AN4115");
0254   if (hWndPrev != NULL)        /* if another app named AN4115 of... */
0255     {                   /* class ANIMDEMO is already running, then... */
0256     BringWindowToTop(hWndPrev);           /* ...use it instead... */
0257     return FALSE;                       /* ...and cancel this launch */
0258     }
0259
0260   /* ------------- display the splash signon notice ------------- */
0261   MessageBoxChoice= MessageBox(GetFocus(),
0262   "Animation demo from Windcrest McGraw-Hill book 4115",
0263   "Copyright- 1993 Lee Adams", MB_OKCANCEL);
0264   if (MessageBoxChoice == IDCANCEL) return FALSE;
0265
0266   /* -------------- determine version of Windows --------------- */
0267   Version= (DWORD)GetVersion();
0268   if ((LOBYTE(LOWORD(Version))==3) &&
0269      (HIBYTE(LOWORD(Version))==0))
0270     {                          /* if running Windows version 3.0... */
0271     bUseArial= FALSE;              /* ...use Helv font in client area */
0272     }
0273   else
0274     {                 /* ...else if running Windows 3.1 or newer... */
0275     bUseArial= TRUE;           /* ...use Arial font in client area */
0276     }
0277
0278   /* --------- determine capabilities of screen display ---------- */
0279   hDesktopWnd= GetDesktopWindow();
0280   hDCcaps= GetDC(hDesktopWnd);
0281   DisplayWidth= GetDeviceCaps(hDCcaps,HORZRES);
0282   DisplayHeight= GetDeviceCaps(hDCcaps,VERTRES);
0283   DisplayBits= GetDeviceCaps(hDCcaps,BITSPIXEL);
0284   DisplayPlanes= GetDeviceCaps(hDCcaps,PLANES);
0285   ReleaseDC(hDesktopWnd,hDCcaps);
0286
0287   /* ------------- trap unsupported graphics adapters ------------ */
0288   if (DisplayWidth==720)
0289     {                                     /* if HGA detected... */
0290     LoadString(hInstance,IDS_ReqdHdwr1,lpCaption,Max);
0291     LoadString(hInstance,IDS_ReqdHdwr2,lpMessage,MaxText);
0292     MessageBeep(0); MessageBox(GetFocus(),lpMessage,lpCaption,MB_OK);
0293     return FALSE;
0294     }
0295   if (DisplayWidth==640)
0296     {
0297     if ((DisplayHeight==350)||(DisplayHeight==200))
0298       {                                 /* if EGA or CGA detected... */
0299       LoadString(hInstance,IDS_ReqdHdwr1,lpCaption,Max);
0300       LoadString(hInstance,IDS_ReqdHdwr2,lpMessage,MaxText);
0301       MessageBeep(0);
0302       MessageBox(GetFocus(),lpMessage,lpCaption,MB_OK);
0303       return FALSE;
0304       }
```

```
0305    }
0306
0307    /* ------- calculate screen position to center the window ------ */
0308    WindowX= (DisplayWidth - zWINDOW_WIDTH) / 2;
0309    WindowY= (DisplayHeight - zWINDOW_HEIGHT) /2;
0310    if (WindowX < 0) WindowX= 0;
0311    if (WindowY < 0) WindowY= 0;
0312
0313    /* ---- determine memory mode (enhanced, standard, or real) ---- */
0314    MemoryMode= GetWinFlags();
0315
0316    /* ---------------- create and show the window ----------------- */
0317    hInst = hInstance;          /* store handle to this copy of the app */
0318    if (!zInitClass(hInstance)) return FALSE;     /* initialize class */
0319    MainhWnd = zInitMainWindow(hInstance);       /* initialize window */
0320    if (!MainhWnd) return FALSE;          /* if error, cancel startup */
0321    ShowWindow(MainhWnd, nCmdShow);                /* show the window */
0322    UpdateWindow(MainhWnd);                         /* force a refresh */
0323    hAccel= LoadAccelerators(hInstance,"ANIMKEYS"); /* activate keys */
0324
0325    /* -------------- enforce a 256-by-255 viewport --------------- */
0326    GetClientRect(MainhWnd, &rcClientReqd);       /* get dimensions */
0327    AdjustX=              /* compare actual width to desired width... */
0328              zFRAMEWIDE - (rcClientReqd.right + 1);
0329    AdjustY=             /* compare actual height to desired height... */
0330              zFRAMEHIGH - (rcClientReqd.bottom + 1);
0331    if ((AdjustX != 0)||(AdjustY != 0)) /* if adjustment required... */
0332      {
0333      SetWindowPos(MainhWnd, (HWND)NULL,
0334                  WindowX, WindowY,
0335                  zWINDOW_WIDTH + AdjustX,       /* resize the width */
0336                  zWINDOW_HEIGHT + AdjustY,     /* resize the height */
0337                  SWP_NOZORDER);
0338      }
0339
0340    /* --------------------- check for mouse --------------------- */
0341    MousePresent = GetSystemMetrics(SM_MOUSEPRESENT);
0342    if (!MousePresent)                      /* if no mouse found... */
0343      {                          /* ...display a cautionary warning */
0344      LoadString(hInst,IDS_Warning,lpCaption,Max);
0345      LoadString(hInst,IDS_NoMouse,lpMessage,MaxText);
0346      MessageBox(GetFocus(),lpMessage,lpCaption,MB_OK);
0347      }
0348
0349    /* --------------- initialize the hidden-frame --------------- */
0350    zInitFrame(MainhWnd); /* is used for software-controlled refresh */
0351
0352    /* ---------- begin retrieving messages for the window --------- */
0353    while (GetMessage(&msg,0,0,0))
0354      {
0355      if(TranslateAccelerator(MainhWnd, hAccel, &msg)) continue;
0356      TranslateMessage(&msg);
0357      DispatchMessage(&msg);
0358      }
0359    return(msg.wParam);
0360    }
0361
0362    /*
0363    ------------------------------------------------------------------
0364                     Switcher for incoming messages
0365    ------------------------------------------------------------------
```

```
0366                                                                */
0367   LONG FAR PASCAL zMessageHandler(HWND hWnd, unsigned message,
0368                                   WORD wParam, LONG lParam)
0369   {
0370     HDC hDCpaint;                        /* for Windows-generated refresh */
0371
0372   switch (message)
0373     {
0374     /* -------------- filter incoming timer events ------------- */
0375     case WM_TIMER:    /* slower CPUs need delay so menus can pop up */
0376       TimerCounter--;                   /* decrement the delay mechanism */
0377       if (TimerCounter > 0) break; /* do nothing if still delaying */
0378       TimerCounter++;      /* otherwise restore the mechanism and... */
0379       zShowNextFrame(hWnd); /* ...show the next frame if animating */
0380       break;
0381
0382     /* ----------------- menu system commands ------------------ */
0383     case WM_COMMAND:
0384       switch(wParam)
0385         {
0386         case IDM_New:     break;
0387         case IDM_Open:    break;
0388         case IDM_Save:    break;
0389         case IDM_SaveAs:  break;
0390         case IDM_Exit:
0391             MessageBoxChoice= MessageBox(GetFocus(),
0392               "Exit the 3D animation demo and return to Windows?",
0393               "Please confirm", MB_YESNO);
0394             if (MessageBoxChoice == IDYES) PostQuitMessage(0);
0395             break;
0396         case IDM_Undo:    break;
0397         case IDM_Cut:     break;
0398         case IDM_Copy:    break;
0399         case IDM_Paste:   break;
0400         case IDM_Delete:  break;
0401
0402         /* ------------- manage the animation engine ------------- */
0403         case IDM_RunForward:              /* begin forward playback... */
0404             if (AnimationReady==FALSE)
0405               {
0406               MessageBeep(0);
0407               LoadString(hInst,IDS_NotReady,lpCaption,Max);
0408               LoadString(hInst,IDS_BuildBefore,lpMessage,MaxText);
0409               TimerCounter= zTIMER_PAUSE;
0410               MessageBox(GetFocus(),lpMessage,lpCaption,MB_OK);
0411               break;
0412               }
0413             Pause= FALSE;
0414             PaintImage= zANIMATING;
0415             FrameDirection= zFORWARD;
0416             zShowNextFrame(hWnd);
0417             break;
0418         case IDM_RunReverse:              /* begin reverse playback... */
0419             if (AnimationReady==FALSE)
0420               {
0421               MessageBeep(0);
0422               LoadString(hInst,IDS_NotReady,lpCaption,Max);
0423               LoadString(hInst,IDS_BuildBefore,lpMessage,MaxText);
0424               TimerCounter= zTIMER_PAUSE;
0425               MessageBox(GetFocus(),lpMessage,lpCaption,MB_OK);
0426               break;
```

```
0427                    }
0428              Pause= FALSE;
0429              PaintImage= zANIMATING;
0430              FrameDirection= zREVERSE;
0431              zShowNextFrame(hWnd);
0432              break;
0433          case IDM_StopAnimation:              /* pause the playback... */
0434              if (AnimationReady==FALSE)
0435                 {
0436                 MessageBeep(0);
0437                 LoadString(hInst,IDS_NotReady,lpCaption,Max);
0438                 LoadString(hInst,IDS_BuildBefore,lpMessage,MaxText);
0439                 TimerCounter= zTIMER_PAUSE;
0440                 MessageBox(GetFocus(),lpMessage,lpCaption,MB_OK);
0441                 break;
0442                 }
0443              Pause= TRUE;
0444              zShowNextFrame(hWnd);
0445              break;
0446          case IDM_SaveAnimation:          /* save animation to disk... */
0447              LoadString(hInst,IDS_Build,lpCaption,Max);
0448              LoadString(hInst,IDS_ToCancel,lpMessage,MaxText);
0449              TimerCounter= zTIMER_PAUSE;
0450              MessageBox(GetFocus(),lpMessage,lpCaption,MB_OK);
0451              zInitialize3D(hWnd);
0452              SetCapture(hWnd); hPrevCursor= SetCursor(hHourGlass);
0453              zSaveAnimation(hWnd);
0454              LoadString(hInst,IDS_Caption,lpCaption,Max);
0455              SetWindowText(hWnd,lpCaption);
0456              SetCursor(hPrevCursor); ReleaseCapture();
0457              if (bAnimationSaved==FALSE)
0458                 {
0459                 MessageBeep(0);
0460                 LoadString(hInst,IDS_NotReady,lpCaption,Max);
0461                 LoadString(hInst,IDS_Disk26,lpMessage,MaxText);
0462                 TimerCounter= zTIMER_PAUSE;
0463                 MessageBox(GetFocus(),lpMessage,lpCaption,MB_OK);
0464                 }
0465              break;
0466          case IDM_UseShaded:       /* use fully-shaded 3D objects... */
0467              zInitialize3D(hWnd);
0468              zUseWireframeMode(FALSE);
0469              MessageBox(GetFocus(),
0470                 "Using solid shaded modeling mode.",
0471                 "3D status report", MB_OK);
0472              break;
0473          case IDM_UseWireframe:       /* use wireframe 3D objects... */
0474              zInitialize3D(hWnd);
0475              zUseWireframeMode(TRUE);
0476              MessageBox(GetFocus(),
0477                 "Using wireframe modeling mode.",
0478                 "3D status report", MB_OK);
0479              break;
0480          case IDM_LoadAnimation:       /* load animation from disk... */
0481              LoadString(hInst,IDS_Loading,lpCaption,Max);
0482              SetWindowText(hWnd,lpCaption);
0483              SetCapture(hWnd); hPrevCursor= SetCursor(hHourGlass);
0484              zLoadAnimation(hWnd);
0485              SetCursor(hPrevCursor); ReleaseCapture();
0486              LoadString(hInst,IDS_Caption,lpCaption,Max);
0487              SetWindowText(hWnd,lpCaption);
```

```
0488              break;
0489          case IDM_Clear:                    /* clear the viewport... */
0490              if (Pause==TRUE)
0491                {
0492                zClear(hWnd);
0493                PaintImage= zBLANK;
0494                }
0495              break;
0496
0497          /* -------------- adjust the playback rate -------------- */
0498          case IDM_FPS182:                   /* use 18 frames per second */
0499              wPrevRate= wFrameRate;
0500              wFrameRate= (WORD)55;
0501              zSetFrameRate(hWnd, wFrameRate);
0502              break;
0503          case IDM_FPS91:                    /* use 9 frames per second */
0504              wPrevRate= wFrameRate;
0505              wFrameRate= (WORD)110;
0506              zSetFrameRate(hWnd, wFrameRate);
0507              break;
0508          case IDM_FPS61:                    /* use 6 frames per second */
0509              wPrevRate= wFrameRate;
0510              wFrameRate= (WORD)165;
0511              zSetFrameRate(hWnd, wFrameRate);
0512              break;
0513          case IDM_FPS45:                    /* use 4.5 frames per second */
0514              wPrevRate= wFrameRate;
0515              wFrameRate= (WORD) 220;
0516              zSetFrameRate(hWnd, wFrameRate);
0517              break;
0518          case IDM_FPS36:                    /* use 3.5 frames per second */
0519              wPrevRate= wFrameRate;
0520              wFrameRate= (WORD) 275;
0521              zSetFrameRate(hWnd, wFrameRate);
0522              break;
0523          case IDM_FPS30:                    /* use 3 frames per second */
0524              wPrevRate= wFrameRate;
0525              wFrameRate= (WORD) 330;
0526              zSetFrameRate(hWnd, wFrameRate);
0527              break;
0528
0529          /* ----------- About, License, and How to Use ----------- */
0530          case IDM_About:                    /* copyright information... */
0531            LoadString(hInst,IDS_About,lpCaption,Max);
0532            LoadString(hInst,IDS_AboutText,lpMessage,MaxText);
0533            TimerCounter= zTIMER_PAUSE;
0534            MessageBox(GetFocus(),lpMessage,lpCaption,MB_OK);
0535            break;
0536          case IDM_License:                  /* license information... */
0537            LoadString(hInst,IDS_License,lpCaption,Max);
0538            LoadString(hInst,IDS_LicenseText,lpMessage,MaxText);
0539            TimerCounter= zTIMER_PAUSE;
0540            MessageBox(GetFocus(),lpMessage,lpCaption,MB_OK);
0541            break;
0542          case IDM_GeneralHelp:              /* how to use the demo... */
0543            LoadString(hInst,IDS_Help,lpCaption,Max);
0544            LoadString(hInst,IDS_HelpText,lpMessage,MaxText);
0545            TimerCounter= zTIMER_PAUSE;
0546            MessageBox(GetFocus(),lpMessage,lpCaption,MB_OK);
0547            break;
0548          default:
```

```
0549              return(DefWindowProc(hWnd, message, wParam, lParam));
0550          }
0551       break;
0552
0553    /* ---------- grab handle for menu item checkmark ------------ */
0554    case WM_INITMENUPOPUP:       /* if a menu is about to pop up... */
0555       TimerCounter= zTIMER_PAUSE; /* provide pause for slower CPUs */
0556       if (lParam == 2)       /* and if it is the frame-rate menu... */
0557         hMenu= wParam; /* remember it so check-mark can be tweaked */
0558       break;
0559
0560    /* ------- oversee Windows-generated refresh requests -------- */
0561    case WM_PAINT:
0562       hDCpaint= BeginPaint(hWnd,&ps);
0563       EndPaint(hWnd, &ps);
0564       if (PaintImage==zBLANK) break;          /* if blank do nothing */
0565       if (PaintImage==zPREVIEW)        /* if frame preview mode... */
0566         {
0567         zCopyToDisplay(hWnd);  /* ...copy hidden-frame to viewport */
0568         break;
0569         }
0570       if (Pause==TRUE)                 /* if animation is paused... */
0571         {
0572         Redisplay= TRUE;                     /* reset the token... */
0573         zShowNextFrame(hWnd); /* so current frame is refreshed... */
0574         Redisplay= FALSE;              /* ...then restore the token */
0575         break;
0576         }
0577       zShowNextFrame(hWnd);    /* else if animating show next frame */
0578       break;
0579
0580    /* --- manage incoming keystrokes for single-step playback --- */
0581    case WM_KEYDOWN:
0582       switch (wParam)
0583         {
0584         case VK_LEFT:    /* left direction key: singlestep reverse */
0585           if (Pause==TRUE)                /* if animation paused... */
0586             {
0587             if (FrameDirection==zFORWARD)
0588               {              /* confirm the playback direction... */
0589               FrameDirection= zREVERSE;
0590               }
0591             Pause= FALSE;
0592             zShowNextFrame(hWnd);    /* ...and show the next frame */
0593             Pause= TRUE;
0594             PaintImage= zANIMATING;
0595             }
0596           break;
0597         case VK_RIGHT:  /* right direction key: singlestep forward */
0598           if (Pause==TRUE)
0599             {              /* (control logic is similar to VK_LEFT) */
0600             if (FrameDirection==zREVERSE)
0601               {
0602               FrameDirection= zFORWARD;
0603               }
0604             Pause= FALSE;
0605             zShowNextFrame(hWnd);
0606             Pause= TRUE;
0607             PaintImage= zANIMATING;
0608             }
0609           break;
```

```
0610          default: return(DefWindowProc(hWnd,message,wParam,lParam));
0611          }
0612        break;
0613
0614     /* --------------- ensure a graceful shutdown -------------- */
0615     case WM_DESTROY:
0616       if (FrameReady==TRUE)
0617         {            /* if a hidden-frame was created, destroy it... */
0618         SelectObject(hFrameDC,hPrevFrame);
0619         DeleteObject(hFrame);
0620         DeleteDC(hFrameDC);
0621         KillTimer(hWnd,1);                          /* ...and the timer */
0622         }
0623       if (bAnimationLoaded==TRUE)
0624         {     /* if an animation sequence was loaded into memory... */
0625         SelectObject(hFDC,hPrevF); /* select default bitmap handle */
0626         for (LoopCount= 1; LoopCount<= zNUMCELS; LoopCount++)
0627           {                /* for each bitmap handle in the array... */
0628           DeleteObject(BitmapHandles[LoopCount-1]);   /* ...delete */
0629           }
0630         DeleteDC(hFDC);    /* ...then delete memory display-context */
0631         }
0632       zClose3D();                          /* shut down the 3D engine */
0633       PostQuitMessage(0);
0634       break;
0635
0636     /* ------- intercept attempt to resize or move window -------- */
0637     case WM_SYSCOMMAND:
0638       if ((wParam & 0xfff0)== SC_SIZE)
0639         {
0640         MessageBeep(0); break;
0641         }
0642       if ((wParam & 0xfff0)== SC_MINIMIZE)
0643         {
0644         MessageBeep(0); break;
0645         }
0646       if ((wParam & 0xfff0)== SC_MAXIMIZE)
0647         {
0648         MessageBeep(0); break;
0649         }
0650
0651     /* ----- send all other messages to Windows for handling ----- */
0652     default:
0653       return(DefWindowProc(hWnd, message, wParam, lParam));
0654     }
0655   return FALSE;
0656   }
0657   /*
0658   -------------------------------------------------------------------
0659               Initialize the attributes of the window class
0660   -------------------------------------------------------------------
0661                                                                    */
0662   BOOL zInitClass(HANDLE hInstance)
0663   {
0664     WNDCLASS WndClass;
0665   WndClass.style= 0;
0666   WndClass.lpfnWndProc= zMessageHandler;  /* app's message handler */
0667   WndClass.cbClsExtra= 0;
0668   WndClass.cbWndExtra= 0;
0669   WndClass.hInstance= hInstance;              /* this copy of the app */
0670   WndClass.hIcon= LoadIcon(NULL,IDI_EXCLAMATION);    /* app's icon */
```

```
0671   WndClass.hCursor= LoadCursor(NULL,IDC_ARROW);      /* app's cursor */
0672   WndClass.hbrBackground=                  /* background color for viewport */
0673                       CreateSolidBrush(RGB(255,255,255));
0674   WndClass.lpszMenuName= "ANIMENUS";      /* menu script in .rc file */
0675   WndClass.lpszClassName= "ANIMDEMO";      /* nominal name of class */
0676   return RegisterClass(&WndClass); /* tell Windows about the class */
0677   }
0678   /*
0679   ------------------------------------------------------------------
0680                       Create the main window
0681   ------------------------------------------------------------------
0682                                                                    */
0683   HWND zInitMainWindow(HANDLE hInstance)
0684   {
0685     HWND hWnd;
0686   LoadString(hInstance,IDS_Caption,lpCaption,Max); /* load caption */
0687   hHourGlass= LoadCursor(NULL,IDC_WAIT);  /* load hourglass cursor */
0688   hWnd = CreateWindow("ANIMDEMO",                     /* class name */
0689     lpCaption,                               /* window caption */
0690     WS_OVERLAPPED | WS_THICKFRAME | WS_CLIPCHILDREN,     /* style */
0691     WindowX,WindowY,                         /* location of window */
0692     zWINDOW_WIDTH,zWINDOW_HEIGHT,           /* dimensions of window */
0693     0,                                      /* parent window, if any */
0694     0,                                      /* special menu, if any */
0695     hInstance,                              /* this copy of the app */
0696     (LPSTR)NULL);      /* for multiple-document interface, if any */
0697   return hWnd;    /* return the newly-created handle to the caller */
0698   }
0699
0700   /*
0701   ------------------------------------------------------------------
0702                       Graphics system functions
0703   ------------------------------------------------------------------
0704   ------------------------------------------------------------------
0705                       Create the hidden-frame.
0706   ------------------------------------------------------------------
0707                                                                    */
0708   static void zInitFrame(HWND hWnd)
0709   {
0710     HDC hDisplayDC;
0711
0712   if (FrameReady==TRUE)
0713     {                        /* if a hidden-frame already exists... */
0714     MessageBeep(0);
0715     LoadString(hInst,IDS_Ready,lpCaption,Max);
0716     LoadString(hInst,IDS_Already,lpMessage,MaxText);
0717     TimerCounter= zTIMER_PAUSE;
0718     MessageBox(GetFocus(),lpMessage,lpCaption,MB_OK);
0719     return;
0720     }
0721   GlobalCompact((DWORD)-1L);             /* maximize contiguous memory */
0722
0723   /* ----------------- create a hidden bitmap ------------------- */
0724   hDisplayDC= GetDC(hWnd);                       /* display-context */
0725   hFrameDC= CreateCompatibleDC(hDisplayDC);            /* memory DC */
0726   hFrame= CreateCompatibleBitmap(hDisplayDC,zFRAMEWIDE,zFRAMEHIGH);
0727   if (hFrame==NULL)
0728     {                  /* if unable to create compatible bitmap... */
0729     LoadString(hInst,IDS_NotReady,lpCaption,Max);
0730     LoadString(hInst,IDS_InsufMem1,lpMessage,MaxText);
0731     MessageBox(GetFocus(),lpMessage,lpCaption,MB_OK);
```

```
0732     DeleteDC(hFrameDC);
0733     TimerExists= FALSE; FrameReady= FALSE; AnimationReady= FALSE;
0734     return;
0735     }
0736  hPrevFrame= SelectObject(hFrameDC,hFrame);        /* select bitmap */
0737
0738  /* -------- clear the viewport and copy to hidden-frame -------- */
0739  zClear(hWnd);
0740  BitBlt(hFrameDC,0,0,zFRAMEWIDE,zFRAMEHIGH,hDisplayDC,0,0,SRCCOPY);
0741  ReleaseDC(hWnd,hDisplayDC);        /* release the display-context */
0742
0743  /* -------------------- initialize a timer -------------------- */
0744  TimerID1= SetTimer(hWnd,1,wFrameRate,(FARPROC) NULL);
0745  if (TimerID1 == 0)              /* if no timer was initialized... */
0746     {                            /* ...display a warning */
0747     LoadString(hInst,IDS_NotReady,lpCaption,Max);
0748     LoadString(hInst,IDS_NoTimer,lpMessage,MaxText);
0749     MessageBox(GetFocus(),lpMessage,lpCaption,MB_OK);
0750     SelectObject(hFrameDC,hPrevFrame);
0751     DeleteObject(hFrame);
0752     DeleteDC(hFrameDC);
0753     TimerExists= FALSE;
0754     return;
0755     }
0756  TimerExists= TRUE;
0757  FrameReady= TRUE;
0758  FrameNum= 1;
0759  return;
0760  }
0761  /*
0762  -------------------------------------------------------------------
0763                        Clear the hidden frame.
0764  -------------------------------------------------------------------
0765                                                                    */
0766  static void zClearHiddenFrame(void)
0767  {
0768  if (FrameReady == TRUE)
0769     {
0770     PatBlt(hFrameDC,0,0,zFRAMEWIDE,zFRAMEHIGH,WHITENESS);
0771     }
0772  return;
0773  }
0774  /*
0775  -------------------------------------------------------------------
0776             Copy the hidden frame to the display window.
0777  -------------------------------------------------------------------
0778                                                                    */
0779  static void zCopyToDisplay(HWND hWnd)
0780  {
0781     HDC hDC;
0782  hDC= GetDC(hWnd);
0783  if (FrameReady == TRUE)
0784     {
0785     BitBlt(hDC,0,0,zFRAMEWIDE,zFRAMEHIGH,hFrameDC,0,0,SRCCOPY);
0786     }
0787  ReleaseDC(hWnd,hDC);
0788  return;
0789  }
0790  /*
0791  -------------------------------------------------------------------
0792                      Blank the display window.
```

```
0793   ------------------------------------------------------------
0794                                                             */
0795   static void zClear(HWND hWnd)
0796   {
0797     HDC hDC;
0798   hDC= GetDC(hWnd);
0799   PatBlt(hDC,0,0,zFRAMEWIDE,zFRAMEHIGH,WHITENESS);
0800   ReleaseDC(hWnd,hDC);
0801   return;
0802   }
0803
0804   /*
0805   ------------------------------------------------------------
0806                   Animation authoring functions
0807   ------------------------------------------------------------
0808   ------------------------------------------------------------
0809                 Create the frames and save to disk.
0810   ------------------------------------------------------------
0811                                                             */
0812   static void zSaveAnimation(HWND hWnd)
0813   {
0814   if (FrameReady==FALSE)
0815     {
0816     MessageBeep(0);
0817     LoadString(hInst,IDS_NotReady,lpCaption,Max);
0818     LoadString(hInst,IDS_NoFrame,lpMessage,MaxText);
0819     MessageBox(GetFocus(),lpMessage,lpCaption,MB_OK);
0820     return;
0821     }
0822   if (bAnimationSaved==TRUE)
0823     {
0824     MessageBeep(0);
0825     LoadString(hInst,IDS_Unexpected,lpCaption,Max);
0826     LoadString(hInst,IDS_Disk1,lpMessage,MaxText);
0827     TimerCounter= zTIMER_PAUSE;
0828     MessageBox(GetFocus(),lpMessage,lpCaption,MB_OK);
0829     return;
0830     }
0831   if (bPrevSaveAttempt==TRUE)
0832     {
0833     MessageBeep(0);
0834     LoadString(hInst,IDS_Unexpected,lpCaption,Max);
0835     LoadString(hInst,IDS_Disk8,lpMessage,MaxText);
0836     TimerCounter= zTIMER_PAUSE;
0837     MessageBox(GetFocus(),lpMessage,lpCaption,MB_OK);
0838     return;
0839     }
0840   bPrevSaveAttempt= TRUE;
0841
0842   /* ------------------- initialize the camera ------------------- */
0843   Cam1.Heading= 330; Cam1.Pitch= 320; Cam1.Distance= 356;
0844   zSetCameraDistance(Cam1.Distance);
0845   zSetCameraPitch(Cam1.Pitch);
0846   zSetCameraHeading(Cam1.Heading);
0847
0848   /* -------------- specify the path of the camera -------------- */
0849   Cam1Path1.StartFrame= 1; Cam1Path1.EndFrame= zNUMCELS;
0850   Cam1Path1.ChgHeading= 0;                 /* set to -2 for dolly */
0851   Cam1Path1.ChgPitch= 0;                   /* set to 2 for crane */
0852   Cam1Path1.ChgDistance= 0;
0853
```

```
0854     /* ---------------- initialize the light-source ---------------- */
0855     Lt1.Elevation= 60;
0856     Lt1.Heading= 180;
0857     zSetLightPosition(Lt1.Elevation, Lt1.Heading);
0858
0859     /* ------------ specify the path of the light-source ----------- */
0860     Lt1Path1.StartFrame= 1; Lt1Path1.EndFrame= zNUMCELS;
0861     Lt1Path1.ChgHeading= 0; Lt1Path1.ChgElevation= 0;
0862
0863     /* -------------------- initialize the actor ------------------- */
0864     Actor1.PositionX= 0;           /* position of actor in 3D world... */
0865     Actor1.PositionY= 0;
0866     Actor1.PositionZ= 0;
0867     Actor1.Yaw= 0;                 /* orientation of actor in 3D world... */
0868     Actor1.Roll= 45;
0869     Actor1.Pitch= 0;
0870     zSetSubjectLocation(Actor1.PositionX,
0871                         Actor1.PositionY,
0872                         Actor1.PositionZ);
0873     zSetSubjectAttitude(Actor1.Yaw, Actor1.Roll, Actor1.Pitch);
0874
0875     /* -------------- specify the path of the actor --------------- */
0876     Actor1Path1.StartFrame= 1;
0877     Actor1Path1.EndFrame= zNUMCELS;            /* for frames 1 to 36... */
0878     Actor1Path1.ChgYaw= 0;
0879     Actor1Path1.ChgRoll= 0;
0880     Actor1Path1.ChgPitch= 5;    /* rotate entity 5 degrees each frame */
0881     Actor1Path1.ChgPosX =0;
0882     Actor1Path1.ChgPosY =0;
0883     Actor1Path1.ChgPosZ= 0;
0884
0885     /* ---------------- build and save the cels ------------------ */
0886     for (LoopCount= 1; LoopCount<= zNUMCELS; LoopCount++)
0887       {                         /* for each cel in the animation... */
0888       bFrameSaved= zBuildFrame(LoopCount, hWnd,  /* ... save to disk */
0889                             (LPSTR)FrameFiles[LoopCount-1]);
0890       if (bFrameSaved==FALSE) return; /* cancel loop if error occurs */
0891       }
0892     bAnimationSaved= TRUE;
0893     bPrevLoadAttempt= FALSE;
0894     zClear(hWnd);
0895     MessageBeep(0);
0896     LoadString(hInst,IDS_Status,lpCaption,Max);
0897     LoadString(hInst,IDS_Disk2,lpMessage,MaxText);
0898     MessageBox(GetFocus(),lpMessage,lpCaption,MB_OK);
0899     return;
0900     }
0901     /*
0902     -------------------------------------------------------------------
0903                      Build one cel and save to disk.
0904     -------------------------------------------------------------------
0905                                                                       */
0906     static BOOL zBuildFrame(int Number, HWND hWnd, LPSTR lpFileName)
0907     {
0908       BOOL bDiskResult;
0909       HFONT Font;
0910       HFONT PrevFont;
0911       DWORD PrevFontColor;
0912       DWORD PrevBkColor;
0913       HDC hDC;
0914       struct tm *NewTime;              /* pointer to tm struct of time.h */
```

```
0915    time_t TimeSeconds;               /* long integer time_t of time.h */
0916    MSG msg;                                   /* incoming message */
0917
0918    /* ---------- display progress report on caption bar ---------- */
0919    TextLength= wsprintf(lpCaption,      /* build and save the string */
0920              "Building frame %d...", Number);
0921    SetWindowText(hWnd,lpCaption);        /* display it in caption bar */
0922
0923    /* --------------------- reset all buffers ------------------- */
0924    zClearHiddenFrame();
0925    zClear(hWnd);
0926    zClearHidden3DPage();
0927    zResetZBuffer();
0928
0929    /* ----------------- draw the appropriate cel ---------------- */
0930    zDrawCel(Number);
0931    if (FrameReady==TRUE)
0932      {
0933      hDC= GetDC(hWnd);
0934      BitBlt(hFrameDC,0,0,zFRAMEWIDE,zFRAMEHIGH,hDC,0,0,SRCCOPY);
0935      ReleaseDC(hWnd,hDC);
0936      }
0937
0938    /* ------------ check for user-requested cancel -------------- */
0939    if (PeekMessage(&msg,NULL,0,0,PM_REMOVE))
0940      {                      /* if a message is waiting in the queue... */
0941      if (msg.message == WM_RBUTTONDOWN)
0942        {                    /* ...if right mouse button pressed... */
0943        return FALSE;        /* ...then cancel the build sequence */
0944        }
0945      }
0946
0947    /* --------- display the titles, labels, and timestamp -------- */
0948    if ((DisplayBits==1)&&(DisplayPlanes==1))
0949      {                      /* if a mono display use black typeface... */
0950      PrevFontColor= SetTextColor(hFrameDC,RGB(0,0,0));
0951      PrevBkColor=  SetBkColor(hFrameDC,RGB(255,255,255));
0952      }
0953    else
0954      {    /* else if a color display use any solid color typeface... */
0955      PrevFontColor= SetTextColor(hFrameDC,RGB(0,0,0));
0956      PrevBkColor=  SetBkColor(hFrameDC,RGB(255,255,255));
0957      }
0958    SetBkMode(hFrameDC,TRANSPARENT);
0959
0960    if (bUseArial == FALSE)
0961      {                      /* if running Windows 3.0 use Helv font... */
0962      Font= CreateFont(24, 0, 0, 0, FW_BOLD, FALSE, FALSE, FALSE,
0963           ANSI_CHARSET, OUT_DEFAULT_PRECIS, CLIP_DEFAULT_PRECIS,
0964           DRAFT_QUALITY, VARIABLE_PITCH | FF_SWISS, "Helv");
0965      PrevFont= SelectObject(hFrameDC,Font);
0966      TextOut(hFrameDC,10,6,"A Lee Adams tutorial:",21);
0967      Font= CreateFont(36, 0, 0, 0, FW_BOLD, FALSE, FALSE, FALSE,
0968           ANSI_CHARSET, OUT_DEFAULT_PRECIS, CLIP_DEFAULT_PRECIS,
0969           DRAFT_QUALITY, VARIABLE_PITCH | FF_SWISS, "Helv");
0970      SelectObject(hFrameDC,Font);
0971      TextOut(hFrameDC,8,24,"3D animation",12);
0972      }
0973    else   /* else if running Windows 3.1 or newer use Arial font... */
0974      {
0975      Font= CreateFont(24, 0, 0, 0, FW_BOLD, FALSE, FALSE, FALSE,
```

```
0976          ANSI_CHARSET, OUT_DEFAULT_PRECIS, CLIP_DEFAULT_PRECIS,
0977          DRAFT_QUALITY, VARIABLE_PITCH | FF_SWISS, "Arial");
0978   PrevFont= SelectObject(hFrameDC,Font);
0979   TextOut(hFrameDC,10,6,"A Lee Adams tutorial:",21);
0980   Font= CreateFont(36, 0, 0, 0, FW_BOLD, FALSE, FALSE, FALSE,
0981          ANSI_CHARSET, OUT_DEFAULT_PRECIS, CLIP_DEFAULT_PRECIS,
0982          DRAFT_QUALITY, VARIABLE_PITCH | FF_SWISS, "Arial");
0983   SelectObject(hFrameDC,Font);
0984   TextOut(hFrameDC,8,24,"3D animation",12);
0985   }
0986
0987 SelectObject(hFrameDC,PrevFont);
0988 TextOut(hFrameDC,10,220,"Animation production timestamp",30);
0989 time(&TimeSeconds);
0990 NewTime= localtime(&TimeSeconds);
0991 TextOut(hFrameDC,10,235,(LPSTR)asctime(NewTime),24);
0992 SetBkMode(hFrameDC,OPAQUE);
0993 SetBkColor(hFrameDC,PrevBkColor);
0994 SetTextColor(hFrameDC,PrevFontColor);
0995
0996 /* ---------- check again for user-requested cancel ---------- */
0997 if (PeekMessage(&msg,NULL,0,0,PM_REMOVE))
0998   {
0999   if (msg.message == WM_RBUTTONDOWN)
1000     {
1001     return FALSE;
1002     }
1003   }
1004
1005 /* ---------- display the cel and save it to disk ------------ */
1006 zCopyToDisplay(hWnd);
1007 bDiskResult= zSaveFrame(hFrame,lpFileName);
1008 if (bDiskResult==FALSE) return FALSE;
1009 return TRUE;
1010 }
1011 /*
1012 --------------------------------------------------------------------
1013                          Draw a cel.
1014 --------------------------------------------------------------------
1015                                                                    */
1016 static void zDrawCel(int Number)
1017 {
1018   int PartID;              /* counter is used in the drawing loop */
1019
1020 /* -------------------- update the camera -------------------- */
1021 if ((Number > Cam1Path1.StartFrame) &&
1022     (Number <= Cam1Path1.EndFrame))
1023   {              /* if a frame num specified in the path struct... */
1024   Cam1.Distance= Cam1.Distance + Cam1Path1.ChgDistance;
1025   Cam1.Heading= Cam1.Heading + Cam1Path1.ChgHeading;
1026   Cam1.Pitch= Cam1.Pitch + Cam1Path1.ChgPitch;
1027   }
1028 if (Cam1.Heading < 0) Cam1.Heading= Cam1.Heading + 360;
1029 if (Cam1.Heading > 360) Cam1.Heading= Cam1.Heading - 360;
1030 if (Cam1.Pitch < 0) Cam1.Pitch= Cam1.Pitch + 360;
1031 if (Cam1.Pitch > 360) Cam1.Pitch= Cam1.Pitch - 360;
1032 zSetCameraDistance(Cam1.Distance);
1033 zSetCameraPitch(Cam1.Pitch);
1034 zSetCameraHeading(Cam1.Heading);
1035
1036 /* ------------------ update the light-source ---------------- */
```

```
1037  if ((Number > Lt1Path1.StartFrame) &&
1038     (Number <= Lt1Path1.EndFrame))
1039  {              /* if a frame num specified in the path struct... */
1040    Lt1.Heading= Lt1.Heading + Lt1Path1.ChgHeading;
1041    Lt1.Elevation= Lt1.Elevation + Lt1Path1.ChgElevation;
1042  }
1043  if (Lt1.Elevation > 90) Lt1.Elevation= 90;
1044  if (Lt1.Elevation < 0) Lt1.Elevation= 0;
1045  if (Lt1.Heading > 360) Lt1.Heading= Lt1.Heading - 360;
1046  if (Lt1.Heading < 0) Lt1.Heading= Lt1.Heading + 360;
1047  zSetLightPosition(Lt1.Elevation, Lt1.Heading);
1048
1049  /* --------------------- update the actor --------------------- */
1050  if ((Number > Actor1Path1.StartFrame) &&
1051     (Number <= Actor1Path1.EndFrame))
1052  {              /* if a frame num specified in the path struct... */
1053    Actor1.PositionX=  Actor1.PositionX + Actor1Path1.ChgPosX;
1054    Actor1.PositionY=  Actor1.PositionY + Actor1Path1.ChgPosY;
1055    Actor1.PositionZ=  Actor1.PositionZ + Actor1Path1.ChgPosZ;
1056    Actor1.Yaw=   Actor1.Yaw + Actor1Path1.ChgYaw;
1057    Actor1.Roll=  Actor1.Roll + Actor1Path1.ChgRoll;
1058    Actor1.Pitch= Actor1.Pitch + Actor1Path1.ChgPitch;
1059  }
1060  if (Actor1.Yaw < 0) Actor1.Yaw= Actor1.Yaw + 360;
1061  if (Actor1.Yaw > 360) Actor1.Yaw= Actor1.Yaw - 360;
1062  if (Actor1.Roll < 0) Actor1.Roll= Actor1.Roll + 360;
1063  if (Actor1.Roll > 360) Actor1.Roll= Actor1.Roll - 360;
1064  if (Actor1.Pitch < 0) Actor1.Pitch= Actor1.Pitch + 360;
1065  if (Actor1.Pitch > 360) Actor1.Pitch= Actor1.Pitch - 360;
1066
1067  zSetSubjectLocation(Actor1.PositionX,
1068                      Actor1.PositionY,
1069                      Actor1.PositionZ);
1070  zSetSubjectAttitude(Actor1.Yaw, Actor1.Roll, Actor1.Pitch);
1071
1072  /* ---- render actor (could also put these params in struct) --- */
1073  zSetSubjectSize(25,25,25);          /* dimensions 50-by-50-by-50 */
1074  zSetShadingColor(zRED);                        /* entity's color */
1075  zDrawCube();                                   /* draw the entity */
1076  return;
1077  }
1078
1079  /*
1080  --------------------------------------------------------------------
1081                    Animation playback functions
1082  --------------------------------------------------------------------
1083            Display the next frame of the animation.
1084  --------------------------------------------------------------------
1085                                                                   */
1086  static void zShowNextFrame(HWND hWnd)
1087  {
1088    HDC hDC;
1089  if (bUseDisk==TRUE) goto DISK_PLAYBACK; /* using memory or disk? */
1090
1091  /* ------------ manage memory-based frame animation ----------- */
1092  MEMORY_PLAYBACK:
1093  if (AnimationReady==FALSE) return;
1094  if (bAnimationLoaded==FALSE) return;
1095  if (Redisplay==TRUE) goto DISPLAY_FRAME;
1096  if (Pause==TRUE) return;
1097  if (FrameDirection==zFORWARD)             /* if a forward loop... */
```

```
1098    {
1099    FrameNum++;                              /* increment the frame number */
1100    if (FrameNum > zFINALFRAME)              /* if at end of loop... */
1101      FrameNum= zFIRSTFRAME;                    /* ...wraparound */
1102    }
1103    if (FrameDirection==zREVERSE)            /* if a reverse loop... */
1104    {
1105    FrameNum--;                              /* decrement the frame number */
1106    if (FrameNum < zFIRSTFRAME)             /* but if at end of loop... */
1107      FrameNum= zFINALFRAME;                    /* ...wraparound */
1108    }
1109    DISPLAY_FRAME:
1110    hDC= GetDC(hWnd);                        /* grab a display-context */
1111    SelectObject(hFDC,BitmapHandles[FrameNum-1]);   /* select handle */
1112    BitBlt(hDC,0,0,                          /* copy the bitmap to the display */
1113            zFRAMEWIDE,zFRAMEHIGH,hFDC,0,0,SRCCOPY);
1114    ReleaseDC(hWnd,hDC);                     /* release the display-context */
1115    return;
1116
1117    /* ------------ manage disk-based frame animation ------------ */
1118    DISK_PLAYBACK:
1119    if (bAnimationHalted==TRUE) return;
1120    if (Redisplay==TRUE) goto SAME_FRAME;
1121    if (Pause==TRUE) return;
1122    if (FrameDirection==zFORWARD)            /* if a forward loop... */
1123    {
1124    FrameNum++;
1125    if (FrameNum > zFINALFRAME) FrameNum= zFIRSTFRAME;
1126    }
1127    if (FrameDirection==zREVERSE)            /* if a reverse loop... */
1128    {
1129    FrameNum--;
1130    if (FrameNum < zFIRSTFRAME) FrameNum= zFINALFRAME;
1131    }
1132    SAME_FRAME:
1133    hDC= GetDC(hWnd);                        /* grab a display-context */
1134    bFrameLoaded= zLoadFrame(hFrame,   /* load the binary image file */
1135                        (LPSTR)FrameFiles[FrameNum-1]);
1136    if (bFrameLoaded==FALSE)                 /* if an error occurred... */
1137    {
1138    bAnimationHalted= TRUE;
1139    MessageBeep(0);
1140    LoadString(hInst,IDS_Unexpected,lpCaption,Max);
1141    LoadString(hInst,IDS_Disk3,lpMessage,MaxText);
1142    TimerCounter= zTIMER_PAUSE;
1143    MessageBox(GetFocus(),lpMessage,lpCaption,MB_OK);
1144    return;
1145    }
1146    BitBlt(hDC,0,0,                          /* copy the bitmap to the display */
1147            zFRAMEWIDE,zFRAMEHIGH,hFrameDC,0,0,SRCCOPY);
1148    ReleaseDC(hWnd,hDC);                     /* release the display-context */
1149    return;
1150    }
1151    /*
1152    -------------------------------------------------------------------
1153                Load the animation sequence from disk.
1154    -------------------------------------------------------------------
1155                                                                      */
1156    static void zLoadAnimation(HWND hWnd)
1157    {
1158      HDC hDC;
```

```
1159    int Bitmaps;
1160
1161  if (FrameReady==FALSE)
1162    {
1163    MessageBeep(0);
1164    LoadString(hInst,IDS_NotReady,lpCaption,Max);
1165    LoadString(hInst,IDS_NoFrame,lpMessage,MaxText);
1166    MessageBox(GetFocus(),lpMessage,lpCaption,MB_OK);
1167    return;
1168    }
1169  if (bAnimationLoaded==TRUE)
1170    {
1171    MessageBeep(0);
1172    LoadString(hInst,IDS_Unexpected,lpCaption,Max);
1173    LoadString(hInst,IDS_Disk4,lpMessage,MaxText);
1174    TimerCounter= zTIMER_PAUSE;
1175    MessageBox(GetFocus(),lpMessage,lpCaption,MB_OK);
1176    return;
1177    }
1178  if (bPrevLoadAttempt==TRUE)
1179    {
1180    MessageBeep(0);
1181    LoadString(hInst,IDS_Unexpected,lpCaption,Max);
1182    LoadString(hInst,IDS_Disk5,lpMessage,MaxText);
1183    TimerCounter= zTIMER_PAUSE;
1184    MessageBox(GetFocus(),lpMessage,lpCaption,MB_OK);
1185    return;
1186    }
1187  bPrevLoadAttempt= TRUE;
1188
1189  /* -------------- create bitmaps to hold the frames ------------ */
1190  GlobalCompact((DWORD)-1L);
1191  hDC= GetDC(hWnd);
1192  hFDC= CreateCompatibleDC(hDC);
1193  for (LoopCount= 1; LoopCount<= zNUMCELS; LoopCount++)
1194    {                          /* for each cel in the animation... */
1195    BitmapHandles[LoopCount-1]=          /* create a bitmap... */
1196         CreateCompatibleBitmap(hDC,zFRAMEWIDE,zFRAMEHIGH);
1197    if (BitmapHandles[LoopCount-1]==NULL)    /* if error occurs... */
1198      goto BITMAPS_NOT_OK;       /* ...jump out of loop and tidy up */
1199    }
1200  goto BITMAPS_OK;                /* if OK, jump past error-handler */
1201
1202  /* ------------------- bitmap error-handler -------------------- */
1203  BITMAPS_NOT_OK:
1204  for (Bitmaps= LoopCount-1; Bitmaps>= 1; Bitmaps--)
1205    {          /* for each bitmap that was successfully created... */
1206    DeleteObject(BitmapHandles[Bitmaps-1]);        /* ...delete it */
1207    }
1208  DeleteDC(hFDC);                      /* delete the compatible DC */
1209  ReleaseDC(hWnd,hDC);              /* release the display-context */
1210  bUseDisk= TRUE; AnimationReady= TRUE;       /* reset the tokens */
1211  LoadString(hInst,IDS_Status,lpCaption,Max);
1212  LoadString(hInst,IDS_Disk6,lpMessage,MaxText);
1213  MessageBox(GetFocus(),lpMessage,lpCaption,MB_OK); /* message box */
1214  return;                             /* ...and return to caller */
1215
1216  BITMAPS_OK: ReleaseDC(hWnd,hDC);  /* release the display-context */
1217
1218  /* ------------- load frame files into the bitmaps ------------- */
1219  for (LoopCount= 1; LoopCount<= zNUMCELS; LoopCount++)
```

```
1220    {                            /* for each cel in the animation... */
1221      bFrameLoaded= zLoadFrame(BitmapHandles[LoopCount-1],   /* load */
1222                          (LPSTR)FrameFiles[LoopCount-1]);
1223      if (bFrameLoaded==FALSE)              /* if disk error occurred... */
1224        goto DISK_ERROR;                   /* jump to error-handler */
1225    }
1226    goto DISK_OK;                  /* if OK, jump past the error-handler */
1227
1228    /* -------------------- disk error-handler -------------------- */
1229    DISK_ERROR:
1230      for (LoopCount= 1; LoopCount<= zNUMCELS; LoopCount++)
1231        {                     /* for each bitmap handle in the animation... */
1232        DeleteObject(BitmapHandles[LoopCount-1]);     /* delete it... */
1233        }
1234      DeleteDC(hFDC);      /* ...and delete the memory display-context */
1235      return;
1236
1237    /* -------------------- tidy up and return -------------------- */
1238    DISK_OK:
1239    hPrevF= SelectObject(hFDC,BitmapHandles[0]);
1240    bAnimationLoaded= TRUE;
1241    AnimationReady= TRUE;
1242    bAnimationSaved= TRUE;
1243    MessageBeep(0);
1244    LoadString(hInst,IDS_AnimReady,lpCaption,Max);
1245    LoadString(hInst,IDS_Disk7,lpMessage,MaxText);
1246    MessageBox(GetFocus(),lpMessage,lpCaption,MB_OK);
1247    return;
1248    }
1249    /*
1250    ----------------------------------------------------------------
1251                    Reset the animation frame rate.
1252    ----------------------------------------------------------------
1253                                                                    */
1254    static void zSetFrameRate(HWND hWnd, WORD wNewRate)
1255    {
1256    if (TimerExists==FALSE)
1257      {
1258      wFrameRate= wPrevRate;
1259      MessageBeep(0);
1260      LoadString(hInst,IDS_NotReady,lpCaption,Max);
1261      LoadString(hInst,IDS_NoReset,lpMessage,MaxText);
1262      MessageBox(GetFocus(),lpMessage,lpCaption,MB_OK);
1263      return;
1264      }
1265
1266    /* ----------- remove the check-mark from the menu ------------ */
1267    switch (wPrevRate)
1268      {   /* use hMenu from case WM_INITMENUPOPUP in message handler */
1269      case 55:  CheckMenuItem(hMenu,IDM_FPS182,MF_UNCHECKED); break;
1270      case 110: CheckMenuItem(hMenu,IDM_FPS91, MF_UNCHECKED); break;
1271      case 165: CheckMenuItem(hMenu,IDM_FPS61, MF_UNCHECKED); break;
1272      case 220: CheckMenuItem(hMenu,IDM_FPS45, MF_UNCHECKED); break;
1273      case 275: CheckMenuItem(hMenu,IDM_FPS36, MF_UNCHECKED); break;
1274      case 330: CheckMenuItem(hMenu,IDM_FPS30, MF_UNCHECKED); break;
1275      }
1276
1277    /* --------- destroy existing timer, create new timer --------- */
1278    KillTimer(hWnd,1);
1279    TimerID1= SetTimer(hWnd,1,wNewRate,(FARPROC) NULL);
1280    if (TimerID1==0)
```

```
1281   {
1282   LoadString(hInst,IDS_NotReady,lpCaption,Max);
1283   LoadString(hInst,IDS_CannotReset,lpMessage,MaxText);
1284   MessageBox(GetFocus(),lpMessage,lpCaption,MB_OK);
1285   TimerExists= FALSE;
1286   return;
1287   }
1288
1289   /* ----------------- add check-mark to menu ----------------- */
1290   switch (wFrameRate)
1291   {
1292   case 55:  CheckMenuItem(hMenu,IDM_FPS182,MF_CHECKED); break;
1293   case 110: CheckMenuItem(hMenu,IDM_FPS91, MF_CHECKED); break;
1294   case 165: CheckMenuItem(hMenu,IDM_FPS61, MF_CHECKED); break;
1295   case 220: CheckMenuItem(hMenu,IDM_FPS45, MF_CHECKED); break;
1296   case 275: CheckMenuItem(hMenu,IDM_FPS36, MF_CHECKED); break;
1297   case 330: CheckMenuItem(hMenu,IDM_FPS30, MF_CHECKED); break;
1298   }
1299   return;
1300   }
1301   /*
1302   ------------------------------------------------------------------
1303                     End of the C source file
1304   ------------------------------------------------------------------
1305                                                                  */
```

C-4 Source listings for the interactive, animated, 3D hierarchical model application, assembly.c, consisting of .def, .h, .rc, and .c files. See Appendix B for the toolkits which must be linked in to build this application. See Appendix A for instructions on building the demo.

```
0001   NAME          HRA4115
0002   DESCRIPTION   'Copyright 1993 Lee Adams.  All rights reserved.'
0003   EXETYPE       WINDOWS
0004   STUB          'WINSTUB.EXE'
0005   CODE          PRELOAD MOVEABLE
0006   DATA          PRELOAD MOVEABLE MULTIPLE
0007   HEAPSIZE      1024
0008   STACKSIZE     8192
0009   EXPORTS       zMessageHandler
0001   /*
0002   ------------------------------------------------------------------
0003                     Include file assembly.h
0004            Copyright 1993 Lee Adams.  All rights reserved.
0005     Include this file in the .RC resource script file and in the
0006     .C source file.  It contains function prototypes, menu ID
0007     constants, and string ID constants.
0008   ------------------------------------------------------------------
0009   ------------------------------------------------------------------
0010                     Function prototypes
0011   ------------------------------------------------------------------
0012                                                                  */
0013   #if !defined(zRCFILE)                /* if not an .rc file... */
0014     LONG FAR PASCAL zMessageHandler(HWND, unsigned, WORD, LONG);
0015     int PASCAL WinMain(HANDLE,HANDLE,LPSTR,int);
0016     HWND zInitMainWindow(HANDLE);
0017     BOOL zInitClass(HANDLE);
0018   static void zClear(HWND);              /* blank the display window */
0019   static void zInitFrame(HWND);             /* creates hidden frame */
0020   static void zShowNextFrame(HWND);          /* the playback engine */
0021   static void zSetFrameRate(HWND,WORD);         /* resets the timer */
```

```
0022    static void zSaveAnimation(HWND);       /* saves animation sequence */
0023    static BOOL zBuildFrame(int,HWND,LPSTR);         /* builds a frame */
0024    static void zDrawCel(int);                          /* draws a cel */
0025    static void zLoadAnimation(HWND);     /* loads animation sequence */
0026    static void zCopyToDisplay(HWND);      /* copies frame to display */
0027    static void zClearHiddenFrame(void);       /* clears hidden frame */
0028    #endif
0029    /*
0030    -------------------------------------------------------------------
0031                            Menu ID constants
0032    -------------------------------------------------------------------
0033                                                                      */
0034    #define IDM_New                 1
0035    #define IDM_Open                2
0036    #define IDM_Save                3
0037    #define IDM_SaveAs              4
0038    #define IDM_Exit                5
0039
0040    #define IDM_Undo                6
0041    #define IDM_Cut                 7
0042    #define IDM_Copy                8
0043    #define IDM_Paste               9
0044    #define IDM_Delete              10
0045
0046    #define IDM_LoadAnimation       11
0047    #define IDM_RunForward          12
0048    #define IDM_RunReverse          13
0049    #define IDM_Clear               14
0050    #define IDM_StopAnimation       15
0051    #define IDM_SaveAnimation       16
0052    #define IDM_UseShaded           17
0053    #define IDM_UseWireframe        18
0054
0055    #define IDM_FPS182              19
0056    #define IDM_FPS91               20
0057    #define IDM_FPS61               21
0058    #define IDM_FPS45               22
0059    #define IDM_FPS36               23
0060    #define IDM_FPS30               24
0061
0062    #define IDM_About               25
0063    #define IDM_License             26
0064    #define IDM_GeneralHelp         27
0065    /*
0066    -------------------------------------------------------------------
0067                            String ID constants
0068    -------------------------------------------------------------------
0069                                                                      */
0070    #define IDS_Caption     1
0071    #define IDS_Warning     2
0072    #define IDS_NoMouse     3
0073    #define IDS_About       4
0074    #define IDS_AboutText   5
0075    #define IDS_License     6
0076    #define IDS_LicenseText 7
0077    #define IDS_Help        8
0078    #define IDS_HelpText    9
0079    #define IDS_Completed   10
0080    #define IDS_Error       11
0081    #define IDS_NotReady    12
0082    #define IDS_Ready       13
```

```
0083    #define IDS_BuildBefore 14
0084    #define IDS_Already     15
0085    #define IDS_InsufMem1   16
0086
0087    #define IDS_InsufMem2   17
0088    #define IDS_NoTimer     18
0089    #define IDS_NoReset     19
0090    #define IDS_CannotReset 20
0091    #define IDS_NoFrame     21
0092    #define IDS_AnimReady   22
0093
0094    #define IDS_Unexpected  44
0095    #define IDS_Status      45
0096    #define IDS_Disk1       46
0097    #define IDS_Disk2       47
0098    #define IDS_Disk3       48
0099    #define IDS_Disk4       49
0100    #define IDS_Disk5       50
0101    #define IDS_Disk6       51
0102    #define IDS_Disk7       52
0103    #define IDS_Disk8       53
0104    #define IDS_Disk9       54
0105    #define IDS_Disk10      55
0106    #define IDS_Disk11      56
0107    #define IDS_Disk12      57
0108    #define IDS_Disk13      58
0109    #define IDS_Disk14      59
0110    #define IDS_Disk15      60
0111    #define IDS_Disk16      61
0112    #define IDS_Disk17      62
0113    #define IDS_Disk18      63
0114    #define IDS_Disk19      64
0115    #define IDS_Disk20      65
0116    #define IDS_Disk21      66
0117    #define IDS_Disk22      67
0118    #define IDS_Disk23      68
0119    #define IDS_Disk24      69
0120    #define IDS_Disk25      70
0121    #define IDS_Disk26      71
0122    #define IDS_NoBg        72
0123    #define IDS_BgAlready   73
0124    #define IDS_InsufMemBg  74
0125    #define IDS_ReqdHdwr1   75
0126    #define IDS_ReqdHdwr2   76
0127    #define IDS_Build       77
0128    #define IDS_ToCancel    78
0129    #define IDS_Loading     79
0130    /*
0131    -------------------------------------------------------------------
0132                         End of include file
0133    -------------------------------------------------------------------
0134                                                                   */
0001    /*
0002    -------------------------------------------------------------------
0003                  Resource script file assembly.rc
0004            Copyright 1993 Lee Adams.  All rights reserved.
0005      This file defines the menu resources, the accelerator key
0006      resources, and the string resources that will be used by the
0007      demonstration application at runtime.
0008    -------------------------------------------------------------------
0009                                                                   */
```

```
0010    #define zRCFILE
0011    #include <WINDOWS.H>
0012    #include "ASSEMBLY.H"
0013    /*
0014    ----------------------------------------------------------------
0015                              Script for menus
0016    ----------------------------------------------------------------
0017                                                                  */
0018    HRAMENUS MENU
0019      BEGIN
0020      POPUP "&File"
0021        BEGIN
0022          MENUITEM  "&New", IDM_New, GRAYED
0023          MENUITEM  "&Open...", IDM_Open, GRAYED
0024          MENUITEM  "&Save", IDM_Save, GRAYED
0025          MENUITEM  "Save &As...", IDM_SaveAs, GRAYED
0026          MENUITEM SEPARATOR
0027          MENUITEM  "E&xit", IDM_Exit
0028        END
0029      POPUP "&Edit"
0030        BEGIN
0031          MENUITEM  "&Undo\tAlt+BkSp", IDM_Undo, GRAYED
0032          MENUITEM SEPARATOR
0033          MENUITEM  "Cu&t\tShift+Del", IDM_Cut, GRAYED
0034          MENUITEM  "&Copy\tCtrl+Ins", IDM_Copy, GRAYED
0035          MENUITEM  "&Paste\tShift+Ins", IDM_Paste, GRAYED
0036          MENUITEM  "&Delete\tDel", IDM_Delete, GRAYED
0037        END
0038      POPUP "&Run"
0039        BEGIN
0040          MENUITEM "&Load Animation", IDM_LoadAnimation
0041          MENUITEM SEPARATOR
0042          MENUITEM "Run &Forward", IDM_RunForward
0043          MENUITEM "Run &Reverse", IDM_RunReverse
0044          MENUITEM "Free&zeframe", IDM_StopAnimation
0045          POPUP "S&et Speed..."
0046            BEGIN
0047              MENUITEM "&18 fps", IDM_FPS182, CHECKED
0048              MENUITEM " &9 fps", IDM_FPS91
0049              MENUITEM " &6 fps", IDM_FPS61
0050              MENUITEM " &5 fps", IDM_FPS45
0051              MENUITEM " &4 fps", IDM_FPS36
0052              MENUITEM " &3 fps", IDM_FPS30
0053            END
0054          MENUITEM SEPARATOR
0055          MENUITEM "&Clear Viewport", IDM_Clear
0056          MENUITEM SEPARATOR
0057          POPUP "&Production..."
0058            BEGIN
0059              MENUITEM "&Build Animation", IDM_SaveAnimation
0060              MENUITEM SEPARATOR
0061              MENUITEM "Use &shaded solids", IDM_UseShaded
0062              MENUITEM "Use &wireframe mode", IDM_UseWireframe
0063            END
0064        END
0065      POPUP "&Using"
0066        BEGIN
0067          MENUITEM "&About", IDM_About
0068          MENUITEM "&License", IDM_License
0069          MENUITEM SEPARATOR
0070          MENUITEM "&How to Use", IDM_GeneralHelp
```

```
0071      END
0072    END
0073  /*
0074  --------------------------------------------------------------
0075                     Script for accelerator keys
0076  --------------------------------------------------------------
0077                                                              */
0078  HRAKEYS ACCELERATORS
0079    BEGIN
0080    VK_BACK, IDM_Undo, VIRTKEY, ALT
0081    VK_DELETE, IDM_Cut, VIRTKEY, SHIFT
0082    VK_INSERT, IDM_Copy, VIRTKEY, CONTROL
0083    VK_INSERT, IDM_Paste, VIRTKEY, SHIFT
0084    VK_DELETE, IDM_Delete,VIRTKEY
0085    END
0086  /*
0087  --------------------------------------------------------------
0088                       Script for strings
0089    If you are typing this listing, set your right margin to 255
0090    characters so you can create lengthy strings without embedded
0091    carriage returns.  The line wraparounds in the following
0092    STRINGTABLE listing are used only for readability.
0093  --------------------------------------------------------------
0094                                                              */
0095  STRINGTABLE
0096    BEGIN
0097      IDS_Caption      "Animated 3D subassemblies"
0098      IDS_Warning      "Warning"
0099      IDS_NoMouse      "No mouse found.  Some features of this
                demonstration program may require a mouse."
0100      IDS_About        "About this program"
0101      IDS_AboutText    "This is a demo from Windcrest McGraw-Hill
                book 4115.  Copyright~ 1993 Lee Adams.  All rights reserved."
0102      IDS_License      "License Agreement"
0103      IDS_LicenseText "You can use this code as part of your own
                software product subject to the License Agreement and
                Limited Warranty in Windcrest McGraw-Hill book 4115 and on
                its companion disk."
0104      IDS_Help         "How to use this animated 3D demo"
0105      IDS_HelpText     "For animation playback pick Load Animation
                then Run Forward from the Run menu.  To build and save an
                animation, choose the Production submenu.  Also see the
                book."
0106      IDS_Completed    "Task completed OK"
0107      IDS_Error        "Runtime error"
0108      IDS_NotReady     "Animation not ready"
0109      IDS_Ready        "Animation ready"
0110      IDS_BuildBefore "Animation frames not ready for playback."
0111      IDS_Already      "The hidden frame has already been created."
0112      IDS_InsufMem1    "Unable to create hidden-frame because
                insufficient global memory.  Animation functions
                unavailable.  Close other applications before restarting
                this demo."
0113      IDS_NoTimer      "Unable to create a timer.  Animation
                functions unavailable.  Restart this demo after closing
                other applications that may be using timers."
0114      IDS_NoReset      "Create hidden frame before attempting to
                reset timer."
0115      IDS_CannotReset "Unable to reset the timer."
0116      IDS_NoFrame      "Hidden frame not yet created."
0117      IDS_AnimReady    "Animation ready"
```

```
0118    IDS_Unexpected  "Unexpected animation condition"
0119    IDS_Status      "Animation status"
0120    IDS_Disk1       "Animation sequence already saved to disk."
0121    IDS_Disk2       "Animation sequence saved to disk."
0122    IDS_Disk3       "Unable to load next frame from disk.
        Animation halted."
0123    IDS_Disk4       "Animation sequence already loaded from disk."
0124    IDS_Disk5       "Previous load failed.  Cancelling this
        attempt."
0125    IDS_Disk6       "Not enough memory available to store
        animation sequence in memory.  Each frame will be loaded as
        needed from disk during playback."
0126    IDS_Disk7       "Animation sequence loaded in memory."
0127    IDS_Disk8       "Previous save failed.  Cancelling this
        attempt."
0128    IDS_Disk9       "No hidden-frame exists.  No frame saved to
        disk."
0129    IDS_Disk10      "Unable to retrieve bitmap data structure."
0130    IDS_Disk11      "Bit array is too long to save to disk in a
        single pass."
0131    IDS_Disk12      "Cannot create memory buffer for disk write."
0132    IDS_Disk13      "Unable to copy bits from bitmap to buffer."
0133    IDS_Disk14      "File already exists.  Overwrite existing
        file?"
0134    IDS_Disk15      "Unable to open the file for writing."
0135    IDS_Disk16      "Unable to write to the opened file."
0136    IDS_Disk17      "Unable to close the file after writing."
0137    IDS_Disk18      "No memory bitmap exists.  Unable to load from
        disk."
0138    IDS_Disk19      "Image file is larger than animation frame.
        No file loaded."
0139    IDS_Disk20      "Cannot create memory buffer for file read."
0140    IDS_Disk21      "Unable to open the file for reading.  Be sure
        you have saved an animation sequence to disk before
        attempting to load it."
0141    IDS_Disk22      "An error occurred while reading the file."
0142    IDS_Disk23      "Windows must be using same color mode as when
        this animation was saved, either 2, 16, or 256 colors.  To
        run the existing animation, use Windows Setup to switch
        color modes.  Otherwise rebuild the animation in the current
        mode."
0143    IDS_Disk24      "Unable to close the file after reading."
0144    IDS_Disk25      "Unable to copy bits from buffer to bitmap."
0145    IDS_Disk26      "Not all frames saved to disk because
        insufficient space available on disk or because the frames
        have already been saved to disk or because you interrupted
        the build process."
0146    IDS_NoBg        "Hidden background image not yet created."
0147    IDS_BgAlready   "The hidden background bitmap has already been
        created."
0148    IDS_InsufMemBg  "Insufficient global memory for background
        bitmap."
0149    IDS_ReqdHdwr1   "Graphics hardware not supported"
0150    IDS_ReqdHdwr2   "CGA, HGA, or EGA graphics adapter detected.
        This application requires either an industry-standard VGA, a
        VESA-standard SuperVGA, an 8514/a, or an XGA graphics
        adapter and compatible display."
0151    IDS_Build       "Animation build process"
0152    IDS_ToCancel    "Ready to begin building the animation
        sequence.  To interrupt a build session in progress, click
        the right mouse button.  To begin the build, select OK now.
```

```
                See the book for further information."
0153     IDS_Loading      "Loading animation..."
0154   END
0155 /*
0156 ------------------------------------------------------------------
0157                 End of resource script file
0158 ------------------------------------------------------------------
0159                                                              */
0001 /*
0002 ------------------------------------------------------------------
0003            3D hierarchical modeling for animation
0004 ------------------------------------------------------------------
0005   Source file: assembly.c
0006   Release version:  1.2              Programmer:  Lee Adams
0007   Type:  C source file for Windows application development.
0008   Supported compilers:  Explicit compatibility with Microsoft
0009     QuickC for Windows v1.00 and Borland Turbo C++ for Windows
0010     v3.0.  Nominal compatibility with all Windows-compatible C
0011     and C++ compilers such as Borland C++, Zortech C++, Watcom C,
0012     and Microsoft C/C++.
0013   Memory model:  medium.
0014   Build notes:  Do not use the load optimization feature of the
0015     Resource Compiler (or use the command-line -K switch).
0016     For trouble-free compiling follow the tips in the book.
0017   Project notes:  Load the assembly.mak project file if you are
0018     using QuickC for Windows.  Load the assembly.prj project file
0019     if you are using Turbo C++ for Windows.  Refer to the book if
0020     you are using another compiler.  The following files are
0021     needed to build the executable:
0022       assembly.def      module definition file
0023       assembly.h        include file
0024       assembly.rc       resource script file
0025       assembly.c        C source file
0026       engine3d.h        include file for 3D functions
0027       engine3d.c        3D toolkit
0028       shapes3d.h        include file for 3D solids
0029       shapes3d.c        3D shapes toolkit
0030       deform3d.h        include file for deformed solids
0031       deform3d.c        3D deformation toolkit
0032       assemb3d.h        include file for hierarchical modeling
0033       assemb3d.c        3D hierarchical modeling toolkit
0034       lights3d.h        include file for light-source functions
0035       lights3d.c        light-source toolkit
0036       disk3d.h          include file for disk functions
0037       disk3d.c          image save/load toolkit
0038   Output and features:  Demonstrates 3D hierarchical modeling for
0039     animation sequences and storage of frames on disk as binary
0040     image files.  Demonstrates loading of frames from disk and
0041     interactive playback of animation sequence from RAM or from
0042     disk if insufficient memory available.  The startup code
0043     automatically sizes the window to yield a client area with
0044     dimensions of 256-by-255 pixels in any graphics mode.  You
0045     can use the menu system to toggle between wireframe and
0046     shaded modes.
0047       NUMBER OF FRAMES:  In its current implementation, the
0048     application produces an animation sequence of 36 frames.
0049     To create a sequence that uses fewer frames or more frames,
0050     you can edit lines 00150 and 00151, and then remove or add
0051     filenames as required at lines 00169 to 00177.
0052   Publication: Contains material from Windcrest/McGraw-Hill book
0053     4115 published by TAB BOOKS Division of McGraw-Hill Inc.
```

C-4 Continued.

```
0054    License: As purchaser of the book you are granted a royalty-
0055       free license to distribute executable files generated using
0056       this code provided you accept the conditions of the License
0057       Agreement and Limited Warranty described in the book and on
0058       the companion disk.  Government users: This software and
0059       documentation are subject to restrictions set forth in The
0060       Rights in Technical Data and Computer Software clause at
0061       252.227-7013 and elsewhere.
0062    ------------------------------------------------------------------
0063       (c) Copyright 1991-1993 Lee Adams.  All rights reserved.
0064          Lee Adams(tm) is a trademark of Lee Adams.
0065    ------------------------------------------------------------------
0066
0067    ------------------------------------------------------------------
0068                           Include files
0069    ------------------------------------------------------------------
0070                                                                     */
0071    #include <WINDOWS.H>            /* declarations for Windows API */
0072    #include "ASSEMBLY.H"       /* declares function prototypes, etc. */
0073    #include "DISK3D.H"           /* declares functions in disk engine */
0074    #include "ENGINE3D.H"            /* declares functions in 3D engine */
0075    #include "SHAPES3D.H"   /* declares functions in 3D shapes module */
0076    #include "DEFORM3D.H"          /* functions in deformation module */
0077    #include "LIGHTS3D.H"    /* declares functions in lighting module */
0078    #include "ASSEMB3D.H"   /* declares functions in hierarchy module */
0079    #include <time.h>                     /* supports date and time */
0080
0081    /*
0082    ------------------------------------------------------------------
0083             Static variables visible throughout this file
0084    ------------------------------------------------------------------
0085                                                                     */
0086    /* ------------------- window specifications ----------------- */
0087    #define zWINDOW_WIDTH 263                       /* width of window */
0088    #define zWINDOW_HEIGHT 300                      /* depth of window */
0089    #define zFRAMEWIDE 256                        /* width of viewport */
0090    #define zFRAMEHIGH 255                        /* depth of viewport */
0091    static int WindowX, WindowY;               /* location of window */
0092
0093    /* ------------------- instance operations -------------------- */
0094    HANDLE hInst;                /* handle to this copy of the app */
0095    static HWND MainhWnd;               /* handle to the app's window */
0096    static HANDLE hAccel;          /* handle to the accelerator keys */
0097    static HMENU hMenu;      /* handle to an active menu at runtime */
0098    static PAINTSTRUCT ps;   /* used for Windows-generated refreshes */
0099
0100    /* ------------------- mouse and cursor -------------------- */
0101    static HCURSOR hPrevCursor;             /* handle to arrow cursor */
0102    static HCURSOR hHourGlass;          /* handle to hourglass cursor */
0103    static int MousePresent;             /* indicates if mouse found */
0104
0105    /* ------------------- runtime conditions -------------------- */
0106    static int DisplayWidth, DisplayHeight; /* resolution of display */
0107    static int DisplayBits;             /* number of bits per pixel */
0108    static int DisplayPlanes;              /* number of bitplanes */
0109    static DWORD MemoryMode;               /* runtime memory mode */
0110    static DWORD Version;                  /* version of Windows */
0111    static BOOL bUseArial= TRUE;   /* FALSE, use Helv if Windows 3.0 */
0112
0113    /* ------------------- message box operations ----------------- */
0114    char lpCaption[51];             /* stores caption for message box */
```

```
0115    int Max= 50;                           /* max length of caption */
0116    char lpMessage[250];               /* stores text for message box */
0117    int MaxText= 249;                      /* max length of text */
0118    static short TextLength= 0;          /* stores wsprintf() string */
0119    static int MessageBoxChoice= 0;        /* user's selection, if any */
0120
0121    /* ---------------- persistent image operations --------------- */
0122    #define zBLANK 0
0123    #define zANIMATING  1
0124    #define zPREVIEW  2
0125    static int PaintImage= zBLANK;       /* indicates viewport status */
0126
0127    /* --------------------- timer operations -------------------- */
0128    #define zTIMER_PAUSE 3
0129    static int TimerCounter= zTIMER_PAUSE; /* timing delay mechanism */
0130    static BOOL TimerExists= FALSE;              /* timer active? */
0131    static WORD TimerID1;                          /* timer ID */
0132
0133    /* ----------------- hidden-frame operations ----------------- */
0134    static HDC hFrameDC;          /* display-context of hidden-frame */
0135    static HBITMAP hFrame;             /* bitmap of hidden-frame */
0136    static HBITMAP hPrevFrame;              /* default bitmap */
0137    BOOL FrameReady= FALSE;               /* hidden-frame ready? */
0138
0139    /* --------------------- animation engine -------------------- */
0140    static BOOL Pause= TRUE;                /* animation paused? */
0141    static WORD wFrameRate= 55;              /* animation rate */
0142    static WORD wPrevRate= 55;         /* remembers previous rate */
0143    #define zFORWARD 1
0144    #define zREVERSE 0
0145    static int FrameDirection= zFORWARD;     /* animation direction */
0146    static BOOL Redisplay= FALSE;      /* for refresh when paused */
0147    static BOOL AnimationReady= FALSE;  /* animation sequence ready? */
0148    static int FrameNum= 1;                  /* current frame */
0149    #define zFIRSTFRAME 1      /* first frame of animation sequence */
0150    #define zFINALFRAME 36     /* final frame of animation sequence */
0151    #define zNUMCELS 36     /* number of cels in animation sequence */
0152    static int LoopCount;                    /* loop counter */
0153
0154    /* ---------------- disk save/load operations ---------------- */
0155    int RetVal;                    /* value returned by functions */
0156    static BOOL bFrameSaved= FALSE;                /* frame saved? */
0157    static BOOL bFrameLoaded= FALSE;              /* frame loaded? */
0158    static BOOL bAnimationSaved= FALSE;        /* animation saved? */
0159    static BOOL bAnimationLoaded= FALSE;      /* animation loaded? */
0160    static BOOL bPrevSaveAttempt= FALSE; /* previous save attempted? */
0161    static BOOL bPrevLoadAttempt= FALSE; /* previous load attempted? */
0162    static BOOL bUseDisk= FALSE;     /* use RAM or disk for playback? */
0163    static BOOL bAnimationHalted= FALSE;      /* playback paused? */
0164    static HDC hFDC;       /* memory display-context for hidden bitmaps */
0165    static HBITMAP hPrevF;                       /* default bitmap */
0166    static HBITMAP BitmapHandles[zNUMCELS];    /* array of bitmaps */
0167    static char *FrameFiles[zNUMCELS]=
0168        {   /* array of pointers to filenames for animation frames... */
0169        "HRA01.BIT", "HRA02.BIT", "HRA03.BIT", "HRA04.BIT",
0170        "HRA05.BIT", "HRA06.BIT", "HRA07.BIT", "HRA08.BIT",
0171        "HRA09.BIT", "HRA10.BIT", "HRA11.BIT", "HRA12.BIT",
0172        "HRA13.BIT", "HRA14.BIT", "HRA15.BIT", "HRA16.BIT",
0173        "HRA17.BIT", "HRA18.BIT", "HRA19.BIT", "HRA20.BIT",
0174        "HRA21.BIT", "HRA22.BIT", "HRA23.BIT", "HRA24.BIT",
0175        "HRA25.BIT", "HRA26.BIT", "HRA27.BIT", "HRA28.BIT",
```

```
0176     "HRA29.BIT", "HRA30.BIT", "HRA31.BIT", "HRA32.BIT",
0177     "HRA33.BIT", "HRA34.BIT", "HRA35.BIT", "HRA36.BIT",
0178     };
0179
0180  /* --------- declare data types for animation script --------- */
0181  static struct CameraPath
0182     {                       /* camera movement during specified frames... */
0183     int StartFrame;
0184     int EndFrame;
0185     int ChgHeading;
0186     int ChgPitch;
0187     int ChgDistance;
0188     };
0189  static struct LightPath
0190     {            /* light-source movement during specified frames... */
0191     int StartFrame;
0192     int EndFrame;
0193     int ChgHeading;
0194     int ChgElevation;
0195     };
0196  static struct ActorPath
0197     {  /* actor movement & deformation during specified frames... */
0198     int StartFrame;
0199     int EndFrame;
0200     int ChgYaw;
0201     int ChgRoll;
0202     int ChgPitch;
0203     int ChgPosX;
0204     int ChgPosY;
0205     int ChgPosZ;
0206     };
0207
0208  static struct SubAssyPath
0209     {                /* subassembly movement during specified frames... */
0210     int StartFrame;
0211     int EndFrame;
0212     int ChgYaw;
0213     int ChgRoll;
0214     int ChgPitch;
0215     };
0216
0217  static struct CameraDefine
0218     {                                /* camera startup parameters... */
0219     int Heading;
0220     int Pitch;
0221     int Distance;
0222     };
0223  static struct LightDefine
0224     {                                /* light-source startup parameters... */
0225     int Heading;
0226     int Elevation;
0227     };
0228
0229  static struct ActorDefine
0230     {                                /* actor startup parameters... */
0231     int PositionX;          /* position of actor in 3D world... */
0232     int PositionY;
0233     int PositionZ;
0234     int Yaw;                /* orientation of actor in 3D world... */
0235     int Roll;
0236     int Pitch;
```

```
0237    };
0238
0239    static struct AssemblyDefine
0240       {                            /* assembly startup parameters... */
0241       unsigned char Solid;                     /* type of 3D solid */
0242       int Level;                             /* hierarchy level */
0243       int Color;                             /* rendering color */
0244       int SizeX;                          /* width of subobject */
0245       int SizeY;                          /* height of subobject */
0246       int SizeZ;                          /* depth of subobject */
0247       int PositionX;    /* position of subobject in assembly-space... */
0248       int PositionY;
0249       int PositionZ;
0250       int Yaw;        /* orientation of subobject in assembly-space... */
0251       int Roll;
0252       int Pitch;
0253       int DeformRightX;      /* extrusion deformation of subobject... */
0254       int DeformLeftX;
0255       int DeformUpY;
0256       int DeformDownY;
0257       int PivotX;                     /* subassembly pivot-point... */
0258       int PivotY;
0259       int PivotZ;
0260       int SubAssyYaw;/* subassembly orientation in assembly-space... */
0261       int SubAssyRoll;
0262       int SubAssyPitch;
0263       int SubAssyX;      /* subassembly position in assembly-space... */
0264       int SubAssyY;
0265       int SubAssyZ;
0266       };
0267
0268    /* --------- camera, light, actor, subassembly structs --------- */
0269    static struct CameraDefine    Cam1;                       /* camera */
0270    static struct CameraPath      Cam1Path1;            /* camera path */
0271    static struct LightDefine     Lt1;                /* light-source */
0272    static struct LightPath       Lt1Path1;      /* light-source path */
0273
0274    static struct ActorDefine     Actor1;              /* an actor... */
0275    static struct ActorPath       Actor1Path1;   /* ...and its path */
0276    static struct AssemblyDefine  Assembly1[10]; /* a subassembly... */
0277    static struct SubAssyPath     Assembly1Path1; /* ...and its path */
0278
0279    #define zROBOT_START  0        /* parameters for rendering loop... */
0280    #define zROBOT_FINISH 9
0281    #define zBOX          1                     /* available solids... */
0282    #define zSPHERE       2
0283    #define zCYLINDER     3
0284    #define zCONE         4
0285    #define zWEDGE        5
0286    #define zCURVE        6
0287    #define zHEMISPHERE   7
0288    #define zDEFORMBOX    8
0289    #define zHALFCYL      9
0290    #define zBULGE        10
0291    #define zNULL         11
0292    #define zLEVEL1       1                 /* progeny in 3D hierarchy... */
0293    #define zLEVEL2       2
0294    #define zLEVEL3       3
0295
0296    /*
0297    --------------------------------------------------------------
```

```
0298                   Entry point for the application
0299   -------------------------------------------------------------------
0300                                                                     */
0301   int PASCAL WinMain(HANDLE hInstance, HANDLE hPrevInstance,
0302                      LPSTR lpCmdLine, int nCmdShow)
0303   {
0304     MSG msg;                           /* holds incoming messages */
0305     HWND hWndPrev;                  /* handle to previous copy of app */
0306     HWND hDesktopWnd;                /* handle to the entire display */
0307     HDC hDCcaps;             /* display-context for the entire display */
0308     RECT rcClientReqd;           /* size of viewport before adjustment */
0309     int AdjustX, AdjustY; /* amount to adjust to ensure 256-by-255 */
0310
0311   /* ------------- ensure only one copy is running ------------- */
0312   hWndPrev = FindWindow("HRADEMO", "HRA4115");
0313   if (hWndPrev != NULL)        /* if another app named HRA4115 of... */
0314     {                         /* class HRADEMO is already running, then... */
0315     BringWindowToTop(hWndPrev);              /* ...use it instead... */
0316     return FALSE;                      /* ...and cancel this launch */
0317     }
0318
0319   /* ------------- display the splash signon notice ------------- */
0320   MessageBoxChoice= MessageBox(GetFocus(),
0321   "3D hierarchical sampler from Windcrest McGraw-Hill book 4115",
0322   "Copyright- 1993 Lee Adams", MB_OKCANCEL);
0323   if (MessageBoxChoice == IDCANCEL) return FALSE;
0324
0325   /* --------------- determine version of Windows --------------- */
0326   Version= (DWORD)GetVersion();
0327   if ((LOBYTE(LOWORD(Version))==3) &&
0328      (HIBYTE(LOWORD(Version))==0))
0329     {                          /* if running Windows version 3.0... */
0330     bUseArial= FALSE;              /* ...use Helv font in client area */
0331     }
0332   else
0333     {                 /* ...else if running Windows 3.1 or newer... */
0334     bUseArial= TRUE;             /* ...use Arial font in client area */
0335     }
0336
0337   /* --------- determine capabilities of screen display ---------- */
0338   hDesktopWnd= GetDesktopWindow();
0339   hDCcaps= GetDC(hDesktopWnd);
0340   DisplayWidth= GetDeviceCaps(hDCcaps,HORZRES);
0341   DisplayHeight= GetDeviceCaps(hDCcaps,VERTRES);
0342   DisplayBits= GetDeviceCaps(hDCcaps,BITSPIXEL);
0343   DisplayPlanes= GetDeviceCaps(hDCcaps,PLANES);
0344   ReleaseDC(hDesktopWnd,hDCcaps);
0345
0346   /* ------------- trap unsupported graphics adapters ------------ */
0347   if (DisplayWidth==720)
0348     {                                        /* if HGA detected... */
0349     LoadString(hInstance,IDS_ReqdHdwr1,lpCaption,Max);
0350     LoadString(hInstance,IDS_ReqdHdwr2,lpMessage,MaxText);
0351     MessageBeep(0); MessageBox(GetFocus(),lpMessage,lpCaption,MB_OK);
0352     return FALSE;
0353     }
0354   if (DisplayWidth==640)
0355     {
0356     if ((DisplayHeight==350)||(DisplayHeight==200))
0357       {                             /* if EGA or CGA detected... */
0358       LoadString(hInstance,IDS_ReqdHdwr1,lpCaption,Max);
```

```
0359        LoadString(hInstance,IDS_ReqdHdwr2,lpMessage,MaxText);
0360        MessageBeep(0);
0361        MessageBox(GetFocus(),lpMessage,lpCaption,MB_OK);
0362        return FALSE;
0363      }
0364    }
0365
0366    /* ------ calculate screen position to center the window ------ */
0367    WindowX= (DisplayWidth - zWINDOW_WIDTH) / 2;
0368    WindowY= (DisplayHeight - zWINDOW_HEIGHT) /2;
0369    if (WindowX < 0) WindowX= 0;
0370    if (WindowY < 0) WindowY= 0;
0371
0372    /* ---- determine memory mode (enhanced, standard, or real) ---- */
0373    MemoryMode= GetWinFlags();
0374
0375    /* ---------------- create and show the window ---------------- */
0376    hInst = hInstance;          /* store handle to this copy of the app */
0377    if (!zInitClass(hInstance)) return FALSE;   /* initialize class */
0378    MainhWnd = zInitMainWindow(hInstance);        /* initialize window */
0379    if (!MainhWnd) return FALSE;          /* if error, cancel startup */
0380    ShowWindow(MainhWnd, nCmdShow);              /* show the window */
0381    UpdateWindow(MainhWnd);                      /* force a refresh */
0382    hAccel= LoadAccelerators(hInstance,"HRAKEYS");  /* activate keys */
0383
0384    /* ------------- enforce a 256-by-255 viewport --------------- */
0385    GetClientRect(MainhWnd, &rcClientReqd);        /* get dimensions */
0386    AdjustX=              /* compare actual width to desired width... */
0387            zFRAMEWIDE - (rcClientReqd.right + 1);
0388    AdjustY=            /* compare actual height to desired height... */
0389            zFRAMEHIGH - (rcClientReqd.bottom + 1);
0390    if ((AdjustX != 0)||(AdjustY != 0)) /* if adjustment required... */
0391      {
0392      SetWindowPos(MainhWnd, (HWND)NULL,
0393                  WindowX, WindowY,
0394                  zWINDOW_WIDTH + AdjustX,      /* resize the width */
0395                  zWINDOW_HEIGHT + AdjustY,     /* resize the height */
0396                  SWP_NOZORDER);
0397      }
0398
0399    /* --------------------- check for mouse --------------------- */
0400    MousePresent = GetSystemMetrics(SM_MOUSEPRESENT);
0401    if (!MousePresent)                       /* if no mouse found... */
0402      {                         /* ...display a cautionary warning */
0403      LoadString(hInst,IDS_Warning,lpCaption,Max);
0404      LoadString(hInst,IDS_NoMouse,lpMessage,MaxText);
0405      MessageBox(GetFocus(),lpMessage,lpCaption,MB_OK);
0406      }
0407
0408    /* --------------- initialize the hidden-frame --------------- */
0409    zInitFrame(MainhWnd); /* is used for software-controlled refresh */
0410
0411    /* --------- begin retrieving messages for the window --------- */
0412    while (GetMessage(&msg,0,0,0))
0413      {
0414      if(TranslateAccelerator(MainhWnd, hAccel, &msg)) continue;
0415      TranslateMessage(&msg);
0416      DispatchMessage(&msg);
0417      }
0418    return(msg.wParam);
0419  }
```

```
0420
0421   /*
0422   -------------------------------------------------------------------
0423                     Switcher for incoming messages
0424   -------------------------------------------------------------------
0425                                                                   */
0426   LONG FAR PASCAL zMessageHandler(HWND hWnd, unsigned message,
0427                                   WORD wParam, LONG lParam)
0428   {
0429     HDC hDCpaint;                       /* for Windows-generated refresh */
0430
0431   switch (message)
0432     {
0433     /* -------------- filter incoming timer events ------------- */
0434     case WM_TIMER:   /* slower CPUs need delay so menus can pop up */
0435        TimerCounter--;              /* decrement the delay mechanism */
0436        if (TimerCounter > 0) break; /* do nothing if still delaying */
0437        TimerCounter++;      /* otherwise restore the mechanism and... */
0438        zShowNextFrame(hWnd); /* ...show the next frame if animating */
0439        break;
0440
0441     /* ----------------- menu system commands ------------------ */
0442     case WM_COMMAND:
0443       switch(wParam)
0444         {
0445         case IDM_New:    break;
0446         case IDM_Open:   break;
0447         case IDM_Save:   break;
0448         case IDM_SaveAs: break;
0449         case IDM_Exit:
0450             MessageBoxChoice= MessageBox(GetFocus(),
0451               "Exit the 3D hierarchy demo and return to Windows?",
0452               "Please confirm", MB_YESNO);
0453             if (MessageBoxChoice == IDYES) PostQuitMessage(0);
0454             break;
0455         case IDM_Undo:   break;
0456         case IDM_Cut:    break;
0457         case IDM_Copy:   break;
0458         case IDM_Paste:  break;
0459         case IDM_Delete: break;
0460
0461         /* ------------- manage the animation engine ------------ */
0462         case IDM_RunForward:            /* begin forward playback... */
0463             if (AnimationReady==FALSE)
0464               {
0465               MessageBeep(0);
0466               LoadString(hInst,IDS_NotReady,lpCaption,Max);
0467               LoadString(hInst,IDS_BuildBefore,lpMessage,MaxText);
0468               TimerCounter= zTIMER_PAUSE;
0469               MessageBox(GetFocus(),lpMessage,lpCaption,MB_OK);
0470               break;
0471               }
0472             Pause= FALSE;
0473             PaintImage= zANIMATING;
0474             FrameDirection= zFORWARD;
0475             zShowNextFrame(hWnd);
0476             break;
0477         case IDM_RunReverse:              /* begin reverse playback... */
0478             if (AnimationReady==FALSE)
0479               {
0480               MessageBeep(0);
```

```
0481              LoadString(hInst,IDS_NotReady,lpCaption,Max);
0482              LoadString(hInst,IDS_BuildBefore,lpMessage,MaxText);
0483              TimerCounter= zTIMER_PAUSE;
0484              MessageBox(GetFocus(),lpMessage,lpCaption,MB_OK);
0485              break;
0486              }
0487            Pause= FALSE;
0488            PaintImage= zANIMATING;
0489            FrameDirection= zREVERSE;
0490            zShowNextFrame(hWnd);
0491            break;
0492        case IDM_StopAnimation:            /* pause the playback... */
0493            if (AnimationReady==FALSE)
0494              {
0495              MessageBeep(0);
0496              LoadString(hInst,IDS_NotReady,lpCaption,Max);
0497              LoadString(hInst,IDS_BuildBefore,lpMessage,MaxText);
0498              TimerCounter= zTIMER_PAUSE;
0499              MessageBox(GetFocus(),lpMessage,lpCaption,MB_OK);
0500              break;
0501              }
0502            Pause= TRUE;
0503            zShowNextFrame(hWnd);
0504            break;
0505        case IDM_SaveAnimation:        /* save animation to disk... */
0506            LoadString(hInst,IDS_Build,lpCaption,Max);
0507            LoadString(hInst,IDS_ToCancel,lpMessage,MaxText);
0508            TimerCounter= zTIMER_PAUSE;
0509            MessageBox(GetFocus(),lpMessage,lpCaption,MB_OK);
0510            zInitialize3D(hWnd);
0511            SetCapture(hWnd); hPrevCursor= SetCursor(hHourGlass);
0512            zSaveAnimation(hWnd);
0513            LoadString(hInst,IDS_Caption,lpCaption,Max);
0514            SetWindowText(hWnd,lpCaption);
0515            SetCursor(hPrevCursor); ReleaseCapture();
0516            if (bAnimationSaved==FALSE)
0517              {
0518              MessageBeep(0);
0519              LoadString(hInst,IDS_NotReady,lpCaption,Max);
0520              LoadString(hInst,IDS_Disk26,lpMessage,MaxText);
0521              TimerCounter= zTIMER_PAUSE;
0522              MessageBox(GetFocus(),lpMessage,lpCaption,MB_OK);
0523              }
0524            break;
0525        case IDM_UseShaded:      /* use fully-shaded 3D objects... */
0526            zInitialize3D(hWnd);
0527            zUseWireframeMode(FALSE);
0528            MessageBox(GetFocus(),
0529              "Using shaded solids.",
0530              "3D status report", MB_OK);
0531            break;
0532        case IDM_UseWireframe:        /* use wireframe 3D objects... */
0533            zInitialize3D(hWnd);
0534            zUseWireframeMode(TRUE);
0535            MessageBox(GetFocus(),
0536              "Using wireframe modeling mode.",
0537              "3D status report", MB_OK);
0538            break;
0539        case IDM_LoadAnimation:      /* load animation from disk... */
0540            LoadString(hInst,IDS_Loading,lpCaption,Max);
0541            SetWindowText(hWnd,lpCaption);
```

```
0542                SetCapture(hWnd); hPrevCursor= SetCursor(hHourGlass);
0543                zLoadAnimation(hWnd);
0544                SetCursor(hPrevCursor); ReleaseCapture();
0545                LoadString(hInst,IDS_Caption,lpCaption,Max);
0546                SetWindowText(hWnd,lpCaption);
0547                break;
0548          case IDM_Clear:                        /* clear the viewport... */
0549                if (Pause==TRUE)
0550                  {
0551                  zClear(hWnd);
0552                  PaintImage= zBLANK;
0553                  }
0554                break;
0555
0556          /* ------------- adjust the playback rate -------------- */
0557          case IDM_FPS182:                 /* use 18 frames per second */
0558                wPrevRate= wFrameRate;
0559                wFrameRate= (WORD)55;
0560                zSetFrameRate(hWnd, wFrameRate);
0561                break;
0562          case IDM_FPS91:                  /* use 9 frames per second */
0563                wPrevRate= wFrameRate;
0564                wFrameRate= (WORD)110;
0565                zSetFrameRate(hWnd, wFrameRate);
0566                break;
0567          case IDM_FPS61:                  /* use 6 frames per second */
0568                wPrevRate= wFrameRate;
0569                wFrameRate= (WORD)165;
0570                zSetFrameRate(hWnd, wFrameRate);
0571                break;
0572          case IDM_FPS45:                  /* use 4.5 frames per second */
0573                wPrevRate= wFrameRate;
0574                wFrameRate= (WORD) 220;
0575                zSetFrameRate(hWnd, wFrameRate);
0576                break;
0577          case IDM_FPS36:                  /* use 3.5 frames per second */
0578                wPrevRate= wFrameRate;
0579                wFrameRate= (WORD) 275;
0580                zSetFrameRate(hWnd, wFrameRate);
0581                break;
0582          case IDM_FPS30:                  /* use 3 frames per second */
0583                wPrevRate= wFrameRate;
0584                wFrameRate= (WORD) 330;
0585                zSetFrameRate(hWnd, wFrameRate);
0586                break;
0587
0588          /* ----------- About, License, and How to Use ----------- */
0589          case IDM_About:                      /* copyright information... */
0590            LoadString(hInst,IDS_About,lpCaption,Max);
0591            LoadString(hInst,IDS_AboutText,lpMessage,MaxText);
0592            TimerCounter= zTIMER_PAUSE;
0593            MessageBox(GetFocus(),lpMessage,lpCaption,MB_OK);
0594            break;
0595          case IDM_License:                    /* license information... */
0596            LoadString(hInst,IDS_License,lpCaption,Max);
0597            LoadString(hInst,IDS_LicenseText,lpMessage,MaxText);
0598            TimerCounter= zTIMER_PAUSE;
0599            MessageBox(GetFocus(),lpMessage,lpCaption,MB_OK);
0600            break;
0601          case IDM_GeneralHelp:                 /* how to use the demo... */
0602            LoadString(hInst,IDS_Help,lpCaption,Max);
```

```
0603              LoadString(hInst,IDS_HelpText,lpMessage,MaxText);
0604              TimerCounter= zTIMER_PAUSE;
0605              MessageBox(GetFocus(),lpMessage,lpCaption,MB_OK);
0606              break;
0607          default:
0608              return(DefWindowProc(hWnd, message, wParam, lParam));
0609          }
0610       break;
0611
0612    /* ---------- grab handle for menu item checkmark ----------- */
0613    case WM_INITMENUPOPUP:        /* if a menu is about to pop up... */
0614       TimerCounter= zTIMER_PAUSE; /* provide pause for slower CPUs */
0615       if (lParam == 2)      /* and if it is the frame-rate menu... */
0616         hMenu= wParam; /* remember it so check-mark can be tweaked */
0617       break;
0618
0619    /* ------- oversee Windows-generated refresh requests -------- */
0620    case WM_PAINT:
0621       hDCpaint= BeginPaint(hWnd,&ps);
0622       EndPaint(hWnd, &ps);
0623       if (PaintImage==zBLANK) break;          /* if blank do nothing */
0624       if (PaintImage==zPREVIEW)        /* if frame preview mode... */
0625         {
0626         zCopyToDisplay(hWnd);  /* ...copy hidden-frame to viewport */
0627         break;
0628         }
0629       if (Pause==TRUE)                   /* if animation is paused... */
0630         {
0631         Redisplay= TRUE;                      /* reset the token... */
0632         zShowNextFrame(hWnd); /* so current frame is refreshed... */
0633         Redisplay= FALSE;             /* ...then restore the token */
0634         break;
0635         }
0636       zShowNextFrame(hWnd);    /* else if animating show next frame */
0637       break;
0638
0639    /* --- manage incoming keystrokes for single-step playback --- */
0640    case WM_KEYDOWN:
0641       switch (wParam)
0642         {
0643         case VK_LEFT:    /* left direction key: singlestep reverse */
0644           if (Pause==TRUE)                 /* if animation paused... */
0645             {
0646             if (FrameDirection==zFORWARD)
0647               {               /* confirm the playback direction... */
0648               FrameDirection= zREVERSE;
0649               }
0650             Pause= FALSE;
0651             zShowNextFrame(hWnd);    /* ...and show the next frame */
0652             Pause= TRUE;
0653             PaintImage= zANIMATING;
0654             }
0655           break;
0656         case VK_RIGHT:  /* right direction key: singlestep forward */
0657           if (Pause==TRUE)
0658             {                /* (control logic is similar to VK_LEFT) */
0659             if (FrameDirection==zREVERSE)
0660               {
0661               FrameDirection= zFORWARD;
0662               }
0663             Pause= FALSE;
```

```
0664                zShowNextFrame(hWnd);
0665                Pause= TRUE;
0666                PaintImage= zANIMATING; ·
0667                }
0668            break;
0669          default: return(DefWindowProc(hWnd,message,wParam,lParam));
0670          }
0671        break;
0672
0673      /* --------------- ensure a graceful shutdown -------------- */
0674      case WM_DESTROY:
0675        if (FrameReady==TRUE)
0676          {            /* if a hidden-frame was created, destroy it... */
0677          SelectObject(hFrameDC,hPrevFrame);
0678          DeleteObject(hFrame);
0679          DeleteDC(hFrameDC);
0680          KillTimer(hWnd,1);                      /* ...and the timer */
0681          }
0682        if (bAnimationLoaded==TRUE)
0683          {    /* if an animation sequence was loaded into memory... */
0684          SelectObject(hFDC,hPrevF); /* select default bitmap handle */
0685          for (LoopCount= 1; LoopCount<= zNUMCELS; LoopCount++)
0686            {                /* for each bitmap handle in the array... */
0687            DeleteObject(BitmapHandles[LoopCount-1]);   /* ...delete */
0688            }
0689          DeleteDC(hFDC);   /* ...then delete memory display-context */
0690          }
0691        zClose3D();                        /* shut down the 3D engine */
0692        PostQuitMessage(0);
0693        break;
0694
0695      /* ------- intercept attempt to resize or move window -------- */
0696      case WM_SYSCOMMAND:
0697        if ((wParam & 0xfff0)== SC_SIZE)
0698          {
0699          MessageBeep(0); break;
0700          }
0701        if ((wParam & 0xfff0)== SC_MINIMIZE)
0702          {
0703          MessageBeep(0); break;
0704          }
0705        if ((wParam & 0xfff0)== SC_MAXIMIZE)
0706          {
0707          MessageBeep(0); break;
0708          }
0709
0710      /* ----- send all other messages to Windows for handling ----- */
0711      default:
0712        return(DefWindowProc(hWnd, message, wParam, lParam));
0713      }
0714    return FALSE;
0715    }
0716    /*
0717    -----------------------------------------------------------------
0718                Initialize the attributes of the window class
0719    -----------------------------------------------------------------
0720                                                                    */
0721    BOOL zInitClass(HANDLE hInstance)
0722    {
0723      WNDCLASS WndClass;
0724    WndClass.style= 0;
```

```
0725  WndClass.lpfnWndProc= zMessageHandler;  /* app's message handler */
0726  WndClass.cbClsExtra= 0;
0727  WndClass.cbWndExtra= 0;
0728  WndClass.hInstance= hInstance;                  /* this copy of the app */
0729  WndClass.hIcon= LoadIcon(NULL,IDI_EXCLAMATION);     /* app's icon */
0730  WndClass.hCursor= LoadCursor(NULL,IDC_ARROW);      /* app's cursor */
0731  WndClass.hbrBackground=            /* background color for viewport */
0732                          CreateSolidBrush(RGB(255,255,255));
0733  WndClass.lpszMenuName= "HRAMENUS";    /* menu script in .rc file */
0734  WndClass.lpszClassName= "HRADEMO";     /* nominal name of class */
0735  return RegisterClass(&WndClass); /* tell Windows about the class */
0736  }
0737  /*
0738  ----------------------------------------------------------------
0739                        Create the main window
0740  ----------------------------------------------------------------
0741                                                                 */
0742  HWND zInitMainWindow(HANDLE hInstance)
0743  {
0744    HWND hWnd;
0745  LoadString(hInstance,IDS_Caption,lpCaption,Max); /* load caption */
0746  hHourGlass= LoadCursor(NULL,IDC_WAIT);  /* load hourglass cursor */
0747  hWnd = CreateWindow("HRADEMO",                      /* class name */
0748    lpCaption,                              /* window caption */
0749    WS_OVERLAPPED | WS_THICKFRAME | WS_CLIPCHILDREN,     /* style */
0750    WindowX,WindowY,                      /* location of window */
0751    zWINDOW_WIDTH,zWINDOW_HEIGHT,         /* dimensions of window */
0752    0,                                   /* parent window, if any */
0753    0,                                    /* special menu, if any */
0754    hInstance,                          /* this copy of the app */
0755    (LPSTR)NULL);       /* for multiple-document interface, if any */
0756  return hWnd;    /* return the newly-created handle to the caller */
0757  }
0758
0759  /*
0760  ----------------------------------------------------------------
0761                      Graphics system functions
0762  ----------------------------------------------------------------
0763  ----------------------------------------------------------------
0764                      Create the hidden-frame.
0765  ----------------------------------------------------------------
0766                                                                 */
0767  static void zInitFrame(HWND hWnd)
0768  {
0769    HDC hDisplayDC;
0770
0771  if (FrameReady==TRUE)
0772    {                    /* if a hidden-frame already exists... */
0773    MessageBeep(0);
0774    LoadString(hInst,IDS_Ready,lpCaption,Max);
0775    LoadString(hInst,IDS_Already,lpMessage,MaxText);
0776    TimerCounter= zTIMER_PAUSE;
0777    MessageBox(GetFocus(),lpMessage,lpCaption,MB_OK);
0778    return;
0779    }
0780  GlobalCompact((DWORD)-1L);           /* maximize contiguous memory */
0781
0782  /* ----------------- create a hidden bitmap ------------------ */
0783  hDisplayDC= GetDC(hWnd);                     /* display-context */
0784  hFrameDC= CreateCompatibleDC(hDisplayDC);             /* memory DC */
0785  hFrame= CreateCompatibleBitmap(hDisplayDC,zFRAMEWIDE,zFRAMEHIGH);
```

```
0786   if (hFrame==NULL)
0787     {                        /* if unable to create compatible bitmap... */
0788     LoadString(hInst,IDS_NotReady,lpCaption,Max);
0789     LoadString(hInst,IDS_InsufMem1,lpMessage,MaxText);
0790     MessageBox(GetFocus(),lpMessage,lpCaption,MB_OK);
0791     DeleteDC(hFrameDC);
0792     TimerExists= FALSE; FrameReady= FALSE; AnimationReady= FALSE;
0793     return;
0794     }
0795   hPrevFrame= SelectObject(hFrameDC,hFrame);       /* select bitmap */
0796
0797   /* -------- clear the viewport and copy to hidden-frame -------- */
0798   zClear(hWnd);
0799   BitBlt(hFrameDC,0,0,zFRAMEWIDE,zFRAMEHIGH,hDisplayDC,0,0,SRCCOPY);
0800   ReleaseDC(hWnd,hDisplayDC);              /* release the display-context */
0801
0802   /* -------------------- initialize a timer -------------------- */
0803   TimerID1= SetTimer(hWnd,1,wFrameRate,(FARPROC) NULL);
0804   if (TimerID1 == 0)                    /* if no timer was initialized... */
0805     {                                   /* ...display a warning */
0806     LoadString(hInst,IDS_NotReady,lpCaption,Max);
0807     LoadString(hInst,IDS_NoTimer,lpMessage,MaxText);
0808     MessageBox(GetFocus(),lpMessage,lpCaption,MB_OK);
0809     SelectObject(hFrameDC,hPrevFrame);
0810     DeleteObject(hFrame);
0811     DeleteDC(hFrameDC);
0812     TimerExists= FALSE;
0813     return;
0814     }
0815   TimerExists= TRUE;
0816   FrameReady= TRUE;
0817   FrameNum= 1;
0818   return;
0819   }
0820   /*
0821   ----------------------------------------------------------------
0822                    Clear the hidden frame.
0823   ----------------------------------------------------------------
0824                                                                  */
0825   static void zClearHiddenFrame(void)
0826   {
0827   if (FrameReady == TRUE)
0828     {
0829     PatBlt(hFrameDC,0,0,zFRAMEWIDE,zFRAMEHIGH,WHITENESS);
0830     }
0831   return;
0832   }
0833   /*
0834   ----------------------------------------------------------------
0835            Copy the hidden frame to the display window.
0836   ----------------------------------------------------------------
0837                                                                  */
0838   static void zCopyToDisplay(HWND hWnd)
0839   {
0840     HDC hDC;
0841   hDC= GetDC(hWnd);
0842   if (FrameReady == TRUE)
0843     {
0844     BitBlt(hDC,0,0,zFRAMEWIDE,zFRAMEHIGH,hFrameDC,0,0,SRCCOPY);
0845     }
0846   ReleaseDC(hWnd,hDC);
```

```
0847   return;
0848   }
0849   /*
0850   ---------------------------------------------------------------
0851                     Blank the display window.
0852   ---------------------------------------------------------------
0853                                                               */
0854   static void zClear(HWND hWnd)
0855   {
0856     HDC hDC;
0857   hDC= GetDC(hWnd);
0858   PatBlt(hDC,0,0,zFRAMEWIDE,zFRAMEHIGH,WHITENESS);
0859   ReleaseDC(hWnd,hDC);
0860   return;
0861   }
0862
0863   /*
0864   ---------------------------------------------------------------
0865                   Animation authoring functions
0866   ---------------------------------------------------------------
0867   ---------------------------------------------------------------
0868                   Create the frames and save to disk.
0869   ---------------------------------------------------------------
0870                                                               */
0871   static void zSaveAnimation(HWND hWnd)
0872   {
0873   if (FrameReady==FALSE)
0874     {
0875     MessageBeep(0);
0876     LoadString(hInst,IDS_NotReady,lpCaption,Max);
0877     LoadString(hInst,IDS_NoFrame,lpMessage,MaxText);
0878     MessageBox(GetFocus(),lpMessage,lpCaption,MB_OK);
0879     return;
0880     }
0881   if (bAnimationSaved==TRUE)
0882     {
0883     MessageBeep(0);
0884     LoadString(hInst,IDS_Unexpected,lpCaption,Max);
0885     LoadString(hInst,IDS_Disk1,lpMessage,MaxText);
0886     TimerCounter= zTIMER_PAUSE;
0887     MessageBox(GetFocus(),lpMessage,lpCaption,MB_OK);
0888     return;
0889     }
0890   if (bPrevSaveAttempt==TRUE)
0891     {
0892     MessageBeep(0);
0893     LoadString(hInst,IDS_Unexpected,lpCaption,Max);
0894     LoadString(hInst,IDS_Disk8,lpMessage,MaxText);
0895     TimerCounter= zTIMER_PAUSE;
0896     MessageBox(GetFocus(),lpMessage,lpCaption,MB_OK);
0897     return;
0898     }
0899   bPrevSaveAttempt= TRUE;
0900
0901   /* ------------------ initialize the camera ------------------ */
0902   Cam1.Heading= 330; Cam1.Pitch= 320; Cam1.Distance= 356;
0903   zSetCameraDistance(Cam1.Distance);
0904   zSetCameraPitch(Cam1.Pitch);
0905   zSetCameraHeading(Cam1.Heading);
0906
0907   /* ------------- specify the path of the camera -------------- */
```

```
0908   Cam1Path1.StartFrame= 1; Cam1Path1.EndFrame= 18;
0909   Cam1Path1.ChgHeading= 0;                        /* set to -2 for dolly */
0910   Cam1Path1.ChgPitch= 0;                          /* set to -2 for crane */
0911   Cam1Path1.ChgDistance= 0;
0912
0913   /* --------------- initialize the light-source --------------- */
0914   Lt1.Elevation= 60;
0915   Lt1.Heading= 180;
0916   zSetLightPosition(Lt1.Elevation, Lt1.Heading);
0917
0918   /* ----------- specify the path of the light-source ---------- */
0919   Lt1Path1.StartFrame= 1; Lt1Path1.EndFrame= 18;
0920   Lt1Path1.ChgHeading= 0; Lt1Path1.ChgElevation= 0;
0921
0922   /* ------------------- initialize the actor ------------------ */
0923   Actor1.PositionX= 0;            /* position of actor in 3D world... */
0924   Actor1.PositionY= 0;
0925   Actor1.PositionZ= 0;
0926   Actor1.Yaw= 360;             /* orientation of actor in 3D world... */
0927   Actor1.Roll= 360;
0928   Actor1.Pitch= 360;
0929   zSetSubjectLocation(Actor1.PositionX,
0930                       Actor1.PositionY,
0931                       Actor1.PositionZ);
0932   zSetSubjectAttitude(Actor1.Yaw, Actor1.Roll, Actor1.Pitch);
0933
0934   /* ------------- specify the path of the actor --------------- */
0935   Actor1Path1.StartFrame= 1;
0936   Actor1Path1.EndFrame= 18;
0937   Actor1Path1.ChgYaw= 0;
0938   Actor1Path1.ChgRoll= 0;
0939   Actor1Path1.ChgPitch= 0;
0940   Actor1Path1.ChgPosX =0;
0941   Actor1Path1.ChgPosY =0;
0942   Actor1Path1.ChgPosZ= 0;
0943
0944   /* ---- initialize the 3D assembly that comprises the actor ---- */
0945   Assembly1[0].Solid= zBOX;                    /* arm extensor (1 of 1) */
0946   Assembly1[0].Level= zLEVEL1;
0947   Assembly1[0].Color= zGREEN;
0948   Assembly1[0].SizeX= 20;
0949   Assembly1[0].SizeY= 20;
0950   Assembly1[0].SizeZ= 30;
0951   Assembly1[0].Yaw= 0;
0952   Assembly1[0].Roll= 0;
0953   Assembly1[0].Pitch= 0;
0954   Assembly1[0].PositionX= 0;
0955   Assembly1[0].PositionY= 0;
0956   Assembly1[0].PositionZ= -50;
0957   Assembly1[0].DeformRightX= 0;
0958   Assembly1[0].DeformLeftX= 0;
0959   Assembly1[0].DeformUpY= 0;
0960   Assembly1[0].DeformDownY= 0;
0961   Assembly1[0].PivotX= 0;
0962   Assembly1[0].PivotY= 0;
0963   Assembly1[0].PivotZ= 0;
0964   Assembly1[0].SubAssyYaw= 0;
0965   Assembly1[0].SubAssyRoll= 0;
0966   Assembly1[0].SubAssyPitch= 0;
0967   Assembly1[0].SubAssyX= 0;
0968   Assembly1[0].SubAssyY= 0;
```

```
0969    Assembly1[0].SubAssyZ= 0;
0970
0971    Assembly1[1].Solid= zBOX;            /* arm swivel extensor (1 of 2) */
0972    Assembly1[1].Level= zLEVEL1;
0973    Assembly1[1].Color= zGREEN;
0974    Assembly1[1].SizeX= Assembly1[0].SizeX / 4;
0975    Assembly1[1].SizeY= Assembly1[0].SizeY;
0976    Assembly1[1].SizeZ= 10;
0977    Assembly1[1].Yaw= 0;
0978    Assembly1[1].Roll= 0;
0979    Assembly1[1].Pitch= 0;
0980    Assembly1[1].PositionX= Assembly1[0].SizeX - Assembly1[1].SizeX;
0981    Assembly1[1].PositionY= Assembly1[0].PositionY;
0982    Assembly1[1].PositionZ=
0983                    (Assembly1[0].PositionZ+Assembly1[0].SizeZ) +
0984                    Assembly1[1].SizeZ;
0985    Assembly1[1].DeformRightX= 0;
0986    Assembly1[1].DeformLeftX= 0;
0987    Assembly1[1].DeformUpY= 0;
0988    Assembly1[1].DeformDownY= 0;
0989    Assembly1[1].PivotX= 0;
0990    Assembly1[1].PivotY= 0;
0991    Assembly1[1].PivotZ= 0;
0992    Assembly1[1].SubAssyYaw= 0;
0993    Assembly1[1].SubAssyRoll= 0;
0994    Assembly1[1].SubAssyPitch= 0;
0995    Assembly1[1].SubAssyX= 0;
0996    Assembly1[1].SubAssyY= 0;
0997    Assembly1[1].SubAssyZ= 0;
0998
0999    Assembly1[2].Solid= zBOX;            /* arm swivel extensor (2 of 2) */
1000    Assembly1[2].Level= zLEVEL1;
1001    Assembly1[2].Color= zGREEN;
1002    Assembly1[2].SizeX= Assembly1[0].SizeX / 4;
1003    Assembly1[2].SizeY= Assembly1[0].SizeY;
1004    Assembly1[2].SizeZ= 10;
1005    Assembly1[2].Yaw= 0;
1006    Assembly1[2].Roll= 0;
1007    Assembly1[2].Pitch= 0;
1008    Assembly1[2].PositionX=
1009                    ((-1)*Assembly1[0].SizeX)+Assembly1[2].SizeX;
1010    Assembly1[2].PositionY= Assembly1[0].PositionY;
1011    Assembly1[2].PositionZ=
1012                    (Assembly1[0].PositionZ+Assembly1[0].SizeZ) +
1013                    Assembly1[2].SizeZ;;
1014    Assembly1[2].DeformRightX= 0;
1015    Assembly1[2].DeformLeftX= 0;
1016    Assembly1[2].DeformUpY= 0;
1017    Assembly1[2].DeformDownY= 0;
1018    Assembly1[2].PivotX= 0;
1019    Assembly1[2].PivotY= 0;
1020    Assembly1[2].PivotZ= 0;
1021    Assembly1[2].SubAssyYaw= 0;
1022    Assembly1[2].SubAssyRoll= 0;
1023    Assembly1[2].SubAssyPitch= 0;
1024    Assembly1[2].SubAssyX= 0;
1025    Assembly1[2].SubAssyY= 0;
1026    Assembly1[2].SubAssyZ= 0;
1027
1028    Assembly1[3].Solid= zHALFCYL;        /* arm swivel bracket (1 of 2) */
1029    Assembly1[3].Level= zLEVEL1;
```

```
1030   Assembly1[3].Color= zGREEN;
1031   Assembly1[3].SizeX= Assembly1[0].SizeX;
1032   Assembly1[3].SizeY= Assembly1[0].SizeY;
1033   Assembly1[3].SizeZ= Assembly1[1].SizeX;
1034   Assembly1[3].Yaw= 90;
1035   Assembly1[3].Roll= 0;
1036   Assembly1[3].Pitch= 0;
1037   Assembly1[3].PositionX= Assembly1[1].PositionX;
1038   Assembly1[3].PositionY= Assembly1[1].PositionY;
1039   Assembly1[3].PositionZ=
1040               Assembly1[1].PositionZ + Assembly1[1].SizeZ;
1041   Assembly1[3].DeformRightX= 0;
1042   Assembly1[3].DeformLeftX= 0;
1043   Assembly1[3].DeformUpY= 0;
1044   Assembly1[3].DeformDownY= 0;
1045   Assembly1[3].PivotX= 0;
1046   Assembly1[3].PivotY= 0;
1047   Assembly1[3].PivotZ= 0;
1048   Assembly1[3].SubAssyYaw= 0;
1049   Assembly1[3].SubAssyRoll= 0;
1050   Assembly1[3].SubAssyPitch= 0;
1051   Assembly1[3].SubAssyX= 0;
1052   Assembly1[3].SubAssyY= 0;
1053   Assembly1[3].SubAssyZ= 0;
1054
1055   Assembly1[4].Solid= zHALFCYL;       /* arm swivel bracket (2 of 2) */
1056   Assembly1[4].Level= zLEVEL1;
1057   Assembly1[4].Color= zGREEN;
1058   Assembly1[4].SizeX= Assembly1[0].SizeX;
1059   Assembly1[4].SizeY= Assembly1[0].SizeY;
1060   Assembly1[4].SizeZ= Assembly1[2].SizeX;
1061   Assembly1[4].Yaw= 90;
1062   Assembly1[4].Roll= 0;
1063   Assembly1[4].Pitch= 0;
1064   Assembly1[4].PositionX= Assembly1[2].PositionX;
1065   Assembly1[4].PositionY= Assembly1[2].PositionY;
1066   Assembly1[4].PositionZ=
1067               Assembly1[2].PositionZ + Assembly1[2].SizeZ;
1068   Assembly1[4].DeformRightX= 0;
1069   Assembly1[4].DeformLeftX= 0;
1070   Assembly1[4].DeformUpY= 0;
1071   Assembly1[4].DeformDownY= 0;
1072   Assembly1[4].PivotX= 0;
1073   Assembly1[4].PivotY= 0;
1074   Assembly1[4].PivotZ= 0;
1075   Assembly1[4].SubAssyYaw= 0;
1076   Assembly1[4].SubAssyRoll= 0;
1077   Assembly1[4].SubAssyPitch= 0;
1078   Assembly1[4].SubAssyX= 0;
1079   Assembly1[4].SubAssyY= 0;
1080   Assembly1[4].SubAssyZ= 0;
1081
1082   Assembly1[5].Solid= zCYLINDER;                  /* swivel pin (1) */
1083   Assembly1[5].Level= zLEVEL1;
1084   Assembly1[5].Color= zRED;
1085   Assembly1[5].SizeX= 10;
1086   Assembly1[5].SizeY= 10;
1087   Assembly1[5].SizeZ= Assembly1[0].SizeX + 5;
1088   Assembly1[5].Yaw= 90;
1089   Assembly1[5].Roll= 0;
1090   Assembly1[5].Pitch= 0;
```

```
1091    Assembly1[5].PositionX= Assembly1[0].PositionX;
1092    Assembly1[5].PositionY= Assembly1[3].PositionY;
1093    Assembly1[5].PositionZ= Assembly1[3].PositionZ;
1094    Assembly1[5].DeformRightX= 0;
1095    Assembly1[5].DeformLeftX= 0;
1096    Assembly1[5].DeformUpY= 0;
1097    Assembly1[5].DeformDownY= 0;
1098    Assembly1[5].PivotX= 0;
1099    Assembly1[5].PivotY= 0;
1100    Assembly1[5].PivotZ= 0;
1101    Assembly1[5].SubAssyYaw= 0;
1102    Assembly1[5].SubAssyRoll= 0;
1103    Assembly1[5].SubAssyPitch= 0;
1104    Assembly1[5].SubAssyX= 0;
1105    Assembly1[5].SubAssyY= 0;
1106    Assembly1[5].SubAssyZ= 0;
1107
1108    Assembly1[6].Solid= zHALFCYL;           /* wrist swivel bracket (1) */
1109    Assembly1[6].Level= zLEVEL2;
1110    Assembly1[6].Color= zBROWN;
1111    Assembly1[6].SizeX= Assembly1[4].SizeX;
1112    Assembly1[6].SizeY= Assembly1[4].SizeY;
1113    Assembly1[6].SizeZ= Assembly1[4].SizeZ;
1114    Assembly1[6].Yaw= 270;                      /* reorient half-cylinder */
1115    Assembly1[6].Roll= 0;
1116    Assembly1[6].Pitch= 0;
1117    Assembly1[6].PositionX= Assembly1[5].PositionX;
1118    Assembly1[6].PositionY= Assembly1[5].PositionY;
1119    Assembly1[6].PositionZ= Assembly1[5].PositionZ;
1120    Assembly1[6].DeformRightX= 0;
1121    Assembly1[6].DeformLeftX= 0;
1122    Assembly1[6].DeformUpY= 0;
1123    Assembly1[6].DeformDownY= 0;
1124    Assembly1[6].PivotX= 0;
1125    Assembly1[6].PivotY= 0;
1126    Assembly1[6].PivotZ= 0;
1127    Assembly1[6].SubAssyYaw= 0;
1128    Assembly1[6].SubAssyRoll= 0;
1129    Assembly1[6].SubAssyPitch= 0;
1130    Assembly1[6].SubAssyX= 0;
1131    Assembly1[6].SubAssyY= 0;
1132    Assembly1[6].SubAssyZ= 0;
1133
1134    Assembly1[7].Solid= zBOX;                     /* wrist extensor (1) */
1135    Assembly1[7].Level= zLEVEL2;
1136    Assembly1[7].Color= zBROWN;
1137    Assembly1[7].SizeX= Assembly1[6].SizeZ;
1138    Assembly1[7].SizeY= Assembly1[6].SizeX;
1139    Assembly1[7].SizeZ= 30;
1140    Assembly1[7].Yaw= 0;
1141    Assembly1[7].Roll= 0;
1142    Assembly1[7].Pitch= 0;
1143    Assembly1[7].PositionX= Assembly1[6].PositionX;
1144    Assembly1[7].PositionY= Assembly1[6].PositionY;
1145    Assembly1[7].PositionZ=
1146                    Assembly1[6].PositionX + Assembly1[7].SizeZ;
1147    Assembly1[7].DeformRightX= 0;
1148    Assembly1[7].DeformLeftX= 0;
1149    Assembly1[7].DeformUpY= 0;
1150    Assembly1[7].DeformDownY= 0;
1151    Assembly1[7].PivotX= 0;
```

```
1152    Assembly1[7].PivotY= 0;
1153    Assembly1[7].PivotZ= 0;
1154    Assembly1[7].SubAssyYaw= 0;
1155    Assembly1[7].SubAssyRoll= 0;
1156    Assembly1[7].SubAssyPitch= 0;
1157    Assembly1[7].SubAssyX= 0;
1158    Assembly1[7].SubAssyY= 0;
1159    Assembly1[7].SubAssyZ= 0;
1160
1161    Assembly1[8].Solid= zHALFCYL;          /* wrist swivel bracket (1) */
1162    Assembly1[8].Level= zLEVEL2;
1163    Assembly1[8].Color= zBROWN;
1164    Assembly1[8].SizeX= Assembly1[6].SizeX;
1165    Assembly1[8].SizeY= Assembly1[6].SizeY;
1166    Assembly1[8].SizeZ= Assembly1[6].SizeZ;
1167    Assembly1[8].Yaw= 90;
1168    Assembly1[8].Roll= 0;
1169    Assembly1[8].Pitch= 0;
1170    Assembly1[8].PositionX= Assembly1[7].PositionX;
1171    Assembly1[8].PositionY= Assembly1[7].PositionY;
1172    Assembly1[8].PositionZ=
1173                    Assembly1[7].PositionZ + Assembly1[7].SizeZ;
1174    Assembly1[8].DeformRightX= 0;
1175    Assembly1[8].DeformLeftX= 0;
1176    Assembly1[8].DeformUpY= 0;
1177    Assembly1[8].DeformDownY= 0;
1178    Assembly1[8].PivotX= 0;
1179    Assembly1[8].PivotY= 0;
1180    Assembly1[8].PivotZ= 0;
1181    Assembly1[8].SubAssyYaw= 0;
1182    Assembly1[8].SubAssyRoll= 0;
1183    Assembly1[8].SubAssyPitch= 0;
1184    Assembly1[8].SubAssyX= 0;
1185    Assembly1[8].SubAssyY= 0;
1186    Assembly1[8].SubAssyZ= 0;
1187
1188    Assembly1[9].Solid= zCYLINDER;                    /* swivel pin (1) */
1189    Assembly1[9].Level= zLEVEL2;
1190    Assembly1[9].Color= zCYAN;
1191    Assembly1[9].SizeX= Assembly1[5].SizeX;
1192    Assembly1[9].SizeY= Assembly1[5].SizeY;
1193    Assembly1[9].SizeZ= Assembly1[8].SizeZ + 15;
1194    Assembly1[9].Yaw= 90;
1195    Assembly1[9].Roll= 0;
1196    Assembly1[9].Pitch= 0;
1197    Assembly1[9].PositionX= Assembly1[8].PositionX;
1198    Assembly1[9].PositionY= Assembly1[8].PositionY;
1199    Assembly1[9].PositionZ= Assembly1[8].PositionZ;
1200    Assembly1[9].DeformRightX= 0;
1201    Assembly1[9].DeformLeftX= 0;
1202    Assembly1[9].DeformUpY= 0;
1203    Assembly1[9].DeformDownY= 0;
1204    Assembly1[9].PivotX= 0;
1205    Assembly1[9].PivotY= 0;
1206    Assembly1[9].PivotZ= 0;
1207    Assembly1[9].SubAssyYaw= 0;
1208    Assembly1[9].SubAssyRoll= 0;
1209    Assembly1[9].SubAssyPitch= 0;
1210    Assembly1[9].SubAssyX= 0;
1211    Assembly1[9].SubAssyY= 0;
1212    Assembly1[9].SubAssyZ= 0;
```

```
1214   /* ------------ specify the path of the subassembly ------------ */
1215   Assembly1Path1.StartFrame= 1;                    /* from frame 1 to... */
1216   Assembly1Path1.EndFrame= 18;                     /* ...frame 18... */
1217   Assembly1Path1.ChgYaw= 0;
1218   Assembly1Path1.ChgRoll= 0;
1219   Assembly1Path1.ChgPitch= 3;      /* ...raise subassembly 3 degrees */
1220
1221   /* ----------------- build and save the cels ------------------- */
1222   for (LoopCount= 1; LoopCount<= zNUMCELS; LoopCount++)
1223     {                              /* for each cel in the animation... */
1224       bFrameSaved= zBuildFrame(LoopCount, hWnd,  /* ... save to disk */
1225                             (LPSTR)FrameFiles[LoopCount-1]);
1226       if (bFrameSaved==FALSE) return; /* cancel loop if error occurs */
1227     }
1228   bAnimationSaved= TRUE;
1229   bPrevLoadAttempt= FALSE;
1230   zClear(hWnd);
1231   MessageBeep(0);
1232   LoadString(hInst,IDS_Status,lpCaption,Max);
1233   LoadString(hInst,IDS_Disk2,lpMessage,MaxText);
1234   MessageBox(GetFocus(),lpMessage,lpCaption,MB_OK);
1235   return;
1236   }
1237   /*
1238   ---------------------------------------------------------------
1239                   Build one cel and save to disk.
1240   ---------------------------------------------------------------
1241                                                                  */
1242   static BOOL zBuildFrame(int Number, HWND hWnd, LPSTR lpFileName)
1243   {
1244     BOOL bDiskResult;
1245     HFONT Font;
1246     HFONT PrevFont;
1247     DWORD PrevFontColor;
1248     DWORD PrevBkColor;
1249     HDC hDC;
1250     struct tm *NewTime;          /* pointer to tm struct of time.h */
1251     time_t TimeSeconds;          /* long integer time_t of time.h */
1252     MSG msg;                                /* incoming message */
1253
1254   /* ---------- display progress report on caption bar ----------- */
1255   TextLength= wsprintf(lpCaption,      /* build and save the string */
1256               "Building frame %d...", Number);
1257   SetWindowText(hWnd,lpCaption);       /* display it in caption bar */
1258
1259   /* -------------------- reset all buffers -------------------- */
1260   zClearHiddenFrame();
1261   zClear(hWnd);
1262   zClearHidden3DPage();
1263   zResetZBuffer();
1264
1265   /* ----------------- draw the appropriate cel --------------- */
1266   zDrawCel(Number);
1267   if (FrameReady==TRUE)
1268     {
1269     hDC= GetDC(hWnd);
1270     BitBlt(hFrameDC,0,0,zFRAMEWIDE,zFRAMEHIGH,hDC,0,0,SRCCOPY);
1271     ReleaseDC(hWnd,hDC);
1272     }
1273
```

C-4 Continued.

```
1274    /* ------------ check for user-requested cancel -------------- */
1275    if (PeekMessage(&msg,NULL,0,0,PM_REMOVE))
1276      {                        /* if a message is waiting in the queue... */
1277      if (msg.message == WM_RBUTTONDOWN)
1278        {                           /* ...if right mouse button pressed... */
1279        return FALSE;               /* ...then cancel the build sequence */
1280        }
1281      }
1282
1283    /* --------- display the titles, labels, and timestamp --------- */
1284    if ((DisplayBits==1)&&(DisplayPlanes==1))
1285      {                        /* if a mono display use black typeface... */
1286      PrevFontColor= SetTextColor(hFrameDC,RGB(0,0,0));
1287      PrevBkColor=  SetBkColor(hFrameDC,RGB(255,255,255));
1288      }
1289    else
1290      {   /* else if a color display use any solid color typeface... */
1291      PrevFontColor= SetTextColor(hFrameDC,RGB(0,0,0));
1292      PrevBkColor=  SetBkColor(hFrameDC,RGB(255,255,255));
1293      }
1294    SetBkMode(hFrameDC,TRANSPARENT);
1295
1296    if (bUseArial == FALSE)
1297      {                        /* if running Windows 3.0 use Helv font... */
1298      Font= CreateFont(24, 0, 0, 0, FW_BOLD, FALSE, FALSE, FALSE,
1299           ANSI_CHARSET, OUT_DEFAULT_PRECIS, CLIP_DEFAULT_PRECIS,
1300           DRAFT_QUALITY, VARIABLE_PITCH | FF_SWISS, "Helv");
1301      PrevFont= SelectObject(hFrameDC,Font);
1302      TextOut(hFrameDC,10,6,"A Lee Adams tutorial:",21);
1303      Font= CreateFont(36, 0, 0, 0, FW_BOLD, FALSE, FALSE, FALSE,
1304           ANSI_CHARSET, OUT_DEFAULT_PRECIS, CLIP_DEFAULT_PRECIS,
1305           DRAFT_QUALITY, VARIABLE_PITCH | FF_SWISS, "Helv");
1306      SelectObject(hFrameDC,Font);
1307      TextOut(hFrameDC,8,24,"3D subassembly",14);
1308      }
1309    else   /* else if running Windows 3.1 or newer use Arial font... */
1310      {
1311      Font= CreateFont(24, 0, 0, 0, FW_BOLD, FALSE, FALSE, FALSE,
1312           ANSI_CHARSET, OUT_DEFAULT_PRECIS, CLIP_DEFAULT_PRECIS,
1313           DRAFT_QUALITY, VARIABLE_PITCH | FF_SWISS, "Arial");
1314      PrevFont= SelectObject(hFrameDC,Font);
1315      TextOut(hFrameDC,10,6,"A Lee Adams tutorial:",21);
1316      Font= CreateFont(36, 0, 0, 0, FW_BOLD, FALSE, FALSE, FALSE,
1317           ANSI_CHARSET, OUT_DEFAULT_PRECIS, CLIP_DEFAULT_PRECIS,
1318           DRAFT_QUALITY, VARIABLE_PITCH | FF_SWISS, "Arial");
1319      SelectObject(hFrameDC,Font);
1320      TextOut(hFrameDC,8,24,"3D subassembly",14);
1321      }
1322
1323    SelectObject(hFrameDC,PrevFont);
1324    TextOut(hFrameDC,10,220,"Animation production timestamp",30);
1325    time(&TimeSeconds);
1326    NewTime= localtime(&TimeSeconds);
1327    TextOut(hFrameDC,10,235,(LPSTR)asctime(NewTime),19);
1328    SetBkMode(hFrameDC,OPAQUE);
1329    SetBkColor(hFrameDC,PrevBkColor);
1330    SetTextColor(hFrameDC,PrevFontColor);
1331
1332    /* ----------- check again for user-requested cancel ---------- */
1333    if (PeekMessage(&msg,NULL,0,0,PM_REMOVE))
1334      {
```

```
1335    if (msg.message == WM_RBUTTONDOWN)
1336      {
1337      return FALSE;
1338      }
1339    }
1340
1341    /* ----------- display the cel and save it to disk ------------ */
1342    zCopyToDisplay(hWnd);
1343    bDiskResult= zSaveFrame(hFrame,lpFileName);
1344    if (bDiskResult==FALSE) return FALSE;
1345    return TRUE;
1346    }
1347    /*
1348    ------------------------------------------------------------------
1349                            Draw a cel.
1350    ------------------------------------------------------------------
1351                                                                    */
1352    static void zDrawCel(int Number)
1353    {
1354      int PartID;                /* counter is used in the drawing loop */
1355
1356    /* -------------------- update the camera -------------------- */
1357    if ((Number > Cam1Path1.StartFrame) &&
1358        (Number <= Cam1Path1.EndFrame))
1359      {              /* if a frame num specified in the path struct... */
1360      Cam1.Distance= Cam1.Distance + Cam1Path1.ChgDistance;
1361      Cam1.Heading= Cam1.Heading + Cam1Path1.ChgHeading;
1362      Cam1.Pitch= Cam1.Pitch + Cam1Path1.ChgPitch;
1363      }
1364    zSetCameraDistance(Cam1.Distance);
1365    zSetCameraPitch(Cam1.Pitch);
1366    zSetCameraHeading(Cam1.Heading);
1367
1368    /* ----------------- update the light-source ----------------- */
1369    if ((Number > Lt1Path1.StartFrame) &&
1370        (Number <= Lt1Path1.EndFrame))
1371      {              /* if a frame num specified in the path struct... */
1372      Lt1.Heading= Lt1.Heading + Lt1Path1.ChgHeading;
1373      Lt1.Elevation= Lt1.Elevation + Lt1Path1.ChgElevation;
1374      }
1375    zSetLightPosition(Lt1.Elevation, Lt1.Heading);
1376
1377    /* --------------------- update the actor -------------------- */
1378    if ((Number > Actor1Path1.StartFrame) &&
1379        (Number <= Actor1Path1.EndFrame))
1380      {              /* if a frame num specified in the path struct... */
1381      Actor1.PositionX= Actor1.PositionX + Actor1Path1.ChgPosX;
1382      Actor1.PositionY= Actor1.PositionY + Actor1Path1.ChgPosY;
1383      Actor1.PositionZ= Actor1.PositionZ + Actor1Path1.ChgPosZ;
1384      Actor1.Yaw= Actor1.Yaw + Actor1Path1.ChgYaw;
1385      Actor1.Roll= Actor1.Roll + Actor1Path1.ChgRoll;
1386      Actor1.Pitch= Actor1.Pitch + Actor1Path1.ChgPitch;
1387      }
1388    zSetSubjectLocation(Actor1.PositionX,
1389                        Actor1.PositionY,
1390                        Actor1.PositionZ);
1391    zSetSubjectAttitude(Actor1.Yaw, Actor1.Roll, Actor1.Pitch);
1392
1393    /* ------------- build actor, update subassembly -------------- */
1394    for (PartID= zROBOT_START; PartID<= zROBOT_FINISH; PartID++)
1395      {                      /* for each subobject in the assembly... */
```

```
1396    zSetShadingColor(Assembly1[PartID].Color);           /* set color */
1397    zSetSubjectSize(Assembly1[PartID].SizeX,                  /* resize */
1398                    Assembly1[PartID].SizeY,
1399                    Assembly1[PartID].SizeZ);
1400    zSetSubobjectAttitude(Assembly1[PartID].Yaw,          /* reorient */
1401                    Assembly1[PartID].Roll,
1402                    Assembly1[PartID].Pitch);
1403    zSetSubobjectLocation(Assembly1[PartID].PositionX,      /* repos */
1404                    Assembly1[PartID].PositionY,
1405                    Assembly1[PartID].PositionZ);
1406    if (Assembly1[PartID].Level == zLEVEL1)
1407      {          /* if subobject is part of a top-level assembly... */
1408      zSetHierarchyLevel(zLEVEL1);
1409      }
1410    else if (Assembly1[PartID].Level == zLEVEL2)
1411      {          /* else if subobject is part of a subassembly... */
1412      if ((Number > Assembly1Path1.StartFrame) &&
1413        (Number <= Assembly1Path1.EndFrame))
1414        {                           /* ...raise the subassembly */
1415        Assembly1[PartID].SubAssyYaw=
1416          Assembly1[PartID].SubAssyYaw + Assembly1Path1.ChgYaw;
1417        Assembly1[PartID].SubAssyRoll=
1418          Assembly1[PartID].SubAssyRoll + Assembly1Path1.ChgRoll;
1419        Assembly1[PartID].SubAssyPitch=
1420          Assembly1[PartID].SubAssyPitch + Assembly1Path1.ChgPitch;
1421        }
1422      else if (Number > Assembly1Path1.EndFrame)
1423        {                           /* ...else lower the subassembly */
1424        Assembly1[PartID].SubAssyYaw=
1425          Assembly1[PartID].SubAssyYaw - Assembly1Path1.ChgYaw;
1426        Assembly1[PartID].SubAssyRoll=
1427          Assembly1[PartID].SubAssyRoll - Assembly1Path1.ChgRoll;
1428        Assembly1[PartID].SubAssyPitch=
1429          Assembly1[PartID].SubAssyPitch - Assembly1Path1.ChgPitch;
1430        }
1431      zSetSubAssyPivot(Assembly1[PartID].PivotX,
1432                    Assembly1[PartID].PivotY,
1433                    Assembly1[PartID].PivotZ);
1434      zSetSubAssyRotation(Assembly1[PartID].SubAssyYaw,
1435                    Assembly1[PartID].SubAssyRoll,
1436                    Assembly1[PartID].SubAssyPitch);
1437      zSetSubAssyPosition(Assembly1[PartID].SubAssyX,
1438                    Assembly1[PartID].SubAssyY,
1439                    Assembly1[PartID].SubAssyZ);
1440      zSetHierarchyLevel(zLEVEL2);
1441      }
1442
1443    zSetHierarchyMode(TRUE);              /* enable hierarchy modeling */
1444    switch (Assembly1[PartID].Solid)                          /* render */
1445      {
1446      case zBOX:        zDrawCube();        break;
1447      case zSPHERE:     zDrawSphere();      break;
1448      case zCYLINDER:   zDrawCylinder();    break;
1449      case zCONE:       zDrawCone();        break;
1450      case zWEDGE:      zDrawWedge();       break;
1451      case zCURVE:      zDrawCurve();       break;
1452      case zHEMISPHERE: zDrawHemisphere();  break;
1453      case zDEFORMBOX:
1454        zDrawDeformBox(Assembly1[PartID].DeformRightX,
1455                                  Assembly1[PartID].DeformLeftX,
                                    Assembly1[PartID].DeformUpY,
```

```
1456
            Assembly1[PartID].DeformDownY);
1457                                         break;
1458      case zHALFCYL:     zDrawHalfCylinder(); break;
1459      case zBULGE:       zDrawBulge();        break;
1460      case zNULL: break;
1461      default:    break;
1462      }                                /* end of switch() block */
1463   zSetHierarchyMode(FALSE);       /* disable hierarchy modeling */
1464   }                        /* end of subassembly rendering loop */
1465 return;
1466 }
1467
1468 /*
1469 --------------------------------------------------------------------
1470                    Animation playback functions
1471 --------------------------------------------------------------------
1472            Display the next frame of the animation.
1473 --------------------------------------------------------------------
1474                                                                  */
1475 static void zShowNextFrame(HWND hWnd)
1476 {
1477    HDC hDC;
1478 if (bUseDisk==TRUE) goto DISK_PLAYBACK; /* using memory or disk? */
1479
1480 /* ----------- manage memory-based frame animation ----------- */
1481 MEMORY_PLAYBACK:
1482 if (AnimationReady==FALSE) return;
1483 if (bAnimationLoaded==FALSE) return;
1484 if (Redisplay==TRUE) goto DISPLAY_FRAME;
1485 if (Pause==TRUE) return;
1486 if (FrameDirection==zFORWARD)              /* if a forward loop... */
1487    {
1488    FrameNum++;                         /* increment the frame number */
1489    if (FrameNum > zFINALFRAME)             /* if at end of loop... */
1490      FrameNum= zFIRSTFRAME;                      /* ...wraparound */
1491    }
1492 if (FrameDirection==zREVERSE)              /* if a reverse loop... */
1493    {
1494    FrameNum--;                         /* decrement the frame number */
1495    if (FrameNum < zFIRSTFRAME)         /* but if at end of loop... */
1496      FrameNum= zFINALFRAME;                      /* ...wraparound */
1497    }
1498 DISPLAY_FRAME:
1499 hDC= GetDC(hWnd);                          /* grab a display-context */
1500 SelectObject(hFDC,BitmapHandles[FrameNum-1]);   /* select handle */
1501 BitBlt(hDC,0,0,                    /* copy the bitmap to the display */
1502          zFRAMEWIDE,zFRAMEHIGH,hFDC,0,0,SRCCOPY);
1503 ReleaseDC(hWnd,hDC);                  /* release the display-context */
1504 return;
1505
1506 /* ------------ manage disk-based frame animation ------------ */
1507 DISK_PLAYBACK:
1508 if (bAnimationHalted==TRUE) return;
1509 if (Redisplay==TRUE) goto SAME_FRAME;
1510 if (Pause==TRUE) return;
1511 if (FrameDirection==zFORWARD)              /* if a forward loop... */
1512    {
1513    FrameNum++;
1514    if (FrameNum > zFINALFRAME) FrameNum= zFIRSTFRAME;
1515    }
```

```
1516    if (FrameDirection==zREVERSE)                    /* if a reverse loop... */
1517      {
1518      FrameNum--;
1519      if (FrameNum < zFIRSTFRAME) FrameNum= zFINALFRAME;
1520      }
1521    SAME_FRAME:
1522    hDC= GetDC(hWnd);                                /* grab a display-context */
1523    bFrameLoaded= zLoadFrame(hFrame,    /* load the binary image file */
1524                        (LPSTR)FrameFiles[FrameNum-1]);
1525    if (bFrameLoaded==FALSE)                         /* if an error occurred... */
1526      {
1527      bAnimationHalted= TRUE;
1528      MessageBeep(0);
1529      LoadString(hInst,IDS_Unexpected,lpCaption,Max);
1530      LoadString(hInst,IDS_Disk3,lpMessage,MaxText);
1531      TimerCounter= zTIMER_PAUSE;
1532      MessageBox(GetFocus(),lpMessage,lpCaption,MB_OK);
1533      return;
1534      }
1535    BitBlt(hDC,0,0,                          /* copy the bitmap to the display */
1536           zFRAMEWIDE,zFRAMEHIGH,hFrameDC,0,0,SRCCOPY);
1537    ReleaseDC(hWnd,hDC);                     /* release the display-context */
1538    return;
1539    }
1540    /*
1541    ------------------------------------------------------------------
1542                 Load the animation sequence from disk.
1543    ------------------------------------------------------------------
1544                                                                      */
1545    static void zLoadAnimation(HWND hWnd)
1546    {
1547      HDC hDC;
1548      int Bitmaps;
1549
1550    if (FrameReady==FALSE)
1551      {
1552      MessageBeep(0);
1553      LoadString(hInst,IDS_NotReady,lpCaption,Max);
1554      LoadString(hInst,IDS_NoFrame,lpMessage,MaxText);
1555      MessageBox(GetFocus(),lpMessage,lpCaption,MB_OK);
1556      return;
1557      }
1558    if (bAnimationLoaded==TRUE)
1559      {
1560      MessageBeep(0);
1561      LoadString(hInst,IDS_Unexpected,lpCaption,Max);
1562      LoadString(hInst,IDS_Disk4,lpMessage,MaxText);
1563      TimerCounter= zTIMER_PAUSE;
1564      MessageBox(GetFocus(),lpMessage,lpCaption,MB_OK);
1565      return;
1566      }
1567    if (bPrevLoadAttempt==TRUE)
1568      {
1569      MessageBeep(0);
1570      LoadString(hInst,IDS_Unexpected,lpCaption,Max);
1571      LoadString(hInst,IDS_Disk5,lpMessage,MaxText);
1572      TimerCounter= zTIMER_PAUSE;
1573      MessageBox(GetFocus(),lpMessage,lpCaption,MB_OK);
1574      return;
1575      }
1576    bPrevLoadAttempt= TRUE;
```

```
1577
1578   /* ------------- create bitmaps to hold the frames ------------ */
1579   GlobalCompact((DWORD)-1L);
1580   hDC= GetDC(hWnd);
1581   hFDC= CreateCompatibleDC(hDC);
1582   for (LoopCount= 1; LoopCount<= zNUMCELS; LoopCount++)
1583     {                            /* for each cel in the animation... */
1584     BitmapHandles[LoopCount-1]=              /* create a bitmap... */
1585        CreateCompatibleBitmap(hDC,zFRAMEWIDE,zFRAMEHIGH);
1586     if (BitmapHandles[LoopCount-1]==NULL)   /* if error occurs... */
1587       goto BITMAPS_NOT_OK;       /* ...jump out of loop and tidy up */
1588     }
1589   goto BITMAPS_OK;               /* if OK, jump past error-handler */
1590
1591   /* ------------------ bitmap error-handler ------------------ */
1592   BITMAPS_NOT_OK:
1593   for (Bitmaps= LoopCount-1; Bitmaps>= 1; Bitmaps--)
1594     {          /* for each bitmap that was successfully created... */
1595     DeleteObject(BitmapHandles[Bitmaps-1]);          /* ...delete it */
1596     }
1597   DeleteDC(hFDC);                    /* delete the compatible DC */
1598   ReleaseDC(hWnd,hDC);              /* release the display-context */
1599   bUseDisk= TRUE; AnimationReady= TRUE;        /* reset the tokens */
1600   LoadString(hInst,IDS_Status,lpCaption,Max);
1601   LoadString(hInst,IDS_Disk6,lpMessage,MaxText);
1602   MessageBox(GetFocus(),lpMessage,lpCaption,MB_OK); /* message box */
1603   return;                          /* ...and return to caller */
1604
1605   BITMAPS_OK: ReleaseDC(hWnd,hDC);  /* release the display-context */
1606
1607   /* ------------ load frame files into the bitmaps ------------ */
1608   for (LoopCount= 1; LoopCount<= zNUMCELS; LoopCount++)
1609     {                            /* for each cel in the animation... */
1610     bFrameLoaded= zLoadFrame(BitmapHandles[LoopCount-1],   /* load */
1611                           (LPSTR)FrameFiles[LoopCount-1]);
1612     if (bFrameLoaded==FALSE)         /* if disk error occurred... */
1613       goto DISK_ERROR;               /* jump to error-handler */
1614     }
1615   goto DISK_OK;                /* if OK, jump past the error-handler */
1616
1617   /* -------------------- disk error-handler -------------------- */
1618   DISK_ERROR:
1619     for (LoopCount= 1; LoopCount<= zNUMCELS; LoopCount++)
1620       {               /* for each bitmap handle in the animation... */
1621       DeleteObject(BitmapHandles[LoopCount-1]);    /* delete it... */
1622       }
1623     DeleteDC(hFDC);      /* ...and delete the memory display-context */
1624     return;
1625
1626   /* -------------------- tidy up and return -------------------- */
1627   DISK_OK:
1628   hPrevF= SelectObject(hFDC,BitmapHandles[0]);
1629   bAnimationLoaded= TRUE;
1630   AnimationReady= TRUE;
1631   bAnimationSaved= TRUE;
1632   MessageBeep(0);
1633   LoadString(hInst,IDS_AnimReady,lpCaption,Max);
1634   LoadString(hInst,IDS_Disk7,lpMessage,MaxText);
1635   MessageBox(GetFocus(),lpMessage,lpCaption,MB_OK);
1636   return;
1637   }
```

```
1638   /*
1639   -------------------------------------------------------------------
1640                     Reset the animation frame rate.
1641   -------------------------------------------------------------------
1642                                                                   */
1643   static void zSetFrameRate(HWND hWnd, WORD wNewRate)
1644   {
1645   if (TimerExists==FALSE)
1646     {
1647     wFrameRate= wPrevRate;
1648     MessageBeep(0);
1649     LoadString(hInst,IDS_NotReady,lpCaption,Max);
1650     LoadString(hInst,IDS_NoReset,lpMessage,MaxText);
1651     MessageBox(GetFocus(),lpMessage,lpCaption,MB_OK);
1652     return;
1653     }
1654
1655   /* ---------- remove the check-mark from the menu ------------- */
1656   switch (wPrevRate)
1657     {   /* use hMenu from case WM_INITMENUPOPUP in message handler */
1658     case 55:  CheckMenuItem(hMenu,IDM_FPS182,MF_UNCHECKED); break;
1659     case 110: CheckMenuItem(hMenu,IDM_FPS91, MF_UNCHECKED); break;
1660     case 165: CheckMenuItem(hMenu,IDM_FPS61, MF_UNCHECKED); break;
1661     case 220: CheckMenuItem(hMenu,IDM_FPS45, MF_UNCHECKED); break;
1662     case 275: CheckMenuItem(hMenu,IDM_FPS36, MF_UNCHECKED); break;
1663     case 330: CheckMenuItem(hMenu,IDM_FPS30, MF_UNCHECKED); break;
1664     }
1665
1666   /* --------- destroy existing timer, create new timer ---------- */
1667   KillTimer(hWnd,1);
1668   TimerID1= SetTimer(hWnd,1,wNewRate,(FARPROC) NULL);
1669   if (TimerID1==0)
1670     {
1671     LoadString(hInst,IDS_NotReady,lpCaption,Max);
1672     LoadString(hInst,IDS_CannotReset,lpMessage,MaxText);
1673     MessageBox(GetFocus(),lpMessage,lpCaption,MB_OK);
1674     TimerExists= FALSE;
1675     return;
1676     }
1677
1678   /* ------------------ add check-mark to menu ------------------ */
1679   switch (wFrameRate)
1680     {
1681     case 55:  CheckMenuItem(hMenu,IDM_FPS182,MF_CHECKED); break;
1682     case 110: CheckMenuItem(hMenu,IDM_FPS91, MF_CHECKED); break;
1683     case 165: CheckMenuItem(hMenu,IDM_FPS61, MF_CHECKED); break;
1684     case 220: CheckMenuItem(hMenu,IDM_FPS45, MF_CHECKED); break;
1685     case 275: CheckMenuItem(hMenu,IDM_FPS36, MF_CHECKED); break;
1686     case 330: CheckMenuItem(hMenu,IDM_FPS30, MF_CHECKED); break;
1687     }
1688   return;
1689   }
1690   /*
1691   -------------------------------------------------------------------
1692                     End of the C source file
1693   -------------------------------------------------------------------
1694                                                                   */
```

C-5 Source listings for the interactive, animated, forward kinematics editor, kinematx.c, consisting of .def, .h, .rc, and .c files. See Appendix B for the toolkits which must be linked in to build this application. See Appendix A for instructions on building the demo.

```
0001   NAME          DEMO4115
0002   DESCRIPTION   'Copyright 1993 Lee Adams.  All rights reserved.'
0003   EXETYPE       WINDOWS
0004   STUB          'WINSTUB.EXE'
0005   CODE          PRELOAD MOVEABLE
0006   DATA          PRELOAD MOVEABLE MULTIPLE
0007   HEAPSIZE      1024
0008   STACKSIZE     8192
0009   EXPORTS       zMessageHandler
0001   /*
0002   ------------------------------------------------------------------
0003                     Include file kinematx.h
0004           Copyright 1993 Lee Adams.  All rights reserved.
0005      Include this file in the .RC resource script file and in the
0006      .C source file.  It contains function prototypes, menu ID
0007      constants, and string ID constants.
0008   ------------------------------------------------------------------
0009   ------------------------------------------------------------------
0010                        Function prototypes
0011   ------------------------------------------------------------------
0012                                                                  */
0013   #if !defined(zRCFILE)               /* if not an .rc file... */
0014      LONG FAR PASCAL zMessageHandler(HWND, unsigned, WORD, LONG);
0015      int PASCAL WinMain(HANDLE,HANDLE,LPSTR,int);
0016      HWND zInitMainWindow(HANDLE);
0017      BOOL zInitClass(HANDLE);
0018   static void zClear(HWND);                /* blank the display window */
0019   static void zInitFrame(HWND);               /* creates hidden frame */
0020   static void zShowNextFrame(HWND);            /* the playback engine */
0021   static void zSetFrameRate(HWND,WORD);        /* resets the timer */
0022   static void zSaveAnimation(HWND);     /* saves animation sequence */
0023   static void zPreviewFirstFrame(HWND);        /* previews frame 1 */
0024   static void zPreviewFinalFrame(HWND);        /* previews frame 36 */
0025   static void zSelectPreviewFrame(int);     /* select preview frame */
0026   static BOOL zBuildFrame(int,HWND,LPSTR);      /* builds a frame */
0027   static void zDrawCel(int);                    /* draws a cel */
0028   static void zInitializeModel(void);     /* initialize kinematics */
0029   static void zLoadAnimation(HWND);     /* loads animation sequence */
0030   static void zCopyToDisplay(HWND);      /* copies frame to display */
0031   static void zClearHiddenFrame(void);       /* clears hidden frame */
0032   static BOOL zSaveScript(LPSTR);           /* saves script database */
0033   static BOOL zLoadScript(LPSTR);           /* loads script database */
0034   #endif
0035   /*
0036   ------------------------------------------------------------------
0037                       Menu ID constants
0038   ------------------------------------------------------------------
0039                                                                  */
0040   #define IDM_New            1
0041   #define IDM_Open           2
0042   #define IDM_Save           3
0043   #define IDM_SaveAs         4
0044   #define IDM_Exit           5
0045
0046   #define IDM_Undo           6
0047   #define IDM_Cut            7
0048   #define IDM_Copy           8
0049   #define IDM_Paste          9
```

```
0050    #define IDM_Delete              10
0051
0052    #define IDM_LoadAnimation       11
0053    #define IDM_RunForward          12
0054    #define IDM_RunReverse          13
0055    #define IDM_Clear               14
0056    #define IDM_StopAnimation       15
0057    #define IDM_SaveAnimation       16
0058    #define IDM_PreviewFirst        17
0059    #define IDM_PreviewFinal        18
0060    #define IDM_UseShaded           19
0061    #define IDM_UseWireframe        20
0062    #define IDM_SaveScript1         21
0063    #define IDM_SaveScript2         22
0064    #define IDM_SaveScript3         23
0065    #define IDM_SaveScript4         24
0066    #define IDM_SaveScript5         25
0067    #define IDM_LoadScript1         26
0068    #define IDM_LoadScript2         27
0069    #define IDM_LoadScript3         28
0070    #define IDM_LoadScript4         29
0071    #define IDM_LoadScript5         30
0072
0073    #define IDM_FPS182              31
0074    #define IDM_FPS91               32
0075    #define IDM_FPS61               33
0076    #define IDM_FPS45               34
0077    #define IDM_FPS36               35
0078    #define IDM_FPS30               36
0079
0080    #define IDM_About               37
0081    #define IDM_License             38
0082    #define IDM_GeneralHelp         39
0083    /*
0084    ----------------------------------------------------------------
0085                                      String ID constants
0086    ----------------------------------------------------------------
0087                                                                  */
0088    #define IDS_Caption         1
0089    #define IDS_Warning         2
0090    #define IDS_NoMouse         3
0091    #define IDS_About           4
0092    #define IDS_AboutText       5
0093    #define IDS_License         6
0094    #define IDS_LicenseText     7
0095    #define IDS_Help            8
0096    #define IDS_HelpText        9
0097    #define IDS_Completed       10
0098    #define IDS_Error           11
0099    #define IDS_NotReady        12
0100    #define IDS_Ready           13
0101    #define IDS_BuildBefore     14
0102    #define IDS_Already         15
0103    #define IDS_InsufMem1       16
0104
0105    #define IDS_InsufMem2       17
0106    #define IDS_NoTimer         18
0107    #define IDS_NoReset         19
0108    #define IDS_CannotReset     20
0109    #define IDS_NoFrame         21
0110    #define IDS_AnimReady       22
```

```
0111
0112    #define IDS_Unexpected   44
0113    #define IDS_Status       45
0114    #define IDS_Disk1        46
0115    #define IDS_Disk2        47
0116    #define IDS_Disk3        48
0117    #define IDS_Disk4        49
0118    #define IDS_Disk5        50
0119    #define IDS_Disk6        51
0120    #define IDS_Disk7        52
0121    #define IDS_Disk8        53
0122    #define IDS_Disk9        54
0123    #define IDS_Disk10       55
0124    #define IDS_Disk11       56
0125    #define IDS_Disk12       57
0126    #define IDS_Disk13       58
0127    #define IDS_Disk14       59
0128    #define IDS_Disk15       60
0129    #define IDS_Disk16       61
0130    #define IDS_Disk17       62
0131    #define IDS_Disk18       63
0132    #define IDS_Disk19       64
0133    #define IDS_Disk20       65
0134    #define IDS_Disk21       66
0135    #define IDS_Disk22       67
0136    #define IDS_Disk23       68
0137    #define IDS_Disk24       69
0138    #define IDS_Disk25       70
0139    #define IDS_Disk26       71
0140    #define IDS_NoBg         72
0141    #define IDS_BgAlready    73
0142    #define IDS_InsufMemBg   74
0143    #define IDS_ReqdHdwr1    75
0144    #define IDS_ReqdHdwr2    76
0145    #define IDS_Build        77
0146    #define IDS_ToCancel     78
0147    #define IDS_Loading      79
0148    #define IDS_Previewing   80
0149    /*
0150    ----------------------------------------------------------------
0151                        End of include file
0152    ----------------------------------------------------------------
0153                                                                  */
0001    /*
0002    ----------------------------------------------------------------
0003                    Resource script file kinematx.rc
0004              Copyright 1993 Lee Adams.  All rights reserved.
0005         This file defines the menu resources, the accelerator key
0006         resources, and the string resources that will be used by the
0007         demonstration application at runtime.
0008    ----------------------------------------------------------------
0009                                                                  */
0010    #define zRCFILE
0011    #include <WINDOWS.H>
0012    #include "KINEMATX.H"
0013    /*
0014    ----------------------------------------------------------------
0015                            Script for menus
0016    ----------------------------------------------------------------
0017                                                                  */
0018    KTXMENUS MENU
```

```
0019    BEGIN
0020    POPUP "&File"
0021      BEGIN
0022        MENUITEM "&New", IDM_New, GRAYED
0023        MENUITEM "&Open...", IDM_Open, GRAYED
0024        MENUITEM "&Save", IDM_Save, GRAYED
0025        MENUITEM "Save &As...", IDM_SaveAs, GRAYED
0026        MENUITEM SEPARATOR
0027        MENUITEM "E&xit", IDM_Exit
0028      END
0029    POPUP "&Edit"
0030      BEGIN
0031        MENUITEM "&Undo\tAlt+BkSp", IDM_Undo, GRAYED
0032        MENUITEM SEPARATOR
0033        MENUITEM "Cu&t\tShift+Del", IDM_Cut, GRAYED
0034        MENUITEM "&Copy\tCtrl+Ins", IDM_Copy, GRAYED
0035        MENUITEM "&Paste\tShift+Ins", IDM_Paste, GRAYED
0036        MENUITEM "&Delete\tDel", IDM_Delete, GRAYED
0037      END
0038    POPUP "&Run"
0039      BEGIN
0040        MENUITEM "&Load Animation", IDM_LoadAnimation
0041        MENUITEM SEPARATOR
0042        MENUITEM "Run &Forward", IDM_RunForward
0043        MENUITEM "Run &Reverse", IDM_RunReverse
0044        MENUITEM "Free&zeframe", IDM_StopAnimation
0045        POPUP "S&et Speed..."
0046          BEGIN
0047            MENUITEM "&18 fps", IDM_FPS182, CHECKED
0048            MENUITEM " &9 fps", IDM_FPS91
0049            MENUITEM " &6 fps", IDM_FPS61
0050            MENUITEM " &5 fps", IDM_FPS45
0051            MENUITEM " &4 fps", IDM_FPS36
0052            MENUITEM " &3 fps", IDM_FPS30
0053          END
0054        MENUITEM SEPARATOR
0055        MENUITEM "&Clear Viewport", IDM_Clear
0056        MENUITEM SEPARATOR
0057        POPUP "&Production..."
0058          BEGIN
0059            MENUITEM "&Build Animation", IDM_SaveAnimation
0060            MENUITEM SEPARATOR
0061            MENUITEM "Pre&view First Frame", IDM_PreviewFirst
0062            MENUITEM "Prev&iew Final Frame", IDM_PreviewFinal
0063            MENUITEM SEPARATOR
0064            MENUITEM "Use &shaded solids", IDM_UseShaded
0065            MENUITEM "Use &wireframe mode", IDM_UseWireframe
0066          END
0067        POPUP "&Scripts..."
0068          BEGIN
0069            MENUITEM "Save Script &1", IDM_SaveScript1
0070            MENUITEM "Save Script &2", IDM_SaveScript2
0071            MENUITEM "Save Script &3", IDM_SaveScript3
0072            MENUITEM "Save Script &4", IDM_SaveScript4
0073            MENUITEM "Save Script &5", IDM_SaveScript5
0074            MENUITEM SEPARATOR
0075            MENUITEM "Load &Script 1", IDM_LoadScript1
0076            MENUITEM "Load S&cript 2", IDM_LoadScript2
0077            MENUITEM "Load Sc&ript 3", IDM_LoadScript3
0078            MENUITEM "Load Scr&ipt 4", IDM_LoadScript4
0079            MENUITEM "Load Scrip&t 5", IDM_LoadScript5
```

```
0080          END
0081       END
0082    POPUP "&Using"
0083       BEGIN
0084          MENUITEM "&About", IDM_About
0085          MENUITEM "&License", IDM_License
0086          MENUITEM SEPARATOR
0087          MENUITEM "&How to Use", IDM_GeneralHelp
0088       END
0089    END
0090  /*
0091  -----------------------------------------------------------------
0092                    Script for accelerator keys
0093  -----------------------------------------------------------------
0094                                                                  */
0095  KTXKEYS ACCELERATORS
0096    BEGIN
0097    VK_BACK, IDM_Undo, VIRTKEY, ALT
0098    VK_DELETE, IDM_Cut, VIRTKEY, SHIFT
0099    VK_INSERT, IDM_Copy, VIRTKEY, CONTROL
0100    VK_INSERT, IDM_Paste, VIRTKEY, SHIFT
0101    VK_DELETE, IDM_Delete,VIRTKEY
0102    END
0103  /*
0104  -----------------------------------------------------------------
0105                         Script for strings
0106    If you are typing this listing, set your right margin to 255
0107    characters so you can create lengthy strings without embedded
0108    carriage returns.  The line wraparounds in the following
0109    STRINGTABLE listing are used only for readability.
0110  -----------------------------------------------------------------
0111                                                                  */
0112  STRINGTABLE
0113    BEGIN
0114       IDS_Caption      "Kinematics Editor"
0115       IDS_Warning      "Warning"
0116       IDS_NoMouse      "No mouse found.  Some features of this
                  demonstration program may require a mouse."
0117       IDS_About        "About this program"
0118       IDS_AboutText    "This is a demo from Windcrest McGraw-Hill
                  book 4115.  Copyright- 1993 Lee Adams.  All rights reserved."
0119       IDS_License      "License Agreement"
0120       IDS_LicenseText "You can use this code as part of your own
                  software product subject to the License Agreement and
                  Limited Warranty in Windcrest McGraw-Hill book 4115 and on
                  its companion disk."
0121       IDS_Help         "How to use this kinematics demo"
0122       IDS_HelpText     "For animation playback pick Load Animation
                  then Run Forward from the Run menu.  To build and save an
                  animation, choose the Production submenu.  To save or load a
                  kinematics script choose the Scripts submenu.  Also see the
                  book."
0123       IDS_Completed    "Task completed OK"
0124       IDS_Error        "Runtime error"
0125       IDS_NotReady     "Animation not ready"
0126       IDS_Ready        "Animation ready"
0127       IDS_BuildBefore "Animation frames not ready for playback."
0128       IDS_Already      "The hidden frame has already been created."
0129       IDS_InsufMem1    "Unable to create hidden-frame because
                  insufficient global memory.  Animation functions
                  unavailable.  Close other applications before restarting
```

```
        this demo."
0130    IDS_NoTimer      "Unable to create a timer.  Animation
        functions unavailable.  Restart this demo after closing
        other applications that may be using timers."
0131    IDS_NoReset      "Create hidden frame before attempting to
        reset timer."
0132    IDS_CannotReset "Unable to reset the timer."
0133    IDS_NoFrame      "Hidden frame not yet created."
0134    IDS_AnimReady    "Animation ready"
0135    IDS_Unexpected   "Unexpected animation condition"
0136    IDS_Status       "Animation status"
0137    IDS_Disk1        "Animation sequence already saved to disk."
0138    IDS_Disk2        "Animation sequence saved to disk."
0139    IDS_Disk3        "Unable to load next frame from disk.
        Animation halted."
0140    IDS_Disk4        "Animation sequence already loaded from disk."
0141    IDS_Disk5        "Previous load failed.  Cancelling this
        attempt."
0142    IDS_Disk6        "Not enough memory available to store
        animation sequence in memory.  Each frame will be loaded as
        needed from disk during playback."
0143    IDS_Disk7        "Animation sequence loaded in memory."
0144    IDS_Disk8        "Previous save failed.  Cancelling this
        attempt."
0145    IDS_Disk9        "No hidden-frame exists.  No frame saved to
        disk."
0146    IDS_Disk10       "Unable to retrieve bitmap data structure."
0147    IDS_Disk11       "Bit array is too long to save to disk in a
        single pass."
0148    IDS_Disk12       "Cannot create memory buffer for disk write."
0149    IDS_Disk13       "Unable to copy bits from bitmap to buffer."
0150    IDS_Disk14       "File already exists.  Overwrite existing
        file?"
0151    IDS_Disk15       "Unable to open the file for writing."
0152    IDS_Disk16       "Unable to write to the opened file."
0153    IDS_Disk17       "Unable to close the file after writing."
0154    IDS_Disk18       "No memory bitmap exists.  Unable to load from
        disk."
0155    IDS_Disk19       "Image file is larger than animation frame.
        No file loaded."
0156    IDS_Disk20       "Cannot create memory buffer for file read."
0157    IDS_Disk21       "Unable to open the file for reading.  Be sure
        you have saved an animation sequence to disk before
        attempting to load it."
0158    IDS_Disk22       "An error occurred while reading the file."
0159    IDS_Disk23       "Windows must be using same color mode as when
        this animation was saved, either 2, 16, or 256 colors.  To
        run the existing animation, use Windows Setup to switch
        color modes.  Otherwise rebuild the animation in the current
        mode."
0160    IDS_Disk24       "Unable to close the file after reading."
0161    IDS_Disk25       "Unable to copy bits from buffer to bitmap."
0162    IDS_Disk26       "Not all frames saved to disk because
        insufficient space available on disk or because the frames
        have already been saved to disk or because you interrupted
        the build process."
0163    IDS_NoBg         "Hidden background image not yet created."
0164    IDS_BgAlready    "The hidden background bitmap has already been
        created."
0165    IDS_InsufMemBg "Insufficient global memory for background
        bitmap."
```

```
0166      IDS_ReqdHdwr1   "Graphics hardware not supported"
0167      IDS_ReqdHdwr2   "CGA, HGA, or EGA graphics adapter detected.
          This application requires either an industry-standard VGA, a
          VESA-standard SuperVGA, an 8514/a, or an XGA graphics
          adapter and compatible display."
0168      IDS_Build       "Animation build process"
0169      IDS_ToCancel    "Ready to begin building the animation
          sequence.  To interrupt a build session in progress, click
          the right mouse button.  To begin the build, select OK now.
          See the book for further information."
0170      IDS_Loading     "Loading animation..."
0171      IDS_Previewing  "Building preview frame..."
0172   END
0173 /*
0174 -------------------------------------------------------------------
0175                      End of resource script file
0176 -------------------------------------------------------------------
0177                                                                  */
0001 /*
0002 -------------------------------------------------------------------
0003                      3D kinematics animation editor
0004 -------------------------------------------------------------------
0005    Source file:  kinematx.c
0006    Release version:  1.2                    Programmer:  Lee Adams
0007    Type:  C source file for Windows application development.
0008    Supported compilers:  Explicit compatibility with Microsoft
0009      QuickC for Windows v1.00 and Borland Turbo C++ for Windows
0010      v3.0.  Nominal compatibility with all Windows-compatible C
0011      and C++ compilers such as Borland C++, Zortech C++, Watcom C,
0012      and Microsoft C/C++.
0013    Memory model:  medium.
0014    Build notes:  Do not use the load optimization feature of the
0015      Resource Compiler (or use the command-line -K switch).
0016      For trouble-free compiling follow the tips in the book.
0017    Project notes:  Load the kinematx.mak project file if you are
0018      using QuickC for Windows.  Load the kinematx.prj project file
0019      if you are using Turbo C++ for Windows.  Refer to the book if
0020      you are using another compiler.  The following files are
0021      needed to build the executable:
0022        kinematx.def    module definition file
0023        kinematx.h      include file
0024        kinematx.rc     resource script file
0025        kinematx.c      C source file
0026        engine3d.h      include file for 3D functions
0027        engine3d.c      3D toolkit
0028        shapes3d.h      include file for 3D solids
0029        shapes3d.c      3D shapes toolkit
0030        deform3d.h      include file for deformed solids
0031        deform3d.c      3D deformation toolkit
0032        assemb3d.h      include file for hierarchical modeling
0033        assemb3d.c      3D hierarchical modeling toolkit
0034        knmatx3d.h      include file for kinematics functions
0035        knmatx3d.c      3D kinematics toolkit
0036        disk3d.h        include file for disk functions
0037        disk3d.c        image save/load toolkit
0038        lights3d.h      include file for light-source functions
0039        lights3d.c      light-source toolkit
0040    Output and features:  Demonstrates kinematics-based control of
0041      animation sequences and storage of frames on disk as binary
0042      image files.  Demonstrates loading of frames from disk and
0043      interactive playback of animation sequence from RAM or from
```

```
0044        disk if insufficient memory available.  Demonstrates saving
0045        and loading of script files to/from disk.  The startup code
0046        automatically sizes the window to yield a client area with
0047        dimensions of 256-by-255 pixels in any graphics mode.  The
0048        menu system provides a preview mode for the first frame and
0049        final frame of the kinematics animation sequence.  You can use
0050        the menu system to toggle between wireframe and shaded modes.
0051          NUMBER OF FRAMES:  In its current implementation, the
0052        application produces an animation sequence of 36 frames.
0053        To create a sequence that uses fewer frames or more frames,
0054        you can edit lines 00159 and 00160, and then remove or add
0055        filenames as required at lines 00178 to 00186.
0056          KINEMATICS EDITING:  To experiment with kinematics by
0057        manipulating the camera position, light-source, and 3D bodies,
0058        edit the kinematics description at lines 01162 to 01305.  Then
0059        compile and run the program so you can choose Save Script
0060        from the Script... submenu of the Run menu to save your
0061        script to disk.  See the book for further guidance.
0062    Publication: Contains material from Windcrest/McGraw-Hill book
0063        4115 published by TAB BOOKS Division of McGraw-Hill Inc.
0064    License:  As purchaser of the book you are granted a royalty-
0065        free license to distribute executable files generated using
0066        this code provided you accept the conditions of the License
0067        Agreement and Limited Warranty described in the book and on
0068        the companion disk.  Government users:  This software and
0069        documentation are subject to restrictions set forth in The
0070        Rights in Technical Data and Computer Software clause at
0071        252.227-7013 and elsewhere.
0072    -----------------------------------------------------------------
0073        (c) Copyright 1991-1993 Lee Adams.  All rights reserved.
0074            Lee Adams(tm) is a trademark of Lee Adams.
0075    -----------------------------------------------------------------
0076
0077    -----------------------------------------------------------------
0078                              Include files
0079    -----------------------------------------------------------------
0080                                                                   */
0081    #include <WINDOWS.H>              /* declarations for Windows API */
0082    #include "KINEMATX.H"      /* declares function prototypes, etc. */
0083    #include "DISK3D.H"         /* declares functions in disk engine */
0084    #include "ENGINE3D.H"         /* declares functions in 3D engine */
0085    #include "SHAPES3D.H"  /* declares functions in 3D shapes module */
0086    #include "DEFORM3D.H"        /* functions in deformation module */
0087    #include "LIGHTS3D.H"   /* declares functions in lighting module */
0088    #include "ASSEMB3D.H"  /* declares functions in hierarchy module */
0089    #include "KNMATX3D.H" /* declares functions in kinematics module */
0090    #include <time.h>                   /* supports date and time */
0091
0092    /*
0093    -----------------------------------------------------------------
0094            Static variables visible throughout this file
0095    -----------------------------------------------------------------
0096                                                                   */
0097    /* ----------------- window specifications ----------------- */
0098    #define zWINDOW_WIDTH 263                    /* width of window */
0099    #define zWINDOW_HEIGHT 300                   /* depth of window */
0100    #define zFRAMEWIDE 256                     /* width of viewport */
0101    #define zFRAMEHIGH 255                     /* depth of viewport */
0102    static int WindowX, WindowY;             /* location of window */
0103
0104    /* ----------------- instance operations ----------------- */
```

```
0105   HANDLE hInst;                       /* handle to this copy of the app */
0106   static HWND MainhWnd;                   /* handle to the app's window */
0107   static HANDLE hAccel;               /* handle to the accelerator keys */
0108   static HMENU hMenu;         /* handle to an active menu at runtime */
0109   static PAINTSTRUCT ps;     /* used for Windows-generated refreshes */
0110
0111   /* -------------------- mouse and cursor --------------------- */
0112   static HCURSOR hPrevCursor;               /* handle to arrow cursor */
0113   static HCURSOR hHourGlass;            /* handle to hourglass cursor */
0114   static int MousePresent;               /* indicates if mouse found */
0115
0116   /* -------------------- runtime conditions ------------------- */
0117   static int DisplayWidth, DisplayHeight; /* resolution of display */
0118   static int DisplayBits;                 /* number of bits per pixel */
0119   static int DisplayPlanes;                 /* number of bitplanes */
0120   static DWORD MemoryMode;                   /* runtime memory mode */
0121   static DWORD Version;                     /* version of Windows */
0122   static BOOL bUseArial= TRUE;   /* FALSE, use Helv if Windows 3.0 */
0123
0124   /* ----------------- message box operations ----------------- */
0125   char lpCaption[51];             /* stores caption for message box */
0126   int Max= 50;                         /* max length of caption */
0127   char lpMessage[250];            /* stores text for message box */
0128   int MaxText= 249;                     /* max length of text */
0129   static short TextLength= 0;         /* stores wsprintf() string */
0130   static int MessageBoxChoice= 0;       /* user's selection, if any */
0131
0132   /* ---------------- persistent image operations -------------- */
0133   #define zBLANK 0
0134   #define zANIMATING  1
0135   #define zPREVIEW  2
0136   static int PaintImage= zBLANK;       /* indicates viewport status */
0137
0138   /* -------------------- timer operations -------------------- */
0139   #define zTIMER_PAUSE 3
0140   static int TimerCounter= zTIMER_PAUSE; /* timing delay mechanism */
0141   static BOOL TimerExists= FALSE;               /* timer active? */
0142   static WORD TimerID1;                            /* timer ID */
0143
0144   /* ---------------- hidden-frame operations ----------------- */
0145   static HDC hFrameDC;         /* display-context of hidden-frame */
0146   static HBITMAP hFrame;               /* bitmap of hidden-frame */
0147   static HBITMAP hPrevFrame;               /* default bitmap */
0148   BOOL FrameReady= FALSE;               /* hidden-frame ready? */
0149
0150   /* --------------------- animation engine -------------------- */
0151   static BOOL Pause= TRUE;                     /* animation paused? */
0152   static WORD wFrameRate= 55;                 /* animation rate */
0153   static WORD wPrevRate= 55;         /* remembers previous rate */
0154   #define zFORWARD 1
0155   #define zREVERSE 0
0156   static int FrameDirection= zFORWARD;       /* animation direction */
0157   static BOOL Redisplay= FALSE;         /* for refresh when paused */
0158   static BOOL AnimationReady= FALSE;  /* animation sequence ready? */
0159   static int FrameNum= 1;                     /* current frame */
0160   #define zFIRSTFRAME 1       /* first frame of animation sequence */
0161   #define zFINALFRAME 36     /* final frame of animation sequence */
0162   #define zNUMCELS 36     /* number of cels in animation sequence */
0163   static int LoopCount;                       /* loop counter */
0164
0165   /* ---------------- disk save/load operations ---------------- */
```

```
0166    int RetVal;                         /* value returned by functions */
0167    static BOOL bFrameSaved= FALSE;                  /* frame saved? */
0168    static BOOL bFrameLoaded= FALSE;                 /* frame loaded? */
0169    static BOOL bAnimationSaved= FALSE;          /* animation saved? */
0170    static BOOL bAnimationLoaded= FALSE;         /* animation loaded? */
0171    static BOOL bPrevSaveAttempt= FALSE; /* previous save attempted? */
0172    static BOOL bPrevLoadAttempt= FALSE; /* previous load attempted? */
0173    static BOOL bUseDisk= FALSE;      /* use RAM or disk for playback? */
0174    static BOOL bAnimationHalted= FALSE;         /* playback paused? */
0175    static HDC hFDC;    /* memory display-context for hidden bitmaps */
0176    static HBITMAP hPrevF;                        /* default bitmap */
0177    static HBITMAP BitmapHandles[zNUMCELS];     /* array of bitmaps */
0178    static char *FrameFiles[zNUMCELS]=
0179      {   /* array of pointers to filenames for animation frames... */
0180      "KTX01.BIT", "KTX02.BIT", "KTX03.BIT", "KTX04.BIT",
0181      "KTX05.BIT", "KTX06.BIT", "KTX07.BIT", "KTX08.BIT",
0182      "KTX09.BIT", "KTX10.BIT", "KTX11.BIT", "KTX12.BIT",
0183      "KTX13.BIT", "KTX14.BIT", "KTX15.BIT", "KTX16.BIT",
0184      "KTX17.BIT", "KTX18.BIT", "KTX19.BIT", "KTX20.BIT",
0185      "KTX21.BIT", "KTX22.BIT", "KTX23.BIT", "KTX24.BIT",
0186      "KTX25.BIT", "KTX26.BIT", "KTX27.BIT", "KTX28.BIT",
0187      "KTX29.BIT", "KTX30.BIT", "KTX31.BIT", "KTX32.BIT",
0188      "KTX33.BIT", "KTX34.BIT", "KTX35.BIT", "KTX36.BIT",
0189      };
0190
0191    /* ------------- declare data types for the script ------------- */
0192    #define zNUM_ACTORS  25 /* maximum number of objects in database */
0193
0194    static struct Header              /* data type for database header */
0195      {
0196      double FPS;                             /* frames per second */
0197      int NumBodies;                    /* number of active objects */
0198      int FirstFrame;                              /* first frame */
0199      int FinalFrame;                              /* final frame */
0200      };
0201
0202    static struct CameraDefine           /* data type for camera specs */
0203      {
0204      int Heading;                               /* camera heading */
0205      int Pitch;                                 /* camera pitch */
0206      int Distance;                /* distance from camera to target */
0207      };
0208
0209    static struct CameraPath             /* data type for camera script */
0210      {
0211      int StartFrame;                                /* start cue */
0212      int EndFrame;                                  /* stop cue */
0213      int ChgHeading;              /* camera heading change per frame */
0214      int ChgPitch;                 /* camera pitch change per frame */
0215      int ChgDistance; /* camera-to-target distance change per frame */
0216      };
0217
0218    static struct LightDefine    /* data type for light-source specs */
0219      {
0220      int Heading;                          /* light-source heading */
0221      int Elevation;                          /* light-source pitch */
0222      };
0223
0224    static struct LightPath      /* data type for light-source script */
0225      {
0226      int StartFrame;                                /* start cue */
```

```
0227     int EndFrame;                                        /* stop cue */
0228     int ChgHeading;        /* light-source heading change per frame */
0229     int ChgElevation;       /* light-source pitch change per frame */
0230     };
0231
0232   static struct ActorParams /* data type for object specifications */
0233     {
0234     int TypeOfSubobject;        /* box, cylinder, sphere, other... */
0235     int Color;                                    /* shading color */
0236     double DimensionX;                              /* dimensions... */
0237     double DimensionY;
0238     double DimensionZ;
0239     double LocationX;                                 /* location... */
0240     double LocationY:
0241     double LocationZ;
0242     double OrientationYaw;                         /* orientation... */
0243     double OrientationRoll;
0244     double OrientationPitch;
0245     double LinearVelocityDirection;           /* linear velocity... */
0246     double LinearVelocityPitch;
0247     double LinearVelocitySpeed;
0248     double RotationalVelocityYawSpeed;    /* rotational velocity... */
0249     double RotationalVelocityRollSpeed;
0250     double RotationalVelocityPitchSpeed;
0251     double LinearAccelUnitsPerSecSqd;     /* linear acceleration... */
0252     double LinearAccelSeconds;
0253     double RotationalAccelYaw;        /* rotational acceleration... */
0254     double RotationalAccelRoll;
0255     double RotationalAccelPitch;
0256     double RotationalAccelSeconds;
0257     double HeadingChangeDegreesPerSec;    /* velocity direction... */
0258     double HeadingChangeSeconds;
0259     double PitchChangeDegreesPerSec;
0260     double PitchChangeSeconds;
0261     };
0262
0263   static struct ScriptDatabase      /* data type for script database */
0264     {           /* database of 25 bodies requires 5142 bytes storage */
0265     struct Header Kinematics;                       /* 14-byte header */
0266     struct CameraDefine Cam1;         /* 6-byte camera specifications */
0267     struct CameraPath Cam1Path1;            /* 10-byte camera path */
0268     struct LightDefine Lt1;  /* 4-byte light-source specifications */
0269     struct LightPath Lt1Path1;          /* 8-byte light-source path */
0270     struct ActorParams Actor[zNUM_ACTORS];   /* 25 204-byte bodies */
0271     };
0272
0273   /* ------------ pointers and handles for script -------------- */
0274   static struct ScriptDatabase far *Script;    /* ptr to structure */
0275   static GLOBALHANDLE ScriptHandle;      /* handle to memory buffer */
0276   static char *ScriptFiles[5]=
0277     {              /* array of pointers to filenames for scripts... */
0278     "SCRIPT01.SCR", "SCRIPT02.SCR", "SCRIPT03.SCR",
0279     "SCRIPT04.SCR", "SCRIPT05.SCR",
0280     };
0281   static BOOL bScriptLoaded= FALSE;          /* script file loaded? */
0282   static BOOL bScriptSaved= FALSE;            /* script file saved? */
0283
0284   /*
0285   -------------------------------------------------------------------
0286                   Entry point for the application
0287   -------------------------------------------------------------------
```

```
0288                                                                   */
0289    int PASCAL WinMain(HANDLE hInstance, HANDLE hPrevInstance,
0290                       LPSTR lpCmdLine, int nCmdShow)
0291    {
0292      MSG msg;                              /* holds incoming messages */
0293      HWND hWndPrev;                 /* handle to previous copy of app */
0294      HWND hDesktopWnd;                 /* handle to the entire display */
0295      HDC hDCcaps;           /* display-context for the entire display */
0296      RECT rcClientReqd;       /* size of viewport before adjustment */
0297      int AdjustX, AdjustY; /* amount to adjust to ensure 256-by-255 */
0298
0299    /* -------------- ensure only one copy is running -------------- */
0300    hWndPrev = FindWindow("KTXDEMO", "DEMO4115");
0301    if (hWndPrev != NULL)      /* if another app named DEMO4115 of... */
0302       {                 /* class KTXDEMO is already running, then... */
0303       BringWindowToTop(hWndPrev);              /* ...use it instead... */
0304       return FALSE;                     /* ...and cancel this launch */
0305       }
0306
0307    /* ------------- display the splash signon notice ------------- */
0308    MessageBoxChoice= MessageBox(GetFocus(),
0309    "Animated kinematics sampler from Windcrest McGraw-Hill book 4115",
0310    "Copyright- 1993 Lee Adams", MB_OKCANCEL);
0311    if (MessageBoxChoice == IDCANCEL) return FALSE;
0312
0313    /* --------------- determine version of Windows --------------- */
0314    Version= (DWORD)GetVersion();
0315    if ((LOBYTE(LOWORD(Version))==3) &&
0316       (HIBYTE(LOWORD(Version))==0))
0317       {                       /* if running Windows version 3.0... */
0318       bUseArial= FALSE;            /* ...use Helv font in client area */
0319       }
0320    else
0321       {              /* ...else if running Windows 3.1 or newer... */
0322       bUseArial= TRUE;            /* ...use Arial font in client area */
0323       }
0324
0325    /* --------- determine capabilities of screen display ---------- */
0326    hDesktopWnd= GetDesktopWindow();
0327    hDCcaps= GetDC(hDesktopWnd);
0328    DisplayWidth= GetDeviceCaps(hDCcaps,HORZRES);
0329    DisplayHeight= GetDeviceCaps(hDCcaps,VERTRES);
0330    DisplayBits= GetDeviceCaps(hDCcaps,BITSPIXEL);
0331    DisplayPlanes= GetDeviceCaps(hDCcaps,PLANES);
0332    ReleaseDC(hDesktopWnd,hDCcaps);
0333
0334    /* ------------- trap unsupported graphics adapters ------------ */
0335    if (DisplayWidth==720)
0336       {                                          /* if HGA detected... */
0337       LoadString(hInstance,IDS_ReqdHdwr1,lpCaption,Max);
0338       LoadString(hInstance,IDS_ReqdHdwr2,lpMessage,MaxText);
0339       MessageBeep(0); MessageBox(GetFocus(),lpMessage,lpCaption,MB_OK);
0340       return FALSE;
0341       }
0342    if (DisplayWidth==640)
0343       {
0344       if ((DisplayHeight==350)||(DisplayHeight==200))
0345          {                     /* if EGA or CGA detected... */
0346          LoadString(hInstance,IDS_ReqdHdwr1,lpCaption,Max);
0347          LoadString(hInstance,IDS_ReqdHdwr2,lpMessage,MaxText);
0348          MessageBeep(0);
```

```
0349       MessageBox(GetFocus(),lpMessage,lpCaption,MB_OK);
0350       return FALSE;
0351       }
0352    }
0353
0354    /* ------- calculate screen position to center the window ------ */
0355    WindowX= (DisplayWidth - zWINDOW_WIDTH) / 2;
0356    WindowY= (DisplayHeight - zWINDOW_HEIGHT) /2;
0357    if (WindowX < 0) WindowX= 0;
0358    if (WindowY < 0) WindowY= 0;
0359
0360    /* ---- determine memory mode (enhanced, standard, or real) ---- */
0361    MemoryMode= GetWinFlags();
0362
0363    /* ---------------- create and show the window ---------------- */
0364    hInst = hInstance;         /* store handle to this copy of the app */
0365    if (!zInitClass(hInstance)) return FALSE;    /* initialize class */
0366    MainhWnd = zInitMainWindow(hInstance);      /* initialize window */
0367    if (!MainhWnd) return FALSE;         /* if error, cancel startup */
0368    ShowWindow(MainhWnd, nCmdShow);          /* show the window */
0369    UpdateWindow(MainhWnd);                 /* force a refresh */
0370    hAccel= LoadAccelerators(hInstance,"KTXKEYS");  /* activate keys */
0371
0372    /* -------------- enforce a 256-by-255 viewport --------------- */
0373    GetClientRect(MainhWnd, &rcClientReqd);          /* get dimensions */
0374    AdjustX=           /* compare actual width to desired width... */
0375            zFRAMEWIDE - (rcClientReqd.right + 1);
0376    AdjustY=            /* compare actual height to desired height... */
0377            zFRAMEHIGH - (rcClientReqd.bottom + 1);
0378    if ((AdjustX != 0)||(AdjustY != 0)) /* if adjustment required... */
0379       {
0380       SetWindowPos(MainhWnd, (HWND)NULL,
0381                   WindowX, WindowY,
0382                   zWINDOW_WIDTH + AdjustX,       /* resize the width */
0383                   zWINDOW_HEIGHT + AdjustY,    /* resize the height */
0384                   SWP_NOZORDER);
0385       }
0386
0387    /* --------------------- check for mouse --------------------- */
0388    MousePresent = GetSystemMetrics(SM_MOUSEPRESENT);
0389    if (!MousePresent)                          /* if no mouse found... */
0390       {                      /* ...display a cautionary warning */
0391       LoadString(hInst,IDS_Warning,lpCaption,Max);
0392       LoadString(hInst,IDS_NoMouse,lpMessage,MaxText);
0393       MessageBox(GetFocus(),lpMessage,lpCaption,MB_OK);
0394       }
0395
0396    /* ---------------- initialize the hidden-frame --------------- */
0397    zInitFrame(MainhWnd); /* is used for software-controlled refresh */
0398
0399    /* ---------- allocate memory for the script database ---------- */
0400    ScriptHandle=               /* allocate a buffer in global heap */
0401       GlobalAlloc(GMEM_MOVEABLE, sizeof (struct ScriptDatabase));
0402    if (ScriptHandle == 0)        /* if memory allocation failed... */
0403       {
0404       MessageBeep(0);
0405       MessageBox(GetFocus(),
0406         "Unable to allocate memory for kinematics script.",
0407         "Insufficient system memory", MB_OK);
0408       PostQuitMessage(0);
0409       }
```

```
0410
0411    /* ---------- begin retrieving messages for the window --------- */
0412    while (GetMessage(&msg,0,0,0))
0413      {
0414      if(TranslateAccelerator(MainhWnd, hAccel, &msg)) continue;
0415      TranslateMessage(&msg);
0416      DispatchMessage(&msg);
0417      }
0418    return(msg.wParam);
0419    }
0420
0421    /*
0422    -------------------------------------------------------------------
0423                        Switcher for incoming messages
0424    -------------------------------------------------------------------
0425                                                                     */
0426    LONG FAR PASCAL zMessageHandler(HWND hWnd, unsigned message,
0427                                    WORD wParam, LONG lParam)
0428    {
0429      HDC hDCpaint;                       /* for Windows-generated refresh */
0430
0431    switch (message)
0432      {
0433      /* -------------- filter incoming timer events ------------- */
0434      case WM_TIMER:   /* slower CPUs need delay so menus can pop up */
0435         TimerCounter--;                  /* decrement the delay mechanism */
0436         if (TimerCounter > 0) break; /* do nothing if still delaying */
0437         TimerCounter++;      /* otherwise restore the mechanism and... */
0438         zShowNextFrame(hWnd); /* ...show the next frame if animating */
0439         break;
0440
0441      /* ---------------- menu system commands ---------------- */
0442      case WM_COMMAND:
0443        switch(wParam)
0444          {
0445          case IDM_New:    break;
0446          case IDM_Open:   break;
0447          case IDM_Save:   break;
0448          case IDM_SaveAs: break;
0449          case IDM_Exit:
0450              MessageBoxChoice= MessageBox(GetFocus(),
0451                "Exit the kinematics editor and return to Windows?",
0452                "Please confirm", MB_YESNO);
0453              if (MessageBoxChoice == IDYES) PostQuitMessage(0);
0454              break;
0455          case IDM_Undo:   break;
0456          case IDM_Cut:    break;
0457          case IDM_Copy:   break;
0458          case IDM_Paste:  break;
0459          case IDM_Delete: break;
0460
0461          /* ------------ manage the animation engine ------------ */
0462          case IDM_RunForward:             /* begin forward playback... */
0463              if (AnimationReady==FALSE)
0464                {
0465                MessageBeep(0);
0466                LoadString(hInst,IDS_NotReady,lpCaption,Max);
0467                LoadString(hInst,IDS_BuildBefore,lpMessage,MaxText);
0468                TimerCounter= zTIMER_PAUSE;
0469                MessageBox(GetFocus(),lpMessage,lpCaption,MB_OK);
0470                break;
```

```
0471                    }
0472                    Pause= FALSE;
0473                    PaintImage= zANIMATING;
0474                    FrameDirection= zFORWARD;
0475                    zShowNextFrame(hWnd);
0476                    break;
0477           case IDM_RunReverse:              /* begin reverse playback... */
0478                    if (AnimationReady==FALSE)
0479                      {
0480                      MessageBeep(0);
0481                      LoadString(hInst,IDS_NotReady,lpCaption,Max);
0482                      LoadString(hInst,IDS_BuildBefore,lpMessage,MaxText);
0483                      TimerCounter= zTIMER_PAUSE;
0484                      MessageBox(GetFocus(),lpMessage,lpCaption,MB_OK);
0485                      break;
0486                      }
0487                    Pause= FALSE;
0488                    PaintImage= zANIMATING;
0489                    FrameDirection= zREVERSE;
0490                    zShowNextFrame(hWnd);
0491                    break;
0492           case IDM_StopAnimation:           /* pause the playback... */
0493                    if (AnimationReady==FALSE)
0494                      {
0495                      MessageBeep(0);
0496                      LoadString(hInst,IDS_NotReady,lpCaption,Max);
0497                      LoadString(hInst,IDS_BuildBefore,lpMessage,MaxText);
0498                      TimerCounter= zTIMER_PAUSE;
0499                      MessageBox(GetFocus(),lpMessage,lpCaption,MB_OK);
0500                      break;
0501                      }
0502                    Pause= TRUE;
0503                    zShowNextFrame(hWnd);
0504                    break;
0505           case IDM_SaveAnimation:        /* save animation to disk... */
0506                    LoadString(hInst,IDS_Build,lpCaption,Max);
0507                    LoadString(hInst,IDS_ToCancel,lpMessage,MaxText);
0508                    TimerCounter= zTIMER_PAUSE;
0509                    MessageBox(GetFocus(),lpMessage,lpCaption,MB_OK);
0510                    zInitialize3D(hWnd);
0511                    SetCapture(hWnd); hPrevCursor= SetCursor(hHourGlass);
0512                    zSaveAnimation(hWnd);
0513                    LoadString(hInst,IDS_Caption,lpCaption,Max);
0514                    SetWindowText(hWnd,lpCaption);
0515                    SetCursor(hPrevCursor); ReleaseCapture();
0516                    if (bAnimationSaved==FALSE)
0517                      {
0518                      MessageBeep(0);
0519                      LoadString(hInst,IDS_NotReady,lpCaption,Max);
0520                      LoadString(hInst,IDS_Disk26,lpMessage,MaxText);
0521                      TimerCounter= zTIMER_PAUSE;
0522                      MessageBox(GetFocus(),lpMessage,lpCaption,MB_OK);
0523                      }
0524                    break;
0525           case IDM_PreviewFirst:        /* preview the first frame... */
0526                    SetCapture(hWnd);
0527                    hPrevCursor= SetCursor(hHourGlass);
0528                    LoadString(hInst,IDS_Previewing,lpCaption,Max);
0529                    SetWindowText(hWnd,lpCaption);
0530                    zPreviewFirstFrame(hWnd);
0531                    LoadString(hInst,IDS_Caption,lpCaption,Max);
```

```
0532              SetWindowText(hWnd,lpCaption);
0533              SetCursor(hPrevCursor);
0534              ReleaseCapture();
0535              PaintImage= zPREVIEW;
0536              break;
0537          case IDM_PreviewFinal:         /* preview the final frame... */
0538              SetCapture(hWnd);
0539              hPrevCursor= SetCursor(hHourGlass);
0540              LoadString(hInst,IDS_Previewing,lpCaption,Max);
0541              SetWindowText(hWnd,lpCaption);
0542              zPreviewFinalFrame(hWnd);
0543              LoadString(hInst,IDS_Caption,lpCaption,Max);
0544              SetWindowText(hWnd,lpCaption);
0545              SetCursor(hPrevCursor);
0546              ReleaseCapture();
0547              PaintImage= zPREVIEW;
0548              break;
0549          case IDM_UseShaded:        /* use fully-shaded 3D objects... */
0550              zInitialize3D(hWnd);
0551              zUseWireframeMode(FALSE);
0552              MessageBox(GetFocus(),
0553                "Using shaded solids.",
0554                "3D status report", MB_OK);
0555              break;
0556          case IDM_UseWireframe:         /* use wireframe 3D objects... */
0557              zInitialize3D(hWnd);
0558              zUseWireframeMode(TRUE);
0559              MessageBox(GetFocus(),
0560                "Using wireframe modeling mode.",
0561                "3D status report", MB_OK);
0562              break;
0563          case IDM_LoadAnimation:     /* load animation from disk... */
0564              LoadString(hInst,IDS_Loading,lpCaption,Max);
0565              SetWindowText(hWnd,lpCaption);
0566              SetCapture(hWnd); hPrevCursor= SetCursor(hHourGlass);
0567              zLoadAnimation(hWnd);
0568              SetCursor(hPrevCursor); ReleaseCapture();
0569              LoadString(hInst,IDS_Caption,lpCaption,Max);
0570              SetWindowText(hWnd,lpCaption);
0571              break;
0572          case IDM_Clear:                   /* clear the viewport... */
0573              if (Pause==TRUE)
0574                {
0575                zClear(hWnd);
0576                PaintImage= zBLANK;
0577                }
0578              break;
0579
0580          /* ----------- manage the kinematics scripts ----------- */
0581          case IDM_SaveScript1:             /* save script to disk... */
0582              zInitialize3D(hWnd);
0583              bScriptSaved= zSaveScript((LPSTR)ScriptFiles[0]);
0584              break;
0585          case IDM_SaveScript2:
0586              zInitialize3D(hWnd);
0587              bScriptSaved= zSaveScript((LPSTR)ScriptFiles[1]);
0588              break;
0589          case IDM_SaveScript3:
0590              zInitialize3D(hWnd);
0591              bScriptSaved= zSaveScript((LPSTR)ScriptFiles[2]);
0592              break;
```

```
0593        case IDM_SaveScript4:
0594              zInitialize3D(hWnd);
0595              bScriptSaved= zSaveScript((LPSTR)ScriptFiles[3]);
0596              break;
0597        case IDM_SaveScript5:
0598              zInitialize3D(hWnd);
0599              bScriptSaved= zSaveScript((LPSTR)ScriptFiles[4]);
0600              break;
0601        case IDM_LoadScript1:            /* load script from disk... */
0602              zInitialize3D(hWnd);
0603              bScriptLoaded= zLoadScript((LPSTR)ScriptFiles[0]);
0604              zInitializeModel();
0605              break;
0606        case IDM_LoadScript2:
0607              zInitialize3D(hWnd);
0608              bScriptLoaded= zLoadScript((LPSTR)ScriptFiles[1]);
0609              zInitializeModel();
0610              break;
0611        case IDM_LoadScript3:
0612              zInitialize3D(hWnd);
0613              bScriptLoaded= zLoadScript((LPSTR)ScriptFiles[2]);
0614              zInitializeModel();
0615              break;
0616        case IDM_LoadScript4:
0617              zInitialize3D(hWnd);
0618              bScriptLoaded= zLoadScript((LPSTR)ScriptFiles[3]);
0619              zInitializeModel();
0620              break;
0621        case IDM_LoadScript5:
0622              zInitialize3D(hWnd);
0623              bScriptLoaded= zLoadScript((LPSTR)ScriptFiles[4]);
0624              zInitializeModel();
0625              break;
0626
0627        /* ------------- adjust the playback rate -------------- */
0628        case IDM_FPS182:                 /* use 18 frames per second */
0629              wPrevRate= wFrameRate;
0630              wFrameRate= (WORD)55;
0631              zSetFrameRate(hWnd, wFrameRate);
0632              break;
0633        case IDM_FPS91:                  /* use 9 frames per second */
0634              wPrevRate= wFrameRate;
0635              wFrameRate= (WORD)110;
0636              zSetFrameRate(hWnd, wFrameRate);
0637              break;
0638        case IDM_FPS61:                  /* use 6 frames per second */
0639              wPrevRate= wFrameRate;
0640              wFrameRate= (WORD)165;
0641              zSetFrameRate(hWnd, wFrameRate);
0642              break;
0643        case IDM_FPS45:                  /* use 4.5 frames per second */
0644              wPrevRate= wFrameRate;
0645              wFrameRate= (WORD) 220;
0646              zSetFrameRate(hWnd, wFrameRate);
0647              break;
0648        case IDM_FPS36:                  /* use 3.5 frames per second */
0649              wPrevRate= wFrameRate;
0650              wFrameRate= (WORD) 275;
0651              zSetFrameRate(hWnd, wFrameRate);
0652              break;
0653        case IDM_FPS30:                  /* use 3 frames per second */
```

```
0654              wPrevRate= wFrameRate;
0655              wFrameRate= (WORD) 330;
0656              zSetFrameRate(hWnd, wFrameRate);
0657              break;
0658
0659        /* ----------- About, License, and How to Use ----------- */
0660        case IDM_About:                    /* copyright information... */
0661          LoadString(hInst,IDS_About,lpCaption,Max);
0662          LoadString(hInst,IDS_AboutText,lpMessage,MaxText);
0663          TimerCounter= zTIMER_PAUSE;
0664          MessageBox(GetFocus(),lpMessage,lpCaption,MB_OK);
0665          break;
0666        case IDM_License:                  /* license information... */
0667          LoadString(hInst,IDS_License,lpCaption,Max);
0668          LoadString(hInst,IDS_LicenseText,lpMessage,MaxText);
0669          TimerCounter= zTIMER_PAUSE;
0670          MessageBox(GetFocus(),lpMessage,lpCaption,MB_OK);
0671          break;
0672        case IDM_GeneralHelp:              /* how to use the demo... */
0673          LoadString(hInst,IDS_Help,lpCaption,Max);
0674          LoadString(hInst,IDS_HelpText,lpMessage,MaxText);
0675          TimerCounter= zTIMER_PAUSE;
0676          MessageBox(GetFocus(),lpMessage,lpCaption,MB_OK);
0677          break;
0678        default:
0679          return(DefWindowProc(hWnd, message, wParam, lParam));
0680        }
0681      break;
0682
0683    /* ---------- grab handle for menu item checkmark ----------- */
0684    case WM_INITMENUPOPUP:          /* if a menu is about to pop up... */
0685      TimerCounter= zTIMER_PAUSE; /* provide pause for slower CPUs */
0686      if (lParam == 2)       /* and if it is the frame-rate menu... */
0687        hMenu= wParam; /* remember it so check-mark can be tweaked */
0688      break;
0689
0690    /* ------- oversee Windows-generated refresh requests -------- */
0691    case WM_PAINT:
0692      hDCpaint= BeginPaint(hWnd,&ps);
0693      EndPaint(hWnd, &ps);
0694      if (PaintImage==zBLANK) break;         /* if blank do nothing */
0695      if (PaintImage==zPREVIEW)          /* if frame preview mode... */
0696        {
0697        zCopyToDisplay(hWnd);   /* ...copy hidden-frame to viewport */
0698        break;
0699        }
0700      if (Pause==TRUE)                      /* if animation is paused... */
0701        {
0702        Redisplay= TRUE;                     /* reset the token... */
0703        zShowNextFrame(hWnd);  /* so current frame is refreshed... */
0704        Redisplay= FALSE;             /* ...then restore the token */
0705        break;
0706        }
0707      zShowNextFrame(hWnd);    /* else if animating show next frame */
0708      break;
0709
0710    /* --- manage incoming keystrokes for single-step playback --- */
0711    case WM_KEYDOWN:
0712      switch (wParam)
0713        {
0714        case VK_LEFT:     /* left direction key: singlestep reverse */
```

```
0715          if (Pause==TRUE)                    /* if animation paused... */
0716            {
0717            if (FrameDirection==zFORWARD)
0718              {                       /* confirm the playback direction... */
0719              FrameDirection= zREVERSE;
0720              }
0721            Pause= FALSE;
0722            zShowNextFrame(hWnd);     /* ...and show the next frame */
0723            Pause= TRUE;
0724            PaintImage= zANIMATING;
0725            }
0726          break;
0727        case VK_RIGHT:  /* right direction key: singlestep forward */
0728          if (Pause==TRUE)
0729            {                       /* (control logic is similar to VK_LEFT) */
0730            if (FrameDirection==zREVERSE)
0731              {
0732              FrameDirection= zFORWARD;
0733              }
0734            Pause= FALSE;
0735            zShowNextFrame(hWnd);
0736            Pause= TRUE;
0737            PaintImage= zANIMATING;
0738            }
0739          break;
0740        default: return(DefWindowProc(hWnd,message,wParam,lParam));
0741        }
0742      break;
0743
0744    /* --------------- ensure a graceful shutdown -------------- */
0745    case WM_DESTROY:
0746      if (FrameReady==TRUE)
0747        {             /* if a hidden-frame was created, destroy it... */
0748        SelectObject(hFrameDC,hPrevFrame);
0749        DeleteObject(hFrame);
0750        DeleteDC(hFrameDC);
0751        KillTimer(hWnd,1);                    /* ...and the timer */
0752        }
0753      if (bAnimationLoaded==TRUE)
0754        {   /* if an animation sequence was loaded into memory... */
0755        SelectObject(hFDC,hPrevF); /* select default bitmap handle */
0756        for (LoopCount= 1; LoopCount<= zNUMCELS; LoopCount++)
0757          {               /* for each bitmap handle in the array... */
0758          DeleteObject(BitmapHandles[LoopCount-1]);   /* ...delete */
0759          }
0760        DeleteDC(hFDC);   /* ...then delete memory display-context */
0761        }
0762      zClose3D();                        /* shut down the 3D engine */
0763      if (ScriptHandle != 0)
0764        {                       /* if script handle is valid... */
0765        GlobalFree(ScriptHandle); /* ...discard the memory buffer */
0766        }
0767      PostQuitMessage(0);
0768      break;
0769
0770    /* ------- intercept attempt to resize or move window -------- */
0771    case WM_SYSCOMMAND:
0772      if ((wParam & 0xfff0)== SC_SIZE)
0773        {
0774        MessageBeep(0); break;
0775        }
```

```
0776       if ((wParam & 0xfff0)== SC_MINIMIZE)
0777          {
0778          MessageBeep(0); break;
0779          }
0780       if ((wParam & 0xfff0)== SC_MAXIMIZE)
0781          {
0782          MessageBeep(0); break;
0783          }
0784
0785     /* ----- send all other messages to Windows for handling ----- */
0786     default:
0787        return(DefWindowProc(hWnd, message, wParam, lParam));
0788     }
0789  return FALSE;
0790  }
0791  /*
0792  ------------------------------------------------------------------
0793               Initialize the attributes of the window class
0794  ------------------------------------------------------------------
0795                                                                  */
0796  BOOL zInitClass(HANDLE hInstance)
0797  {
0798     WNDCLASS WndClass;
0799  WndClass.style= 0;
0800  WndClass.lpfnWndProc= zMessageHandler;  /* app's message handler */
0801  WndClass.cbClsExtra= 0;
0802  WndClass.cbWndExtra= 0;
0803  WndClass.hInstance= hInstance;               /* this copy of the app */
0804  WndClass.hIcon= LoadIcon(NULL,IDI_EXCLAMATION);     /* app's icon */
0805  WndClass.hCursor= LoadCursor(NULL,IDC_ARROW);      /* app's cursor */
0806  WndClass.hbrBackground=            /* background color for viewport */
0807                     CreateSolidBrush(RGB(255,255,255));
0808  WndClass.lpszMenuName= "KTXMENUS";     /* menu script in .rc file */
0809  WndClass.lpszClassName= "KTXDEMO";        /* nominal name of class */
0810  return RegisterClass(&WndClass); /* tell Windows about the class */
0811  }
0812  /*
0813  ------------------------------------------------------------------
0814                        Create the main window
0815  ------------------------------------------------------------------
0816                                                                  */
0817  HWND zInitMainWindow(HANDLE hInstance)
0818  {
0819     HWND hWnd;
0820  LoadString(hInstance,IDS_Caption,lpCaption,Max); /* load caption */
0821  hHourGlass= LoadCursor(NULL,IDC_WAIT); /* load hourglass cursor */
0822  hWnd = CreateWindow("KTXDEMO",                       /* class name */
0823     lpCaption,                               /* window caption */
0824     WS_OVERLAPPED | WS_THICKFRAME | WS_CLIPCHILDREN,      /* style */
0825     WindowX,WindowY,                        /* location of window */
0826     zWINDOW_WIDTH,zWINDOW_HEIGHT,         /* dimensions of window */
0827     0,                                  /* parent window, if any */
0828     0,                                   /* special menu, if any */
0829     hInstance,                           /* this copy of the app */
0830     (LPSTR)NULL);       /* for multiple-document interface, if any */
0831  return hWnd;    /* return the newly-created handle to the caller */
0832  }
0833
0834  /*
0835  ------------------------------------------------------------------
0836                       Graphics system functions
```

```
0837   ------------------------------------------------------------------
0838   ------------------------------------------------------------------
0839                          Create the hidden-frame.
0840   ------------------------------------------------------------------
0841                                                                    */
0842   static void zInitFrame(HWND hWnd)
0843   {
0844     HDC hDisplayDC;
0845
0846   if (FrameReady==TRUE)
0847     {                          /* if a hidden-frame already exists... */
0848     MessageBeep(0);
0849     LoadString(hInst,IDS_Ready,lpCaption,Max);
0850     LoadString(hInst,IDS_Already,lpMessage,MaxText);
0851     TimerCounter= zTIMER_PAUSE;
0852     MessageBox(GetFocus(),lpMessage,lpCaption,MB_OK);
0853     return;
0854     }
0855   GlobalCompact((DWORD)-1L);            /* maximize contiguous memory */
0856
0857   /* ----------------- create a hidden bitmap ------------------- */
0858   hDisplayDC= GetDC(hWnd);                     /* display-context */
0859   hFrameDC= CreateCompatibleDC(hDisplayDC);           /* memory DC */
0860   hFrame= CreateCompatibleBitmap(hDisplayDC,zFRAMEWIDE,zFRAMEHIGH);
0861   if (hFrame==NULL)
0862     {                    /* if unable to create compatible bitmap... */
0863     LoadString(hInst,IDS_NotReady,lpCaption,Max);
0864     LoadString(hInst,IDS_InsufMem1,lpMessage,MaxText);
0865     MessageBox(GetFocus(),lpMessage,lpCaption,MB_OK);
0866     DeleteDC(hFrameDC);
0867     TimerExists= FALSE; FrameReady= FALSE; AnimationReady= FALSE;
0868     return;
0869     }
0870   hPrevFrame= SelectObject(hFrameDC,hFrame);        /* select bitmap */
0871
0872   /* -------- clear the viewport and copy to hidden-frame -------- */
0873   zClear(hWnd);
0874   BitBlt(hFrameDC,0,0,zFRAMEWIDE,zFRAMEHIGH,hDisplayDC,0,0,SRCCOPY);
0875   ReleaseDC(hWnd,hDisplayDC);         /* release the display-context */
0876
0877   /* -------------------- initialize a timer -------------------- */
0878   TimerID1= SetTimer(hWnd,1,wFrameRate,(FARPROC) NULL);
0879   if (TimerID1 == 0)              /* if no timer was initialized... */
0880     {                                    /* ...display a warning */
0881     LoadString(hInst,IDS_NotReady,lpCaption,Max);
0882     LoadString(hInst,IDS_NoTimer,lpMessage,MaxText);
0883     MessageBox(GetFocus(),lpMessage,lpCaption,MB_OK);
0884     SelectObject(hFrameDC,hPrevFrame);
0885     DeleteObject(hFrame);
0886     DeleteDC(hFrameDC);
0887     TimerExists= FALSE;
0888     return;
0889     }
0890   TimerExists= TRUE;
0891   FrameReady= TRUE;
0892   FrameNum= 1;
0893   return;
0894   }
0895   /*
0896   ------------------------------------------------------------------
0897                          Clear the hidden frame.
```

```
0898    -------------------------------------------------------------
0899                                                                */
0900    static void zClearHiddenFrame(void)
0901    {
0902    if (FrameReady == TRUE)
0903      {
0904      PatBlt(hFrameDC,0,0,zFRAMEWIDE,zFRAMEHIGH,WHITENESS);
0905      }
0906    return;
0907    }
0908    /*
0909    -------------------------------------------------------------
0910              Copy the hidden frame to the display window.
0911    -------------------------------------------------------------
0912                                                                */
0913    static void zCopyToDisplay(HWND hWnd)
0914    {
0915      HDC hDC;
0916    hDC= GetDC(hWnd);
0917    if (FrameReady == TRUE)
0918      {
0919      BitBlt(hDC,0,0,zFRAMEWIDE,zFRAMEHIGH,hFrameDC,0,0,SRCCOPY);
0920      }
0921    ReleaseDC(hWnd,hDC);
0922    return;
0923    }
0924    /*
0925    -------------------------------------------------------------
0926                     Blank the display window.
0927    -------------------------------------------------------------
0928                                                                */
0929    static void zClear(HWND hWnd)
0930    {
0931      HDC hDC;
0932    hDC= GetDC(hWnd);
0933    PatBlt(hDC,0,0,zFRAMEWIDE,zFRAMEHIGH,WHITENESS);
0934    ReleaseDC(hWnd,hDC);
0935    return;
0936    }
0937
0938    /*
0939    -------------------------------------------------------------
0940                   Animation authoring functions
0941    -------------------------------------------------------------
0942    -------------------------------------------------------------
0943              Create the frames and save to disk.
0944    -------------------------------------------------------------
0945                                                                */
0946    static void zSaveAnimation(HWND hWnd)
0947    {
0948    if (FrameReady==FALSE)
0949      {
0950      MessageBeep(0);
0951      LoadString(hInst,IDS_NotReady,lpCaption,Max);
0952      LoadString(hInst,IDS_NoFrame,lpMessage,MaxText);
0953      MessageBox(GetFocus(),lpMessage,lpCaption,MB_OK);
0954      return;
0955      }
0956    if (bAnimationSaved==TRUE)
0957      {
0958      MessageBeep(0);
```

```
0959    LoadString(hInst,IDS_Unexpected,lpCaption,Max);
0960    LoadString(hInst,IDS_Disk1,lpMessage,MaxText);
0961    TimerCounter= zTIMER_PAUSE;
0962    MessageBox(GetFocus(),lpMessage,lpCaption,MB_OK);
0963    return;
0964    }
0965    if (bPrevSaveAttempt==TRUE)
0966    {
0967    MessageBeep(0);
0968    LoadString(hInst,IDS_Unexpected,lpCaption,Max);
0969    LoadString(hInst,IDS_Disk8,lpMessage,MaxText);
0970    TimerCounter= zTIMER_PAUSE;
0971    MessageBox(GetFocus(),lpMessage,lpCaption,MB_OK);
0972    return;
0973    }
0974    bPrevSaveAttempt= TRUE;
0975
0976    /* ---- initialize the camera, light-source, and kinematics ---- */
0977    zInitializeModel();
0978
0979    /* ----------------- build and save the cels ------------------ */
0980    for (LoopCount= 1; LoopCount<= zNUMCELS; LoopCount++)
0981    {                               /* for each cel in the animation... */
0982    bFrameSaved= zBuildFrame(LoopCount, hWnd,  /* ... save to disk */
0983                            (LPSTR)FrameFiles[LoopCount-1]);
0984    if (bFrameSaved==FALSE) return; /* cancel loop if error occurs */
0985    }
0986    bAnimationSaved= TRUE;
0987    bPrevLoadAttempt= FALSE;
0988    zClear(hWnd);
0989    MessageBeep(0);
0990    LoadString(hInst,IDS_Status,lpCaption,Max);
0991    LoadString(hInst,IDS_Disk2,lpMessage,MaxText);
0992    MessageBox(GetFocus(),lpMessage,lpCaption,MB_OK);
0993    return;
0994    }
0995    /*
0996    ------------------------------------------------------------------
0997                       Build one cel and save to disk.
0998    ------------------------------------------------------------------
0999                                                                    */
1000    static BOOL zBuildFrame(int Number, HWND hWnd, LPSTR lpFileName)
1001    {
1002       BOOL bDiskResult;
1003       HFONT Font;
1004       HFONT PrevFont;
1005       DWORD PrevFontColor;
1006       DWORD PrevBkColor;
1007       HDC hDC;
1008       struct tm *NewTime;          /* pointer to tm struct of time.h */
1009       time_t TimeSeconds;          /* long integer time_t of time.h */
1010       MSG msg;                              /* incoming message */
1011
1012    /* ---------- display progress report on caption bar ----------- */
1013    TextLength= wsprintf(lpCaption,      /* build and save the string */
1014              "Building frame %d...", Number);
1015    SetWindowText(hWnd,lpCaption);       /* display it in caption bar */
1016
1017    /* -------------------- reset all buffers -------------------- */
1018    zClearHiddenFrame();
1019    zClear(hWnd);
```

```
1020   zClearHidden3DPage();
1021   zResetZBuffer();
1022
1023   /* ---------------- draw the appropriate cel ---------------- */
1024   zDrawCel(Number);
1025   if (FrameReady==TRUE)
1026     {
1027     hDC= GetDC(hWnd);
1028     BitBlt(hFrameDC,0,0,zFRAMEWIDE,zFRAMEHIGH,hDC,0,0,SRCCOPY);
1029     ReleaseDC(hWnd,hDC);
1030     }
1031
1032   /* ------------ check for user-requested cancel -------------- */
1033   if (PeekMessage(&msg,NULL,0,0,PM_REMOVE))
1034     {                      /* if a message is waiting in the queue... */
1035     if (msg.message == WM_RBUTTONDOWN)
1036       {                        /* ...if right mouse button pressed... */
1037       return FALSE;            /* ...then cancel the build sequence */
1038       }
1039     }
1040
1041   /* --------- display the titles, labels, and timestamp --------- */
1042   if ((DisplayBits==1)&&(DisplayPlanes==1))
1043     {                      /* if a mono display use black typeface... */
1044     PrevFontColor= SetTextColor(hFrameDC,RGB(0,0,0));
1045     PrevBkColor=  SetBkColor(hFrameDC,RGB(255,255,255));
1046     }
1047   else
1048     {  /* else if a color display use any solid color typeface... */
1049     PrevFontColor= SetTextColor(hFrameDC,RGB(0,0,0));
1050     PrevBkColor=  SetBkColor(hFrameDC,RGB(255,255,255));
1051     }
1052   SetBkMode(hFrameDC,TRANSPARENT);
1053
1054   if (bUseArial == FALSE)
1055     {                      /* if running Windows 3.0 use Helv font... */
1056     Font= CreateFont(24, 0, 0, 0, FW_BOLD, FALSE, FALSE, FALSE,
1057           ANSI_CHARSET, OUT_DEFAULT_PRECIS, CLIP_DEFAULT_PRECIS,
1058           DRAFT_QUALITY, VARIABLE_PITCH | FF_SWISS, "Helv");
1059     PrevFont= SelectObject(hFrameDC,Font);
1060     TextOut(hFrameDC,10,6,"A Lee Adams tutorial:",21);
1061     Font= CreateFont(36, 0, 0, 0, FW_BOLD, FALSE, FALSE, FALSE,
1062           ANSI_CHARSET, OUT_DEFAULT_PRECIS, CLIP_DEFAULT_PRECIS,
1063           DRAFT_QUALITY, VARIABLE_PITCH | FF_SWISS, "Helv");
1064     SelectObject(hFrameDC,Font);
1065     TextOut(hFrameDC,8,24,"Kinematics",10);
1066     }
1067   else   /* else if running Windows 3.1 or newer use Arial font... */
1068     {
1069     Font= CreateFont(24, 0, 0, 0, FW_BOLD, FALSE, FALSE, FALSE,
1070           ANSI_CHARSET, OUT_DEFAULT_PRECIS, CLIP_DEFAULT_PRECIS,
1071           DRAFT_QUALITY, VARIABLE_PITCH | FF_SWISS, "Arial");
1072     PrevFont= SelectObject(hFrameDC,Font);
1073     TextOut(hFrameDC,10,6,"A Lee Adams tutorial:",21);
1074     Font= CreateFont(36, 0, 0, 0, FW_BOLD, FALSE, FALSE, FALSE,
1075           ANSI_CHARSET, OUT_DEFAULT_PRECIS, CLIP_DEFAULT_PRECIS,
1076           DRAFT_QUALITY, VARIABLE_PITCH | FF_SWISS, "Arial");
1077     SelectObject(hFrameDC,Font);
1078     TextOut(hFrameDC,8,24,"Kinematics",10);
1079     }
1080
```

```
1081   SelectObject(hFrameDC,PrevFont);
1082   TextOut(hFrameDC,10,220,"Kinematics production timestamp",31);
1083   time(&TimeSeconds);
1084   NewTime= localtime(&TimeSeconds);
1085   TextOut(hFrameDC,10,235,(LPSTR)asctime(NewTime),19);
1086   SetBkMode(hFrameDC,OPAQUE);
1087   SetBkColor(hFrameDC,PrevBkColor);
1088   SetTextColor(hFrameDC,PrevFontColor);
1089
1090   /* ---------- check again for user-requested cancel ---------- */
1091   if (PeekMessage(&msg,NULL,0,0,PM_REMOVE))
1092     {
1093     if (msg.message == WM_RBUTTONDOWN)
1094       {
1095       return FALSE;
1096       }
1097     }
1098
1099   /* ---------- display the cel and save it to disk ------------ */
1100   zCopyToDisplay(hWnd);
1101   bDiskResult= zSaveFrame(hFrame,lpFileName);
1102   if (bDiskResult==FALSE) return FALSE;
1103   return TRUE;
1104   }
1105   /*
1106   -------------------------------------------------------------------
1107                             Draw a cel.
1108   -------------------------------------------------------------------
1109                                                                    */
1110   static void zDrawCel(int Number)
1111   {
1112   /* ----------------- lock the memory buffer ----------------- */
1113   Script= (struct ScriptDatabase far * )GlobalLock(ScriptHandle);
1114
1115   /* -------------------- update the camera -------------------- */
1116   if ((Number > Script->Cam1Path1.StartFrame) &&
1117       (Number <= Script->Cam1Path1.EndFrame))
1118     {
1119     Script->Cam1.Distance=
1120       Script->Cam1.Distance + Script->Cam1Path1.ChgDistance;
1121     Script->Cam1.Heading=
1122       Script->Cam1.Heading + Script->Cam1Path1.ChgHeading;
1123     Script->Cam1.Pitch=
1124       Script->Cam1.Pitch + Script->Cam1Path1.ChgPitch;
1125     }
1126   if (Script->Cam1.Heading > 360)
1127       Script->Cam1.Heading= Script->Cam1.Heading - 360;
1128   if (Script->Cam1.Heading < 0)
1129       Script->Cam1.Heading= Script->Cam1.Heading + 360;
1130   if (Script->Cam1.Pitch > 360) Script->Cam1.Pitch= 360;
1131   if (Script->Cam1.Pitch < 270) Script->Cam1.Pitch= 270;
1132   zSetCameraDistance(Script->Cam1.Distance);
1133   zSetCameraPitch(Script->Cam1.Pitch);
1134   zSetCameraHeading(Script->Cam1.Heading);
1135
1136   /* ----------------- update the light-source ----------------- */
1137   if ((Number > Script->Lt1Path1.StartFrame) &&
1138       (Number <= Script->Lt1Path1.EndFrame))
1139     {
1140     Script->Lt1.Heading=
1141       Script->Lt1.Heading + Script->Lt1Path1.ChgHeading;
```

```
1142    Script->Lt1.Elevation=
1143       Script->Lt1.Elevation + Script->Lt1Path1.ChgElevation;
1144    }
1145    zSetLightPosition(Script->Lt1.Elevation, Script->Lt1.Heading);
1146
1147    /* ---------------- unlock the memory buffer ---------------- */
1148    GlobalUnlock(ScriptHandle);     /* discard ptr and unlock buffer */
1149
1150    /* -------------- update the kinematics bodies --------------- */
1151    kmRenderScene();                        /* call the kinematics engine */
1152    return;
1153    }
1154    /*
1155    ------------------------------------------------------------------
1156          Initialize or re-initialize the kinematics interface.
1157    ------------------------------------------------------------------
1158                                                                      */
1159    static void zInitializeModel(void)
1160    {
1161    /* ----------------- lock the memory buffer ------------------ */
1162    Script= (struct ScriptDatabase far * )GlobalLock(ScriptHandle);
1163
1164    /* ----------------- initialize the camera ------------------ */
1165    if (bScriptLoaded == FALSE)
1166    {    /* use defaults if no script has been loaded from disk... */
1167      Script->Cam1.Heading= 340;
1168      Script->Cam1.Pitch= 350;
1169      Script->Cam1.Distance= 356;
1170    }
1171    zSetCameraDistance(Script->Cam1.Distance);
1172    zSetCameraPitch(Script->Cam1.Pitch);
1173    zSetCameraHeading(Script->Cam1.Heading);
1174
1175    /* -------------- specify the path of the camera -------------- */
1176    if (bScriptLoaded == FALSE)
1177    {
1178      Script->Cam1Path1.StartFrame= 1;
1179      Script->Cam1Path1.EndFrame= zNUMCELS;
1180      Script->Cam1Path1.ChgHeading= 0;
1181      Script->Cam1Path1.ChgPitch= 0;
1182      Script->Cam1Path1.ChgDistance= 0;
1183    }
1184
1185    /* ---------------- initialize the light-source --------------- */
1186    if (bScriptLoaded == FALSE)
1187    {
1188      Script->Lt1.Elevation= 60;
1189      Script->Lt1.Heading= 180;
1190    }
1191    zSetLightPosition(Script->Lt1.Elevation, Script->Lt1.Heading);
1192
1193    /* ----------- specify the path of the light-source ---------- */
1194    if (bScriptLoaded == FALSE)
1195    {
1196      Script->Lt1Path1.StartFrame= 1;
1197      Script->Lt1Path1.EndFrame= zNUMCELS;
1198      Script->Lt1Path1.ChgHeading= 0;
1199      Script->Lt1Path1.ChgElevation= 0;
1200    }
1201
1202    /* ----------------- initialize the kinematics --------------- */
```

```
1203    if (bScriptLoaded == FALSE)
1204      {
1205      Script->Kinematics.FPS= 18.2;   /* 36 frames at 18 fps = 2 secs */
1206      Script->Kinematics.NumBodies= 3;          /* number of bodies */
1207      Script->Kinematics.FirstFrame= 1;             /* first frame */
1208      Script->Kinematics.FinalFrame= zNUMCELS;      /* final frame */
1209      }
1210    kmInitializeKinematics(Script->Kinematics.FPS,
1211                           Script->Kinematics.NumBodies,
1212                           Script->Kinematics.FirstFrame,
1213                           Script->Kinematics.FinalFrame);
1214
1215    /* ------------- specify kinematics for first body ------------- */
1216    if (bScriptLoaded == FALSE)
1217      {    /* use defaults if no script has been loaded from disk... */
1218      Script->Actor[0].TypeOfSubobject= zCYLINDER;
1219      Script->Actor[0].Color= zRED;
1220      Script->Actor[0].DimensionX= 30;
1221      Script->Actor[0].DimensionY= 30;
1222      Script->Actor[0].DimensionZ= 30;
1223      Script->Actor[0].LocationX= 60;
1224      Script->Actor[0].LocationY= 0;
1225      Script->Actor[0].LocationZ= 0;
1226      Script->Actor[0].OrientationYaw= 0;
1227      Script->Actor[0].OrientationRoll= 0;
1228      Script->Actor[0].OrientationPitch= 0;
1229      Script->Actor[0].LinearVelocityDirection= zWEST;
1230      Script->Actor[0].LinearVelocityPitch= zHORIZONTAL;
1231      Script->Actor[0].LinearVelocitySpeed= 0;
1232      Script->Actor[0].RotationalVelocityYawSpeed= 90;
1233      Script->Actor[0].RotationalVelocityRollSpeed= 0;
1234      Script->Actor[0].RotationalVelocityPitchSpeed= 0;
1235      Script->Actor[0].LinearAccelUnitsPerSecSqd= 0;
1236      Script->Actor[0].LinearAccelSeconds= 0;
1237      Script->Actor[0].RotationalAccelYaw= 0;
1238      Script->Actor[0].RotationalAccelRoll= 0;
1239      Script->Actor[0].RotationalAccelPitch= 0;
1240      Script->Actor[0].RotationalAccelSeconds= 0;
1241      Script->Actor[0].HeadingChangeDegreesPerSec= 0;
1242      Script->Actor[0].HeadingChangeSeconds= 0;
1243      Script->Actor[0].PitchChangeDegreesPerSec= 0;
1244      Script->Actor[0].PitchChangeSeconds= 0;
1245      }
1246    /* ------------- specify kinematics for second body ------------- */
1247    if (bScriptLoaded == FALSE)
1248      {    /* use defaults if no script has been loaded from disk... */
1249      Script->Actor[1].TypeOfSubobject= zBOX;
1250      Script->Actor[1].Color= zRED;
1251      Script->Actor[1].DimensionX= 26;
1252      Script->Actor[1].DimensionY= 26;
1253      Script->Actor[1].DimensionZ= 26;
1254      Script->Actor[1].LocationX= -50;
1255      Script->Actor[1].LocationY= -60;
1256      Script->Actor[1].LocationZ= 0;
1257      Script->Actor[1].OrientationYaw= 0;
1258      Script->Actor[1].OrientationRoll= 45;
1259      Script->Actor[1].OrientationPitch= 0;
1260      Script->Actor[1].LinearVelocityDirection= zEAST;
1261      Script->Actor[1].LinearVelocityPitch= zHORIZONTAL;
1262      Script->Actor[1].LinearVelocitySpeed= 0;
1263      Script->Actor[1].RotationalVelocityYawSpeed= 0;
```

```
1264     Script->Actor[1].RotationalVelocityRollSpeed= 0;
1265     Script->Actor[1].RotationalVelocityPitchSpeed= 90;
1266     Script->Actor[1].LinearAccelUnitsPerSecSqd= 0;
1267     Script->Actor[1].LinearAccelSeconds= 0;
1268     Script->Actor[1].RotationalAccelYaw= 0;
1269     Script->Actor[1].RotationalAccelRoll= 0;
1270     Script->Actor[1].RotationalAccelPitch= 0;
1271     Script->Actor[1].RotationalAccelSeconds= 0;
1272     Script->Actor[1].HeadingChangeDegreesPerSec= 0;
1273     Script->Actor[1].HeadingChangeSeconds= 0;
1274     Script->Actor[1].PitchChangeDegreesPerSec= 0;
1275     Script->Actor[1].PitchChangeSeconds= 0;
1276     }
1277  /* ------------ specify kinematics for third body ------------- */
1278  if (bScriptLoaded == FALSE)
1279     {    /* use defaults if no script has been loaded from disk... */
1280     Script->Actor[2].TypeOfSubobject= zWEDGE;
1281     Script->Actor[2].Color= zRED;
1282     Script->Actor[2].DimensionX= 30;
1283     Script->Actor[2].DimensionY= 30;
1284     Script->Actor[2].DimensionZ= 30;
1285     Script->Actor[2].LocationX= -50;
1286     Script->Actor[2].LocationY= 30;
1287     Script->Actor[2].LocationZ= 0;
1288     Script->Actor[2].OrientationYaw= 0;
1289     Script->Actor[2].OrientationRoll= 0;
1290     Script->Actor[2].OrientationPitch= 0;
1291     Script->Actor[2].LinearVelocityDirection= zEAST;
1292     Script->Actor[2].LinearVelocityPitch= zHORIZONTAL;
1293     Script->Actor[2].LinearVelocitySpeed= 0;
1294     Script->Actor[2].RotationalVelocityYawSpeed= -90;
1295     Script->Actor[2].RotationalVelocityRollSpeed= 0;
1296     Script->Actor[2].RotationalVelocityPitchSpeed= 0;
1297     Script->Actor[2].LinearAccelUnitsPerSecSqd= 0;
1298     Script->Actor[2].LinearAccelSeconds= 0;
1299     Script->Actor[2].RotationalAccelYaw= 0;
1300     Script->Actor[2].RotationalAccelRoll= 0;
1301     Script->Actor[2].RotationalAccelPitch= 0;
1302     Script->Actor[2].RotationalAccelSeconds= 0;
1303     Script->Actor[2].HeadingChangeDegreesPerSec= 0;
1304     Script->Actor[2].HeadingChangeSeconds= 0;
1305     Script->Actor[2].PitchChangeDegreesPerSec= 0;
1306     Script->Actor[2].PitchChangeSeconds= 0;
1307     }
1308
1309  /* -------------- initialize the kinematics engine ------------- */
1310  for (LoopCount= 0; LoopCount < Script->Kinematics.NumBodies;
1311       LoopCount++)              /* for each body being animated... */
1312     {                 /* ...initialize it in the kinematics engine... */
1313     kmSetSolid(LoopCount + 1,
1314              Script->Actor[LoopCount].TypeOfSubobject);
1315     kmSetColor(LoopCount + 1,Script->Actor[LoopCount].Color);
1316     kmSetDimensions(LoopCount + 1,
1317        Script->Actor[LoopCount].DimensionX,
1318        Script->Actor[LoopCount].DimensionY,
1319        Script->Actor[LoopCount].DimensionZ);
1320     kmSetLocation(LoopCount + 1,
1321        Script->Actor[LoopCount].LocationX,
1322        Script->Actor[LoopCount].LocationY,
1323        Script->Actor[LoopCount].LocationZ);
1324     kmSetOrientation(LoopCount + 1,
```

```
1325        Script->Actor[LoopCount].OrientationYaw,
1326        Script->Actor[LoopCount].OrientationRoll,
1327        Script->Actor[LoopCount].OrientationPitch);
1328     kmSetLinearVelocity(LoopCount + 1,
1329        Script->Actor[LoopCount].LinearVelocityDirection,
1330        Script->Actor[LoopCount].LinearVelocityPitch,
1331        Script->Actor[LoopCount].LinearVelocitySpeed);
1332     kmSetRotationalVelocity(LoopCount + 1,
1333        Script->Actor[LoopCount].RotationalVelocityYawSpeed,
1334        Script->Actor[LoopCount].RotationalVelocityRollSpeed,
1335        Script->Actor[LoopCount].RotationalVelocityPitchSpeed);
1336     kmSetLinearAcceleration(LoopCount + 1,
1337        Script->Actor[LoopCount].LinearAccelUnitsPerSecSqd,
1338        Script->Actor[LoopCount].LinearAccelSeconds);
1339     kmSetRotationalAcceleration(LoopCount + 1,
1340        Script->Actor[LoopCount].RotationalAccelYaw,
1341        Script->Actor[LoopCount].RotationalAccelRoll,
1342        Script->Actor[LoopCount].RotationalAccelPitch,
1343        Script->Actor[LoopCount].RotationalAccelSeconds);
1344     kmSetHeadingChange(LoopCount + 1,
1345        Script->Actor[LoopCount].HeadingChangeDegreesPerSec,
1346        Script->Actor[LoopCount].HeadingChangeSeconds);
1347     kmSetPitchChange(LoopCount + 1,
1348        Script->Actor[LoopCount].PitchChangeDegreesPerSec,
1349        Script->Actor[LoopCount].PitchChangeSeconds);
1350     }                             /* loop back to do next body... */
1351
1352  /* ----------------- unlock the memory buffer ----------------- */
1353  GlobalUnlock(ScriptHandle);     /* discard ptr and unlock buffer */
1354  return;
1355  }
1356  /*
1357  -------------------------------------------------------------------
1358              Preview the first frame of the animation.
1359  -------------------------------------------------------------------
1360                                                                   */
1361  static void zPreviewFirstFrame(HWND hWnd)
1362  {
1363     HDC hDC;
1364  zInitialize3D(hWnd);                    /* clear various buffers... */
1365  zClearHiddenFrame();
1366  zClear(hWnd);
1367  zClearHidden3DPage();
1368  zResetZBuffer();
1369  zInitializeModel();                     /* reset kinematics interface... */
1370  kmReset();
1371  zDrawCel(1);                                     /* draw the frame */
1372  if (FrameReady==TRUE)
1373     {
1374     hDC= GetDC(hWnd);
1375     BitBlt(hFrameDC,0,0,zFRAMEWIDE,zFRAMEHIGH,hDC,0,0,SRCCOPY);
1376     ReleaseDC(hWnd,hDC);
1377     }
1378  zInitializeModel();                     /* tidy up and return... */
1379  kmReset();
1380  zCopyToDisplay(hWnd);
1381  return;
1382  }
1383  /*
1384  -------------------------------------------------------------------
1385              Preview the final frame of the animation.
```

```
1386  -------------------------------------------------------------------
1387                                                                     */
1388  static void zPreviewFinalFrame(HWND hWnd)
1389  {
1390    HDC hDC;
1391  zInitialize3D(hWnd);
1392  zClearHiddenFrame();
1393  zClear(hWnd);
1394  zClearHidden3DPage();
1395  zResetZBuffer();
1396  zInitializeModel();
1397  kmReset();
1398  zSelectPreviewFrame(zNUMCELS);
1399  kmSelectPreviewFrame(zNUMCELS);
1400  zDrawCel(zNUMCELS);
1401  if (FrameReady==TRUE)
1402    {
1403    hDC= GetDC(hWnd);
1404    BitBlt(hFrameDC,0,0,zFRAMEWIDE,zFRAMEHIGH,hDC,0,0,SRCCOPY);
1405    ReleaseDC(hWnd,hDC);
1406    }
1407  zInitializeModel();
1408  kmReset();
1409  zCopyToDisplay(hWnd);
1410  return;
1411  }
1412  /*
1413  -------------------------------------------------------------------
1414            Adjust camera and light-source for a preview frame.
1415  -------------------------------------------------------------------
1416                                                                     */
1417  static void zSelectPreviewFrame(int WhichFrame)
1418  {
1419    int Count;
1420  /* ----------------- lock the memory buffer ------------------ */
1421  Script= (struct ScriptDatabase far * )GlobalLock(ScriptHandle);
1422
1423  for (Count= 1; Count< WhichFrame; Count++)
1424    {     /* for each frame preceding the desired preview frame... */
1425    if ((Count> Script->Cam1Path1.StartFrame) &&  /* update camera */
1426        (Count<= Script->Cam1Path1.EndFrame))
1427      {
1428      Script->Cam1.Distance=
1429        Script->Cam1.Distance + Script->Cam1Path1.ChgDistance;
1430      Script->Cam1.Heading=
1431        Script->Cam1.Heading + Script->Cam1Path1.ChgHeading;
1432      Script->Cam1.Pitch=
1433        Script->Cam1.Pitch + Script->Cam1Path1.ChgPitch;
1434      }
1435    if (Script->Cam1.Heading > 360)
1436      Script->Cam1.Heading= Script->Cam1.Heading - 360;
1437    if (Script->Cam1.Heading < 0)
1438      Script->Cam1.Heading= Script->Cam1.Heading + 360;
1439    if (Script->Cam1.Pitch > 360) Script->Cam1.Pitch= 360;
1440    if (Script->Cam1.Pitch < 270) Script->Cam1.Pitch= 270;
1441    if ((Count> Script->Lt1Path1.StartFrame) &&    /* update light */
1442        (Count<= Script->Lt1Path1.EndFrame))
1443      {
1444      Script->Lt1.Heading=
1445        Script->Lt1.Heading + Script->Lt1Path1.ChgHeading;
1446      Script->Lt1.Elevation=
```

```
1447          Script->Lt1.Elevation + Script->Lt1Path1.ChgElevation;
1448      }
1449    }
1450
1451  /* ---------------- unlock the memory buffer ------------------ */
1452  GlobalUnlock(ScriptHandle);     /* discard ptr and unlock buffer */
1453  return;
1454  }
1455  /*
1456  ----------------------------------------------------------------
1457                  Save a script database to disk.
1458  ----------------------------------------------------------------
1459                                                                 */
1460  static BOOL zSaveScript(LPSTR lpFileName)
1461  {
1462    LPSTR ScriptBuffer;      /* will point to script memory buffer */
1463    WORD NumBytes;             /* number of bytes to write to disk */
1464    int hFile;                                     /* file handle */
1465    OFSTRUCT FileStruct;              /* data structure for file */
1466    int UserChoice;            /* value returned by MessageBox() */
1467    int DiskResult;           /* value returned by disk functions */
1468
1469  /* ---- initialize the camera, light-source, and kinematics ---- */
1470  zInitializeModel();
1471
1472  /* ----------------- lock the memory buffer ------------------- */
1473  ScriptBuffer= (LPSTR)GlobalLock(ScriptHandle);   /* grab pointer */
1474
1475  /* --------------- write the database to disk ---------------- */
1476  NumBytes= sizeof(struct ScriptDatabase);
1477  if (NumBytes > 65534)
1478      {
1479      MessageBeep(0);
1480      MessageBox(GetFocus(),
1481        "Script too large.  Cannot save to disk.",
1482        "Script save", MB_OK);
1483      GlobalUnlock(ScriptHandle);
1484      return FALSE;
1485      }
1486  hFile= OpenFile(lpFileName,&FileStruct,OF_EXIST);
1487  if (hFile >= 0)          /* if the file already exists on disk... */
1488      {
1489      MessageBeep(0);
1490      UserChoice= MessageBox(GetFocus(),
1491        "That script already exists on disk.  Overwrite?",
1492        "Script save", MB_YESNO);
1493      if (UserChoice == IDNO)
1494          {
1495          GlobalUnlock(ScriptHandle);
1496          return FALSE;
1497          }
1498      }
1499  hFile= OpenFile(lpFileName,&FileStruct,OF_CREATE|OF_WRITE);
1500  if (hFile == -1)
1501      {
1502      MessageBeep(0);
1503      MessageBox(GetFocus(),
1504        "Unable to open file for writing.",
1505        "Script file error", MB_OK);
1506      GlobalUnlock(ScriptHandle);
1507      return FALSE;
```

```
1508    }
1509  DiskResult= _lwrite(hFile,ScriptBuffer,NumBytes);
1510  if (DiskResult == -1)
1511    {
1512    MessageBeep(0);
1513    MessageBox(GetFocus(),
1514      "Unable to write to the file.",
1515      "Script file error", MB_OK);
1516    _lclose(hFile);
1517    GlobalUnlock(ScriptHandle);
1518    return FALSE;
1519    }
1520  DiskResult= _lclose(hFile);
1521  if (DiskResult == -1)
1522    {
1523    MessageBeep(0);
1524    MessageBox(GetFocus(),
1525      "Unable to close the file.",
1526      "Script file error", MB_OK);
1527    GlobalUnlock(ScriptHandle);
1528    return FALSE;
1529    }
1530
1531  /* ---------------- unlock the memory buffer ---------------- */
1532  GlobalUnlock(ScriptHandle);     /* discard ptr and unlock buffer */
1533
1534  /* --------------------- status report --------------------- */
1535  MessageBox(GetFocus(),
1536    "The script file has been saved.",
1537    "Script file save", MB_OK);
1538  return TRUE;
1539  }
1540  /*
1541  ------------------------------------------------------------------
1542                    Load a script database from disk.
1543  ------------------------------------------------------------------
1544                                                                  */
1545  static BOOL zLoadScript(LPSTR lpFileName)
1546  {
1547    LPSTR ScriptBuffer;
1548    WORD NumBytes;
1549    int hFile;
1550    OFSTRUCT FileStruct;
1551    int DiskResult;
1552
1553  /* ------------------ lock the memory buffer ------------------ */
1554  ScriptBuffer= (LPSTR)GlobalLock(ScriptHandle);   /* grab pointer */
1555
1556  /* ---------------- load the database from disk ---------------- */
1557  NumBytes= sizeof(struct ScriptDatabase);
1558  hFile= OpenFile(lpFileName,&FileStruct,OF_EXIST);
1559  if (hFile < 0)          /* if the file does not exist on disk... */
1560    {
1561    MessageBeep(0);
1562    MessageBox(GetFocus(),
1563      "There is no script of that name on the disk.",
1564      "Script file error", MB_OK);
1565    GlobalUnlock(ScriptHandle);
1566    return FALSE;
1567    }
1568  hFile= OpenFile(lpFileName,&FileStruct,OF_READ);
```

```
1569   if (hFile == -1)
1570     {
1571     MessageBeep(0);
1572     MessageBox(GetFocus(),
1573       "Unable to open script file for reading.",
1574       "Script load error", MB_OK);
1575     GlobalUnlock(ScriptHandle);
1576     return FALSE;
1577     }
1578   DiskResult= _lread(hFile,ScriptBuffer,NumBytes);
1579   if (DiskResult == -1)
1580     {
1581     MessageBeep(0);
1582     MessageBox(GetFocus(),
1583       "Unable to read from the file.",
1584       "Script load error", MB_OK);
1585     _lclose(hFile);
1586     GlobalUnlock(ScriptHandle);
1587     return FALSE;
1588     }
1589   if (DiskResult != (int)NumBytes)
1590     {   /* if incoming data is not same size as script database... */
1591     MessageBeep(0);
1592     MessageBox(GetFocus(),
1593       "Unexpected script file length.  See book for further help.",
1594       "Script load error", MB_OK);
1595     _lclose(hFile);
1596     GlobalUnlock(ScriptHandle);
1597     return FALSE;
1598     }
1599   DiskResult= _lclose(hFile);
1600   if (DiskResult == -1)
1601     {
1602     MessageBeep(0);
1603     MessageBox(GetFocus(),
1604       "Unable to close the file.",
1605       "Script load error", MB_YESNO);
1606     GlobalUnlock(ScriptHandle);
1607     return FALSE;
1608     }
1609
1610   /* ---------------- unlock the memory buffer ------------------ */
1611   GlobalUnlock(ScriptHandle);      /* discard ptr and unlock buffer */
1612
1613   /* ---------------------- status report --------------------- */
1614   MessageBox(GetFocus(),
1615     "The script file has been loaded.",
1616     "Script file load", MB_OK);
1617   return TRUE;
1618   }
1619
1620   /*
1621   ------------------------------------------------------------------
1622                       Animation playback functions
1623   ------------------------------------------------------------------
1624               Display the next frame of the animation.
1625   ------------------------------------------------------------------
1626                                                                   */
1627   static void zShowNextFrame(HWND hWnd)
1628   {
1629     HDC hDC;
```

```
1630   if (bUseDisk==TRUE) goto DISK_PLAYBACK; /* using memory or disk? */
1631
1632   /* ----------- manage memory-based frame animation ----------- */
1633   MEMORY_PLAYBACK:
1634   if (AnimationReady==FALSE) return;
1635   if (bAnimationLoaded==FALSE) return;
1636   if (Redisplay==TRUE) goto DISPLAY_FRAME;
1637   if (Pause==TRUE) return;
1638   if (FrameDirection==zFORWARD)                    /* if a forward loop... */
1639     {
1640     FrameNum++;                                /* increment the frame number */
1641     if (FrameNum > zFINALFRAME)                    /* if at end of loop... */
1642       FrameNum= zFIRSTFRAME;                             /* ...wraparound */
1643     }
1644   if (FrameDirection==zREVERSE)                    /* if a reverse loop... */
1645     {
1646     FrameNum--;                                /* decrement the frame number */
1647     if (FrameNum < zFIRSTFRAME)                    /* but if at end of loop... */
1648       FrameNum= zFINALFRAME;                            /* ...wraparound */
1649     }
1650   DISPLAY_FRAME:
1651   hDC= GetDC(hWnd);                                  /* grab a display-context */
1652   SelectObject(hFDC,BitmapHandles[FrameNum-1]);    /* select handle */
1653   BitBlt(hDC,0,0,                             /* copy the bitmap to the display */
1654         zFRAMEWIDE,zFRAMEHIGH,hFDC,0,0,SRCCOPY);
1655   ReleaseDC(hWnd,hDC);                              /* release the display-context */
1656   return;
1657
1658   /* ------------ manage disk-based frame animation ------------ */
1659   DISK_PLAYBACK:
1660   if (bAnimationHalted==TRUE) return;
1661   if (Redisplay==TRUE) goto SAME_FRAME;
1662   if (Pause==TRUE) return;
1663   if (FrameDirection==zFORWARD)                    /* if a forward loop... */
1664     {
1665     FrameNum++;
1666     if (FrameNum > zFINALFRAME) FrameNum= zFIRSTFRAME;
1667     }
1668   if (FrameDirection==zREVERSE)                    /* if a reverse loop... */
1669     {
1670     FrameNum--;
1671     if (FrameNum < zFIRSTFRAME) FrameNum= zFINALFRAME;
1672     }
1673   SAME_FRAME:
1674   hDC= GetDC(hWnd);                  -                /* grab a display-context */
1675   bFrameLoaded= zLoadFrame(hFrame,    /* load the binary image file */
1676                     (LPSTR)FrameFiles[FrameNum-1]);
1677   if (bFrameLoaded==FALSE)                          /* if an error occurred... */
1678     {
1679     bAnimationHalted= TRUE;
1680     MessageBeep(0);
1681     LoadString(hInst,IDS_Unexpected,lpCaption,Max);
1682     LoadString(hInst,IDS_Disk3,lpMessage,MaxText);
1683     TimerCounter= zTIMER_PAUSE;
1684     MessageBox(GetFocus(),lpMessage,lpCaption,MB_OK);
1685     return;
1686     }
1687   BitBlt(hDC,0,0,                             /* copy the bitmap to the display */
1688         zFRAMEWIDE,zFRAMEHIGH,hFrameDC,0,0,SRCCOPY);
1689   ReleaseDC(hWnd,hDC);                              /* release the display-context */
1690   return;
```

```
1691  }
1692  /*
1693  -------------------------------------------------------------------
1694                   Load the animation sequence from disk.
1695  -------------------------------------------------------------------
1696                                                                   */
1697  static void zLoadAnimation(HWND hWnd)
1698  {
1699    HDC hDC;
1700    int Bitmaps;
1701
1702  if (FrameReady==FALSE)
1703    {
1704    MessageBeep(0);
1705    LoadString(hInst,IDS_NotReady,lpCaption,Max);
1706    LoadString(hInst,IDS_NoFrame,lpMessage,MaxText);
1707    MessageBox(GetFocus(),lpMessage,lpCaption,MB_OK);
1708    return;
1709    }
1710  if (bAnimationLoaded==TRUE)
1711    {
1712    MessageBeep(0);
1713    LoadString(hInst,IDS_Unexpected,lpCaption,Max);
1714    LoadString(hInst,IDS_Disk4,lpMessage,MaxText);
1715    TimerCounter= zTIMER_PAUSE;
1716    MessageBox(GetFocus(),lpMessage,lpCaption,MB_OK);
1717    return;
1718    }
1719  if (bPrevLoadAttempt==TRUE)
1720    {
1721    MessageBeep(0);
1722    LoadString(hInst,IDS_Unexpected,lpCaption,Max);
1723    LoadString(hInst,IDS_Disk5,lpMessage,MaxText);
1724    TimerCounter= zTIMER_PAUSE;
1725    MessageBox(GetFocus(),lpMessage,lpCaption,MB_OK);
1726    return;
1727    }
1728  bPrevLoadAttempt= TRUE;
1729
1730  /* ------------- create bitmaps to hold the frames ------------ */
1731  GlobalCompact((DWORD)-1L);
1732  hDC= GetDC(hWnd);
1733  hFDC= CreateCompatibleDC(hDC);
1734  for (LoopCount= 1; LoopCount<= zNUMCELS; LoopCount++)
1735    {                              /* for each cel in the animation... */
1736    BitmapHandles[LoopCount-1]=              /* create a bitmap... */
1737        CreateCompatibleBitmap(hDC,zFRAMEWIDE,zFRAMEHIGH);
1738    if (BitmapHandles[LoopCount-1]==NULL)    /* if error occurs... */
1739      goto BITMAPS_NOT_OK;        /* ...jump out of loop and tidy up */
1740    }
1741  goto BITMAPS_OK;                 /* if OK, jump past error-handler */
1742
1743  /* ------------------ bitmap error-handler ------------------- */
1744  BITMAPS_NOT_OK:
1745  for (Bitmaps= LoopCount-1; Bitmaps>= 1; Bitmaps--)
1746    {          /* for each bitmap that was successfully created... */
1747    DeleteObject(BitmapHandles[Bitmaps-1]);         /* ...delete it */
1748    }
1749  DeleteDC(hFDC);                         /* delete the compatible DC */
1750  ReleaseDC(hWnd,hDC);                 /* release the display-context */
1751  bUseDisk= TRUE; AnimationReady= TRUE;         /* reset the tokens */
```

```
1752  LoadString(hInst,IDS_Status,lpCaption,Max);
1753  LoadString(hInst,IDS_Disk6,lpMessage,MaxText);
1754  MessageBox(GetFocus(),lpMessage,lpCaption,MB_OK); /* message box */
1755  return;                                  /* ...and return to caller */
1756
1757  BITMAPS_OK: ReleaseDC(hWnd,hDC);  /* release the display-context */
1758
1759  /* ------------- load frame files into the bitmaps ------------- */
1760  for (LoopCount= 1; LoopCount<= zNUMCELS; LoopCount++)
1761    {                              /* for each cel in the animation... */
1762     bFrameLoaded= zLoadFrame(BitmapHandles[LoopCount-1],   /* load */
1763                            (LPSTR)FrameFiles[LoopCount-1]);
1764     if (bFrameLoaded==FALSE)              /* if disk error occurred... */
1765       goto DISK_ERROR;                      /* jump to error-handler */
1766    }
1767  goto DISK_OK;               /* if OK, jump past the error-handler */
1768
1769  /* -------------------- disk error-handler -------------------- */
1770  DISK_ERROR:
1771    for (LoopCount= 1; LoopCount<= zNUMCELS; LoopCount++)
1772      {               /* for each bitmap handle in the animation... */
1773       DeleteObject(BitmapHandles[LoopCount-1]);     /* delete it... */
1774      }
1775    DeleteDC(hFDC);     /* ...and delete the memory display-context */
1776    return;
1777
1778  /* -------------------- tidy up and return -------------------- */
1779  DISK_OK:
1780  hPrevF= SelectObject(hFDC,BitmapHandles[0]);
1781  bAnimationLoaded= TRUE;
1782  AnimationReady= TRUE;
1783  bAnimationSaved= TRUE;
1784  MessageBeep(0);
1785  LoadString(hInst,IDS_AnimReady,lpCaption,Max);
1786  LoadString(hInst,IDS_Disk7,lpMessage,MaxText);
1787  MessageBox(GetFocus(),lpMessage,lpCaption,MB_OK);
1788  return;
1789  }
1790  /*
1791  -----------------------------------------------------------------
1792                    Reset the animation frame rate.
1793  -----------------------------------------------------------------
1794                                                                  */
1795  static void zSetFrameRate(HWND hWnd, WORD wNewRate)
1796  {
1797  if (TimerExists==FALSE)
1798    {
1799     wFrameRate= wPrevRate;
1800     MessageBeep(0);
1801     LoadString(hInst,IDS_NotReady,lpCaption,Max);
1802     LoadString(hInst,IDS_NoReset,lpMessage,MaxText);
1803     MessageBox(GetFocus(),lpMessage,lpCaption,MB_OK);
1804     return;
1805    }
1806
1807  /* ----------- remove the check-mark from the menu ------------ */
1808  switch (wPrevRate)
1809    {  /* use hMenu from case WM_INITMENUPOPUP in message handler */
1810    case 55:  CheckMenuItem(hMenu,IDM_FPS182,MF_UNCHECKED); break;
1811    case 110: CheckMenuItem(hMenu,IDM_FPS91, MF_UNCHECKED); break;
1812    case 165: CheckMenuItem(hMenu,IDM_FPS61, MF_UNCHECKED); break;
```

```
1813    case 220: CheckMenuItem(hMenu,IDM_FPS45, MF_UNCHECKED); break;
1814    case 275: CheckMenuItem(hMenu,IDM_FPS36, MF_UNCHECKED); break;
1815    case 330: CheckMenuItem(hMenu,IDM_FPS30, MF_UNCHECKED); break;
1816    }
1817
1818  /* --------- destroy existing timer, create new timer ---------- */
1819  KillTimer(hWnd,1);
1820  TimerID1= SetTimer(hWnd,1,wNewRate,(FARPROC) NULL);
1821  if (TimerID1==0)
1822    {
1823    LoadString(hInst,IDS_NotReady,lpCaption,Max);
1824    LoadString(hInst,IDS_CannotReset,lpMessage,MaxText);
1825    MessageBox(GetFocus(),lpMessage,lpCaption,MB_OK);
1826    TimerExists= FALSE;
1827    return;
1828    }
1829
1830  /* ----------------- add check-mark to menu ------------------ */
1831  switch (wFrameRate)
1832    {
1833    case 55:  CheckMenuItem(hMenu,IDM_FPS182,MF_CHECKED); break;
1834    case 110: CheckMenuItem(hMenu,IDM_FPS91, MF_CHECKED); break;
1835    case 165: CheckMenuItem(hMenu,IDM_FPS61, MF_CHECKED); break;
1836    case 220: CheckMenuItem(hMenu,IDM_FPS45, MF_CHECKED); break;
1837    case 275: CheckMenuItem(hMenu,IDM_FPS36, MF_CHECKED); break;
1838    case 330: CheckMenuItem(hMenu,IDM_FPS30, MF_CHECKED); break;
1839    }
1840  return;
1841  }
1842  /*
1843  ------------------------------------------------------------------
1844                      End of the C source file
1845  ------------------------------------------------------------------
1846                                                                  */
```

C-6 Source listings for the interactive, animated, virtual reality sampler, maze.c, consisting of .def, .h, .rc, and .c files. See Appendix B for the toolkits which must be linked in to build this application. See Appendix A for instructions on building the demo.

```
0001  NAME          VIRTDEMO
0002  DESCRIPTION   'Copyright 1993 Lee Adams.  All rights reserved.'
0003  EXETYPE       WINDOWS
0004  STUB          'WINSTUB.EXE'
0005  CODE          PRELOAD MOVEABLE
0006  DATA          PRELOAD MOVEABLE MULTIPLE
0007  HEAPSIZE      1024
0008  STACKSIZE     8192
0009  EXPORTS       zMessageHandler
0001  /*
0002  ------------------------------------------------------------------
0003                      Include file maze.h
0004          Copyright 1993 Lee Adams. All rights reserved.
0005    Include this file in the .RC resource script file and in the
0006    .C source file.  It contains function prototypes, menu ID
0007    constants, and string ID constants.
0008  ------------------------------------------------------------------
0009  ------------------------------------------------------------------
0010                      Function prototypes
0011  ------------------------------------------------------------------
0012                                                                  */
```

```
0013   #if !defined(zRCFILE)                        /* if not an .rc file... */
0014      LONG FAR PASCAL zMessageHandler(HWND, unsigned, WORD, LONG);
0015      int PASCAL WinMain(HANDLE,HANDLE,LPSTR,int);
0016      HWND zInitMainWindow(HANDLE);
0017      BOOL zInitClass(HANDLE);
0018   static void zClear(HWND);                    /* blank the display window */
0019   static void zInitFrame(HWND);                   /* creates hidden frame */
0020   static void zSaveAnimation(HWND);        /* saves animation sequence */
0021   static void zPreviewFirstFrame(HWND);           /* previews frame 1 */
0022   static void zPreviewFinalFrame(HWND);          /* previews frame 36 */
0023   static BOOL zBuildFrame(int,HWND,LPSTR);          /* builds a frame */
0024   static void zDrawCel(int);                            /* draws a cel */
0025   static void zLoadAnimation(HWND);        /* loads animation sequence */
0026   static void zCopyToDisplay(HWND);       /* copies frame to display */
0027   static void zClearHiddenFrame(void);         /* clears hidden frame */
0028   static void vrWalkthrough(unsigned char,              /* VR player */
0029                             unsigned char, HWND);
0030   #endif
0031   /*
0032   -------------------------------------------------------------------
0033                            Menu ID constants
0034   -------------------------------------------------------------------
0035                                                                    */
0036   #define IDM_New               1
0037   #define IDM_Open              2
0038   #define IDM_Save              3
0039   #define IDM_SaveAs            4
0040   #define IDM_Exit              5
0041
0042   #define IDM_Undo              6
0043   #define IDM_Cut               7
0044   #define IDM_Copy              8
0045   #define IDM_Paste             9
0046   #define IDM_Delete            10
0047
0048   #define IDM_VirtualReality    11
0049   #define IDM_SaveAnimation     12
0050   #define IDM_PreviewFirst      13
0051   #define IDM_PreviewFinal      14
0052   #define IDM_LoadAnimation     15
0053   #define IDM_UseShaded         16
0054   #define IDM_UseWireframe      17
0055
0056   #define IDM_About             18
0057   #define IDM_License           19
0058   #define IDM_GeneralHelp       20
0059   /*
0060   -------------------------------------------------------------------
0061                           String ID constants
0062   -------------------------------------------------------------------
0063                                                                    */
0064   #define IDS_Caption       1
0065   #define IDS_Warning       2
0066   #define IDS_NoMouse       3
0067   #define IDS_About         4
0068   #define IDS_AboutText     5
0069   #define IDS_License       6
0070   #define IDS_LicenseText   7
0071   #define IDS_Help          8
0072   #define IDS_HelpText      9
0073   #define IDS_Completed     10
```

```
0074    #define IDS_Error          11
0075    #define IDS_NotReady       12
0076    #define IDS_Ready          13
0077    #define IDS_BuildBefore    14
0078    #define IDS_Already        15
0079    #define IDS_InsufMem1      16
0080
0081    #define IDS_InsufMem2      17
0082    #define IDS_NoTimer        18
0083    #define IDS_NoReset        19
0084    #define IDS_CannotReset    20
0085    #define IDS_NoFrame        21
0086    #define IDS_AnimReady      22
0087    #define IDS_VRStart        23
0088    #define IDS_VRKeys         24
0089
0090    #define IDS_Unexpected     44
0091    #define IDS_Status         45
0092    #define IDS_Disk1          46
0093    #define IDS_Disk2          47
0094    #define IDS_Disk3          48
0095    #define IDS_Disk4          49
0096    #define IDS_Disk5          50
0097    #define IDS_Disk6          51
0098    #define IDS_Disk7          52
0099    #define IDS_Disk8          53
0100    #define IDS_Disk9          54
0101    #define IDS_Disk10         55
0102    #define IDS_Disk11         56
0103    #define IDS_Disk12         57
0104    #define IDS_Disk13         58
0105    #define IDS_Disk14         59
0106    #define IDS_Disk15         60
0107    #define IDS_Disk16         61
0108    #define IDS_Disk17         62
0109    #define IDS_Disk18         63
0110    #define IDS_Disk19         64
0111    #define IDS_Disk20         65
0112    #define IDS_Disk21         66
0113    #define IDS_Disk22         67
0114    #define IDS_Disk23         68
0115    #define IDS_Disk24         69
0116    #define IDS_Disk25         70
0117    #define IDS_Disk26         71
0118    #define IDS_NoBg           72
0119    #define IDS_BgAlready      73
0120    #define IDS_InsufMemBg     74
0121    #define IDS_ReqdHdwr1      75
0122    #define IDS_ReqdHdwr2      76
0123    #define IDS_Build          77
0124    #define IDS_ToCancel       78
0125    #define IDS_Loading        79
0126    #define IDS_Previewing     80
0127    /*
0128    ------------------------------------------------------------
0129                      End of include file
0130    ------------------------------------------------------------
0131                                                            */
0001    /*
0002    ------------------------------------------------------------
0003                  Resource script file maze.rc
```

```
0004              Copyright 1993 Lee Adams.  All rights reserved.
0005       This file defines the menu resources, the accelerator key
0006       resources, and the string resources that will be used by the
0007       demonstration application at runtime.
0008       -------------------------------------------------------------------
0009                                                                        */
0010       #define zRCFILE
0011       #include <WINDOWS.H>
0012       #include "MAZE.H"
0013       /*
0014       -------------------------------------------------------------------
0015                                Script for menus
0016       -------------------------------------------------------------------
0017                                                                        */
0018       VIRTMENUS MENU
0019         BEGIN
0020         POPUP "&File"
0021           BEGIN
0022             MENUITEM   "&New", IDM_New, GRAYED
0023             MENUITEM   "&Open...", IDM_Open, GRAYED
0024             MENUITEM   "&Save", IDM_Save, GRAYED
0025             MENUITEM   "Save &As...", IDM_SaveAs, GRAYED
0026             MENUITEM SEPARATOR
0027             MENUITEM   "E&xit virtual reality", IDM_Exit
0028           END
0029         POPUP "&Edit"
0030           BEGIN
0031             MENUITEM   "&Undo\tAlt+BkSp", IDM_Undo, GRAYED
0032             MENUITEM SEPARATOR
0033             MENUITEM   "Cu&t\tShift+Del", IDM_Cut, GRAYED
0034             MENUITEM   "&Copy\tCtrl+Ins", IDM_Copy, GRAYED
0035             MENUITEM   "&Paste\tShift+Ins", IDM_Paste, GRAYED
0036             MENUITEM   "&Delete\tDel", IDM_Delete, GRAYED
0037           END
0038         POPUP "&VR"
0039           BEGIN
0040             MENUITEM "&Load universe", IDM_LoadAnimation
0041             MENUITEM "&Run universe", IDM_VirtualReality
0042             MENUITEM SEPARATOR
0043             MENUITEM "&Build universe", IDM_SaveAnimation
0044             MENUITEM "Use &shaded solids", IDM_UseShaded
0045             MENUITEM "Use &wireframe mode", IDM_UseWireframe
0046             MENUITEM SEPARATOR
0047             MENUITEM "Preview s&tart position", IDM_PreviewFirst
0048             MENUITEM "Preview go&al position", IDM_PreviewFinal
0049           END
0050         POPUP "&Using"
0051           BEGIN
0052             MENUITEM "&About", IDM_About
0053             MENUITEM "&License", IDM_License
0054             MENUITEM SEPARATOR
0055             MENUITEM "&How to Use", IDM_GeneralHelp
0056           END
0057         END
0058       /*
0059       -------------------------------------------------------------------
0060                          Script for accelerator keys
0061       -------------------------------------------------------------------
0062                                                                        */
0063       VIRTKEYS ACCELERATORS
0064         BEGIN
```

```
0065    VK_BACK, IDM_Undo, VIRTKEY, ALT
0066    VK_DELETE, IDM_Cut, VIRTKEY, SHIFT
0067    VK_INSERT, IDM_Copy, VIRTKEY, CONTROL
0068    VK_INSERT, IDM_Paste, VIRTKEY, SHIFT
0069    VK_DELETE, IDM_Delete,VIRTKEY
0070    END
0071    /*
0072    ----------------------------------------------------------------
0073                        Script for strings
0074    If you are typing this listing, set your right margin to 255
0075    characters so you can create lengthy strings without embedded
0076    carriage returns.  The line wraparounds in the following
0077    STRINGTABLE listing are used only for readability.
0078    ----------------------------------------------------------------
0079                                                                 */
0080    STRINGTABLE
0081      BEGIN
0082        IDS_Caption     "Virtual Reality Sampler"
0083        IDS_Warning     "Warning"
0084        IDS_NoMouse     "No mouse found.  Some features of this
                demonstration program may require a mouse."
0085        IDS_About       "About this program"
0086        IDS_AboutText   "This is a demo from Windcrest McGraw-Hill
                book 4115.  Copyright- 1993 Lee Adams.  All rights reserved."
0087        IDS_License     "License Agreement"
0088        IDS_LicenseText "You can use this code as part of your own
                software product subject to the License Agreement and
                Limited Warranty in Windcrest McGraw-Hill book 4115 and on
                its companion disk."
0089        IDS_Help        "How to use this virtual reality demo"
0090        IDS_HelpText    "The VR menu manages the virtual reality
                player.  Select Build Universe to create viewpoint nodes and
                save virtual reality sequence to disk.  Select Load
                Universe, then Run Universe, to start a virtual reality
                simulation."
0091        IDS_Completed   "Task completed OK"
0092        IDS_Error       "Runtime error"
0093        IDS_NotReady    "Virtual reality not ready"
0094        IDS_Ready       "Virtual reality ready"
0095        IDS_BuildBefore "Universe images not ready for playback."
0096        IDS_Already     "The hidden frame has already been created."
0097        IDS_InsufMem1   "Insufficient global memory for frame bitmap."
0098        IDS_NoTimer     "Unable to create a timer.  Animation
                functions unavailable.  Restart this demo after closing
                other applications that may be using timers."
0099        IDS_NoReset     "Create hidden frame before attempting to
                reset timer."
0100        IDS_CannotReset "Unable to reset the timer."
0101        IDS_NoFrame     "Hidden frame not yet created."
0102        IDS_AnimReady   "Virtual reality ready"
0103        IDS_Unexpected  "Unexpected virtual reality condition"
0104        IDS_Status      "Virtual reality status"
0105        IDS_Disk1       "Virtual reality sequence already saved to
                disk."
0106        IDS_Disk2       "Virtual reality sequence saved to disk."
0107        IDS_Disk3       "Unable to load next frame from disk.  Virtual
                reality simulation halted."
0108        IDS_Disk4       "Virtual reality sequence already loaded from
                disk."
0109        IDS_Disk5       "Previous load failed.  Cancelling this
                attempt."
```

```
0110      IDS_Disk6        "Not enough memory available to store the
          entire virtual reality universe in memory.  Software will
          dynamically load each image from disk during playback.  To
          begin the virtual reality session select Run Universe from
          the VR menu."
0111      IDS_Disk7        "Virtual reality sequence loaded in memory.
          For optimum performance please wait for your hard disk to
          settle before starting the virtual reality session by
          selecting Run Universe from the VR menu."
0112      IDS_Disk8        "Previous save failed.  Cancelling this
          attempt."
0113      IDS_Disk9        "No hidden-frame exists.  No frame saved to
          disk."
0114      IDS_Disk10       "Unable to retrieve bitmap data structure."
0115      IDS_Disk11       "Bit array is too long to save to disk in a
          single pass."
0116      IDS_Disk12       "Cannot create memory buffer for disk write."
0117      IDS_Disk13       "Unable to copy bits from bitmap to buffer."
0118      IDS_Disk14       "File already exists.  Overwrite existing
          file?"
0119      IDS_Disk15       "Unable to open the file for writing."
0120      IDS_Disk16       "Unable to write to the opened file."
0121      IDS_Disk17       "Unable to close the file after writing."
0122      IDS_Disk18       "No memory bitmap exists.  Unable to load from
          disk."
0123      IDS_Disk19       "Image file is larger than animation frame.
          No file loaded."
0124      IDS_Disk20       "Cannot create memory buffer for file read."
0125      IDS_Disk21       "Unable to open the file for reading.  Be sure
          you have saved a virtual reality universe sequence to disk
          before attempting to load it."
0126      IDS_Disk22       "An error occurred while reading the file."
0127      IDS_Disk23       "Windows must be using same color mode as when
          this universe was saved, either 2, 16, or 256 colors.  To
          run existing virtual reality, use Windows Setup to switch
          color modes.  Otherwise rebuild this sequence in the current
          mode."
0128      IDS_Disk24       "Unable to close the file after reading."
0129      IDS_Disk25       "Unable to copy bits from buffer to bitmap."
0130      IDS_Disk26       "Not all frames saved to disk because
          insufficient space available on disk or because the frames
          have already been saved to disk or because you interrupted
          the build process."
0131      IDS_NoBg         "Hidden background image not yet created."
0132      IDS_BgAlready    "The hidden background bitmap has already been
          created."
0133      IDS_InsufMemBg   "Insufficient global memory for background
          bitmap."
0134      IDS_ReqdHdwr1    "Graphics hardware"
0135      IDS_ReqdHdwr2    "CGA, HGA, or EGA graphics card has been
          detected.  This demo requires an industry-standard VGA or a
          VESA-standard SuperVGA and compatible display -- or a
          graphics accelerator card (16-bit or 24-bit) and appropriate
          display."
0136      IDS_Build        "Cyberspace build process"
0137      IDS_ToCancel     "Ready to begin building the virtual reality
          sequence.  To interrupt a build session in progress, click
          the right mouse button.  To begin the build, select OK now.
          See the book for further information."
0138      IDS_Loading      "Loading universe..."
0139      IDS_Previewing   "Building preview node..."
```

```
0140     IDS_VRStart     "Universe startup"
0141     IDS_VRKeys      "You can use the keyboard to navigate the
         virtual reality environment.  The arrow keys to move you
         ahead, back, left, right.  Use the arrow keys with NumLock
         toggled on to look North, East, South, West.  Also refer to
         the book."
0142   END
0143 /*
0144 -------------------------------------------------------------------
0145                      End of resource script file
0146 -------------------------------------------------------------------
0147                                                               */
0001 /*
0002 -------------------------------------------------------------------
0003                      3D virtual reality sampler
0004 -------------------------------------------------------------------
0005   Source file:  maze.c
0006   Release version:  1.5                    Programmer:  Lee Adams
0007   Type:  C source file for Windows application development.
0008   Supported compilers:  Explicit compatibility with Microsoft
0009     QuickC for Windows v1.00 and Borland Turbo C++ for Windows
0010     v3.0.  Nominal compatibility with all Windows-compatible C
0011     and C++ compilers such as Borland C++, Zortech C++, Watcom C,
0012     and Microsoft C/C++.
0013   Memory model:  medium.
0014   Build notes:  This project relies on the 3D functions in
0015     engine3d.c.  Before building the executable, you must edit
0016     lines 01165, 01166, and 01167 in engine3d.c by changing each
0017     occurrence of && to ||.  You must also use remark tokens to
0018     disable lines 01191 through 01198 in engine3d.c.  In order to
0019     ensure that all virtual objects are rendered, you must also
0020     use remark tokens to disable lines 01594, 01595, and 01598
0021     in engine3d.c so that lines 01598 and 01597 will always
0022     execute in spite of any spurious settings for the near and
0023     far clipping planes.
0024     If you subsequently use engine3d.c to build another demo in
0025     this book you must undo the changes and restore engine3d.c
0026     to its original state.
0027     Do not use the load optimization feature of the Resource
0028     Compiler (or use the command-line -K switch).
0029     For trouble-free compiling follow the tips in the book.
0030   Project notes:  Load the kinematx.mak project file if you are
0031     using QuickC for Windows.  Load the kinematx.prj project file
0032     if you are using Turbo C++ for Windows.  Refer to the book if
0033     you are using another compiler.  The following files are
0034     needed to build the executable:
0035       maze.def        module definition file
0036       maze.h          include file
0037       maze.rc         resource script file
0038       maze.c          C source file
0039       engine3d.h      include file for 3D functions
0040       engine3d.c      3D toolkit
0041       shapes3d.h      include file for 3D solids
0042       shapes3d.c      3D shapes toolkit
0043       lights3d.h      include file for light-source functions
0044       lights3d.c      light-source toolkit
0045       assemb3d.h      include file for hierarchical modeling
0046       assemb3d.c      3D hierarchical modeling toolkit
0047       disk3d.h        include file for disk functions
0048       disk3d.c        image save/load toolkit
0049   Output and features:  Demonstrates cyberspace-based control of
```

```
0050            virtual reality animation sequences.  The interactive demo
0051            provides a maze environment which can be traversed by the
0052            player, who uses the arrow keys to move from node to node
0053            in the artifical environment.  The viewpoint images require
0054            3.2 MB of storage.  If insufficient memory is available for
0055            RAM-based playback, then each frame will be loaded from disk
0056            as needed during an interactive virtual reality session.
0057        Publication: Contains material from Windcrest/McGraw-Hill book
0058            4115 published by TAB BOOKS Division of McGraw-Hill Inc.
0059        License:  As purchaser of the book you are granted a royalty-
0060            free license to distribute executable files generated using
0061            this code provided you accept the conditions of the License
0062            Agreement and Limited Warranty described in the book and on
0063            the companion disk.  Government users:  This software and
0064            documentation are subject to restrictions set forth in The
0065            Rights in Technical Data and Computer Software clause at
0066            252.227-7013 and elsewhere.
0067     -------------------------------------------------------------------
0068            (c) Copyright 1991-1993 Lee Adams.  All rights reserved.
0069              Lee Adams(tm) is a trademark of Lee Adams.
0070     -------------------------------------------------------------------
0071
0072     -------------------------------------------------------------------
0073                            Include files
0074     -------------------------------------------------------------------
0075                                                                       */
0076     #include <WINDOWS.H>              /* declarations for Windows API */
0077     #include "MAZE.H"           /* declares function prototypes, etc. */
0078     #include "DISK3D.H"          /* declares functions in disk engine */
0079     #include "ENGINE3D.H"          /* declares functions in 3D engine */
0080     #include "SHAPES3D.H"   /* declares functions in 3D shapes module */
0081     #include "LIGHTS3D.H"     /* declares functions in lighting module */
0082     #include "ASSEMB3D.H"   /* declares functions in hierarchy module */
0083     #include <time.h>                   /* supports date and time */
0084
0085     /*
0086     -------------------------------------------------------------------
0087            Static variables visible throughout this file
0088     -------------------------------------------------------------------
0089                                                                       */
0090     /* ------------------- window specifications ----------------- */
0091     #define zWINDOW_WIDTH 263                      /* width of window */
0092     #define zWINDOW_HEIGHT 300                     /* depth of window */
0093     #define zFRAMEWIDE 256                       /* width of viewport */
0094     #define zFRAMEHIGH 255                       /* depth of viewport */
0095     static int WindowX, WindowY;               /* location of window */
0096
0097     /* ------------------- instance operations ------------------- */
0098     HANDLE hInst;                  /* handle to this copy of the app */
0099     static HWND MainhWnd;              /* handle to the app's window */
0100     static HANDLE hAccel;          /* handle to the accelerator keys */
0101     static HMENU hMenu;       /* handle to an active menu at runtime */
0102     static PAINTSTRUCT ps;   /* used for Windows-generated refreshes */
0103
0104     /* ------------------- mouse and cursor --------------------- */
0105     static HCURSOR hPrevCursor;            /* handle to arrow cursor */
0106     static HCURSOR hHourGlass;         /* handle to hourglass cursor */
0107     static int MousePresent;           /* indicates if mouse found */
0108
0109     /* ------------------- runtime conditions ----------------- */
0110     static int DisplayWidth, DisplayHeight; /* resolution of display */
```

```
0111   static int DisplayBits;                    /* number of bits per pixel */
0112   static int DisplayPlanes;                    /* number of bitplanes */
0113   static DWORD MemoryMode;                    /* runtime memory mode */
0114   static DWORD Version;                         /* version of Windows */
0115   static BOOL bUseArial= TRUE;    /* FALSE, use Helv if Windows 3.0 */
0116
0117   /* ------------------ message box operations ------------------ */
0118   char lpCaption[51];                 /* stores caption for message box */
0119   int Max= 50;                            /* max length of caption */
0120   char lpMessage[250];                   /* stores text for message box */
0121   int MaxText= 249;                          /* max length of text */
0122   static short TextLength= 0;           /* stores wsprintf() string */
0123   static int MessageBoxChoice= 0;        /* user's selection, if any */
0124
0125   /* ---------------- persistent image operations -------------- */
0126   #define zBLANK 0
0127   #define zANIMATING  1
0128   #define zPREVIEW  2
0129   static int PaintImage= zBLANK;       /* indicates viewport status */
0130
0131   /* ----------------- hidden-frame operations ----------------- */
0132   static HDC hFrameDC;             /* display-context of hidden-frame */
0133   static HBITMAP hFrame;                   /* bitmap of hidden-frame */
0134   static HBITMAP hPrevFrame;                   /* default bitmap */
0135   BOOL FrameReady= FALSE;                   /* hidden-frame ready? */
0136
0137   /* ------------------- animation operations ------------------- */
0138   static BOOL bUsingVR= FALSE;    /* TRUE if using interactive mode */
0139   static WORD wFrameRate= 55;
0140   static WORD wPrevRate= 55;
0141   #define zFORWARD 1
0142   #define zREVERSE 0
0143   static int FrameDirection= zFORWARD;
0144   static BOOL Redisplay= FALSE;
0145   static BOOL AnimationReady= FALSE;
0146   static int FrameNum= 1;
0147   #define zFIRSTFRAME 1
0148   #define zFINALFRAME 100
0149   #define zNUMCELS 100
0150   static int LoopCount;
0151
0152   /* ------ virtual reality extensions to animation engine ------- */
0153   #define vrVIEW000       1                /* directions of view... */
0154   #define vrVIEW090       2
0155   #define vrVIEW180       3
0156   #define vrVIEW270       4
0157   #define vrSTATIONARY    5                /* viewpoint movements... */
0158   #define vrMOVE_FORWARD  6
0159   #define vrMOVE_RIGHT    7
0160   #define vrMOVE_BACKWARD 8
0161   #define vrMOVE_LEFT     9
0162   #define vrMAX_ROW       4 /* maximum, minimum viewpoint nodes... */
0163   #define vrMAX_COLUMN    4
0164   #define vrMIN_ROW       0
0165   #define vrMIN_COLUMN    0
0166   #define vrNUM_COLUMNS   5       /* number of columns in each array */
0167   #define vrNUM_NODES     25      /* number of nodes in each array */
0168   #define vrFIRST_ARRAY   0          /* index into array of ptrs... */
0169   #define vrSECOND_ARRAY  25
0170   #define vrTHIRD_ARRAY   50
0171   #define vrFOURTH_ARRAY  75
```

```
0172    static HBITMAP *vrCurrentHandle;        /* ptr to array of handles */
0173    static char * (*vrCurrentFile);         /* ptr to array of pointers */
0174    static unsigned char vrMove= vrSTATIONARY; /* viewpoint movement */
0175    static unsigned char vrView= vrVIEW000;    /* direction of view */
0176    static unsigned char vrRow= 4;             /* for view matrix */
0177    static unsigned char vrColumn= 2;          /* for view matrix */
0178    static unsigned char vrArrayOffset= vrFIRST_ARRAY;
0179    static int vrFrameID= 0;                 /* index into array of pointers */
0180
0181    /* ---------------- disk save/load operations ---------------- */
0182    int RetVal;                             /* value returned by functions */
0183    static BOOL bFrameSaved= FALSE;                 /* frame saved? */
0184    static BOOL bFrameLoaded= FALSE;                /* frame loaded? */
0185    static BOOL bAnimationSaved= FALSE;          /* animation saved? */
0186    static BOOL bAnimationLoaded= FALSE;         /* animation loaded? */
0187    static BOOL bPrevSaveAttempt= FALSE; /* previous save attempted? */
0188    static BOOL bPrevLoadAttempt= FALSE; /* previous load attempted? */
0189    static BOOL bUseDisk= FALSE;       /* use RAM or disk for playback? */
0190    static BOOL bAnimationHalted= FALSE;         /* playback paused? */
0191    static HDC hFDC;   /* memory display-context for hidden bitmaps */
0192    static HBITMAP hPrevF;                     /* default bitmap */
0193    static HBITMAP BitmapHandles[zNUMCELS];   /* array of bitmaps */
0194    static char *FrameFiles[zNUMCELS]= /* array of ptrs to filenames */
0195    {                /* Viewpoint nodes */
0196    /* Row 0      Row 1       Row 2       Row 3       Row 4 */
0197              /* ---- 000 degree view angle --- */
0198    "VR01.BIT","VR02.BIT","VR03.BIT","VR04.BIT","VR05.BIT", /* Col 0 */
0199    "VR06.BIT","VR07.BIT","VR08.BIT","VR09.BIT","VR10.BIT", /* Col 1 */
0200    "VR11.BIT","VR12.BIT","VR13.BIT","VR14.BIT","VR15.BIT", /* Col 2 */
0201    "VR16.BIT","VR17.BIT","VR18.BIT","VR19.BIT","VR20.BIT", /* Col 3 */
0202    "VR21.BIT","VR22.BIT","VR23.BIT","VR24.BIT","VR25.BIT", /* Col 4 */
0203
0204              /* ---- 090 degree view angle --- */
0205    "VR26.BIT","VR27.BIT","VR28.BIT","VR29.BIT","VR30.BIT", /* Col 0 */
0206    "VR31.BIT","VR32.BIT","VR33.BIT","VR34.BIT","VR35.BIT", /* Col 1 */
0207    "VR36.BIT","VR37.BIT","VR38.BIT","VR39.BIT","VR40.BIT", /* Col 2 */
0208    "VR41.BIT","VR42.BIT","VR43.BIT","VR44.BIT","VR45.BIT", /* Col 3 */
0209    "VR46.BIT","VR47.BIT","VR48.BIT","VR49.BIT","VR50.BIT", /* Col 4 */
0210
0211              /* ---- 180 degree view angle --- */
0212    "VR51.BIT","VR52.BIT","VR53.BIT","VR54.BIT","VR55.BIT", /* Col 0 */
0213    "VR56.BIT","VR57.BIT","VR58.BIT","VR59.BIT","VR60.BIT", /* Col 1 */
0214    "VR61.BIT","VR62.BIT","VR63.BIT","VR64.BIT","VR65.BIT", /* Col 2 */
0215    "VR66.BIT","VR67.BIT","VR68.BIT","VR69.BIT","VR70.BIT", /* Col 3 */
0216    "VR71.BIT","VR72.BIT","VR73.BIT","VR74.BIT","VR75.BIT", /* Col 4 */
0217
0218              /* ---- 270 degree view angle --- */
0219    "VR76.BIT","VR77.BIT","VR78.BIT","VR79.BIT","VR80.BIT", /* Col 0 */
0220    "VR81.BIT","VR82.BIT","VR83.BIT","VR84.BIT","VR85.BIT", /* Col 1 */
0221    "VR86.BIT","VR87.BIT","VR88.BIT","VR89.BIT","VR90.BIT", /* Col 2 */
0222    "VR91.BIT","VR92.BIT","VR93.BIT","VR94.BIT","VR95.BIT", /* Col 3 */
0223    "VR96.BIT","VR97.BIT","VR98.BIT","VR99.BIT","VR00.BIT", /* Col 4 */
0224    };
0225
0226    /*
0227    -----------------------------------------------------------------
0228                      Entry point for the application
0229    -----------------------------------------------------------------
0230                                                                    */
0231    int PASCAL WinMain(HANDLE hInstance, HANDLE hPrevInstance,
0232                    LPSTR lpCmdLine, int nCmdShow)
```

```
0233   {
0234     MSG msg;                                    /* holds incoming messages */
0235     HWND hWndPrev;                       /* handle to previous copy of app */
0236     HWND hDesktopWnd;                    /* handle to the entire display */
0237     HDC hDCcaps;            /* display-context for the entire display */
0238     RECT rcClientReqd;           /* size of viewport before adjustment */
0239     int AdjustX, AdjustY; /* amount to adjust to ensure 256-by-255 */
0240
0241   /* ------------- ensure only one copy is running ------------- */
0242   hWndPrev = FindWindow("VIRT4115", "VIRTDEMO");
0243   if (hWndPrev != NULL)     /* if another app named VIRTDEMO of... */
0244     {                 /* class VIRT4115 is already running, then... */
0245     BringWindowToTop(hWndPrev);                /* ...use it instead... */
0246     return FALSE;                      /* ...and cancel this launch */
0247     }
0248
0249   /* ------------- display the splash signon notice ------------- */
0250   MessageBoxChoice= MessageBox(GetFocus(),
0251   "Virtual reality sampler from Windcrest McGraw-Hill book 4115",
0252   "Copyright- 1993 Lee Adams", MB_OKCANCEL);
0253   if (MessageBoxChoice == IDCANCEL) return FALSE;
0254
0255   /* -------------- determine version of Windows --------------- */
0256   Version= (DWORD)GetVersion();
0257   if ((LOBYTE(LOWORD(Version))==3) &&
0258      (HIBYTE(LOWORD(Version))==0))
0259     {                         /* if running Windows version 3.0... */
0260     bUseArial= FALSE;         /* ...use Helv font in client area */
0261     }
0262   else
0263     {                 /* ...else if running Windows 3.1 or newer... */
0264     bUseArial= TRUE;            /* ...use Arial font in client area */
0265     }
0266
0267   /* --------- determine capabilities of screen display ---------- */
0268   hDesktopWnd= GetDesktopWindow();
0269   hDCcaps= GetDC(hDesktopWnd);
0270   DisplayWidth= GetDeviceCaps(hDCcaps,HORZRES);
0271   DisplayHeight= GetDeviceCaps(hDCcaps,VERTRES);
0272   DisplayBits= GetDeviceCaps(hDCcaps,BITSPIXEL);
0273   DisplayPlanes= GetDeviceCaps(hDCcaps,PLANES);
0274   ReleaseDC(hDesktopWnd,hDCcaps);
0275
0276   /* ------------- trap unsupported graphics adapters ----------- */
0277   if (DisplayWidth==720)
0278     {                                        /* if HGA detected... */
0279     LoadString(hInstance,IDS_ReqdHdwr1,lpCaption,Max);
0280     LoadString(hInstance,IDS_ReqdHdwr2,lpMessage,MaxText);
0281     MessageBeep(0); MessageBox(GetFocus(),lpMessage,lpCaption,MB_OK);
0282     return FALSE;
0283     }
0284   if (DisplayWidth==640)
0285     {
0286     if ((DisplayHeight==350)||(DisplayHeight==200))
0287       {                              /* if EGA or CGA detected... */
0288       LoadString(hInstance,IDS_ReqdHdwr1,lpCaption,Max);
0289       LoadString(hInstance,IDS_ReqdHdwr2,lpMessage,MaxText);
0290       MessageBeep(0);
0291       MessageBox(GetFocus(),lpMessage,lpCaption,MB_OK);
0292       return FALSE;
0293       }
```

C-6 Continued.

```
0294      }
0295
0296      /* ------- calculate screen position to center the window ------ */
0297      WindowX= (DisplayWidth - zWINDOW_WIDTH) / 2;
0298      WindowY= (DisplayHeight - zWINDOW_HEIGHT) /2;
0299      if (WindowX < 0) WindowX= 0;
0300      if (WindowY < 0) WindowY= 0;
0301
0302      /* ---- determine memory mode (enhanced, standard, or real) ---- */
0303      MemoryMode= GetWinFlags();
0304
0305      /* ---------------- create and show the window ---------------- */
0306      hInst = hInstance;          /* store handle to this copy of the app */
0307      if (!zInitClass(hInstance)) return FALSE;    /* initialize class */
0308      MainhWnd = zInitMainWindow(hInstance);       /* initialize window */
0309      if (!MainhWnd) return FALSE;          /* if error, cancel startup */
0310      ShowWindow(MainhWnd, nCmdShow);                /* show the window */
0311      UpdateWindow(MainhWnd);                         /* force a refresh */
0312      hAccel= LoadAccelerators(hInstance,"VIRTKEYS"); /* activate keys */
0313
0314      /* --------------- enforce a 256-by-255 viewport --------------- */
0315      GetClientRect(MainhWnd, &rcClientReqd);        /* get dimensions */
0316      AdjustX=              /* compare actual width to desired width... */
0317              zFRAMEWIDE - (rcClientReqd.right + 1);
0318      AdjustY=              /* compare actual height to desired height... */
0319              zFRAMEHIGH - (rcClientReqd.bottom + 1);
0320      if ((AdjustX != 0)||(AdjustY != 0)) /* if adjustment required... */
0321         {
0322         SetWindowPos(MainhWnd, (HWND)NULL,
0323                   WindowX, WindowY,
0324                   zWINDOW_WIDTH + AdjustX,      /* resize the width */
0325                   zWINDOW_HEIGHT + AdjustY,     /* resize the height */
0326                   SWP_NOZORDER);
0327         }
0328
0329      /* ---------------------- check for mouse ---------------------- */
0330      MousePresent = GetSystemMetrics(SM_MOUSEPRESENT);
0331         if (!MousePresent)             /* if no mouse found... */
0332         {                        /* ...display a cautionary warning */
0333         LoadString(hInst,IDS_Warning,lpCaption,Max);
0334         LoadString(hInst,IDS_NoMouse,lpMessage,MaxText);
0335         MessageBox(GetFocus(),lpMessage,lpCaption,MB_OK);
0336         }
0337
0338      /* ---------------- initialize the hidden-frame ---------------- */
0339      zInitFrame(MainhWnd); /* is used for software-controlled refresh */
0340
0341      /* --------- initialize the virtual reality extensions --------- */
0342      vrCurrentHandle= &BitmapHandles[0]; /* point to array of handles */
0343      vrCurrentFile= &FrameFiles[0];      /* point to array of pointers */
0344
0345      /* ---------- begin retrieving messages for the window ---------- */
0346      while (GetMessage(&msg,0,0,0))
0347         {
0348         if(TranslateAccelerator(MainhWnd, hAccel, &msg)) continue;
0349         TranslateMessage(&msg);
0350         DispatchMessage(&msg);
0351         }
0352      return(msg.wParam);
0353      }
0354
```

```
0355   /*
0356   ------------------------------------------------------------------
0357                     Switcher for incoming messages
0358   ------------------------------------------------------------------
0359                                                                   */
0360   LONG FAR PASCAL zMessageHandler(HWND hWnd, unsigned message,
0361                                   WORD wParam, LONG lParam)
0362   {
0363     HDC hDCpaint;                    /* for Windows-generated refresh */
0364
0365   switch (message)
0366     {
0367     /* ----------------- menu system commands ------------------ */
0368     case WM_COMMAND:
0369       switch(wParam)
0370         {
0371         case IDM_New:    break;
0372         case IDM_Open:   break;
0373         case IDM_Save:   break;
0374         case IDM_SaveAs: break;
0375         case IDM_Exit:
0376             MessageBoxChoice= MessageBox(GetFocus(),
0377               "Exit virtual reality and return to Windows?",
0378               "Please confirm", MB_YESNO);
0379             if (MessageBoxChoice == IDYES) PostQuitMessage(0);
0380             break;
0381         case IDM_Undo:   break;
0382         case IDM_Cut:    break;
0383         case IDM_Copy:   break;
0384         case IDM_Paste:  break;
0385         case IDM_Delete: break;
0386
0387         /* ------------------- VR menu --------------------- */
0388         case IDM_VirtualReality:         /* interactive walkthrough */
0389             if (bUsingVR == TRUE)
0390               {                /* if virtual reality already running... */
0391               MessageBox(GetFocus(),
0392                 "The virtual reality universe is already running.",
0393                 "Virtual reality status", MB_OK);
0394               break;
0395               }
0396             if (AnimationReady==FALSE)
0397               {
0398               MessageBeep(0);
0399               LoadString(hInst,IDS_NotReady,lpCaption,Max);
0400               LoadString(hInst,IDS_BuildBefore,lpMessage,MaxText);
0401               MessageBox(GetFocus(),lpMessage,lpCaption,MB_OK);
0402               break;
0403               }
0404             bUsingVR= TRUE;
0405             LoadString(hInst,IDS_VRstart,lpCaption,Max);
0406             LoadString(hInst,IDS_VRKeys,lpMessage,MaxText);
0407             MessageBox(GetFocus(),lpMessage,lpCaption,MB_OK);
0408             /* -------- display the virtual reality scene -------- */
0409             vrMove= vrSTATIONARY;        /* reset viewpoint movement */
0410             vrView= vrVIEW000;           /* reset direction of view */
0411             vrRow= 4; vrColumn= 2;              /* reselect view node */
0412             vrWalkthrough(vrMove, vrView, hWnd);  /* display scene */
0413             break;
0414         case IDM_SaveAnimation:   /* build images and save to disk */
0415             if (bUsingVR == TRUE)
```

```
0416                    {
0417                    MessageBox(GetFocus(),
0418                      "The virtual reality universe is already running.",
0419                      "No build available", MB_OK);
0420                    break;
0421                    }
0422                  LoadString(hInst,IDS_Build,lpCaption,Max);
0423                  LoadString(hInst,IDS_ToCancel,lpMessage,MaxText);
0424                  MessageBox(GetFocus(),lpMessage,lpCaption,MB_OK);
0425                  zInitialize3D(hWnd); zSetNearClippingPlane(10);
0426                  SetCapture(hWnd); hPrevCursor= SetCursor(hHourGlass);
0427                  zSaveAnimation(hWnd);
0428                  LoadString(hInst,IDS_Caption,lpCaption,Max);
0429                  SetWindowText(hWnd,lpCaption);
0430                  SetCursor(hPrevCursor); ReleaseCapture();
0431                  if (bAnimationSaved==FALSE)
0432                    {
0433                    MessageBeep(0);
0434                    LoadString(hInst,IDS_NotReady,lpCaption,Max);
0435                    LoadString(hInst,IDS_Disk26,lpMessage,MaxText);
0436                    MessageBox(GetFocus(),lpMessage,lpCaption,MB_OK);
0437                    }
0438                break;
0439            case IDM_PreviewFirst:          /* preview startup position */
0440                if (bUsingVR == TRUE)
0441                    {
0442                    MessageBeep(0);
0443                    MessageBox(GetFocus(),
0444                      "The virtual reality universe is already running.",
0445                      "No preview available", MB_OK);
0446                    break;
0447                    }
0448                  SetCapture(hWnd);
0449                  hPrevCursor= SetCursor(hHourGlass);
0450                  LoadString(hInst,IDS_Previewing,lpCaption,Max);
0451                  SetWindowText(hWnd,lpCaption);
0452                  zPreviewFirstFrame(hWnd);
0453                  LoadString(hInst,IDS_Caption,lpCaption,Max);
0454                  SetWindowText(hWnd,lpCaption);
0455                  SetCursor(hPrevCursor);
0456                  ReleaseCapture();
0457                  PaintImage= zPREVIEW;
0458                  bUsingVR= FALSE;
0459                break;
0460            case IDM_PreviewFinal:              /* preview goal position */
0461                if (bUsingVR == TRUE)
0462                    {
0463                    MessageBeep(0);
0464                    MessageBox(GetFocus(),
0465                      "The virtual reality universe is already running.",
0466                      "No preview available", MB_OK);
0467                    break;
0468                    }
0469                  SetCapture(hWnd);
0470                  hPrevCursor= SetCursor(hHourGlass);
0471                  LoadString(hInst,IDS_Previewing,lpCaption,Max);
0472                  SetWindowText(hWnd,lpCaption);
0473                  zPreviewFinalFrame(hWnd);
0474                  LoadString(hInst,IDS_Caption,lpCaption,Max);
0475                  SetWindowText(hWnd,lpCaption);
0476                  SetCursor(hPrevCursor);
```

```
0477                ReleaseCapture();
0478                bUsingVR= FALSE;
0479                PaintImage= zPREVIEW;
0480                break;
0481            case IDM_LoadAnimation:              /* load images from disk */
0482                if (bUsingVR == TRUE)
0483                    {           /* if virtual reality already running... */
0484                     MessageBeep(0);
0485                     MessageBox(GetFocus(),
0486                       "The virtual reality universe is already running.",
0487                       "Already loaded", MB_OK);
0488                     break;
0489                    }
0490                LoadString(hInst,IDS_Loading,lpCaption,Max);
0491                SetWindowText(hWnd,lpCaption);
0492                SetCapture(hWnd); hPrevCursor= SetCursor(hHourGlass);
0493                zLoadAnimation(hWnd);
0494                SetCursor(hPrevCursor); ReleaseCapture();
0495                LoadString(hInst,IDS_Caption,lpCaption,Max);
0496                SetWindowText(hWnd,lpCaption);
0497                break;
0498            case IDM_UseShaded:              /* use fully-shaded universe */
0499                if (bUsingVR == TRUE)
0500                    {
0501                     MessageBeep(0);
0502                     MessageBox(GetFocus(),
0503                       "The virtual reality universe is already running.",
0504                       "Mode already set", MB_OK);
0505                     break;
0506                    }
0507                zInitialize3D(hWnd);
0508                zUseWireframeMode(FALSE);
0509                MessageBox(GetFocus(),
0510                  "Using shaded solids production mode.",
0511                  "Virtual reality report", MB_OK);
0512                break;
0513            case IDM_UseWireframe:              /* use wireframe universe */
0514                if (bUsingVR == TRUE)
0515                    {
0516                     MessageBeep(0);
0517                     MessageBox(GetFocus(),
0518                       "The virtual reality universe is already running.",
0519                       "Mode already set", MB_OK);
0520                     break;
0521                    }
0522                zInitialize3D(hWnd);
0523                zUseWireframeMode(TRUE);
0524                MessageBox(GetFocus(),
0525                  "Using wireframe prototyping mode.",
0526                  "Virtual reality report", MB_OK);
0527                break;
0528
0529            /* ----------- About, License, and How to Use ----------- */
0530            case IDM_About:                    /* copyright information... */
0531              LoadString(hInst,IDS_About,lpCaption,Max);
0532              LoadString(hInst,IDS_AboutText,lpMessage,MaxText);
0533              MessageBox(GetFocus(),lpMessage,lpCaption,MB_OK);
0534              break;
0535            case IDM_License:                  /* license information... */
0536              LoadString(hInst,IDS_License,lpCaption,Max);
0537              LoadString(hInst,IDS_LicenseText,lpMessage,MaxText);
```

```
0538              MessageBox(GetFocus(),lpMessage,lpCaption,MB_OK);
0539              break;
0540           case IDM_GeneralHelp:                    /* how to use the demo... */
0541              LoadString(hInst,IDS_Help,lpCaption,Max);
0542              LoadString(hInst,IDS_HelpText,lpMessage,MaxText);
0543              MessageBox(GetFocus(),lpMessage,lpCaption,MB_OK);
0544              break;
0545           default:
0546              return(DefWindowProc(hWnd, message, wParam, lParam));
0547           }
0548        break;
0549
0550      /* ------- oversee Windows-generated refresh requests -------- */
0551      case WM_PAINT:
0552        hDCpaint= BeginPaint(hWnd,&ps);
0553        EndPaint(hWnd, &ps);
0554        if (PaintImage==zBLANK) break;           /* if blank do nothing */
0555        if (PaintImage==zPREVIEW)                 /* if in preview mode... */
0556           {
0557           zCopyToDisplay(hWnd);        /* copy hidden frame to viewport */
0558           break;
0559           }
0560        if (bUsingVR==TRUE)            /* if in virtual reality mode... */
0561           {
0562           vrWalkthrough(vrMove, vrView, hWnd);   /* redisplay scene */
0563           break;
0564           }
0565        break;
0566
0567      /* ---- manage keystrokes for interactive virtual reality ---- */
0568      case WM_KEYDOWN:
0569        switch (wParam)                    /* check for supported keys... */
0570           {
0571           /* ----- the arrow keys manage the viewpoint movement ---- */
0572           case VK_LEFT:            /* VR participant wants to move left */
0573              if (bUsingVR==TRUE)
0574                 {
0575                 vrMove= vrMOVE_LEFT;        /* set viewpoint movement */
0576                 vrWalkthrough(vrMove, vrView, hWnd);     /* call VR */
0577                 vrMove= vrSTATIONARY;    /* reset viewpoint movement */
0578                 PaintImage= zANIMATING;   /* animation housekeeping */
0579                 }
0580              break;
0581
0582           case VK_RIGHT:          /* VR participant wants to move right */
0583              if (bUsingVR==TRUE)
0584                 {
0585                 vrMove= vrMOVE_RIGHT;
0586                 vrWalkthrough(vrMove, vrView, hWnd);
0587                 vrMove= vrSTATIONARY;
0588                 PaintImage= zANIMATING;
0589                 }
0590              break;
0591
0592           case VK_UP:          /* VR participant wants to move forward */
0593              if (bUsingVR==TRUE)
0594                 {
0595                 vrMove= vrMOVE_FORWARD;
0596                 vrWalkthrough(vrMove, vrView, hWnd);
0597                 vrMove= vrSTATIONARY;
0598                 PaintImage= zANIMATING;
```

```
0599                        }
0600                  break;
0601
0602         case VK_DOWN:        /* VR participant wants to move backward */
0603              if (bUsingVR==TRUE)
0604                  {
0605                  vrMove= vrMOVE_BACKWARD;
0606                  vrWalkthrough(vrMove, vrView, hWnd);
0607                  vrMove= vrSTATIONARY;
0608                  PaintImage= zANIMATING;
0609                  }
0610              break;
0611
0612         /* ---- the keyboard keys manage the viewing direction --- */
0613         case VK_NUMPAD8:      /* VR participant wants to look North */
0614              if (bUsingVR==TRUE)
0615                  {
0616                  vrView= vrVIEW000;
0617                  vrWalkthrough(vrMove, vrView, hWnd);
0618                  PaintImage= zANIMATING;
0619                  }
0620              break;
0621
0622         case VK_NUMPAD6:        /* VR participant wants to look East */
0623              if (bUsingVR==TRUE)
0624                  {
0625                  vrView= vrVIEW090;
0626                  vrWalkthrough(vrMove, vrView, hWnd);
0627                  PaintImage= zANIMATING;
0628                  }
0629              break;
0630
0631         case VK_NUMPAD2:      /* VR participant wants to look South */
0632              if (bUsingVR==TRUE)
0633                  {
0634                  vrView= vrVIEW180;
0635                  vrWalkthrough(vrMove, vrView, hWnd);
0636                  PaintImage= zANIMATING;
0637                  }
0638              break;
0639
0640         case VK_NUMPAD4:        /* VR participant wants to look West */
0641              if (bUsingVR==TRUE)
0642                  {
0643                  vrView= vrVIEW270;
0644                  vrWalkthrough(vrMove, vrView, hWnd);
0645                  PaintImage= zANIMATING;
0646                  }
0647              break;
0648
0649         /* ------ pass all other keystrokes back to Windows ------ */
0650         default:
0651                  return(DefWindowProc(hWnd,message,wParam,lParam));
0652          }
0653      break;
0654
0655     /* --------------- ensure a graceful shutdown --------------- */
0656     case WM_DESTROY:
0657       if (FrameReady==TRUE)
0658         {              /* if a hidden-frame was created, destroy it... */
0659         SelectObject(hFrameDC,hPrevFrame);
```

```
0660        DeleteObject(hFrame);
0661        DeleteDC(hFrameDC);
0662        }
0663    if (bAnimationLoaded==TRUE)
0664        {    /* if an animation sequence was loaded into memory... */
0665        SelectObject(hFDC,hPrevF); /* select default bitmap handle */
0666        for (LoopCount= 1; LoopCount<= zNUMCELS; LoopCount++)
0667            {                /* for each bitmap handle in the array... */
0668            DeleteObject(BitmapHandles[LoopCount-1]);   /* ...delete */
0669            }
0670        DeleteDC(hFDC);   /* ...then delete memory display-context */
0671        }
0672    zClose3D();                        /* shut down the 3D engine */
0673    PostQuitMessage(0);
0674    break;
0675
0676    /* ------- intercept attempt to resize or move window -------- */
0677    case WM_SYSCOMMAND:
0678      if ((wParam & 0xfff0)== SC_SIZE)
0679        {
0680        MessageBeep(0); break;
0681        }
0682      if ((wParam & 0xfff0)== SC_MINIMIZE)
0683        {
0684        MessageBeep(0); break;
0685        }
0686      if ((wParam & 0xfff0)== SC_MAXIMIZE)
0687        {
0688        MessageBeep(0); break;
0689        }
0690
0691    /* ----- send all other messages to Windows for handling ----- */
0692    default:
0693      return(DefWindowProc(hWnd, message, wParam, lParam));
0694    }
0695 return FALSE;
0696 }
0697 /*
0698 ------------------------------------------------------------------
0699           Initialize the attributes of the window class
0700 ------------------------------------------------------------------
0701                                                                 */
0702 BOOL zInitClass(HANDLE hInstance)
0703 {
0704   WNDCLASS WndClass;
0705 WndClass.style= 0;
0706 WndClass.lpfnWndProc= zMessageHandler;  /* app's message handler */
0707 WndClass.cbClsExtra= 0;
0708 WndClass.cbWndExtra= 0;
0709 WndClass.hInstance= hInstance;                /* this copy of the app */
0710 WndClass.hIcon= LoadIcon(NULL,IDI_EXCLAMATION);    /* app's icon */
0711 WndClass.hCursor= LoadCursor(NULL,IDC_ARROW);     /* app's cursor */
0712 WndClass.hbrBackground=            /* background color for viewport */
0713                    CreateSolidBrush(RGB(255,255,255));
0714 WndClass.lpszMenuName= "VIRTMENUS";   /* menu script in .rc file */
0715 WndClass.lpszClassName= "VIRT4115";     /* nominal name of class */
0716 return RegisterClass(&WndClass); /* tell Windows about the class */
0717 }
0718 /*
0719 ------------------------------------------------------------------
0720                     Create the main window
```

```
0721   ------------------------------------------------------------
0722                                                             */
0723   HWND zInitMainWindow(HANDLE hInstance)
0724   {
0725     HWND hWnd;
0726   LoadString(hInstance,IDS_Caption,lpCaption,Max); /* load caption */
0727   hHourGlass= LoadCursor(NULL,IDC_WAIT);  /* load hourglass cursor */
0728   hWnd = CreateWindow("VIRT4115",                   /* class name */
0729     lpCaption,                               /* window caption */
0730     WS_OVERLAPPED | WS_THICKFRAME | WS_CLIPCHILDREN,    /* style */
0731     WindowX,WindowY,                        /* location of window */
0732     zWINDOW_WIDTH,zWINDOW_HEIGHT,         /* dimensions of window */
0733     0,                                   /* parent window, if any */
0734     0,                                   /* special menu, if any */
0735     hInstance,                           /* this copy of the app */
0736     (LPSTR)NULL);         /* for multiple-document interface, if any */
0737   return hWnd;     /* return the newly-created handle to the caller */
0738   }
0739
0740   /*
0741   ------------------------------------------------------------------
0742                      Graphics system functions
0743   ------------------------------------------------------------------
0744   ------------------------------------------------------------------
0745                      Create the hidden-frame.
0746   ------------------------------------------------------------------
0747                                                                   */
0748   static void zInitFrame(HWND hWnd)
0749   {
0750     HDC hDisplayDC;
0751
0752   if (FrameReady==TRUE)
0753     {                       /* if a hidden-frame already exists... */
0754     MessageBeep(0);
0755     LoadString(hInst,IDS_Ready,lpCaption,Max);
0756     LoadString(hInst,IDS_Already,lpMessage,MaxText);
0757     MessageBox(GetFocus(),lpMessage,lpCaption,MB_OK);
0758     return;
0759     }
0760   GlobalCompact((DWORD)-1L);          /* maximize contiguous memory */
0761
0762   /* ----------------- create a hidden bitmap ------------------- */
0763   hDisplayDC= GetDC(hWnd);                     /* display-context */
0764   hFrameDC= CreateCompatibleDC(hDisplayDC);           /* memory DC */
0765   hFrame= CreateCompatibleBitmap(hDisplayDC,zFRAMEWIDE,zFRAMEHIGH);
0766   if (hFrame==NULL)
0767     {               /* if unable to create compatible bitmap... */
0768     LoadString(hInst,IDS_NotReady,lpCaption,Max);
0769     LoadString(hInst,IDS_InsufMem1,lpMessage,MaxText);
0770     MessageBox(GetFocus(),lpMessage,lpCaption,MB_OK);
0771     DeleteDC(hFrameDC);
0772     FrameReady= FALSE; AnimationReady= FALSE;
0773     return;
0774     }
0775   hPrevFrame= SelectObject(hFrameDC,hFrame);          /* select bitmap */
0776
0777   /* -------- clear the viewport and copy to hidden-frame -------- */
0778   zClear(hWnd);
0779   BitBlt(hFrameDC,0,0,zFRAMEWIDE,zFRAMEHIGH,hDisplayDC,0,0,SRCCOPY);
0780   ReleaseDC(hWnd,hDisplayDC);          /* release the display-context */
0781
```

C-6 Continued.

```
0782  FrameReady= TRUE;
0783  FrameNum= 1;
0784  return;
0785  }
0786  /*
0787  -----------------------------------------------------------------
0788                        Clear the hidden frame.
0789  -----------------------------------------------------------------
0790                                                                  */
0791  static void zClearHiddenFrame(void)
0792  {
0793  if (FrameReady == TRUE)
0794    {
0795    PatBlt(hFrameDC,0,0,zFRAMEWIDE,zFRAMEHIGH,WHITENESS);
0796    }
0797  return;
0798  }
0799  /*
0800  -----------------------------------------------------------------
0801            Copy the hidden frame to the display window.
0802  -----------------------------------------------------------------
0803                                                                  */
0804  static void zCopyToDisplay(HWND hWnd)
0805  {
0806    HDC hDC;
0807  hDC= GetDC(hWnd);
0808  if (FrameReady == TRUE)
0809    {
0810    BitBlt(hDC,0,0,zFRAMEWIDE,zFRAMEHIGH,hFrameDC,0,0,SRCCOPY);
0811    }
0812  ReleaseDC(hWnd,hDC);
0813  return;
0814  }
0815  /*
0816  -----------------------------------------------------------------
0817                      Blank the display window.
0818  -----------------------------------------------------------------
0819                                                                  */
0820  static void zClear(HWND hWnd)
0821  {
0822    HDC hDC;
0823  hDC= GetDC(hWnd);
0824  PatBlt(hDC,0,0,zFRAMEWIDE,zFRAMEHIGH,WHITENESS);
0825  ReleaseDC(hWnd,hDC);
0826  return;
0827  }
0828
0829  /*
0830  -----------------------------------------------------------------
0831                 Virtual realityauthoring functions
0832  -----------------------------------------------------------------
0833  -----------------------------------------------------------------
0834         Create the virtual reality frames and save to disk.
0835  -----------------------------------------------------------------
0836                                                                  */
0837  static void zSaveAnimation(HWND hWnd)
0838  {
0839  if (FrameReady==FALSE)
0840    {
0841    MessageBeep(0);
0842    LoadString(hInst,IDS_NotReady,lpCaption,Max);
```

```
0843    LoadString(hInst,IDS_NoFrame,lpMessage,MaxText);
0844    MessageBox(GetFocus(),lpMessage,lpCaption,MB_OK);
0845    return;
0846    }
0847  if (bAnimationSaved==TRUE)
0848    {
0849    MessageBeep(0);
0850    LoadString(hInst,IDS_Unexpected,lpCaption,Max);
0851    LoadString(hInst,IDS_Disk1,lpMessage,MaxText);
0852    MessageBox(GetFocus(),lpMessage,lpCaption,MB_OK);
0853    return;
0854    }
0855  if (bPrevSaveAttempt==TRUE)
0856    {
0857    MessageBeep(0);
0858    LoadString(hInst,IDS_Unexpected,lpCaption,Max);
0859    LoadString(hInst,IDS_Disk8,lpMessage,MaxText);
0860    MessageBox(GetFocus(),lpMessage,lpCaption,MB_OK);
0861    return;
0862    }
0863  bPrevSaveAttempt= TRUE;
0864
0865  /* ---------------- build and save the cels ------------------ */
0866  for (LoopCount= 1; LoopCount<= zNUMCELS; LoopCount++)
0867    {           /* for each node in the virtual reality universe... */
0868    bFrameSaved= zBuildFrame(LoopCount, hWnd,  /* ... save to disk */
0869                           (LPSTR)FrameFiles[LoopCount-1]);
0870    if (bFrameSaved==FALSE) return; /* cancel loop if error occurs */
0871    }
0872  bAnimationSaved= TRUE;
0873  bPrevLoadAttempt= FALSE;
0874  zClear(hWnd);
0875  MessageBeep(0);
0876  LoadString(hInst,IDS_Status,lpCaption,Max);
0877  LoadString(hInst,IDS_Disk2,lpMessage,MaxText);
0878  MessageBox(GetFocus(),lpMessage,lpCaption,MB_OK);
0879  return;
0880  }
0881  /*
0882  -----------------------------------------------------------------
0883                    Build one image and save to disk.
0884  -----------------------------------------------------------------
0885                                                                  */
0886  static BOOL zBuildFrame(int Number, HWND hWnd, LPSTR lpFileName)
0887  {
0888    BOOL bDiskResult;
0889    HFONT Font;
0890    HFONT PrevFont;
0891    DWORD PrevFontColor;
0892    DWORD PrevBkColor;
0893    HDC hDC;
0894    struct tm *NewTime;            /* pointer to tm struct of time.h */
0895    time_t TimeSeconds;            /* long integer time_t of time.h */
0896    MSG msg;                                    /* incoming message */
0897
0898  /* ---------- display progress report on caption bar ----------- */
0899  TextLength= wsprintf(lpCaption,     /* build and save the string */
0900            "Building image %d...", Number);
0901  SetWindowText(hWnd,lpCaption);      /* display it in caption bar */
0902
0903  /* ---------------------- reset all buffers -------------------- */
```

```
0904   zClearHiddenFrame();
0905   zClear(hWnd);
0906   zClearHidden3DPage();
0907   zResetZBuffer();
0908
0909   /* ---------------- draw the appropriate image --------------- */
0910   zDrawCel(Number);
0911   if (FrameReady==TRUE)
0912     {
0913     hDC= GetDC(hWnd);
0914     BitBlt(hFrameDC,0,0,zFRAMEWIDE,zFRAMEHIGH,hDC,0,0,SRCCOPY);
0915     ReleaseDC(hWnd,hDC);
0916     }
0917
0918   /* ------------- check for user-requested cancel -------------- */
0919   if (PeekMessage(&msg,NULL,0,0,PM_REMOVE))
0920     {                       /* if a message is waiting in the queue... */
0921     if (msg.message == WM_RBUTTONDOWN)
0922       {                     /* ...if right mouse button pressed... */
0923       return FALSE;         /* ...then cancel the build sequence */
0924       }
0925     }
0926
0927   /* --------- display the titles, labels, and timestamp --------- */
0928   if ((DisplayBits==1)&&(DisplayPlanes==1))
0929     {                       /* if a mono display use black typeface... */
0930     PrevFontColor= SetTextColor(hFrameDC,RGB(0,0,0));
0931     PrevBkColor=  SetBkColor(hFrameDC,RGB(255,255,255));
0932     }
0933   else
0934     {   /* else if a color display use any solid color typeface... */
0935     PrevFontColor= SetTextColor(hFrameDC,RGB(0,0,0));
0936     PrevBkColor=  SetBkColor(hFrameDC,RGB(255,255,255));
0937     }
0938   SetBkMode(hFrameDC,TRANSPARENT);
0939
0940   if (bUseArial == FALSE)
0941     {                       /* if running Windows 3.0 use Helv font... */
0942     Font= CreateFont(24, 0, 0, 0, FW_BOLD, FALSE, FALSE, FALSE,
0943           ANSI_CHARSET, OUT_DEFAULT_PRECIS, CLIP_DEFAULT_PRECIS,
0944           DRAFT_QUALITY, VARIABLE_PITCH | FF_SWISS, "Helv");
0945     PrevFont= SelectObject(hFrameDC,Font);
0946     TextOut(hFrameDC,10,6,"A Lee Adams tutorial:",21);
0947     Font= CreateFont(36, 0, 0, 0, FW_BOLD, FALSE, FALSE, FALSE,
0948           ANSI_CHARSET, OUT_DEFAULT_PRECIS, CLIP_DEFAULT_PRECIS,
0949           DRAFT_QUALITY, VARIABLE_PITCH | FF_SWISS, "Helv");
0950     SelectObject(hFrameDC,Font);
0951     TextOut(hFrameDC,8,24,"Virtual reality",15);
0952     }
0953   else   /* else if running Windows 3.1 or newer use Arial font... */
0954     {
0955     Font= CreateFont(24, 0, 0, 0, FW_BOLD, FALSE, FALSE, FALSE,
0956           ANSI_CHARSET, OUT_DEFAULT_PRECIS, CLIP_DEFAULT_PRECIS,
0957           DRAFT_QUALITY, VARIABLE_PITCH | FF_SWISS, "Arial");
0958     PrevFont= SelectObject(hFrameDC,Font);
0959     TextOut(hFrameDC,10,6,"A Lee Adams tutorial:",21);
0960     Font= CreateFont(36, 0, 0, 0, FW_BOLD, FALSE, FALSE, FALSE,
0961           ANSI_CHARSET, OUT_DEFAULT_PRECIS, CLIP_DEFAULT_PRECIS,
0962           DRAFT_QUALITY, VARIABLE_PITCH | FF_SWISS, "Arial");
0963     SelectObject(hFrameDC,Font);
0964     TextOut(hFrameDC,8,24,"Virtual reality",15);
```

```
0965    }
0966
0967    SelectObject(hFrameDC,PrevFont);
0968    TextOut(hFrameDC,10,220,"Find the exit from the maze.",28);
0969    time(&TimeSeconds);
0970    NewTime= localtime(&TimeSeconds);
0971    TextOut(hFrameDC,10,235,(LPSTR)asctime(NewTime),19);
0972    SetBkMode(hFrameDC,OPAQUE);
0973    SetBkColor(hFrameDC,PrevBkColor);
0974    SetTextColor(hFrameDC,PrevFontColor);
0975
0976    /* ---------- check again for user-requested cancel ---------- */
0977    if (PeekMessage(&msg,NULL,0,0,PM_REMOVE))
0978      {
0979      if (msg.message == WM_RBUTTONDOWN)
0980        {
0981        return FALSE;
0982        }
0983      }
0984
0985    /* ---------- display the image and save it to disk ---------- */
0986    zCopyToDisplay(hWnd);
0987    bDiskResult= zSaveFrame(hFrame,lpFileName);
0988    if (bDiskResult==FALSE) return FALSE;
0989    return TRUE;
0990    }
0991    /*
0992    ------------------------------------------------------------------
0993                            Draw one node.
0994    ------------------------------------------------------------------
0995                                                                    */
0996    static void zDrawCel(int Number)
0997    {
0998    zDisableTarget();               /* unlock camera from fixed target */
0999    zSetLightPosition(60,180);         /* set light-source position */
1000    zSetVRCameraPitch(360);                    /* set camera pitch */
1001
1002    /* ---------- set node-dependent camera parameters ---------- */
1003    if (Number <= 25)                /* if view angle = 0 degrees... */
1004      {
1005      zSetVRCameraHeading(360);              /* set the camera heading */
1006      switch (Number)         /* set the appropriate node location... */
1007        {
1008        case 1: zSetVRCameraLocation(-60,0,296);  break;
1009        case 2: zSetVRCameraLocation(-30,0,296);  break;
1010        case 3: zSetVRCameraLocation(0,0,296);    break;
1011        case 4: zSetVRCameraLocation(30,0,296);   break;
1012        case 5: zSetVRCameraLocation(60,0,296);   break;
1013        case 6: zSetVRCameraLocation(-60,0,326);  break;
1014        case 7: zSetVRCameraLocation(-30,0,326);  break;
1015        case 8: zSetVRCameraLocation(0,0,326);    break;
1016        case 9: zSetVRCameraLocation(30,0,326);   break;
1017        case 10: zSetVRCameraLocation(60,0,326);  break;
1018        case 11: zSetVRCameraLocation(-60,0,356); break;
1019        case 12: zSetVRCameraLocation(-30,0,356); break;
1020        case 13: zSetVRCameraLocation(0,0,356);   break;
1021        case 14: zSetVRCameraLocation(30,0,356);  break;
1022        case 15: zSetVRCameraLocation(60,0,356);  break;
1023        case 16: zSetVRCameraLocation(-60,0,386); break;
1024        case 17: zSetVRCameraLocation(-30,0,386); break;
1025        case 18: zSetVRCameraLocation(0,0,386);   break;
```

C-6 Continued.

```
1026        case 19: zSetVRCameraLocation(30,0,386);   break;
1027        case 20: zSetVRCameraLocation(60,0,386);   break;
1028        case 21: zSetVRCameraLocation(-60,0,416);  break;
1029        case 22: zSetVRCameraLocation(-30,0,416);  break;
1030        case 23: zSetVRCameraLocation(0,0,416);    break;
1031        case 24: zSetVRCameraLocation(30,0,416);   break;
1032        case 25: zSetVRCameraLocation(60,0,416);   break;
1033        }
1034     goto CAMERA_UPDATED;                 /* jump past other view angles */
1035     }
1036   if (Number <= 50)                      /* if view angle = 90 degrees... */
1037     {
1038     zSetVRCameraHeading(90);
1039     switch (Number)
1040        {
1041        case 26: zSetVRCameraLocation(-60,0,296);  break;
1042        case 27: zSetVRCameraLocation(-30,0,296);  break;
1043        case 28: zSetVRCameraLocation(0,0,296);    break;
1044        case 29: zSetVRCameraLocation(30,0,296);   break;
1045        case 30: zSetVRCameraLocation(60,0,296);   break;
1046        case 31: zSetVRCameraLocation(-60,0,326);  break;
1047        case 32: zSetVRCameraLocation(-30,0,326);  break;
1048        case 33: zSetVRCameraLocation(0,0,326);    break;
1049        case 34: zSetVRCameraLocation(30,0,326);   break;
1050        case 35: zSetVRCameraLocation(60,0,326);   break;
1051        case 36: zSetVRCameraLocation(-60,0,356);  break;
1052        case 37: zSetVRCameraLocation(-30,0,356);  break;
1053        case 38: zSetVRCameraLocation(0,0,356);    break;
1054        case 39: zSetVRCameraLocation(30,0,356);   break;
1055        case 40: zSetVRCameraLocation(60,0,356);   break;
1056        case 41: zSetVRCameraLocation(-60,0,386);  break;
1057        case 42: zSetVRCameraLocation(-30,0,386);  break;
1058        case 43: zSetVRCameraLocation(0,0,386);    break;
1059        case 44: zSetVRCameraLocation(30,0,386);   break;
1060        case 45: zSetVRCameraLocation(60,0,386);   break;
1061        case 46: zSetVRCameraLocation(-60,0,416);  break;
1062        case 47: zSetVRCameraLocation(-30,0,416);  break;
1063        case 48: zSetVRCameraLocation(0,0,416);    break;
1064        case 49: zSetVRCameraLocation(30,0,416);   break;
1065        case 50: zSetVRCameraLocation(60,0,416);   break;
1066        }
1067     goto CAMERA_UPDATED;
1068     }
1069   if (Number <= 75)                      /* if view angle = 180 degrees... */
1070     {
1071     zSetVRCameraHeading(180);
1072     switch (Number)
1073        {
1074        case 51: zSetVRCameraLocation(-60,0,296);  break;
1075        case 52: zSetVRCameraLocation(-30,0,296);  break;
1076        case 53: zSetVRCameraLocation(0,0,296);    break;
1077        case 54: zSetVRCameraLocation(30,0,296);   break;
1078        case 55: zSetVRCameraLocation(60,0,296);   break;
1079        case 56: zSetVRCameraLocation(-60,0,326);  break;
1080        case 57: zSetVRCameraLocation(-30,0,326);  break;
1081        case 58: zSetVRCameraLocation(0,0,326);    break;
1082        case 59: zSetVRCameraLocation(30,0,326);   break;
1083        case 60: zSetVRCameraLocation(60,0,326);   break;
1084        case 61: zSetVRCameraLocation(-60,0,356);  break;
1085        case 62: zSetVRCameraLocation(-30,0,356);  break;
1086        case 63: zSetVRCameraLocation(0,0,356);    break;
```

```
1087        case 64: zSetVRCameraLocation(30,0,356);  break;
1088        case 65: zSetVRCameraLocation(60,0,356);  break;
1089        case 66: zSetVRCameraLocation(-60,0,386); break;
1090        case 67: zSetVRCameraLocation(-30,0,386); break;
1091        case 68: zSetVRCameraLocation(0,0,386);   break;
1092        case 69: zSetVRCameraLocation(30,0,386);  break;
1093        case 70: zSetVRCameraLocation(60,0,386);  break;
1094        case 71: zSetVRCameraLocation(-60,0,416); break;
1095        case 72: zSetVRCameraLocation(-30,0,416); break;
1096        case 73: zSetVRCameraLocation(0,0,416);   break;
1097        case 74: zSetVRCameraLocation(30,0,416);  break;
1098        case 75: zSetVRCameraLocation(60,0,416);  break;
1099        }
1100     goto CAMERA_UPDATED;
1101     }
1102   if (Number <= 100)              /* if view angle = 270 degrees... */
1103     {
1104     zSetVRCameraHeading(270);
1105     switch (Number)
1106       {
1107       case 76: zSetVRCameraLocation(-60,0,296); break;
1108       case 77: zSetVRCameraLocation(-30,0,296); break;
1109       case 78: zSetVRCameraLocation(0,0,296);   break;
1110       case 79: zSetVRCameraLocation(30,0,296);  break;
1111       case 80: zSetVRCameraLocation(60,0,296);  break;
1112       case 81: zSetVRCameraLocation(-60,0,326); break;
1113       case 82: zSetVRCameraLocation(-30,0,326); break;
1114       case 83: zSetVRCameraLocation(0,0,326);   break;
1115       case 84: zSetVRCameraLocation(30,0,326);  break;
1116       case 85: zSetVRCameraLocation(60,0,326);  break;
1117       case 86: zSetVRCameraLocation(-60,0,356); break;
1118       case 87: zSetVRCameraLocation(-30,0,356); break;
1119       case 88: zSetVRCameraLocation(0,0,356);   break;
1120       case 89: zSetVRCameraLocation(30,0,356);  break;
1121       case 90: zSetVRCameraLocation(60,0,356);  break;
1122       case 91: zSetVRCameraLocation(-60,0,386); break;
1123       case 92: zSetVRCameraLocation(-30,0,386); break;
1124       case 93: zSetVRCameraLocation(0,0,386);   break;
1125       case 94: zSetVRCameraLocation(30,0,386);  break;
1126       case 95: zSetVRCameraLocation(60,0,386);  break;
1127       case 96: zSetVRCameraLocation(-60,0,416); break;
1128       case 97: zSetVRCameraLocation(-30,0,416); break;
1129       case 98: zSetVRCameraLocation(0,0,416);   break;
1130       case 99: zSetVRCameraLocation(30,0,416);  break;
1131       case 100: zSetVRCameraLocation(60,0,416); break;
1132       }
1133     goto CAMERA_UPDATED;
1134     }
1135
1136   /* ------------------ render the scenery ------------------ */
1137   CAMERA_UPDATED:              /* jump to here after camera updated */
1138   zSetHierarchyMode(FALSE);        /* disable hierarchical modeling */
1139
1140   /* ---------------- draw the exterior walls ------------------ */
1141   zSetSubjectSize(15,15,2);              /* set subobject extrusion */
1142   zSetSubjectAttitude(0,0,0);           /* set subobject orientation */
1143   zSetShadingColor(zRED);                        /* North wall... */
1144   zSetSubjectLocation(-60,0,281); zDrawCube();
1145   zSetSubjectLocation(-30,0,281); zDrawCube();
1146   zSetSubjectLocation(0,0,281);   zDrawCube();
1147   zSetSubjectLocation(30,0,281);  zDrawCube();
```

```
1148    zSetSubjectLocation(60,0,281);  zDrawCube();
1149
1150    zSetShadingColor(zRED);                /* all exterior walls are red */
1151    zSetSubjectAttitude(90,0,0);                        /* East wall... */
1152    zSetSubjectLocation(75,0,296);  zDrawCube();
1153    zSetSubjectLocation(75,0,326);  zDrawCube();
1154    zSetSubjectLocation(75,0,356);  zDrawCube();
1155    zSetSubjectLocation(75,0,386);  zDrawCube();
1156    zSetSubjectLocation(75,0,416);  zDrawCube();
1157
1158    zSetShadingColor(zRED);
1159    zSetSubjectAttitude(0,0,0);                        /* South wall... */
1160    zSetSubjectLocation(-60,0,431); zDrawCube();
1161    zSetSubjectLocation(-30,0,431); zDrawCube();
1162    zSetSubjectLocation(0,0,431);   zDrawCube();
1163    zSetSubjectLocation(30,0,431);  zDrawCube();
1164    zSetSubjectLocation(60,0,431);  zDrawCube();
1165
1166    zSetShadingColor(zRED);
1167    zSetSubjectAttitude(90,0,0);                        /* West wall... */
1168    zSetSubjectLocation(-75,0,296); zDrawCube();
1169    zSetSubjectLocation(-75,0,326); zDrawCube();
1170    zSetSubjectLocation(-75,0,356); zDrawCube();
1171    zSetSubjectLocation(-75,0,386); zDrawCube();
1172 /* zSetSubjectLocation(-75,0,416); zDrawCube();       the doorway */
1173
1174 /* ----------------- draw the interior walls ----------------- */
1175    zSetShadingColor(zBROWN);     /* all North-South walls are yellow */
1176    zSetSubjectAttitude(90,0,0);
1177    zSetSubjectLocation(-45,0,296); zDrawCube();
1178    zSetSubjectLocation(-45,0,356); zDrawCube();
1179    zSetSubjectLocation(-45,0,386); zDrawCube();
1180    zSetSubjectLocation(-45,0,416); zDrawCube();
1181
1182    zSetShadingColor(zGREEN);         /* all East-West walls are green */
1183    zSetSubjectAttitude(0,0,0);
1184    zSetSubjectLocation(-30,0,311); zDrawCube();
1185    zSetShadingColor(zBROWN);
1186    zSetSubjectAttitude(90,0,0);
1187    zSetSubjectLocation(-15,0,326); zDrawCube();
1188    zSetSubjectLocation(-15,0,356); zDrawCube();
1189    zSetSubjectLocation(-15,0,386); zDrawCube();
1190
1191    zSetShadingColor(zBROWN);
1192    zSetSubjectAttitude(90,0,0);
1193    zSetSubjectLocation(15,0,296);  zDrawCube();
1194    zSetSubjectLocation(15,0,356);  zDrawCube();
1195    zSetSubjectLocation(15,0,386);  zDrawCube();
1196
1197    zSetShadingColor(zGREEN);
1198    zSetSubjectAttitude(0,0,0);
1199    zSetSubjectLocation(30,0,311);  zDrawCube();
1200    zSetShadingColor(zBROWN);
1201    zSetSubjectAttitude(90,0,0);
1202    zSetSubjectLocation(45,0,326);  zDrawCube();
1203    zSetSubjectLocation(45,0,356);  zDrawCube();
1204    zSetSubjectLocation(45,0,386);  zDrawCube();
1205    zSetShadingColor(zGREEN);
1206    zSetSubjectAttitude(0,0,0);
1207    zSetSubjectLocation(30,0,401);  zDrawCube();
1208
```

```
1209  /* -------------------- tidy up and return ------------------- */
1210  zEnableTarget();              /* restore fixed-target camera mode */
1211  return;
1212  }
1213  /*
1214  -------------------------------------------------------------------
1215        Preview the first node of the virtual reality sequence.
1216  -------------------------------------------------------------------
1217                                                                  */
1218  static void zPreviewFirstFrame(HWND hWnd)
1219  {                  /* previews the player's starting position... */
1220    HDC hDC;
1221  zInitialize3D(hWnd);                  /* clear various buffers... */
1222  zClearHiddenFrame();
1223  zClear(hWnd);
1224  zClearHidden3DPage();
1225  zResetZBuffer();
1226  zDrawCel(23);                              /* draw the frame */
1227  if (FrameReady==TRUE)
1228    {
1229    hDC= GetDC(hWnd);
1230    BitBlt(hFrameDC,0,0,zFRAMEWIDE,zFRAMEHIGH,hDC,0,0,SRCCOPY);
1231    ReleaseDC(hWnd,hDC);
1232    }
1233  zCopyToDisplay(hWnd);
1234  return;
1235  }
1236  /*
1237  -------------------------------------------------------------------
1238        Preview the final node of the virtual reality sequence.
1239  -------------------------------------------------------------------
1240                                                                  */
1241  static void zPreviewFinalFrame(HWND hWnd)
1242  {  /* previews the doorway when in wireframe prototyping mode... */
1243    HDC hDC;
1244  zInitialize3D(hWnd);
1245  zClearHiddenFrame();
1246  zClear(hWnd);
1247  zClearHidden3DPage();
1248  zResetZBuffer();
1249  zDrawCel(zNUMCELS);
1250  if (FrameReady==TRUE)
1251    {
1252    hDC= GetDC(hWnd);
1253    BitBlt(hFrameDC,0,0,zFRAMEWIDE,zFRAMEHIGH,hDC,0,0,SRCCOPY);
1254    ReleaseDC(hWnd,hDC);
1255    }
1256  zCopyToDisplay(hWnd);
1257  return;
1258  }
1259  /*
1260  -------------------------------------------------------------------
1261        Display next frame in interactive virtual reality mode.
1262  -------------------------------------------------------------------
1263                                                                  */
1264  static void vrWalkthrough(unsigned char CameraMove,
1265                            unsigned char CameraAngle,
1266                            HWND hWndVR)
1267  {
1268    HDC hDC;
1269  /* -------------- update the direction of view --------------- */
```

```
1270    if (CameraMove == vrSTATIONARY) /* if viewpoint is stationary... */
1271       {              /* ...then the direction of view is being changed */
1272       switch (CameraAngle)
1273          {
1274          case vrVIEW000: vrArrayOffset= vrFIRST_ARRAY; break;
1275          case vrVIEW090: vrArrayOffset= vrSECOND_ARRAY; break;
1276          case vrVIEW180: vrArrayOffset= vrTHIRD_ARRAY; break;
1277          case vrVIEW270: vrArrayOffset= vrFOURTH_ARRAY; break;
1278          }
1279       goto DISPLAY_VR;            /* jump past viewpoint movement code */
1280       }
1281    /* --- marry the movement direction to the direction of view --- */
1282    if (CameraAngle == vrVIEW090)
1283       {
1284       switch (CameraMove)
1285          {
1286          case vrMOVE_FORWARD: CameraMove= vrMOVE_RIGHT; break;
1287          case vrMOVE_RIGHT: CameraMove= vrMOVE_BACKWARD; break;
1288          case vrMOVE_LEFT: CameraMove= vrMOVE_FORWARD; break;
1289          case vrMOVE_BACKWARD: CameraMove= vrMOVE_LEFT; break;
1290          }
1291       }
1292    if (CameraAngle == vrVIEW180)
1293       {
1294       switch (CameraMove)
1295          {
1296          case vrMOVE_FORWARD: CameraMove= vrMOVE_BACKWARD; break;
1297          case vrMOVE_RIGHT:  CameraMove= vrMOVE_LEFT; break;
1298          case vrMOVE_LEFT:   CameraMove= vrMOVE_RIGHT; break;
1299          case vrMOVE_BACKWARD: CameraMove= vrMOVE_FORWARD; break;
1300          }
1301       }
1302    if (CameraAngle == vrVIEW270)
1303       {
1304       switch (CameraMove)
1305          {
1306          case vrMOVE_FORWARD: CameraMove= vrMOVE_LEFT; break;
1307          case vrMOVE_RIGHT: CameraMove= vrMOVE_FORWARD; break;
1308          case vrMOVE_LEFT: CameraMove= vrMOVE_BACKWARD; break;
1309          case vrMOVE_BACKWARD: CameraMove= vrMOVE_RIGHT; break;
1310          }
1311       }
1312
1313    /* -------- inhibit any attempt to move through a wall -------- */
1314    if (CameraMove == vrMOVE_FORWARD)
1315       {                            /* if attempting to move North... */
1316       if (vrRow == vrMIN_ROW) goto PROHIBIT;
1317       if ((vrRow == 1) && (vrColumn == 1)) goto PROHIBIT;
1318       if ((vrRow == 1) && (vrColumn == 3)) goto PROHIBIT;
1319       if ((vrRow == vrMAX_ROW) && (vrColumn == 3)) goto PROHIBIT;
1320       }
1321    if (CameraMove == vrMOVE_BACKWARD)
1322       {                            /* if attempting to move South... */
1323       if (vrRow == vrMAX_ROW) goto PROHIBIT;
1324       if ((vrRow == vrMIN_ROW) && (vrColumn == 1)) goto PROHIBIT;
1325       if ((vrRow == vrMIN_ROW) && (vrColumn == 3)) goto PROHIBIT;
1326       if ((vrRow == 3) && (vrColumn == 3)) goto PROHIBIT;
1327       }
1328    if (CameraMove == vrMOVE_RIGHT)
1329       {                            /* if attempting to move East... */
1330       if (vrColumn == vrMAX_COLUMN) goto PROHIBIT;
```

```
1331    if ((vrColumn == vrMIN_COLUMN) && (vrRow != 1)) goto PROHIBIT;
1332    if ((vrColumn == 1) && (vrRow == 1)) goto PROHIBIT;
1333    if ((vrColumn == 1) && (vrRow == 2)) goto PROHIBIT;
1334    if ((vrColumn == 1) && (vrRow == 3)) goto PROHIBIT;
1335    if ((vrColumn == 2) && (vrRow == 0)) goto PROHIBIT;
1336    if ((vrColumn == 2) && (vrRow == 2)) goto PROHIBIT;
1337    if ((vrColumn == 2) && (vrRow == 3)) goto PROHIBIT;
1338    if ((vrColumn == 3) && (vrRow == 1)) goto PROHIBIT;
1339    if ((vrColumn == 3) && (vrRow == 2)) goto PROHIBIT;
1340    if ((vrColumn == 3) && (vrRow == 3)) goto PROHIBIT;
1341    }
1342  if (CameraMove == vrMOVE_LEFT)
1343    {                          /* if attempting to move West... */
1344    if ((vrColumn == vrMIN_COLUMN) && (vrRow != vrMAX_ROW))
1345      goto PROHIBIT;
1346    if ((vrColumn == 1) && (vrRow == 0)) goto PROHIBIT;
1347    if ((vrColumn == 1) && (vrRow == 2)) goto PROHIBIT;
1348    if ((vrColumn == 1) && (vrRow == 3)) goto PROHIBIT;
1349    if ((vrColumn == 1) && (vrRow == 4)) goto PROHIBIT;
1350    if ((vrColumn == 2) && (vrRow == 1)) goto PROHIBIT;
1351    if ((vrColumn == 2) && (vrRow == 2)) goto PROHIBIT;
1352    if ((vrColumn == 2) && (vrRow == 3)) goto PROHIBIT;
1353    if ((vrColumn == 3) && (vrRow == 0)) goto PROHIBIT;
1354    if ((vrColumn == 3) && (vrRow == 2)) goto PROHIBIT;
1355    if ((vrColumn == 3) && (vrRow == 3)) goto PROHIBIT;
1356    if ((vrColumn == vrMAX_COLUMN) && (vrRow == 1)) goto PROHIBIT;
1357    if ((vrColumn == vrMAX_COLUMN) && (vrRow == 2)) goto PROHIBIT;
1358    if ((vrColumn == vrMAX_COLUMN) && (vrRow == 3)) goto PROHIBIT;
1359    }
1360
1361  /* ----------------- detect a winning position --------------- */
1362  if (CameraMove == vrMOVE_LEFT)
1363    {                          /* if attempting to move West and... */
1364    if ((vrColumn == vrMIN_COLUMN) && (vrRow == vrMAX_ROW))
1365      {                  /* ...if located at row 0 column 4... */
1366      MessageBeep(0);
1367      MessageBox(GetFocus(),
1368      "You have found the maze's exit.",
1369      "Congratulations!", MB_OK);
1370      return;
1371      }
1372    }
1373
1374  /* -------------- update the viewpoint location -------------- */
1375  switch (CameraMove)
1376    {
1377    case vrMOVE_FORWARD:  if (vrRow> vrMIN_ROW) vrRow--;
1378                          break;
1379    case vrMOVE_RIGHT:    if (vrColumn< vrMAX_COLUMN) vrColumn++;
1380                          break;
1381    case vrMOVE_LEFT:     if (vrColumn> vrMIN_COLUMN) vrColumn--;
1382                          break;
1383    case vrMOVE_BACKWARD: if (vrRow< vrMAX_ROW) vrRow++;
1384                          break;
1385    }
1386
1387  /* -- use bitmaps resident in RAM to display appropriate view -- */
1388  DISPLAY_VR:
1389  vrFrameID=         /* 3-dimensional index into 1-dimensional array */
1390        (int)(vrArrayOffset + ((vrNUM_COLUMNS * vrRow) + vrColumn));
1391  if (bUseDisk==TRUE) goto LOAD_FROM_DISK;   /* jump if using disk */
```

```
1392   hDC= GetDC(hWndVR);                          /* grab display-context */
1393   SelectObject(hFDC,BitmapHandles[vrFrameID]);    /* select handle */
1394   BitBlt(hDC,0,0,                          /* copy bitmap to viewport */
1395          zFRAMEWIDE,zFRAMEHIGH,hFDC,0,0,SRCCOPY);
1396   ReleaseDC(hWndVR,hDC);                   /* release display-context */
1397   goto DISPLAY_POSITION;              /* jump past disk-based code... */
1398
1399   /* ----- load bitmap from disk to display appropriate view ----- */
1400   LOAD_FROM_DISK:
1401   hDC= GetDC(hWndVR);                          /* grab display-context */
1402   bFrameLoaded= zLoadFrame(hFrame,    /* load the binary image file */
1403                    (LPSTR)FrameFiles[vrFrameID]);
1404   if (bFrameLoaded==FALSE)                    /* if an error occurred... */
1405     {
1406     bUsingVR= FALSE;
1407     MessageBeep(0);
1408     MessageBox(GetFocus(),
1409       "Unable to load next image from disk.",
1410       "Unexpected virtual reality condition", MB_OK);
1411     return;
1412     }
1413   BitBlt(hDC,0,0,                          /* copy bitmap to viewport */
1414          zFRAMEWIDE,zFRAMEHIGH,hFrameDC,0,0,SRCCOPY);
1415   ReleaseDC(hWndVR,hDC);                   /* release display-context */
1416
1417   /* --------------- display the viewpoint status --------------- */
1418   DISPLAY_POSITION:
1419   switch (CameraAngle)
1420     {
1421     case vrVIEW000:
1422       TextLength= wsprintf(lpCaption,"Looking North from node %d,%d",
1423                    (int)vrRow, (int)vrColumn); break;
1424     case vrVIEW090:
1425       TextLength= wsprintf(lpCaption,"Looking East from node %d,%d",
1426                    (int)vrRow, (int)vrColumn); break;
1427     case vrVIEW180:
1428       TextLength= wsprintf(lpCaption,"Looking South from node %d,%d",
1429                    (int)vrRow, (int)vrColumn); break;
1430     case vrVIEW270:
1431       TextLength= wsprintf(lpCaption,"Looking West from node %d,%d",
1432                    (int)vrRow, (int)vrColumn); break;
1433     }
1434   SetWindowText(hWndVR,lpCaption);    /* display it in caption bar */
1435   return;
1436
1437   /* ---------- prohibit any movement through walls ------------ */
1438   PROHIBIT:  /* jump to here if user attempts to move through wall */
1439   MessageBeep(0);
1440   MessageBox(GetFocus(),
1441   "Movement through walls prohibited.  Please select another move.",
1442   "Virtual reality rule", MB_OK);
1443   return;
1444   }
1445   /*
1446   -----------------------------------------------------------------
1447               Load the virtual reality sequence from disk.
1448   -----------------------------------------------------------------
1449                                                                   */
1450   static void zLoadAnimation(HWND hWnd)
1451   {
1452     HDC hDC;
```

```
1453     int Bitmaps;
1454
1455  if (FrameReady==FALSE)
1456     {
1457     MessageBeep(0);
1458     LoadString(hInst,IDS_NotReady,lpCaption,Max);
1459     LoadString(hInst,IDS_NoFrame,lpMessage,MaxText);
1460     MessageBox(GetFocus(),lpMessage,lpCaption,MB_OK);
1461     return;
1462     }
1463  if (bAnimationLoaded==TRUE)
1464     {
1465     MessageBeep(0);
1466     LoadString(hInst,IDS_Unexpected,lpCaption,Max);
1467     LoadString(hInst,IDS_Disk4,lpMessage,MaxText);
1468     MessageBox(GetFocus(),lpMessage,lpCaption,MB_OK);
1469     return;
1470     }
1471  if (bPrevLoadAttempt==TRUE)
1472     {
1473     MessageBeep(0);
1474     LoadString(hInst,IDS_Unexpected,lpCaption,Max);
1475     LoadString(hInst,IDS_Disk5,lpMessage,MaxText);
1476     MessageBox(GetFocus(),lpMessage,lpCaption,MB_OK);
1477     return;
1478     }
1479  bPrevLoadAttempt= TRUE;
1480
1481  /* ------------- create bitmaps to hold the frames ----------- */
1482  GlobalCompact((DWORD)-1L);
1483  hDC= GetDC(hWnd);
1484  hFDC= CreateCompatibleDC(hDC);
1485  for (LoopCount= 1; LoopCount<= zNUMCELS; LoopCount++)
1486     {                          /* for each cel in the animation... */
1487     BitmapHandles[LoopCount-1]=                /* create a bitmap... */
1488        CreateCompatibleBitmap(hDC,zFRAMEWIDE,zFRAMEHIGH);
1489     if (BitmapHandles[LoopCount-1]==NULL)    /* if error occurs... */
1490       goto BITMAPS_NOT_OK;        /* ...jump out of loop and tidy up */
1491     }
1492  goto BITMAPS_OK;                 /* if OK, jump past error-handler */
1493
1494  /* ----------------- bitmap error-handler ------------------- */
1495  BITMAPS_NOT_OK:
1496  for (Bitmaps= LoopCount-1; Bitmaps>= 1; Bitmaps--)
1497     {            /* for each bitmap that was successfully created... */
1498     DeleteObject(BitmapHandles[Bitmaps-1]);        /* ...delete it */
1499     }
1500  DeleteDC(hFDC);                        /* delete the compatible DC */
1501  ReleaseDC(hWnd,hDC);              /* release the display-context */
1502  bUseDisk= TRUE; AnimationReady= TRUE;        /* reset the tokens */
1503  LoadString(hInst,IDS_Status,lpCaption,Max);
1504  LoadString(hInst,IDS_Disk6,lpMessage,MaxText);
1505  MessageBox(GetFocus(),lpMessage,lpCaption,MB_OK); /* message box */
1506  return;                              /* ...and return to caller */
1507
1508  BITMAPS_OK: ReleaseDC(hWnd,hDC);  /* release the display-context */
1509
1510  /* ------------- load frame files into the bitmaps ------------- */
1511  for (LoopCount= 1; LoopCount<= zNUMCELS; LoopCount++)
1512     {                          /* for each cel in the animation... */
1513     bFrameLoaded= zLoadFrame(BitmapHandles[LoopCount-1],    /* load */
```

```
1514                              (LPSTR)FrameFiles[LoopCount-1]);
1515    if (bFrameLoaded==FALSE)              /* if disk error occurred... */
1516      goto DISK_ERROR;                     /* jump to error-handler */
1517    }
1518  goto DISK_OK;                 /* if OK, jump past the error-handler */
1519
1520  /* -------------------- disk error-handler -------------------- */
1521  DISK_ERROR:
1522    for (LoopCount= 1; LoopCount<= zNUMCELS; LoopCount++)
1523      {                     /* for each bitmap handle in the animation... */
1524      DeleteObject(BitmapHandles[LoopCount-1]);    /* delete it... */
1525      }
1526    DeleteDC(hFDC);    /* ...and delete the memory display-context */
1527    return;
1528
1529  /* -------------------- tidy up and return -------------------- */
1530  DISK_OK:
1531  hPrevF= SelectObject(hFDC,BitmapHandles[0]);
1532  bAnimationLoaded= TRUE;
1533  AnimationReady= TRUE;
1534  bAnimationSaved= TRUE;
1535  MessageBeep(0);
1536  LoadString(hInst,IDS_AnimReady,lpCaption,Max);
1537  LoadString(hInst,IDS_Disk7,lpMessage,MaxText);
1538  MessageBox(GetFocus(),lpMessage,lpCaption,MB_OK);
1539  return;
1540  }
1541  /*
1542  ----------------------------------------------------------------
1543                      End of the C source file
1544  ----------------------------------------------------------------
1545                                                                */
```

Appendix D
Math primer for graphics programming

Graphics programmers tend to use mathematics more often than other programmers do. But that doesn't mean you need to be a mathematician to be a graphics programmer. Quite the opposite is true. All you usually need to help you solve a particular problem is a quick primer or thumbnail synopsis of the relevant math. That's what this appendix provides.

2D vectors

A 2D vector is a line with both magnitude and direction. A vector is defined by its offsets from the XY origin. For example, a vector described as (1,1) would have one endpoint at 0,0 and the other endpoint at 1,1. As a consequence of its attributes, a vector defined as (1,1) would possess a magnitude (length) of 1 and a direction of 45 degrees. A vector defined as (-1,1) would possess a direction of 315 degrees, of course. The length of a vector is the square root of the sum of the squares of its two components. This means a vector defined as (10,10) would be 14 units in length.

Addition and subtraction When you add or subtract 2D vectors, you perform the operations on the corresponding components of the two vectors:

$$\vec{u} = (a,b)$$

$$\vec{v} = (c,d)$$

$$\vec{u} + \vec{v} = (a+c, b+d)$$

$$\vec{u} - \vec{v} = (a-c, b-d)$$

Scalar multiplication   When you multiply a 2D vector by a scalar (regular) number, you multiply each of the vector's components by the scalar value:

$$\vec{u} = (a,b)$$

$$t\vec{u} = t(a,b)$$

$$\therefore t\vec{u} = (ta,tb)$$

Dot products   A *dot product* is the result of a special way of multiplying two 2D vectors in order to produce a scalar number. A dot product of two vectors is the sum of the multiplication of the vectors' individual components:

$$\vec{u} = (a,b)$$

$$\vec{v} = (c,d)$$

$$\vec{u} \bullet v = (a,b) \bullet (c,d) = ac + bd$$

2D vector representation of lines   You can use 2D vector subtraction and scalar multiplication to represent lines, as shown here:

$$\vec{u} = \vec{w} - \vec{v}$$

If $\vec{x}$ is a vector extending from (0,0) to a point on a line that contains points P and Q then $\vec{x} - \vec{v}$ will be a multiple of $\vec{u}$.

$$\vec{x} - \vec{v} = t\vec{u}$$

$$\therefore \vec{x} = \vec{v} + t\vec{u}$$

Each choice of t will result in a specific point (x,y) that lies on the line.

3D vectors

A 3D vector is a line in 3D-space with both magnitude and direction. A 3D vector is defined by its offsets from the XYZ origin. For example, a vector described as (1,1,1) would have one endpoint at 0,0,0 and the other endpoint at 1,1,1. As a consequence of its attributes, a vector defined as (1,1,1) would possess a magnitude of 1 and a yaw-right of 45 degrees and a pitch-up of

45 degrees. A vector defined as (-1,1,1) would possess a yaw direction of 315 degrees and a pitch of 45 degrees, of course. The length of a 3D vector is the square root of the sum of the squares of its three components. This means a vector defined as (10,10,10) would be 17 units in length.

Addition and subtraction When you add or subtract 3D vectors, you perform the operations on the corresponding components of the two vectors:

$$\vec{v} = (2,1,7)$$

$$\vec{w} = (3,2,-5)$$

$$\therefore \vec{v} + \vec{w} = (2,1,7) + (3,2,-5) = (5,3,2)$$

$$\therefore \vec{v} - \vec{w} = (2,1,7) - (3,2,-5) = (-1,-1,12)$$

Scalar multiplication When you multiply a 3D vector by a scalar (regular) number, you multiply each of the vector's components by the scalar value:

$$\vec{v} = (2,1,7)$$

$$4\vec{v} = 4(2,1,7) = (8,4,28)$$

Dot products A 3D dot product results from a special way of multiplying two 3D vectors in order to produce a scalar number. A dot product of two 3D vectors is the sum of the multiplication of the vectors' individual components:

$$\vec{u} = (a,b,c)$$

$$\vec{v} = (d,e,f)$$

$$\vec{u} \bullet \vec{v} = (a,b,c) \bullet (d,e,f) = ad + be + cf$$

$$\text{length of } \vec{v} = |v| \quad \text{length of } \vec{u} = |u|$$

$$\vec{u} \bullet \vec{v} = |u||v| \cos\Theta \text{ where } \cos\Theta \text{ is the angle between } \vec{u} \text{ and } \vec{v}$$

If the angle between the two vectors is between 0° and 90°, then the dot product is a positive value. If the angle is between 90° and 180° degrees, then the dot product is a negative value. Cosine and arc cosine can be used to calculate the angle between two vectors using their dot product:

$$\cos\theta = \frac{\vec{u} \bullet \vec{v}}{|\vec{u}||\vec{v}|}$$

The angle between the two vectors is:

$$\arccos\frac{\vec{u} \bullet \vec{v}}{|\vec{u}||\vec{v}|}$$

This capability is important for 3D shading.

Cross products The cross product of two 3D vectors is a vector that is *normal* (perpendicular) to the plane in which the two 3D vectors reside, as shown here:

$$\vec{u} = (a,b,c)$$

$$\vec{v} = (d,e,f)$$

$$\vec{u} \times \vec{v} = (bf-ce,cd-af,ae,bd)$$

This is essentially how 3D shading works. First, the software calculates the surface normal by computing the cross product of two 3D vectors (two half-edges) from the facet being considered. Next, the software uses dot products (see the previous paragraph) to calculate the angle between the surface normal and the incoming light ray (a vector). The size of the angle determines how much light is striking the facet, which in turn determines how brightly the facet should be shaded by the software.

Cross products are useful for back-face culling of facets because of the opposite direction nature of some cross products. Note in the previous example that $\vec{u} \times \vec{v}$ and $\vec{v} \times \vec{u}$ have opposite directions.

3D vector representation of lines You can use 3D vector subtraction and scalar multiplication to represent lines. The line that passes through (2,1,7) and (3,2,5) can be represented as $\vec{x} = \vec{v} + t\vec{u}$

$$\vec{u} = \vec{w} - \vec{v} = (3,2,-5) - (2,1,7) = (1,1,-12)$$

This means that the vector form of the equation of the line is:

$$(x,y,z) = (2,1,7) + t(1,1,-12)$$
$$\text{or } (x,y,z) = (2,1,7) + t((3,2,-5) - (2,1,7))$$
$$\text{or } (x,y,z) = \vec{v} + t\vec{u} \text{ where } \vec{u} = \vec{w} - \vec{v}$$

Matrix math

A *matrix* is a mathematical array of values. A matrix with 3 rows and 4 columns is usually depicted as:

$$A = \begin{bmatrix} a_{11} & a_{12} & a_{13} & a_{14} \\ a_{21} & a_{22} & a_{23} & a_{24} \\ a_{31} & a_{32} & a_{33} & a_{34} \end{bmatrix}$$

Special notation is used to identify specific members of a matrix, similar to the way in which an index is used by software to identify members of an array.

Multiplying two matrices Use this template when you want to multiply two matrices:

$$\begin{bmatrix} a_{11} & a_{12} \\ a_{21} & a_{22} \end{bmatrix} \begin{bmatrix} b_{11} & b_{12} \\ b_{21} & b_{22} \end{bmatrix} = \begin{bmatrix} a_{11}b_{11}+a_{12}b_{21} & a_{11}b_{12}+a_{12}b_{22} \\ a_{21}b_{11}+a_{22}b_{21} & a_{21}b_{12}+a_{22}b_{22} \end{bmatrix}$$

You'll want to pay careful attention to the fact that matrix multiplication is not commutative ($AB \neq BA$), but rather is associative: $A(BC) = (AB)C$. In other words, the order of the matrices being multiplied is important.

Transformation matrices

A *transformation matrix* can transform a point to another location, provided that the point has first been associated with its own matrix. Consider matrix A:

$$\text{matrix } A = \begin{bmatrix} a & b \\ c & d \end{bmatrix}$$

Any matrix A provides a means to associate a point (x,y) with the point $(ax + cy, bx + dy)$.

$$(x,y) \begin{bmatrix} 4 & 2 \\ 8 & 9 \end{bmatrix} = (4x + 8y, 2x + 9y)$$

Point (x,y) can be transformed to point $(ax + ay, bx + dy)$ using the matrix of transformation:

$$\begin{bmatrix} a & b \\ c & d \end{bmatrix}$$

What are homogeneous coordinates Homogeneous coordinates are XYZ coordinates with a nominal fourth coordinate added. This fourth axis makes it possible to use a 4 × 4 matrix to transform the XYZ coordinates, as shown in Fig. D-10. This transformation matrix can be designed to translate, to rotate, or to scale the XYZ coordinates. For example, this four-dimensional representation can be scaled by multiplying each coordinate by the same factor, because the XYZ formulas preserve the ratios:

$$x = \frac{x^1}{w} \quad y = \frac{y^1}{w} \quad z = \frac{z^1}{w}$$

Points located at infinity can be represented by $w = 0$.

Translation in 3D space Use the template provided here to translate 3D XYZ coordinates to a new location in 3D-space:

$$[x \ y \ z \ w \ ] \begin{bmatrix} 1 & 0 & 0 & 0 \\ 0 & 1 & 0 & 0 \\ 0 & 0 & 1 & 0 \\ t_x & t_y & t_z & 1 \end{bmatrix} = [x+t_zw \ \ y+t_yw \ \ z+t_zw \ \ w]$$

Rotation in 3D space Use the three templates provided here to rotate a set of XYZ coordinates around the X-axis, Y-axis, or Z-axis in 3D-space.

For rotation around the Z-axis, adjusting roll by A radians:

$$\begin{bmatrix} cosA & sinA & 0 & 0 \\ -sinA & cosA & 0 & 0 \\ 0 & 0 & 1 & 0 \\ 0 & 0 & 0 & 1 \end{bmatrix}$$

For rotation around the X-axis, adjusting pitch by A radians:

$$\begin{bmatrix} 1 & 0 & 0 & 0 \\ 0 & cosA & sinA & 0 \\ 0 & -sinA & cosA & 0 \\ 0 & 0 & 0 & 1 \end{bmatrix}$$

For rotation around the Y-axis, adjusting pitch by A radians:

$$\begin{bmatrix} cosA & 0 & -sinA & 0 \\ 0 & 1 & 0 & 0 \\ sinA & 0 & cosA & 0 \\ 0 & 0 & 0 & 1 \end{bmatrix}$$

Scaling in 3D space Use this template if you want to scale a set of XYZ coordinates in 3D-space:

$$\begin{bmatrix} S_x & 0 & 0 & 0 \\ 0 & S_y & 0 & 0 \\ 0 & 0 & S_z & 0 \\ 0 & 0 & 0 & 1 \end{bmatrix}$$

Vector math for ray tracing

3D math for ray-tracing uses parametric representation of vectors to compute different points along the path of the light ray (which is a vector). The template provided here shows how to calculate a particular XYZ location along the light-ray by varying the parameter variable. By inspecting the resulting XYZ location, you can determine if the light-ray (a vector) has intersected a 3D entity (a facet) in the scene.

Assume that x_0, y_0, z_0 is the location of the camera. Assume that x_1, y_1, z_1 is a point on the viewplane window that represents the center of a pixel on the raster viewport. Then each point along the vector adheres to a parametric representation where the parameter t ranges from 0 to 1. In particular, $t = 0$ at the origin (the camera location) and $t = 1$ at the surface of the viewplane window:

$$x = x_0 + t(x_1 - x_0)$$
$$y = y_0 + t(y_1 - y_0)$$
$$z = z_0 + t(z_1 - z_0)$$

Assume that $\Delta x = x_1 - x_0$
$$\Delta y = y_1 - y_0$$
$$\Delta z = z_1 - z_0$$

Then $x = x_0 + t(\Delta x)$
$$y = y_0 + t(\Delta y)$$
$$z = z_0 + t(\Delta z)$$

To calculate the intersection of a vector with a facet, use the equation for a plane and the parametric representation for a 3D line to calculate the intersection of a vector with a facet, as shown in the previous discussion.

Glossary

accelerator table   A list of accelerator keystrokes and their corresponding menu IDS. The table is a part of the resource script file for a Windows application.

actor   A movable 2D or 3D object in procedural animation and physically-based animation. Also called a cast member in procedural animation.

additive operators   The + operator and the - operator.

aggregate type   A C or C++ array, structure, or union.

algorithm   A method for solving a problem.

alias   (1) The jagged effect, or jaggies, produced by diagonal or curved lines on monitors with coarse resolution. See supersampling. (2) The awkward jumping effect present in animations where the frame display rate is too slow to smoothly simulate actors moving at speed across the image. See motion blur. See anti-aliasing. (3) One of several names which refer to the same memory location or variable. See union.

alphanumeric   A set of characters containing both letters and numbers.

ampersand   The & character.

animate on ones   Animating by displaying each frame no longer than the frame rate, usually 1/30th second (TV and VTR) or 1/24th second (film). On personal computers the system timer chip issues an interrupt at 55 ms intervals (about 18.2 times per second), thereby limiting computer animation to animating on twos. See animate on twos.

animate on twos   Animating by display each frame for a length of time that is twice the frame rate. TV and VTR animation is usually played at 30 frames per second. If an animation sequence is animated on twos, each frame is held on display for 1/15th second instead of 1/30th second (66.7

ms). The system timer chip in personal computers issues an interrupt at 55 ms intervals, permitting a close approximation of animating on twos.

animation   A rapid display of separate images that deceives the human eye into perceiving motion. Animation is based on an optical illusion called image retention that is characteristic of all human eyes. Rather than seeing two separate images, the first image is retained long enough by the rods and cones of the eye to blur the transition to the next image when viewing film animation, television animation, or computer animation.

animation control   The process of managing the objects and events that are being animated. See also animation implementation.

animation engine   A block of code or a module that loads and manages the playback of an animation sequence.

animation implementation   The mechanics of creating the illusion of movement on the computer screen. See also animation control.

anti-aliasing   The process of reducing the visual impact of jagged lines or jumpy animation movement. See aliasing, motion blur.

area fill   To fill a specified region with a specified color or pattern. The color attribute surrounding the region to be filled is called the boundary.

area process   An image-processing function that modifies an individual pixel or picture element as a result of considering the surrounding pixels (the neighborhood). See point process, neighborhood.

argument   A value passed to a C function or to a C++ method by the caller. The value received by a function or method is called a parameter.

argument-type list   The list of arguments found in a C function prototype or C++ method definition.

arithmetic operator   A mathematical operator such as addition (+), multiplication (*), and others.

array   A set of data elements of similar type grouped together under a single name, usually arranged in rows and columns. An array can be scalar (consisting of numeric or string data) or graphic (consisting of pixel attributes).

articulated motion   Movement of individual parts of a complex 3D assembly.

articulated motion editor   An interactive, 3D application that can be used to specify the local motion and positioning of articulated entities (progeny and parent) in an animation sequence. See also staging editor and hierarchical modeling.

artificial reality   Virtual reality.

assignment   To assign a value to a variable. The C and C++ assignment operator is =. Avoid confusion with the equality operator ==. An arithmetic operation can be performed during the assignment process using the += addition assignment operator, the − = subtraction assignment operator, the *= multiplication assignment operator, the /= division assignment operator, and the %= remainder assignment operator. Other assignment variations include the <<= left-shift assignment operator, the >>= right-shift assignment operator, the &= bitwise-AND assignment operator, and the ^= bitwise-XOR assignment operator.

atom table A table of strings and corresponding integer ID numbers (atoms).

audio track the sound component of an animation sequence or multimedia presentation. Microsoft Windows provides support for audio from a wave audio sound file, a musical MIDI file, or directly from CD-ROM or videodisc.

authoring Designing, creating, and testing an animation sequence, multimedia presentation, or virtual reality application.

authoring platform The personal computer system on which an animation sequence, multimedia presentation, or virtual reality application is prototyped and tested. See delivery platform.

AVI Acronym for audio-video interleaved, a Microsoft Windows animation standard supporting a 160-by-120 pixel viewport at 15 frames-per-second in 256-color mode using 8-bit palettized color, with audio at 11,025 Hz sampling rate at 8 bits-per-sample.

back-face culling Backplane removal. Also see culling.

background color The underlying color over which the graphics are drawn. The GDI sets the default background color for a new window to white.

backplane removal The elimination of backward-facing facets from convex polyhedra like cubes, spheres, and cylinders in 3D scenes. Also called backface culling.

bar sheet A written, visual representation of the sound track for an animation sequence. Used to synchronize character movement with dialog and sound effects. See lip sync.

binary file A file stored in binary format, as opposed to ASCII or ANSI format (text). Sometimes called a binary image in graphics programming.

binary operator A C or C++ operator used in binary expressions. Binary operators include multiplicative operators ($*,/$), additive operators ($+,-$), shift operators ($<<,>>$), relational operators ($<,>,<=,>=,==,!=,$), bitwise operators ($\&,|,\wedge$), logical operators ($\&\&,||$), and the sequential-evaluation operator ($,$).

bit array A graphic array or bitblt image.

bitblt An acronym for bit block transfer. Also called block graphics and graphic array.

bitblt animation Graphic array animation.

bitblt image A graphic array.

bit block transfer See bitblt.

bitmap An arrangement of bytes in display memory or conventional memory representing a virtual display surface upon which graphics can be drawn. A device-dependent bitmap can be displayed on a particular device (ie a graphics adapter). A device-independent bitmap contains a generalized description of its contents, enabling the application (or Windows GDI) to modify it for display on a diverse range of devices.

bitplane One of four separate buffers that are sandwiched together by VGA,

EGA, Super VGA, and other graphics adapters in order to drive video output. Also called a color plane.

bit tiling   Mixing pixels of different colors to create patterns or shades. Windows' built-in bit tiling is called dithering.

bitwise operators   &, |, and ^, which compare bits to check for true and false conditions. C's bitwise operators are AND (&), OR (|), and XOR (^). Also see C's logical operators AND (&&), OR (||), and NOT (!).

black box   A block of code that has been previously tested and debugged and is assumed to operate correctly. The programmer is unconcerned with the algorithm or processes used by the black box code, but rather with the input and output. See white box.

black-box testing   Program testing that is concerned with input and output, not with the inner functioning of code. See white-box testing.

blitting   Using bitblts (graphic arrays) in a graphics program.

block   A cohesive sequence of C or C++ statements, instructions, declarations, or definitions that are enclosed within braces { }.

block graphics   Same as graphic array. See bitblt.

body suit   Data suit.

Boolean logic   Logic calculus employing operators such as NOT, AND, OR, XOR, and others.

bounding-box   (1) In 3D computer graphics, a parallelepiped (a six-sided box) that encompasses all the vertices of a 3D model or subobject; (2) In 2D computer graphics, a rectangle that surrounds the vertices of an object. Also called a stand-in.

bounding-box test   Using the bounding boxes of two objects to determine if a potential conflict exists.

braces   The { } tokens that enclose a block in a C or C++ program. See also parentheses and brackets.

brackets   The [ ] tokens that are used to initialize and access the elements of arrays.

b-rep   Boundary representation, a method of creating images of 3D models by using planes, polygons, and facets. The outer surfaces or skin are used to model the so-called boundaries of the 3D object. See CSG.

buffer   An area of memory used for temporary storage of data or images.

bump mapping   The intentional random displacement of surface normals to simulate a rough surface on a 3D model.

callback function   A function in an application that is called by the Windows operating system. For example, the window function in an application is a callback function. See window function.

camera coordinates   The XYZ coordinates that describe how a 3D model will appear to a hypothetical viewer at a given location in the 3D scene. Also called view coordinates.

camera instruction sheet   See dope sheet.

canonical view-volume   A 3D view-volume derived from a cube whose vertices are located within a -1 to 1 range. Also called a normalized view-volume.

caption bar The title bar of an application's main window. Usually contains the name of the application.

caret The ^ character.

cast-based animation An object-oriented form of animation control whereby multiple actors are independently animated in front of a scene. Also called procedural animation.

cast member See actor.

CATA An acronym for computer-assisted traditional animation.

CD-ROM An acronym for compact disk read-only memory. A 4.7-inch diameter plastic disc that stores digital data by pits and lands (bumps) that are etched into its surface. The data is read by interpreting the plastic surface with a laser beam. A CD-ROM disk can store 600Mb of data, representing numeric, text, sound, or graphic information.

cel (1) An image painted on acetate as used in traditional film animation studios. (2) The rectangular space occupied by a single character in a particular font. (3) A bitblt or bitmap used for computer animation sequences.

cel animation Computer animation that emulates traditional methods of cel animation, where actors or scenic elements painted on transparent acetate are manipulated in front of static background art while being filmed using a single-exposure camera.

char A C or C++ variable stored in one byte of memory, capable of representing values from −128 to +127. An unsigned char can represent values from 0 to 255. By default, char is signed. A char type is often used to store the integer value of a member of the ASCII or ANSI alphanumeric character set.

chroma-key see key color.

CGI computer-generated image.

CGM The ANSI computer graphics metafile format for exchanging images between application programs or between computer systems.

claymation A form of pixilation animation in which clay and plasticine models are used as actors and scenery. See pixilation, stop-motion photography.

client area The interior image space of a Windows application's main window that is available for use by the application. Also called the window viewport.

clipboard A block of global memory that is managed by Windows in order to permit applications to pass data and images to other applications.

clock tick An interrupt issued at intervals of 54.925 ms (about 18.2 times each second) by the system timer chip. See INT 08H.

CMY model The cyan-magenta-yellow color model used primarily by printers and publishers using offset lithography.

clipping See line clipping.

cognitive computing Software processes that mimic human thinking by means of neural-based, fuzzy-based, or genetic-based algorithms.

collision detection Detecting the moment when a vertex or facet of one solid

3D model conflicts with the space occupied by another solid 3D model. Collision response refers to the action taken by the software after collision is detected.

color cycling A method for producing animation by swapping palette values.

color interpolation Determining the color of a pixel from its neighbors or from its distance between two pixels whose colors are known.

computer visualization Using graphics to interpret, manipulate, or create data. Specialized fields of computer visualization include scientific visualization, 3D modeling and rendering, computer animation, biomedicine, fluid dynamics, tomography, computer vision, image processing, and others.

constructive solid geometry See CSG.

conventional memory RAM up to 640K.

coordinate system The arrangement of x axis and y axis in a 2D graphics environment or the arrangement of x axis, y axis, and z axis in a 3D graphics environment.

copy To provide a handle to the Windows clipboard.

cosine The cosine of an angle in a right-angle triangle defines the relationship between the hypotenuse and the adjacent side.

cross-compiler development Application development that ensures compatibility on different compilers.

CSG Constructive solid geometry, a method of creating images of 3D models by using primitives (subobjects) such as cubes, cylinders, spheres, and cones. See b-rep.

culling (1) A 3D modeling paradigm that discards an entity that would occupy only a few pixels; (2) A 3D modeling algorithm that detects and discards backward-facing facets from 3D solids. Also see backface culling.

cut to instantly change from one full-frame image to another during animation playback. See also dissolve.

cyberspace A virtual environment consisting of multiple computers, databases, and users. Sometimes used to mean artificial reality.

cycle See loop.

data suit A full-body suit used in virtual reality applications to provide input representing the positions and orientation of various parts of the user's body.

declaration The statements that define the name and attributes of a C or C++ variable, function, structure, or class.

decrement To make smaller by a specified number of units.

default A condition assumed to exist unless defined otherwise by the user or developer.

definition The instructions that comprise a C function or a C++ method.

deformation See squashing-and-stretching.

degrees-of-freedom The translation and rotation input values permitted by a virtual reality input device. A mouse provides two degrees-of-freedom or 2D input. A bat provides 3D input (XYZ translation or yaw-roll-pitch rotation). A bird provides 6D input (XYZ translation and yaw-roll-pitch rotation).

delivery platform The personal computer system(s) on which a finished animation sequence, multimedia presentation, or virtual reality application is intended to be played. Also called a playback platform. See authoring platform.

depth cuing The use of colors or line styles to assist the viewer in interpreting depth in a computer-generated 3D image.

depth sort Ordering (sorting) the visible facets of a 3D scene into a sequence so that the 3D modeler draws the facets in farthest-to-nearest order (the so-called painter's algorithm).

detail polygon A two-dimensional facet containing line and color detailing that is mapped to a corresponding facet on a 3D entity in order to provide enhanced visual detail.

development platform The configuration of hardware and software used to build a software product. See target platform.

digital camera A still camera that stores imagery in digital format instead of on photographic film. Dedicated software permits the image data to be exported to a personal computer via the parallel or serial port.

digital video interactive A combination of hardware and software methods for combining graphics, video, audio, titling, and other multimedia components into a computer-controlled presentation. See multimedia.

digitize To convert an analog image or signal to a corresponding series of bits and bytes.

dirty rectangle animation Refresh animation.

display context A Windows data structure that defines an output device and the various drawing attributes associated with it, such as drawing tools, colors, dimensions, and others.

display coordinates Screen coordinates. Refers primarily to the converted camera coordinates of a 3D modeling application.

display-independent Refers to algorithms, functional code, graphics, and Windows applications that perform consistently across a diverse range of different display modes and display hardware.

display schedule A script that manages the playback of an animation sequence.

dissolve To smoothly replace one image with another by fading out the first image while fading up the second image. Also called a crossfade.

dithering The bit tiling or patterning of pixels used to implement a shading or coloring scheme. Windows uses dithering to simulate colors beyond the limited selection available in the 16-color VGA mode. See bit tiling.

DLL See dynamic link library.

do-nothing routine A routine that simply returns control to the caller. Do-nothing routines are used during preliminary program development and debugging. Also called a stub.

dope sheet A camera instruction sheet for animation production.

double-buffer animation A method of animation whereby the software builds the next frame on a hidden bitmap while displaying the current frame on the application's display window. To display the next finished image the application copies the hidden bitmap to the screen. Double-buffer animation is implemented differently in applications running under DOS.

dpi   Dots per inch. Often used to describe the graphics resolution of laser printers and scanners.

DVI   An acronym for digital video interactive.

dynamic link library   A library of routines and data that can be called or accessed by any Windows application. The Graphics Device Interface (GDI) is a dynamic link library (DLL). A DLL file might use either the dll or exe filename extension.

dynamics   The study of motion as it relates to force, mass, and other constraints in animation sequences.

electronic darkroom   Refers to image-processing routines that manipulate images to produce results otherwise obtained by sending negatives, transparencies, or prints to professional photography labs or retouching services.

elegant   See optimize.

elision   A 3D modeling paradigm that refrains from rendering entities past a specified distance in order to avoid cluttering a 3D image.

EMB   Extended memory blocks.

emulation   (1) Simulation of unavailable hardware by available hardware and software; (2) Simulation of a real-world situation or event by software.

EMS   Expanded memory specification. Expanded memory is used to provide additional physical RAM for computers which are otherwise limited to 640K RAM. Access is through a page manager. See XMS.

enhanced mode   Windows runtime memory mode requiring an 80286, 80386, 80486 or higher processor with more than 2Mb RAM running in protected mode and providing virtual memory via disk swapping when physical memory is exhausted.

ensemble animation   refresh animation.

ensemble processing   An image-processing function whereby the content of two images is compared. See also ensemble animation and refresh animation.

ergonomics   Refers to compatibility of hardware or software with human psychology and physiology.

error-handler   An algorithm or routine used to handle exceptions occurring at runtime.

error trapping   Using a programmer-defined routine to detect and respond to errors caused by hardware or software exceptions at runtime.

Euler operators   Logical and arithmetic operators for the manipulation of 3D solids. The standard operations are join, intersection, and subtraction.

expanded memory   See EMS.

exploratory VR   A virtual reality environment that allows the user to actively explore but not otherwise interact with the environment. See also passive VR and interactive VR.

expression   A combination of operators acting on variables.

extended memory   See XMS.

extrusion   Stretching or deforming an object in a 3D scene. See rotation. See translation.

4D   Four dimensional. Often used to refer to animated 3D computer graphics because the fourth dimension of time has been added to the image. Usually represented by (x,y,z,t) notation.

4D space-time   A display of 3D-space over time. See 4D.

facet   A polygonal plane surface used to create solid 3D models constructed by the B-rep method.

file pointer   A variable that indicates the current position of read and write operations on a file. See stream.

filtering   A method of color interpolation useful for anti-aliasing (removal of jaggies).

fitted curve   A computer-generated curve.

fixed-loop animation   An animation sequence driven by a block of code that executes repeatedly for a fixed number of iterations. See idle-loop animation.

font   A cohesive set of alphanumeric characters in a particular point size (ie 12 pt.) of a particular typeface (ie Arial) in a particular type style (ie bold).

font file   A file containing the bitmap data or vector formulas required to generate and display a particular font. See font.

force constraints   The forces acting upon actors in a physically-based animation sequence. See geometric constraints.

forensic animation   Computer-generated animation used as evidence in criminal proceedings or civil litigation, often in motor vehicle collision cases.

forward dynamics   The process of calculating the result of the application of force, loads, or constraints on an object. See inverse dynamics.

forward kinematics   The process of calculating the result of the application of velocity or acceleration on an object. See inverse kinematics.

fourier analysis   Using rate of change as the discriminating factor to analyze image data.

fourier window   A method of anti-aliasing.

fps   Frames per second, used to express the display rate of animation programs. Traditional film animation uses 24 frames per second (25 fps in Europe). North American NTSC television animation uses 30 frames per second (25 fps in Europe). See NTSC.

frame   (1) A single image in an animation sequence, usually intended to mean a full screen image. (2) A complete image that is being interpreted or manipulated by an image-processing function.

frame animation   The rapid display of previously created graphic images (frames). Frames can be stored as metafiles or as bitmaps in convention memory, extended memory, or on hard disk. See animation engine.

frame buffer   The bitmap or viewport where the color values or image of a Z-buffer-rendered 3D scene is stored. The corresponding depth-values are stored in the Z-buffer.

frame grab   Capturing a graphic image from an external source and storing it in a buffer or on disk. Typical external sources include scanners, live video, videotape players, and others.

frame process   An image-processing function that manipulates or combines two input images to produce a third image. Each image is called a frame.

frames per second   The rate of animation, expressed as new images per second. Also called fps.

freeze-frame   To display over a period of time a single frame from an animated sequence.

frequency   The rate of change found by fourier analysis.

frisket   (1) A paper or cellophane shield used by graphic artists and film animators to protect portions of artwork from being inadvertently colored during airbrushing; (2) A bitmap matte used to protect an existing background during a transparent put operation. See transparent put.

function declaration   Statements that define the name, return type, storage class, and parameter list of a C or C++ function. See declaration.

function definition   Statements that define the name, return type, storage class, parameter list, and the executable instructions which comprise a C or C++ function. See definition.

GDI   Graphics Device Interface, the host graphics engine built into Windows as a dynamic link library (DLL) whose routines can be called by any Windows application.

gdi.exe   The Windows dynamic link library that provides device-independent graphics functions for Windows applications. See user.exe and kernel.exe.

geometric constraints   The dimensional conditions affecting physically-based animation. See also force constraints.

geometric model   A mathematical definition of an object.

geometric processing   Image processing functions such as move, copy, shear, stretch, and others.

geometry   Mathematics concerned with points, lines, angles, shapes, solids, and surfaces.

global variable   A variable in a C or C++ source file that is available to all functions in that file. A variable declared outside of any function is global by default.

gnomon   A visual representation of the XYZ axis system in a 3D application.

Gouraud shading   Smooth shading.

gradient   A subtle transition between two hues. Also called a ramp.

graphics device interface   See GDI.

granular   Refers to the size of the smallest linkable element of a library, a set of routines, or a collection of data.

granularity   See granular.

graphic array   A rectangular image that has been saved in RAM as a bit array (bitblt) for later retrieval and display. Also called a block. See bitblt.

graphic array animation   Placing one or more graphic arrays (bitblts) onto the display in order to produce animation. Also called bitblt animation and block animation.

graphics driver   A module of executable code designed to interact directly with the graphics hardware. The VGA graphics driver shipped with the retail version of Windows is named VGA.DRV.

gray scale   Refers to images or to the palette scheme used by images displayed as a range of gray tones.

groundplane   A graphic representation of the orientation of the 3D environment in modeling and shading software.

GUI   Graphical user interface.

handle   An identifier that is provided by Windows to an application at runtime that permits the application to use or manipulate a window, display context, bitmap, data, or other object identified by the handle.

hexadecimal   The base 16 numbering system. The decimal system uses base 10. The base is also called the radix.

hex   Same as hexadecimal. A hexadecimal value is prefixed by the 0x symbol in C and C++. It is followed by the H symbol in assembly language.

hidden line   A line that is hidden by another graphic.

hidden surface   A plane or facet that is hidden by other surfaces.

hidden surface elimination   See hidden surface removal.

hidden surface removal   The process of removing from a 3D scene all surfaces that should be hidden from view. Visible surface algorithms falls into two broad categories: image-space methods and object-space methods.

hierarchical modeler   An interactive, 3D application that can be used to design and construct complex assemblies of subobjects (primitives). See also primitives modeler.

hierarchical modeling   A 3D modeling paradigm that uses hierarchies of related subobjects to built complex assemblies and subassemblies. Also see parent. Also see progeny.

hierarchy   A database of related 3D subobjects or entities (parents and progeny). See hierarchical modeling.

high memory   The first 64K segment of memory in RAM physically located above 1Mb on an 80286, 80386, 80486, or newer computer. Through an addressing idiosyncrasy DOS applications can access this portion of memory and can use it as a page to access simulated EMS, which is actually located in XMS.

histogram   A table describing the distribution of gray values or color in an image being manipulated by image-processing software.

HLS   The hue-luminance-saturation color model.

HMA   High memory area.

HMD Head-mounted display used in virtual reality.

host graphics engine The runtime graphics library being used. Windows applications use the Graphics Device Interface (GDI) as the host engine.

HSV The hue-saturation-value color model.

Hungarian notation A convention of rules for naming and capitalization of functions, variables, and constants in Windows applications source files.

HVC The hue-value-chroma color model.

icon A miniature bitmap image that represents a minimized Windows application.

idle-loop animation An animation sequence driven by a block of code that executes repeatedly, but only when there are no other demands on the Windows operating environment. See fixed-loop animation.

illumination model A paradigm that explains the process whereby a computer-generated 3D scene is lighted.

image file A binary file that contains a graphic image or the algorithm for recreating the image.

image-precision algorithms Refers to 3D hidden-surface and illumination routines that perform their calculations on pixels rather than on the 3D coordinates. Also called image-space methods. Also see object-precision algorithms.

image processing Analyzing, interpreting, and modifying a digitized image with a computer. Typical applications include photo retouching and enhancement, blur removal, edge detection, geometric processing (stretch, invert, mirror, flop), contrast adjustment, cut and paste, computer vision, morphing and tweening, pattern recognition, target-recognition, ensemble processing, and others.

image-space methods Image-precision algorithms.

include file A text file that is logically but not physically merged into the source code at compile time.

increment To make larger by a specified number of units.

indirection Refers generally to the act of addressing a variable in memory. Specifically refers to the indirection operator (*) which is used in C and C++ to declare a pointer to another variable. See pointer.

ink and paint In traditional film animation, refers to the final rendering (or inking and painting) of cels derived from the pencil sketches used to prototype the animation sequence. In computer animation, refers to coloring the frames, whether by interactive paint software or by computer-controlled automatic methods.

instance (1) A single occurrence of a graphical entity in an image or scene. (2) A running copy of a Windows application.

instancing Creating a complex 2D or 3D model by multiple occurrences of the same entity at different locations in the scene.

int 08H An interrupt issued 18.2 times each second (once each 54.925 milliseconds) by the computer's system timer chip. Used by Windows' virtual timer. See clock tick.

integer A whole number with no fractional parts or decimal point.

interactive   Responds to input from the user at runtime.

interactive graphics   Software that creates or modifies a graphical display in timely response to user input.

interactive VR   A virtual reality environment that allows the user to explore and interact with the environment. See also passive VR and exploratory VR.

interop   Interoperability, the ability of software to operate on and share data across different hardware platforms.

intersection   See Euler operators.

inverse dynamics   The process of calculating the forces or constraints required to move an object of a certain mass from one position to another over a fixed period of time. See forward dynamics.

inverse kinematics   The process of calculating the velocity or acceleration required to move an object from one position to another over a fixed period of time. See forward kinematics.

iterative   See loop.

jiffy   The shortest time interval between two frames during playback of an animation sequence. Conversely, frames per second refers to the number of frames displayed per second during playback. See fps.

join   See Euler operators.

kernel.exe   The Windows dynamic link library that provides system resources such as memory management and resource management to Windows applications at runtime. See user.exe and gdi.exe.

key color   a color that will appear transparent when the image is overlaid on another image or background. Called chroma-key by the broadcast television industry.

keyframe   A significant frame in an animation script, tweening session, or morphing sequence. Typically, the developer or the user provides a set of keyframes and the software provides the in-between images (tweens).

kinematics   The study of motion as it relates to the positions and velocities of objects in animation sequences.

kinematic animation   Computer animation that is managed by algorithms conforming more or less to the laws of physics. See procedural animation. See kinematics.

lamina   A 3D plane of null thickness that can be viewed from either side.

language binding   A module that calls compiler-dependent routines in a graphics library or runtime library.

lens distortion error field   A bitmap schematic that indicates the areas of lens distortion in images grabbed from a live video camera attached to a computer.

lerping   Linear interpolation.

library   A file containing modules of object code representing functions available for use by the developer's C or C++ program.

line clipping   Deletion of a line segment that exceeds the physical range of the viewport.

line styling   Dotted or dashed lines.

linear interpolation An algorithm for generating in-between images from keyframes whereby the movement of a vertex is assumed to follow a straight line. Also called lerping. See spline interpolation.

lip sync Synchronization of a cartoon character's mouth movements to a sound track. See bar sheet.

local variable Same as static variable. See also global variable.

logical operators && and ||, which perform logical operations on bytes being compared. The && token is used to AND two bytes (the resulting bit will be on only if both the bits being evaluated were on). The || token is used to OR two bytes (the resulting bit will be on if either of the bits being evaluated were on).

logical palette A table of colors defined by a Windows application for its own use. Where possible the colors in a logical palette are mapped by Windows to matching hues in the system palette (hardware palette). If no match is possible, Windows uses dithering to simulate the color requested by the logical palette. See system palette.

lookup table The logical table used by the graphics adapter to match color index numbers (used by the application software) to RGB gun settings (used by the display monitor). Windows sets the values of the lookup table at startup.

loop A repeating set of frames that comprises an animation cycle, as in a run cycle. In traditional film animation, lengths of film were spliced end to end to form repeating loops. See idle loop.

LUT Lookup table.

mach band An optical illusion whereby the human eye emphasizes the subtle differences between two adjacent shaded areas.

matte A bitblt mask that is used in conjunction with GDI raster operations to permit an irregularly shaped, multicolor bitblt image to be cleanly placed onto a multicolored background. Also called a key matte. In traditional filmmaking a matte is a black mask that prevents a designated part of each frame from being exposed, thereby permitting other images to be added later. See travelling matte.

MDK Multimedia development kit.

memory model One of the memory-management schemes used by C and C++ to set up memory space for executable code and addressable data. Windows applications usually employ the small model or the medium memory model.

message loop The block of statements in a Windows application that retrieves input messages from the application queue maintained by the Windows operating system.

metafile The GDI statements and the data necessary to reconstruct an image. A Windows metafile can exist in RAM, can be stored on disk for later use, and can be passed to the clipboard for use by other Windows applications.

millisecond 1/1000th of a second. Windows applications wishing to define a timer interval must do so using milliseconds (ms).

model photography   See stop-motion photography.

model sheet   A set of reference design drawings showing a cartoon character in typical poses.

modeling   Creating a geometric shape representing a 3D object.

module   The block of C or C++ code contained in a separate source file. Can also mean a cohesive block of code that performs a specific function.

morgue   A collection of reference photographs and drawings used by artists, animators, designers, and writers.

morphing   A gradual transformation of a graphics object to a different object. Derived from the term metamorphosis.

motion-control model photography   See stop-motion photography.

motion blur   In traditional film photography, image fuzziness caused by the subject moving faster than the frame rate of the camera. Animation software often employs intentional image blurring (temporal anti-aliasing) to overcome temporal aliasing. See temporal aliasing.

motion dynamics   Changes in location, orientation, and juxtaposition of objects during an animation sequence. See update dynamics and viewing dynamics.

motion test   A prototype animation sequence used to test timing, pacing, and movement before producing the final images. Traditional film animators used an animation pencil-test for the same purpose.

MPC   Acronym for multimedia personal computer.

MSC   Microsoft C.

multimedia   A collection of hardware and software methods for combining graphics, full-motion video, audio, titling, and other components from diverse sources into a computer-controlled presentation. See digital video interactive.

multimedia personal computer   A PC with multimedia-capable hardware components.

multi-module programming   Using separately compiled source files to build an executable file.

multiplicative operators   The * and / operators, which are multiplication and division.

native code   Executable code that is processor-specific.

neighborhood   The grouping of picture elements (pixels) that surrounds the subject picture element being analyzed. Neighborhoods are considered by image-processing software functions when manipulating an image or when detecting edges. See spatial filter.

nested loop   A program loop contained within another loop.

normalized coordinates   coordinates that have been scaled to the range -1 to $+(1)$ Normalized coordinates are considered device-independent. Also see canonical view-volume.

normalized view-volume   Canonical view-volume.

NTSC   A video signal that adheres to the accepted technical standards of the broadcast industry in the United States, Canada, Mexico, Central

America, and Japan. NTSC is defined as 525 lines refreshed 30 frames per second. The PAL standard, used in Europe, Australia, and New Zealand, is 625 lines at 25 fps. See VTR.

NULL   A constant that means undefined. NULL is defined as 0 by windows.h.

null pointer   A pointer to nothing. An undefined pointer.

nybble   half a byte, or four bits.

object   A cohesive 2D or 3D graphical entity.

object file   A file containing object code. Also called an OBJ file.

object-precision algorithms   Refers to 3D hidden-surface and illumination routines that perform their calculations on the 3D coordinates rather than on pixels. Also called object-space methods. Also see image-precision algorithms.

object-space methods   Object-precision algorithms.

objectification   Representing a phenomenon as form, color, texture, motion, and time. See visualization.

onion skin   A feature provided by animation software, whereby the previous three or four cels can be superimposed over the current cel. See cel animation.

OOP   Object-oriented programming, whereby each independent module contains both executable code and the data upon which it operates.

operand   A constant or a variable operated on by operators in an expression.

optimize   To improve a program's execution speed or to reduce its memory requirements at runtime.

overlay   A module of data or executable code that is loaded from disk at runtime over an existing block of code or data.

painter's algorithm   A method of 3D hidden object removal. See Z-buffer method.

PAL   See NTSC.

pan   To move an image left or right. See scroll.

parameter   A value that a function expects to receive when called. Also called an argument, but many technical writers and developers make a distinction between the two.

parent   A subobject in a 3D hierarchical modeling environment that serves as a reference point for other subobjects (progeny) whose position and orientation are expressed relative to the parent. Also see progeny.

passive VR   A virtual reality environment that allows the user to observe but not interactive. See also exploratory VR and interactive VR.

paste   To retrieve a handle from the Windows clipboard.

pencil-test   See motion test.

persistent image   Refers to graphics displayed in the client area of a window that are preserved when the window is moved, clipped or unclipped by the edge of the screen, covered or uncovered by another application's window, or resized.

physically-based animation   An animation sequence managed according to laws of physics. See forward kinematics, inverse kinematics, forward dynamics, and inverse dynamics.

pipe The | character.

pixel Picture element. A pixel is the smallest addressable graphic on a display screen. In RGB systems, a pixel is a triad comprised of a red dot, a green dot, and a blue dot.

pixilation Animation created by single-frame exposures of inanimate models. Claymation is a form of pixilation. See stop-motion photography. See claymation.

plane equation A vector formula that describes the qualities of a plane, including the location of a given point relative to the surface of the plane. Plane equations are useful for hidden surface removal.

plane equation test Testing to determine if a given point is located on the inside or outside of a given facet in a 3D scene.

platform-independent Refers to applications able to execute on a diverse range of hardware configurations.

point process An image-processing function that modifies an individual pixel or a single picture element as a result of considering the value or location of the pixel. Neighboring pixels are not considered. See area process. See neighborhood.

pointer A variable that contains the address of another variable. See null pointer.

polygon Usually intended to mean a plane surface used to create a 3D solid model constructed by the B-rep method. Also used to describe a multi-sided, closed geometric shape.

POV Point of view, also called viewpoint.

preprocessor directive An instruction that modifies the behavior of a C or C++ compiler at compile time. Common preprocessor directives are #if, #elseif, #endif, and #include.

primitive A fundamental 3D solid such as a sphere, cylinder, cone, parallelepiped, wedge, and others. Also called a subobject.

primitives modeler An interactive, 3D application that can be used to design and construct 3D primitives (subobjects) and simple assemblies. See also hierarchical modeler.

procedural animation Object-oriented animation. See cast-based animation.

progeny A subobject in a 3D hierarchical modeling environment whose position and orientation are expressed relative to another subobject (parent). Also see parent.

prototype (1) The initial declaration of a function in a C or C++ program, usually containing the return type and argument list of the function. (2) A tentative mock-up of a program for project-planning purposes.

pruning A 3D modeling paradigm that discards an entity if it falls wholly outside the view-volume.

quadric primitive A 3D subobject.

RAD Rapid applications development, a method of efficient software development that stresses preliminary prototypes, client feedback, and clearly defined goals.

radian A length of arc based upon the relationship between elements of a unit circle (whose radius equals one unit).

radiosity An algorithm that considers the overall energy levels from different light sources in a 3D scene.

radix The base of a numbering system. The radix of the hexadecimal numbering system is 16, of the decimal system is 10.

ramp See gradient.

rapid applications development See RAD.

raster operations Boolean operators that affect bitmap operations performed by GDI functions. Some common raster operations are XOR, AND, OR, and overwrite.

ray tracing An algorithm that calculates the illumination level of a model by tracing a ray of light back from the viewer's eye to the model and eventually to the light source.

real mode Windows runtime memory mode using an 8086, 8088 or higher processor with 1Mb RAM maximum, using EMS as a global heap for applications.

real-time animation (1) An animation sequence that is being created and displayed at runtime; (2) An animation sequence intended to correspond to or react to events occuring in the real world at runtime.

reflection mapping Mathematically projecting onto the surface of a 3D model a previously defined bitmap containing a visual reflection of other objects in the scene. The reflection bitmap is acquired by temporarily placing the viewpoint on the surface of the mirrored object.

refresh animation Computer animation that detects corrupted portions of a hidden frame and refreshes only those corresponding rectangles on the display image. Also called dirty rectangle animation and ensemble animation.

refresh buffer The display buffer. The display hardware uses the display buffer to refresh the display monitor.

regen Regeneration of a graphic entity or image. The instructions necessary to implement regen are sometimes stored in a metafile.

registration points The user-specified coordinates in keyframes that will be used to create tweens. See tweening.

relational operators The operators $<$, $>$, $<=$, $>=$, $==$, and $!=$, which in C and C++ mean less-than, greater-than, less-than-or-equal-to, greater-than-or-equal-to, equal-to, and not-equal-to. A relational operator compares the relationship between two values.

rendering Adding illumination, shading, and color to a 3D scene.

reveal See wipe.

RGB model The color model used by most personal computer graphics adapters and monitors.

rotation Adjusting the yaw, roll, or pitch attitude of an object in a 3D scene. See translation. See Extrusion.

rotoscoping Deriving realistic images for use in animated sequences by tracing the shapes found in live-action films.

rubberbanding The rapid erasing and redrawing of guidelines that represent the shape and position of a graphical entity to be drawn by the software if the user's current selection were used.

run-cycle A loop of frames that can be repeated in order to produce a running actor in an animated sequence. Static run cycles are usually overlayed on a panning background. Dynamic run cycles often use bitblts to move the actor across a static background.

runtime The time when the application is executing.

scalar A mathematical quantity that has quantity but not direction. A vector has quantity and direction.

scanner A peripheral device capable of grabbing a continuous tone hard-copy image and storing it in computer memory as a digitized image.

scientific visualization The graphical representation of formulas or phenomena for the purpose of scientific research.

scripted animation The computer-assisted equivalent of traditional cel animation.

scroll To move an image upwards or downwards. See pan.

SDK The Microsoft Windows Software Development Kit.

section A cross-section, cutaway view of a 3D object.

semantically implemented A phrase used by compiler manufacturers to indicate that their compiler recognizes a keyword but does not implement it. Syntactically implemented keywords are fully functional.

sensor Program code or virtual trigger-spot that manages how an entity responds to the user or to other entities in a virtual reality environment.

sequential-evaluation operator (,) used to separate a series of sequentially evaluated expressions.

sfx Sound effects.

shading Adding the effects of illumination, shadow, and color to a 3D model. Sometimes called rendering.

shadow map A two-dimensional image of a 3D scene from the viewpoint of the light-source. Entities which are not visible to the light-source will be cloaked in shadow in the frame buffer (viewport display).

shift operators << and >>, which shift the bits in a byte to the left or to the right.

simulation An imitation of a real-world event.

simulation manager The software engine that manages a virtual reality session.

simulator A program that imitates a real-world event.

sine The sine of an angle in a right-angle triangle defines the relationship between the hypotenuse and the side opposite.

single-step To advance to and pause at the next frame of an animation sequence after receiving explicit input (usually a keystroke) from the user. See freeze frame.

6D Six-dimensional. Usually refers to virtual reality input devices offering six degrees-of-freedom (x,y,z translation and yaw, roll, pitch rotation).

slow-in/slow-out The avoidance of unnatural instant-start and instant-stop events in computer animation sequences.

solid model A 3D model with hidden surfaces removed. It can be constructed by the constructive solid geometry method (CSG) or the boundary representation method (B-rep).

spatial filter A matrix calculation used by image- processing routines to manipulate images. See neighborhood.

specular reflection A highlight on the surface of a 3D model.

spline interpolation An algorithm for generating in-between images from keyframes whereby the movement of a vertex is assumed to follow a fitted curve or freeform curve. See linear interpolation.

squashing-and-stretching Deformation of an object or actor as a result of movement, acceleration, deceleration, collision, or other events.

staging Choreographing or directing an animation sequence or an individual frame.

staging editor An interactive, 3D application that can be used to specify the movement and positioning of entities (actors) in an animation sequence. See also articulated motion editor.

stamp A field of data in the header of a Windows application file. The resource compiler stamps each application with the Windows version for which the executable file is intended. Windows will not launch any application that does not contain the appropriate stamp.

standard mode Windows runtime memory mode requiring an 80286, 80386, 80486 or higher processor with less than 2Mb RAM, running in protected mode.

stand-in A bounding-box.

statement A C or C++ instruction. Sometimes called an expression.

static variable A variable that is available to only the function in which it has been declared. Also called a local variable. See global variable.

stereo vision Computer vision implemented with two video cameras.

stereolithography A process that uses 3D software to drive lasers that sculpt prototype solids from plastic, acrylic, wood, or light metal. Used for industrial prototyping.

stock font A font that is built into the retail versions of Windows. Stock fonts are guaranteed to be available for use by an application at runtime. See font.

stop-motion photography a method for production animation whereby inanimate models are photographed a few frames at a time and manually moved between each exposure. Also called model animation and motion-control model animation. See claymation. See pixellation.

stream The flow of data to or from a file or other output device.

structure   A set of items grouped under a single name. The elements might be of different types. In an array, the elements must be of similar type.

stub   See do-nothing routine.

subobject   A fundamental 3D solid such as a sphere, cylinder, cone, parallelepiped, wedge, and others. Also called a primitive.

subtraction   See Euler operators.

supersampling   Creating an image at a resolution that is greater than the actual screen resolution. When the image is scaled down to fit into the display buffer, many digital artifacts like jagged lines are suppressed as a convenient by-product of the scaling mathematics.

Super VGA   Graphics adapters that extend the capabilities of the standard VGA.

surface normal   A line that is perpendicular to the surface of a plane in a 3D environment. The illumination level of a surface can be derived by comparing the surface normal to the angle of incidence of incoming light rays.

swish pan   A rapid pan. Also called a zip pan.

syntactically implemented   The full functional implementation of a particular keyword or statement by a C or C++ compiler. See semantically implemented.

system palette   The current hardware palette, composed of a lookup table (LUT) that correlates a specified color index (usually an integer) with a particular triad of voltage settings for the RGB guns of the display monitor. A VGA running Windows can provide a system palette of 16 distinct and simultaneously displayable hues. A Super VGA, 8514/A, or XGA running Windows can provide a system palette of 256 hues. See logical palette.

3D   Three dimensional. Refers to computer images representing objects possessing the three dimensions of width, height, and depth. See 4D.

target platform   The group of personal computers and operating system configuration versions for which a software product is developed.

temporal aliasing   Refers to an awkward jumping effect present in computer-animated sequences when the frame rate is too slow to smoothly simulate actors moving at speed across the image. See motion blur. See anti-aliasing.

tilde   The ~ character, which C and C++ use to mean one's complement.

timer   A logical timing device maintained by Windows in order to send a WM_TIMER message to the application at an interval defined by the application. See the entry for animate on twos.

timer-based animation   An animation sequence driven by WM_TIMER timer messages from the Windows API.

titling   adding titles, production credits, and labels to an animated sequence or multimedia presentation.

toon   An actor (cartoon character) in a computer-animated cartoon sequence.

touring   See walkthrough.

traceback   The portion of an animation frame that is unchanged from the previous frame.

translation   Repositioning of an object in a 3D scene. See rotation. See Extrusion.

transparent put   The graphics effect of cleanly placing a random-shaped, multicolored bitblt image over a multicolored background scene. See frisket.

travelling matte   A matte whose shape changes as it accompanies a moving image. See matte.

trigonometry   Mathematics concerned with the relationship of two sides opposite a specific angle in a right-angle triangle. Sine and cosine are particularly useful for 3D computer graphics.

tween   An in-between image that software has interpolated from keyframes provided by the user or developer. See keyframe.

tweening   Generating tweens.

UMB   Upper memory blocks.

unary operator   An operator that manipulates a single variable. C and C++ provide the following unary operators: logical NOT (!), bitwise compliment (~), arithmetic negation (−), indirection (*), address-of (&), and unary plus (or arithmetic increment) (+).

union   A C or C++ structure that allocates the same memory space to different variables. The variables are often of different types.

universe   The collection of entities, scripts, and rules that comprise a particular virtual reality environment or session.

update dynamics   Changes in shape, color, and texture during an animation sequence. See motion dynamics and viewing dynamics.

user.exe   The Windows dynamic link library that provides window management functions for Windows applications at runtime. See kernel.exe and gdi.exe.

vector   A mathematical value that has quantity and direction. A scalar value has only quantity.

VGA   Video graphics array. Windows runs in the 640×480×16-color mode on VGA adapters.

videodisc   A large-format plastic disc used to store digital or analog information. Read by laser beam. Often used to store and play full-motion video and audio. Similar in concept to CD-ROM.

view coordinates   See camera coordinates.

viewing dynamics   Changes in lighting, camera, and viewpoint during an animation sequence. See motion dynamics and update dynamics.

viewport   A subset of the display screen.

view-volume   The volume of space visible to the camera in a 3D modeling environment, generally taken to be a frustum (a decapitated pyramid). Also see canonical view-volume.

virtual reality   Generally, a field of computer science concerned with real-time, interactive, 3D simulations that mimic the real world or fictional worlds by providing a virtual environment with which a user can interact.

Specifically, the particular environment being modeled and simulated. Virtual reality sessions can be passive, exploratory, or interactive. See cyberspace.

visibility   Describes whether or not a function or a variable can be used by other parts of a C or C++ program.

visual algorithm   The graphical representation of a computer function or algorithm.

visualization   Using graphics to interpret, manipulate, or create data. Specialized fields of computer visualization include scientific visualization, 3D modeling and rendering, computer animation, biomedicine, fluid dynamics, tomography, computer vision, image processing, and others. See objectification.

visualization graphics   The graphics used for computer visualization. See visualization.

void   Undefined. See NULL.

volume visualization   Using 3D objects to represent data. See scientific visualization.

VR   Acronym for virtual reality.

VR rules   The specific rules and protocol that govern a particular virtual reality environment or session.

vtr   videotape recorder or videotape recording. See NTSC.

waldo   A facial input device used in virtual reality applications.

walk-through   Animation of a 3D architectural model, intended to simulate a walk-through by the viewer. Also called touring.

weighted sum   An image-processing operation whereby the sum of values of a pixel and its neighbors are calculated in compliance with a spatial filter.

white box   A block of code currently under development and whose algorithms and processes are being adjusting during testing. See black box.

white-box testing   Program testing that requires access to the inner workings of a block of code. See black-box testing.

window   (1) The display space used by a Windows application. (2) A viewport on the display screen. (3) The logical relationship between the display screen and the world coordinates in 3D graphics programming.

window class   A logical definition describing the attributes of a window. A window class is used to create the main window of a Windows application.

window function   A callback function in a Windows application, responsible for interpreting incoming messages and directing program flow to the appropriate core functions of the application. See callback function.

windows.h   The include file that contains definitions and declarations for Windows variables, data structures, functions, and constants that are available for use by a Windows application.

WinMain()   The entry-point function of a Windows application. WinMain() contains the message loop.

wipe   Revealing the next image by selectively manipulating the image buffer. Similar in concept to opening a set of venetian blinds to reveal a scene or opening a sliding door to reveal a room. Also called a reveal.

wire-frame   A 3D object modeled with edges, with no hidden surfaces removed.

WM_COMMAND   The runtime variable that contains an incoming message that identifies the user's actions in navigating through and selecting from the application's menus.

world coordinates   The XYZ coordinates that describe the position and orientation of an object in a 3D environment.

XGA   Extended graphics adapter. As defined by IBM, an XGA adapter provides a 640×480×256-color mode, 1024×768×256-color mode, a 640×480×65,536-color mode, and all VGA modes.

XMS   Extended memory specification. XMS memory is physical memory located above 1Mb which can be accessed by an 80286, 80386, 80486, or newer microprocessor. See EMS.

YIQ model   The color model used by commercial television components.

z-buffer   A buffer containing the depth values for each pixel in a 3D scene, allowing the software to draw only the nearest entity at any particular location. The corresponding color values for each pixel are stored in a frame buffer. Also see frame buffer.

z-buffer method   A method of hidden surface removal whereby depth-values for each non-obstructed pixel are stored in a Z-buffer and the corresponding color values for each visible pixel are stored in a frame buffer. Also called the painter's algorithm. Also see Z-buffer.

zip pan   See swish pan.

zoom   To move the camera closer to or farther away from the objects in a 3D scene.

zoom axis   The 3D axis that represents the near/far context in a 3D scene. The zoom axis is perpendicular to the image plane. The 3D routines in the demonstration programs in this book use the z axis to represent near/far.

Index

Boldface numbers refer to art

modeling and modeling geometry
continued
hierarchical modeling/operations, 3D, 48, 91-94, 110
meshes, **90**-91
modeling geometry, 46, 53-54, 68, 82-91
parallelpipeds, 83-84, **83-84**
pitch, 82, **84**
primitives, 53, 82
primitives modeler, 91-92
pruning, 93-94
roll, 82, **84**
spheres, 84-86, **85-86**
   half-spheres, 84-86, **85-86**
spherical coordinate system, 82
staging editors, 91-92
structure coordinates, 91
structures, 48, 91
subassemblies, 48, 91, 92-94, **93**, **94**
subassembly modeling pipeline, 92-94, **93**, **94**
subobjects, 82
sweeps, 90, **90**
transformations in 3D, 82
vertices, 53
wedges, 87, **88**, **89**
yaw, 82, **84**
modes, drawing mode
   raster-operation codes, 21
   drawing mode, SetROP2(), 21
module definition files, 10
monitor requirements, 240, 242
   color, xxi
   color depth, 242
   resolution, xxi, 242
   RGB color, 7, 17, 22, 27
motion dynamics, 133
motion-control programming (*see* Assembly application)
MoveTo(), 23
multiplication
   2D vectors, 526
   3D vectors, 527
   matrices, 529
multitasking, 15

N

neural networks, 166
nonzero-sum games, 164, 177-180
normalized 3D perspective view-volume (*see* canonical)
numeric coprocessor requirements, compiling companion disk/samples, 241, 242

O

object coordinates, 47, 54-56, **55**, 82

Objects application (*see also* 3D programming), xxiv, 94-95, 97-118, 358-395
3D functions, 111
3D menu, 98, 99-102, **99-102**
accelerator keys, 107
assemb3d toolkit operation, 117
back-face culling, 114
boxes, 115
C code file, objects.c, 107-111
camera manipulation, 102, **105**, **106**
centering of window, 108
clipping plane demonstration, 101, **104**
clipping-planes, 113
color selection, Use menu, 99
complex solids, 101
cones, 116
constants, 111-112
core functions, 111
curved surfaces, 102, **104**, 116
customizing the application, 118
cylinders, 116
declarations, 107
deform3d toolkit operation, 116-117
display adapter support, 108
display-contexts, 108
Edit menu, 98
engine3d toolkit operation, 111-115
entry point, 108
facet functions, 114
facet shading, 114
File menu, 98
fixed-target camera functions, 113
function prototypes, 112
header file, objects.h, 106
hidden workspace, 114-115
hierarchical mode, 117
hierarchical modeling, 110
include files, 107, 112
initialization, 112-113
instancing, 113, 117
keyboard use, 99
lighting demonstration, 101, **104**
lights3d toolkit operation, 117
menus in the applications, 98, 106-107
   3D menu, 98, 99-102, **99-102**
   Edit menu, 98
   File menu, 98
   mouse vs. keyboard commands, 99
   Use menu, 98, 99
message handler, 109
mouse use, 99
multiple-copy protection, 108
nested menus, 3D menu, 99-100, **100**
parents and progeny, 117
persistent graphics, 110-111
primitives, 101, **103**
programmer's guide, 103-117

Other Books by Author

C FOR WINDOWS ANIMATION PROGRAMMING—Lee Adams

Use high-powered animation techniques in Windows® with this practical guide. Learn how to perform 2D cel animation, 3D behavioral animation, and 3D cinematic animation. You get comprehensive coverage of: major animation techniques, keyboard- and mouse-based control techniques, memory and storage considerations, and graphics application programming. 496 pages, illustrated. Book No. 4114, $39.95 paperback only

HIGH-PERFORMANCE C GRAPHICS PROGRAMMING FOR WINDOWS—Lee Adams

Take advantage of the explosive popularity of Windows with the help of computer graphics ace Lee Adams. Adams gives you a detailed introduction to a wide range of C graphics programming topics, including powerful programming techniques for 2D cel animation . . . 3D behavioral animation . . . and 3D kinetic animation. You get dozens of hands-on programming examples, including manipulating 3D objects, performing surface mapping, handling image processing, and valuable, ready-to-use sourcecode. 528 pages, 224 illustrations. Book No. 4103, $34.95 hardcover only

VISUAL BASIC ANIMATION PROGRAMMING—Lee Adams

Discover the true meaning of leading-edge animation techniques in the Visual Basic and Windows environment. Ready-to-use programs on disk show you how to tap into Window's GDI graphics library. Full instructions help you to achieve run-cycles, background pans, motion blur, animated images, and adjustable timers. Have all the techniques of animation graphics programming in your hand—and create behavioral, 2-D, 3-D, kinematic, real-time, and frame animations. 496 pages, 150 illustrations, includes FREE 3.5" disk. Book No. 4224, $39.95 paperback only

HIGH PERFORMANCE GRAPHICS IN C: ANIMATION AND SIMULATION—Lee Adams

Create realistic simulations, high-speed animation, and 3-dimensional computer graphics—this book will show you how. Using these ready-to-run program listings and Quick C and Turbo C, you'll learn how to: coax the best possible graphics out of your particular hardware and software . . . animate 3-D models and business graphics . . . test-fly a working flight simulator . . . perform walkthroughs of architectural images . . . and more. 552 pages, 235 illustrations. Book No. 3049, $37.95 hardcover only

LEE ADAMS' VISUALIZATION GRAPHICS IN C—Lee Adams

Create computer visualization graphics in programs for real-world applications with Quick C® and Turbo C® and this step-by-step programming guide. Going beyond 2D and 3D modeling and rendering, this revolutionary guide shows you how to use bitmaps, work with movement and hues, use process images, cel animation, photorealistic rendering, and more. Includes valuable source code you can use as is or customize to meet your needs. 506 pages, 100 illustrations. Book No. 3487, $36.95 hardcover only

LEE ADAMS' SUPERCHARGED C+ + GRAPHICS—Lee Adams

Get your C+ + programs up and running smoothly right from the start—and get them on the market sooner. This guide combines step-by-step instructions, computer-generated output tips, and complete program listings to give you the edge you need. You'll find tools, techniques, and programs for desktop publishing, 2D paint and draw, 3D CAD modeling, and many other applications. The easy-to-follow text includes over 10,000 lines of original source code. 512 pages, 100 illustrations. Book No. 3489, $34.95 hardcover only

Prices Subject to Change Without Notice.

Look for These and Other TAB Books at Your Local Bookstore

To Order Call Toll Free 1-800-822-8158
(24-hour telephone service available.)

or write to TAB Books, Blue Ridge Summit, PA 17294-0840.

Title	Product No.	Quantity	Price

☐ Check or money order made payable to TAB Books

Charge my ☐ VISA ☐ MasterCard ☐ American Express

Acct. No. _____ Exp. _____

Signature: _____

Name: _____

Address: _____

City: _____

State: _____ Zip: _____

Subtotal	$ _____
Postage and Handling ($3.00 in U.S., $5.00 outside U.S.)	$ _____
Add applicable state and local sales tax	$ _____
TOTAL	$ _____

TAB Books catalog free with purchase; otherwise send $1.00 in check or money order and receive $1.00 credit on your next purchase.

Orders outside U.S. must pay with international money in U.S. dollars drawn on a U.S. bank.

TAB Guarantee: If for any reason you are not satisfied with the book(s) you order, simply return it (them) within 15 days and receive a full refund.

BC

Order Form for Books
Requiring a Single 3.5" Disk

This Windcrest/McGraw-Hill software product is also available on a 3.5"/720K disk. If you need the software in 3.5" format, simply follow these instructions:

- Complete the order form below. Be sure to include the exact title of the Windcrest/McGraw-Hill book for which you are requesting a replacement disk.

- Make check or money order made payable to *Glossbrenner's Choice*. The cost is **$5.00** (**$8.00** for shipments outside the U.S.) to cover media, postage, and handling. Pennsylvania residents, please add 6% sales tax.

- Foreign orders: please send an international money order or a check drawn on a bank with a U.S. clearing branch. We cannot accept foreign checks.

- Mail order form and payment to:

   Glossbrenner's Choice
   Attn: Windcrest/McGraw-Hill Disk Replacement
   699 River Road
   Yardley, PA 19067-1965

Your disks will be shipped via First Class Mail. Please allow one to two weeks for delivery.

 ....

Windcrest/McGraw-Hill
Disk Replacement

Please send me a replacement disk in 3.5"/720K format for the following Windcrest/McGraw-Hill book:

Book Title _____

Name _____

Address _____

City/State/ZIP _____

DISK WARRANTY

This software is protected by both United States copyright law and international copyright treaty provision. You must treat this software just like a book, except that you may copy it into a computer in order to be used and you may make archival copies of the software for the sole purpose of backing up our software and protecting your investment from loss.

By saying "just like a book," McGraw-Hill means, for example, that this software may be used by any number of people and may be freely moved from one computer location to another, so long as there is no possibility of its being used at one location or on one computer while it also is being used at another. Just as a book cannot be read by two different people in two different places at the same time, neither can the software be used by two different people in two different places at the same time (unless, of course, McGraw-Hill's copyright is being violated).

LIMITED WARRANTY

Windcrest/McGraw-Hill takes great care to provide you with top-quality software, thoroughly checked to prevent virus infections. McGraw-Hill warrants the physical diskette(s) contained herein to be free of defects in materials and workmanship for a period of sixty days from the purchase date. If McGraw-Hill receives written notification within the warranty period of defects in materials or workmanship, and such notification is determined by McGraw-Hill to be correct, McGraw-Hill will replace the defective diskette(s). Send requests to:

> Customer Service
> Windcrest/McGraw-Hill
> 13311 Monterey Lane
> Blue Ridge Summit, PA 17294-0850

The entire and exclusive liability and remedy for breach of this Limited Warranty shall be limited to replacement of defective diskette(s) and shall not include or extend to any claim for or right to cover any other damages, including but not limited to, loss of profit, data, or use of the software, or special, incidental, or consequential damages or other similar claims, even if McGraw-Hill has been specifically advised of the possibility of such damages. In no event will McGraw-Hill's liability for any damages to you or any other person ever exceed the lower of suggested list price or actual price paid for the license to use the software, regardless of any form of the claim.

McGRAW-HILL, INC. SPECIFICALLY DISCLAIMS ALL OTHER WARRANTIES, EXPRESS OR IMPLIED, INCLUDING, BUT NOT LIMITED TO, ANY IMPLIED WARRANTY OF MERCHANTABILITY OR FITNESS FOR A PARTICULAR PURPOSE.

Specifically, McGraw-Hill makes no representation or warranty that the software is fit for any particular purpose and any implied warranty of merchantability is limited to the sixty-day duration of the Limited Warranty covering the physical diskette(s) only (and not the software) and is otherwise expressly and specifically disclaimed.

This limited warranty gives you specific legal rights; you may have others which may vary from state to state. Some states do not allow the exclusion of incidental or consequential damages, or the limitation on how long an implied warranty lasts, so some of the above may not apply to you.

If you need help
with the enclosed disk . . .

This enclosed 5¼-inch diskette contains one self-extracting file named 4115DISK.EXE. Make a subdirectory on your hard drive to copy the file to:

```
C:\> MD directory_name
```

where *directory_name* is the name of the directory that you want to create. Next, make this new directory the current directory:

```
C:\> CD directory_name
```

where *directory_name* is the name of the directory that you just created. Then, copy the self-extracting file to this directory:

```
C:\> COPY d:4115DISK.EXE
```

where *d* is the letter of the floppy drive containing the companion diskette.

To uncompress the files in 4115DISK.EXE, simply type the name at the DOS prompt:

```
C:\> 4115DISK
```

The file will expand to the 69 program files that are contained in the self-extracting file.

Important

Read the Disk Warranty terms on the previous page before opening the disk envelope. Opening the envelope constitutes acceptance of these terms and renders this entire book-disk package nonreturnable except for re-placement in kind due to material defects.